Early Human Life on the Southeastern Coastal Plain

Florida Museum of Natural History: Ripley P. Bullen Series

FLORIDA MUSEUM®

EARLY HUMAN LIFE ON THE SOUTHEASTERN COASTAL PLAIN

Edited by Albert C. Goodyear
and Christopher R. Moore

University of Florida Press
Gainesville

First cloth printing, 2018
First paperback printing, 2021

26 25 24 23 22 21   6 5 4 3 2 1

Library of Congress Cataloging-in-Publication Data
Names: Goodyear, Albert C., editor. | Moore, Christopher R., editor.
Title: Early human life on the southeastern coastal plain / edited by Albert C.
    Goodyear and Christopher R. Moore.
Other titles: Ripley P. Bullen series.
Description: Gainesville : University of Florida Press, 2018. | Series:
    Florida Museum of Natural History: Ripley P. Bullen series | Includes
    bibliographical references and index.
Identifiers: LCCN 2017032240 | ISBN 9781683400349 (cloth : alk. paper) |
    ISBN 9781683402480 (pbk.)
Subjects: LCSH: Archaeology—Southern States. | Prehistoric peoples—Southern
    States. | Indians of North America—Southern States. | Southern
    States—Antiquities.
Classification: LCC E78.S65 G66 2018 | DDC 975/.01—dc23
LC record available at https://lccn.loc.gov/2017032240

UF PRESS

UNIVERSITY
OF FLORIDA

University of Florida Press
2046 NE Waldo Road
Suite2100
Gainesville, FL 32609
http://upress.ufl.edu

CONTENTS

FIGURES

Tables

Preface and Acknowledgments

This volume is the cumulative product of numerous colleagues both professional and avocational, students all of the ancient past. The studies and findings herein are a testament to the curiosity and perseverance of archaeologists, geoscientists, and members of the public so necessary to reveal such a vast subject, often based on highly elusive and ephemeral remains. Institutional support was provided by the South Carolina Institute of Archaeology and Anthropology, University of South Carolina, the Savannah River Archaeological Research Program, and the Southeastern Paleoamerican Survey.

The chapters in this volume were originally papers presented at the 2014 Southeastern Archaeological Conference in Greenville, South Carolina. These authors were specifically solicited for their contributions, seeing that taken all together, good coverage by time, space, and topic could be assembled. The editors are most grateful to the authors for providing their contributions, and we believe their value speaks for itself. We would like to acknowledge the University of Florida Press and the assistance of Judith Knight and two reviewers in helping produce this book, and the opportunity to publish in the Ripley P. Bullen Series.

1

Introduction

ALBERT C. GOODYEAR AND CHRISTOPHER R. MOORE

The physiographic unit known as the Southeastern Coastal Plain runs like a ribbon along the eastern seaboard of the Atlantic Ocean, joining the Gulf of Mexico for its western margin. Composed of unconsolidated sediments ultimately transported from the South Appalachians, the Coastal Plain bears evidence of numerous marine transgressions over the past several million years that left terraces of different ages and elevations all capped by late Quaternary cover sands. Within these sands lie artifacts from several millennia, ranging in age from the Last Glacial Maximum (LGM) and before to latest prehistory. The Coastal Plain with its seashore resources and immense spatially extensive wetland features, as well as the floodplains of major rivers originating from the mountains, provided the highest carrying capacity on the Atlantic Slope for human foragers due to the abundance of surface water. The extensive archaeological record of the Coastal Plain is made more comprehensible by the resulting natural abundance of plants and animals dependent upon wetland habitats and their margins.

Nearly geographically coextensive with this landform are Tertiary-age marine cherts occurring as outcrops of silicified limestones from south of Tampa Bay to the Santee River in South Carolina. These cherts provided high-quality tool stone, which was intensively exploited by prehistoric inhabitants throughout all time periods. Nature, as it were, not only provided abundant biotic resources for food and fiber but also provided the tool stone necessary for their extraction. While organic artifacts can be found in certain wetland sites such as in Florida (Dunbar 2016; Webb 2006), the bulk of the evidence available to archaeologists continues to be chipped stone technologies. The chapters in this volume show how archaeologists can derive anthropologically relevant information using these various lithic data sets.

Over the past 50,000 years, the Coastal Plain was in a real sense a stage on which a number of dramatic climatic and environmental changes took place accompanied by distinct human responses to these conditions. Except for the larger rivers that originate in the South Appalachians, no major physical barriers existed over a transect 1,000 km or more north and south to inhibit human interactions. To this end, two major cultural systems, first with the Late Pleistocene Clovis peoples, and later the early Holocene Early Archaic makers of notched points, show considerable cultural continuities and connections over the entire Coastal Plain. Understanding human decision making by past inhabitants throughout prehistory over this dynamic landscape is the ultimate goal of paleoanthropology.

The earliest evidence of human occupation to date would be that of the Topper site along the banks of the Savannah River in South Carolina (Goodyear 2005a). Here, examples of humanly manufactured stone artifacts have been found in Pleistocene deposits dating from about 50,000 to 25,000 radiocarbon years ago. As such, Topper would be the earliest known archaeological site in North America, rivaled only by the famous South American site of Pedra Furada in Brazil with comparably old dates (Boeda et al. 2013; Guidon and Delibrias 1986). In their chapter Goodyear and Sain present the results of recent analyses that have been conducted on the pre-Clovis lithic assemblages of Topper drawing on the master's thesis work of Megan King (2016) and the dissertation of Douglas Sain (Sain 2015). Topper appears to be a non-bifacial, core and flake technology dating prior to the LGM. A number of late glacial pre-Clovis sites dating from 16,000 to 12,000 radiocarbon years have been reported from the eastern seaboard, including Myles Point (Lowery et al. 2010), Cactus Hill (McAvoy and McAvoy 2015), and Page-Ladson (Dunbar 2016; Halligan et al. 2016). These sites are contemporary with before-Clovis sites in western North America (Gilbert et al. 2008; Waters et al. 2011) and South America (Boeda et al. 2013; Dillehay 2000).

In his chapter, Blaine Ensor presents an assemblage of lithic artifacts that are noticeably different from Holocene age stone technology typical of this area of the Southeast. Because they are characterized as relatively thick bifacially shaped discoidal cores, he refers to them as Levallois-like, to emphasize how different they are compared to the usually thinner Holocene age bifaces made in preparation for bifacial projectile points. While not recovered from closed stratigraphic contexts, they are highly weathered, similar to Paleoindian stone tools made from the Coastal Plain cherts so prone to weathering through time (Purdy 1981). Given the growing evidence of pre-Clovis sites in the Americas, it seems prudent to pay attention to such weathered and technologically atypical assemblages, particularly in the event they are excavated in Pleistocene contexts.

When evaluating Pleistocene and early Holocene archaeological deposits on the Coastal Plain, refined excavation techniques and multiple analytic tools are needed. In their presentation of the ongoing work at the famous Old Vero site, C. Andrew Hemmings et al. (2014) illustrate the great care required in excavation for context documentation and the necessary roles of related disciplines such as soil morphology, ^{14}C chemistry, and faunal analysis. While excavations are still in progress, they are getting hints of pre-Clovis-age surfaces with potential human presence. Similarly, the chapter by Christopher Moore and his colleagues provides solid evidence of how the typically shallow sandy sites of the Coastal Plain can be studied with refined excavation methods to yield archaeostratigraphy and chronology with AMS radiocarbon dating and optically stimulated luminescence. They provide examples of stratified Coastal Plain sites buried in alluvium, colluvium, and aeolian deposits such as Carolina bays, and suggest that site burial processes are driven in part by penecontemporaneous hydrological and vegetation changes in response to periods of rapid climate change and ecosystem stress.

Even more challenging is the prospecting for and data recovery from possible Pleistocene-age sites now drowned by sea level rise. It is widely acknowledged that Florida was nearly twice its present size during the lowest sea levels of the LGM. Sea level reconstructions for the last 22,000 years are becoming available (Anderson and Bissett 2015; Harris et al. 2013), allowing prospecting by potential age and depth. The work of Harris et al. (2013) in the South Atlantic region, for example, would suggest that Clovis peoples would have had full access to the continental shelf, with the Atlantic Ocean breaching the shelf sometime after that. The mapping of ancient river channels, bedrock highs, and other formerly subaerial landscape features will hopefully provide specific targets for underwater archaeological surveys. Scott Harris' chapter herein reviews the potential for discovering sites on the South Atlantic shelf and beyond.

When considering the ice age of the Late Pleistocene, it is important to realize that even during the coldest period elsewhere in North America, the lower Southeast was not directly affected by glaciers as was the case farther north. Rather, it is better conceived as a chronological period meaning contemporary with the Wisconsin, the last major period of glaciation. During this time period paleontological and palynological studies have shown that the climate was optimal for a great variety of plants and animals. The Late Pleistocene of the Southeast has been shown to exhibit disharmonious faunas (Lundelius et al. 1983), which included animal species native to the northern latitudes existing alongside more southern subtropical species (Webb 1981a). Likewise, a Late Pleistocene forest type described by Watts (1980) as cool, mesic, broadleaf hardwoods has been referred to as "no analogue," expressing its uniqueness to the period from 16,000 to 10,000 years ago. These phenomena have been brought together under the rubric of what Russell et al. (2009) refer to as a warm thermal enclave. They hypothesize that the Gulf Stream flowing close to the coasts of the Gulf of Mexico and the Atlantic Ocean thermally subsidized the Southeast, creating a more temperate climate. They argue that this enclave was in existence during the entire Rancholabrean period, for several thousand years before the LGM. Thus, these optimal climatic conditions prevailing for tens of thousands of years created highly desirable environments for early humans colonizing this part of North America. For the purposes of archaeology in searching for early Paleoamericans, the Southeast should have an exceptionally high potential for early human occupation and, hopefully, site discovery.

The end of the Late Pleistocene is marked by a dramatic reversion to ice age temperatures known as the Younger Dryas. At a time when the world was warming and glaciers melting, this reversion came on very suddenly in geological time scales (Alley 2000). Compared to previous stadials, it is almost freakish, considering how rapidly it occurred and compared to later Heinrich events. Two chapters (LeCompte and others and Kennett and others) deal with what is termed the Younger Dryas Boundary (YDB) with reference to an extraterrestrial impact or the YDB impact hypothesis and the potential effects on fauna, including human life. A Bayesian chronological analysis shows that from 23 stratigraphic sections and 354 dates from 12 countries, a remarkable synchronicity exists with the event with a modeled YDB age range of 12,835–12,735 cal B.P. at 95 percent probability (Kennett et al. 2015). This time frame would be contemporary with Clovis people, who disappeared from the archaeological record about this time, as well as mammoths and mastodons. The demise of Clovis culture and the extinction of the last of the Pleistocene megafauna have long posed a mystery to paleontologists and archaeologists alike. While they are still controversial to some, a variety of other independent researchers at different sites continue to find the diagnostic impact markers at that boundary. To these can be added recent evidence for a widespread platinum (Pt) anomaly at the Younger Dryas onset across the North American continent (Moore et al.

2017). The controversy surrounding such a dramatic event will no doubt continue in the near future. One comprehensive study of the frequency of post-Clovis projectile points for the Southeast has identified a sharp drop in points as well as radiocarbon dates (Anderson et al. 2011), suggesting some kind of demographic reorganization and/or collapse.

In Smallwood and others' chapter, treatment is given to the traditional Paleoindian cultures using projectile point data collected from South Carolina. With Clovis as a point of departure, then moving through time with non-Clovis and presumably post-Clovis projectile points, and ending with Dalton conceived as the end of the Paleoindian lanceolates, significant differences can be seen in raw material selection and landscape usage over some 1,500 years. The role of sea level rise is considered, as it would have removed much of the lower Coastal Plain, with its prime biotic resources. Clovis is seen as focusing on the Coastal Plain with their distinctive use of Coastal Plain cherts as recognized from the extensive work done at the quarry-related sites of Topper and Big Pine Tree (Goodyear 1999; Smallwood 2010; Smallwood et al. 2013). A parallel study for the state of Georgia (Smallwood et al. 2015) revealed a similar pattern for Clovis. The Clovis use of the Coastal Plain, while not exclusively so, has been summarized as the Allendale–Brier Creek Clovis Complex (Goodyear 2018), providing some insights into their stone tool technologies and settlement systems beyond just points.

The use of raw material types and the plotting of degree of usage through time is coming of age in much of the Southeastern Coastal Plain. The landmark work of Sam Upchurch (Upchurch et al. 1982a) for Florida cherts, organized by the concept of quarry clusters throughout that state, has been updated in recent years as presented by Robert Austin and others in their chapter. The similarly conceived work of Upchurch in the central Savannah River region of the Allendale County, South Carolina, chert quarries and the adjacent counties in southeastern Georgia (Upchurch 1984b), has provided a baseline petrologic study of the northern extension of these Tertiary-age marine cherts which begin south of Tampa Bay. The work of Daniel and Butler (1996) in the Uwharrie Mountain sources of North Carolina with the various metavolcanic tool stones, updated by Steponaitis et al. (2006), provide more geographic information on the sources and dispersion of time sensitive tools so critical to mapping foraging ranges through time.

Three chapters examine the Early Archaic of the Coastal Plain with data sets spanning from Florida to South Carolina. The chapters by David

Thulman and Kara Bridgman Sweeney look at notched points on the basis of haft attributes over space rather than just by traditional cultural historic types. Thulman finds significant patterning using geometric morphometrics, which is concerned with shapes rather than size and angle measurements. He emphasizes that craft production takes place in social contexts, which should result in discernible patterning amongst hafted bifaces. Using this new methodology, he is able to detect what he regards as socially produced patterning in Bolen points from adjacent river valleys in Florida. Bridgman Sweeney takes a geographically broad perspective based on her dissertation work (Bridgman Sweeney 2013), using data from a transect up the Coastal Plain from Tampa Bay to the southern Coastal Plain of South Carolina. She reworks her dissertation data using social network analysis theory, revealing what may be numerous overlapping scales of interaction. Her concept of "Bandscapes" is provocative, in that it explicitly brings into focus the social reality of multiple contemporary human groups as part of the "environment," rather than just the natural environment in the more ecological sense. The chapter by Wilkinson looks at the Early Archaic at yet another scale: that of the nature of sites located in the extensive inter-riverine zones between the major rivers such as the Savannah and the Santee. Previous formulations of the Early Archaic in the South Atlantic Slope area, such as that of Anderson and Hanson (1988), concentrated on settlement analysis and ultimately bands and macrobands centered around habitation sites on the major rivers. Unlike previous analyses, Wilkinson's analysis utilizes Early Archaic stone tools besides just points and provides our first insights into activities in the inter-riverine zones. He takes advantage of progress now realized in lithic raw material types and sources for this part of South Carolina, revealing significant patterning in local versus exotic types, which has implications for possible band interactions.

The final chapters, by David Anderson and Joe Schuldenrein, are valuable contributions to the volume based on their nearly 40 years of work in the Southeast in both Paleoindian and Early Archaic archaeology. This includes surveys and excavations of important sites such as those in the Savannah River basin and beyond with their early use of geoarchaeological approaches to site discovery and environmental reconstruction. Anderson was a pioneer in synthesizing Paleoindian and Early Archaic archaeology in the Southeast (Anderson and Sassaman 1996), which he continues to this day (Anderson and Sassaman 2012). Schuldenrein in his chapter reviews the progress of geoarchaeology from his work in the Southeast and the East as well as from an Old World perspective. Both of these chapters should have a beneficial effect as archaeologists continue to probe into the often rare and at times ephemeral sites that could be described as early human archaeology.

The research conducted for these chapters spans a period of over 50 years, with some projects still under way. In the ensuing decades, major changes have been realized, ranging from the discovery of pre-Clovis sites to the application of optically stimulated luminescence dating of sandy sediments often bereft of charcoal for radiocarbon dating. Enough statewide Paleoindian point databases are now available to begin reconstructing settlement systems, and coupled with the identification of lithic raw materials and their sources, they are enabling the mapping of foraging ranges and possible evidence for exchange. The increasing capability of offshore surveying technology is giving rise to the expectation that archaeologists and marine geologists alike will soon be finding prehistoric sites now inundated on the continental shelf. Other major issues, such as the sudden demise of the Clovis technoculture and the Pleistocene megafauna, along with the recognition of the mysterious "Middle Paleoindian" period, should indicate that more fascinating research developments are on the way. Hopefully, this volume will provide some consolidation of knowledge gained thus far and serve as a point of departure to guide future inquiry.

2

THE PRE-CLOVIS OCCUPATION OF THE TOPPER SITE, ALLENDALE COUNTY, SOUTH CAROLINA

ALBERT C. GOODYEAR AND DOUGLAS A. SAIN

The Topper site is a multicomponent prehistoric site located on the east bank of the Savannah River in Allendale County, South Carolina. The site is composed of an alluvial terrace bordered on the west by a chute channel of the Savannah River and the upland of the Coastal Plain (Figure 2.1). The upland, which slopes down to the terrace, has also been referred to as the Hillside or Hilltop by the various investigators. A bed of high-quality chert known as Allendale Coastal Plain chert is exposed at the base of the uplands, which was extensively quarried during pre-Clovis, Clovis, and later Holocene times. This chert, in its terrestrial exposure and in the bottom of the adjacent Savannah River (Goodyear and Charles 1984), was the primary resource that drew people to the site for several millennia.

Archaeological excavations have taken place at Topper every year since 1998, when the first evidence of pre-Clovis artifacts was discovered. Extensive geological fieldwork was conducted from 1999 to 2004, primarily in the terrace portion of the site, to determine its stratigraphy and age (Waters et al. 2009). Based on the negative results of test excavations on the Hillside, the pre-Clovis occupation is thus far restricted to the terrace portion of the site (Goodyear 2005a; Sain 2015). Clovis has been identified both on the terrace (Goodyear and Steffy 2003) and on the Hillside (Goodyear et al. 2007; Miller 2010; Sain 2011; Smallwood 2010; Smallwood et al. 2013). Approximately 130 contiguous square meters have been hand excavated in the pre-Clovis Pleistocene-age sediments. Altogether some 860 m^2 of Clovis-age deposits on both the terrace and Hillside (Figure 2.2) have been excavated, and the stratigraphic occurrence of Clovis-age material throughout the site has been well documented.

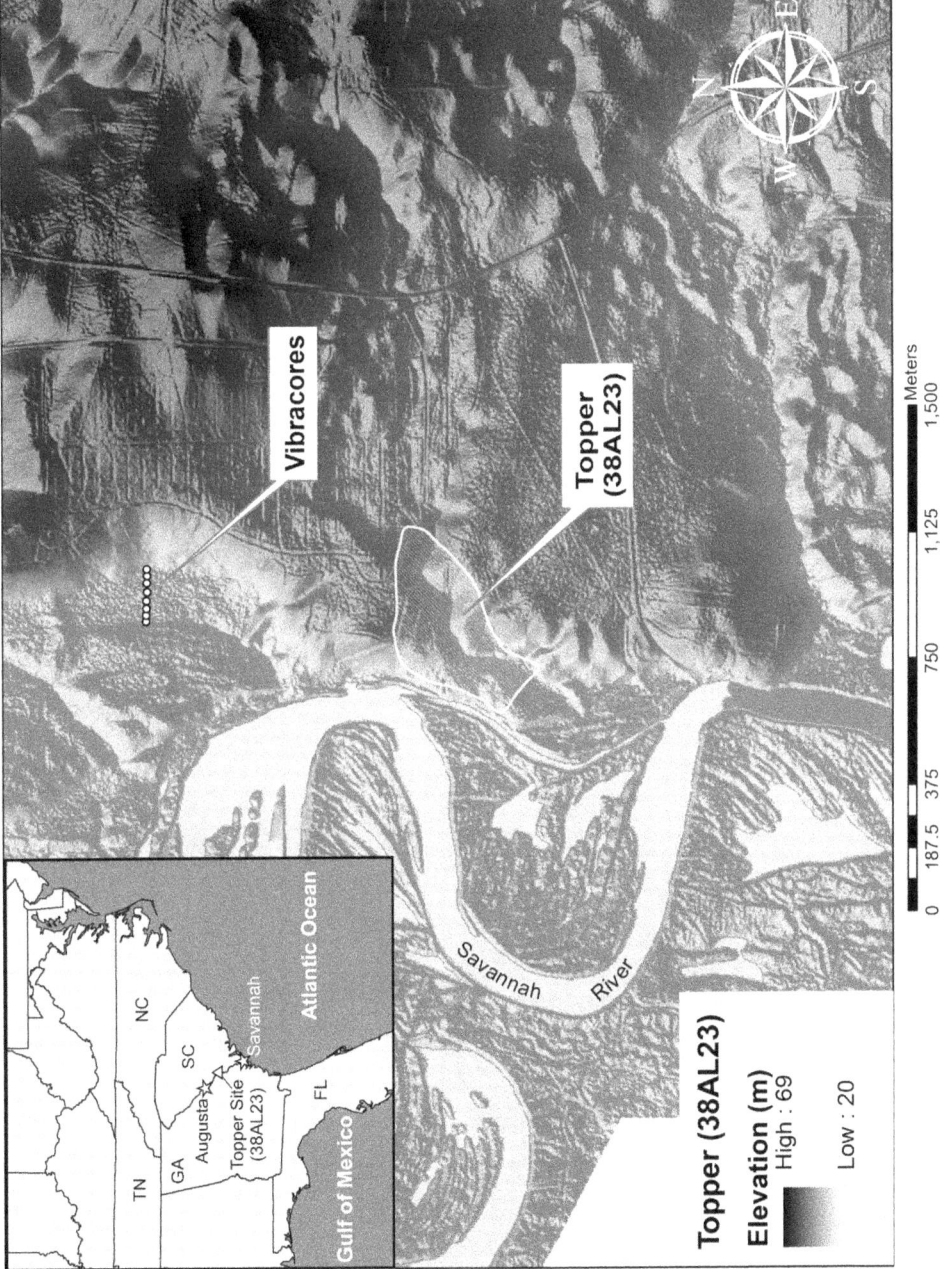

Figure 2.1. Digital elevation map of Topper site and immediate environs, including vibracores (courtesy of Christopher R. Moore).

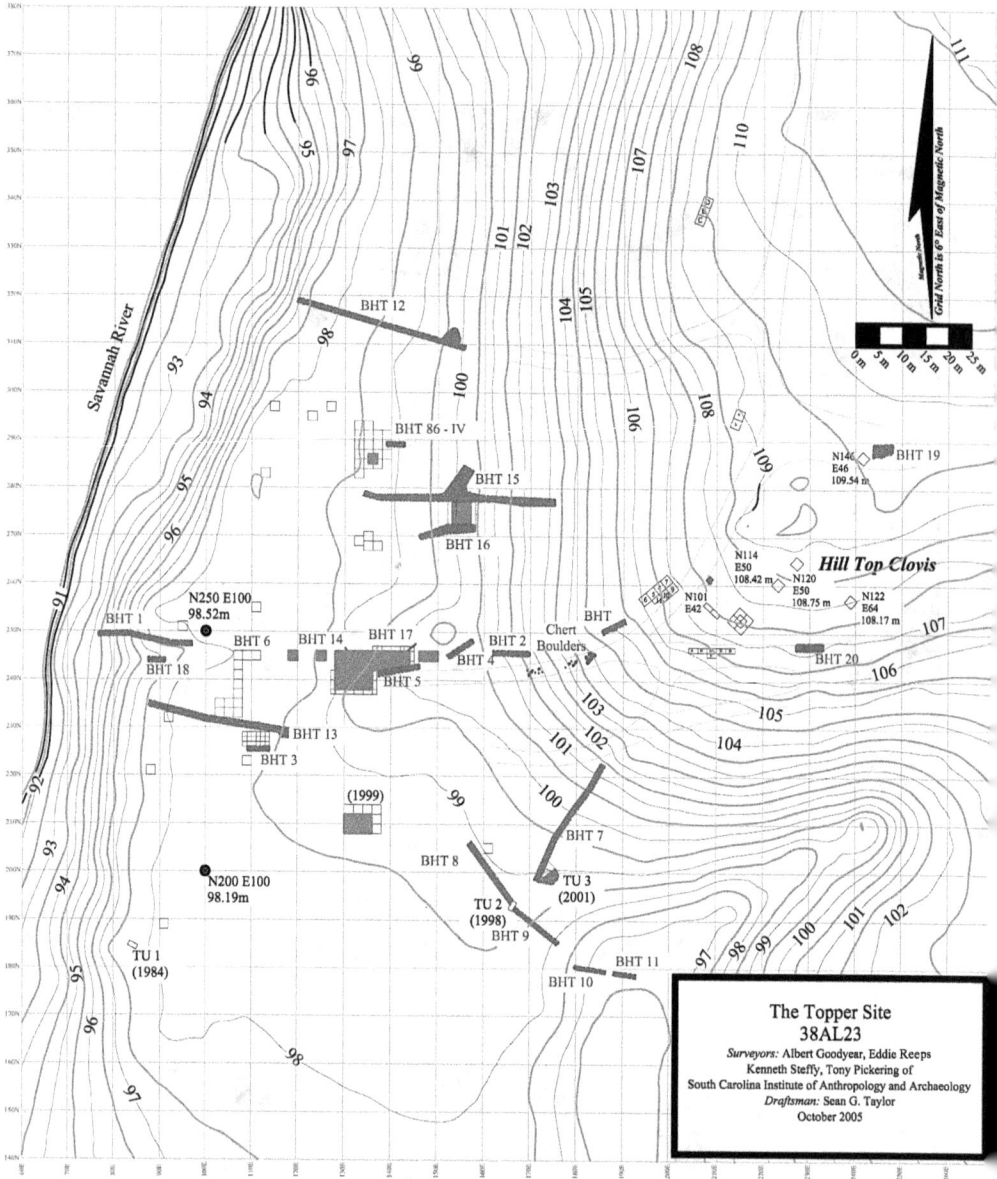

Figure 2.2. Site map of Topper showing topography and excavation units on the terrace and hillside.

On the terrace the geological layers bearing artifacts are well known, based on the work of a team of geoscientists (Goodyear 2005a:Figure 7; Waters et al. 2009). The upper layer from the ground surface down to about 1.0 m consists of colluvium eroding off the adjacent hillside (Figure 2.3). A nearly complete Holocene archaeological sequence from Mississippian to Clovis is present in proper order. From 1.0 to 2.0 m is a zone of white Pleistocene alluvial sands, which has produced abundant pre-Clovis artifacts. From 2.0 m to at least 4.0 m below the surface exists the Pleistocene alluvial terrace, which also produces artifacts similar to those of the zone above. Radiocarbon dates for this unit are ca. 50,000 years old or greater (Figure 2.3).

The Stratigraphic Position of Clovis on the Terrace

The stratigraphic position of Clovis on the terrace has been established in the base of the colluvium. On the northern end of the site, as seen in the profile of backhoe trench 15 (Figure 2.2), Clovis artifacts related to an extensive industrial floor can be seen as a line at the bottom of the colluvium (Figure 2.4; Goodyear 2005b:Figures 1–3). Below this was a reddish-brown Bw soil horizon, 3a, in the geologist's nomenclature (Waters et al. 2009:1304), which was sterile of artifacts. In this area of the site, this soil separates the Holocene-age colluvium from the white Pleistocene sands. In the pre-Clovis excavation block around backhoe trench 17 (Figure 2.2), an optically stimulated luminescence (*OSL*) date of 13,200 ± 1300 B.P. was obtained for the Clovis zone. Also in a block excavation immediately north of BHT 15 (Figure 2.2), another Clovis-age OSL date of 13,000 ± 900 B.P. was obtained above a buried Clovis artifact layer (Waters et al. 2009). Within the Hillside excavations, an AMS radiocarbon date of 10,958 ± 65 B.P. was obtained within a dense floor of Clovis lithics (Anderson et al. 2016; Goodyear 2013). Clovis point preforms are found throughout the terrace area at the bottom of the Holocene archaeological sequence, as are three Clovis points found in situ (Goodyear and Steffy 2003; Smallwood 2010). Clovis macroblades are also present throughout the site (Sain 2011; Sain and Goodyear 2012).

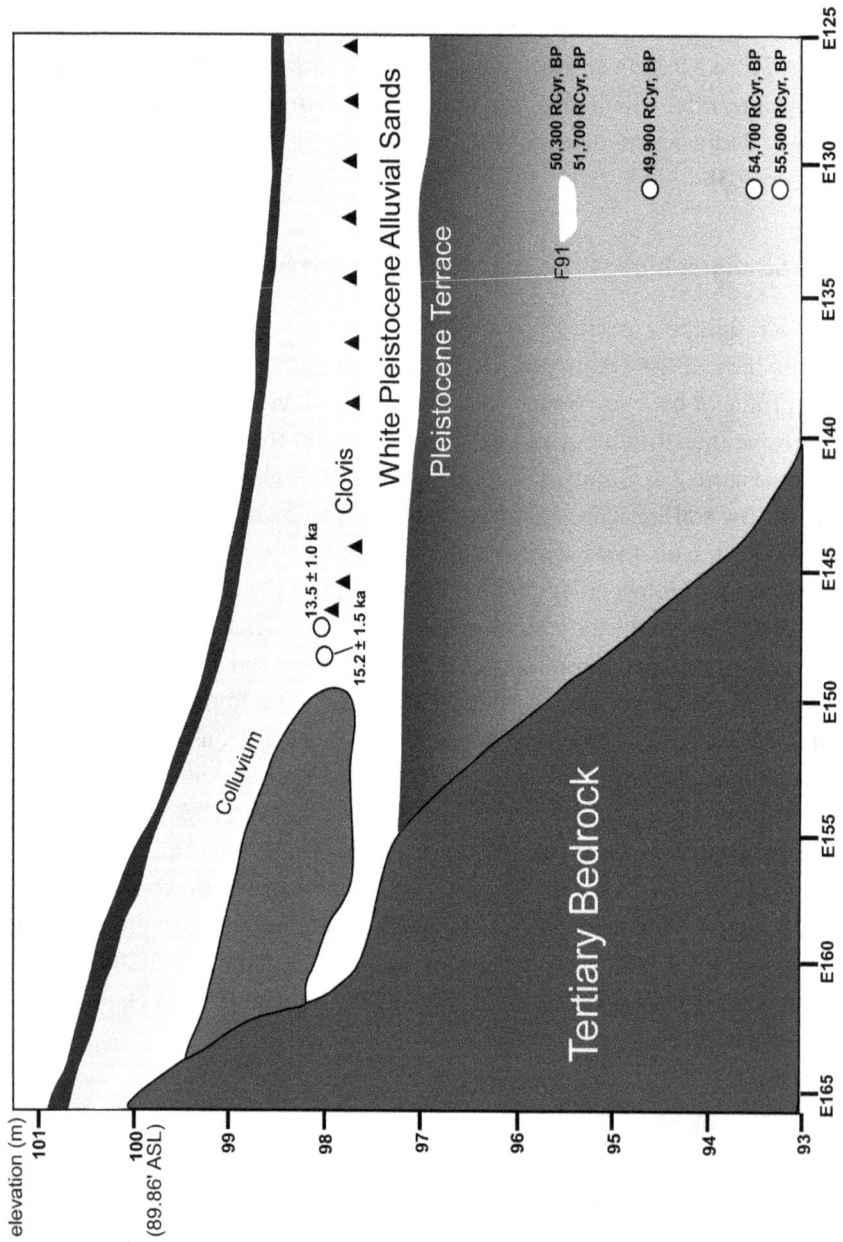

Figure 2.3. Schematic profile of terrace stratigraphy at Topper (after Goodyear 2005a).

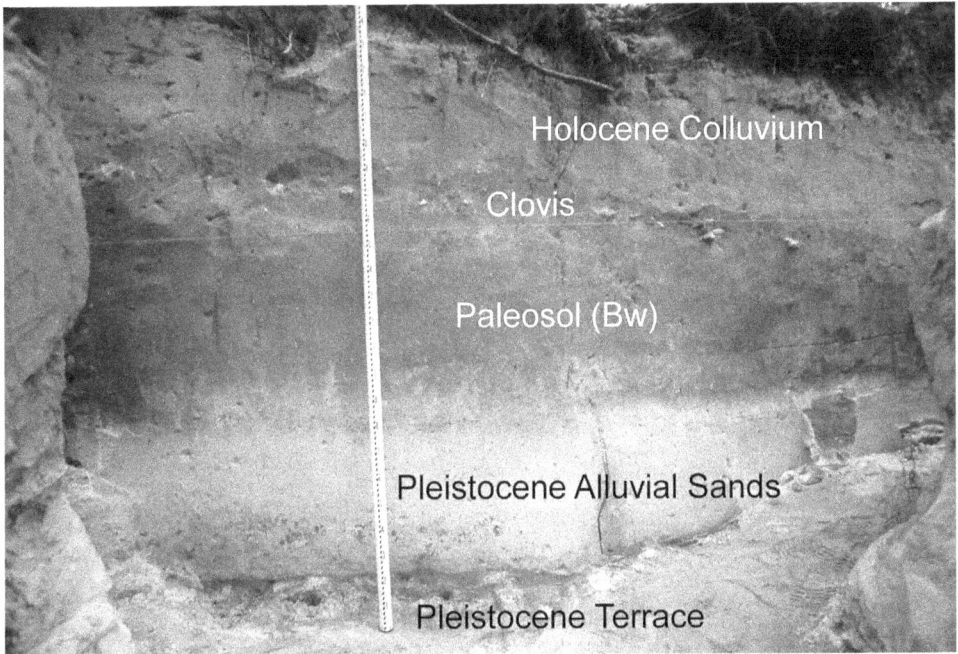

Figure 2.4. Photograph of complete stratigraphic profile exposed in BHT 15 from surface to the top of the Pleistocene terrace at the Topper site.

The Pre-Clovis Lithic Assemblage in the White Pleistocene Alluvial Sands

The initial discovery of lithic artifacts below the Clovis level occurred in 1998 (Goodyear 2005a); they were located within the white Pleistocene alluvial sands (WPAS) (Figure 2.3). These sands were deposited by the ice age Savannah River when it flowed at higher elevations than today, known as the second terrace (T2). These sediments are characterized by coarse sands and small pebbles probably related to a braided stream regime (Waters et al. 2009:1304), known for the late Pleistocene rivers of the Atlantic Coastal Plain region (Leigh 2008; Leigh et al. 2004). The stratigraphic break between the colluvium originating from the Hillside and the alluvial sands, while visually indistinct, is fairly evident, as revealed by textural analysis (Figure 2.5; Harris et al. 2010). These sands are designated as Unit 2b in the geology study (Waters et al. 2009:Figure 2).

The artifacts in the WPAS represent an assemblage characterized by small flake tools such as side and end scrapers, spokeshaves, utilized flakes,

Profile Photo

Sediment Analyses

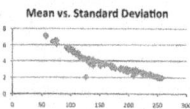

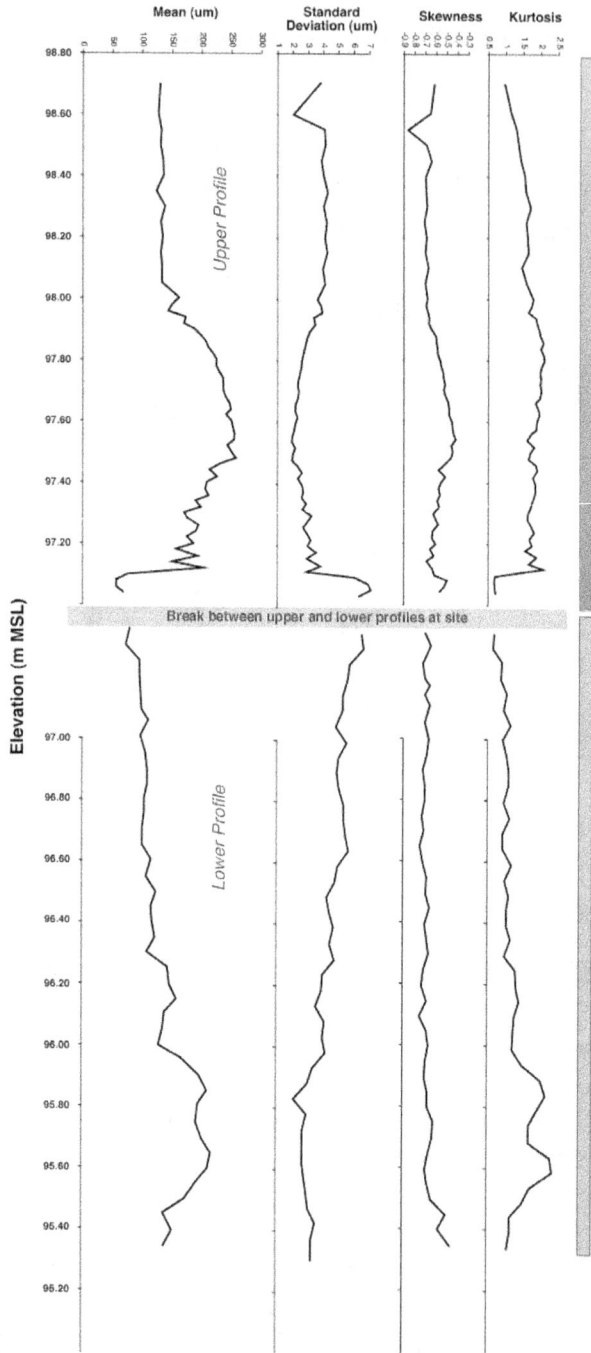

Figure 2.5. Particle size analysis from surface through the Pleistocene terrace: *top profile*, Holocene through Pleistocene sands to top of Pleistocene terrace; *bottom profile*, top of Pleistocene terrace down to top of Unit 1a of Waters et al. (2009) (from Harris et al. 2010).

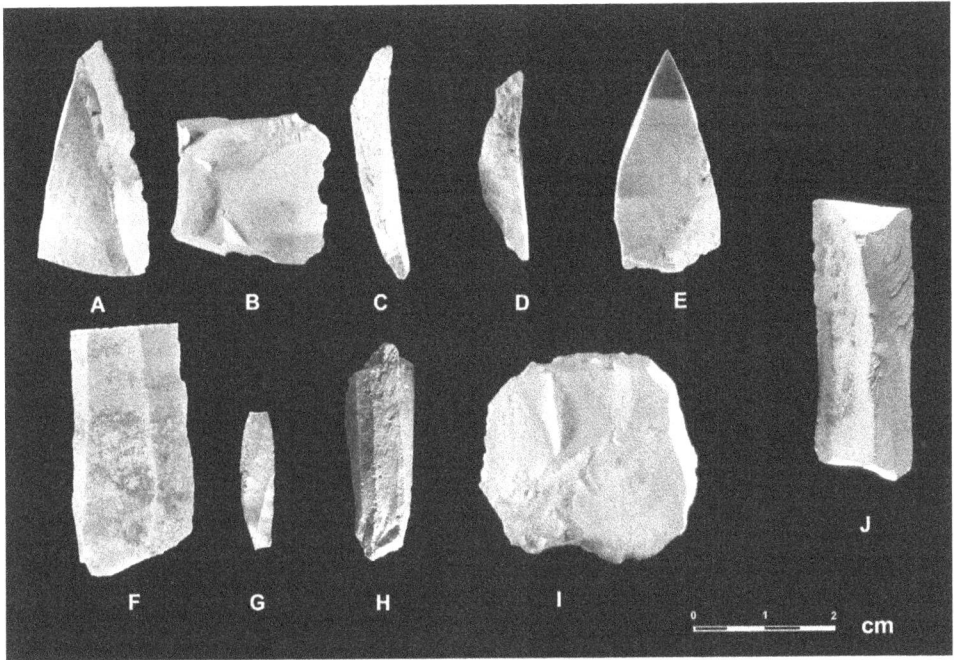

Figure 2.6. Pre-Clovis lithic artifacts from the white Pleistocene alluvial sands: *A*, *B*, *E*, bend-break tools; *C*, *D*, bend-break spalls; *F*, *G*, blades; *H*, probable bipolar core; *I*, scraper; *J*, bladelike tool (SCIAA photo by Daryl P. Miller).

gravers, prismatic blades, and bend-breaks (Figure 2.6), and by larger artifacts such as cores, choppers, and planes. A summary of tools and lithic debris from the WPAS and the Pleistocene terrace beneath are provided in Tables 2.1 and 2.2 as summarized from Sain (2015). Because of their relatively small size, the flake tools have been described as microlithic (Goodyear 2005a). The most common artifact is a bend-break piece, which number in the hundreds (Goodyear 2005a; Sain 2015). A bend-break is a flake modified by breaking or snapping yielding fractures formed by tension and compression versus a Hertzian cone (Cotterell and Kamminga 1987; Wiederhold and Pevny 2013). They are also known as pseudo-burins for the chisel-like corners where two broken edges meet. They have been recognized in Clovis (McAvoy and McAvoy 1997; Ferring 2001), Folsom (Root et al. 1999), and pre-Clovis sites (Waters et al. 2011; Wiederhold and Pevny 2013).

In identifying early human lithic artifacts, especially in assemblages without highly formalized artifacts such as bifaces and prismatic blades, issues concerning the possible role of nature in creating pseudo-artifacts

Table 2.1. Stone Tools and Debitage Found in situ by Stratigraphic Units

	Core Tools	Biface Tools	Flake Tools	Bend-Breaks	Debitage	Split Quartz	Total
Clovis	48	75	79	8	172	12	394
Pleistocene sands	109	3[a]	188	39	562	42	943
Pleistocene terrace	64	0	255	236	2,245	436	3,236
Total	221	78	522	283	2,979	490	4,573

[a]One artifact is a biface from the upper WPAS that may indicate a Late Glacial occupation. Two small basal portions were found in deeper WPAS and may represent intrusions.

Table 2.2. Debitage and Lithic Debris Found in Excavation Levels

	Complete Flakes	Broken Flakes	Flake Fragments	Debris	Amorphous Debris	Total
Clovis (64 m² area)	4,538	1,842	2,143	2,305	810	11,638
Pleistocene sands (64 m² area)	5,248	4,954	12,278	11,261	8,743	42,484
Pleistocene terrace (14 m² area)	1,047	647	3,254	4,862	6,142	15,952
Total	10,833	7,443	17,675	18,428	15,695	70,074

must be considered. Given proper agencies, nature can beak siliceous materials in ways that sometimes can mimic simple human implements. The geologists, who were unfamiliar with bipolar, core, and flake technologies, suggested that the "Topper assemblage," as it was neutrally referred to, may have been produced by agencies such as forest fires, freezing and thawing, and stream transport (Waters et al. 2009:1304, 1309). In the case of Topper, natural agencies have been examined to determine their possible effect, if any.

Regarding stream transport, excavations were conducted into the WPAS in the northern part of the terrace, which would have been the upstream portion of the site. The chert cobbles and cortical debris such as seen in dense concentrations in the main excavation block were not present. It is evident that the source of the chert cobbles is coming from bedrock deposits observable on the hillslope immediately to the east of the main excavation block (Figure 2.2). In the excavation block area, lenticular lenses of gravels some 50 to 140 cm wide and 5 to 30 cm in depth were noted (Waters et al. 2009:1304). During excavation it could be seen that gravels, pieces of cortex, and flakes were entrained in these shallow channels. It is likely that some artifacts and pieces of cortex were transported a few meters by stream flow. The edges of retouched flake tools and debitage are sharp and not stream abraded or rolled, indicating minimal movement within the deposit. The energy of stream flow also seems minimal, as the cobble clusters found in the lower portion of the WPAS in many cases were not disturbed, with items arranged in small piles, with items still stacked upon one another (Figure 2.7). The cobbles in these clusters were found on common surfaces and not in depressions or potholes as from stream flow.

As for chert nodules rolling down the hillslope and fracturing into "artifacts," there are many factors that render this improbable. The present slope from the exposed bedrock to the present ground surface at the closest terrace area (Figure 2.2) is not steep, with a total drop in elevation of 6 m, from 105.5 m to 99.50 m over a 35-m distance, or about 17 percent. Below that, down 2.5 m to the top of the Pleistocene terrace at the same location would be about 97.00 m, or 8.5 m, or about 24 percent. From the bedrock out 55 m to the terrace at ground surface at 98.50 m, the drop is 7 m, or 12.7 percent. At the same location to the top of the Pleistocene terrace at 96.50 m is 9 m, or about 16 percent. The natural shape of the nodules is not spherical but oblong and flattish, and not conducive to rolling. The weathered cortex of the nodules is rough-textured limestone, providing friction with the sandy substrate. Repeated examination of the insides of nodules has not indicated any flaws such as cracks or variability in silicification that would create natural tendencies of breakage.

Contemporary attempts to break open the natural chert nodules have shown that it can be done only with highly concentrated force. Hurling nodules against each other usually did not result in cracking them open but merely bruised the thick, tough cortex. As shown by replication, cortex-on-cortex percussion has a strong tendency to cushion and diffuse the energy. The Topper assemblage was replicated by Scott Jones and Steve Watts (Jones 2002) without a hammer stone by first placing a nodule on a larger boulder and repeatedly smashing it with another boulder size nodule to break it open. From there they were able to take bipolar and anvil-struck flakes and create the flake tool forms. In another experiment to break open chert nodules, cobbles and boulders were recovered from nearby Smiths Lake Creek in the Savannah River floodplain to evaluate the quality of silicification. Repeated blows with an eight-pound sledgehammer were necessary to break them open. The relevant question here is not how nature could have broken open the nodules but how humans were able to do so.

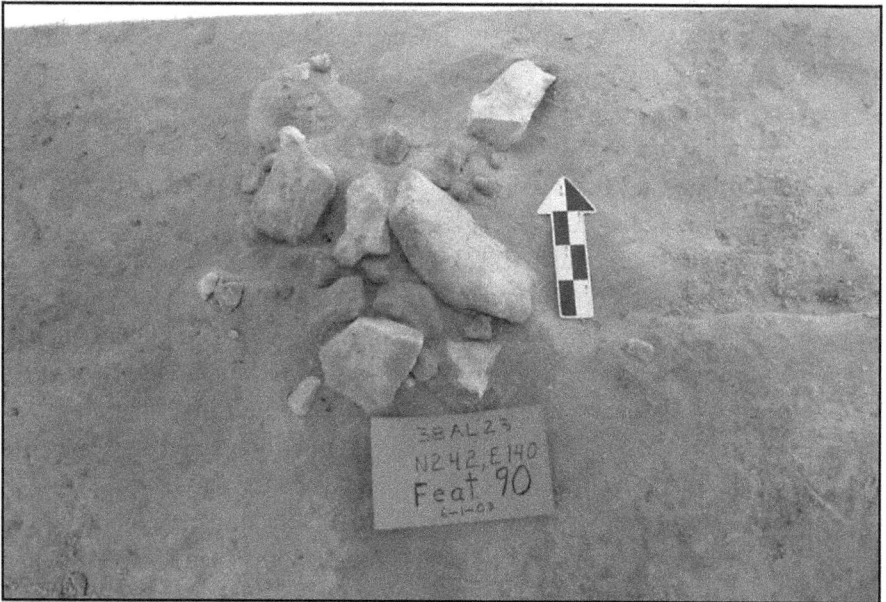

Figure 2.7. Examples of chert clusters in the white Pleistocene alluvial sands from Topper: *top*, Feature 61; *bottom*, Feature 90.

Table 2.3. Analysis of Pre-Clovis Cobble and Boulder-Size Cores, Core Tools, and Nodules

Category	Frequency	Percentage	Thermal Alteration	
			Definitive	Possible
Core	119	52.89	1	7
Core fragment	8	3.56	0	0
Core-chopper	28	12.44	0	0
Core-tool	3	1.33	0	0
Retouched				
Tested	41	18.22	0	0
Nodule	26	11.56	0	0
Totals	225	99.9	1	7

Notes: 88.46% are modified.
3.56% or less thermally altered. No indication of thermal fracture.

A study of 225 cobble- and boulder-size nodules and artifacts drawn from both the WPAS and the Pleistocene terrace revealed that nearly 90 percent of them have some flake removals (Goodyear et al. 2013). The most common category was core and core fragments, defined as having three or more detachments, with 127 examples, or about 56 percent (Table 2.3). Some had unifacial and bifacial retouch, indicating modification for tools. It should be noted that of the 225 cobbles and boulders examined, only one had evidence of thermal alteration, with another possible seven, thus eliminating fire as an agency of fracture for the nodules. The detachment scars show strong force lines and hinge terminations indicative of percussion flaking. Cores typically do not exhibit negative bulbs resulting from hard hammer percussion, and no hammer stones of sufficient size have been found in the assemblage. Small (< 6 cm) quartz pebbles are a natural part of the alluvium that do not have sufficient mass to break the cobbles. Sain (2015) conducted freezing and thawing experiments using local Allendale Coastal Plain chert and found that such mechanical weathering processes are unlikely to produce detachments with lithic attributes characteristic of conchoidal or bend fractures.

The archaeostratigraphy of the pre-Clovis deposit in the WPAS is apparent from back plotting (Figure 2.8). A separate deposit can be seen predominantly in the lower 50 cm of the alluvium. Within this zone are found the chert cobble clusters (cf. Figure 2.7), concentrations of large pieces of cortex and chert that in some cases still have items stacked on top of one

Mapped Artifacts from Ground Surface to Top of Alluvial Terrace

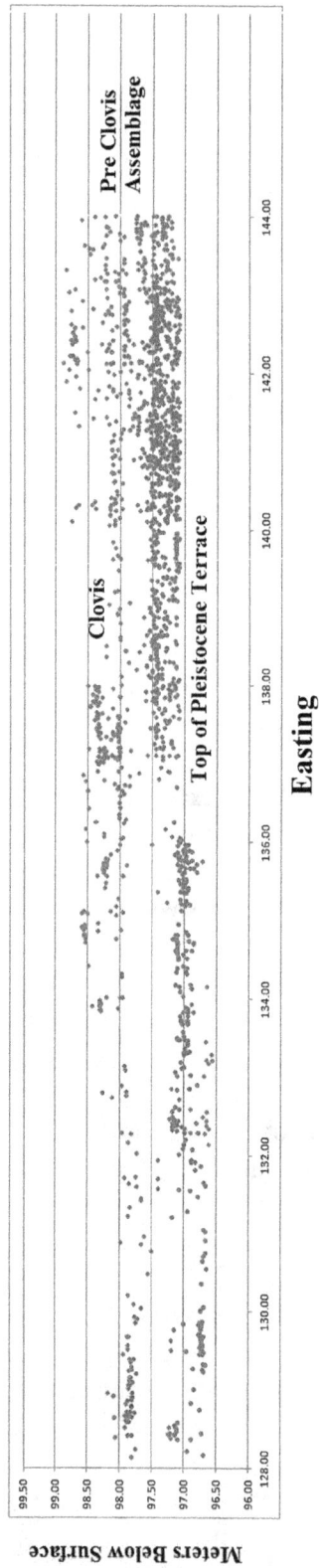

Figure 2.8. Backplot of artifacts showing Clovis zone and pre-Clovis zone with chert clusters.

Figure 2.9. Photograph of systematic retouch on pre-Clovis scraper-plane from the white Pleistocene alluvial sands.

another. While regarded as of human creation, their purpose is not known. Although fluvial disturbances are present in the WPAS, these cobble clusters indicate some original occupational surfaces, indicating that human occupation took place within this zone and that the cobbles were not re-deposited from somewhere else. Flakes with striking platforms and bulbs of force are common in the deposit (King 2016; Goodyear et al. 2013; Sain 2015), resulting from retouching flake tools and core choppers and planes. Compared to Archaic and Clovis age flakes from above, these flakes tend to be small, a result of retouching flake and core tools rather than reducing cores. The larger of these flakes (2 to 3 cm in length) are from retouching choppers and planes such as the scraper-plane illustrated in Figure 2.9.

The question of artifacts being donated from the Clovis zone above has been dealt with by examining the condition of cherts represented in each deposit (Sain 2015). Starting at least by Clovis times and continuing through the Holocene, prehistoric occupants of Topper had access to the chert cobbles found in the bottom of the Savannah River today. The river cut down into its meandering period at least, by Clovis times if not a few thousand years earlier (Waters et al. 2009:1308). The chert nodules found in the river are typically water worn and have a dark stain from tannin in the water. As much as 9.5 percent of the debitage from the Clovis layer has the characteristic river cortex and stain (Sain 2015), the same percentage Small-wood (2015:76) obtained for Clovis on the Hillside. The chert sources in the pre-Clovis deposits are from the terrestrial bedrock outcrops observed at the escarpment (Goodyear and Charles 1984; Goodyear et al. 2013). Chert nodules from the uplands are characterized by thick, chemically weathered cortical surfaces from being in the atmosphere for tens of thousands of years. A few tiny river cortex flakes are found at the contact of the Clovis zone and the top of the WPAS. River cortex debitage is not found in the bottom 60 cm of the WPAS, which is the primary deposit of the pre-Clovis (Figure 2.8). Thus, if the relatively numerous flakes with river cortex are not moving down into the WPAS, it is highly unlikely that later finished tools were moving either.

Last, the refitting work of Derek Anderson on both the terrace (Ander-son 2011) and the Hillside (Anderson 2018; Anderson et al. 2016) has shown minimal vertical movement of Clovis artifacts. Refitting analysis in a 4-×-4-m unit immediately north of the main excavation block on the terrace showed that refitted items were conjoined in less than an average of 5 cm vertically (Anderson 2011). Whether on the terrace or Hillside, excavations have shown that when the Clovis layer of tools and debitage ends, there are only a few small flakes a few centimeters below that zone, resulting no doubt from bioturbation. The Clovis lithic floors regardless of where found on the Topper site are remarkably stable horizontally and vertically (Figure 2.4; Anderson et al. 2016; Miller 2010; Smallwood 2015).

Direct dating of the WPAS has proven problematic. Charcoal for radio-carbon dating has not been recovered. The two OSL dates of 14,400 ± 1200 yr B.P. (UIC763) and 15,200 ± 1500 yr B.P. (UIC764) were taken from the top of the alluvium (Waters et al. 2009:1308) and may have had some col-luvium mixed in. In their interpretation of the stratigraphy, the geologists concluded that these two dates represent a provisional minimum age for the Pre-Clovis material below. OSL samples taken in the artifact-producing zone of the WPAS were nonfinite and incalculable. These resulted in dates of < 37,200 (UIC695) and >37,200 (UIC781) (Waters 2009 et al.:Table 2, Figure 5c). All of the OSL dating was done using the single-aliquot method (Waters et al. 2009). However, dating of the sandy alluvium was provided by another team of geologists about 1,000 m up the tread of the Pleisto-cene Savannah River with a series of vibracores cross sectioning the T2 channel (Figure 2.1). They correlated the alluvium there with the Topper stratigraphy (Karabanov et al. 2002). They also obtained ^{14}C dates of 25,330 ± 130 B.P., 34, 210 ± 370 B.P., and 37,810 ± 570 B.P., providing an estimate of the age for the WPAS between about 25,000 and 38,000 RCYBP.

The Pre-Clovis Artifacts in the Pleistocene Terrace

Immediately below the WPAS is what we have called the Pleistocene terrace (Figure 2.3), also designated unit 1b by the geologists (Waters et al. 2009:Figure 4). This artifact-bearing zone sits unconformably at the contact of the alluvial sands, having been scoured by the latter. The color and textural change is dramatic, and because of the fine sediments, it is also referred to as muds (Harris et al. 2010). The Pleistocene terrace represents a meander condition of the Savannah River like that of the present with overbank deposition and creation of back swamps. Compared to the point bar sediments in the WPAS, there is much lower energy represented in flood deposition (Harris et al. 2010). The top of this terrace has two argillic paleosols (Btb1 and Btb2) present (West 2004), with the upper soil truncated by erosion. The upper 2.0 m of the terrace exhibits a clear fining-up sequence as part of terrace building (Figure 2.5), capped by a period of landform stability culminating with pedogenesis (Harris et al. 2010; Waters et al. 2009). Artifacts like those in the WPAS are found throughout the upper 2.0 meters of the terrace. Two infinite ^{14}C dates were obtained about 2.0 m down in the terrace from F91 dating at least 50,000 RCYBP (Figure 2.3; Waters et al. 2009:Figure 4).

The age of the Pleistocene terrace is not constrained by radiocarbon or OSL dating. The two dates mentioned above are minimal ages and could be older. No charcoal suitable for dating was observed in the terrace until the concentrated lens of carbonized plant remains was found in what was designated Feature 91 (Figure 2.3). This charcoal is considered humified plant remains (Waters et al. 2009:Table 1) and not a result of fire. Micromorphological analysis of the enclosing sediment yielded no evidence of thermal alteration typical of hearths (Sherwood and Goldberg 2006). Thus, it represents a date of the sediments at that depth. Two radiocarbon dates on humic acids obtained from alluvial sediments in BHT 1 closer to the river (Figure 2.2) dated 19,280 ± 140 RCYRBP and 20,860 ± 90 RCYRBP (Waters et al. 2009:Table 1). These samples were taken from deposits that are lower than the top of the Pleistocene terrace and lap onto the terrace. As such, they represent minimal ages for the terrace. The dates from the vibracores farther up the paleo river channel, however, would also indicate they are

Figure 2.10. Large boulder used as anvil in the top of the Pleistocene terrace.

too young to date the terrace. In all likelihood the entire terrace is beyond radiocarbon dating. The 2 m above the F91 dates to the terrace top could have been deposited within a few thousand years or less. Holocene alluvial sections in the Piedmont portion of the Savannah River under meander conditions deposited up to 6 m at Gregg Shoals in about 12,000 years. Farther downstream, near Augusta, up to 4.0 m accumulated in about 10,000 years at Rae's Creek (Goodyear 1999:453, 455).

Because of the evident erosional contact of the terrace and WPAS, it is highly likely that some artifacts from the terrace have been donated to the sands as lag deposits. An illustration of this situation can be seen in Figure 2.10, where a large chert boulder used as an anvil is partially exposed in the terrace with several definitive artifacts associated (Figure 2.11). The anvil and the artifacts are discolored gray from being housed in the dark gray moist terrace. Artifacts in the WPAS are typically light colored from weathering and being in well-drained sands. Some of these may have originally been stained from being in the terrace but have been bleached in the oxidized sands.

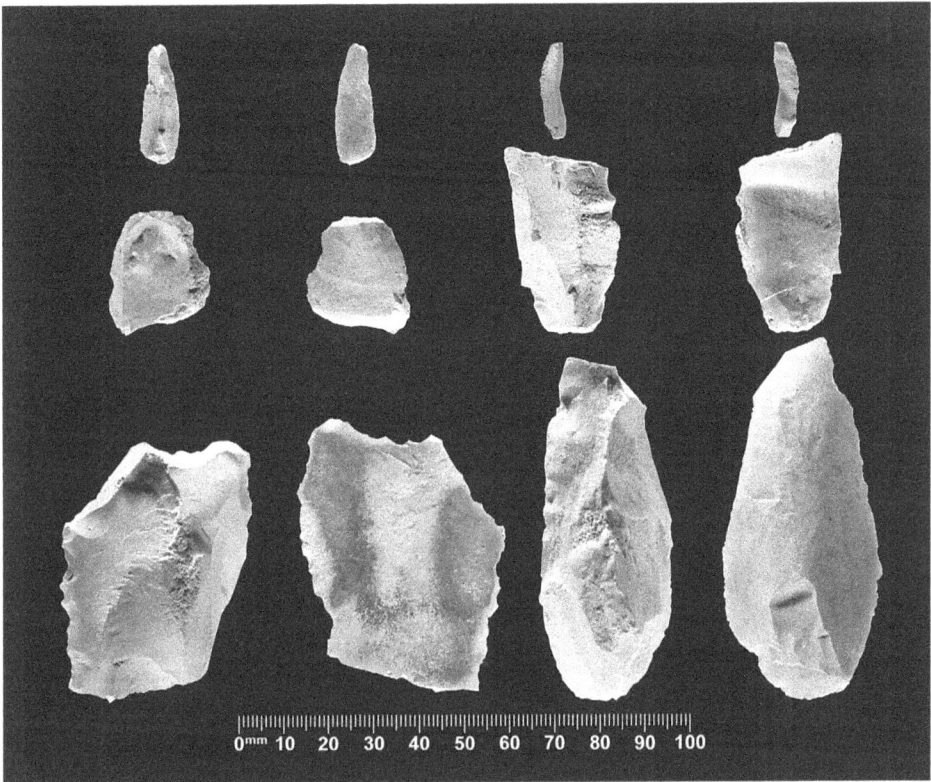

Figure 2.11. Front and back photographs of pre-Clovis flake tools associated with anvil in the top of the Pleistocene terrace: *top row*, bladelets; *middle row*, whole flake with striking platform and bulb of force, endscraper on flake; *bottom row*, uniface-denticulate, uniface-sidescraper (SCIAA photo by Daryl P. Miller).

The artifacts in the terrace are the same as those in WPAS although not as dense (Sain 2015). That is, they represent the same type of technology with cores and flake tools, including bend-break pieces. At least two artifacts merit special mention. The first is a bend-break piece with an obvious graver spur fashioned on it (Figure 2.12). This piece was found in situ 22 cm into the terrace. At least two other flakes with graver spurs were found in the WPAS with similar spurs. The second artifact is a large core found deep in the terrace at 96.05 m (Figure 2.13). It was recovered in situ about 50 cm above F91 with the infinite radiocarbon dates. It has multiple detachments and three separate areas exhibiting battering from repeated unsuccessful blows. Unlike the highly oxidized, well-drained WPAS, chert artifacts found in the terrace exhibit little or no weathering, due to the

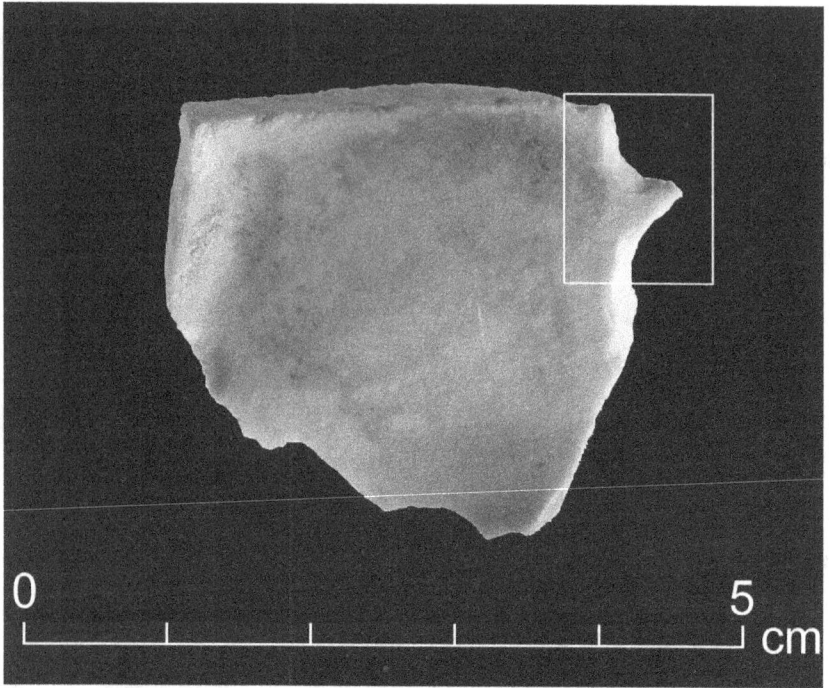

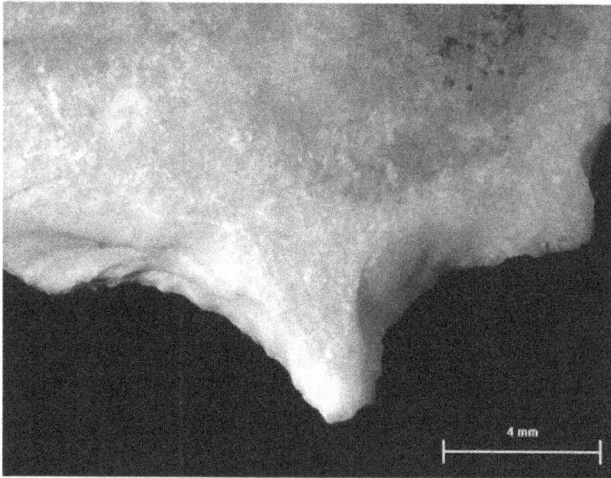

Figure 2.12. *Top*: bend-break piece with graver spur; *bottom*: photomicrograph of graver spur showing flaking details (SCIAA photo).

Figure 2.13. Large, heavily flaked core in situ in the Pleistocene terrace of Topper.

relatively permanent moisture of the sediments, which retards and even prevents weathering.

To check for the possibility of artifacts somehow moving down into the terrace from the WPAS, the mean weight of all artifacts was calculated by 5-cm levels. This revealed no down-profile reduction of artifact size (Figure 2.14). Furthermore, while artifacts are found continuously down through the terrace, it is apparent that three major artifact modes are present, representing denser zones. These zones are composed of both flakes and flake tools as well as large cobble and boulder-size cores (Figure 2.15). It appears that artifacts large and small are being deposited into the terrace as it is accreting vertically. No cracks were observed in the sediments from 2004 through the present, except for those appearing in 2007 when the roof was constructed over the main excavation block. This had the effect of shutting off rainfall to the sediments and artificially exposing the terrace to air in the walls of excavation units. These cracks were a centimeter or less in width and clearly a result of the roofed building. While silt and clay increase up the terrace profile, sand always dominates the percentage and acts as temper, inhibiting cracking in the sediment (David Leigh, personal communication 2007). In addition to this, no evidence of seismically induced liquefaction has been observed in the pre-Clovis stratigraphy (Talwani 2003) that might account for artifacts in the terrace.

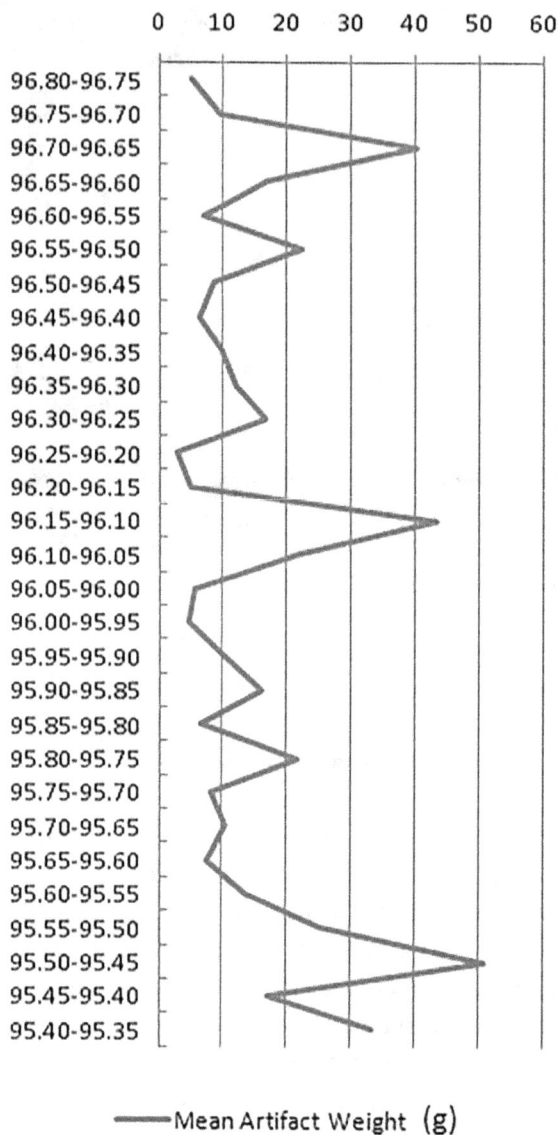

Figure 2.14. Distribution of mean artifact weights by 5-cm levels in the Pleistocene Terrace, showing no down-profile reduction in size and tri-layers.

In the terrace, artifacts, even large ones, are often found turned vertically, probably due to root pressure. Redoxification features are present, extending down about a meter into the terrace, a result of wetting and drying of roots due to a fluctuating water table. These red discolorations indicate that the top of the terrace was vegetated, probably toward the end of its formation. Such root activity was not sufficient to obliterate the tri-layer zones but likely blurred them to some extent with root pressure.

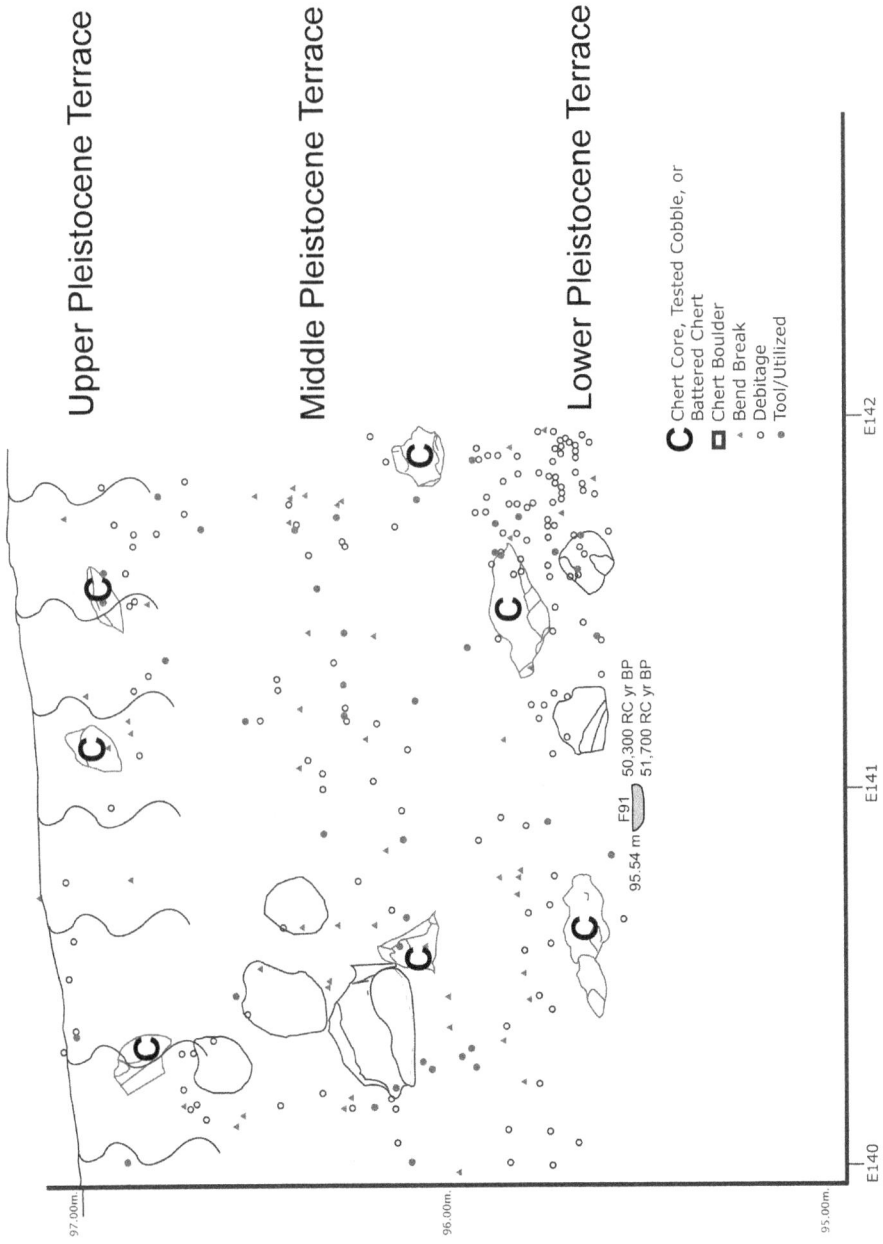

Figure 2.15. Back-plot of pre-Clovis artifacts, including large-boulder-size artifacts and nodules showing stratigraphic tri-layering down to 50,000 yr B.P. radiocarbon dates in Feature 91.

Upper Pleistocene Terrace

Middle Pleistocene Terrace

Lower Pleistocene Terrace

C Chert Core, Tested Cobble, or
Battered Chert
☐ Chert Boulder
▲ Bend Break
○ Debitage
● Tool/Utilized

F91 50,300 RC yr BP
95.54 m 51,700 RC yr BP

E140   E141   E142

97.00m.

96.00m.

95.00m.

Conclusions

The Topper site is an unusual Pleistocene-age site thus far seen in the Western Hemisphere. Besides its apparent great age, it is characterized by a non-bifacial type of lithic technology based on bipolar and other forms of smash core reduction. The presence of artifacts such as unifacially flaked side and end scrapers, spokeshaves, and denticulates, plus small prismatic blades, are typical of Upper Paleolithic assemblages around the world. However, because of their unusually small size, including the numerous bend-break pieces, the Topper site has been referred to as microlithic (Goodyear 2005a). It also has a heavy industry in the form of large choppers, cores, and planes, typical of prehistoric lithic assemblages found on chert quarries of all ages. Altogether such an assemblage seems likely devoted to working organic media such as wood, ivory, bone, and antler in order to manufacture tools for hunting and fishing as well as other subsistence activities. Accordingly, it has been named the Clariant Complex, for the former owner of site who supported so much of this research (Goodyear et al. 2013).

The artifacts conform to categories common to Paleolithic and even some Paleoindian assemblages. That they are humanly created and not somehow a product of nature seems self-evident. The great energy required to break open the nodules plus the systematic flaking of cores, core tools, and flake tools are all well beyond what has been loosely called "geofacts." Their clear association with two different geological deposits, the upper one in sandy sediments typical of braided streams, the lower one in the top of a terrace formed by overbank flooding when the Savannah River was in a meander phase, indicates they are essentially in place and represent intact interpretable assemblages. The people responsible for the Clariant Complex existed over a substantial amount of time that transcended two major phases of the Late Pleistocene Savannah River.

In their appraisal of the dating of Topper, Waters et al. (2009:1309) reported that it dated diachronously, from minimally about 15,000 yrs B.P. to at least 50,000 or more years. The radiocarbon dating of the WPAS deposit with the cores farther up the terrace ranging from 25,330 B.P. to 38,810 B.P. is the probable minimal age of the upper pre-Clovis assemblage. That being the case, the beginning of the site as found in the Pleistocene terrace would still be minimally about 50,000 yrs B.P. or more. A time span of 25,000 to 50,000 B.P. or longer is still a remarkable amount of time for a lithic technology to persist, at least by New World standards. The use of single-grain OSL dating on these sediments will be necessary to try to date the beginning of human occupation at Topper. For now it clearly dates well before the Last Glacial Maximum (LGM) and joins other sites, such as Pedra Furada, Monte Verde I, and Burnham in Oklahoma (Wyckoff et al. 2003), all of which give strong hints that the peopling of the Americas had a much earlier beginning than the currently recognized Late Pleistocene sites of North America such as Meadowcroft Rockshelter, Cactus Hill, and Friedkin, to name a few (Goodyear 2005a; Waters et al. 2011).

Trying to imagine settlement systems with predictable site locations for other sites in the Clariant Complex is challenging. If the focus of pre-LGM adaptations was more coastal-riverine than on the interior of the North American continent as seen in Clovis and Folsom, those sites will be largely drowned by sea level rise (Harris et al. 2013). If Topper was a part of such a system, it could represent the interior riverine portion of a coastal system where forays up the Savannah River for aquatic resources and tool stone sources were a regular migration, thus leaving the distinctive artifacts of the Topper site. Finding artifacts like those at Topper seaward would be an indication of this use. Topper at least gives us something that could be looked for.

Acknowledgments

We would like to thank Archroma, the owner of the Topper site, and previous owners, including Sandoz Chemical and the Clariant Corporation for the great assistance they have provided over several years for our work at the Topper site. The archaeologists and geoscientists who have contributed to this study are many and acknowledged in most cases by citing their publications on Topper. The volunteers and donors supporting field and lab work are too numerous to recount here. To all of you who helped out, our sincere thanks; it literally could not have been done without you. You have given new meaning to the term *public archaeology* in a very hands-on way. Doug Sain would like to acknowledge the help and encouragement of his dissertation committee at the University of Tennessee. The many colleagues who visited our excavations over the years are also thanked for their interest and insights. All interpretations herein are ours, as are any errors.

3

Capps

A Levallois-Like Flaked Stone Technology
in North America

H. BLAINE ENSOR

The question of when and why the first Americans arrived in the Americas, and just who they were, remains an open question among researchers (Anderson et al. 2015; Dillehay 2009; Goebel et al. 2008; Meltzer 2009). Although consensus and evidence have been building that Clovis groups were not the first inhabitants of North America, the timing and sequence of the earliest arrivals in the Americas are not well understood and most likely occurred as a process, not an event, over a significant period of time (Collins et al. 2013). Attempts to estimate the timing of human dispersal across North America from Siberia have been put forth based on genetic models; however, very little in the way of archaeological data is available to independently test those models. Even the search for viable antecedents to Clovis lithic technology in the Americas and elsewhere has proven both elusive and controversial (Anderson et al. 2015). Despite the contributions of genetics, geomorphology, and environmental reconstruction, the empirical basis for our understanding of the initial settlement of North America and the Americas in general must ultimately be grounded in artifacts and the archaeological record (Goebel et al. 2008) and thus remains problematic. Toward this end, the present study represents an exploratory attempt to describe a stone-working technology known as Capps that has not been previously described in North American prehistory. This initial effort to make sense of the technology, given the nature of the data, can in no way be construed as anything approaching "definitive." Rather, it is an attempt to understand and learn about this technology and promote interest and further research. Before proceeding with the present analysis it is important to provide a sense of context by reviewing some of the studies and rebuttals put forth over the years related to earliest-American research.

Previous Research Regarding the Earliest Americans

It is a fact that during the late nineteenth, twentieth, and twenty-first centuries there have been numerous claims of pre-Clovis or Paleolithic-like implements reportedly found at sites in North America. Some of these appear to mimic Old World Paleolithic types (Abbott 1872; Carter 1957; Dixon 1983; Dragoo 1973; Hibben 1941; Josselyn 1965; Krieger 1964; Leakey 1979; Lee 1957; Minshall 1976; Raemsch 1977a, 1977b; Renaud 1936; Simpson 1989), among others. Sometimes the advocates had considerable experience with Old World technologies, such as Leakey (1935) and Bordes (1961). François Bordes examined pebble tools from Alabama in the 1960s and reacted favorably toward them being a "pebble tool industry," not just the result of haphazard use of naturally occurring pebbles as "expedient tools" over many millennia during the North American Holocene (Josselyn 1965). Leakey (1979) identified supposed Pleistocene-age artifacts from the controversial Calico Hills site in southern California. In each case there were swift negative reactions and attempts to discredit any notion that historical connections may have existed between the Old and the New World during glacial times (Cole et al. 1977; Haynes 1973; Ritchie 1977; Sharrock 1966).

The study traditionally used to refute the idea of American Paleolithic tools has been the extensive early work published by William Henry Holmes during the late nineteenth and early twentieth centuries (Holmes 1919; see also Meltzer and Dunnell 1992). Johnson (1981) has provided a general summary of Holmes' quarry-workshop related work as well as an evaluation of various critiques of Holmes' "quarry blank" theory, such as Bryan (1950) and Ives (1975). The general paucity of work at quarry/workshop sites in North America has been noted by Ives (1975), and Johnson's (1981) work at quarry/workshop sites at Yellow Creek remains one of the most extensive studies to date. Today it is generally recognized that a wide variety of prehistoric activities took place at raw material sources (Odell 1996). These activities may have included primary extraction (mining) or collection of naturally occurring material with subsequent initial modification prior to transport as well as a considerable range of tool manufacture and use.

Regardless of the total range of activities performed at quarry/workshop sites, the most critical aspect of Holmes' work that has been used to deny the presence of Paleolithic-like implements in North America is the quarry blank model of biface manufacture (also see Sharrock 1966). Problems still linger in accepting Holmes' premise that all quarry "blanks" represent early-to-intermediate stages in thin-biface manufacture. As noted by Callahan (1979) during early-to-intermediate prehistoric biface manufacture in North America, common biface width-thickness ratios range between 2.0 and 4.0, which are the same ranges evident for Old World Paleolithic "handaxe" manufacture. The potential for confusion is obviously great when attempting to separate an "early stage" biface of Holocene age from a potential Paleolithic biface among literally thousands of specimens at a workshop site when the technique of manufacture can result in virtually indistinguishable formal characteristics. So, does the fact that the full range of Clovis or later Holocene biface manufacture has been documented at a quarry/workshop site mean that other bifaces that may be significantly older cannot be present assuming the raw material was available? In other words, Holmes' quarry blank model whereby thick bifaces are gradually thinned to finished form may be valid in many instances (Johnson 1981; Callahan 1979; Bradley et al. 2010). However, just because it is valid at one site or series of sites does not negate the possibility that bifaces were also designed to be finished tools that did not necessarily pass through successive "stages" before completion. Despite the claims and rebuttals, very little systematic archaeological analysis has been conducted that would validate or invalidate the claims of Paleolithic-like artifacts in North America (Haynes 2015). While Holmes (1919) and Hrdlicka (1917), among many others, denied the existence of any Old World Paleolithic technologies or Pleistocene skeletal remains in the Americas, Willey (1966) left the door open to a "Lower Lithic Stage" along the lines of Krieger's (1964) "Pre-Projectile Point Horizon" that hypothetically may have consisted of simple core and flake tools.

Consequently, American archaeologists have continued their pursuit of potential pre-Clovis North American lithic technologies/sites into the present. Prospective pre-Clovis artifacts have been recovered from a number of sites in Eastern North America and elsewhere. Sites such as Meadowcroft Rockshelter, Pennsylvania (Adovasio et al. 1999) include "thin bifaces, including one lanceolate point, the Miller Lanceolate, small prismatic blades; retouched flake tools and blades" (Goodyear 2005a:103). At the Saltville locality in Virginia potential pre-Clovis artifacts include bone tools and chert debitage (McDonald 2000). Another site in Virginia known as Cactus Hill (44SX202) (McAvoy and McAvoy 1997) has produced evidence of pre-Clovis occupation in the form of quartzite artifacts including "prismatic blades, polyhedral cores, and tringuloid-to-lanceolate bifaces" (Goodyear 2005a:107). Goodyear (2000, 2005a) reports the discovery of potential pre-Clovis bend-break tools and spalls as well as micro-blade cores/blades, scrapers, spokeshaves, and core choppers at the Topper site (38AL23) in South Carolina. A sampling of other potential North American pre-Clovis sites recently reviewed by Haynes (2015) includes the Debra L. Friedkin and Gault sites in central Texas, Page-Ladson in Florida, Paisley Caves in Oregon, sites in the Delmarva Peninsula, and a host of East Beringian Tradition locations. Goebel et al. (2008) also provide their view on possible pre-Clovis archaeological data from New World sites such as Monte Verde (Chile), Pedra Furada (Brazil), Schaefer and Hebior sites (Wisconsin), and Pendejo Cave (New Mexico), among others. Haynes (2015) and Goebel et al. (2008) indicate overall weak evidence for pre-Clovis occupation based on material remains, with the best evidence coming from sites dating after 15 kya. Other researchers (Anderson et al. 2015; Collins et al. 2013) acknowledge genetic evidence that may support a post–Late Glacial Maximum timing for the first Americans but leave the door open for earlier Pleistocene arrivals.

The Sites

The Capps site (1HE178) and the Shelley site (1HE105) are located in southeastern Alabama in Henry County about 20 miles north of Dothan (Figure 3.1). These sites are located on flat upland terrain where marine Tertiary-age (Eocene residuum) sediments are present at the surface of the Gulf Coastal Plain. The Capps site covers approximately 200 m by 300 m of cultivated peanut fields just north of the farm community of Capps, while the Shelley site (also known as the Tumbleton Flint Quarry) occupies about half of a square-mile section near the town of Abbeville just north of Tumbleton. The Shelley site (Tumbleton Flint Quarry) was first reported in the 1940s by Wesley Hurt as part of David DeJarnette's Lake Walter F. George impoundment survey along the Chattahoochee River (DeJarnette 1975). The site was later surface collected and investigated by members of the Alabama Archaeological Society in the mid-to-late 1960s. The only record of the Capps site prior to the present investigation came from articles published by William Emanuel and Daniel Josselyn (Emanuel 1968), a sketch map on file at the University of Alabama-Birmingham, and the artifacts surface collected from the site by members of the Alabama Archaeological Society,

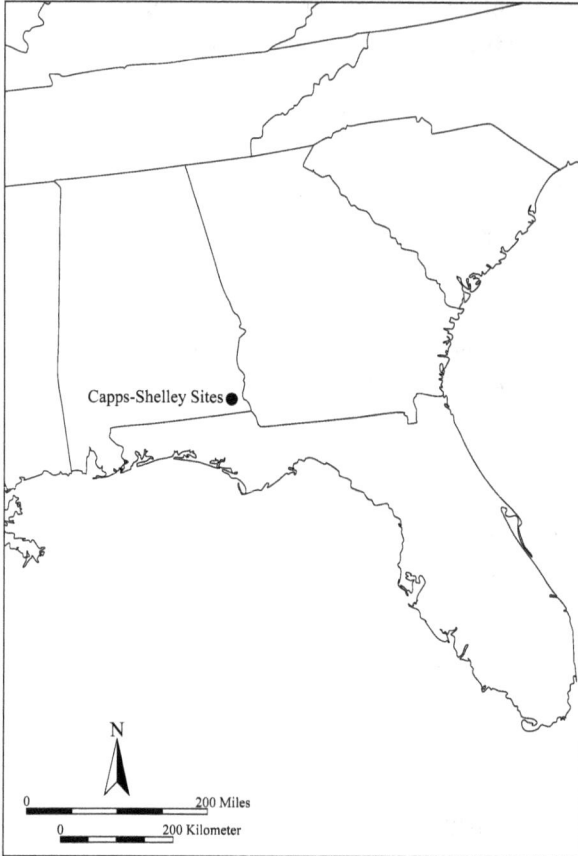

Figure 3.1. Location of Capps-Shelley Sites in Southeastern Alabama.

primarily during the 1960s. The Capps and Shelley sites now have been officially recorded with the Alabama state site files, and the site locations have been field verified. A representative sample (N = 235) of heavily patinated flaked stone artifacts surface collected from the Capps (1HE178) and Shelley (1HE105) sites were chosen for analysis. Surface collection of the Capps site produced almost exclusively heavily patinated Capps technology cores and flakes/spalls with thin bifaces, biface manufacturing rejects, biface thinning flakes, pressure flakes, prismatic blades and heat treatment of Ocala chert absent. The Shelley site, on the other hand, produced a wide array of cultural materials from the surface, including heated projectile points/knives and evidence of thin biface manufacture, with numerous biface-thinning flakes present. However, the Shelley site also produced heavily patinated

Capps technology cores and flakes/spalls, duplicating those from the Capps site and providing further evidence of this prepared core technology.

The purpose of the current study is to provide a description of a flaked stone core and flake technology, designated as Capps, that has been found at the Capps-Shelley sites and at a number of geographically divergent sites/locales across North America over the past decade or so (Ensor 2008, 2013, 2014). The technology appears to differ significantly from Clovis and later Holocene technologies that have been described in the North American literature over the past half century or more—yet placing an age or cultural affiliation with the technology has proven elusive. Capps technology apparently lacks traditional Clovis and later Holocene thin-biface technology, that is, the production of hafted bifaces or projectile points/knives and their by-products such as bifacial thinning flakes and thin biface manufacturing rejects (width/thickness ratio generally in excess of 4.0) (Callahan 1979). Capps technology instead relies primarily on a percussion-based, well-controlled flat flaking technique (Witthoft 1967) to produce various pre-determined flake forms from prepared cores. This technique was used to shape cores and to produce the desired flake or end-products in a Levallois-like manner. Retouch of end-products appears to have been accomplished solely by percussion flaking, with no evidence of pressure flaking.

The representative sample of 235 lithic artifacts from the Capps (N = 156) and Shelley (N = 79) sites was selected for analysis based on its perceived ability to impart useful information regarding a previously unrecognized prepared core technology in North America. The consistent degree of patination, coloration, and weathering on Capps-technology artifacts, coupled with distinctive core preparation and associated end-products, as well as the lack of traditional thin-biface technology, pressure flaking, and intentional thermal alteration (as demonstrated by surface collections from the Capps site, which produced almost exclusively heavily weathered and patinated Capps-technology artifacts) made selection of a sample relatively straightforward. Since the artifacts are from the surface, there can be no assurance that every artifact was produced during a specific time period or by a particular cultural group. However, for the reasons noted above, there is a high degree of confidence that a previously unknown North American stone-working technology is being revealed. Ultimately, this technology must be found in datable context so that an age assessment can be made and claims regarding historical connections or cultural affinity examined.

Capps Flaked Stone Technology

Raw Material

Large Ocala (Coastal Plain) chert nodules occur near the surface of both sites, which were used extensively by site inhabitants for manufacturing stone tools. Numerous "quarry pits" exist at the Shelley site, indicative of intensive exploitation of this chert resource for a very long period of time. No "quarry pits" have been observed at the Capps site, but a road cut that intersects the site revealed the presence of sizable Ocala chert nodules within two meters of the present surface. Moderate-to-heavy prehistoric lithic debris is scattered over almost the entire surface of both sites (Emanuel 1968). Capps and Shelley are designated as quarry/workshop sites or lithic procurement sites since Ocala chert was likely available over a long period of time at both locations. Ocala, or coastal plain, chert outcrops across Henry and Houston counties in southeast Alabama and occurs both in situ as silicified nodules formed most likely in Ocala limestone of the Eocene Jackson group and as residuum weathered from the Ocala Limestone Formation (Copeland 1968). Nodule size ranges from small to large, with an estimated range from less than 10 cm to over one meter. The deeply weathered cortex or rind varies in thickness from a few millimeters up to a centimeter or more, based on Ocala chert nodules from the Capps-Shelley sites.

A light brown, pale brown, and moderate yellowish brown calcareous cortex is common on weathered Capps-related artifacts. The deeply weathered/patinated non-cortical flaked surfaces of Capps-related artifacts are generally very pale orange, to pale yellowish orange, to grayish orange, to dark yellowish orange in color. Although Ocala chert artifacts in southeastern Alabama have been described as having a white/chalky patination (Moon 1999), Capps technology specimens generally take on the colorations mentioned above, most likely due to subsurface staining of the patina from a reddish brown sandy soil matrix. Occasionally a type of reddish brown "varnish" is visible on certain artifacts and a relatively bright orange-brown staining is present on Capps-related artifacts. Chert quality is generally good to excellent based on observations of fresh material eroding from a gray compact clay at the Capps site and limited experimental testing of heavily weathered Ocala chert nodules found at the Shelley site. No heat treatment was noted for any of the Capps technology specimens, although Ocala chert was regularly heated by Gulf Coastal Plain Archaic and Woodland groups (Ensor and Largent 1997; Purdy and Clark 1987; Thomas et al. 2013).

The heavily weathered/patinated surfaces on Capps technology artifacts on occasion inhibit clear recognition of flake scars. Patination on Capps technology artifacts was produced in large part by chemical weathering (Hurst and Kelly 1961; Purdy and Clark 1987), although mechanical processes may also be involved. White patination is the result of selective leaching of cryptocrystalline silicates that produces an increase in the number of reflective surfaces. Subsequent staining of the patinated surfaces often occurs, and this is the case with the Capps-Shelley artifacts. Study of the relationship between patination and age has shown that there is a significant correspondence between the two; however, the observed variability of factors related to patination is likely too great to produce a precise dating method (Frederick et al. 1994).

Methods

During the analysis all linear measurements are to the nearest tenth of a millimeter after (Debénath and Dibble 1994), and striking platform or tool edge angles were taken with a simple goniometer to the nearest plus or minus five degrees. Terminology referencing Old World Levallois stoneworking technology is from Bordes (1961), Van Peer (1992), and Debénath and Dibble (1994) unless otherwise stated. Basic lithic technology terms are derived primarily from Crabtree (1972). Examination of tool/flake edges for evidence of use was aided by a 10x hand lens.

Capps Technology Cores

Heavily patinated and weathered cores from Capps-Shelley exhibit a variety of prepared shaping techniques. A total of 68 cores were analyzed from the surface of the two sites: 50 from Capps and 18 from Shelley. Capps technology core preparation appears to have relied primarily on modification of very thick flakes or spalls that had been obtained from Ocala chert nodules of varying sizes. It is also possible that an entire nodule of the appropriate size may have served as the original blank for core preparation. Nodules were split or otherwise fractured by percussion flaking to obtain the desired flake blank. The precise technique of nodule reduction is unknown and may have included freehand percussion, anvil-assisted, and/or bipolar flaking (Crabtree 1972). There is strong evidence that Ocala chert nodules were procured at or very close to the sites, and that nodule reduction, core preparation, flake/spall production and tool-use occurred on each site. As mentioned above, the heavy patination/weathering present on the cores made identification of technological attributes difficult at times. Sometimes negative flake scar removals, direction and origin of flake scars, and subsequently intent of the knapper were hard to decipher due to these factors. Nonetheless, the sample size and overall visibility were sufficient to grasp the basics of core preparation and reduction and its apparent similarity to Old World Levallois technology (Bordes 1961; Debénath and Dibble 1994; Derev'anko 1998; Van Peer 1992). A typological approach to core analysis was avoided in favor of an attribute approach that attempts to provide basic statistical information regarding the variation present relevant to key core preparation and reduction techniques. While others have mentioned Levallois-like technology with reference to North American flaked stone technologies (Bradley et al. 2010; Bryan 1950; Dixon 1983; Raemsch 1977b; Renaud 1936), there does not appear to have been any systematic attempt to describe a Levallois-like method other than Guy Muto's description of the Levallois-like "Cascade Technique" in Oregon (Muto 1976). This technique produces prismatic blades and bladelike flakes from prepared cores in a Levallois-like manner.

The following discussion of Capps technology recognizes it as a bifacial hierarchical core technology as described by Shea (2013) and Hovers (2009), where a single flake release surface is dedicated to end-product or flake tool production while points or areas along the margin of the opposing prepared surface serve as striking platforms. While a nontypological approach was taken, a general classificatory distinction is drawn between the traditional North American unprepared core type known as expedient or amorphous (Koldehoff 1987; Parry and Kelly 1987) and Old World Mode 3 prepared core types known as Levallois (Bordes 1961; Clark 1969; Van Peer 1992), since the former is considered nonhierarchical and the latter hierarchical.

Nonhierarchical or expedient/amorphous cores (Clark 1969; Shea 2013) are characterized by detachment of a series of percussion flakes in either a systematic or an opportunistic manner, with the requirement that flake release surfaces and platform preparation or flake initiation surfaces be interchangeable throughout core reduction (Hovers 2009; Shea 2013). The overall form of these cores is usually subspherical, cuboid, or amorphous dependent on the extent of core reduction. This is the most common core form described for post-Clovis Archaic, Woodland, and Mississippian societies in North America, notwithstanding certain prepared core technologies associated with Clovis (Bradley et al. 2010; Collins 1999), Late Archaic (Ford et al. 1955), Middle Woodland (Montet-White 1968), and Mississippian cultures (Perino 1960). In contrast, hierarchical or Mode 3 cores (which are divided into bifacial and unifacial) possess two flake release surfaces that serve different purposes (Hovers 2009; Shea 2013). Bifacial hierarchical cores (commonly referred to as Levallois in the Old World) have fracture initiation surfaces characterized by relatively short flake removals that allow for longer flake detachment from the flake release surface. The result is a flake release surface that is generally shallow and convex, and cross sections that are plano-convex to trapezoidal in form. The fracture initiation and flake release surfaces are not interchangeable, since they serve two fundamentally different purposes. While the difference between nonhierarchical and hierarchical cores may seem clear from a conceptual point of view, in reality it obviously cannot be ruled out that a flake removed during platform preparation for a hierarchical core was ultimately used in some fashion as a tool. However, this fact does not diminish the overall interpretive value. Capps core technology consistently produced a flake release surface that was systematically prepared in a variety of configurations to produce preconceived end-products, hence referral to the technology as Levallois-like. Capps technology end-products correspond in a consistent and predetermined manner to the overall form and shape of the prepared flaking surface that released them.

Table 3.1 presents summary statistics recorded for Capps technology cores during the present analysis, and Figures 3.2–3.6 illustrate a representative sample of Capps technology cores. Percussion flaking with an apparent high incidence of controlled flat flaking as opposed to free flaking (Witthoft 1967) is a critical component of Capps technology. Often core shaping involves removal of large, thick, flat flakes that create broad, smooth facets along core margins, creating a "sculpted" effect in some instances. Lateral, proximal, and distal shaping of core margins results in relatively steep angles between core margins and flake release surfaces. The facets or ridges serve as striking platforms for radial, unidirectional, bidirectional or centripetal flaking. The location of contact between the precursor and the striking platform is more often an area as opposed to a point, and flakes routinely travel across the entire core surface, sometimes removing a portion of the opposite core margin. Many flakes retain smooth facets along the lateral or distal edges that represent remnant core margins; some of these resemble éclats débordants, including triangular-shaped "pseudo-Levallois points." Core cross sections are biconvex to plano-convex, while

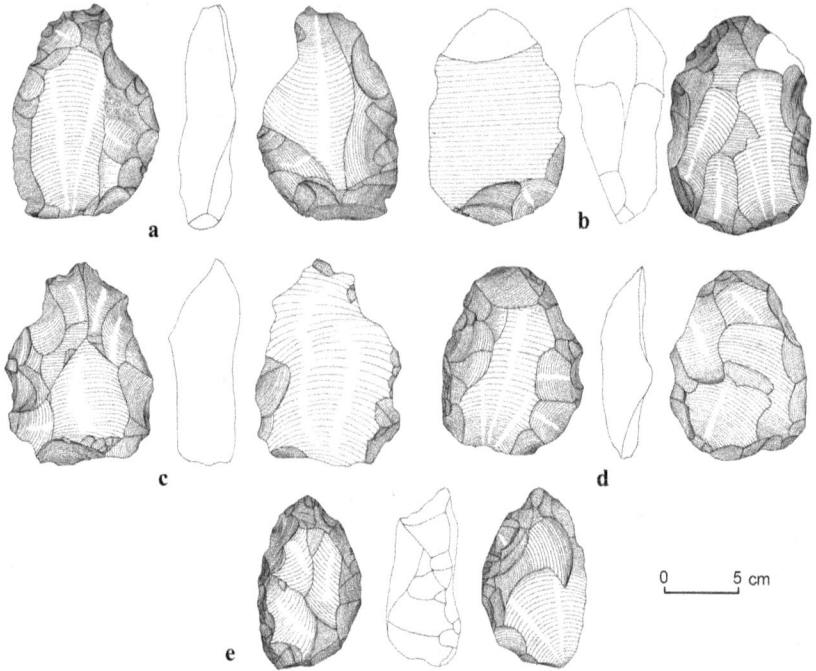

Figure 3.2. Capps technology cores: (*a*) Capps site; (*b–c*) Shelley site; (*d–e*) Capps site.

plan views include triangular, rectilinear, oval, disk, or asymmetrical. No evidence of heat treatment has been detected on analyzed specimens, and there is no pressure flaking or grinding/abrasion involved with platform preparation.

Observations recorded include the presence or absence of linear flake (bladelike) removals, location and patterning of core preparation scars, relative amount of cortex, estimated striking platform angle, and maximum length, width, and thickness. The cores have a mean length of 81.7 mm (N = 66), a mean width of 60.0 mm (N = 68), a mean thickness of 36.0 mm (N = 68), and a mean striking platform angle of 82 degrees. Core length

Table 3.1. Summary Statistics for Capps Technology Cores

	N	Mean	STD	Min	Max
Core length	66	81.7	20.5	38	139.2
Core width	68	60.0	13.7	30.5	97.2
Core thickness	68	36.0	11.3	14	60.0
Est. striking platform angle	54	82	13.3	30	110

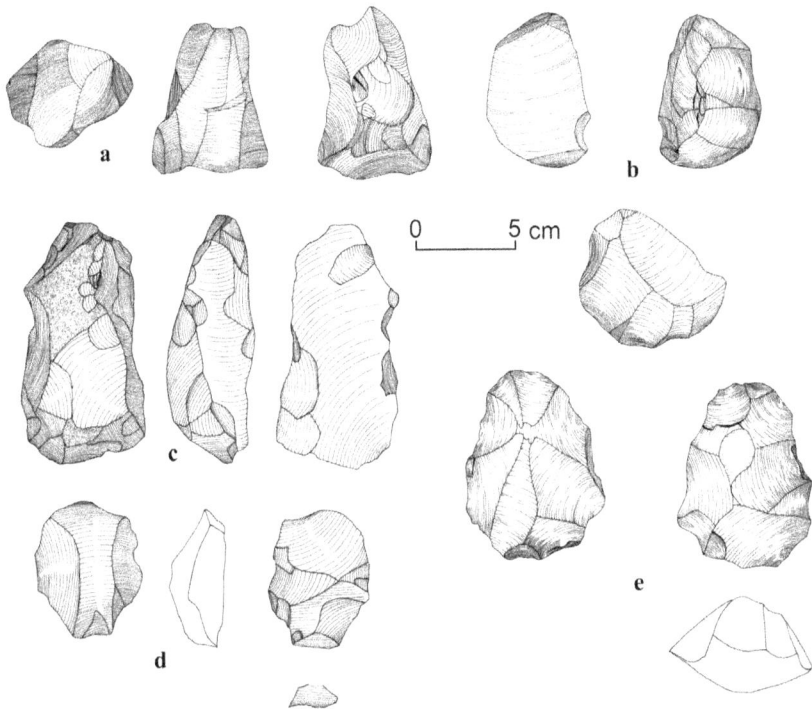

Figure 3.3. Capps technology Cores: (*a–c*) Capps site; (*d*) Shelley site; (*e*) Capps site.

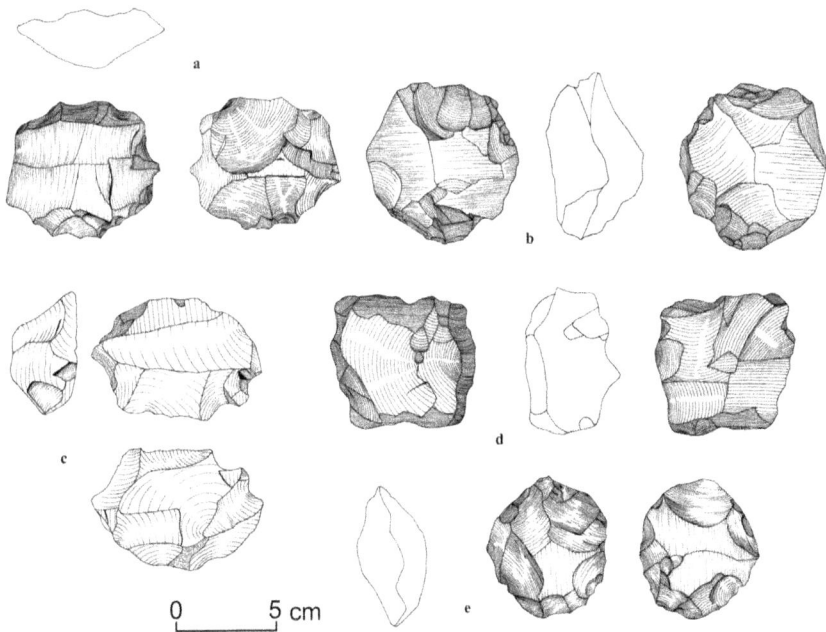

Figure 3.4. Capps technology cores: (*a–e*) Capps site.

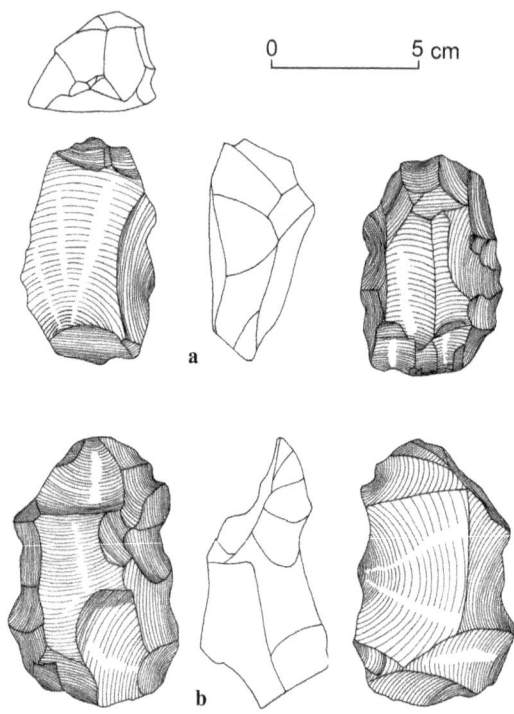

0   5 cm

a

b

Figure 3.5. Capps technology cores: (a–b) Capps site.

a

b

c

d

Figure 3.6. Capps technology cores: (a–d) Capps site.

ranges from 38 mm to 139 mm, core width ranges from 30 to 97 mm, core thickness ranges from 14 to 60 mm, and striking platform angles range from 30 to 110 degrees. A total of 12 cores (18 percent) exhibit core preparation and negative flake scars suggesting linear flake or bladelike removals (Figures 3.2a, b, d, 3.3a, d, 3.4a, c, 3.5b), seven (10 percent) show core preparation/flake removal on primarily one surface (Figures 3.2b, c, 3.3c, 3.5a), 26 (38 percent) have two surfaces with bifacial preparatory/flake removal scars (Figures 3.3d, e, 3.4a–e, 3.5b), and seven (10 percent) have multiple surfaces flaked (Figure 3.3a, b). Five cores (6 percent) have multiple surfaces flaked, resulting in a globular multifaceted form; 11 (16 percent) are circular or disc-shaped and show bifacial core preparation/flake removals (Figure 3.4 a, b, e), while one large bifacial core (1.5 percent) exhibits Levallois-like preparation and/or flake removals on two surfaces (Figure 3.2d). In terms of naturally weathered cortex, the vast majority of 64 (94 percent) have less than 25 percent cortex present, while four (6 percent) exhibit between 25 and 75 percent cortex.

The location and patterning of core surface scar morphology (after Dibble 1995) includes four (6 percent) where a single flake removal dominates the flake release surface (Figure 3.4d), three (4 percent) exhibit unidirectional or bidirectional preparation exclusively (Figure 3.3a), 24 (35 percent) have sub-radial flake scar morphology whereby flakes originate from 2–3 directions, including lateral margins (Figures 3.2a, 3.3c, d), and 37 (54 percent) demonstrate radial flaking with flake scars originating from four or more directions, including both lateral margins (Figures 3.2c, 3.3b, e, 3.4a–e, 3.5a). The majority of prepared core surfaces exhibit either radial or subradial flaking. Capps technology flake release surfaces demonstrate lineal (both unidirectional and bidirectional removals) and centripetal removals.

Capps Technology End-Products

A total of 89 flake tools made on end-products drawn from Capps technology cores were analyzed from Capps-Shelley: 34 from Capps and 55 from Shelley. Table 3.2 present summary metric data for the sample of Capps technology end-products recorded during the present analysis. Figures 3.7–3.12 illustrate a representative sample of Capps technology end-products. Observations recorded include platform type, retouch type, flake blank type, any additional modification present, estimated striking platform angle to plus or minus five degrees, maximum flake tool length, maximum flake tool width, maximum flake tool thickness, maximum platform width, and maximum platform thickness. Virtually all of the end-products exhibit the

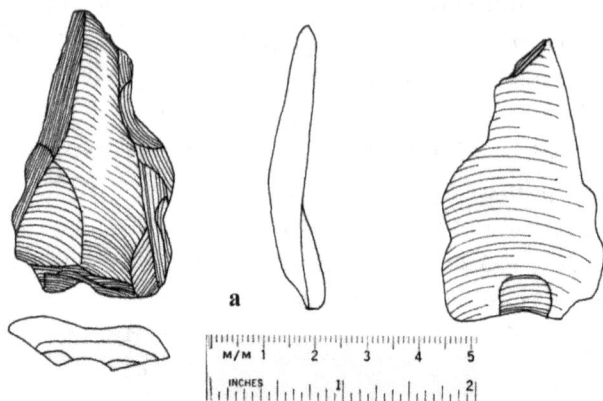

Figure 3.7. Capps technology end-product: (*a*) Capps site.

remnants of core preparation scars and/or previous end-product removals on their dorsal surface.

Capps flake tools or end-products are manufactured on thin-to-thick Levallois-like flakes of various shapes and sizes. Retouch includes direct percussion along margins of the dorsal flake surface, bifacial retouch (both dorsal and ventral surface flaked along the same margin) or a combination of alternating retouch whereby one edge segment is flaked on the dorsal surface while an opposing edge segment is flaked on the ventral surface (Bordes 1961; Debénath and Dibble 1994). Many Levallois-like flake end-products are modified only by use or with little or no evidence of macroscopic retouch or use, and many are roughly triangular-shaped (Figures 3.9a–h, 3.10a, b), while others resemble Old World Levallois/Mousterian points (Figures 3.7a, 3.8b, 3.10b) (Debénath and Dibble 1994; Van Peer 1992). Other Capps technology flake end-products are oval-shaped (Figures 3.8a, 3.10f, 3.11d–g) or rectangle-shaped (Figures 3.8c, 3.10d).

The 89 Capps technology end-products (tools) have a mean length of 79.6 mm, a mean width of 47.2 mm, and a mean thickness of 22.4 mm. Tool length ranges from 42 to 128 mm, tool width from 20 to 122 mm, and tool thickness from 7 to 50 mm. The mean length of end-products is slightly less than the mean length of cores, and the range of end-product lengths corresponds well with the range of core lengths. The mean internal striking platform angle on Capps end-products (tools) is 100 degrees, while platforms have an average width of 19.1 mm and an average thickness of 7.8 mm. Striking platform angles range from 85 to 110 degrees, while platform

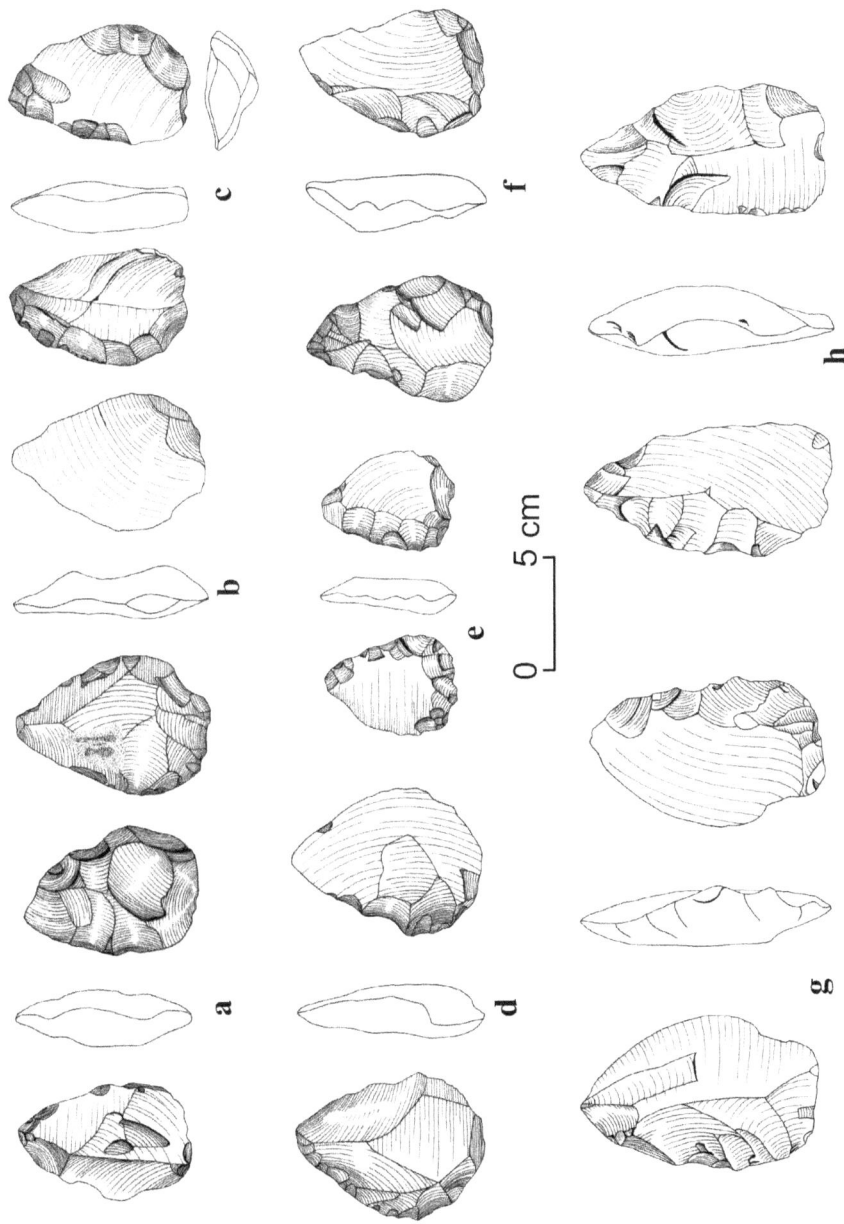

Figure 3.8. Capps technology end-products: (*a*) Capps site; (*b*) Shelley site; (*c*) Capps site; (*d*) Shelley site; (*e*) Capps site; (*f*) Shelley site; (*g*) Capps site; (*h*) Shelley site.

0 5 cm

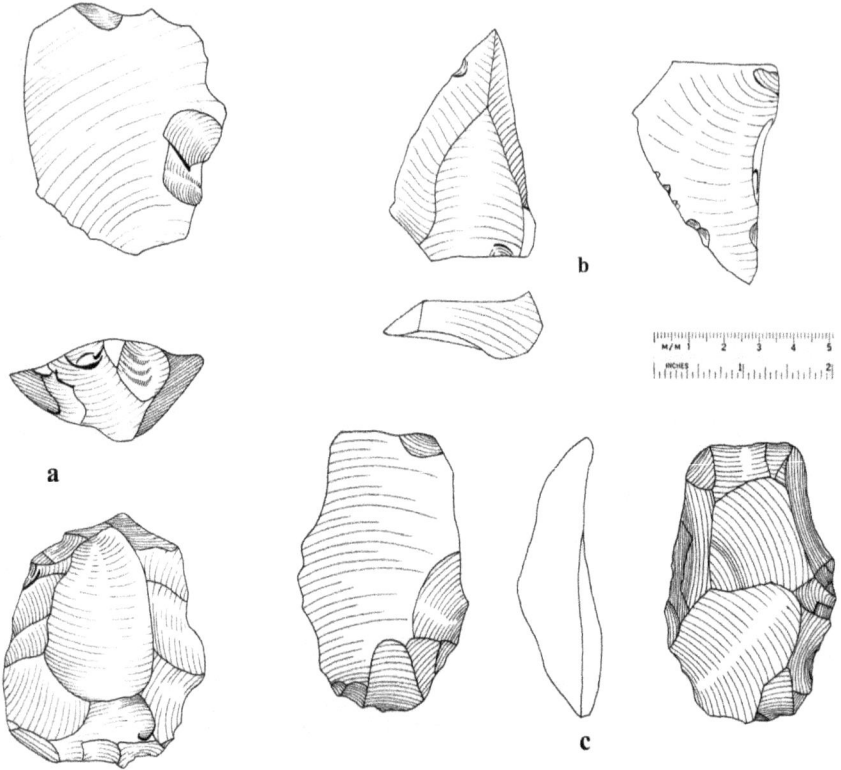

Figure 3.9. Capps technology end-products: (*a*) Shelley site; (*b–c*) Capps site.

width and thickness ranges from 6 to 51 mm and 1.5 to 19 mm, respectively. End-products struck from the prepared cores often possess slightly twisted, straight-to-convex cross sections and plunging distal ends (Figures 3.7–3.10). These flakes are either end-struck (Figures 3.7a, 3.8a, 3.10b, 3.11g), side-struck (Figures 3.9h, 3.10c), or corner-struck (Figures 3.9b, d, 3.10d) (Van Riet-Lowe 1945). Flake terminations are generally clean and smooth, with step fracturing uncommon.

A variety of striking platforms are present on Capps-Shelley end-products (tools), including faceted (Figures 3.8a, 3.10a), plain or simple (Figure 3.10d), dihedral (Figure 3.8b), and cortical. Over 50 percent of the striking platforms are missing on these specimens due to retouch or other factors. Platform types break down as follows: 21, or 24 percent, are simple or plain; nine, or 10 percent, are faceted; five, or 6 percent, are dihedral; seven, or 8 percent, are cortical; one, or 1 percent, is *chapeau de gendarme*, and the

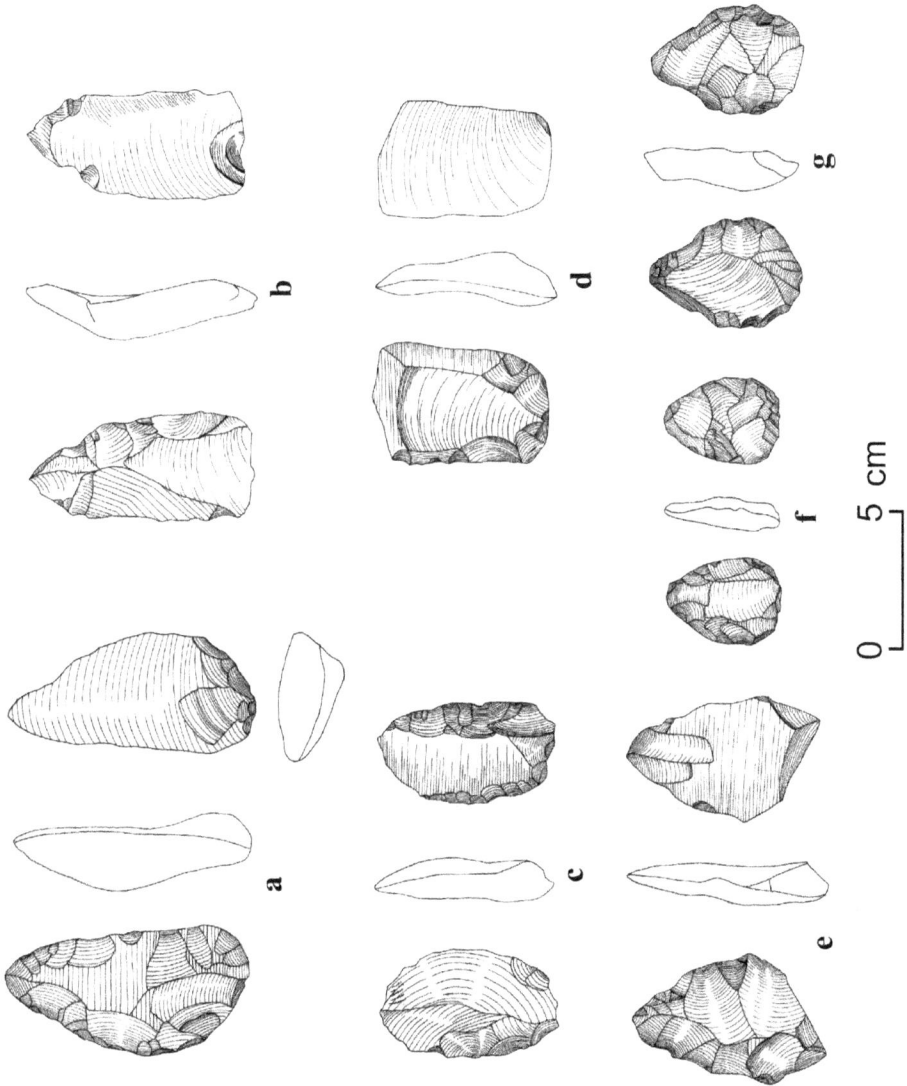

Figure 3.10. Capps technology end-products: (*a–e*) Capps site; (*f–g*) Shelley site.

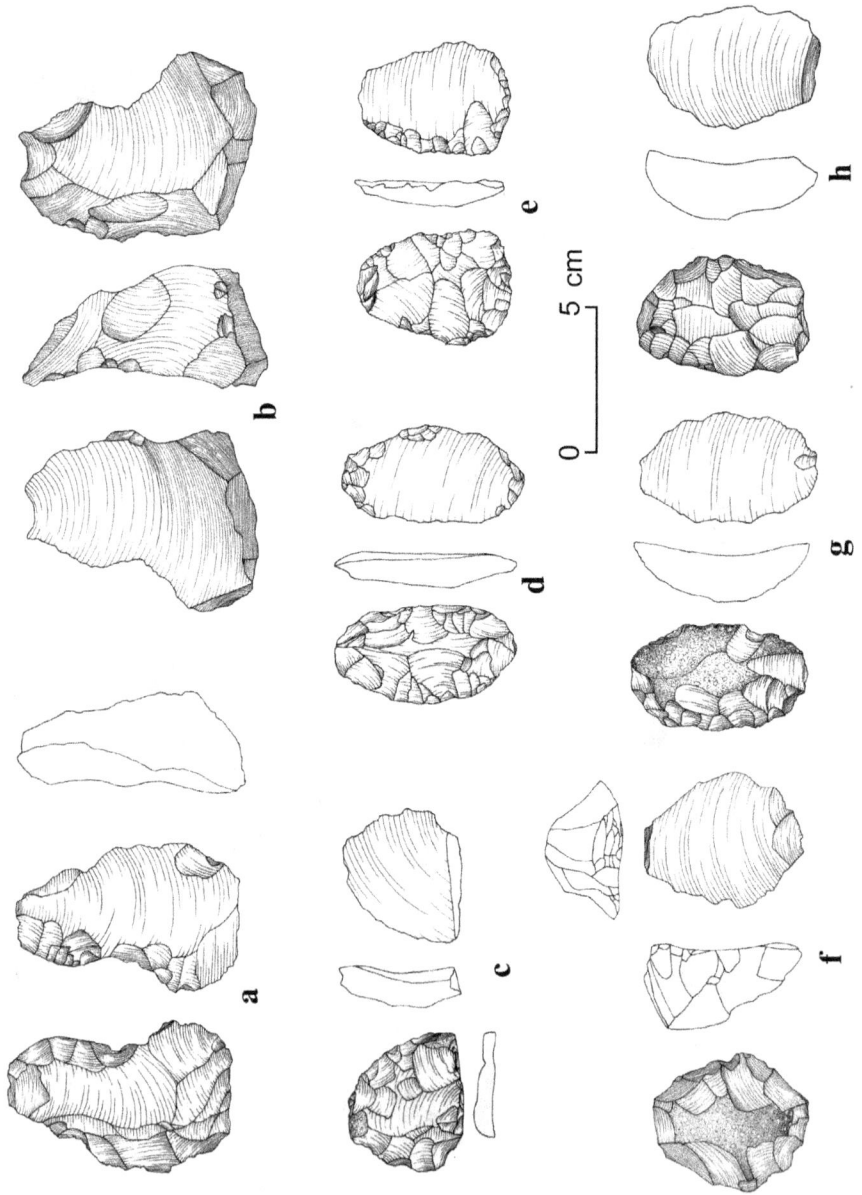

Figure 3.11. Capps technology end-products: (a) Capps site; (b) Shelley site; (c–d) Capps site; (e) Shelley site; (f) Capps site; (g) Shelley site; (h) Capps site.

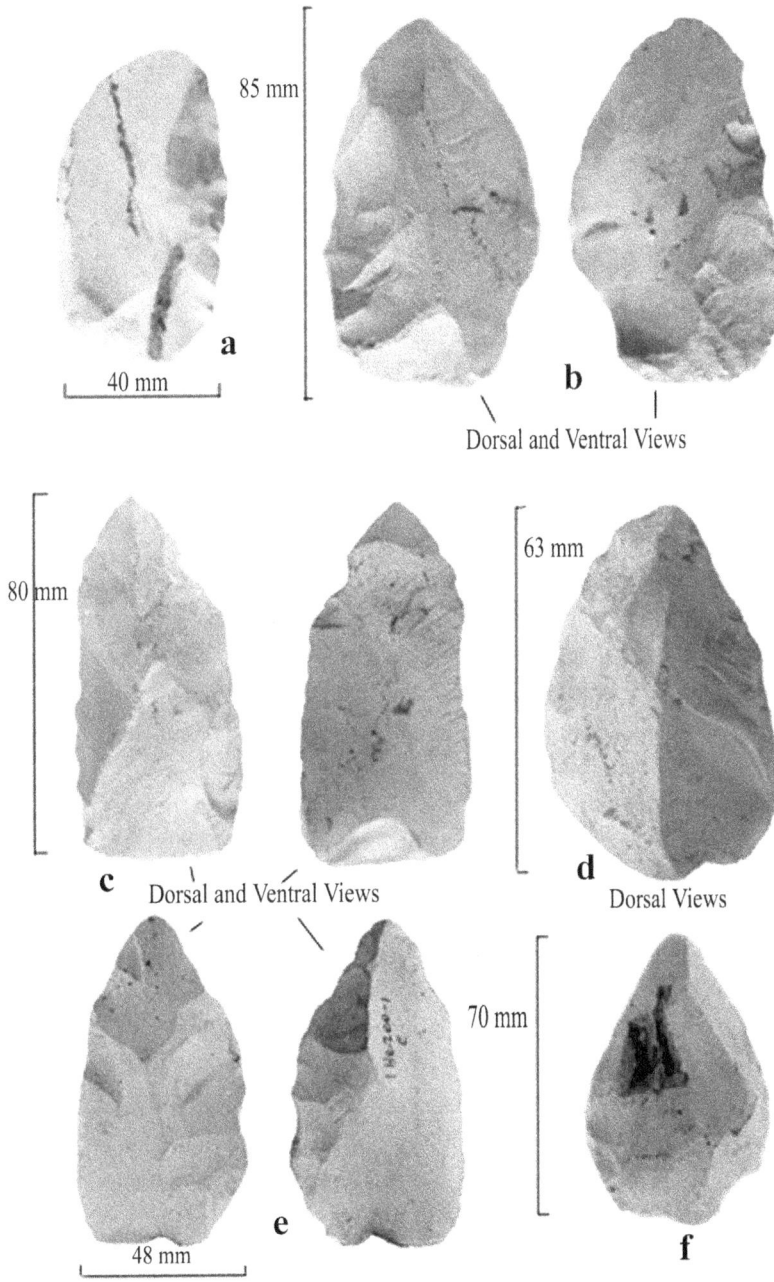

85 mm

40 mm

a

b

Dorsal and Ventral Views

80 mm

63 mm

c

Dorsal and Ventral Views

d

Dorsal Views

70 mm

48 mm

e

f

Figure 3.12. Capps technology end-products: (*a–d*) Capps site; (*e–f*) Shelley site.

Table 3.2. Summary Statistics for Capps Technology End-Products

	N	Mean	STD	Min	Max
Flake tool length	86	79.6	18.0	42.5	128.4
Flake tool width	89	47.2	14.2	20.2	121.5
Flake tool thickness	89	22.4	7.5	7.8	50.1
Est. working edge angle	89	49.0	15.3	25.0	90.0
Est. striking platform angle	41	100	7.2	85	110
Striking platform width	35	19.1	10.1	6.8	50.5
Striking platform thickness	36	7.8	4.2	1.5	19.5

remainder (greater than 50 percent) are indeterminate. The side-struck and corner-struck techniques emphasize removal of the flake end-product from the side of the core, sometimes resulting in a flake that is wider than long (Figure 3.10c). When this technique is applied, the axis of percussion is not parallel to the longest dimension of the flake, due to the orientation of the percussion blow and prior shaping of core surfaces. End-struck flakes exhibit an axis of percussion parallel to the longest dimension of the flake. Analysis of 89 end-products indicates that 30, or 34 percent, are end-struck; 13, or 15 percent, are side-struck; 21, or 24 percent, are corner-struck; and the remainder are indeterminate. Platform grinding is absent, and bulbs of percussion (prominent and diffuse) are present, along with an occasional eraillure scar and Hertzian cone (Figures 3.7a, 3.9b, d, 3.10a, c).

Retouch types present include direct, bifacial, alternate, use-modified, and none. A total of 22, or 25 percent, exhibit direct retouch; 14, or 16 percent, possess bifacial retouch; one shows alternate retouch; 33, or 37 percent, are use-modified at the macroscopic level; and 19, or 21 percent, show no macroscopic evidence of retouch or use. Retouch is both noninvasive and invasive (Figures 3.9–3.11) (Bordes 1961) and may be short, long, or covering (Bordes 1961). The location of retouch normally occurs either exclusively on the dorsal surface (direct) (N = 23) (Figures 3.9d, 3.10a, b, d, 3.11c, f, g, h) or simultaneously on dorsal-ventral surfaces (bifacial) (N = 15) (Figures 3.9c, g, 3.10f, g, 3.11a, e). Retouch is rarely on the ventral surface alone (N = 1) or platform (N = 1), but alternate retouch does occur with direct retouch along one dorsal margin, and inverse retouch along an opposing ventral margin (Figure 3.9e). The remainder have no intentional retouch. In addition to retouch/use modification some of the end-products (N = 19) exhibit secondary modification. One has a burin/tranchet blow (Figure 3.10b), nine are denticulated/notched (Figure 3.11a), one shows intentional platform thinning/removal (Figure 3.9h), three possess a graver/

projected beak, and five have been intentionally truncated (Figure 3.11c). The average working-edge angle on 89 Capps technology end-products or tools is 49 degrees, with a range from 25 to 90 degrees, suggesting that a wide range of subsistence activities occurred on-site (Table 3.2).

Capps Technology Flakes

A representative sample of 64 heavily patinated nonlinear flakes that ex-hibit Levallois-like preparation and attributable to Capps technology were analyzed from the Capps site. Summary metric data for the flakes is pre-sented in Table 3.3, and Figures 3.13–3.17 illustrate a representative flake sample. Capps technology nonlinear flake size is considerably smaller than the flake end-products described above, and most appear to have been pro-duced during core shaping/preparation/surface remodeling by percussion, using a controlled flat flaking technique. Some of the flakes exhibit minor traces of macroscopic use wear (N = 13) (Figure 3.16a), others have been intentionally truncated or snapped to form burin-like tips (Figure 3.14b), and some are notched (Figure 3.14a). Sixteen show no evidence of use at the macroscopic level. The remainder could not be adequately assessed for evidence of use, due to heavy weathering and erosion of flake surfaces. The flakes vary from thick to thin and small to large, with a mean length of 46.6 mm, a mean width of 38.0 mm, and a mean thickness of 12.2 mm. Flake length ranges from 25 mm to 83 mm, flake width from 19 to 74 mm, and flake thickness from 5 to 25 mm (Table 3.3). The estimated average interior striking platform angle is 103 degrees. Mean platform width is 17.0 mm, and mean platform thickness is 7.5 mm. Many of the flakes have an approxi-mate triangular shape with a pointed end (Figures 3.13d, 3.14c, 3.15a, b, d) while other common flake morphologies include square (Figure 3.13f), rectangular (Figures 3.13c, 3.14f, 3.16c), and oval-shaped (Figure 3.14e) due to their removal from a core flake release surface with a similar surface

Table 3.3. Summary Statistics for Capps Technology Nonlinear Flakes

	N	Mean	STD	Min	Max
Flake length	56	46.6	12.4	25.2	83.0
Flake width	60	38.0	10.2	19.5	73.9
Flake thickness	64	12.2	3.9	5.5	24.5
Est. striking platform angle	63	103	8.7	90	120
Striking platform width	56	17.0	8.4	5.5	49.0
Striking platform thickness	60	7.5	3.6	2.0	18.0

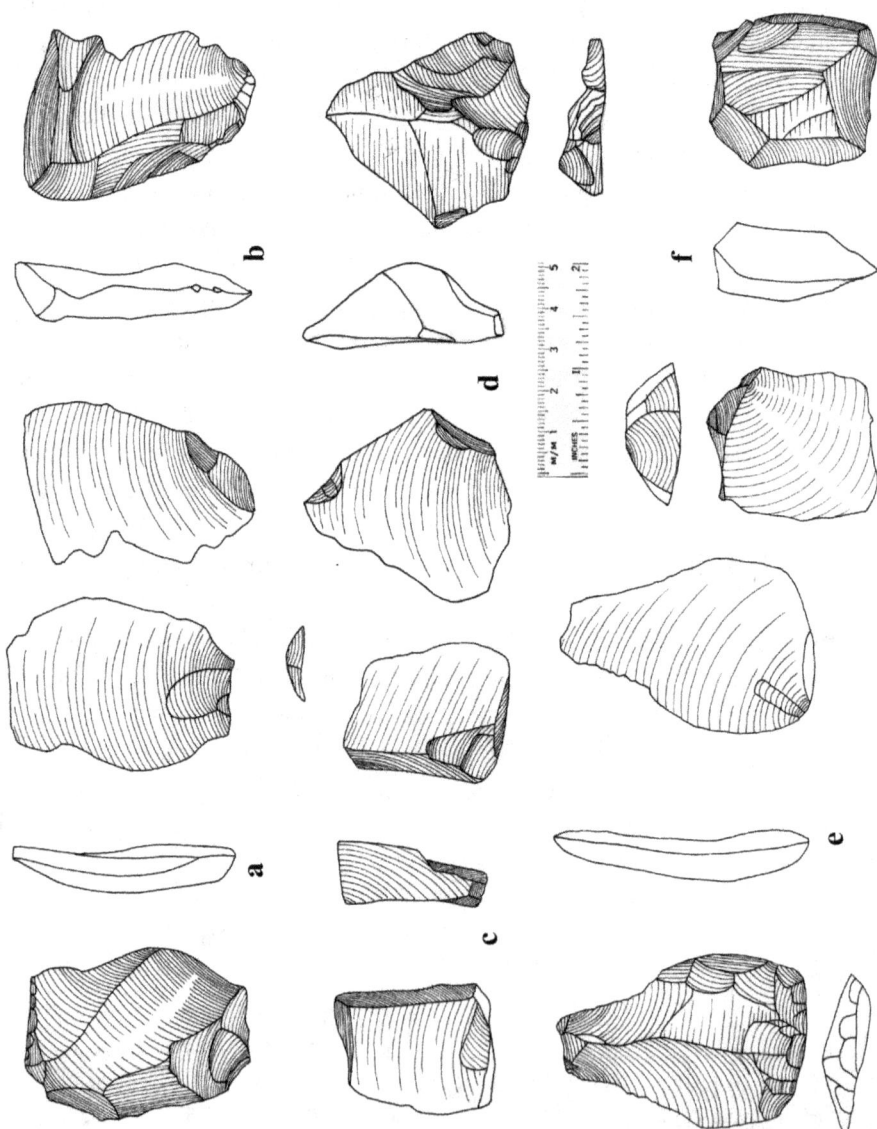

Figure 3.13. Capps technology flakes: (a–f) Capps site.

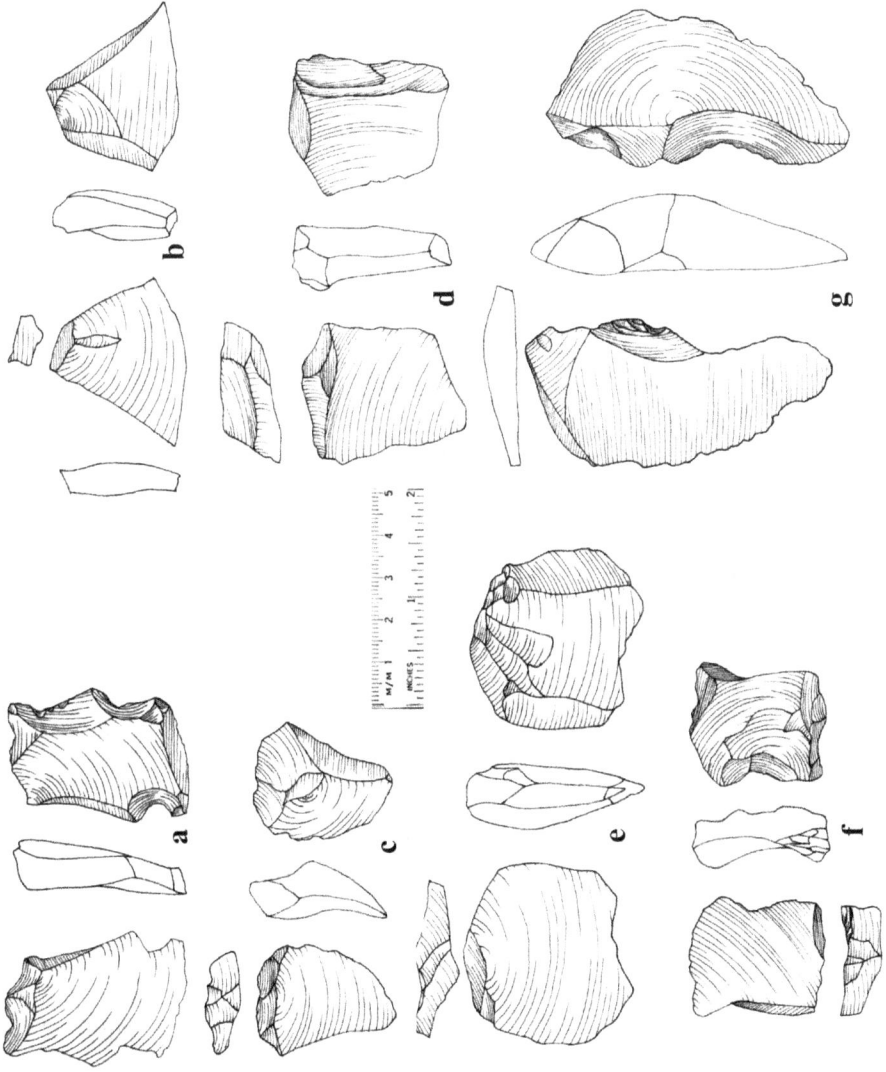

Figure 3.14. Capps technology flakes: (a–g) Capps site.

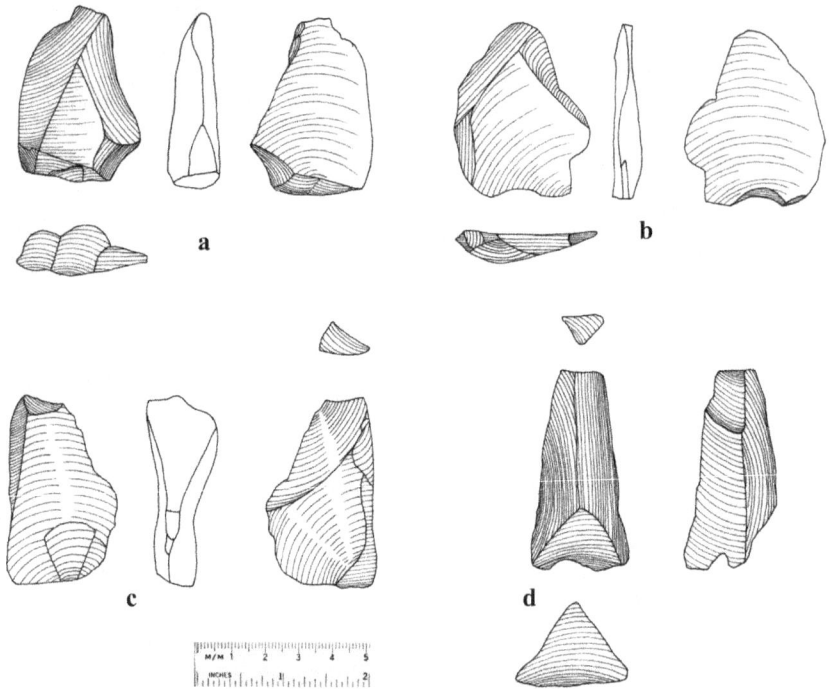

Figure 3.15. Capps technology flakes: (*a–d*) Capps site.

morphology. Some flakes are asymmetrical due to their removal as core shaping, rejuvenation, or maintenance flakes. Platform preparation types in the flake sample consist of plain or simple (N = 34) (Figure 3.14b), faceted (N = 22) (Figures 3.13d, f, 3.14a, c, e, f, 3.15a), and cortical (N = 7). The amount of cortex detected on flakes broke down as follows: 0–25 percent (N = 57), or 89.1 percent; 25–75 percent (N = 5), or 7.8 percent; and >75 percent (N = 2), or 3.1 percent. A total of 63 Capps technology flakes demonstrate the following: 48, or 76.2 percent, are end-struck (Figures 3.13a, 3.14c,3.15a,c); six, or 9.5 percent, are side-struck (Figures 3.14g, 3.16a); and nine, or 14.3 percent, are corner-struck (Figure 3.13b, e, f).

In addition to the nonlinear flakes described above, heavily patinated bladelike or linear flakes recovered from Capps-Shelley (N = 14) are relatively thick, with simple or faceted platforms that are unground (Figure 3.18). Eight of the specimens were recovered from Capps, and the remaining six from Shelley. Many of these linear specimens appear to have been produced during maintenance of core surfaces/striking platforms and in that sense may be termed platform rejuvenation flakes (Figure 3.18e, f). Others

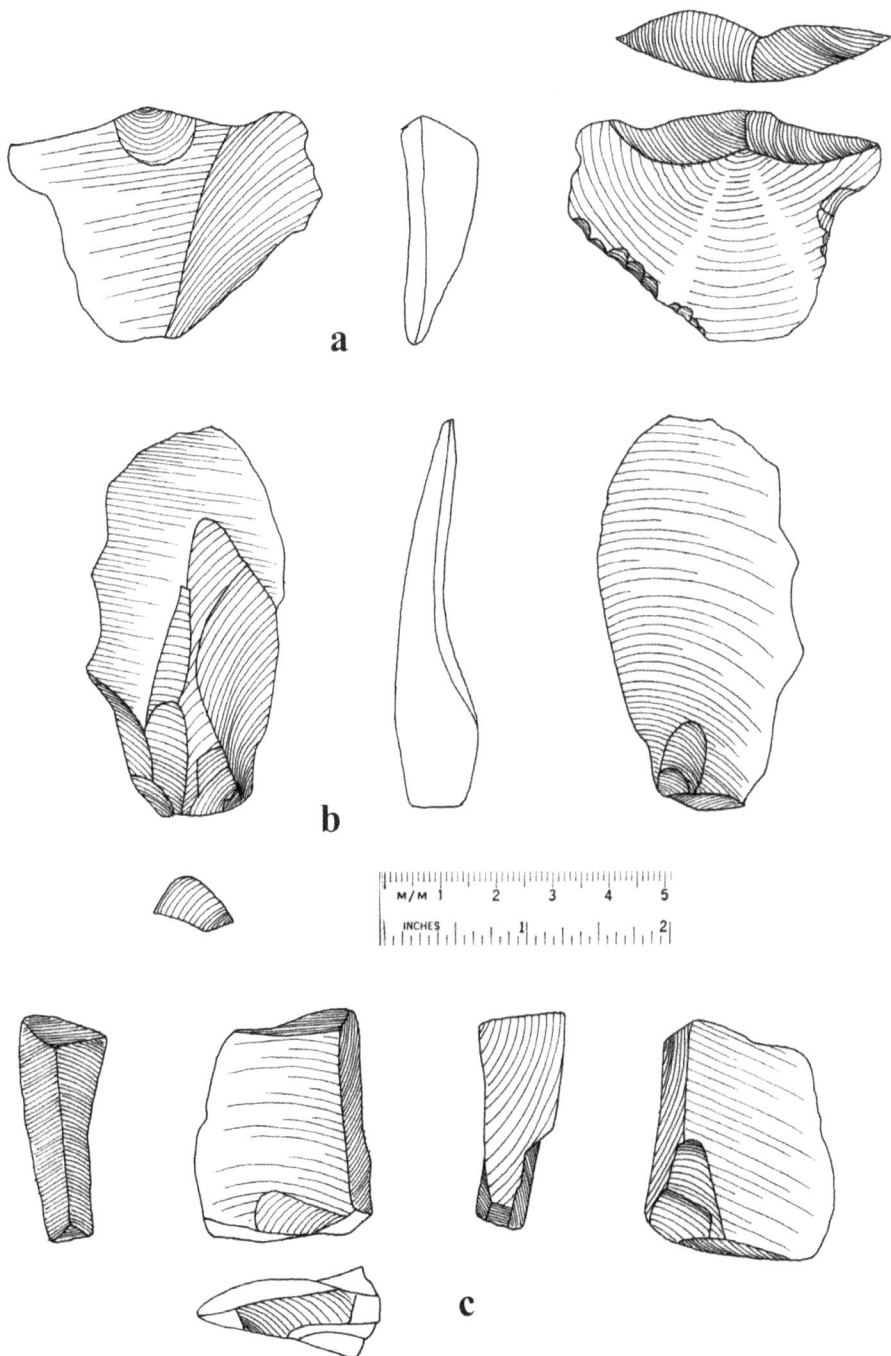

Figure 3.16. Capps technology flakes: (a–c) Capps site.

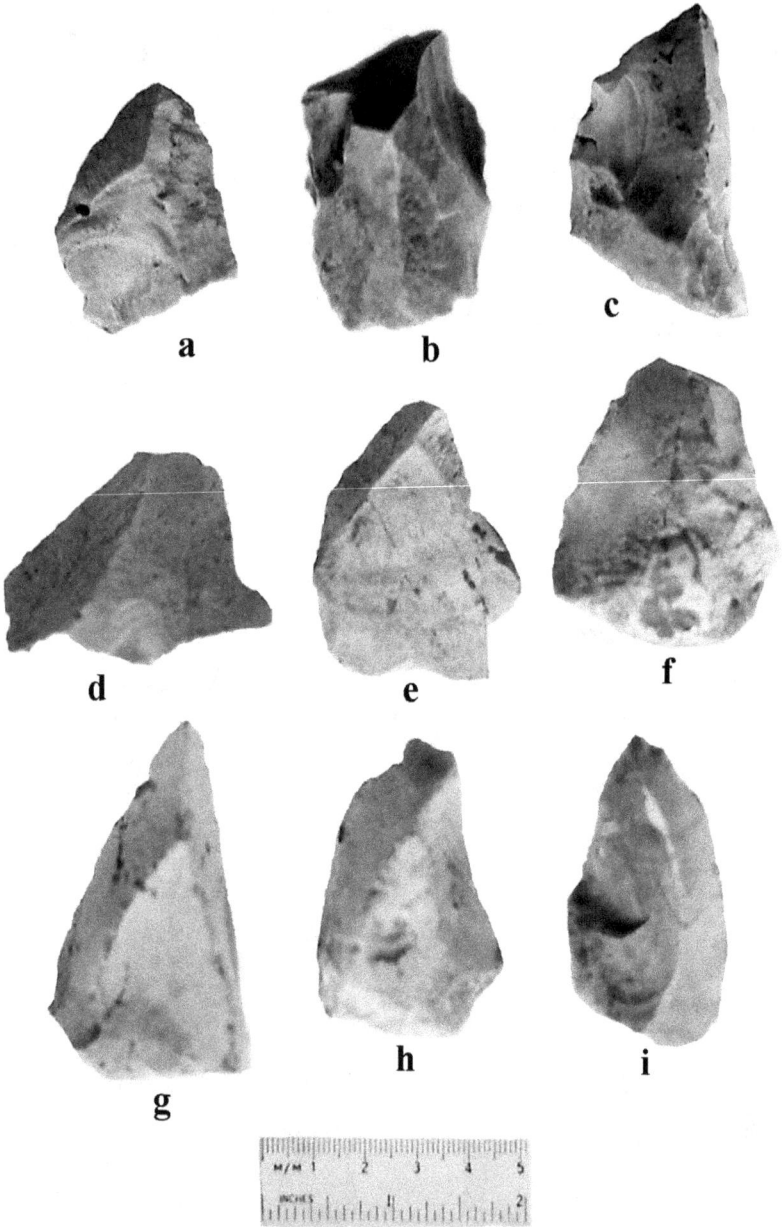

Figure 3.17. Capps technology flakes: (*a–i*) Capps site.

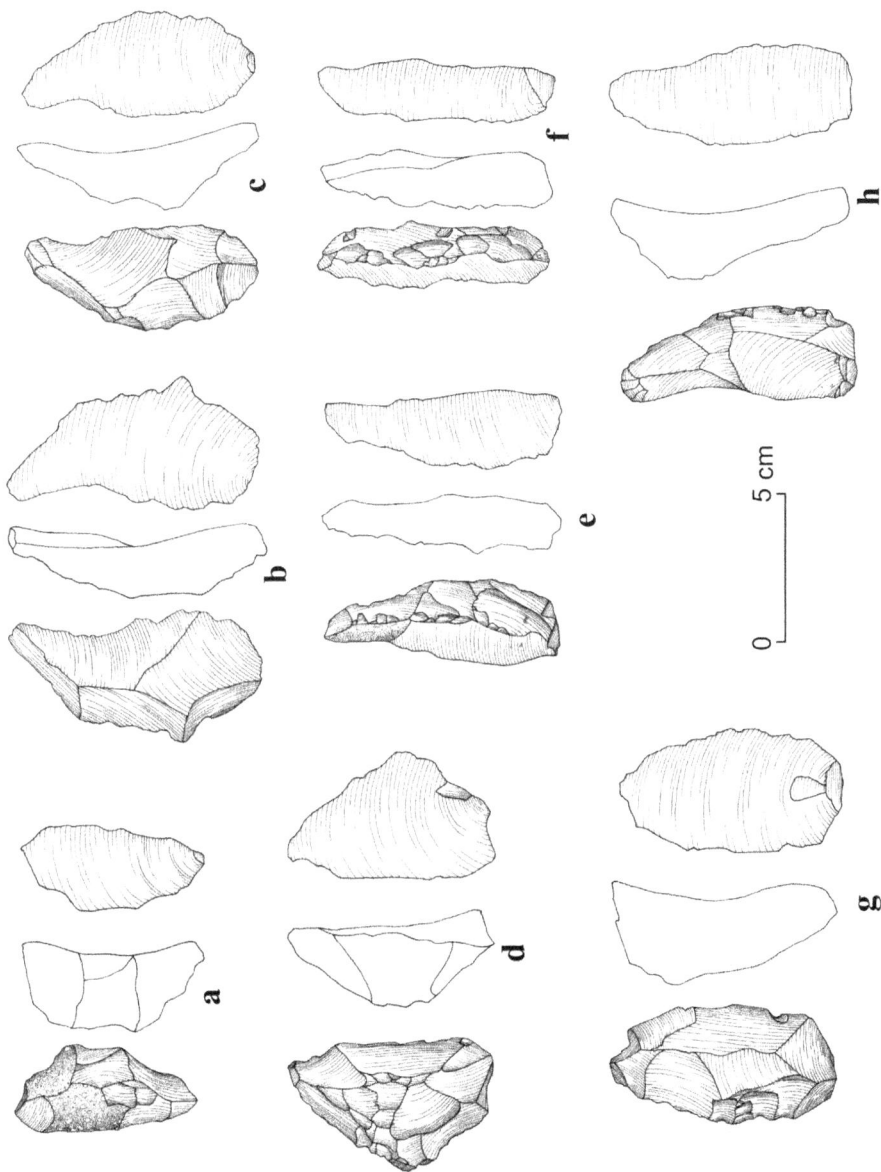

Figure 3.18. Capps technology linear flakes: (a) Capps site; (b) Shelley site; (c–e) Capps site; (f) Shelley site; (g–h) Capps site.

appear to have been systematically removed from a prepared convex core surface (Figure 3.18 b, c, g, h). The lateral margins are generally parallel, and they have an average length of 77.1 mm, an average width of 31 mm, and an average thickness of 19.5 mm. Linear flake length ranges from 47 to 91 mm, width ranges from 20 to 46 mm, and thickness ranges from 9 to 28 mm. Striking platform widths (N = 10) average 19.2 mm (range 7–34 mm), and striking platform thicknesses (N = 11) average 12 mm (range 3–27 mm). The mean internal striking platform angle for nine measurable specimens of 104 degrees (range of 95 to 115 degrees) is almost identical to the mean internal striking platform angle of the nonlinear flakes. A few exhibit evidence of use-retouch, but none appear to have been intentionally worked except for flaking associated with core preparation prior to detachment.

Evidence of core preparation is common in the form of ridges created either by converging flake scars and/or a combination of the intersection of large, linear facets and plain linear segments of core margins. Often the axis of percussion is perpendicular to previous core-shaping scars, indicating that production of the linear flake took advantage of a previously prepared core surface in a Levallois-like manner. Two specimens exhibit prior linear flake removals on the dorsal surface that originate from the same platform, while others have a single ridge on the dorsal surface created either by intersecting core preparation scars or the remnant of previous core striking platforms or both. In cross section the linear flakes are mainly triangular in form, and some are slightly twisted in cross section. Most are end-struck, although one is corner-struck. In lateral view the cross sections of the linear flakes exhibit a more or less straight profile (Figure 3.18 e, f), a slightly convex (curved) profile (Figure 3.18 b, d), or a highly convex (curved) "crested" appearance (Figure 3.18 g, h). Sometimes on curved specimens the distal portion of the linear flake indicates it dove toward the center of the core upon termination (Figure 3.18h).

Summary and Conclusions

The present analysis has described a prepared core technology that appears to compare favorably with Old World Middle Paleolithic technologies such as Levallois. In specific terms, the concept of Levallois technology in the Old World has traditionally been defined as a prepared core technology characterized by initial removal of flakes from the margin of the parent or objective piece by a hammer stone that creates striking platforms. These platforms then serve to shape the core and create a slightly convex upper or "domed" flake release surface. This domed surface is then reduced by removal of either a single large oval-shaped flake (*preferential*) or multiple flakes (*recurrent*). If the recurrent approach was used, flakes were removed from one end of the core only, from opposing ends of the core, or radially from multiple directions around the core periphery (Sandgathe 2005). Further Levallois core preparation may result in a variety of upper (flake release) and lower (flake initiation) surface configurations, such as an unprepared lower surface and a prepared upper surface or prepared upper (flake release) and prepared lower (flake initiation) surfaces, etc. (Van Peer 1992). The Mousterian, or disc core, technique in the Old World (Debénath and Dibble 1994) is characterized by centripetal flaking around the entire core margin and may be included within a broad category of "single surface" cores of which the classic Levallois technique is a member. However, flakes removed from the disc cores may be initiated either from opposing core margins in a bifacial manner or from a single hierarchical surface similar to Levallois (Sandgathe 2005).

End-products produced from Middle Paleolithic prepared cores, including those considered Levallois, include semi-circular and triangular flakes and blades and their form has been interpreted as the result of predetermined core shaping by many analysts. Striking platforms on Levallois flakes and flake end-products may be plain, faceted, dihedral, or *chapeau de gendarme* (Hovers 2009). End-products may be unretouched or retouched on one or more margins, and the retouch may be alternating, bifacial, or inverse retouch and continuous or discontinuous in nature. Retouch may be confined to near the tool margin or invasive and produced by direct percussion (Bordes 1961).

When we examine the results of the present analysis, it is prudent to compare them with Old World core and flake technologies such as Levallois and related Middle Paleolithic single-surface technology to determine similarities and differences. Referring to the results of the present analysis, it may be seen that many of the characteristics of Levallois or single-surface core technologies present in the Old World Middle Paleolithic are also present in the Capps-Shelley artifacts. Capps technology exhibits preparation of upper and lower core surfaces or combinations therein, lateral and distal core shaping, and removal of flakes/blades from a single release surface that are common in Levallois and related single-surface core reduction strategies. Flakes/spalls produced by Capps technology may be semicircular, triangular, or linear with their form directly related to overall core preparation form. Further, Capps technology flake/blade removals may be a single flake/blade or multiple removals from the same surface in a unidirectional, bidirectional, or radial manner similar to Levallois-related core reduction strategies. Disc cores are present in Capps technology as are *éclats débordants*, including pseudo Levallois points, a triangular form produced from Levallois-related single-surface core technologies in the Old World. Striking platforms on Capps technology end-products/flakes exhibit a range from plain to faceted, dihedral, and, rarely, *chapeau de gendarme*. Retouched Capps technology end-products exhibit direct percussion retouch in a manner similar to that described for Old World Levallois end-products (alternating, bifacial, inverse) and are continuous or discontinuous in nature.

The term *Levallois-like* has been used throughout the present analysis in reference to Capps technology because it appears to compare well with various published descriptions of Old World Levallois-related single-surface technologies (cf. Sandgathe 2005). Capps is a prepared core technology recognized in surface collections made at the Capps and Shelley sites. Capps technology cores possess prepared surfaces, and the end-products have a final form that is predetermined or controlled to a large extent by the nature of prior core shaping. Capps Levallois-like cores possess systematic preparation of core surfaces with heavy emphasis on percussion flaking of lateral/peripheral core margins as well as upper and lower core surfaces in a Levallois-like manner. The age and cultural affiliation of Capps technology are presently unknown.

Andrefsky (1987) points out that just because two artifact forms are morphologically or technologically similar it does not mean that one is derived from the other or that a common history is shared. It is clear that a case for independent invention or diffusion must be carefully demonstrated through proper methodology. The purpose of the present study as stated at the beginning is to provide a description of Capps technology and to promote further study. Since no dates are currently available for Capps technology, no direct historical relationship with Old World Levallois-related technologies can be established. Rather, we are faced with relying on the preponderance of evidence to suggest a cultural and chronological placement. The uniform heavy patination and staining of the Capps-Shelley artifacts certainly suggest some antiquity, but they cannot be used to date the artifacts, due to a variety of factors associated with patina formation, as discussed earlier. The apparent lack of heat treatment, expedient or amorphous core production, thin biface technology, prismatic blade technology, and pressure flaking (as indicated by surface collections made at the Capps site) lessens the likelihood that Capps technology is related to Clovis or later Holocene cultures. A number of flaked stone assemblages recovered from well-dated stratified sites across North America, including the southeastern United States, from Clovis through the late Holocene have been documented where the presence of heat treatment, prismatic blade technology, thin biface technology, amorphous or expedient cores, and pressure flaking is common (Bense 1987; Bradley et al. 2010; Coe 1964; Ensor 1981; Kimball 1996; Montet-White 1968; Thomas et al. 2013), among many others. None of these studies have mentioned Levallois-like technology as a principal technique used by site occupants.

Levallois-like technology that resembles Capps technology has been reported from multiple locations across the southeastern United States, in the Midwest, in the northeastern United States, in Arizona, and in Nevada (Figure 3.19). Surface-collected artifacts similar to Capps technology cores and flakes have been observed by the author from the Withlacoochee and Flint River drainages in south Georgia; the Container Corporation of America site in Florida; the Parsons, Tennessee, locality; site 12VG34 in Indiana; and locales in southern Nevada and Arizona (Ensor 2013, 2014). Further, the Timlin site in upstate New York (Figure 3.19) has reportedly produced Levallois-like artifacts from Pleistocene-age till deposits (Raemsch 1977a, 1977b). These examples tend to strengthen the case for Capps technology being a viable Levallois-like technology, since its repeated occurrence across a wide geographic area reduces the chance that Capps-Shelley artifacts represent some isolated, spurious instance of prepared core reduction with no known counterparts.

When the technological and morphological similarities evident in Capps technology with Old World Levallois technology are added to the mix, one is left with a dilemma. Where does Capps technology fit within the grand scheme of New World archaeology and the earliest Americans? Critical to addressing the problem of Capps technology and what types of historical connection(s) may or may not exist with Old World Levallois technology is dating the artifacts in solid archaeological context. This should be given top priority in future research.

Based on the results of the current analysis, it seems that our devotion to projectile point typology, thin biface production, recognition of prismatic blade technologies, and associated aesthetic qualities of carefully flaked specimens may have distracted us from other important issues regarding the flaked stone archaeological record of North America. The apparent lack of pre-Clovis artifacts in North America may have more to do with

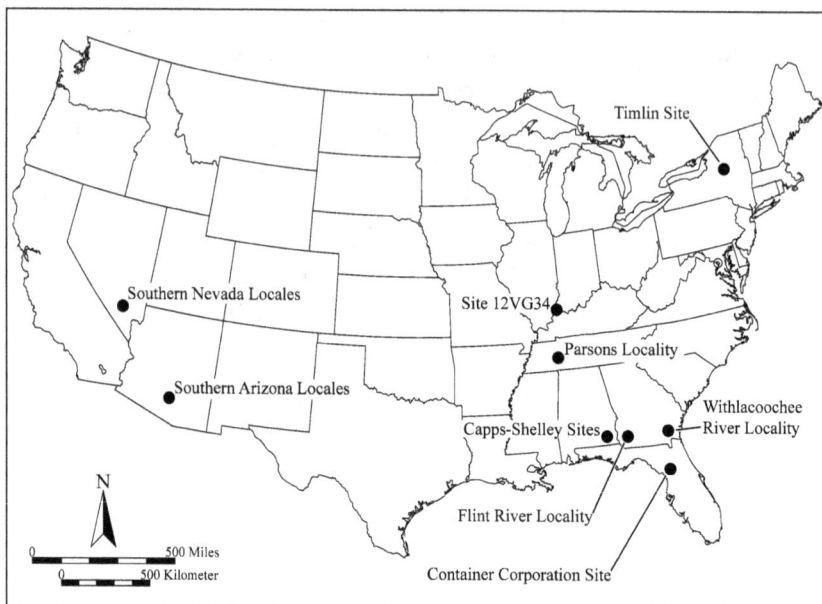

Figure 3.19. Location of sites/locales in North America with Levallois-like flaked stone technology.

artifact (technological) recognition (including mixing or obfuscation by later, more abundant remains) and the identification of appropriate landforms/contexts of proper age that are conducive to site preservation than an actual dearth of older sites. Perhaps the most critical aspect of archaeological interpretation lies not in the objects and their physical attributes, or in their location within the landscape, but within the psychological/cognitive framework of the investigator(s) asking questions about the phenomena under scrutiny. This follows because each individual determines the framework or context within which the remains are interpreted. The manner in which the individual contexts or frameworks are developed depends upon a variety of factors. They include personal training and experience, the capacity for entertaining new ideas, or a conservative approach to the subject matter. In other words, if one has a predefined range of expected outcomes or possibilities, there is a high likelihood that the outcome or determination will fall within this self-imposed universe, and a concomitant danger that the result will be a self-fulfilling prophecy. On the other hand, if the subject matter is approached without such limitations, then the outcome may have a number of possibilities above and beyond traditional interpretation. The difficult part lies in determining the degree to which the "facts" support either the traditional view or perhaps some new alternative. The search for the earliest Americans will undoubtedly continue for many years to come. While the interpretive value of the present analysis and observations is limited by the very nature of the data, it is hoped that the results will provide stimulus to search for evidence of early human occupation wherever it may exist across North America and elsewhere in the New World.

Acknowledgments

Thanks are extended to the late Caryn Hollingsworth and the late Dr. Brian Hesse for providing access to the archaeological collections at the University of Alabama-Birmingham. The artifact illustrations were prepared by Kevin Lomas, and the location maps were drafted by Ron Karl. Margaret Russell aided this study through her knowledge of the Capps and Shelley sites, which is greatly appreciated. Thanks also to two anonymous reviewers for their thoughtful comments and input.

4

THE VERO SITE (8IR009)

CURRENT INVESTIGATIONS SUGGEST
PLEISTOCENE HUMAN OCCUPATION

C. ANDREW HEMMINGS, JAMES M. ADOVASIO, FRANK J. VENTO,
AND ANTHONY J. VEGA

The Vero site (8IR009), also known as the Vero Man site or the Old Vero Man site, is a deeply stratified, multicomponent open site located within the city limits of Vero Beach, Indian River County, Florida (Figure 4.1). New excavations adjacent to the locus of Sellards' 1916 work demonstrate that the stratigraphic sequences across the Vero site are considerably more complex, and better preserved, than have previously been described. Intact strata span the period 22,000–2000 B.P. A flake from a polyhedral core recovered 11 cm above soil humates dated to 9620 ± 30 ^{14}C yr B.P. On a surface 20 cm below the humate date, more than 100 burned fragments of wood, soil, bone, and teeth from extinct taxa were recovered scattered across a 12 m^2 exposure. The unequivocal age of occupation has been pushed to ca. 11,000 B.P., with multiple apparent living surfaces below that level that are bracketed between 11,100 and 14,000 cal B.P.

The Vero site area lies within the Eastern Valley section of the Atlantic Coastal Plain physiographic province (Figure 4.2). The Eastern Valley section lies between the Atlantic Ocean on the east and the terrace riser for the Talbot marine terrace to the west. The Eastern Valley section in the vicinity of the site comprises two distinct marine terraces. The lower and younger is the Silver Bluff terrace, which lies at a nominal elevation of 5.18 m above mean sea level (amsl) and forms the dune, beach, and overwash landforms associated with the Atlantic Coastal Ridges. To the west, the section comprises the higher and older Pamlico terrace, which extends westward to its intersection with the Talbot terrace riser. The Silver Bluff terrace is of

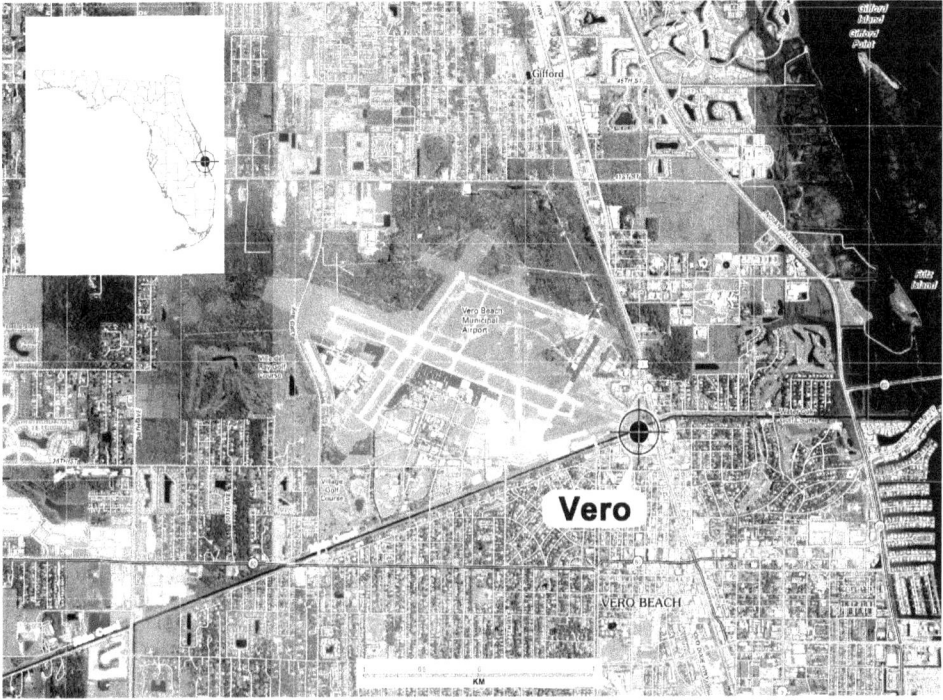

Figure 4.1. Location of the Vero site.

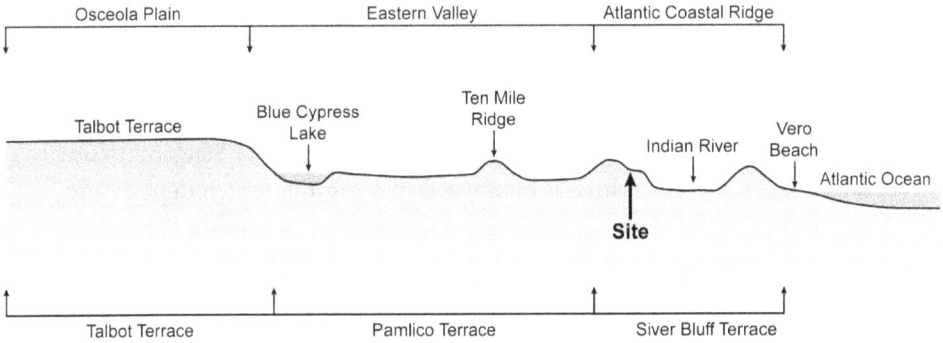

Figure 4.2. Schematic cross section of the Atlantic Coastal Plain physiographic province showing the location of the Vero site.

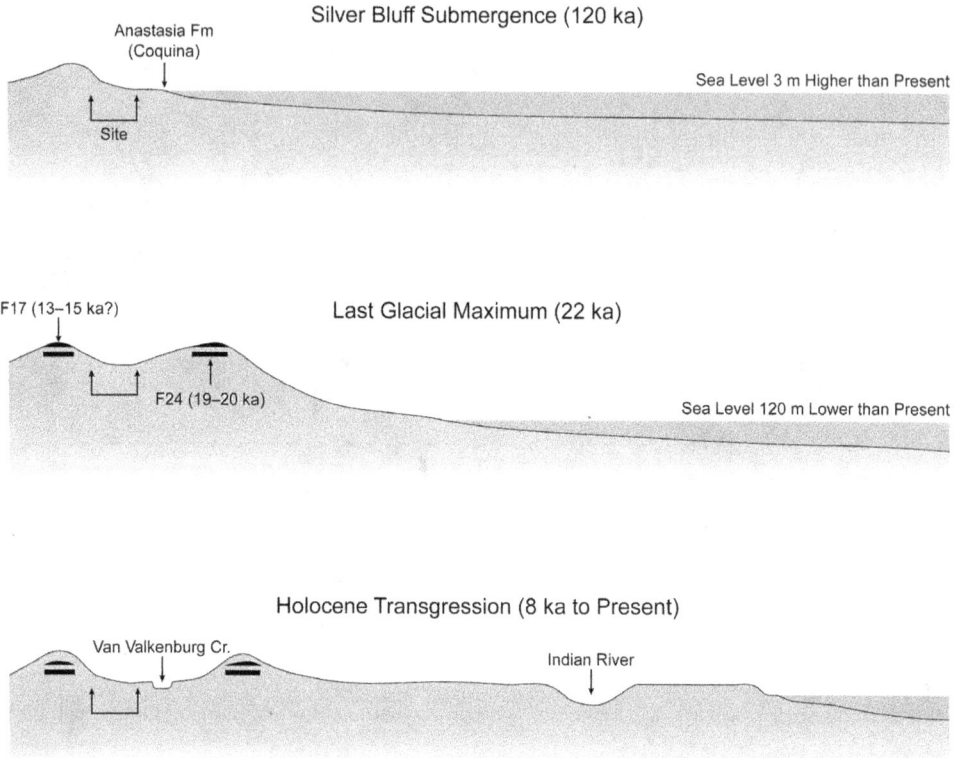

Figure 4.3. Geologic evolution of the general project area from the Sangamon Interglacial to the present.

Sangamon age (120,000 B.P.) and marks a period of time when sea level was 1–3 m higher than the present (Figure 4.3).

Interestingly, the Vero site proper is situated at the stratigraphic boundary between the high sea-level stand associated with the Sangamon-age Anastasia Formation, which is composed of a coquina beach deposit and relict dunes to the west, also of Sangamon age. The Anastasia Formation lies just 5 m east of the site near the active channel of the Lateral E canal. This formation was encountered only in deep auger probes emplaced along the filled margin of the canal and along an east–west 10-m-long backhoe trench that extended from the canal toward the active excavation area. It is interesting to note that between the existing canal and the excavation area, the Anastasia Formation pinches out and grades into aeolian sands that are disconformably capped by alluvial deposits of late Wisconsinan through Holocene age emplaced by overbank deposition from Van Valkenburg

Creek. The Holocene soils thin appreciably to the west, or away from the then-active stream channel.

The general site area encompasses ca. 8,000 m², although the exact site boundaries are unknown due to recent construction. A packing plant, Hogan and Sons, lies to the east and intrudes upon the site, the Indian River Administrative Complex lies directly south and west, and the Vero Beach Municipal Airport lies directly north.

Currently, the elevation of the artificially infilled surface of the site is ca. 6 m above normal canal pool level and ca. 5 m amsl. Prehistorically, the elevation of the site was much higher above the depressed sea levels of the Late Pleistocene. The project area is situated within the Myakka-Holopaw-Pompano soil association. This association consists of soils on broad, low flats, and in sloughs, poorly defined drainage ways, and depressional areas. At the site itself, the soils are mapped to the Pomello series. The Pomello series are classified as sandy, siliceous, hyperthermic Arenic Haplohumods. The Pomello soils are moderately well drained, moderately rapidly permeable soils that form in thick beds of marine sediment (Wettstein et al. 1986). An examination of the soils encountered during excavation at the site indicated that the soil designation is neither accurately mapped nor classified. Rather, the soils at the site have formed in either aeolian sands of Pleistocene through Holocene age or in late Wisconsinan through Holocene-age alluvium associated with overbank deposition and active lateral channel migration of Van Valkenburg Creek. Within the excavation area, these alluvial soils rest disconformably on aeolian sands, while to the east near Lateral E are Anastasia Formation coquina, beach deposits of Sangamon age.

The modern climate of Florida is categorized as humid subtropical, or Cfa in the Koppen climate classification system. The region is characterized as having relatively mild winters and long, hot summers. Much of this is due to the significant maritime influence exerted upon the area by the North Atlantic Ocean and the Gulf of Mexico.

Average cold-month temperatures are ca. 15–16°C. Freezing temperatures, although unexpected in most years, are not uncommon through the state. The coldest month on average is January, the time of most frequent Arctic outbreaks.

In Florida, two general synoptic conditions produce freezing temperatures (Rogers and Rohli 1991; Rohli and Rodgers 1993). The first is associated with migratory cold air masses or Arctic outbreaks, the second involves nighttime radiational cooling. Both situations may result from the same synoptic conditions following a cold front passage. Indeed, radiational cooling may bring further surface cooling to an area already affected by an Arctic outbreak (Vega and Binkley 1994). This may be particularly damaging to the fragile swamp ecosystems that dominate the state. However, considerable modification (warming) of the Arctic air masses is typical as the air masses approach the Gulf of Mexico. Therefore, as noted above, extremely cold temperatures are relatively uncommon.

History of Research

In early 1913 Florida State Geologist Elias H. Sellards appealed to the public for information on fossil finds across the state for a volume the Florida Geological Survey was compiling on the land animals of Florida. In a *St. Lucie Tribune* article (21 February 1913), Sellards alerted readers to the specific species and skeletal elements they might encounter.

Isaac Weills, who assisted Sellards and many other workers at the Vero site, was interviewed by the *Indian River Farmer* (5 November 1914). Weills spoke about the faunal remains he was finding near the spillway of the Vero canal and indicated that several bones had already been identified by Sellards. Weills also noted that he was arranging to have Sellards visit the site. Shortly thereafter, the *Fort Pierce News* (19 February 1915) carried a brief note discussing the Sellards visit and some of the Pleistocene faunal remains they had recovered. This newspaper article chronology confirms that Sellards not only knew of the site but had also visited and collected below the spillway prior to the site becoming a locus of archaeological investigation. Sellards later stated that at the time Vero was brought to his attention, it was one of about 10 sites under study in the area (Sellards 1917a, 1917b).

The first publication of Vero fossil material from the canal excavation also predates the discovery of human remains and artifacts. The Florida Geological Survey Seventh Annual Report includes an article by Sellards (1915:25–116) that provides several pictures and descriptions of extinct horse (*Equus* sp.) and giant armadillo (*Holmesina septentrionalis*) skeletal elements recovered from Vero.

Vero evolved from a Pleistocene fossil locus to an Early Man archaeological site in October 1915, when Frank Ayers found in situ human bones eroding from the canal wall. In early February, Sellards had returned to the site and discovered additional in situ human remains, with the help of Ayers, Weills, and others (*Fort Pierce News* 1916). These discoveries set in motion additional fieldwork throughout the year as well as site visits by a considerable number of the Early Man "authorities" of the time. Sellards announced the Vero site to the world in the 1 July 1916 issue of *Science* and published an open invitation to examine the site (Sellards 1916a).

The first of two small Vero symposia was held in October 1916 and was attended by O. P. Hay, R. Chamberlin, A. Hrdlička, G. G. McCurdy, T. W. Vaughn, E. H. Sellards, and several local individuals. This meeting led to a special January issue of *Geology*, in which the conflicting interpretations of the site's geology, archaeology, and physical anthropology were aired (*Journal of Geology* 1917). A second, smaller conference was held at the site in March 1917, attended by botanist E. W. Berry, E. H. Sellards, H. Gunter, and R. T. Chamberlin.

These conferences were followed by a veritable torrent of claims, counterclaims, and contradictions. Chamberlin correctly described the unrelated, undisturbed, upland geologic sequence west of the fossil and putative human remains bearing pond/creek deposits. Hrdlička created enough doubt in the context of the recovered material to achieve a victory, at least in his own mind. McCurdy and William H. Holmes pronounced the artifacts to be recent. Hay attributed many of the faunal remains from the site to new, previously unknown species and declared the human occupation to be hundreds of thousands of years old. Sellards correctly described the pond/creek basin sediments but did not accurately interpret the extent of post-depositional disturbances. Close examination of the published literature, surviving archival notes, and known collections of materials unequivocally demonstrate that the precise age of all stratigraphic layers at Vero was unknown. Furthermore, the actual age of the human remains and artifacts has remained problematic to the present.

The failure to resolve the age of the Vero deposits can be attributed to several factors. First, Sellards departed for a new position in Texas in 1919 and ceased his investigations at Vero, leaving the site's interpretation somewhat under a cloud. Second, the materials (artifactual, botanical, and faunal) recovered from Vero were dispersed to at least 24 repositories throughout North America and thus were never systematically organized, inventoried, studied, or published. Unfortunately, the human remains recovered during the initial investigations are widely scattered, and some have been missing since 1946 (Stewart 1946). A note card found among Vero casts at the Smithsonian Institution indicated the skull of Vero Man was returned to the Florida Geological Survey in the 1950s. The known materials are being incorporated in our active research.

Despite the failure to resolve the age of the human and artifactual material that Sellards recovered from the site, interest in the site continued, and additional work was sporadically conducted. Nels Nelson dug at Vero for two days in May 1917 and produced a brief summary of his visit (Nelson 1918:100–102). Later visitors included J. Gidley, F. B. Loomis, J. C. Merriam, E. B. Howard, A. Jenks, P. McKellar, H. M. Ami, O. Abel, H. Richards, and I. Rouse, among many others. Most of these visitors did not publish on the site, although Sellards continued to do so until his death in 1961.

Following Nelson's brief excavations, very little work was conducted at Vero until 1956–1957, when University of Florida graduate student Robert Weigel initiated limited horizontal excavations with Sellards in attendance (Weigel 1962). Weigel recovered some 20,000 small amphibian, reptile, and animal bones from creek basin sediments. After Weigel's research, professional interest in the site waned, although collectors still visited the locality in search of fossils. The site continues to be mentioned in discussions of the peopling of the New World.

Interest in the site was renewed in 2008, when plans to develop a water treatment plant threatened negative impacts on a considerable portion of the site. Compliance inquiries by then state archaeologist Ryan Wheeler and research activity by Barbara Purdy prevented the destruction of the site and generated considerable local interest that ultimately initiated new professional archaeological scrutiny. Site coring and trench examinations by Doran, Stafford, and Purdy between 2008 and 2010 indicated that although considerable disturbance had occurred, large pockets of intact sediments still existed (McFadden et al. 2012). In 2010 a citizen group called The Old Vero Ice Age Sites Committee (OVIASC) was formed to promote new research at the site. In 2012 OVIASC contracted with C. Andrew Hemmings and Mercyhurst Archaeological Institute (MAI) to conduct excavations and attendant analyses at the site in 2013–2014. In 2014 Harbor Branch Oceanographic Institute of Florida Atlantic University joined OVIASC and MAI as a third partner in the new ongoing Vero research.

The first season of excavation began on January 6, 2014 and ended on May 30, 2014. An 11-person team composed of trained crewpersons and highly experienced supervisory staff worked 10–12 hours per day, six days per week. Excavation and documentation protocols were exceedingly rigorous and precise. These protocols were initially developed during the multiyear, multidisciplinary excavations at Meadowcroft Rockshelter (36WH297) in southwestern Pennsylvania. The excavations at that National Historic Landmark site are widely considered to be the most carefully excavated of any Paleoindian locality in the entire New World. Refined and enhanced in literally hundreds of excavations throughout the United States and seven foreign countries, the Meadowcroft-developed protocols (see below) were employed throughout both Vero excavation.

The 2015 field season began January 5, 2015, and ended May 6, 2015. Investigations have focused on further exposing and excavating the Late Pleistocene bone veneer and the deeply buried 5A horizon. Although limited, a 25-cm-×-25-cm portion of this stratum was excavated to a depth of 41 cm. Additionally, a 14.1 m² area to the west of the 2014 excavation block was excavated, exposing the 0 cm surface of the 3A horizon, and in three units, exposing the 0 cm floor of F9 (2Bhs).

Research Design

The current investigations at Vero were designed to be a multiyear, multi-disciplinary, empirically oriented research initiative. The strategic project goals include the systematic acquisition, analysis, and integration of any and all data bearing on the archaeology, history, paleoecology, geology, geomorphology, pedology, hydrology, climatology, and floral and faunal succession of the immediate project area and surrounding localities. The specific primary goals of the ongoing field investigations are: (1) detailed documentation of the site stratigraphy, (2) characterization and correlation of the stratigraphic units identified by Sellards with those exposed during the current excavations, and (3) systematic collection of all data utilizing the most precise instrumentation and techniques of which the research staff was cognizant.

The implementation of the basic research strategy, simple though it was in theory, was very complex in practice. Extensive recent and past construction events have significantly modified the landscape in the project area and subsequently buried potentially pristine deposits. The aforementioned coring and trenching succeeded in confirming the presence of potentially intact early Holocene and Late Pleistocene stratigraphic sequences at the site underlying at least 1.8 m of early 1900s canal dump and modern fill. Five specific cores emplaced immediately southwest of the confluence of the Main Drainage Canal and Canal Lateral E and northeast of Indian River County Administrative Complex were of the most interest, as they indicated the presence of at least two deeply buried superimposed paleosols that directly dated to 7060 ± 30 ^{14}C yr B.P. and $17{,}620 \pm 80$ ^{14}C yr B.P.

The 2014 excavations were confined to a relatively small portion of the site measuring ca. 28 m east–west by ca. 16 m north–south. (Formal

Figure 4.4. Field crew assembling WeatherPort Shelter System over the active excavation area.

excavations were confined to an even smaller area measuring ca. 18 m east–west by ca. 7 m north–south.) In 2015 the active excavation block was expanded from 35 m² to a total of 50 m².

In order to expose the apparently intact buried paleosols, the overlying modern fill was excavated to a maximum depth of ca. 2.5 m using two Badger 1085c Cruz-Air mechanical excavators. Excavation was terminated at ca. 20–83 cm above the deposits of interest, and a 60-ft-×-24 ft WeatherPort Shelter System was erected on the exposed surface to protect the formal excavation area, deposits, crew, and equipment during the course of the field investigations. The enclosed site area was equipped with lights, phone and data lines, electricity, and a security system (Figure 4.4). Preparing the site for the formal excavations was extraordinarily complex and time-consuming. These site preparation procedures were extensively documented and photographed with a Nikon D3 digital camera and a variety of lenses.

The sequence of events, processes, and specific excavation and sampling procedures involved in establishing and executing this project are too lengthy to discuss here in detail. They will be exhaustively addressed in future project reports, but a summary of the excavation methodology is warranted.

After the WeatherPort and associated utilities were in place, an arbitrary 1-m-interval grid system, oriented 12 degrees west of magnetic north (348°) was established within the WeatherPort interior. The physical position of the WeatherPort within the project area had been oriented parallel to the southern boundary of the main drainage canal. To maximize the number of excavation units that could be established within the structure, the grid system was not oriented to magnetic north. Horizontal and vertical coordinates were reckoned with a Spectra Precision Focus 10 Total Station setup daily over a permanent bench mark designated Datum A (east 5,000 m, north 5,000 m, 2.85 m amsl). All elevations were recorded in relation to the Carter Associates Benchmark (elevation 16.64 ft, North American Vertical Datum [NAVD] 1988) located at modern ground surface, and also in relation to depth below Datum A. The interior of the WeatherPort was then extensively photographed and mapped via total station. Wooden access platforms were constructed around the interior perimeter of the Weather-Port to allow the field crew and supervisors to move around the site with minimal disturbance to the sediments.

Excavation Methodology

Excavation was conducted within natural strata in 5-cm arbitrary levels and, when required, 2.5-cm arbitrary levels, again, within natural strata. The removal of all sediment was completed with masonry trowels (5.5-in and 4.5-in) and, when warranted and/or feasible, flat-bladed shovels and single-edged razor blades. Arbitrary levels within natural stratigraphy never exceeded 5 cm, even when shovels were employed during the excavation of the stable overbank deposits (labeled F5 between the north 5001 m and 5004 m grid lines [see below, Site Stratigraphy and Dating]). Additionally, shovels were permitted only when it was determined that within the first 7 m², the ca. 50-cm-thick stratum was completely devoid of artifactual or ecofactual material. The crew switched to trowels approximately 10–15 cm above the stratigraphic interface between this stratum and underlying stratum F9, and this entire interface was exposed entirely by hand. Shovel excavation of stratum F5 was terminated prior to the exposure of a piece of flaked stone debitage in situ on the 39-cm floor of the stratum.

Excavation proceeded by determining the vertical relationship of the excavation post-mechanical-removal of the fill to the previously examined stratigraphy in the cores. This necessitated the removal of the remnant fill by hand, moving from the eastern to the western end of the WeatherPort

Above: Figure 4.5. General view of WeatherPort interior after mechanical removal of overburden with grid system emplaced. Active excavation area prior to "cleaning."

Left: Figure 4.6. General view of WeatherPort interior with grid system emplaced. Units within the active excavation area are clean. White string demarcates areas of remnant overburden.

across 80 m² to expose a "clean" surface. These 80 units were then indi-
vidually photographed and mapped prior to further excavation (Figures 4.5
and 4.6).

Visual and tactile observation of the cleaned units and a series of five
3¼-in bucket auger tests around the WeatherPort exterior suggested that
paleosols identified in the cores could be easily reached on the eastern end
of the WeatherPort interior; thus, an east–west trench spanning seven grid
units was opened on the southern end of the WeatherPort. The excavation
proceeded by exposing stratigraphic interfaces within a 7-m-×-1-m trench
between the east 5009 m and west 5016 m grid lines proceeding from the
southern end of the site to the northern end. As interfaces were exposed,
profiles and floors were photographed and mapped. As each interface was
completely exposed across the active excavation area (32.9 m²), a series of
interface photos were taken from various angles with various lenses with
the grid strung and unstrung.

Strata and microstrata were defined by subjective criteria, including
texture, apparent composition, friability, degree of compaction and, on a
much more limited basis, color. Objective, quantifiable verification of the
integrity of these units will be provided by chemical, grain size, and com-
positional analysis.

All fill from all strata was dry processed through stacked 1/8-in and
1/16-in screens. In order to recover materials smaller than that, a constant
volume sample (CVS) of sediment was taken from the southwest corner of
every arbitrary level of every stratum, unless a stratigraphic unit was not
present or had been fully excavated in the southwest corner. If a CVS could
not be taken, a soil sample was collected from a portion of the excavation
unit where the stratum still existed. When possible, the volume of sediment
collected for the soil sample was the same as the CVS. If the same volume
of sediment could not be collected, the total volume available was collected
and recorded. The rationale for collecting these samples is twofold: (1) artifactual and ecofactual remains that pass through the screens are captured
during flotation processing, and (2) only 1,000 cm³ of the collected sediment is processed via flotation, and the remaining "split" is retained for
grain-size analysis, analysis of the silt clay fractions, carbonate analysis,
palynological assay, geochemical composition, trace element scrutiny, mi-
crofaunal study, and at the most minute level, electron microscope analysis
of the digenesis of individual sand grains.

Specific geological sampling procedures employed during the excavation
included the extraction of three pollen columns and one geologic column.

Bulk samples of ca. 362.87 g were collected at 5-cm or 2.5-cm sampling intervals in each column. Where sediment changed composition, that is, at stratum interfaces, samples were taken on both sides of the change. The sample columns were placed to ensure complete coverage of all major strata at the site within the active excavation area. Samples were also collected from the seven bucket augers extracted to the east, west, and north of the active excavation area during the course of the field season.

All notes pertaining to the excavation were recorded on five kinds of standardized MAI forms in electronic format, which were subsequently printed in duplicate. During the 2014 field season, over 1,200 pages of notes were amassed, with another 1,000 added in 2015. Additionally, the excavation was extensively photo-documented prior to, during, and at the end of the field seasons. In all, over 6,000 photographs were taken during the course of the excavation.

Over the 124 working days at Vero, in 2014 an area measuring 32.9 m^2 was hand excavated, removing ca. 46 m^3 of sediment. This area was expanded over 106 work days in 2015. A subset of these units were excavated to a maximum depth of just over 4 m below modern ground surface. In total, over 3,400 samples (^{14}C, soil, CVS, pollen columns) have been collected in two seasons. Of these samples, six AMS samples from the active excavation area have been dated, and several more will be assayed shortly, including materials recovered in the deepest stratigraphic unit (F30).

Site Stratigraphy and Dating

During the course of the archaeological investigations at the Vero site, 15 distinct natural strata were defined (Figures 4.7 and 4.8). These strata comprise four distinct soil generations. The lower two soil generations have formed in aeolian sands of late Wisconsin age, while the overlying three upper soil generations are developed on late Wisconsin through Holocene-age alluvium associated with Van Valkenburg Creek.

The lowermost two soil generations consist of a 41-cm thick, dark brown (10YR3/4) sand cumulic A horizon designated F24 (5A), which was encountered only in the deep hole excavation units (east 5,013 m, north 5,001 m; east 5,014 m, north 5,001 m) and in auger probe excavations lying west of the excavation area. This horizon has been dated to between 19,780 ± 70 ^{14}C B.P. and 21,840 ± 70 ^{14}C B.P. (Table 4.2). The F24(5A) horizon likely formed during a prolonged period of dune stability during the Late Pleistocene in

Figure 4.7. General view of F4 and F5 (in profile along the 5016 m east grid line), and F9, F17, F19, F20, and F22–24 (in profile along the 5015 m east grid line), facing east.

Florida, when sea levels were as much as 120 m lower than today. Vento and Stahlman (2011) have identified multiple late Wisconsin-age paleosols that correspond with the 3A horizon (ca. 13,000 B.P.) and the 5A horizon (ca. 22,000–18,000 B.P.) on St. Catherines Island, Georgia (Figure 4.9). Geoarchaeological investigations in eastern Maryland from the Miles Point site, Elliott Island, Paw Cove, and Oyster Bay have yielded correlative paleosols (ca. 25,000–12,000 B.P.), some of which allegedly contain in situ flaked stone artifacts (Lowery 2005, 2007, 2009; Lowery et al. 2010). At Miles Point a basal loess (Miles Point Loess) was dated 41,000–25,000 B.P. and is overlain conformably by a buried paleosol (Tilghman soil), which contains diagnostic artifacts of Clovis age disconformably overlying the Tilghman soil). The Tilghman soil is dated 25,000–18,000 B.P. and corresponds temporally with the basal 5A horizon at Vero Beach and multiple dated deeply buried paleosols on St. Catherines Island, Georgia (Vento and Stahlman 2011)). This regionally persistent paleosol documents a rather lengthy episode of stability during the Last Glacial Maximum (LGM), when the coastal barrier islands stood as high (>90 m above sea level) hills and were welded to the continent, lying well inland from the shoreline.

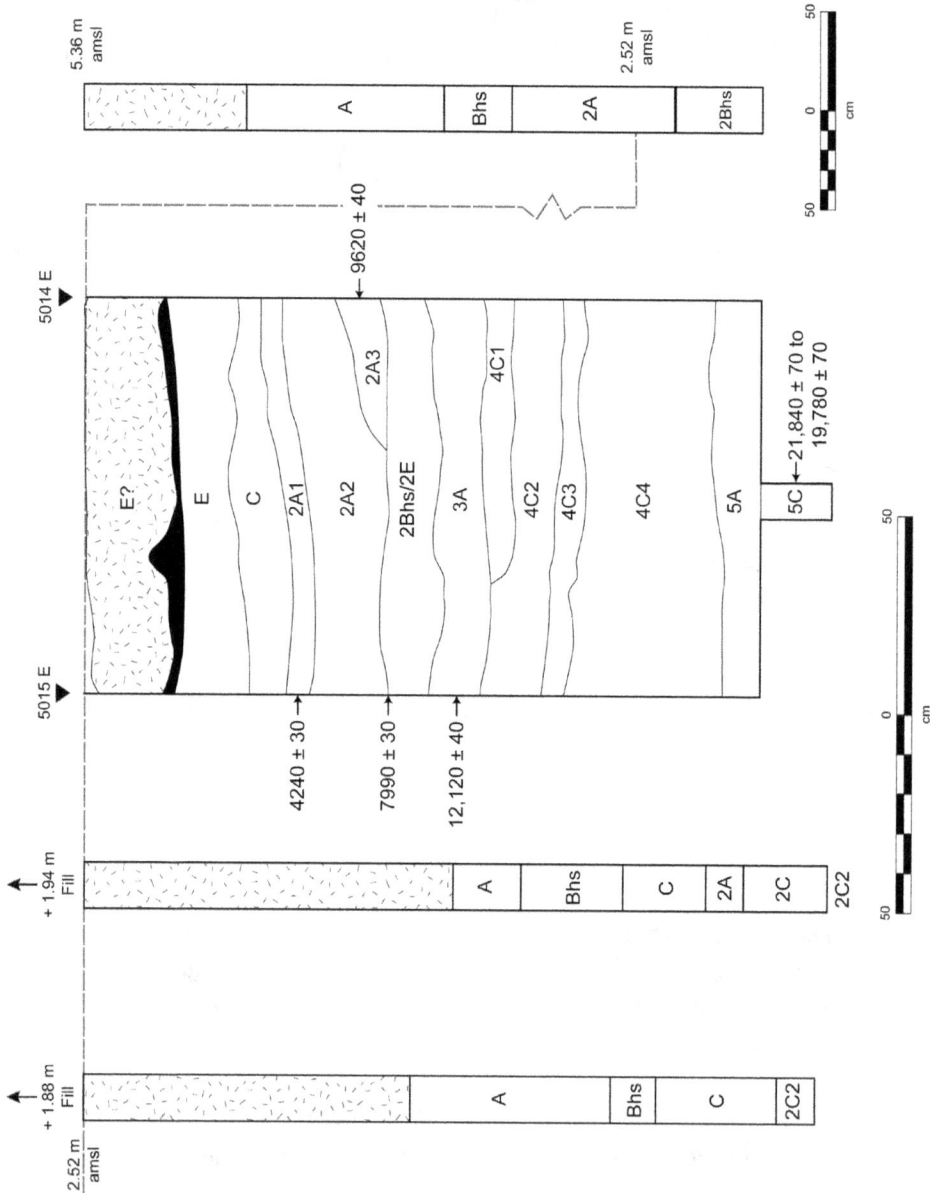

Figure 4.8. Schematic stratigraphic cross section of the project area.

Table 4.1. Aboriginal Flora Recorded at the Vero Site

Species Name	Common Name
Pinus sp.	Unidentified pine
Taxodium distichum	Bald cypress
Carex sp.	Sedge
Serenoa serrulata	Saw palmetto
Sabal palmetto	Cabbage palm
Morella cerifera	Waxmyrtle/southern bayberry
Leitneria floridana	Corkwood
Quercus virginiana	Southern live oak
Quercus laurifolia	Water oak
Quercus chapmani	Chapman white oak
Polygonum sp.	Knotweed (5 fl species)
Magnolia virginiana	Sweetbay magnolia
Annona glabra	Pond apple
Brasenia schreberi-purpurea	Water shield
Ilex glabra	Holly gallberry
Acer rubrum	Southern red maple
Vitis rotundifolia	Muscadine grape
Vitis sp.?	Unidentified grape
Viburnum nudum	Possumhaw viburnum
Xanthium sp.	Cocklebur

Table 4.2. Radiocarbon Dates from the Vero Site

Lab Number	Material	Provenience	Age (^{14}C yr B.P.)
Beta-357933	Organic sediment	Core 16, 272 cm bmgs[a]	6440 ± 40
Beta-357934	Organic sediment	Core 15, 198 cm bmgs	7060 ± 30
Beta-357935	Organic sediment	Core 16, ca. 352.6 cm bmgs	17,620 ± 80
Beta-357936	Organic sediment	Core 15, ca. 427.76 cm bmgs	5180 ± 30
Beta-362859	Organic sediment	Core 15, ca. 375.5 cm bmgs	990 ± 30
Beta-362860	Organic sediment	Core 15, ca. 471.5 cm bmgs	102.5 ± .3 pMC
Beta-362861	Organic sediment	Core 14, ca. 145.0 cm bmgs	410 ± 30
Beta-362862	Organic sediment	Core 14, ca. 174.5 cm bmgs	9030 ± 40
Beta-362863	Organic sediment	Core 14, ca. 403.5 cm bmgs	5100 ± 30
Beta-378226	Organic sediment	Auger 6, 191–199 cm bmgs (A horizon)	2260 ± 30
Beta-378227	Organic sediment	Auger 7, 280 cm bmgs (A horizon)	5570 ± 30
Beta-378228	Organic sediment	Auger 7, 280–290 cm bmgs (A horizon)	7010 ± 30
Beta-378229	Organic sediment	Auger 7, 380–394 cm bmgs (A horizon)	21,840 ± 70
Beta-378230	Organic sediment	5015R5000, F5, .5–5 cm	4240 ± 30
Beta-378231	Organic sediment	5015R5000, F5, 50–55 cm	9620 ± 40
Beta-378232	Organic sediment	5015R5002, F9, 0 cm floor	7780 ± 30
Beta-378233	Organic sediment	5009R5002, F9, 0 cm floor	7990 ± 30
Beta-383037	Organic sediment	5014R5001, F24, 0–1 cm (A horizon)	19,880 ± 70
Beta-383038	Organic sediment	5013R5001, F 24, 0–3 cm (A horizon)	19,780 ± 70

[a] bmgs = below modern ground surface.

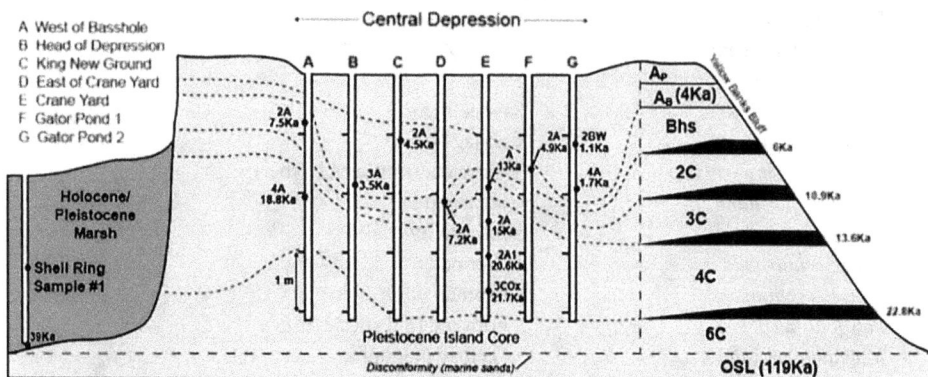

Figure 4.9. Late Wisconsin-age paleosols identified by Vento and Stahlman (2011) on St. Catherines Island, Georgia, that correspond with the 3A and 5A horizons.

At Elliott Island presently buried peat deposits are capped by a variably thick package of terminal Wisconsinan and Holocene aeolian sands. The peat has been dated to calibrated ages of 24,342 ± 305 B.P. and 23,946 ± 318 yr B.P., once again during the height of the LGM (Lowery et al. 2011). At Paw Cove a loess deposit (Paw Loess) has buried Clovis-age lag artifacts and other artifacts older than 132,000 B.P. This loess deposit resulted from reworking and subsequent deposition of nonglacial upland sediments that filled the valley bottom of the lower Susquehanna River ca. 12,700–11,500 B.P. (Lowery 1989, 2002, 2005; Wah 2003).

The 5A horizon was then overlain disconformably by a ca. 40–45-cm-thick white aeolian sand 4C horizon (designated F18, F19, F20, F21, F22, and F23) that was likely emplaced during drier climatic conditions, which promoted aeolian deflation and deposition. The 3C horizon consists of a very fine (0.125–0.063 mm), well-sorted white aeolian sand that lacks any heavy mineral component. Relict root rhizomes from the overlying 3A horizon extend into the 3C horizon and are in-filled with Fe and Mn oxides. The 3C horizon was then disconformably overlain by a significantly coarse-grained (gravelly sand to coarse sand), dark brown (10YR3/3), dense sand cumulic A horizon (3A [designated F17]). This horizon has been dated to 12,120 ± 40 ^{14}C B.P.

Given its stratigraphic position, the 3A horizon likely corresponds with the warmer and moister Bølling-Allerød interval (ca. 15,000–13,000 B.P.) and documents wetter conditions concomitant with increased overbank deposition and active later channel migration of the creek. This same horizon has been identified in buried contexts on the eroding Silver Bluff Island Core along the north shore of St. Catherines Island (Vento and Stahlman 2011). The 3A horizon is the earliest evidence of sediment deposition from Van Valkenburg Creek. The 3A horizon was then overlain by a thin white sand 2C horizon. The 2C horizon was the single autogenic event during Younger Dryas times that terminated the stable conditions and organic activity that allowed for the development of the cumulic A horizon designated as the 3A horizon. Unlike the persistent and horizontally continuous 2A (F5) horizon, the 3A (F17) horizon is discontinuous and is primarily situated on what would have been the relict levee zone of Van Valkenburg Creek.

The 2C horizon was then conformably overlain by a 12.5–22.5 cm thick, reddish brown, iron-rich sand, strongly mottled in its lower part, spodic B horizon which has been emplaced by slow vertical accretion from Van Valkenburg Creek. As detailed below, this horizon is associated with burned bone and several identified faunal elements of Pleistocene age. The 2Bhs horizon contains abundant redoximorphic features created both from a fluctuating groundwater table (illuviation from the overlying organic-rich F5 [2A] horizon) and from bioturbation. As one proceeds north or toward the main canal, the 2Bhs horizon becomes white in color (2E) and reflects intensive eluviation of the B horizon where the overlying 2A (F5) horizon is significantly more organic rich. The 2Bhs and 2E horizons are time equivalent and likely span the period between the end of the Bølling-Allerød and the initiation of hydric soil development associated with the Holocene transgression at 8,000 yr B.P. (Figure 4.10).

The 2Bhs and 2E horizons are then overlain in the western portion of the site by a thick 2A1, 2A2, and 2A3 horizon (F5), which documents a long period of very slow overbank deposition and floodplain stability along Van Valkenburg Creek. The F5 (2A package) horizon ranges from a histic epipedon (northern portion of block excavation) with more than 25 percent organic matter to an ochric less hydric epipedon to the east and southern portions of the excavated block. The F5 (2A) horizon likely began to form when water-table conditions related to rising sea levels allowed for ponding along the stream valley. A radiocarbon date of 9620 ± 40 [14]C B.P. from the base of F5 (2A3) supports the beginning of ponding and wetland conditions.

In the extreme eastern portion of the block excavation closer to the once active channel of Van Valkenburg Creek, the 2A horizon is presently disconformably overlain by a 1-m-thick package of late Holocene age overbank

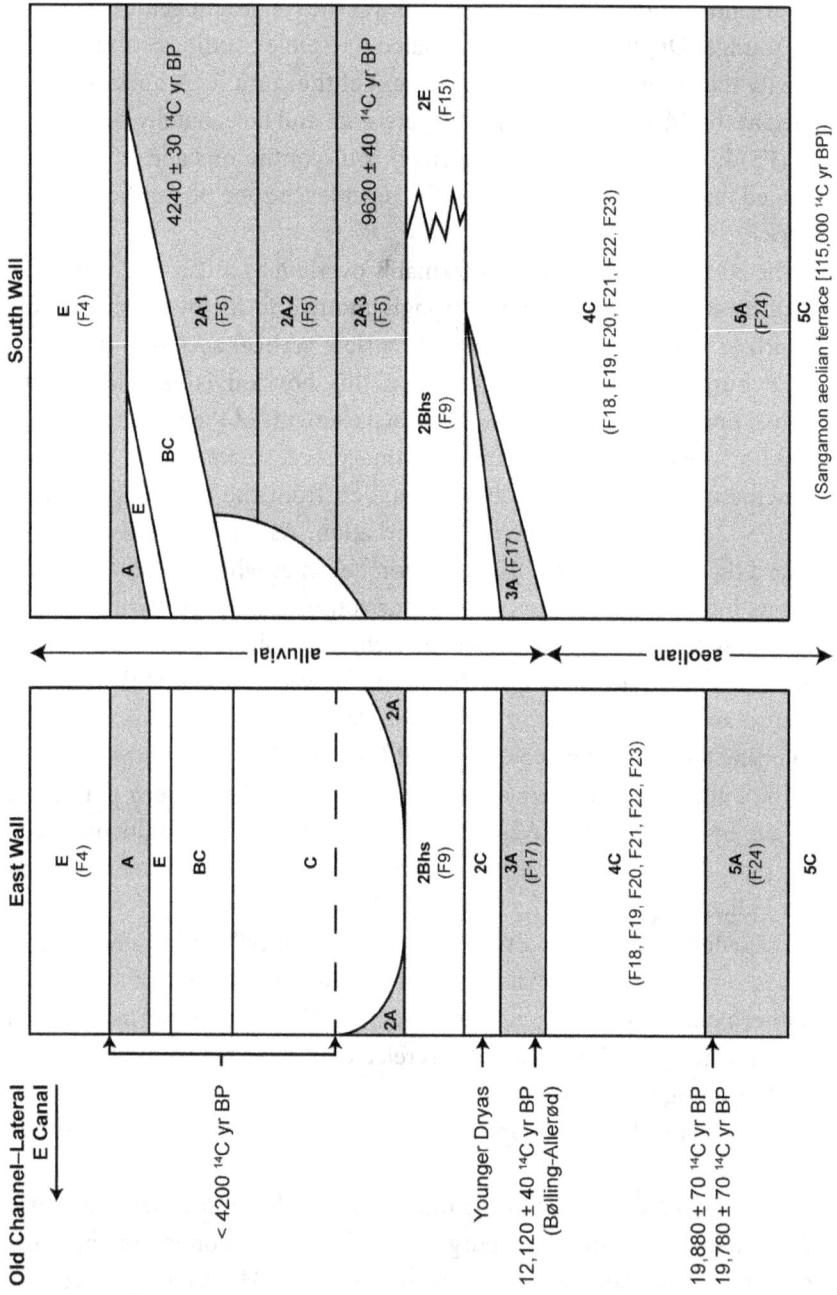

Figure 4.10. Schematic stratigraphic cross section of the Vero site excavation.

Figure 4.11. General view of F18, 0-cm floor, in unit 5010R5001. Arrows indicate in situ charcoal and thermally altered bone fragments.

deposits. Along most of the exposed east wall profile, the 2A horizon has been removed by flood scouring. The soil profile present in the eastern portion of the block excavation is not present to the west or toward the distal margin of the floodplain where it once abutted the lower slope of the dune. The soil profile along the east wall consisted of a thin, organic-rich A horizon which was overlain by canal fill. The A horizon was underlain by a 5–10-cm-thick, grayish white eluviated E horizon. The E horizon was then underlain by a 10–20-cm-thick reddish brown medium to fine sand BC horizon, which in turn was underlain by a 40-cm-thick C horizon, which, as noted above, has incised and removed a portion of the 2A horizon along the eastern portion of the site. The hydric conditions observed in the soil profiles persisted until the ground surface was buried by a 2.5-m-thick package of canal fill emplaced during construction of the main canal and the Lateral E canal throughout the last 100 years (Figure 4.11).

Results

Summary of Cultural Features

No circumscribed cultural features such as pits of known function (e.g., fire, storage, trash) were not encountered during the 2014 excavations. However, as noted in stratigraphy, an apron of dispersed burnt/calcified bone was exposed on the surface and within depositional unit F9, and underlying F18 (Figure 4.12). This phenomenon may well be a downslope occupation surface and/or trash accumulation area, though it is presently devoid of definitive archaeological material.

Artifacts

As of 2015, more than 800 diminutive biface-thinning flakes have been recovered from the intact Holocene sediment package and/or disturbed overburden. A minimum of four different raw lithic material types are represented, including Ocala chert, Brooksville chert, Tampa fossil coral, and Tampa agatized coral. All of these raw materials are exotic to the Vero locality. The nearest known occurrences of these materials are 130, 150, 115, and 115 miles from Vero Beach, respectively.

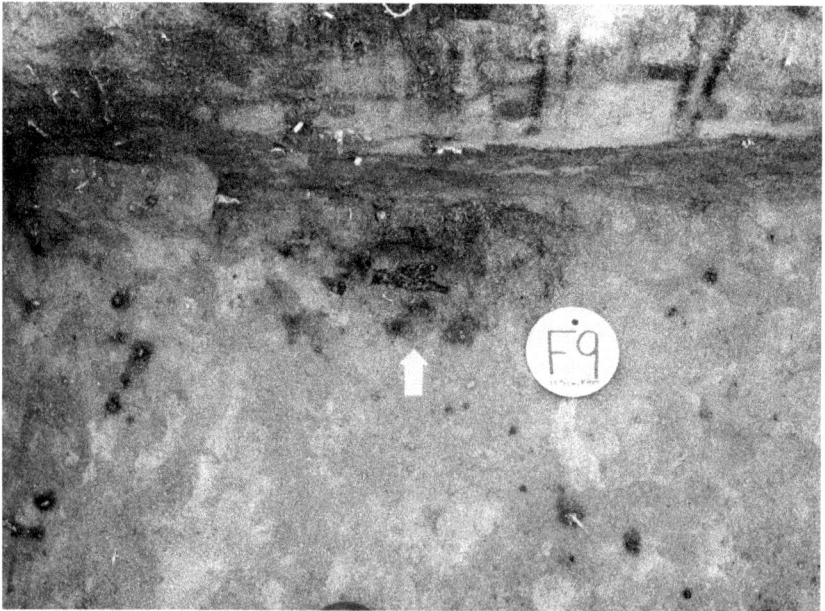

Figure 4.12. General view of F9, 17.5-cm floor, in unit 5010R5001. Arrow indicates in situ thermally altered bone.

The 2014 excavations yielded two late Early Archaic projectile points (one a Kirk Stemmed and the other a Kirk Serrated) from the disturbed overburden as well as an in situ flake from the 39-cm surface of overbank deposit F5. All of these specimens are, like the small flakes, made of nonlocal material from at least 115 miles away.

One item of particular interest, found in 2015, is thought to be a carbonized plant-fiber-derived "string." This item appears to consist of multiple plies of very fine elements of an indeterminate plant species. It was exposed in situ on the 24.5-cm floor of F5 and was removed en bloc. Whatever the raw material source, the specimen is definitely anthropogenic in origin.

Faunal Remains

Twenty-one bone fragments were recovered from the surface of spodic B horizon, F9, and underlying F18 in 2014. At least another 17 bone fragments were recovered in 2015. As noted above, these are thermally altered (Figure 4.12). Two of the pieces have been tentatively identified. One is a lower M1 from a dire wolf (*Canis dirus*), and the other a large molar of an equid (*Equus* sp.).

Floral Remains

To date, most of the CVS samples collected during the 2014–2015 excavations have been screened and are currently being sorted. However, casual scrutiny indicates that both carbonized and uncarbonized floral remains are present. The specimens will be examined and, hopefully, identified in the near future.

In 2015, on the 10-cm floor of F19 (below the layer dated to 12,120 ± 40 ^{14}C B.P.), a large uncarbonized fragment of wood was found with other unburned materials. Stratum F19, in turn, superimposes F24, which was dated by two assays of just younger than 20,000 ^{14}C B.P. (see Table 4.2).

Overview

Though incompletely analyzed at present, the results of the 2014 and 2015 excavations minimally include the following:

- a detailed reconstruction of the depositional history of the site, which redefined the stratigraphic sequence;
- the equation of the observed stratigraphy with the units recognized by Sellards and Chamberlin (Chamberlin 1917), specifically, the

correlation of F5 from 2014 as Sellards' Van Valkenburg S3 and F9/F17, F18, and F15? as Sellards' upper and lower Melbourne S2;

- the implementation of trenching and augering projects designed to identify ancient buried paleosols;
- the identification and delineation of at least three such horizons (F5, F17, and F24);
- the initiation of a broad-based radiocarbon dating project which produced multiple and generally internally consistent ages for the stratigraphic units identified; and
- the collection of a limited suite of artifactual material of early Holocene age and nonlocal origin and, most importantly, the identification and partial exposure of a thermally altered undisturbed bone veneer, which strongly suggests a human presence 14,000–11,100 cal yr B.P. Moreover, as this veneer or apron contains extinct Late Pleistocene species, it indicates the contemporaneity of humans with extinct fauna at this locality.

In short, the 2014 and 2015 projects for the most part resolve the dating conundrum that has plagued the Vero locality since its earliest excavations, thereby demonstrating that Sellards' claims of a contemporaneous human and Late Pleistocene animal presence were indeed correct. We stress that the 2014 and 2015 research did not resolve the provenience of any of the previously recovered human remains from the site, nor did it positively equate any of these remains with Pleistocene fauna. Finally, during 2014 and 2015, concerted efforts have been made to relocate all of the previously excavated Vero site materials and to systematically inventory and analyze these collections.

In January 2016 the third excavation season began will begin at the Vero locality. That project focused on the further exposure of the buried bone apron, as well as the adjacent upland which may well be the "source" of that apron. The deepest paleosol (F24) was also investigated. Results of the 2016 and 2017 field seasons are presently under analysis.

Whenever the multiyear Vero project is ultimately completed, we confidently expect, at the very least, to be able, ultimately, to etch in much sharper relief the inter-relationship of human, animal, and plant populations upon this once highly controversial part of the ancient Florida landscape.

Acknowledgments

The excavation of the Vero site was supervised by Ann E. Marjenin and C. Andrew Hemmings under the direction of James M. Adovasio. Additional field assistance and consultation was provided by Joseph L. Yedlowski and Frank J. Vento. The field crew consisted of Ben C. Wells, Michael D. Way, Jamie E. Badams, Sarah K. Warthen, Patrick C. Rohrer, Alex S. Brown, John S. Duggan, Sarah M. Heuer, Daniel E. Ehrlich, Sabine E. MacMahon, Alix S. Pliven, Kate P. Flor-Stagnato, Lauren A. Urana, Jasper L. McMurtry, J. S. Bailey, Kendall R. Crumpler, S. M. Martz, E. S. Hein, A. H. Bell, Clara M. Summa, and L. E. Osmialowski. Assistance was also provided by M. Harris, J. Vest, K. Johannesen, Michelle L. Farley, Zachary D. Nason, S. A. Martin, Brendan F. Fenerty, University of Central Florida volunteers and numerous OVIASC volunteers. The authors wish to extend our sincere gratitude to David Gunter, Tim, "V" Verlin, John, Devon and the Indian River Farms Water Control District board members, without whom many aspects of this project would not have been possible. Special thanks is also extended to the OVIASC board members: Randy Old, Dick Kerr, Dann Jacobus, Sandra Rawls, Nancy Thayer, Anne Dunn, Carol Fennell, Alan Polackwich, Judi Collins, Ron Rennick, Mary Singer, and Tommye and Rody Johnson for their support and desire to preserve the prehistory of Florida.

We also wish to acknowledge Megan Davis, Patrick Boyles, Greg O'Corry-Crowe, Sarah Rodgers, Tatiana Ferrer, and Heidi Pagan of the Harbor Branch Oceanographic Institute (HBOI) of the Florida Atlantic University, Cathco, Inc., and Piper Aircraft for their consideration and assistance in support of the Vero project. Finally, aerial photography of the site was provided by David Talbot, and this contribution was edited and prepared by David Pedler, who also provided Figures 4.2, 4.3, and 4.10.

5

PALEOGEOGRAPHY AND SEA LEVEL POSITIONS ON THE SOUTHEASTERN U.S. CONTINENTAL MARGIN SINCE THE LGM

IMPLICATIONS TO POTENTIAL HABITATION SITES

M. SCOTT HARRIS

Although the earliest arrival to North America from the Old World may never be known, evidence is clear that pre-Clovis sites were present in North America (Anderson et al. 2015; Goodyear 2005a; Wagner and McAvoy 2004) and that the timing of the arrival of Paleoamericans is being pushed earlier (Halligan et al. 2016) as more and more sites below Clovis horizons are being discovered and studied more closely. The debate is no longer "Clovis First?" but rather "How long before Clovis did Paleoamericans arrive?" Unfortunately, much debate of pre-Clovis peopling of North America is still being driven by the passing paradigm of Clovis First, much like sea level rise is being debated in today's political arena. But where did they come from and when did they first arrive in the southeastern United States (SEUS)? Based on modern and prehistoric human occupation of any known paleogeographic region of the planet, it is a logical conclusion that the varied landscape of the SEUS has been capable of supporting *Homo* spp. since their arrival in the New World, whether after the last glacial maximum (LGM) ~24,000 years ago or much earlier (see Holen et al., 2017). In other regions of the world, *Homo* has crossed large bodies of water to reach new land (Strasser et al. 2010), and based on modern populations using ancient methods, prior to the Beringian journey from Asia humans could have followed the coasts and sea ice from Europe to North America (Bradley and Stanford 2004; Lowery et al. 2012; Stanford and Bradley 2000), although whole-genome DNA comparing modern Native Americans (North,

Central, and South) indicates that the current population descended from a small group only ~12,500 years ago, likely following a North American Pacific coastal route (Skoglund and Reich 2016), as originally hypothesized by Fladmark (1979) where he stated that in lieu of an interior ice-free corridor, "an alternative initial migration route for early man may be offered by a chain of sea-level refugia around the North Pacific coast of North America." Replace *Pacific* with *Atlantic*, and you have the hypothesis of Stanford and Bradley (2000).

Understanding paleolandscapes, from ancient shorelines inland along the fluvial systems, is critical to locating and understanding ancient habitation sites and possible migration routes. This chapter utilizes recent glacial isostatic adjustment models tuned with recent sea level curves and viscosity models to position shorelines on the submerged Continental Shelf from Virginia to the west coast of Florida from the Last Glacial Maximum to approximately 8,000 years ago.

Much of the ancient coastal world is now submerged on the formerly exposed continental shelf (Fenneman 1916) and is receiving a lot of attention (Evans et al. 2014 and articles and references therein) due to the development of the seafloor from many competing needs and the associated legal frameworks (Aplin 2007; Dromgoole 2010; Varmer 2014a, 2014b; Varmer et al. 2010). The modern western North Atlantic margin, the focus of this study, comprises the shoreline at the emerged Coastal Plain margin and features of the submerged Continental Shelf. This region has been emergent uplands ("dry" land) from marine isotope state 4 (MIS-4; ~70 kya) until approximately 11 kya (Harris et al. 2013; Sain 2016). The boundary between the emerged Coastal Plain and submerged Continental Shelf, the shoreline, has migrated across the continental margin in response to sea level changes (Belknap and Kraft 1977, 1981; Blackwelder et al. 1979; Kraft et al. 1977; Mitchell and Huthnance 2008; Schuur et al. 2000), responding to the waxing and waning of continental glaciers throughout the Quaternary (Imbrie and Imbrie 1979; Shackleton and Opdyke 1973). The Coastal Plain, with abundant habitat and resources that could support past human populations (Erlandson 2001), has in the past covered areas much larger than the present due to relative sea level changes across this landscape (see Holliday and Miller 2013 and references therein). This submerged paleolandscape now provides abundant habitat for fisheries (Fraser and Sedberry 2008; Schobernd and Sedberry 2009; Sedberry and Van Dolah 1984), holds sand resources for beach nourishment (Finkl et al. 2008), has a large potential for renewable energy (Galparsoro et al. 2012), and, more important for the focus of this chapter, may preserve a long cultural history of when humans first arrived in North America (Faught and Donoghue 1997; Faught and Gusick 2011). In general, the major research on the continental shelf has been in support of the former resources, with much less expenditures on finding Paleoamerican sites.

Finding likely sites for investigation of coastal populations of Paleoamericans is difficult, due to the inundated system, distances from shore, getting to the seafloor (Garrison et al. 2012; Goodyear et al, 1980), and not knowing where specific coastal and estuarine habitats of a specific age may be located without intense investigation (Faught 2014). Several studies have approached the subject of ancient shorelines in the southeastern United States, relying on compiled local relative sea level curves (Anderson and Bissett 2015; Anderson et al. 2015; Harris et al. 2013; Holliday and Miller 2013), tracing of paleovalleys onto the shelf into appropriate paleolandscapes (Faught and Gusick 2011; Harris et al. 2013), gathering materials under the umbrella of large studies of the other resources (DeVoe 2015; Garrison et al. 2012), and finding sites due to tenacious luck (Lowery et al. 2012; Stanford and Bradley 2000).

Purpose

The purpose of this chapter is to build from the recent continental shelf paleolandscape evolution model of Harris et al. (2013) and more clearly outline the history of inundation since the LGM based on updated glacial isostatic adjustment models (Roy and Peltier 2015) coupled with formerly described (Harris et al. 2013) and recently acquired multibeam bathymetric data sets. The secondary outcome of this manuscript is to provide a clearer and more focused understanding of areas to explore for evidence of past human habitation sites in light of the modern paradigm of "Clovis invaders."

Background

The Coastal Plain and Continental Shelf are bound to the west by the Piedmont and to the east by the continental slope and rise (Emery 1972). The currently emerged Coastal Plain physiographic province extends from the coast to the fall zone, with tides reaching upriver well over a hundred kilometers (Nichols et al. 1991) into the interior uplands (Figure 5.1). Comprising a series of constructional marine ridges and terraces (Colquhoun

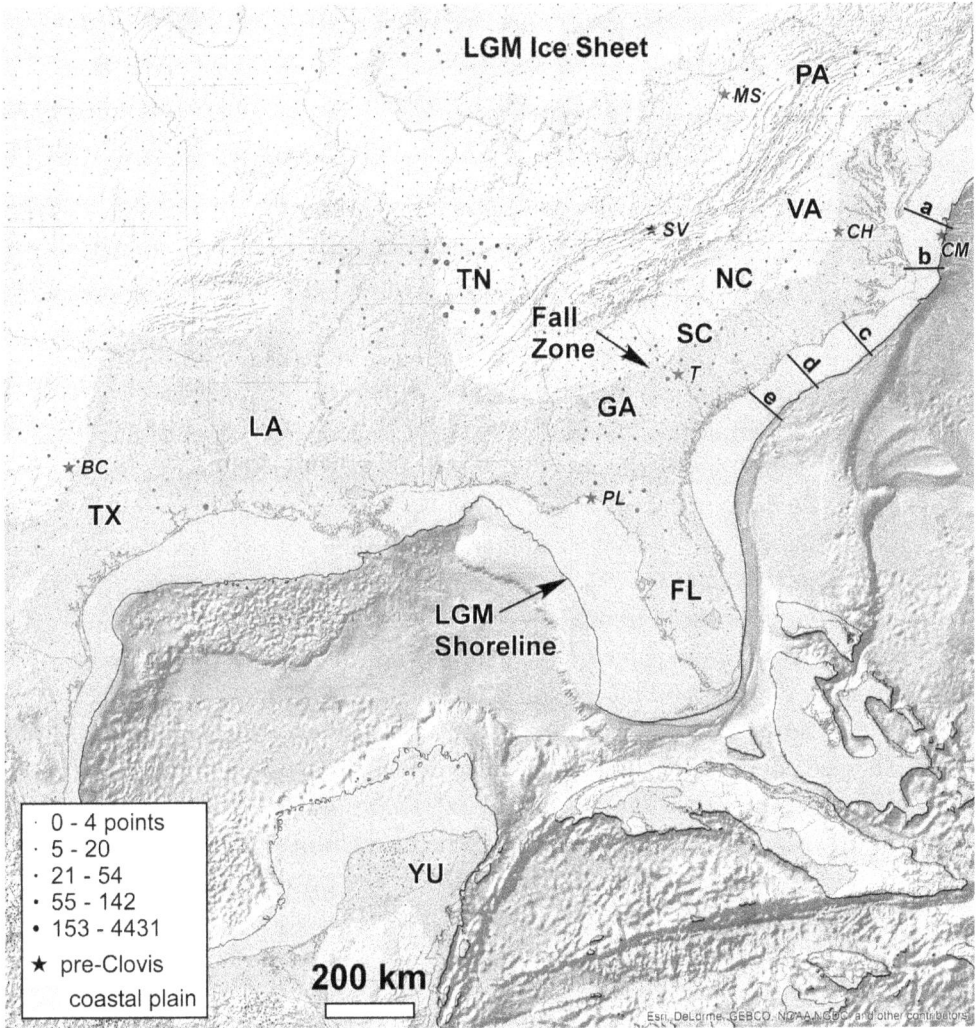

Figure 5.1. General physiography of the southeastern United States, Mexico, and the Caribbean. LGM shoreline corrected for GIA using published models and data (Peltier 2015; Roy and Peltier 2015); *a–e* represent profile locations in Figure 5.2 and correspond to Engelhart et al. (2011) sites 12–16, respectively. *MS* = Meadowcroft Rock Shelter; *SV* = Saltville; *CH* = Cactus Hill; *CM* = CINMAR; *T* = Topper; *BC* = Buttermilk Creek; *PL* = Page-Ladson;. *YU* = Yucatan.

1974; Colquhoun et al. 1991; DuBar et al. 1980; Johnson et al. 1993) and fluvial deposits (Leigh 2006, 2008; Suther et al. 2011), the Coastal Plain is being modified by destructional processes (tidal creek migration, fluvial incision, shoreface ravinement) and major aeolian erosion and deposition in some areas through time (Ivester and Leigh 2003; Markewich et al. 2015).

In many cases, the thickness of Quaternary materials in the SEUS is very small, with tidal creeks incising underlying pre-Quaternary deposits (Harris et al. 2005; Riggs et al. 2000), exposing large chert deposits and other materials suitable for fabrication of tools (Goodyear 2005a; Harris et al. 2013; Nunn 2010).

At the coastline, the area from Virginia to Florida (McBride et al. 2013) ranges from long micro-tidally dominated barrier systems to drumstick barriers with high tidal ranges and wave conditions determining the coastal configurations (Hayes 1994; McBride et al. 2013). In Virginia and North Carolina, Quaternary deposits are much thicker in general (Mallinson et al. 2005; Mixon 1985; Thieler et al. 2014) than off South Carolina, Georgia, or Florida (Colquhoun et al. 1995), except on interfluves (Mallinson et al. 2010; Thieler et al. 2014). Sediment may be thicker in the presence of large fluvial systems where deltas and paleovalleys provide a sediment source (Baldwin et al. 2006; Faught and Donoghue 1997; Garrison et al. 2012; Hayes 1994; Putney et al. 2004). In many areas offshore, hard grounds comprising inundated pre-Quaternary deposits, submerged beachrock, and eroded surfaces are present with little to no Holocene sediment cover (Fraser and Sedberry 2008; Harris et al. 2005; Ojeda et al. 2004; Riggs et al. 1998; Sedberry and Van Dolah 1984). Where sediment is less prevalent, exhumed paleochannels and stumps may remain exposed on the seafloor after coastal transgression migrates inland (Harris et al. 2013). In some regions, the lack of new sediment may be pointed out by the abundance of fossil vs. modern shell materials (Wehmiller et al. 1995).

Understanding the behavior of the marine transgression and alteration of the ancient land surface necessitates a clear understanding of relative sea level rise in a certain location. Global sea level changes have been in general well documented (Fairbanks 1989; Peltier 2002; Potter and Lambeck 2004; Van De Plassche et al. 2014). However, the details for any one area in the SEUS are influenced by the collapse of the ice sheets to the north and northwest, incursion of a mass of water onto the shelf, and tidal variations. Recently, significant effort has been taken to understand tidal gauge data in light of tidal marshes (Kemp et al. 2014; Nikitina et al. 2000) and apply those data as control for better glacial isostatic adjustment (GIA) models (Roy and Peltier 2015) and the subsequent adjustment of local relative sea level curves. Understanding various punctuations in sea level rise rates, such as meltwater pulses (MWP) and cooling events (see references in Bard et al. 2010), will also assist with tuning physical and conceptual models. Natural features on the seafloor have been related to these rapid increases and decreases in sea level rise (Green et al. 2014; Harris et al. 2013), and provide evidence of changes in sea level position against a continental margin.

Superposed on sea level is the change in basin configuration and subsequent variations in tides and tidal masses influencing the local relative sea level change rates. Tide ranges have been calculated for the last 10 ky in the western Atlantic (Hill et al. 2011) based on the ICE-5G (v1.6) GIA model of and are important in understanding sea level studies (Gehrels and Shennan 2015). Primarily, the tidal conditions decreased from the LGM to modern times, with strong amplification around 9 kya (more weakly at 8 kya and 10 kya) in the southeastern United States because of a change in the resonant period due to water depth at that time on the shelf (Hill et al. 2011). Hill et al. (2011) use the ICE-5G (v1.6) GIA model of Peltier (2004).

During transgression since the LGM, ravinement and reworking of shelf sediments has been thought to be the normal process of reworking materials during the marine transgression (Parsons et al. 2003; Swift 1970). However, in light of strong reworking and ravinement processes, preservation of coastal deposits, even aeolianites (Green et al. 2014) and other constructive landforms are well documented (Harris et al. 2013; Ramsay and Cooper 2002; Thieler et al. 2014). Landforms that are being inundated are often climate related (Leigh 2008; Markewich et al. 2015), and their presence on the shelf is important to understand both the climates of the past and the paleolandscapes.

Since the climate shift from the last full interglacial during MIS-5 (125–80 kya) into the glacial at MIS-4 (~70 kya), the climate has changed significantly in the SEUS. In general, the MIS-5 climate was similar to today (Cronin et al. 1981; Otvos 2014) and quickly passed into full glacial conditions by 70 kya (Potter and Lambeck 2004). On land, including the exposed continental shelf at that time, dune development was most active during the drying of the landscape from about 40 kya to the LGM (Brooks et al. 2010; Ivester and Leigh 2003; Markewich et al. 2015). At the same time, river forms were changing from braided with eolian dunes to large scrolling meanders ~16 kya, to large meandering systems at the end of MWP 1-B ~11 kya, and into the modern system of fluvial patterns ~5.5 kya (Leigh 2008; Suther 2013). Pattern changes from the various meander types may not be due to rainfall changes, but rather due to shallow wide river systems and hydraulic inefficiency because of large bedload sand transport from 30 to 17 kya (Suther 2013, p. 86).

With respect specifically to human interactions with the environment, Holliday and Miller (2013) provide an excellent overview of the landscape and climate that Clovis culture peoples had to endure, and the reader is directed there for further reading. Their general characterization of the broad regional characteristics relate to the location of the glacial ice and coastline positions at approximately 13 kya, ranging in elevation below modern sea level from -40 to -60 m in the central Gulf of Mexico off Florida (Faught 2004a, 2004b), approximately -55 m off of Virginia (Lowery et al. 2012), and 60–70 m lower than today off the New England coast (Horton 2007).

In the SEUS, Hussey (1993) identified three major climate zones for the Carolinas based on a core in northeastern South Carolina (near Conway). Between 20.3 and 14.0 kya, the region was dominated by *Pinus* and herbs and was very low in boreal taxa, "probably result[ing] from extreme xeric conditions of soils at Clear Pond" (Hussey 1993:20); between 14 and 8.5 kya, the region was dominated by *Quercus* and *Fagus* and a "reemergence of trees . . . after their near absence during full-glacial time" (Hussey 1993:23); and from 8.5 kya to the present is similar to the present pollen sources. Slightly north of Clear Pond, Goman and Leigh (2004) divide a core from an abandoned river meander in North Carolina into three zones, comparing their results as similar to the Dismal Swamp. Between 10.4 and 10.1 kya, the region was dominated by *Pinus* and *Alnus* (their Zone 3); between 10.1 and 6.1 kya, the region was dominated by *Quercus* and low *Pinus* abundance, with an increase in *Nyssa* and *Betula*; and between 6.1 kya and the present, *Pinus* increases and *Quercus* decreases but are still the dominant species. Increased sand layers from 9.0 to 6.1 kya are attributed to increased flood events in this area. Offshore, the Gulf Stream presence diminished significantly during the Last Glacial Maximum, with what was likely "isotopically depleted riverine input from 17.2 to 15.6 ka BP and 14.9 to 13.6 ka BP" into the Gulf of Mexico (Schmidt and Lynch-Stieglitz 2011:PA4205) or possibly the influence of iceberg discharge along the coast into the Florida Straits (Harris et al. 2013; Hill and Condron 2014).

The predecessor to this analysis (Harris et al. 2013) subdivided the continental shelf into four major bathymetric zones, ranging from the modern coastal zone, to the inner shelf (0 to -25 m), middle and outer shelf (-25 to -80 m), and shelf edge (-80 to -250 m), with a majority focus on the narrow boundary between the shelf edge and the outer shelf; as well as subdividing these four zones into several categories of landforms and landform indicators. Of these, the most interesting follow from a drowned forest (Donahue et al. 1995) and entrenched meanders to the large promontory (Bulls Scarp) at the shelf edge and an outer shelf lobe (Geneva Delta). From approximately 70 kya between MIS 5a and MIS 4 when the sea level dropped below the edge off the shelf until just after the Younger Dryas and meltwater pulse-1B at ~11 kya, this shelf edge was exposed (for almost 60 ky) and provided ample habitat for early Paleoamericans. Since that publication, additional information on GIA has become available (Roy and Peltier 2015), as well as additional paleolandscape indicators on the shelf (this chapter).

Methods and Data

Regional-scale topography and bathymetry data were extracted from the USGS National Map (nationalmap.gov) and NOAA Bathymetry Global Relief model (www.ngdc.noaa.gov) and merged with a prerelease of the Nature Conservancy (Conley et al. 2015) bathymetric data set. Variations between data sets were generally less than 2 m vertical. Depth ranges for the purpose of this chapter extend from the last interglacial shoreline at approximately +2 m (MIS 5a) to approximately -200 m off the shelf edge.

Previously reported multibeam bathymetric datasets (Harris et al., 2011, 2014) collected by NOAA and the College of Charleston at the shelf edge and inshore areas were analyzed separately. In overlap areas, data from multiple cruises over multiple years was generally within one meter and were not corrected for these offsets.

Glacial isostatic adjustment (GIA) TopoDiff data for ICE-6G(VM5a) GIA models from Peltier's website (Peltier 2015) were downloaded and exported from Panoply software (Schmunk 2015) as a georeferenced TIFF image (GeoTIFF) with a 1-degree (~100km) grid spacing. These model outputs were converted to a grid center-point feature class in ArcGIS 10.3. Within ArcGIS, both a TIN and KRIG model were interpolated from the point feature class, resulting in an upsampled 100-m model for the difference in topography from modern. The resulting upsampled TopoDiff layer was added to the modern bathymetry to create a layer where 0 m equals the sea level position at various times provided by Peltier (2015; 1,000-year increments from 26 to 21 kya, and 500-year increments from 20.5 to the modern time). This method provided a smooth GIA model away from the ice edge.

Additional paleochannel data were extracted from the 1976 R/V *Fay* intermediate-resolution mini-sparker seismic data (Paskevich and Soderberg 1997). These data were reviewed and paleochannels marked for some inshore portions of the study area. As our research group converts these from digital scans of original microfiche sources into SEG-Y formats, additional information on paleochannels will be available.

Results

The ICE-6G_C GIA model presented by Roy and Peltier (2015) tuned to sea level curves from Engelhart et al. (2011) are presented on five continental shelf profiles (Figure 5.2, a-3; see Figure 5.1 for locations). On the US East Coast from Virginia to Florida, based on the ICE-6G_C model, local relative sea level did not breach the shelf edge until more recently than 9 kya off Virginia (Figure 5.2a). In South Carolina the shelf edge was inundated at approximately 11 kya just after the Younger Dryas and within a few centuries had migrated inland approximately 20 km. Farther south off Georgia, inundation proceeded more quickly on the wider, less inclined shelf. Paleochannels, most thoroughly mapped off Georgia have been traced to the embayed areas (Figure 5.3; see 10 kya shoreline).

Following from the profiles to the adjusted topographic and bathymetric maps in Figure 5.4, shoreline positions at the LGM 21 kya show a 25–50 percent increase in Coastal Plain area over the current landscape, depending on location north or south. In these panels, the shoreline positions are estimates, as both constructive and destructive processes have been working on the shelf deposits both before and after submergence.

Shoreline positions are shown to overtop the shelf edge and 50-m barrier system (Harris et al. 2013) in the Georgia Bight by 11 kya (see "a" on panel 11 kya in Figure 5.4). In the same panel, the forest of approximately the same age is shown 50 km inland. Shortly after 10 kya, the northern regions off Virginia were overtopped, and the areas farther south to Georgia and Florida continued to migrate rapidly along the gentle shelf slope.

Zooming into some of the available multibeam bathymetry corrected to the GIA model, the shelf break can be more readily studied (Figure 5.5; see Figure 5.4, panel 26 kya for location). At 26 kya (Figure 5.5), sea level is still dropping until 21 kya, exposing more of Bulls Scarp. Sea level starts to rise across the barriers on the northeast side of Bulls Scarp between 14 and 13 kya, and has surrounded the Geneva Delta. By 11 kya the Geneva Delta is completely submerged, with some barrier systems still intact (southwest and center sections; Figure 5.5). By 10 kya, the entire area covered by these multibeam surveys is completely inundated, although water depths on the inland side of the shelf break are only 5–10 m deep at this time.

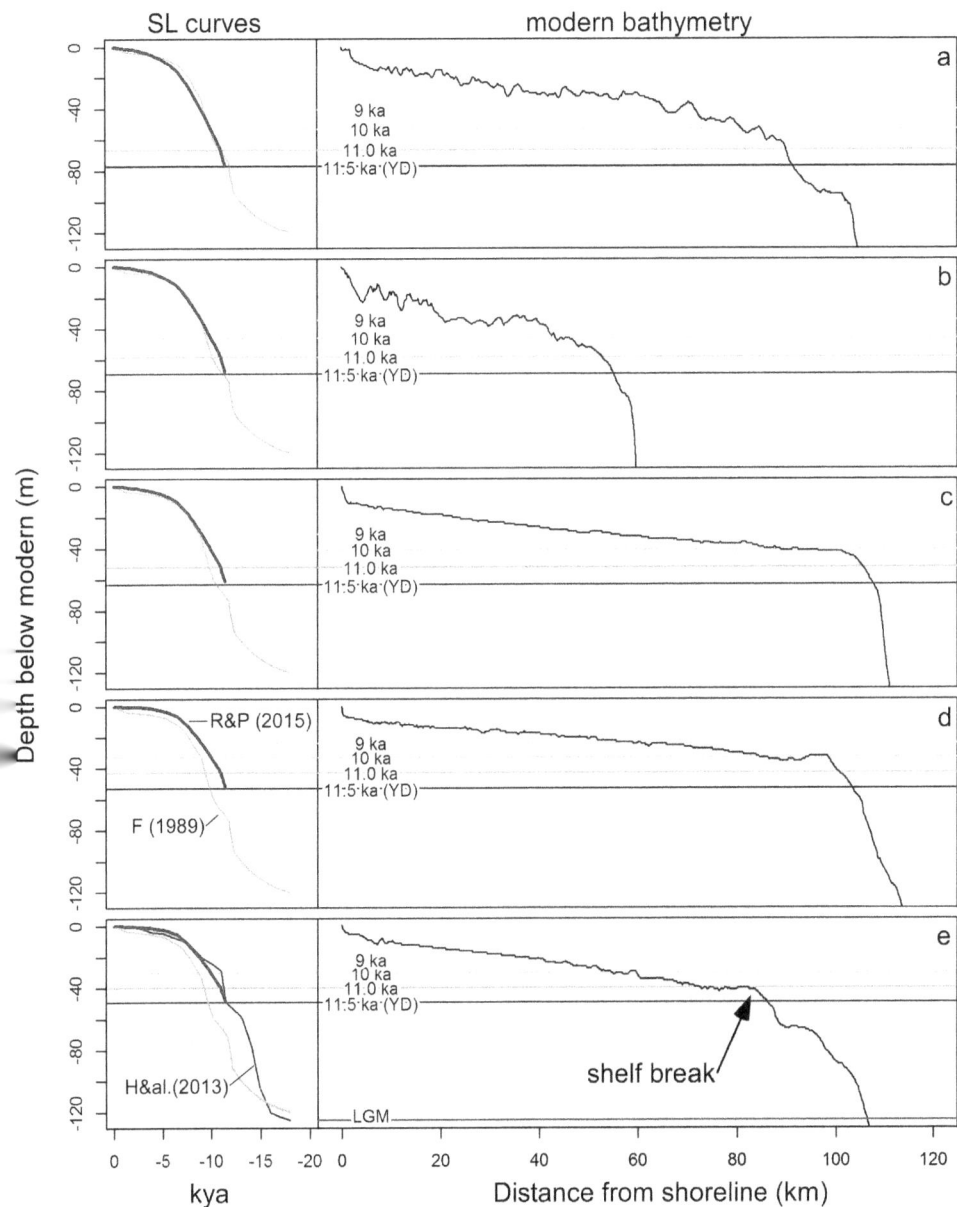

Figure 5.2. GIA-adjusted sea level positions through time (*left column*) are superimposed on modern bathymetric profiles for (*a*) Virginia's Eastern Shore, (*b*) Northern North Carolina, (*c*) Onslow Bay, North Carolina, (*d*) Long Bay, South Carolina, and (*e*) Charleston, South Carolina (locations after Engelhart et al. 2011). The sea level curves presented include profiles used in Roy and Peltier (2015) and this chapter, Fairbanks (1989), and Harris et al. (2013). The shelf is breached first to the south, then farther and farther north in this model.

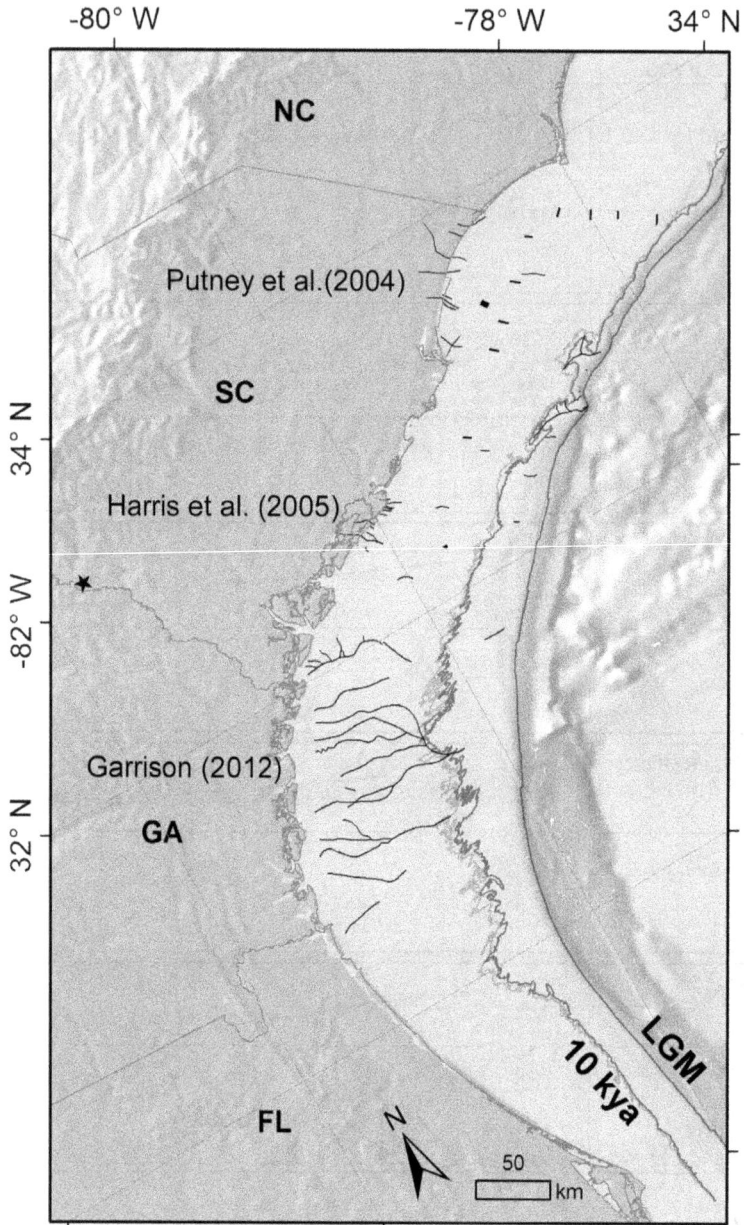

Figure 5.3. Paleochannels mapped within this section of the SEUS. Shorelines for the LGM and 10 kya are shown. Garrison et al. (2012) mapped areas off Georgia; Harris et al. (2005) mapped channel details on the inner shelf of central South Carolina; Putney et al. (2004) mapped inshore of Horry and Georgetown counties in SC; and Harris et al. (2013) have identified shallow channels off central and northern South Carolina; this chapter has further identified Holocene (?) channels in *R/V* Fay (Paskevich and Soderberg 1997) seismic profiles.

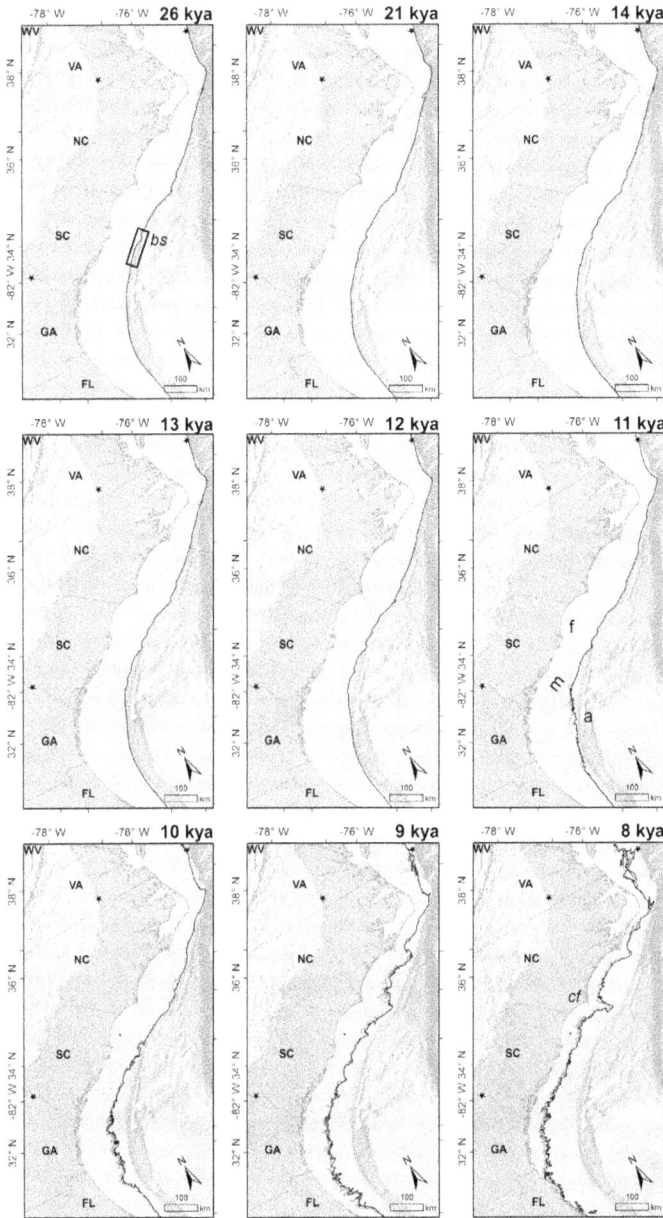

Figure 5.4. Summary of U.S. East Coast shoreline positions from 26 kya, through the LGM, and to 8 kya. Shoreline positions through time using modern bathymetry corrected to recent GIA calculations (Roy and Peltier 2015). Little change is recognized from Virginia to Florida, due to the shoreline abutting the shelf break. Between 12 kya and 11 kya, the shelf edge is breached off Georgia (a). By 10 kya, the coastline is similar in appearance along the SC-GA coasts with large embayments. Black line is 0-m shoreline; gray line (visible after 11 kya) represents approximately +2 m. Stars are documented pre-Clovis sites. f = drowned forest (at cross in *f*); m = entrenched meanders on seafloor. *cf* = Cape Fear; *bs* = Bulls Scarp with inset for MBES analysis.

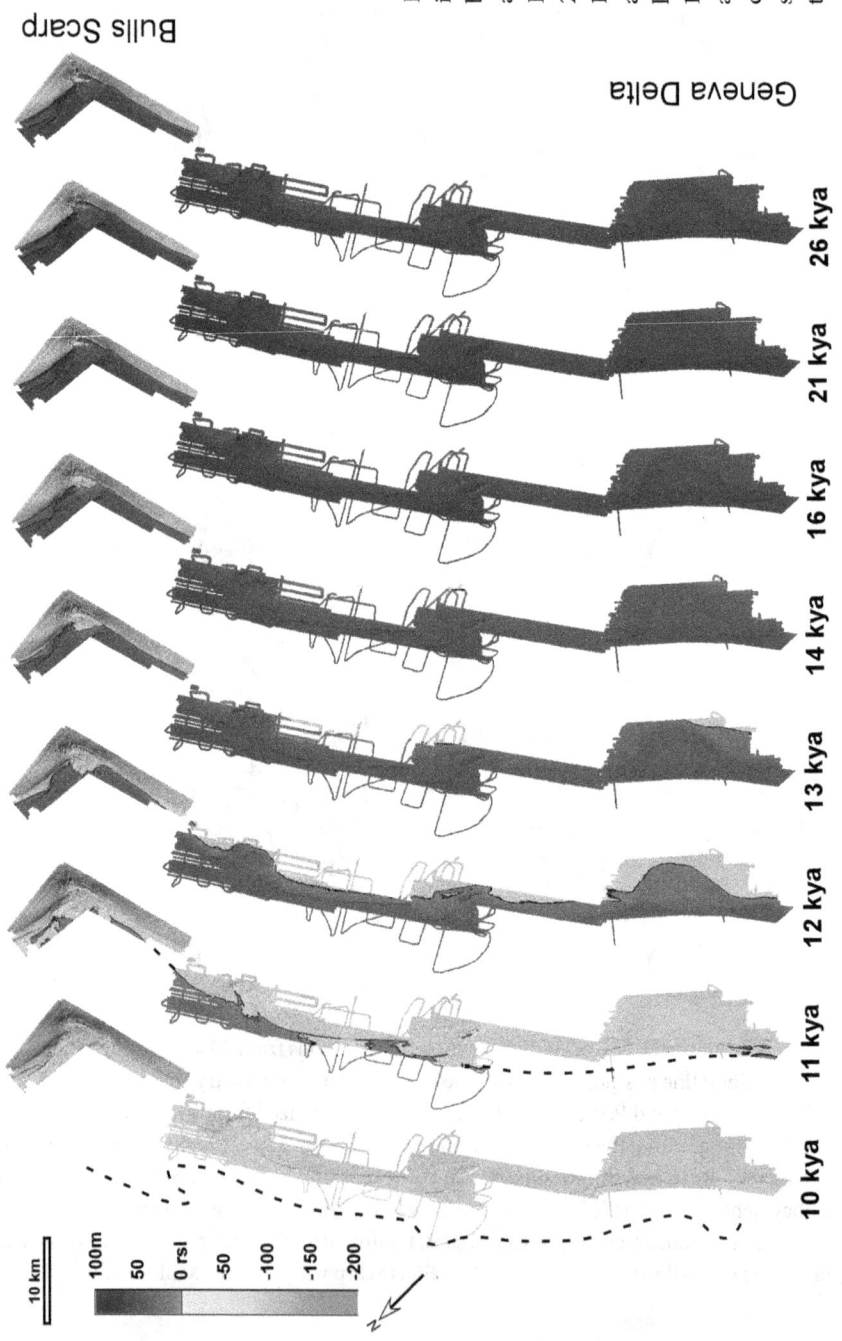

Figure 5.5. Changes in shoreline position between Bulls Scarp and the Geneva Delta (Harris et al. 2013) from 26 kya to 10 kya. Dashed lines approximate shoreline positions for < 11 kya. Light areas are submerged, and darker areas are land surfaces through time.

Bulls Scarp

Geneva Delta

26 kya   21 kya   16 kya   14 kya   13 kya   12 kya   11 kya   10 kya

100m
50
0 rsl
-50
-100
-150
-200

10 km

N

Specific to Bulls Scarp, backscatter imagery has been used to document areas where concentrations of prehistoric materials may be accumulated due to scour and formation of gravel beds (Figure 5.6). In this image, the top image is a perspective view looking south. High backscatter (white) at the base of Bulls Scarp shows the scouring of the exposed Tertiary(?) materials in 220-m water depths. The LGM shoreline is marked with a translucent plane to show above (land) and below (water). Elevations at the top are approximately 45 m. Two profiles with elevation and backscatter show a scoured pocket where high currents keep fine materials from accumulating on the nose of the scarp. Downslope (top image) of this scoured pocket is a mound of sediment apparently being transported into deeper water, where it is being worked to the north by the Gulf Stream into large sand waves (>10 m) with a current reversal, with smaller sand waves traversing back to the south and up the side of the scarp. More recently and until about 8 kya, the overall nature of the shoreline positions on the shelf (Figure 5.7) show these changes along the entire SEUS, including Virginia and parts of the Gulf of Mexico.

Discussion

The primary goal of this chapter has been to more clearly identify the possible and likely age of regions of the submerged Coastal Plain from the shelf edge to the modern shoreline, with the ultimate outcome to identify areas on the shelf where prehistoric sites may be identified. By modeling shoreline positions from modern bathymetric maps that have been corrected by GIA models, this first-cut documentation for the SEUS and vicinity appears to provide an appropriate view. The shelf edge on the East Coast is first breached off Georgia approximately 11 kya, followed to the north and south (figures 5.2 and 5.7), where by approximately 9 kya most East Coast shelves are being covered. The west coast of Florida shelf is not as steep and is inundated fairly consistently and evenly, except for a few areas. These results are similar to Anderson and Bissett (2015) and Anderson et al. (2015), although the Florida sea level curve (Balsillie and Donoghue 2004) positions sea level too high too soon on the coast compared to the GIA model used for this study. Likewise, Harris et al. (2013) overestimate the speed at which the shorelines crossed shelf break and the shelf overall by a few tens of kilometers. Along with continued refinement of the GIA models, several distinct issues are still not resolved. The parameters for the GIA model are continually being modified as new data are discussed, and

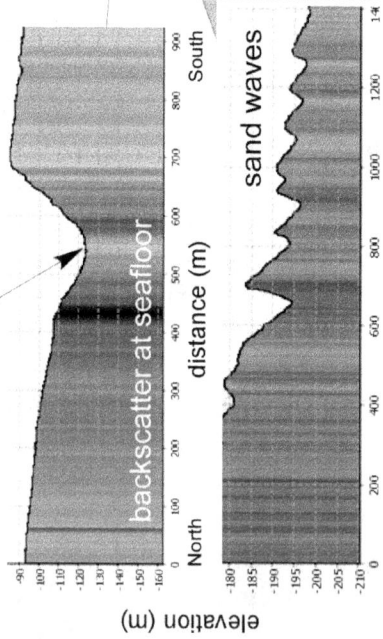

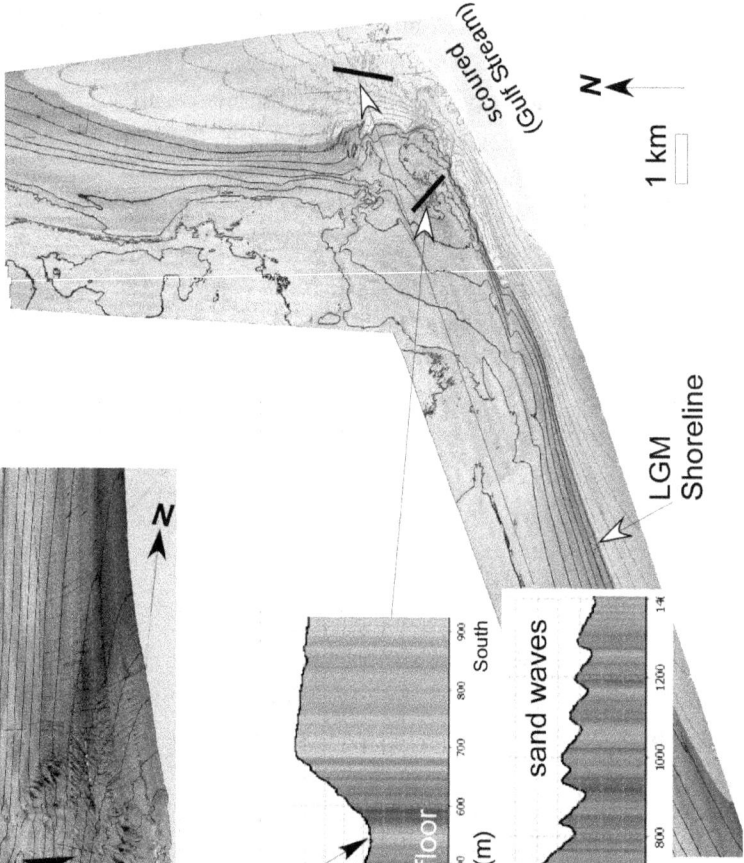

Figure 5.6. Bulls Scarp sticks out into the Gulf Stream, where in the past icebergs passed on their way to south Florida (Harris et al. 2013; Hill and Condron 2014) and likely into the Gulf of Mexico.

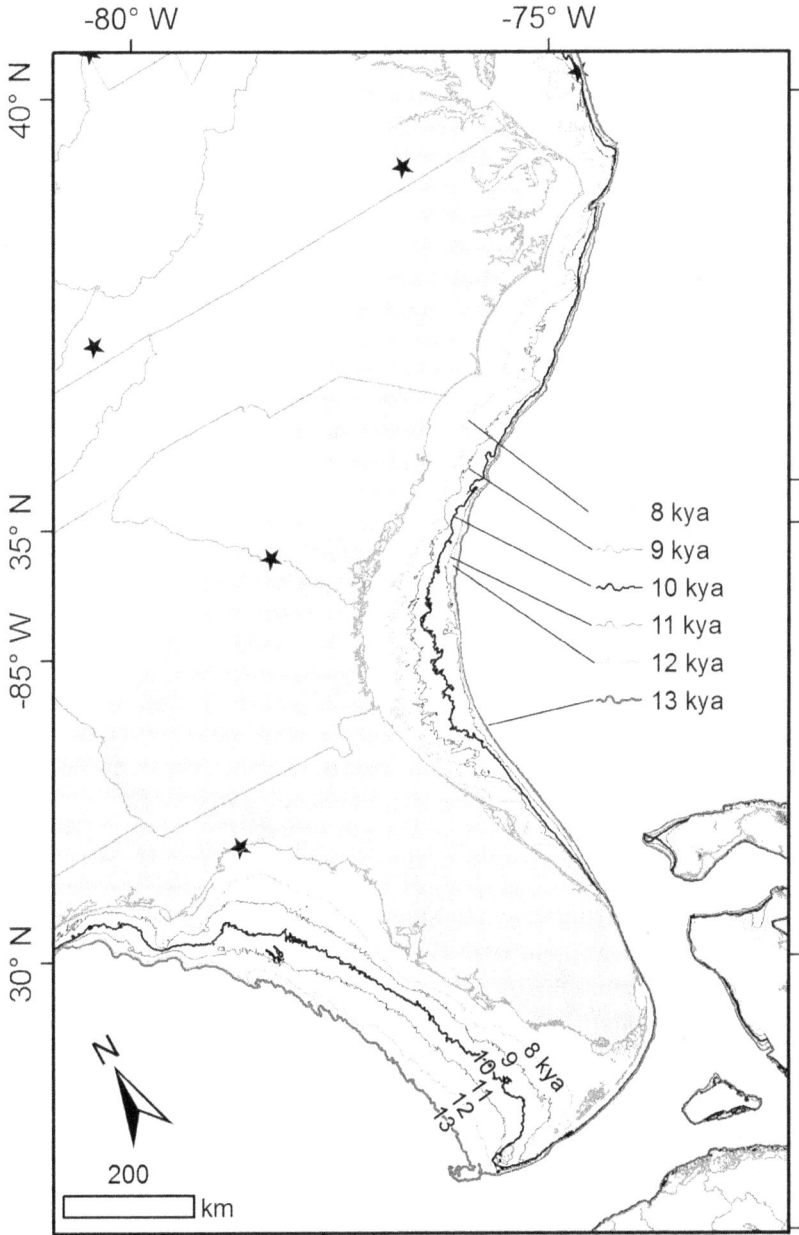

Figure 5.7. Summary of the estimated GIA-model-adjusted shoreline positions for the regions between Virginia and the Gulf of Mexico (including portions of the Bahamas and Cuba) from 13 kya (generally sea level is below shelf break) to 8 kya where modern bathymetry (ravinement and accumulation) needs to be better understood in order to smooth shoreline locations. Stars represent known pre-Clovis sites.

as mantle dynamics are better understood. Likewise, the former landscape and modern bathymetry will need further adjustment as our understanding of surficial processes increase for the continental shelf. In some areas where beach rock formation is apparent (Green et al. 2014), the preservation potential is quite high where rapid inundation after lowstands of sea level. These areas are similar to the 50-m ledges of Harris et al. (2013), indicating that ravinement is not the end to preservation of lithosomes, but rather may leave them exposed and not buried by sweeping more sediments inland and leaving these features exposed on the seafloor. In areas such as Bulls Scarp, currents sweep along and across the surface, cleaning away fine sands and other materials that would normally settle and bury materials. High-backscatter regions in the multibeam bathymetry indicate clear accumulation of gravel patches, providing several areas that were inundated only about 11 kya.

In areas where sediment is prevalent, we may want to further investigate the presence of paleochannels and associated aeolian sand sources. With some shoals being formed by fluvial discharge or tidal inlet associations, broad expanses of the shelf may have had significant aeolian reworking prior to transgression, similar to the discoveries on the modern Coastal Plain (Markewich et al. 2015 and references therein). Close sedimentologic and stratigraphic scrutiny will be required to tease out these associations, as well as the precise timing of shoreline positions (beyond this study), fluvial sediment discharge (e.g., Suther's work on mega-meanders and sediment discharge), and shelf incision (paleochannels and paleovalleys). In particular, the moments when the >1 billion m^3 of sediment in the Geneva Delta were being deposited (Harris et al. 2013) were very likely in sync with increased sediment discharge from the wide and shallow river systems of the time (Suther 2013).

Based on the GIA models used and sea level histories presented for this chapter, the LGM sea level position is supposed to rest at approximately -110 m off South Carolina, in contrary to the position based on the physical sub-bottom profiler evidence at approximately -125 to -135 m (Harris et al. 2013). This discrepancy may be due to the ~1.5-km horizontal range over which sea level changed from 26 kya to 15 kya, and the GIA model resolution (~100 km) that was upsampled with interpolation to match the existing digital elevation model for the regional bathymetry and the multibeam data, or the GIA model underestimates sea level position in this area (it is likely the sampling at fine scale).

The increased tidal amplitude ~9 kya (Hill et al. 2011) likely created more tidal inlets and barrier island segments from North Carolina to Florida, particularly in the embayed section seen in figures 5.3 and 5.7. As Hill et al. (2011) continue to fine-tune their bathymetric layers and tie them to the newer ICE GIA models, our model of shelf paleogeography will also be fine-tuned. Likewise, as our geological understanding of the amount of erosion and deposition during the transgression increases, the bathymetric models will improve.

Conclusions

Using GIA-corrected bathymetry from 26 kya to the present, shoreline positions have been placed for the continental shelf from Virginia to the Gulf of Mexico, building off the models of Harris et al. (2013) and Anderson et al. (2015). For all areas, the shoreline positions provide a clear indication that all Clovis and pre-Clovis cultures could have lived at the edge of the continental shelf from approximately 75 kya to 11 kya, except off the west coast of Florida (Figure 5.7). Climate was such that increased sediment discharge from 30 to 17 kya could have easily fed the Geneva Delta and others yet undiscovered. Using this type of methodology, increasing the possibility of finding and identifying key Paleoamerican sites will continue through science and observation while conducting parallel research initiatives in these critical environments.

Acknowledgments

This work is a continuation from research with my colleague Dr. Leslie Sautter and our students, and our colleagues Dr. George Sedberry (NOAA, retired) and Dr. Marcel Reichart (SC DNR). Funding for portions of the compilation are from the University of Charleston research funds.

6

The Quarry Cluster Approach
to Chert Provenance

A Review of the Method with Examples
from Early Florida Sites

ROBERT J. AUSTIN, SAM B. UPCHURCH, JAMES S. DUNBAR,
RICHARD W. ESTABROOK, JON C. ENDONINO, AND ADAM M. BURKE

The Quarry Cluster concept was developed in the early 1980s by geologist Sam Upchurch and colleagues (Upchurch et al. 1982a) as a way to visually assign lithic artifacts to geographic localities where chert outcrops share similar geological characteristics. It has been used in Florida for over 30 years and has proven to be a robust method for determining chert provenance. In this chapter we discuss the method and some recent improvements, provide examples of its use, and consider current research that has the potential to increase its effectiveness and reliability, particularly as it relates to the early occupation of Florida.

Chert in Florida

Florida chert consists of two major types. The Miocene Hawthorn Group of sediments includes beds of clay with opaline diatoms and other microfossils. Intermixed with the Hawthorn sediments, and formed soon after their deposition, are deposits of sedimentary opal (McFadden 1982; Upchurch et al. 1982b). The appearance of this opaline material is distinctive. It is lustrous, almost greasy-looking, and contains abundant quartz sand inclusions, phosphate pellets, and occasional fossils. Major source areas are the Peace River, Alapaha, and Swift Creek Quarry Clusters (Figure 6.1a), although opaline cherts occur sporadically in other clusters as well. The

A

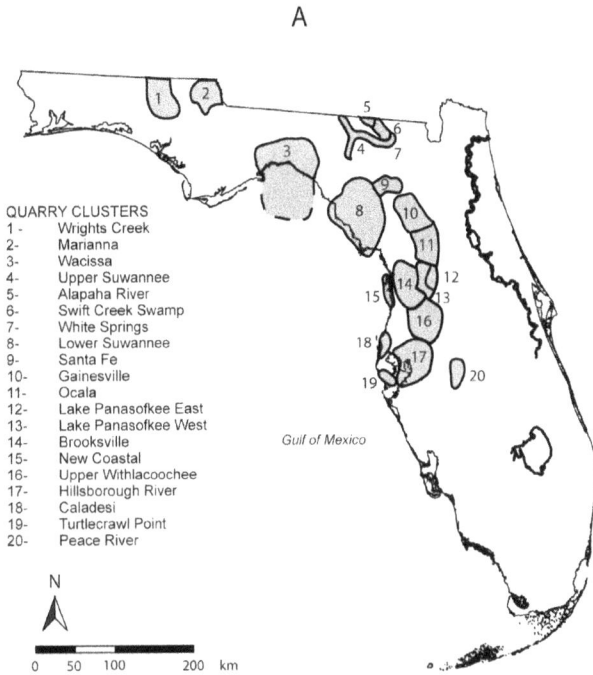

QUARRY CLUSTERS
1 - Wrights Creek
2- Marianna
3- Wacissa
4- Upper Suwannee
5- Alapaha River
6- Swift Creek Swamp
7- White Springs
8- Lower Suwannee
9- Santa Fe
10- Gainesville
11- Ocala
12- Lake Panasofkee East
13- Lake Panasofkee West
14- Brooksville
15- New Coastal
16- Upper Withlacoochee
17- Hillsborough River
18- Caladesi
19- Turtlecrawl Point
20- Peace River

N

0   50   100   200   km

B

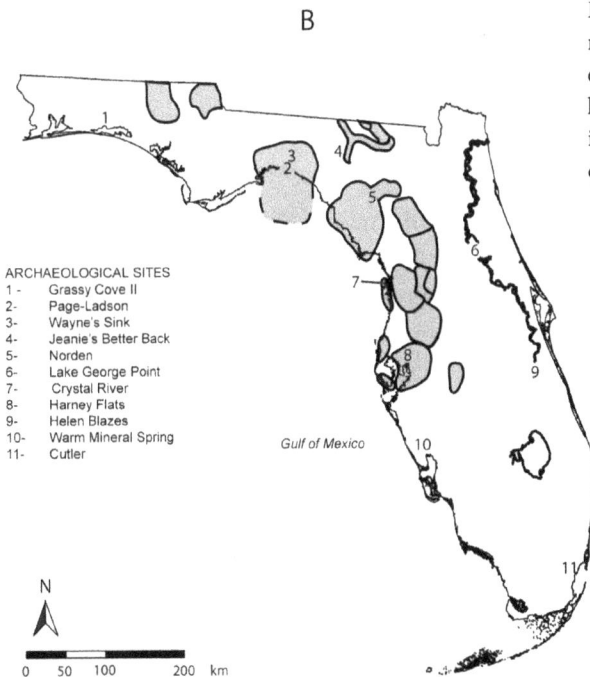

ARCHAEOLOGICAL SITES
1 - Grassy Cove II
2- Page-Ladson
3- Wayne's Sink
4- Jeanie's Better Back
5- Norden
6- Lake George Point
7- Crystal River
8- Harney Flats
9- Helen Blazes
10- Warm Mineral Spring
11- Cutler

N

0   50   100   200   km

Figure 6.1. *A*, Map of chert quarry clusters in Florida showing recent revisions to Upchurch et al. 1982a. *B*, Archaeological sites mentioned in the text in relation to quarry clusters.

cherts tend to be very brittle and weather quickly, because they are less chemically stable than chalcedony and microcrystalline quartz. Although a few Paleoindian and Early Archaic artifacts were made of opaline chert, it was not an important toolstone for early Florida inhabitants.

By far, the most common type of chert in Florida and the southeastern Coastal Plain is silicified limestone. Post-Miocene weathering of the Hawthorn opaline sediments resulted in replacement and void filling of the underlying early Miocene, Oligocene, and Eocene limestone deposits by silica-enriched fluids (Upchurch et al. 1982b). If the silicified limestone was near land surface, all that was needed for a quarry site to develop was exposure by removal of the cover sediments via fluvial or marine erosion and/or sinkhole development.

The Quarry Cluster Concept

Upchurch et al. (1982a) investigated a number of geochemical and petrological methods for determining chert provenance, but use of geochemical criteria proved inconclusive, because all of the silicified limestones and primary chert deposits were deposited under similar tectonic and sedimentologic conditions. Instead, textural and paleontologic criteria were found to be the best tools for determining chert provenance. The limestone strata that were silicified were deposited under different, regional hydrodynamic and diagenetic regimes, and their fossil content varied with the age of the deposit and depositional environment. Therefore, the resulting chert could be differentiated on the basis of its textural and fossil content by visual and nondestructive means.

The relatively flat-lying geological strata of Florida, coupled with silicification of the upper surface of the limestone, suggested that texturally and paleontologically similar cherts were accessible at different exposures at different times within a given geographic area. This concept led to the idea of quarry clusters. The areas of silicification are regional in extent, but the windows through which the chert could have been accessed varied temporally. It was believed that where well-silicified limestone existed near the land surface, one or more quarry sites would be available to Native Americans at any moment in time and that the locations and number of accessible sites would vary with time as a result of changing terrestrial and marine conditions.

Today, some of the aboriginal quarry sites remain exposed at the land surface, others have been discovered through archaeological investigations in terrestrial and inundated contexts, and still others have been exposed as a result of modern earthmoving and construction. A few are inferred from clusters of archaeological sites that contain concentrations of unique chert types. The quarry cluster was therefore defined as an area where (1) regional silicification of a texturally and paleontologically similar rock type occurred, (2) the chert was buried by sediment thin enough for outcrops to be exposed and be buried over time, and (3) fluvial, marine, and karst processes provided access to the chert at differing localities over time.

The goal of chert provenance using the quarry cluster concept is therefore to assign an artifact to an area of origin rather than to a specific quarry or localized outcrop. While locality attribution is, in some cases, possible, the area approach has proven to be reliable and robust. Moreover, the use of visual criteria enables large assemblages of lithic artifacts to be examined and sourced with a minimum of expense. This is important, because it allows for the examination of lithic waste flakes as well as formal tools, increasing the ability of the analyst to identify differential patterns of raw material use within an assemblage.

Since its original formulation, the quarry cluster method has been used in Florida to identify chert provenance at archaeological sites of all time periods, from Paleoindian through the Mississippian (e.g., Austin 1995, 1996, 1997, 1998, 2004, 2013, 2015; Austin and Endonino 2004, 2011; Austin and Estabrook 2000; Austin and Mitchell 1999; Austin et al. 2015; Bridgman Sweeney 2013; Dunbar and Newman 2003; Dunbar et al. 2010; Estabrook 2011; Estabrook and Williams 1992; Goodyear et al. 1980, 1983, 1993; Rink, Dunbar, Doran, et al. 2012; Upchurch 1984a). Figure 6.1a shows an updated map of Upchurch et al.'s (1982a) original quarry clusters, utilizing new data, which are reviewed below. The method also has been used in South Carolina with similar success (Goodyear et al. 1985; Upchurch 1984b).

Recent Research

Quarry Cluster Boundary Revisions

Attempts to improve the method have been devoted primarily to refining the geographic boundaries of existing quarry clusters and the visual criteria used to characterize them. For example, Endonino (2007) sampled 47 locations within and near the Gainesville, Ocala, and Lake Panasoffkee quarry clusters in central Florida, which are characterized by cherts formed in the Eocene-age Ocala Limestone. Upchurch et al. (1982a) originally

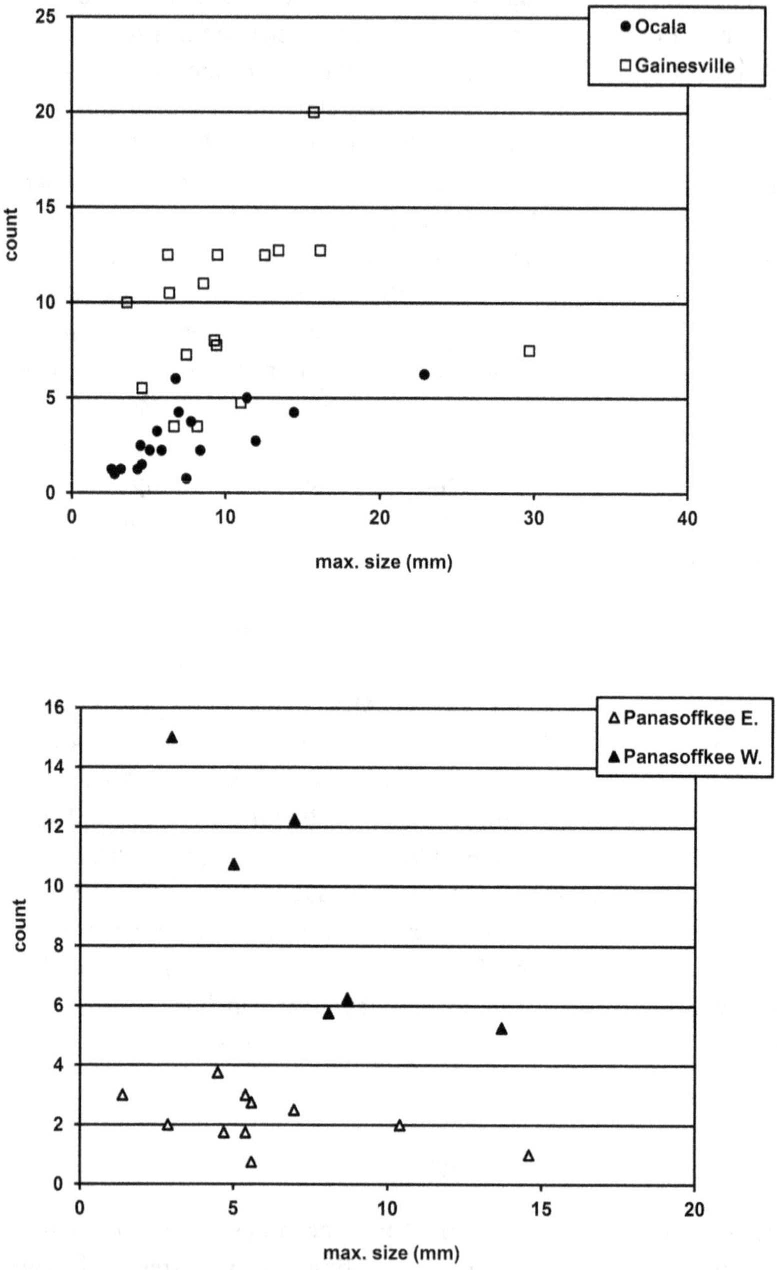

Figure 6.2. Comparison of the size and abundance of Oribitoid foraminifera in the Gainesville and Ocala quarry clusters (*top*) and the Lake Panasoffkee East and Lake Panasoffkee West quarry clusters (*bottom*).

indicated that cherts from these quarry clusters could be distinguished by the size and abundance of diagnostic Orbitoid fossil tests, but operationalizing these criteria was largely subjective. Endonino was able to quantify these differences, reconfirming that size and abundance are reliable as the primary criteria for separating and visually identifying these three quarry clusters (Figure 6.2). Based on his size and abundance data, the geographic extents of the three quarry clusters were revised. Furthermore, the Lake Panasoffkee Quarry Cluster was further subdivided based on the abundance of Orbitoids into Lake Panasoffkee East (fewer Orbitoids) and Lake Panasoffkee West (more Orbitoids).

Austin (1997) expanded the boundaries of the Peace River Quarry Cluster based on a survey of chert exposures in the river, and archaeological projects in the Peace River Valley have identified a wider variety of opaline chert types than was previously known for this cluster (e.g., Austin et al. 2012). Opaline chert outcrops also were identified along the Alafia River near Tampa Bay, and a lanceolate biface recovered from a site adjacent to the river is made from this material.

Dunbar et al. (1991) identified several chert exposures and prehistoric quarries in inundated contexts in the northeastern Gulf of Mexico. The chert is present in both Suwannee and Ocala Limestone exposures. Other offshore quarries have been inferred from the terrestrial distribution of unique chert types (Goodyear et al. 1980, 1993; Goodyear et al. 1983; Upchurch 2015; Upchurch et al. 1982a). One example known to be associated almost exclusively with early sites is a highly fossiliferous chert with abundant, coarse coral and coralgal fossils, which is common at archaeological sites around Tampa Bay (Goodyear et al. 1983). This material is known locally as "Bay Bottom" chert. It frequently occurs in Paleoindian artifact assemblages and is less common in later assemblages. No terrestrial source locations have been identified, and where it is found archaeologically, the material is mostly in the form of worked tools, with few waste flakes or cores. It has been inferred that the source of this chert became inaccessible shortly after Paleoindians found it and that the source location likely is now submerged near the mouth of Tampa Bay, where a well-developed, river-cut valley is located (Figure 6.3). Miocene-age Hawthorn Group cherts have been found in submerged exposures there, and Bay Bottom chert was likely exposed by erosion in the channel of this paleo river. Sea level rise during the early Holocene eventually cut off access to these exposures.

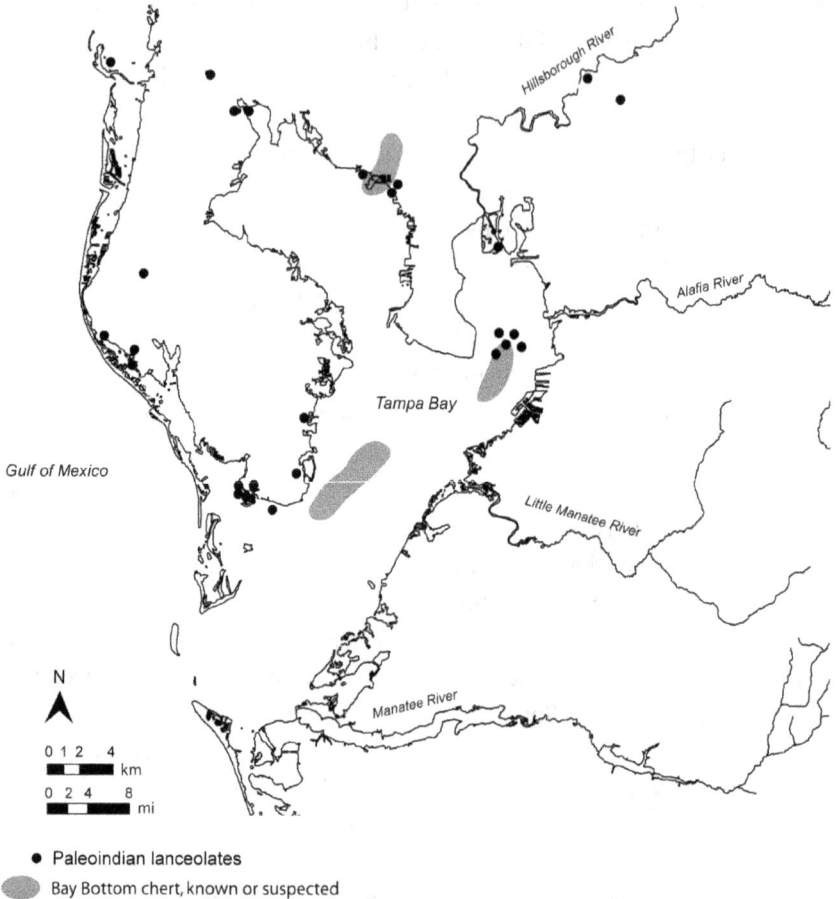

Figure 6.3. Known and suspected locations of Bay Bottom chert in Tampa Bay.

Chert Procurement Patterns

One of the important conclusions from chert provenance studies at Florida Paleoindian and Early Archaic sites is the dependence on mostly local chert sources, implying a relatively restricted foraging range, at least in central and northern Florida, where high-quality chert is abundant. At the Jeanie's Better Back site, an Early Archaic, Bolen site located near the Suwannee River, raw material analysis indicates that the occupants obtained nearly all of their lithic resources from sources located within 30 km of the site, although a few chert samples (< 1 percent) came from as far away as Tampa Bay (Austin and Mitchell 1999). A similar focus on local chert sources was identified for both the Paleoindian and Early Archaic components at

Harney Flats, where all of the tools and debitage examined were made from stone obtainable from sources in the near vicinity of the site (Daniel and Wisenbaker 1987:169; Upchurch 1984a). Similar results have been reported by Goodyear et al. (1983) for Paleoindian lanceolates around Tampa Bay, by Bridgman Sweeney (2013) for Early Archaic Bolen points from northern and west-central Florida, and by Austin et al. (2015) for Early Archaic Bolen and Greenbriar assemblages along the Ocklawaha River in northeastern Florida.

Paleoindian and Early Archaic peoples exploited nearby sources whenever possible, as demonstrated by the association of early sites with Florida's limestone karst region, where both chert exposures and freshwater springs occur (Figure 6.4; see also Dunbar and Waller 1983). There also are examples where cherts from distant quarry clusters were used, as well as truly exotic stone, albeit in comparatively small numbers. Presumably these materials were obtained via exchange, although direct procurement cannot be ruled out completely.

Paleoindians are known for their use of cryptocrystalline stone (Ellis et al. 1998; Goodyear 1983), and this is true in Florida as well; however, other types of stone also were used, particularly in areas located outside of the major chert source areas. The Cutler Ridge site on the southeastern coast has yielded a total of 46 lithic artifacts, including lanceolate Paleoindian and Early Archaic notched points. Twenty-one of the artifacts, including all of the lanceolate points, were manufactured from locally available, hard, fine-grained, micritic limestone, while all of the Bolen points and much of the debitage were made of Suwannee and Ocala Limestone cherts from the Upper Withlacoochee River, Lake Panasoffkee East, and Ocala quarry clusters (Austin 2008; Dunbar 1988). Certain Bolen tools also were made from hard, micritic limestone that visually resembles chert and can fracture conchoidally. It is formed by the dissolution and reprecipitation of the limestone surface, which forms a hard crust. Micritic limestone lenses and strata are associated with the upper Fort Thompson Formation (Krupa and Mullen 2005). While this material flakes relatively easily, it does not hold an edge for very long and would be considered an inferior toolstone if silicified material was available.

At Lake Helen Blazes near Melbourne and farther north at the Lake George Point site, artifacts were made primarily from Ocala Limestone cherts located to the west, but a few were made from Hawthorn Group opaline rock (Dunbar 2012; Dunbar et al. 2010). In addition to Suwannee and Dalton points, the opaline chert was used to make scraping tools. At

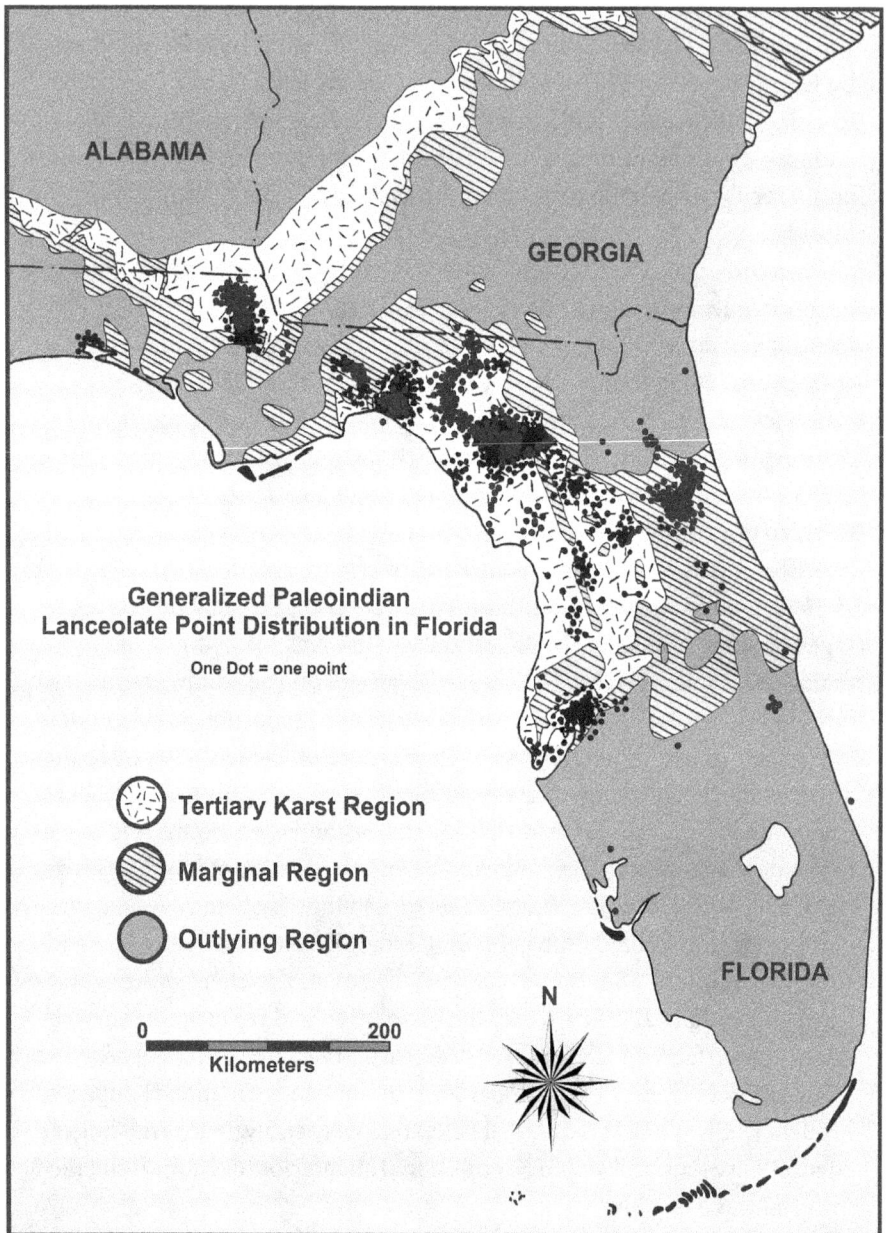

Figure 6.4. Distribution of Paleoindian lanceolate points in relation to Florida's Tertiary karst region.

Warm Mineral Spring near Sarasota, the side-notched points recovered from the 13-m ledge are made from opaline rock. All of these sites are located in areas where no chert exposures exist, and the opaline cherts at Helen Blazes and Warm Mineral Springs are from the Peace River Quarry Cluster.

In the panhandle, Tallahatta Quartzite was identified in the Bolen assemblage at the Grassy Cove II site, located on the northern Gulf Coast (Thomas et al. 2013). This material crops out in southern Alabama, over 100 km away. Suwannee Limestone chert from the slightly closer Marianna and Wright's Creek quarry clusters (ca. 70–80 km northeast) also was used. Cryptocrystalline chert from the nearby Wacissa Quarry Cluster dominated at the Early Archaic Page-Ladson site, but coarse-grained or microgranular chert from the same cluster accounted for about 4 percent of the artifacts (Dunbar 2006:423), and the proportion of coarse-grained chert artifacts from the Santa Fe Quarry Cluster at the Norden site, a waisted Suwannee point site, is essentially the same at 4 percent (Dunbar and Vojnovski 2007:191–194). These microgranular materials crop out locally (i.e., within 1 km from Page-Ladson and within 15 km from Norden). Cryptocrystalline cherts also are located nearby, so these coarse-grained cherts were likely used because they were expedient and close at hand, or because the types of tools that were made from these cherts (scrapers, hammerstones, abraders, and utilized flakes) did not require finer-grained material.

One type of raw material that is noticeably rare at early sites in Florida is silicified coral. The low incidence is probably due to the focus on cryptocrystalline raw materials during these early periods. Silicified coral of the genus *Siderastrea* was used most commonly for tools by prehistoric knappers. These corals grow in large colonies on open seafloors, and silicified *Siderastrea* is common in limestone deposits that formed in Oligocene and Miocene seas that once covered Florida. Because of its structure, silicified coral is extremely difficult to flake without the use of thermal alteration. Increased use of silicified coral during the Middle Archaic period corresponds with a similarly significant increase in the use of thermal alteration (Austin 2006:178; Ste. Claire 1987). The major source for silicified coral is the Upper Withlacoochee Quarry Cluster in the uplands of west-central Florida, where extensive quarries of this material are present in erosional creek banks and sinkholes. Coral-bearing strata crop out in other parts of Florida as well, but it is extremely difficult to assign coral artifacts to specific quarry clusters, because of the near-ubiquitous use of a single genus for tool stone, the difficulty of identifying coral species in well-silicified artifacts, and the geochemical similarities of the various coral exposures.

GIS Predictive Modeling

Most of the analyses discussed here have used relatively subjective measures to determine specific quarry clusters and distance to source areas. Recently, Estabrook (2011) utilized a Weights of Evidence (WofE) approach to predict chert locations in his study of chert use at Crystal River. Although Crystal River is a Woodland period mound and midden complex, the applicability of this approach to chert provenance studies at early sites appears promising. Weights of Evidence is a Bayesian statistical approach framed within a raster-based GIS model (Raines et al. 2000:45). The approach combines a variety of support criteria, or "evidence," which in this case are geological and environmental data, to predict a series of outcome locations—i.e., the locations of chert outcrops. It uses location information about the presence and absence of the event relative to other known features or events to make this prediction.

WofE was employed to update and further evaluate the criteria used by Upchurch et al. (1982a) to create the original quarry cluster designations in a 50-km region surrounding the Crystal River complex in coastal Citrus County. While Estabrook used updated versions of several of the same data sets used in the 1982 investigation, like surface geology and physiographic region, GIS tools allowed for the consideration of many additional data sets known to be associated with chert outcrops in the region, including specific soils, elevation, and distance to various landscape features such as rivers and sinkholes. As shown in Figure 6.5, the WofE analysis was able to predict the possible locations of chert outcrops with a much greater degree of specificity than was possible in Upchurch et al.'s original study.

Since both the WofE analysis and the original quarry cluster boundaries were based on the same data sets, there is a strong spatial relationship between the areas of higher outcrop potential predicted by the model and the boundaries of Upchurch et al.'s quarry clusters. However, the WofE also supported the elimination of the Inverness Quarry Cluster and the possible incorporation of the quarries within the old boundaries of this cluster into adjacent clusters.

The analysis also suggests that there may be a divide between the upland and lowland-coastal portions of the Brooksville Quarry Cluster. The boundaries of this cluster were originally defined primarily within the upland portions of the Brooksville Ridge, but this region appears to be

Elevation Exaggeration 5x

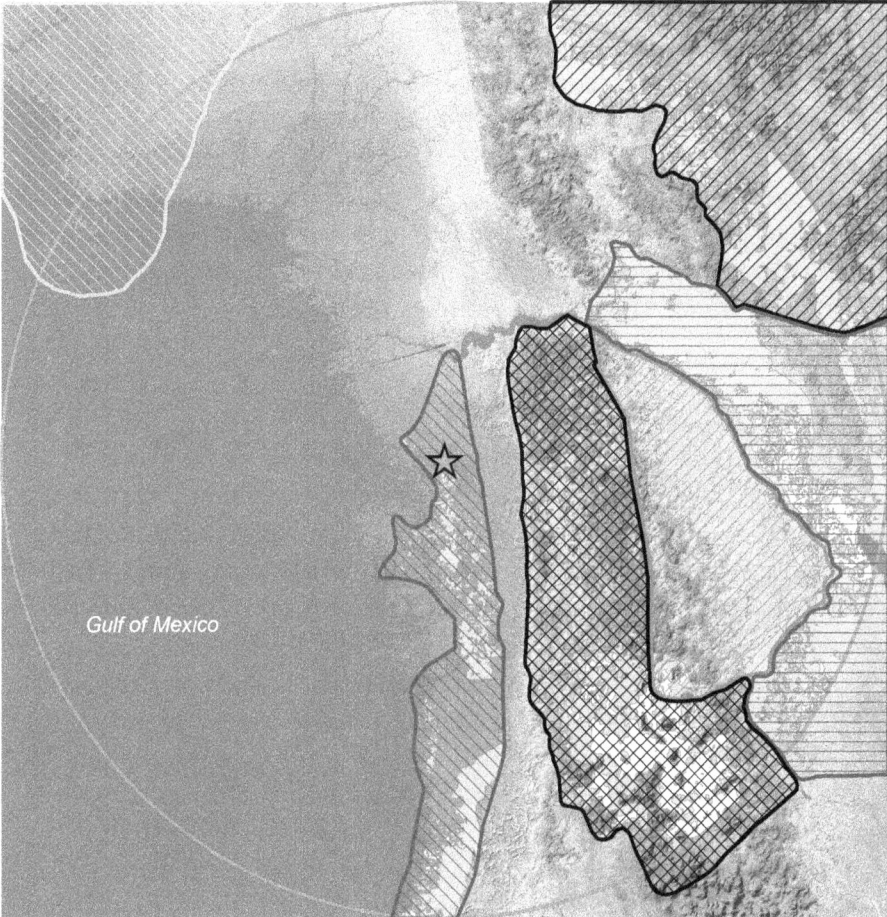

Crystal River Site

Quarry Cluster
Brooksville
Inverness
Lake Panasoffkee
Lower Suwannee
Ocala
New Coastal

Gulf of Mexico

Kilometers
0   5   10   20

Outcrop Potential/Posterior Probabilities

Moderate Outcrop Potential
(.0008 - .0050)

High Outcrop Potential
(.0051 - .0135)

Very High Outcrop Potential
(.0136 - .0355)

Figure 6.5. Chert outcrop potential based on a Weights of Evidence GIS model.

spatially distinct from a series of coastal chert sources along the Gulf of Mexico and adjacent coastal swamps. This series of known coastal out-crops and predicted outcrop locations has been tentatively named the New Coastal Quarry Cluster (Estabrook 2011; see Figure 6.5). These outcrops lie along a band of known Paleoindian and Early Archaic sites. Like other early sites in the Central Florida region, these sites are associated with both the larger sinkhole and chert outcrop features that parallel the coastline in this region. These data, as well as isolated finds of both side-notched and lanceolate points, support the occurrence of Paleo and Early Archaic sites just offshore.

Geochemical Analysis

Although Upchurch et al. (1982a) found that geochemical analysis of Flor-ida cherts is of limited utility, due to a lack of between-site variability, their study suffered from small sample sizes. In a pilot study, Burke (2014) used Portable X-ray Fluorescence Spectrometry (PXRF) to determine if arti-facts from a known quarry, Wayne's Sink, could be traced back to the out-crop that yielded them. Wayne's Sink is located within the Wacissa Quarry Cluster, a Suwannee Limestone chert source area located in the Big Bend region of northwest Florida. The lower Aucilla River provides excellent ac-cess to chert outcrops within this cluster, and the lower karst section of the Aucilla River basin represents a major concentration of Paleoindian and Early Archaic sites. A total of 24 chert samples and 110 lithic artifacts from Wayne's Sink were subjected to PXRF analysis. Through the use of select elements and biplots, the successful sourcing rates of materials back to the Wayne's Sink outcrop range from 48.98 percent for cobalt vs. iron to 91.57 percent for rubidium vs. molybdenum and 96.08 percent for rubidium vs. iron (Figure 6.6).

Ten samples from other quarry clusters that contain Suwannee Lime-stone chert were compared to the Wayne's Sink chert samples. All the ana-lyzed Suwannee chert samples contained iron, strontium, and zirconium, but only chert from Wayne's Sink consistently contained molybdenum, ru-bidium, and cobalt. Thus, iron, strontium, and zirconium may be baseline elements for Suwannee chert, while molybdenum, rubidium, and cobalt seem to characterize chert from a specific outcrop, Wayne's Sink.

While the preliminary results indicate that sampling intensively within individual quarry clusters may lead to successful chert sourcing with in-strument analysis, they need to be verified through additional analysis of a large sample from chert outcrops within other quarry clusters that contain

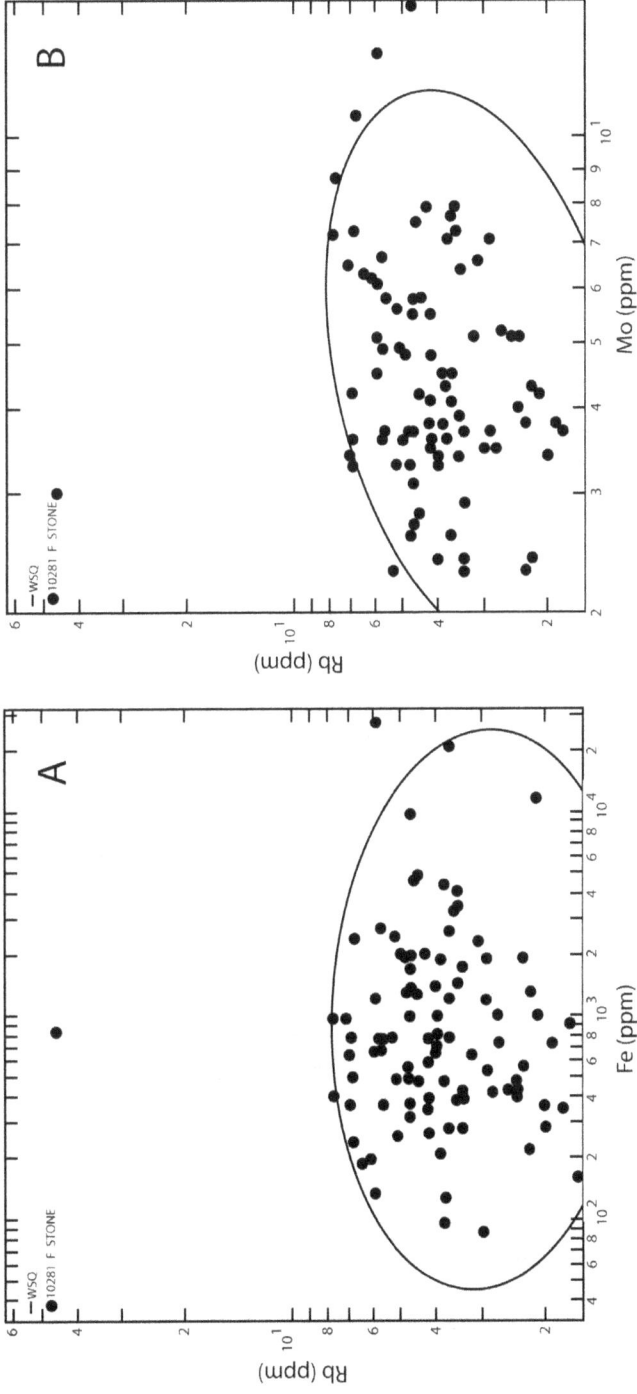

Figure 6.6. Biplots of rubidium versus iron (*A*) and rubidium versus molybdenum (*B*) for chert samples from Wayne's Sink.

Suwannee Limestone chert to determine if individual outcrops can be geo-chemically defined. If so, then geochemical analyses can provide an im-portant independent check on the visual identification approach to chert provenance.

Conclusions

Despite critiques of the visual identification approach (see Parish and Durham 2015 for a recent example), the use of visual criteria will likely continue to be the primary way that most archaeologists assign specific artifacts to a source area. While such an approach may not be suited to all regions where chert was used prehistorically, Florida is fortunate in that the processes resulting in chert formation are well understood and the chert-bearing formations have been accurately mapped. This has contributed to the successful application of the quarry cluster approach, which relies on visual criteria for source area identification. The chert-bearing formations contain fossils and other inclusions that are distinctive enough to assign artifacts to these formations with a high degree of confidence. These forma-tions crop out in relatively restricted geographic locales, which aids in the ability to assign artifacts correctly to a formation of origin.

The problems that have been encountered, such as boundary identifica-tion, quarry clusters that contain cherts with characteristics that are similar to other quarry clusters of the same geological formation, and the difficulty of distinguishing quarry clusters geochemically, continue to be the focus of active research. These problems are offset by the ease of the method's ap-plication, which has led to widespread use and the ability to analyze large samples of artifacts from sites, including debitage as well as tools. This has enabled us to document trade and mobility patterns as well as temporal patterns in the use of different quarry clusters and chert types.

Reducing the potential for committing a Type I error (assigning an arti-fact to a specific quarry cluster when in fact it came from a different quarry cluster) is a major goal of current chert provenance research in Florida. This problem can be mitigated by developing, maintaining, and making widely available a chert database that accurately reflects the range of varia-tion in cherts from all of the identified quarry clusters. Moreover, the simi-lar surficial geology shared by Florida with coastal Alabama, Georgia, and South Carolina makes it feasible to develop a large-scale regional database that incorporates the quarry cluster approach.

The major advantage of such a database lies in standardization. Although Coastal Plain cherts share many attributes, they have been given a variety of names depending on geopolitical boundaries and local custom (e.g., Allendale, Brier Creek, Tallahatta, Ocala, Two Egg, Coastal Plain). With standardized and widely distributed information on the characteristics of cherts from different quarry clusters, one can better evaluate trade and migration vectors, study territoriality, and identify behavioral preferences regarding toolstone selection for activities such as crafting, apprenticeship, symbolic display, and ritual. At present, no such database exists in Florida, and recent attempts to develop a large-scale database for the Southeast (e.g., Parish and Jeu 2016), while worthwhile, have not addressed the issue of standardized terminology for visual characterization.

Instrumental techniques for determining chert provenance also can aid in achieving this goal. The results reported by Burke (2014) on the use of PXRF to identify chert sources are encouraging, as is the use of other techniques elsewhere, such as visible/near-infrared reflectance spectroscopy (Parish 2011; Parish et al. 2012) and laser ablation inductively coupled plasma spectrometry (Roll et al. 2005; Speer 2015). While still costly and not always readily available to all, these techniques potentially can be used to verify quarry cluster assignments made on the basis of visual criteria, increasing reliability of the method.

Acknowledgments

We wish to thank Chris Moore and Al Goodyear for asking us to participate in the 2014 SEAC symposium that formed that basis for this book, and the two anonymous reviewers for their comments.

7

PALEOINDIANS IN
THE SOUTH CAROLINA COASTAL PLAIN

TRACKING PLEISTOCENE–HOLOCENE TRANSITIONS

ASHLEY M. SMALLWOOD, ALBERT C. GOODYEAR,
THOMAS A. JENNINGS, AND DOUGLAS A. SAIN

Evaluating Cultural Change in South Carolina's Coastal Plain

During the Late Pleistocene, Early Paleoindians faced diverse ecological landscapes and ever-changing postglacial environmental conditions. Throughout the interior of the continent, these changes included fluctuations in temperature, precipitation, and seasonality, leading to major extinctions and the reorganization of biotic communities. In the Atlantic Coastal Plain, early human populations faced the additional challenge of significant variation in coastal environments; the melting of once vast continental ice sheets led to significant fluctuations in sea level change (Anderson and Bissett 2015; Harris et al. 2013). Based on the distribution of lanceolate bifaces, it is clear that Paleoindian populations inhabited the Coastal Plain throughout the Late Pleistocene from approximately 13,000 to 11,700 years ago, but how did human use of this landscape change during the Paleoindian period?

In this chapter, we use Clovis, Redstone, Post-Clovis Unfluted, and Dalton Paleoindian points recorded in the Paleoindian Database of the Americas (PIDBA) to explore diachronic changes in Paleoindian settlement in South Carolina's Coastal Plain (Anderson et al. 2010). The Coastal Plain comprises two-thirds of the area of South Carolina. Though it was geographically limited in distribution, the province contains some of the most knappable stone, and the area has produced some of the best-documented evidence of Paleoindian occupation in the American Southeast (Goodyear

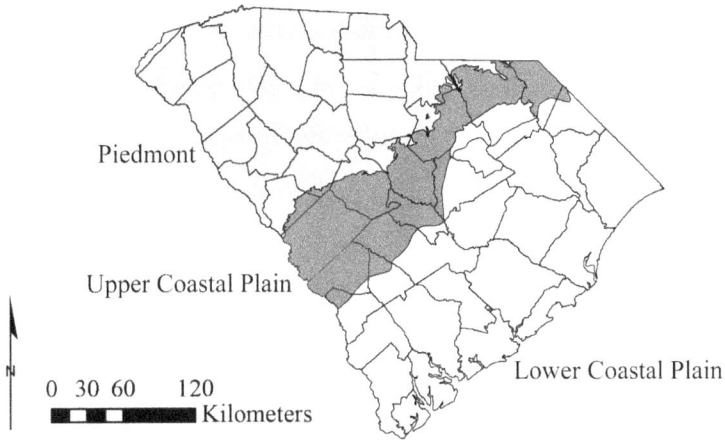

Figure 7.1. Map of South Carolina showing Piedmont, Upper Coastal Plain, and Lower Coastal Plain physiographic provinces.

2013, 2014, 2018; Moore and Brooks 2012a; Smallwood et al. 2013). For these reasons, we focus on this province to compare point distributions across physiographic regions, raw material types, and point transport distances and directions, and we apply these data to ultimately assess changes in settlement over time. We find significant differences in point distributions and raw material use through time that suggest that later Paleoindian populations adjusted their use of the Coastal Plain.

The Environmental Contexts of Paleoindian Cultural Change

To understand how the use of South Carolina's Coastal Plain changed through the Paleoindian period, it is important to consider the area's environmental conditions and resources, as well as those found in adjacent areas. South Carolina encompasses three major physiographic provinces: the Coastal Plain, the Piedmont, and he Blue Ridge. In this study we focus on the two largest geographic areas: the Coastal Plain (represented as the Upper Coastal Plain and Lower Coastal Plain) and the Piedmont to gather a relative understanding of changes in use of the Coastal Plain during the Paleoindian period (Figure 7.1).[1] During the Late Pleistocene, the climate and vegetation of the Coastal Plain and Piedmont were distinct, offering unique resources to populations living there. These environmental distinctions were primarily influenced by latitudinal, and to some extent altitudinal, differences (Russell et al. 2009).

Late Pleistocene Environment of the Coastal Plain

The Coastal Plain is the most expansive area in the state and is character-ized by sand hills and broad, flat coastal terraces. This region had extensive river drainages, large floodplains, and wetlands, including Carolina bays—shallow upland ponds situated throughout the Coastal Plain that formed during the Pleistocene—that were likely critical sources of water and biotic resources for Paleoindian populations (Anderson et al. 1979; Brooks et al. 2010). South Carolina's Coastal Plain can be naturally separated into the Lower Coastal Plain and Upper Coastal Plain. The Lower Coastal Plain is a series of flat coastal terraces with broad river drainages that extend east-ward to the Atlantic Ocean (Cooke 1936). The Upper Coastal Plain includes the Sandhills–Fall Line zone, the macroecotone that runs across South Car-olina separating the low-lying sands of the Lower Coastal Plain from the eroded rocks of the Piedmont (Canouts 1981). During the Pleistocene, as in the present, this Fall Line zone was an environmentally diverse area, with relatively higher relief and more biotic diversity than the coastal terraces of the Lower Coastal Plain (Cable and Cantley 1979; Michie 1980).

Based on reconstructions of paleovegetation, the area south of the 33-de-gree latitude, encompassing much of the Coastal Plain, was comparatively warmer and more temperate than the cool, mesic conditions to the north. Delcourt and Delcourt (1985) broadly reconstruct much of South Caro-lina's Coastal Plain as an oak-hickory-and-southern-pine forest with many modern-day species, such as oak, hickory, sweetgum, and southern pine, present in the area well before the Last Glacial Maximum.

Prior to the Late Pleistocene extinction of megafauna, which was essen-tially complete soon after the onset of the Younger Dryas, approximately 12,850 years ago (Agenbroad 2005; Faith 2011; Faith and Surovell 2009; Fie-del 2009; Fiedel and Haynes 2004; Grayson 1987, 2006; Grayson and Melt-zer 2002, 2003; Guthrie 2003; Haynes 2002, 2009; Martin 1973, 2006; Mead and Meltzer 1984; Meltzer and Mead 1983), the Coastal Plain was home to a diverse population of ungulates, including mammoth, mastodon, bison, and horse (Webb 1981b:79). Recently, Moore et al. (2016) report bison blood residue on Paleoindian-age tools from Flamingo Bay, a Carolina bay situ-ated in the Coastal Plain, providing evidence that populations were exploit-ing bison, and likely other large mammals, during the Paleoindian period. In his paleontological synthesis of the southeastern Coastal Plain, Webb (1981a) concludes based on the ratio of mammoth to mastodon finds that the Coastal Plain had more grasslands than the Piedmont. Thus, during the first few centuries of Paleoindian occupation, the extensive grasslands, wetlands, and broad floodplains likely attracted large grazing mammals and the Paleoindians that hunted them.

The maritime tropical airmass that prevailed during the last 60,000 years kept climate and vegetation communities of the Coastal Plain relatively stable throughout the Pleistocene (Delcourt and Delcourt 1985), but changes in sea levels led to significant environmental instability in the region. Sea level rise began with continental warming and glacial melting during the Bølling-Allerød and continued, with fluctuations that substantially altered shorelines and inundated coastal wetlands, through the Younger Dryas (approximately 12,850–11,700 cal yr B.P.) (Broecker 2006; Broecker and Denton 2012; Broecker et al. 1988; Tarasov and Peltier 2005). In a detailed examination of the influence of changing shorelines on early settlement of the southeastern United States, Anderson and Bissett (2015) use high-resolution topographic data to determine when shorelines were changing most markedly. According to the authors, meltwater pulse-1A (MWP-1A) between approximately 14,308 and 13,928 cal yr B.P. and the initial part of the Younger Dryas between 12,933 and 12,044 cal yr B.P. were two intervals when rapidly changing shorelines would have made coastal margins unfavorable settings for Paleoindian populations. More particularly, in an analysis of the Atlantic Coastal Plain of South Carolina, Harris et al. (2013:19) conclude that by 11,500 years ago, the continental shelf edge was breached and marine transgression rates increased, drowning the Coastal Plain by ca. 60 m/year.

Late Pleistocene Environment of the Adjacent Piedmont

The Lower Coastal Plain rises to the northwest with the Sandhills-Fall Line zone of the Upper Coastal Plain, eventually rising to the Piedmont (Canouts 1981). The Piedmont province has greater relief than the Coastal Plain, and the gently rolling hills and ridges are deeply dissected by major river drainages.

Vegetation communities of the Late Pleistocene indicate that the Piedmont was cooler and wetter than today. According to Delcourt and Delcourt (1985), this area was a mixed hardwood forest.

The palynological sequence from White Pond, located on the 34-degree latitude near the border between the Piedmont and Upper Coastal Plain, most closely reflects environmental conditions of the Piedmont during the Pleistocene (Watts 1980). Based on an associated sequence of radiocarbon dates, during the Paleoindian period the vegetation communities were a mixed forest with hickory, oak, and beech; the latter reflects that cold, moist conditions prevailed (Meeks and Anderson 2012:112; Watts 1980:197). Watts (1980:192) calls this a cool-mesic forest and estimates that 25 percent of the forest community around White Pond was composed of beech and hickory trees. Further, Webb (1981b:79) concludes, based on the ratio of mammoth to mastodon finds, that the Piedmont had comparatively more woodlands than the Coastal Plain to the south.

Based on the paleontological record, the woodland environment of the Piedmont attracted faunal communities adapted for browsing habitats. A Pleistocene-age faunal assemblage from Little Kettle Creek, located in the Piedmont of east-central Georgia, included browsers like American mastodon and deer, as well as some grazers like mammoth and bison (Voorhies 1974). The Piedmont's abundant hickory and oak trees, nut-bearing trees, were likely important food sources for deer as well as Paleoindian populations, especially after megafauna extinctions made deer the primary browser in the region (e.g., Koldehoff and Walthall 2009).

Knappable Stone Sources

While the diverse Pleistocene landscape likely influenced landscape use through time, the location of raw material for tool production was also an important factor in Paleoindian occupation of the Coastal Plain and surrounding regions. Knappable stone occurs throughout South Carolina but in uneven distributions (Figure 7.2), and arguably the highest quality, based on ease of flaking and shaping, occurs in the Coastal Plain. Tertiary-age Coastal Plain chert, often referred to as Allendale Coastal Plain chert, outcrops in Allendale County, South Carolina, in the Lower Coastal Plain as the northernmost quarry exposure of outcrops that also occur in Georgia (Cooke 1936; Goad 1979; Goodyear 2014, 2017; Goodyear and Charles 1984; Goodyear et al. 1985; Upchurch 1984b). These cherts outcrop as beds and as nodules and boulders distributed along streams and ridges. Orthoquartzite occurs in Calhoun, Orangeburg, Clarendon, Williamsburg, and Berkeley counties situated in the Lower Coastal Plain in southeast-central South Carolina (Goodyear 2014; Moore and Brooks 2012b). Based on the distribution of quarry sites, metavolcanic stone (including rhyolite) occurs in four major source areas exploited by prehistoric populations: 1) Saluda, Edgefield, and McCormick counties in western South Carolina in the Piedmont along the Savannah River at the Fall Line, as a part of the Little River Series of the Carolina Slate Belt (Benson 2007; Mittwede 1988; Sassaman et al. 1988; Southerlin 2012); 2) York and Lancaster counties in northern

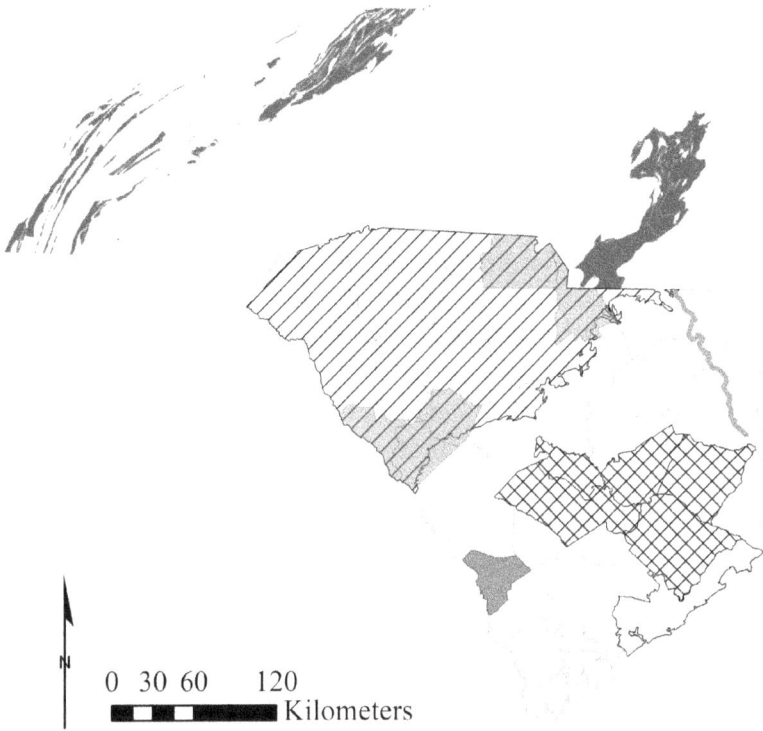

Figure 7.2. Map of South Carolina showing the locations of stone source areas used in this study.

South Carolina in the Piedmont at the border with North Carolina, as a part of the Persimmon Fork Formation of the Slate Belt (Moore et al. 2012; Southerlin 2012); 3) in a portion of the Pee Dee River situated in the Upper Coastal Plain as cobbles (Young 2010, 2012, 2013; Goodyear 2010a); and 4) in North Carolina's Inner Piedmont in the Uwharrie, Cid, and Tillery formations of the Carolina Slate Belt (Daniel 1998, 2001; Daniel and Butler 1996; Steponaitis et al. 2006). Quartz occurs as cobbles throughout the entire Piedmont physiographic province (Novick 1978). In the Ridge and Valley province of eastern Tennessee, cherts from the Knox Group and Fort Payne chert were the most extensively used sources by prehistoric people, and some of this material was used to make points discarded in South Carolina. With this diversity in raw material, hunter-gatherers had alternatives for stone sources throughout the Late Pleistocene landscape and, therefore, analyzing raw material types and tracking the movement of stone in the archaeological record can be used to explore changes in use of the Coastal Plain through time.

South Carolina's Paleoindian Record

South Carolina has a rich Paleoindian record that spans the Late Pleistocene, and the dense archaeological sites and isolated point finds prehistoric peoples left behind are scattered across the Coastal Plain and Piedmont. In South Carolina, much like the greater Southeast, cultural change in the Paleoindian period is marked by morphological and technological changes in discrete bifacially flaked point types (see Anderson et al. 2015 for an overview of the Paleoindian period in the greater Southeast). Only recently have reliable dates helped anchor the chronological placement of the Paleoindian occupation in the state (Anderson et al. 2016; Goodyear 2018; Moore et al. 2012). For this study, we evaluate diachronic changes in landscape use in South Carolina by assessing patterns in the distributions of four major Paleoindian point types recognized in the state: Clovis, Redstone, Post-Clovis Unfluted, and Dalton (Figure 7.3). These point types are morphologically and technologically described and chronologically assigned below.

Clovis

The Clovis period is represented by the Clovis point, a point with a diagnostic flute that initiates at the base and extends about halfway up the biface (Sellards 1952; Stanford 1991; Tankersley 2004; Willig 1991; Wormington 1957). Morphological and technological analyses of Clovis points recovered from the Topper site, in Allendale County, and isolated points in collections have shown that Clovis points in South Carolina have percussion fluting off the base often with slight waisting and ears, making them morphologically more excurvate when compared to Clovis points recovered from the western United States (e.g., Goodyear 2014:Fig. 7.4; Goodyear 2018); however, a geometric morphometric analysis demonstrated that Clovis points from the Southeast still fall within the range of Clovis variation (Smith et al. 2015). Technological studies of Clovis preforms and points from sites like Topper and Big Pine Tree in South Carolina (Goodyear 1999; Goodyear and Steffy 2003; Smallwood 2010, 2012) have demonstrated that Clovis flintknappers used overface flaking (that often produced overshot flakes) and end thinning to produce broad flake removals that narrowed and thinned bifaces for point production (Goodyear 2014; Smallwood 2010, 2012). Based on buried, dated sites, the majority of which are in the western

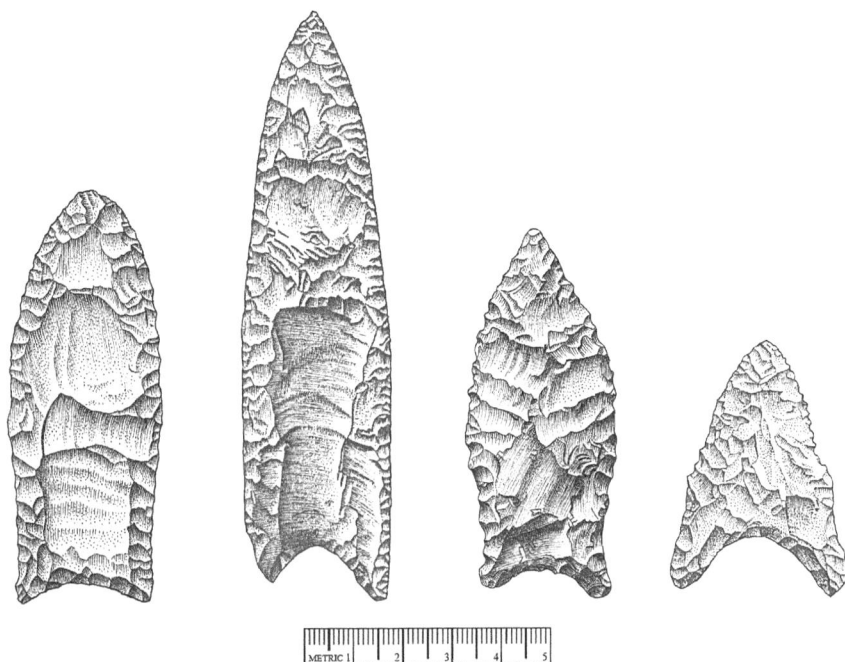

Figure 7.3. Illustrated examples of the four Paleoindian point groups used in this study. *From left to right*: Clovis, Redstone, Post-Clovis Unfluted, Dalton. Drawing by Darby Erd.

United States, Clovis dates to approximately 13,060–12,800 cal B.P. (Waters and Stafford 2007a).[2] Further, a cold-adapted softwood collected from the Clovis component at the Topper site yielded a radiocarbon date of 10,958 ± 65 B.P., chronologically confirming this date range for Clovis in the Southeast (Anderson et al. 2016).

Redstone

The Redstone fluted point was originally defined by avocationalists in northern Alabama in the Tennessee River Valley from surface finds (Cambron and Hulse 1964; Mahan 1964). They are recognized by their narrow, triangular morphology and long flutes, which originate from a characteristically deep basal concavity (Daniel and Goodyear 2006; Goodyear 2006, 2010b). Such flutes were created by instrument-assisted fluting, a technique during which a punch or pressure flaker was placed on a prepared platform in the concavity and pressed or indirectly struck off (Goodyear 2006:100–101). Redstones in South Carolina and the greater Southeast are morphologically similar to types farther north, such as Gainey, Vail, and

Debert (Goodyear 2010b:Fig. 1). In the Midwest and Northeast, these types date immediately after Clovis at approximately 12,770 and 12,600 cal B.P. (Goodyear 2010b:86).

Post-Clovis Unfluted

Post-Clovis Unfluted points represent a provisional category for South Carolina lanceolate points exhibiting waisting in the haft area. They are not fluted but can exhibit minor basal thinning. They are similar to what have been called Suwannee and Simpson points in Florida and south Georgia (e.g., Bullen 1975), although those categories have been redefined by Dunbar and Hemmings (2004). In all likelihood, these points occupy a time period after Clovis and before Dalton (Sherwood et al. 2004).

Dalton

Dalton points are lanceolate points with concave bases. They have characteristic blade resharpening due to knife usage, resulting in a shoulder effect on the blade outside the haft area. The creation of serrations on blade margins and repeated reapplication resulted in a narrowing of blade width, and where resharpening was done on alternate edges, a bevel formed (cf. Lipo et al. 2012; also see Pettigrew et al. 2015). Dalton points in Georgia and the Carolinas, however, appear to have been resharpened bifacially in an effort to create fine serrations. Most Dalton points are basally thinned and rarely fluted (Bradley 1997:57). Radiocarbon-dated Dalton assemblages indicate the Dalton occupation likely ranges from approximately 12,500 to as late as 11,400 cal B.P. (Coleman 1972:154; Crane and Griffin 1972:159; Goodyear 1982; Sherwood et al. 2004), more generally the later Younger Dryas and possibly into the early Holocene (Anderson 1996; Morse 1997; Miller and Gingerich 2013a, 2013b; Walthall 1998). Some researchers classify this technocomplex as transitional Late Paleoindian–Early Archaic because of suggested shifts in mobility and greater reliance on seasonal resources (Koldehoff and Walthall 2009). However, for this chapter, we follow Anderson et al. (2015) and designate Dalton as Late Paleoindian based on point morphology and secure chronological placement during the Younger Dryas.

These distinct point morphologies and technologies are evidence of unique populations with unique adaptations. Clearly, point design, a product of both style and function, changed through time, but did landscape use also shift through the Paleoindian period? Was the Coastal Plain consistently occupied by all Paleoindian populations, or did the importance of this physiographic province change through time?

Materials and Methods

This chapter analyses points from the state of South Carolina; most of these points are reported in the PIDBA (Anderson et al. 2010), and more recently collected points have not yet been submitted to PIDBA, although they are currently being reported (Goodyear 2016). Paleoindian projectile points have been systematically recorded in South Carolina for almost 40 years. Points recorded by type and raw material, with detailed attribute, line drawing, or photographic data, are available online in PIDBA (Charles and Michie 1992; Goodyear et al. 1989, 1990; Michie 1977). In this study, we use 1,227 points that are clearly identified as Paleoindian period points.

To test for changes in landscape use through time, points are grouped into four categories following Anderson et al. (1996, 2010:75–78) and Smallwood et al. (2015) (see also Meeks and Anderson 2012:119–123) and adjusted for point types present in South Carolina (Figure 7.3). These categories are Clovis, Redstone (Post-Clovis Fluted), Post-Clovis Unfluted (Waisted Lanceolates), and Dalton. As noted, questions remain regarding the absolute chronologies of southeastern Paleoindian point types. In this analysis, we use these point groups as indicators of relative chronology and have opted not to correct for proposed calendar year differences given the uncertainties in absolute age ranges for each point type (see Smallwood et al. 2015).

Methods for this analysis closely follow a comparable study of the Georgia Paleoindian record conducted by Smallwood et al. (2015). Points have been spatially provenienced to the county of discovery, and spatial comparisons include county point frequencies and densities. For physiographic province comparisons, counties are grouped into three physiographic categories: Piedmont (including the Blue Ridge, because this province is a minor geographic area and county centroids in this province actually fall within the Piedmont), the Upper Coastal Plain, and the Lower Coastal Plain. We divide the Coastal Plain into these two natural provinces because one of the primary goals of this study is to track changes in use of the Coastal Plain through the Paleoindian period, and these provinces have been recognized as distinct environmental zones

For stone raw material type comparisons, materials are grouped into five source categories. Geographic locations of source areas are mapped in ArcGIS 10.0 according to current known outcrop and gravel distributions as previously discussed (see Figure 7.2). Raw material distances are grouped into three distance categories, local (distance < 20 km), non-local (20 ≤

distance < 100), and exotic (100 ≤ distance) and compared categorically (e.g., Jennings 2008; Ray 1998; Surovell 2009). Calculated distance values for the nonlocal and exotic categories, and transport direction angles for nonlocal and exotic categories, are also compared.

Statistical comparisons of categorical and continuous variables follow procedures outlined by Drennan (2009) and VanPool and Leonard (2011) and are conducted using PASW 18. Chi-square tests are used for categorical comparisons. For individual cells, adjusted residuals greater than or equal to 2 or less than or equal to -2 are considered significant. For normally distributed continuous data, we use ANOVA and post hoc Bonferroni pairwise comparisons. For non-normally distributed continuous data, we use Kruskal-Wallis tests and post hoc pairwise Mann-Whitney/Wilcoxon Ranked Sum tests. Distances and compass directions from the nearest stone source location to the county centroid of each point recovery location were calculated using ArcGIS 10.0. Circular statistical comparisons of stone transport directionality were conducted using Oriana 4.01 (Kovach 2011). The Rayleigh test and Watson's U2 are used to test for randomness and normality, respectively (Fisher 1993). For directional data with von Mises distributions, we use Watson-Williams tests, and for non–von Mises-distributed data, we use Mardia-Watson-Wheeler tests (Mardia and Jupp 2000) to compare point groups.

Results

In the following sections, we present the results of comparisons of point densities and distributions across physiographic regions (Table 7.1). We also present frequencies and point transport distances and directions by raw material types (Table 7.2).

Physiographic Provinces

Of the 1,227 points analyzed in this study, 335 (27.3 percent) are Clovis, 71 (5.8 percent) are Redstone, 35 (2.9 percent) are Post-Clovis Unfluted, and 786 (64.1 percent) are Dalton. Mapping the distribution of point frequencies by county reveals visual similarities and differences in point densities across South Carolina for each point group (Figure 7.4). For each of the four point groups, Allendale County, located along the Savannah River in southwestern South Carolina, is one of the highest-density counties. Beyond this commonality, high-density point distributions appear to vary spatially between the four point groups. To further explore relative

Table 7.1. Counts and Percentages of Points Found in the Three Physiographic Province Groupings

Point Group		Piedmont	Upper Coastal Plain	Lower Coastal Plain	Total
			Province Group		
Clovis	Count	108	70	157	335
	Expected count	87.1	116.0	131.9	335.0
	Percentage within point group	32.2%	20.9%	46.9%	100.0%
	Adjusted Residual	3.1	-6.2	3.3	
Redstone	Count	11	14	46	71
	Expected count	18.5	24.6	27.9	71.0
	Percentage within point group	15.5%	19.7%	64.8%	100.0%
	Adjusted Residual	-2.1	-2.7	4.5	
Post-Clovis Unfluted	Count	6	5	24	35
	Expected count	9.1	12.1	13.8	35.0
	Percentage within point group	17.1%	14.3%	68.6%	100.0%
	Adjusted Residual	-1.2	-2.6	3.6	
Dalton	Count	194	336	256	786
	Expected count	204.3	272.2	309.4	786.0
	Percentage within point group	24.7%	42.7%	32.6%	100.0%

distribution differences, counties are grouped into the three physiographic provinces: Piedmont, Upper Coastal Plain, and Lower Coastal Plain. Between the four Paleoindian point groups, point densities significantly differ by physiographic region (Pearson $\chi^2 = 84.80$, $df = 6$, $p < .001$), although the level of variable association is weak (Cramer's V = .186). Clovis points occur more frequently than expected in the Piedmont (AdjR = 3.1) and Lower Coastal Plain (AdjR = 3.3) and less than expected in the Upper Coastal Plain (AdjR = -6.2). Redstones occur at higher than expected frequencies in the Lower Coastal Plain (AdjR = 4.5) and lower than expected frequencies in the Piedmont (AdjR = -2.1) and Upper Coastal Plain (AdjR = -2.7). Post-Clovis Unfluted points occur at higher than expected frequencies in the Lower Coastal Plain (AdjR = 3.6) and lower than expected frequencies in the Upper Coastal Plain (AdjR = 2.6). Dalton points occur in higher than

Table 7.2. Point Counts, Transport Distances, and Transport Directions by Raw Material Type

Point Group	Total Points within Raw Material Type	Nonlocal and Exotic Count	Percent of Points That Are Nonlocal or Exotic (within Material Type and Point Groups)	Mean Distance (km)	Distance Standard Deviation	Mean Transport Direction (degrees)	Circular Standard Deviation	Raw Material Type
Clovis	8	8	100.0	131.73	24.67	149.56	5.75	Ridge and Valley Chert
Redstone								Ridge and Valley Chert
Post-Clovis Unfluted								Ridge and Valley Chert
Dalton								Ridge and Valley Chert
Clovis	48	14	29.2	71.28	23.71	141.82	12.20	Quartz
Redstone	2	2	100.0	99.51	48.71	145.19	14.64	Quartz
Post-Clovis Unfluted								Quartz
Dalton	90	13	14.4	46.41	20.56	138.92	15.60	Quartz
Clovis	91	49	53.9	59.70	32.51	169.43	82.04	Metavolcanic SC
Redstone	23	15	65.2	60.43	44.78	152.48	63.32	Metavolcanic SC
Post-Clovis Unfluted	4	2	50.0	129.24	60.40	130.70	6.56	Metavolcanic SC

Dalton	316	211	66.8	36.79	26.96	117.40	51.46	Metavolcanic SC
Clovis	91	86	94.6	112.00	56.69	202.19	49.38	Metavolcanic NC
Redstone	23	23	100.0	112.90	67.70	175.04	42.32	Metavolcanic NC
Post-Clovis Unfluted	4	4	100.0	174.65	58.06	208.69	25.51	Metavolcanic NC
Dalton	316	293	92.7	103.27	54.02	195.04	42.75	Metavolcanic NC
Clovis	150	113	75.4	102.99	54.25	48.66	58.53	Coastal Plain Chert
Redstone	31	21	67.8	132.55	60.59	30.46	57.10	Coastal Plain Chert
Post-Clovis Unfluted	29	21	72.4	147.77	34.67	25.07	46.67	Coastal Plain Chert
Dalton	336	192	57.1	68.55	41.63	4.81	41.63	Coastal Plain Chert
Clovis	14	2	14.3	23.54	2.33	282.55	.89	Orthoquartzite
Redstone	3	1	33.3	49.25		208.09		Orthoquartzite
Post-Clovis Unfluted	3	3	100.0	27.77	7.51	252.56	60.92	Orthoquartzite
Dalton	24	0	.0					Orthoquartzite

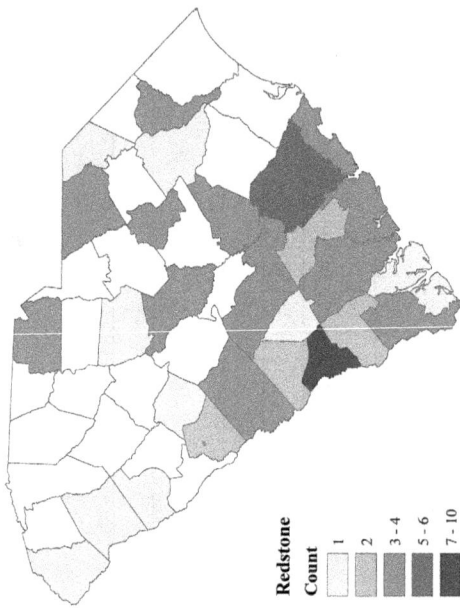

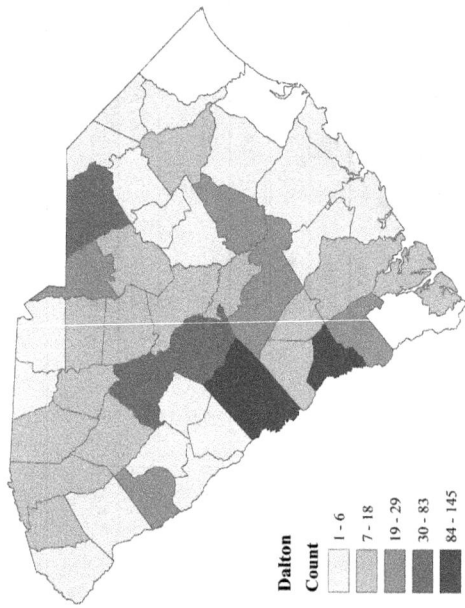

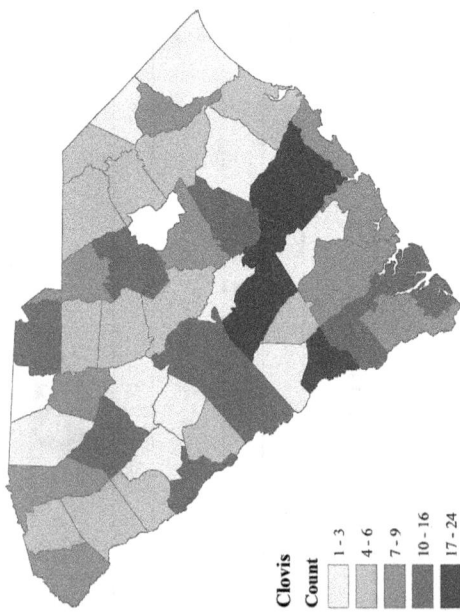

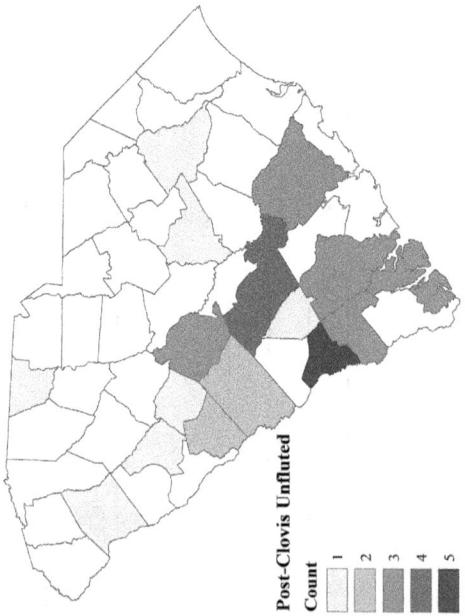

Figure 7.4. Maps of point densities by county for the four point groups.

Clovis
Count
1 - 3
4 - 6
7 - 9
10 - 16
17 - 24

Post-Clovis Unfluted
Count
1
2
3
4
5

Redstone
Count
1
2
3 - 4
5 - 6
7 - 10

Dalton
Count
1 - 6
7 - 18
19 - 29
30 - 83
84 - 145

expected frequencies in the Upper Coastal Plain (AdjR = 8.0) and lower than expected frequencies in the Lower Coastal Plain (AdjR = -6.5).

Coastal Plain Chert

Proportions of points transported local, nonlocal, and exotic distances significantly differ between the point groups (Pearson χ^2 = 99.67, p < .001, Cramer's V = .302). There are more than expected Clovis exotic points (AdjR = 4.8) and fewer than expected local points (AdjR = -3.5). For both the Redstone and Post-Clovis Unfluted groups, more than expected points are exotic (AdjR = 3.5 and 6.1, respectively) and fewer than expected are nonlocal (AdjR = -2.5 and -4.2, respectively). Fewer than expected Dalton points are exotic (AdjR = -8.9), and more than expected are local (AdjR = 3.9) and nonlocal (AdjR = 3.7).

The average distances that nonlocal and exotic points made from Coastal Plain chert were transported also significantly differ (Kruskal-Wallis p < .001). Post-Clovis Unfluted points were transported the farthest, followed by Redstone and Clovis. Dalton points of Coastal Plain chert were transported the shortest average distances.

Among points made from Coastal Plain cherts, Clovis (Z = 39.80, p < .001; U2 = .31, p < .005) and Redstone (Z = 7.78, p < .001; U2 = .109, p < .05) point transport direction angle distributions are nonrandom and non-normal and do not significantly differ from one another (Figure 7.5). Points of each type were transported into the Piedmont, along the Fall Line, and into the Coastal Plain. While not significantly different from these earlier point transport directions and also nonrandomly (Z = 10.82, p < .001) and non-normally (U2 = .14, p < .025) distributed, Post-Clovis Unfluted points were transported north into the Piedmont and east within the Lower Coastal Plain, but not south farther into the Coastal Plain. In a significant departure from Clovis (W = 73.49, p < .001), Redstone (W = 10.75, p < .005), and Post-Clovis Unfluted (W = 18.81, p < .001) point transport directions, Dalton Coastal Plain chert point directions, also nonrandomly (Z = 113.24, p < .001) and nonnormally (U2 = 3.50, p < .005) distributed, are primarily carried north, into the Piedmont and away from the Coastal Plain.

Orthoquartzite

The sample size of points made from orthoquartzite is too small for statistical distance comparisons, because none were transported exotically, and few were transported nonlocally. Most orthoquartzite points for all four point groups were discarded locally near the source area, with the

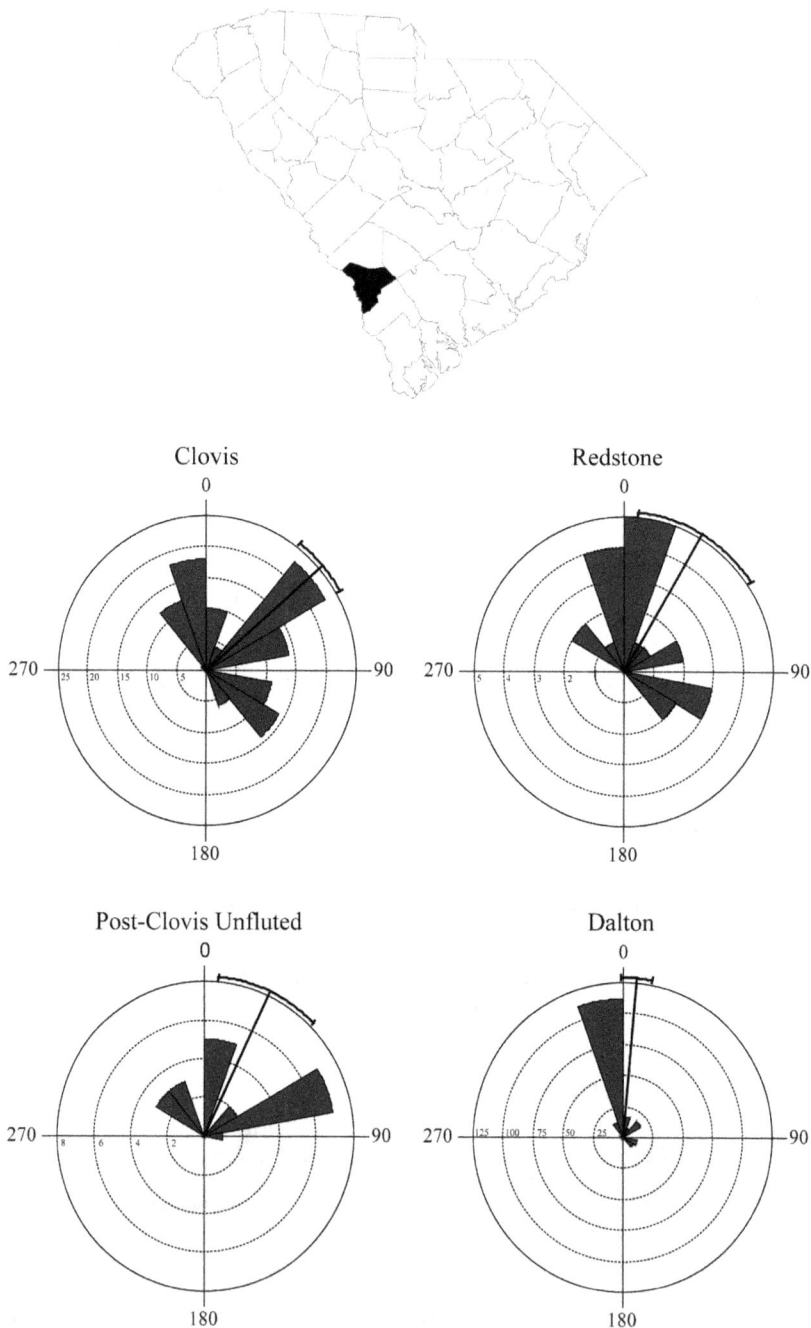

Figure 7.5. Map showing the location of Coastal Plain chert in South Carolina and rose diagrams by point group of non-local and exotic point transport direction angles.

exception that all three Post-Clovis Unfluted orthoquartzite points are nonlocal. All Dalton orthoquartzite points are local.

Frequencies of nonlocal and exotic points made from orthoquartzites are so few for all point groups that no statistical comparisons between transport direction angles could be made. Therefore, we simply present the rose diagrams (Figure 7.6).

Metavolcanic: South Carolina Source Area

If we assume South Carolina outcrops served as the sources for all metavolcanics, the sample size for proportions is too small when the Post-Clovis Unfluted group is included. Excluding this group reveals significant differences (Pearson $\chi^2 = 12.00$, $p = .017$, Cramer's V = .12). The Clovis point group is composed of greater than expected local metavolcanic points

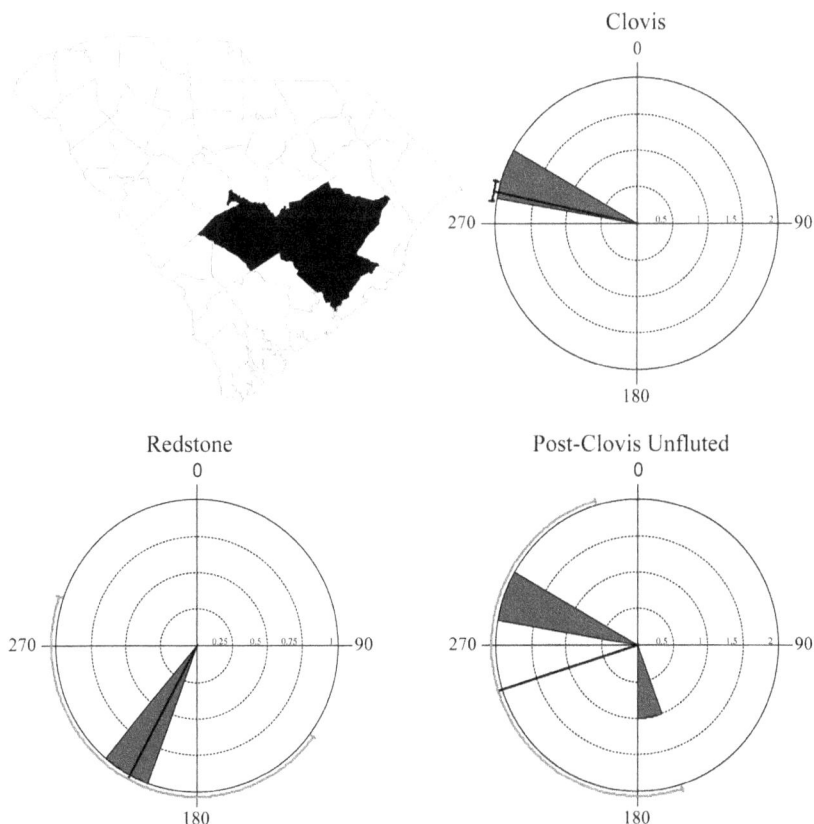

Figure 7.6. Map showing the location of orthoquartzite in South Carolina and rose diagrams by point group of non-local and exotic point transport direction angles.

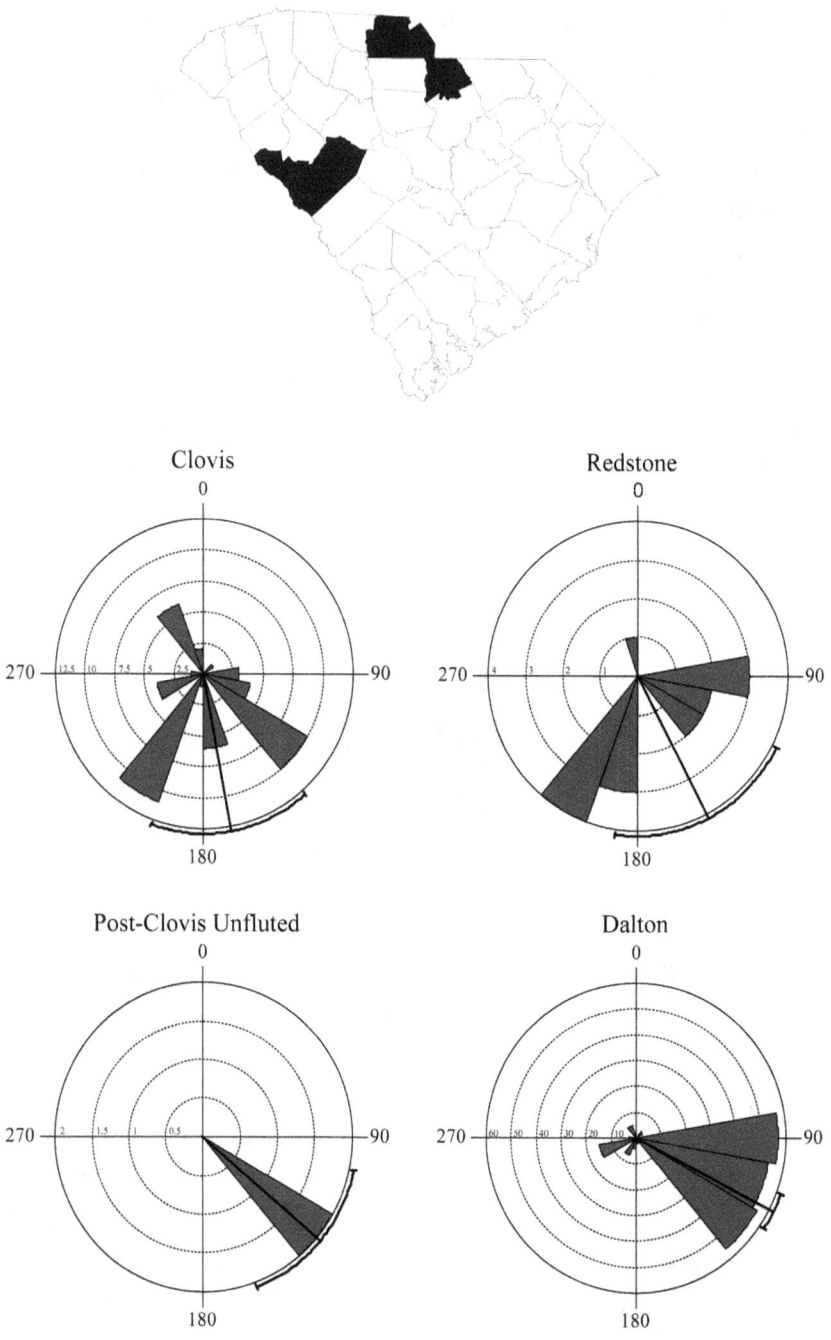

Figure 7.7. Map showing the location of metavolcanics in South Carolina and rose diagrams by point group of non-local and exotic point transport direction angles, assuming South Carolina was the sole source area for metavolcanics.

(AdjR = 2.3) and fewer than expected nonlocal points (AdjR = -2.6). There are more than expected nonlocal metavolcanic Dalton points (AdjR = 2.7) and fewer than expected local (AdjR = -2.0) and exotic (AdjR = -2.1) Dalton points. Average transport distances of nonlocal and exotic points also significantly differ (Kruskal-Wallis p < 0.001). The two Post-Clovis Unfluted points were transported the farthest average distance. Clovis and Redstone points were transported intermediate average distances, and Dalton points were transported the shortest average distance.

Clovis ($Z = 6.31$, $p = .002$; U2 $= .08$, $p < .05$) point angle distributions are nonrandom and non-normal, and Redstone ($Z = 4.42$, $p = .01$; U2 $=$ .07, $.05 < p < 0.10$) point angle distributions are nonrandom and normal. Clovis and Redstone point angles do not significantly differ ($W = .50$, $p =$ .78), with high frequencies of points transported southwest and east of the source area (Figure 7.7). There are too few Post-Clovis Unfluted points of metavolcanics for statistical comparisons, but we note that these points were transported southeast. Dalton angles significantly differ from Clovis ($W = 24.34$, $p < .001$) and nearly significantly differ from Redstone ($W =$ 5.615, $p = .06$). Dalton points, with nonrandom ($Z = 94.17$, $p < .001$) and nonnormal (U2 $= 1.28$, $p < .005$) angle distributions, were transported almost exclusively east and southeast.

Metavolcanic: North Carolina Source Area

If we assume that all metavolcanic points have a source location of North Carolina or the Pee Dee River, a different pattern emerges. The sample size for proportion comparisons is too small when the Post-Clovis Unfluted group is included. Excluding this group, no significant differences are evident in the proportions of local, nonlocal, and exotic metavolcanic points (Pearson $\chi^2 = 6.90$, $p = .141$). Comparing average transport distances between all four point groups also reveals no significant differences (Kruskal-Wallis $p = .109$).

Clovis ($Z = 40.92$, $p < .001$; U2 $= .312$, $p < .005$) and Redstone point direction angle distributions are both nonrandom and nonnormal and do not significantly differ ($W = 2.26$, $p = .323$). Clovis points have predominantly southern and western angles (Figure 7.8), with some southeastern angles. Redstone points have predominantly southern and eastern angles, with some western angles. There are too few Post-Clovis Unfluted points of metavolcanics for statistical comparisons, but we note that these points were transported south and southwest. Dalton direction angle distributions are nonrandom ($Z = 167.90$, $p < .001$) and non-normal (U2 $= 1.44$, $p < .005$)

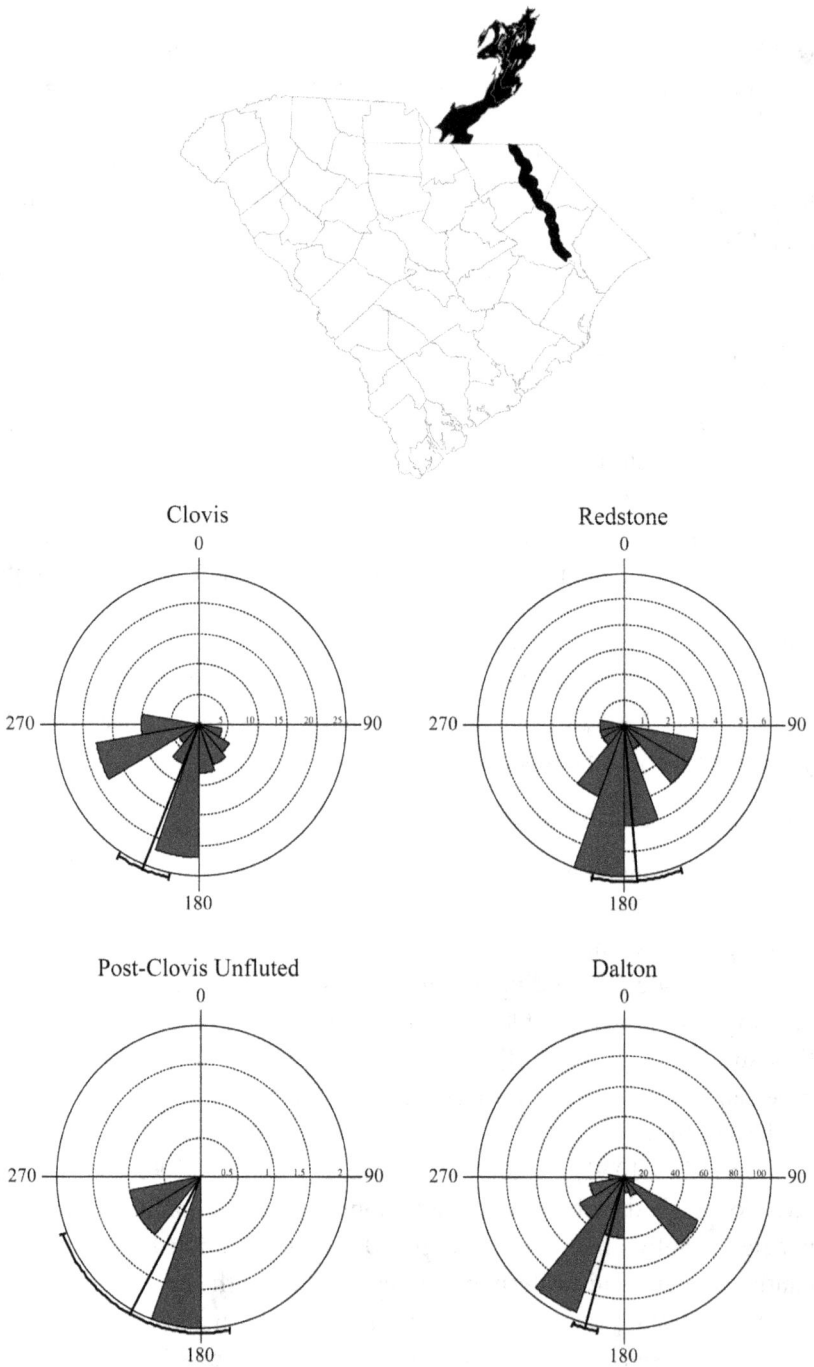

Figure 7.8. Map showing the location of metavolcanics in South and North Carolina and rose diagrams by point group of non-local and exotic point transport direction angles, assuming North Carolina and the Pee Dee River were the source areas for metavolcanics.

and significantly differ from both Clovis (W = 13.76, p = .001) and Redstone (W = 7.21, p = .027). Compared to these earlier point groups, Dalton points were transported less frequently in western and southeastern directions.

Quartz

While the study sample includes many specimens of Clovis and Dalton points made on quartz, only two Redstone and no Post-Clovis Unfluted points are quartz. Comparing Clovis and Dalton point proportions reveals no significant differences (Pearson χ^2 = 3.51, p = .06). Both sample groups are dominated by local quartz points. Exotic and nonlocal transport distances significantly differ (Kruskal-Wallis p = .032), with Dalton quartz points transported the shortest distances.

Among points made from quartz (Figure 7.9), Clovis transport angle distributions are nonrandom (Z = 13.38, p < .001) and normal (U2 = .04), with a predominantly southeastern transport direction. The sample size of

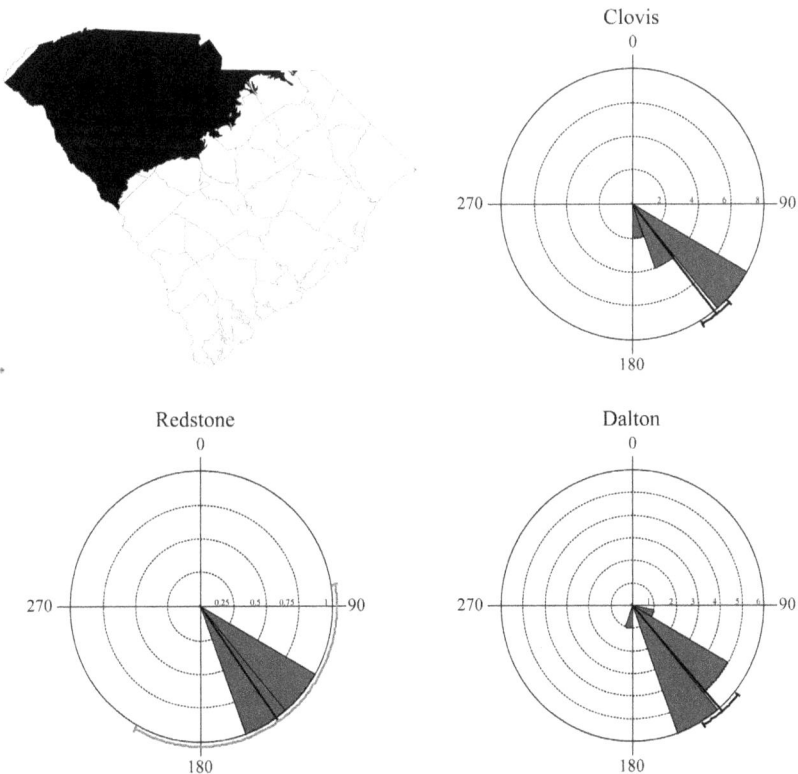

Figure 7.9. Map showing the location of quartz in South Carolina and rose diagrams by point group of non-local and exotic point transport direction angles.

quartz Redstone points is too small for statistical comparisons, but we note that these points were transported to the southeast. There are no recorded quartz Post-Clovis Unfluted points. Dalton quartz point angles are nonrandomly ($Z = 12.07, p < .001$) and nonnormally ($U2 = .16, p < .025$) distributed in a predominantly southeastern direction and do not significantly differ from Clovis angles ($W = .69, p = .707$).

Ridge and Valley

The only recorded points made from Ridge and Valley cherts are Clovis points. All eight of these points are exotic and were transported an average of 131.7 km. These points were transported in a southeastern direction (Figure 7.10).

Discussion: Is There Evidence for Diachronic Changes in Paleoindian Use of the Coastal Plain?

Based on point frequencies by physiographic region, raw material type comparisons, and spatial patterning in distributions, the South Carolina Paleoindian point record provides important insights into changes in how Paleoindians used the Coastal Plain through time. In the following sections, we discuss the evidence for each Paleoindian group and consider the potential relationships between changes in landscape use and environmental change.

Clovis

Clovis populations predominantly occupied the Lower Coastal Plain. Points occur in the highest frequency in this province. In part, Clovis use of the Lower Coastal Plain appears to be associated with the location of Coastal Plain chert in Allendale County; the majority of all Clovis points in the sample were crafted from this raw material (though this number is not significantly greater than in later periods). Another high-density area in the Lower Coastal Plain includes Orangeburg and Berkeley counties. It is interesting to note that these counties are source locations of orthoquartzite. Clovis populations were aware of and sparingly used this material; orthoquartzite points constitute an extremely small percentage of the total Clovis point sample (Goodyear 2014). Clovis points also occur in significantly higher frequency in the Piedmont. Raw material type comparisons show that Clovis people used sources in the Piedmont, though not as extensively as they used Coastal Plain chert. Clovis points chipped from

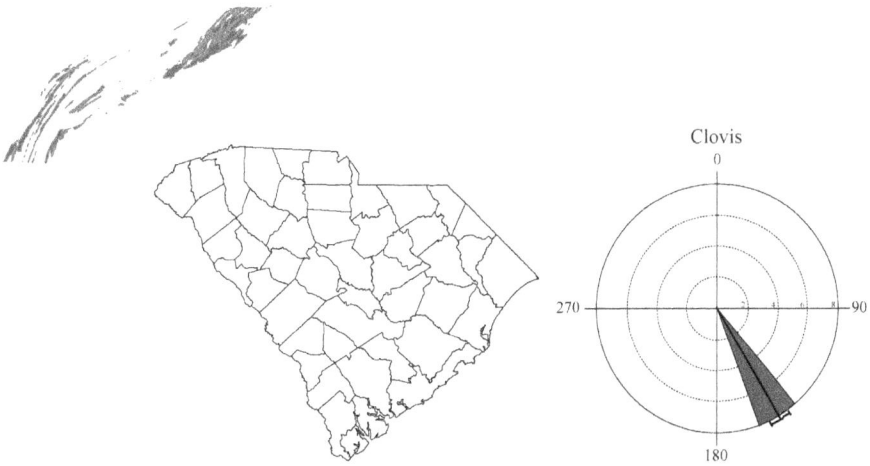

Figure 7.10. Map showing the location of Ridge and Valley cherts in Tennessee and rose diagrams by point group of non-local and exotic point transport direction angles.

quartz and Ridge and Valley cherts occur in greater than expected frequencies. Metavolcanics, also sourced to the Piedmont and Upper Coastal Plain, were frequently used by Clovis people, but to an extent that was less than expected when compared to later periods.

Comparatively, Clovis populations generally remained closer to raw material sources, but some materials were moved away from sources >20 km (nonlocal and exotic). Clovis people discarded more than expected points made on Coastal Plain chert in exotic locations (100 ≤ distance), but when compared to later Redstone and Post-Clovis Unfluted populations, Clovis populations were still staying closer to this source. Coastal Plain chert Clovis points were transported shorter average distances than Redstone and Post-Clovis Unfluted points. These points were transported throughout the Coastal Plain, in the Upper and Lower Coastal Plain, and into the Piedmont. Though they used them minimally, when Clovis people crafted points from orthoquartzite, they were predominantly discarded locally; the two nonlocal orthoquartzite points were transported northwest but still discarded in the Lower Coastal Plain. The second-most frequently used raw material source used by Clovis is metavolcanic. Daniel and Goodyear (2015) observed macroscopic characteristics that suggest most metavolcanic Clovis points discarded in South Carolina can be sourced to outcrops in the Uwharrie Mountains of North Carolina. If this is the source area, then metavolcanic Clovis points were transported great distances, similar to Redstones, and Clovis populations were transporting these points south-west into the Lower Coastal Plain and along the Fall Line. Clovis people used quartz from the Piedmont and predominantly discarded it locally there. Quartz Clovis points that were transported nonlocally were carried southeast through the Upper Coastal Plain to the margins of the Lower Coastal Plain. Finally, all of the points chipped on Ridge and Valley chert are exotic. They were transported great distances to the southeast and dis-carded into the lower Piedmont but not taken into the Coastal Plain. After Clovis, no Paleoindian groups in South Carolina utilized Ridge and Valley cherts.

Clovis populations in South Carolina made extensive use of the Lower Coastal Plain, and perhaps this was their predominant settlement region (also see Goodyear 2018). Dense Clovis deposits have been excavated at the Topper site, a quarry-related site in Allendale County where Coastal Plain chert outcrops along a river terrace (Goodyear 2013; Miller 2010; Smallwood 2010; Smallwood et al. 2013), and Goodyear and Charles (1984) identified a series of additional outcrops along this part of the Savannah River. The presence of high-quality chert likely made this area an important settlement center for Clovis populations. Orthoquartzite also available in the Lower Coastal Plain was relatively minimally used by Clovis popula-tions, suggesting that the presence of this raw material was not driving occupation in the area. An alternative explanation for more-intensive use of this part of the Lower Coastal Plain may be related to the settlement or-ganization of Clovis macrobands. Daniel and Goodyear (2015, 2018) have designated the Congaree and Saluda rivers as a geographic boundary and interaction zone between a Clovis macroband situated on the Uwharrie metavolcanic sources and one situated on Coastal Plain cherts of Allendale County. This might explain the presence of Clovis points in the area, as well as the minimal use of orthoquartzite sources. Interestingly, Clovis people did not extensively use the Upper Coastal Plain when compared with Dal-ton. They did, however, occupy the South Carolina Piedmont. This location is geographically situated near the Uwharrie metavolcanic source locations; thus, the higher frequency of Clovis points discarded in the Piedmont may also relate to the geographic extent of the Uwharrie Clovis macroband (Daniel and Goodyear 2015, 2018; Goodyear 2018). Just before and during the onset of the Younger Dryas, when many megafauna were going extinct, Clovis populations in South Carolina were keying in on research-rich loca-tions with abundant high-quality stone (Daniel and Goodyear 2015; Small-wood 2010).

Redstone

There are decidedly fewer Redstone points compared to Clovis and later Dalton points. Thus, the record in South Carolina also supports hypotheses of a regional population decline or reorganization during the early centuries of the Younger Dryas (Anderson et al. 2011; Meeks and Anderson 2012; Smallwood et al. 2015). Redstone populations continued to most intensively occupy the Lower Coastal Plain. Most of these points occur in the southwestern Lower Coastal Plain in the vicinity of Coastal Plain chert outcrops. Approximately half of the Redstone points in this sample were chipped from Coastal Plain chert. Redstone populations were aware of but, like Clovis groups, made minimal use of orthoquartzite sources in the Lower Coastal Plain. In contrast to Clovis, the Piedmont was less extensively used by Redstone populations, based on overall point frequencies. However, metavolcanic stone, which does outcrop in the Piedmont and Upper Coastal Plain, continued to be utilized by Redstone groups. No studies have yet determined whether Redstone metavolcanic points are made from South Carolina or North Carolina sources, but Goodyear (2010a) states there is a higher frequency of metavolcanic Redstones made from the finer-grained metavolcanics, suggesting a North Carolina source. Redstone populations made significantly less use of quartz, which outcrops throughout the Piedmont, again suggesting decreased settlement emphasis in this region. No Redstone points in the current sample were chipped from Ridge and Valley sources.

Redstone points made from Coastal Plain chert that were transported away from the source area were taken north toward the Piedmont, Upper Coastal Plain, and Lower Coastal Plain, similar to Clovis. Unlike Clovis, transport distances of Coastal Plain chert points are significantly greater for Redstone points. Like Clovis, Redstone orthoquartzite points were not transported great distances from the source. Considering the either/or assumptions of South Carolina or North Carolina as the source area for metavolcanics, Redstone metavolcanic point transport directions and distances do not differ from Clovis. Finally, the two transported quartz points were discarded in Berkeley and Orangeburg counties, the location of orthoquartzite sources on outer margins of the southwestern Lower Coastal Plain.

Redstone populations living during the heart of the Younger Dryas experienced cooler, wetter conditions and increasing sea level variability (Anderson and Bissett 2015). The marked decrease in point frequencies from

Clovis to Redstone is similar to the pattern found in Georgia, though not as extreme (Smallwood et al. 2015), and noted for the greater Southeast (Anderson et al. 2011; Meeks and Anderson 2012). Two of the major post-Clovis fluted point populations in the Southeast are Cumberland and Redstone. Cumberland populations appear to have established a more restricted population center around Ridge and Valley cherts in Tennessee (Anderson et al. 2010; Smallwood et al. 2015). In South Carolina, Redstone populations may have similarly concentrated settlement, in this case, around Coastal Plain chert sources in the southwestern Lower Coastal Plain. Geographically between these two population centers, Georgia appears to have been largely unsettled by post-Clovis fluted point populations (Smallwood et al. 2015). Redstone points have also been identified with some frequency in North Carolina (Daniel and Goodyear 2015), where there also may be an important Redstone population center. Interestingly, exotic transport distances of Redstone Coastal Plain chert points in South Carolina increased compared to Clovis. This could reflect the need for longer-distance travel to connect with more disparate, spatially restricted populations (Anderson 1996; Anderson et al. 2010; Smallwood 2012; Smallwood et al. 2015). In addition to potentially reduced overall population numbers in the region, Redstone populations also stopped using a large portion of the Lower Coastal Plain, perhaps due to increasing coastal instability.

Post-Clovis Unfluted

Post-Clovis Unfluted points are the least common Paleoindian point type recovered in South Carolina. Paleoindian populations that produced Post-Clovis Unfluted points continued to primarily occupy the Lower Coastal Plain, and most of these occur in the southwestern portion of the Lower Coastal Plain. Further, the majority of Post-Clovis Unfluted points were chipped from Coastal Plain chert, but orthoquartzite and metavolcanics were also sparingly used.

The vast majority of Post-Clovis Unfluted points were transported great distances away from the source (100 km ≤ distance), like Redstones, and the farthest average distances when compared to all other Paleoindian periods.

While the small sample size makes reconstructions of settlement difficult, the sheer lack of Post-Clovis Unfluted points suggests a reorganization away from the greater part of South Carolina and especially away from the eastern portion of the Lower Coastal Plain, a trend that began with Redstone. This dearth of points is somewhat surprising, given that in Georgia there are six times as many Post-Clovis Unfluted points (Smallwood et al. 2015). For Georgia, this category includes Quad/Beaver Lake points associated with the Mid-South and Suwannee/Simpson point types commonly found in Florida (Anderson et al. 2011). Perhaps Post-Clovis Unfluted points discarded in South Carolina represent the eastern extent of settlement for an enclave of Suwannee/Simpson pointmakers that occupied central and southwestern Georgia (Smallwood et al. 2015; Thulman 2006).

Dalton

Dalton is the most frequent Paleoindian point type reported in South Carolina and exceeds all other Paleoindian point types combined (n = 786). Although Dalton points are found in all physiographic regions, point densities and distributions indicate that there was a significant shift in landscape use compared to earlier Paleoindian point groups. Dalton populations appear to have shifted focus away from the Lower Coastal Plain and into the Upper Coastal Plain Sandhills–Fall Line zone, a region relatively sparsely occupied by previous Paleoindian populations. As in prior periods, Coastal Plain chert continued to be a key stone source, and orthoquartzite was sparingly used. Dalton populations relied more heavily on metavolcanic materials. Indeed, the number of Coastal Plain chert and metavolcanic Dalton points nearly equal each other, suggesting that these were two equally important stone sources for Dalton populations. Quartz was also substantially used to produce Dalton points. No Dalton points in the current sample were made from the distant Ridge and Valley cherts.

When Dalton populations utilized Coastal Plain cherts, these points were transported the shortest average distance and discarded near the source area within the Lower and Upper Coastal Plains. In a significant departure from Clovis, Redstone, and Post-Clovis Unfluted populations, Dalton groups transported Coastal Plain cherts almost exclusively north into the Upper Coastal Plain and toward the Piedmont. Interestingly, they were not moving this material farther into the Lower Coastal Plain. Dalton points made from orthoquartzite were locally discarded, but this source was not more heavily used than in earlier periods. This differs from the Dalton record in Georgia, which shows that Dalton groups heavily used orthoquartzites (Smallwood et al. 2015), so much so that the material has been termed Daltonite (Waggoner and Jones 2007). This difference likely relates to the location of orthoquartzite source areas. In South Carolina, orthoquartzites occur in counties located in the Lower Coastal Plain, while in Georgia, orthoquartzites are found in the Piedmont. Again, the transport of metavolcanic sources by Dalton populations is difficult to interpret.

However, whether the source area is in South Carolina or North Carolina, Dalton metavolcanic transport directions significantly differ from Clovis and are distinct from Redstone. While chemical sourcing of metavolcanic points would help more specifically distinguish these patterns, these differences provide further evidence that Dalton settlement and landscape use in South Carolina differs from earlier periods. Further, Dalton populations transported quartz the shortest average distances, suggesting this material was primarily used in and near the Piedmont source area, a pattern also found in Georgia (Smallwood et al. 2015).

The Dalton point record in South Carolina reflects a clear and substantial shift in landscape use compared to earlier Paleoindian periods. Three key settlement changes are evident. First, Dalton populations were more intensely occupying the Upper Coastal Plain, with a significantly decreased emphasis on the Lower Coastal Plain. While Dalton populations were readily willing to utilize a variety of stone, landscape use was not heavily influenced by stone sources. Rather, it appears Dalton populations were keying in on other resources within the Upper Coastal Plain and Piedmont. Thus, by the end of the Younger Dryas, populations were shifting settlement away from the coastal terraces and shorelines, perhaps due to increasing instability in coastal environments (Harris et al. 2013). Second, they were significantly more reliant on local stone sources, a pattern observed throughout the Southeast (Goodyear 1999; Jennings 2008, 2010), among smaller assemblages in Georgia (Anderson 1990:184; Anderson et al. 1990:83), and in the previously referenced broader analysis of the Georgia record (Smallwood et al. 2015). Lastly, Dalton populations reduced their range of subsistence-related mobility. They were carrying stone from the source decidedly shorter distances than their Paleoindian predecessors.

Dalton Piedmont Transhumance Hypothesis

The significant changes in Dalton landscape use warrant further discussion on what may have caused this shift to the Upper Coastal Plain and Piedmont. Why would Dalton people transition settlement away from the Coastal Plain, an area once characterized by an enormous amount of surface water, larger floodplains, and extensive wetlands, to the Upper Coastal Plain and Piedmont, areas without large lakes and only rapidly draining creeks and rivers cutting through rock? We propose the answer is twofold. First, sea level change was drowning primary Coastal Plain wetlands (Harris et al. 2013). The loss of this prime foraging zone resulted in pressure to redefine and reorganize subsistence-related settlement strategies.

Second, as a consequence, Dalton populations began to seasonally intensify subsistence in the Fall Line and Piedmont, focusing on the vast fall mast crops of the upland hardwood forests, crops that also supported herds of white-tailed deer. Deer replaced the former Pleistocene browsers, such as mastodon, and became the new primary browser and meat source of the late Paleoindian period. Large deer populations, with even greater numbers due to competitive release following other extinctions, were likely present in the Fall Line and Piedmont especially during the fall, because of acorn production. This increased the biomass in these areas by creating high densities of deer concentrated in predictable and localized areas (Smith 1975:139). To maximize the harvest of deer, group hunting strategies were needed. For example, drives perhaps aided by dogs and forest burning could have exceeded the success of individual hunters. Hunting parties could cover large tracts of the Piedmont, field dressing carcasses and bringing them back to fall season base camps. There, multifamily kin groups could have helped effectively handle large deer kills, processing and storing meat, preparing skins, and extracting bone and antler for tool stock. This may explain the relatively large Dalton sites as defined by high counts of Dalton points and associated unifaces at sites like Manning and Taylor in South Carolina (Michie 1996) and Barnett Shoals on the Oconee River in the Georgia Piedmont (O'Steen 1996).

Conclusions

The South Carolina Coastal Plain, with its plentiful water and water resources and temperate climate, was an important area of settlement for Paleoindians. However, this province underwent dynamic changes at the end of the Pleistocene. Fluctuations in sea level created periods of shoreline instability and flooded primary Coastal Plain wetlands. Further, megafauna that once roamed the grassy Coastal Plain terraces went extinct, reducing large-mammal diversity, but allowing for the competitive release of deer and other smaller mammals. In the midst of these changes, Paleoindian populations altered their use of the Coastal Plain. In this chapter, we used the density and distribution of Paleoindian points and the characteristics of raw material use to evaluate changes in landscape use through time. We demonstrate that the Coastal Plain and its chert resources remained important throughout the Paleoindian period, but the use of this region varied. During the Clovis period, the Lower Coastal Plain was a center of settlement, perhaps for a macroband focused on Allendale Coastal Plain chert resources (Goodyear 2018). During the Redstone period, the intensity of occupation throughout South Carolina, and in the Coastal Plain in particular, decreased. Paleoindians became even more concentrated on high-quality stone sources, and the long-distance movement of points suggests that populations were becoming increasingly regionalized. During the Post-Clovis Unfluted period, regional occupation intensity continued to decrease, and populations were highly restricted to the western portion of the Lower Coastal Plain. These may represent the eastern and northern margins of more inland-based populations centered in Georgia and Florida. The Dalton period is marked by a substantial shift in use of the Coastal Plain. While Dalton populations continued to use chert resources in the Lower Coastal Plain, the Upper Coastal Plain Sandhills–Fall Line zone and Piedmont regions became the foci of Dalton settlement, at least seasonally. In our proposed Dalton Piedmont Transhumance Model, we hypothesize that sea level advance inundated Lower Coastal Plain environments, and, as a response, Dalton groups reorganized their landscape use to target deer and mast resources in more interior regions of South Carolina. Certainly, refining the paleoenvironmental and Paleoindian records, particularly the chronologies of change, will be critical for a further understanding of the complex relationships between reorganizations in Paleoindian landscape use and environmental changes through time.

Acknowledgments

We appreciate the opportunity to participate in the 2014 SEAC symposium that led to this volume. We acknowledge the help from our colleagues, both for this chapter and in times past, including Dave Anderson, Derek Anderson, Mark Brooks, Tommy Charles, Randy Daniel, Scott Harris, Chris Moore, Shane Miller, and Charlotte Pevny. However, any errors and misinterpretations are our own.

Notes

1. We group the Blue Ridge with the Piedmont because this province is a minor geographic area, and county centroids in this province actually fall within the Piedmont. We also separate the Upper and Lower Coastal Plain provinces to investigate the nuances of variation in use of the Coastal Plain through time. The Lower Coastal Plain, as used here, encompasses the Middle and Lower Coastal Plain in other classifications.

2. Dates are calibrated using IntCal13 in Calib 7.1 with 95.4 (2 sigma)(Reimer et al. 2013).

8

BRIEF OVERVIEW OF THE YOUNGER DRYAS COSMIC IMPACT DATUM LAYER 12,800 YEARS AGO AND ITS ARCHAEOLOGICAL UTILITY

MALCOLM A. LECOMPTE, A. VICTOR ADEDEJI, JAMES P. KENNETT, TED E. BUNCH, WENDY S. WOLBACH, AND ALLEN WEST

Firestone et al. (2007) proposed that a major cosmic impact event occurred 12,800 ± 150 calendar years ago (cal B.P.), with major environmental, climatic, biotic, and human consequences. The hypothesized cause is cosmic airburst/impacts, a term referring to atmospheric collisions by extraterrestrial bodies, typically producing explosive, aerial disintegrations, sometimes along with small crater-forming ground impacts. This scenario is part of the Younger Dryas (YD) impact hypothesis that is supported by an increasing body of evidence across multiple continents. As discussed in chapter 9 in this volume, this impact is proposed to have triggered or contributed to the abrupt cooling of the Younger Dryas episode and caused major environmental disruptions. These changes may have also contributed to major extinctions of Pleistocene megafauna and to significant human population declines and cultural changes over broad areas of the Northern Hemisphere (Anderson et al. 2011; Firestone et al. 2007; Kennett et al. 2008; Kennett et al. 2015; Wittke et al. 2013).

The YD impact hypothesis originated from observations of abundance peaks in a variable assemblage of high-temperature, impact-related materials, called proxies, which are found in the Younger Dryas Boundary layer (YDB), a sedimentary stratum typically a few centimeters in thickness (Firestone et al. 2007). Because these proxies have been extensively described and discussed in detail elsewhere, we provide only an overview here. Table 8.1 is a brief, non-exhaustive list of YDB impact-related proxy

Table 8.1. Contributions Related to YDB Proxy Data

Proxy	Proponents	Positive	Negative
Cosmic impact spherules	*Firestone et al. 2007*; Kennett et al. 2008; *Israde et al. 2012*; Bunch et al. 2012; Wittke et al. 2013	Mahaney et al. 2010; Fayek et al. 2012; *LeCompte et al. 2012*; Wu et al. 2013	Surovell et al. 2009; Pinter et al. 2011; Pigati et al. 2012
Meltglass (scoria-like objects)	*Bunch et al. 2012*; Wittke et al. 2013	Mahaney et al. 2010; Fayek et al. 2012; Wu et al. 2013	—
Nanodiamonds	Firestone et al. 2007; Kennett, Kennett, West, Mercer et al. 2009; Kennett, Kennet, A. West, G. J. West 2009b; Kurbatov et al. 2010; Israde et al. 2012; *Kinzie et al. 2014*	Baker et al. 2008; Tian et al. 2011; Bement et al. 2014	Daulton et al. 2010; Pinter et al. 2011; van Hoesel et al. 2012
Anomalous geochemistry	*Firestone et al. 2007*; Kennett et al. 2008	Beets et al. 2008; Haynes et al. 2010; Andronikov et al. 2011, 2014; LeCompte et al. 2012; Petaev et al. 2013; Wu et al. 2013	Paquay et al. 2009; Pinter et al. 2011; Pigati et al. 2012
Aciniform carbon, carbon spherules, glass-like carbon, charcoal	*Firestone et al. 2007*; Kennett et al. 2008; *Israde et al. 2012*	Baker et al. 2008; Mahaney et al. 2010	Scott et al. 2010; Pinter et al. 2011; van Hoesel et al. 2012
Megafaunal extinctions	Firestone et al. 2007; Kennett et al. 2008; Anderson et al. 2011	—	—
Human population changes	Firestone et al. 2007; Kennett et al. 2008; Anderson et al. 2011	—	—

Note: Bold, italicized references contain detailed proxy extraction and analytical protocols.

studies, both by those who reported finding them and others with negative findings. In addition, those contributions providing the extraction and analytical protocols are noted. Although most independent investigations attributed the proxies to a cosmic impact event, some offered alternate explanations (e.g., Haynes et al. 2010; Tian et al. 2011). The studies reporting negative results did not use rigorous dating methods or did not follow the requisite analytical protocol, for example, by not performing crucial analyses using scanning electron microscopy (SEM) and electron diffraction spectroscopy (EDS).

The primary purpose of this chapter is to offer a brief overview of the characteristics, origin, and distribution of the various impact-related proxies that can exhibit peak abundances in the YDB layer, thus allowing its identification as a chronostratigraphic datum that coincides with the YDB cosmic impact event. These include magnetic and glassy impact-related spherules, high-temperature minerals and meltglass, nanodiamonds, carbon spherules, aciniform carbon, platinum, osmium, iridium, and other elements at anomalous concentrations.

The YDB layer has been identified widely in 30 stratigraphic sections in 12 countries on four continents and has a modeled age range of 12,835–12,735 cal B.P. at 95 percent probability (Kennett et al. 2015). The widespread distribution of this now well-dated, synchronous layer makes it of great value as a datum for stratigraphic correlation over wide areas and for chronological underpinning of late Quaternary sequences, including those of interest to archeologists. The YDB layer has been documented in three sites in the U.S. Southeast, including the archeologically important site at Topper, South Carolina (Firestone et al. 2007; Goodyear and Steffy 2003; Kinzie et al. 2014; LeCompte et al. 2012; Waters et al. 2009; Wittke et al. 2013) and should be found in other sites with sediments that span the Younger Dryas onset.

Based on independent dating, the Younger Dryas onset (and hence, the YDB layer) had been already identified in time-series samples collected from stratigraphic sections at many locations. At all sites, cosmic impact-related proxies are generally present in trace quantities and/or as small particles, ranging in size from nanometers to several centimeters. Because of this, quantitatively describing their stratigraphic distribution often requires demanding, labor-intensive analyses. Hence, sampling protocols need to be guided by available age and sedimentary data within a paleontological and archeological context, when possible. The onset of the Younger Dryas episode is often well marked by distinct lithological changes and evidence for environmental degradation; it is synchronous with the upper biostratigraphic limits of many extinct taxa of late Pleistocene megafauna and/or artifacts of the Clovis culture. Prior knowledge of this stratigraphy has often been valuable in guiding sampling for time-series analyses of proxies in stratigraphic sections.

Identification of the YDB Layer

Primary Impact-Related Proxies

The materials described in this section (i.e., primary impact-related proxies) include those that were either directly produced or directly altered by
a YDB impact event, generally due to very high temperatures but also to
high pressures and low-oxygen conditions associated with a cosmic impact.

Spherules (Iron-Rich and Silica-Rich)

Characteristics

YDB spherules are mostly black or brown in color, although a few are red,
blue, green, gray, tan, or white, ranging in clarity from opaque to transparent (Wittke et al. 2013). Although the diameters of spherules range from 5
μm to 5.5 mm, 80 percent of them have diameters of ≤55 μm (avg. 135 μm;
median 30 μm) (Figure 8.1A-B). Most spherules (>95 percent) are rounded,
and the remainder appear as ovoids, aerodynamically shaped teardrops, or
fused clusters of one or more spherules. Concentrations in the YDB layer
range from 5 to 4,900 spherules/kg, averaging 955/kg (median: 388/kg)
(Wittke et al. 2013). The typical composition of YDB spherules is distributed across a continuum from pure iron (FeO) to pure silica ($SiO2$); FeO
ranged from 0 to 100 percent, averaging 44.9 wt percent ; $SiO2$ ranged from
0 to 100 percent and averaged 30.9 wt percent. The abundances of a third
oxide, $Al2O3$, ranged from 0 to 65 percent, averaging 12.2 wt percent. Ten
other oxides collectively constituted < 5 wt percent of the total. A small
percentage of spherules contain osmium and rare earth elements (lanthanum, cerium), ranging from < 1 wt percent to ≈40 wt percent in a few cases
(LeCompte et al. 2012; Wu et al. 2013).

The presence of high-temperature melted minerals in Fe-rich spherules
indicates that minimum formation temperatures were elevated. For example, titanomagnetite melts at ≈1,400 °C; schreibersite at ≈1,400 °C; magnetite at ≈1,550 °C; hercynite at ≈1,700 °C; rutile at ≈1,840 °C; and suessite
at ≈2,300 °C (Bunch et al. 2012; Wu et al. 2013). These melting points can
be slightly lower, depending upon the presence of suitable fluxing agents.
Glassy spherules also often were found to contain high-temperature minerals, including wollastonite, with a melting point of ≈1,500 °C; corundum,
mullite and sillimanite at ≈1,800 °C; and lechatelierite at ≈1,720 °C.

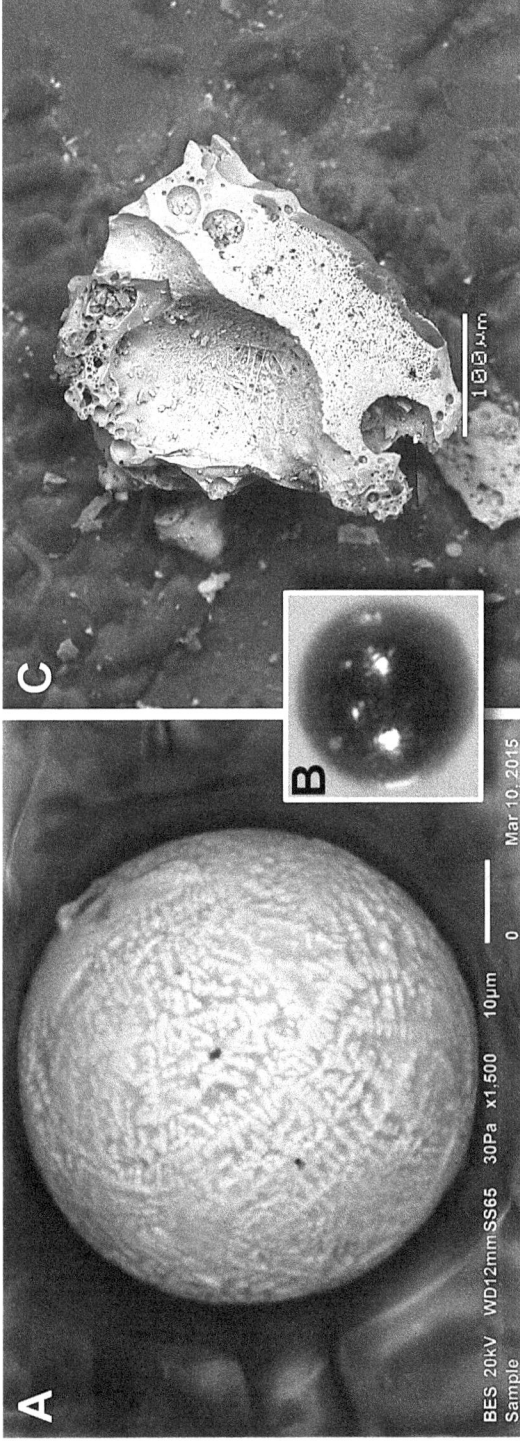

Figure 8.1. (A) SEM image of Fe-rich YDB spherule from Glacial Lake Hind, Manitoba, Canada, showing characteristic dendritic surface pattern. (B) Photomicrograph of 60-μm-wide, Fe-rich spherule from Lake Hind. (C) SEM image of YDB melt-glass from Newtonville, New Jersey, showing vesicular structure resulting from bubbling in molten state.

Distribution

Based on evidence from 27 YDB sites, an estimated 10 million tonnes of melted spherulitic objects are distributed across ≈50 million square kilometers of North and South America, Europe, and Asia (Wittke et al. 2013). They are present in high abundances only in the YDB layer and closely adjacent strata. Workers have also observed abundant unmelted, authigenic framboidal spherules that tend to peak in or near the YDB layer, and thus appear to be secondarily related, perhaps because environmental degradation created anoxic conditions that favored framboidal growth (Wittke et al. 2013).

Inconsistent Origins

(1) Primary cosmic origin: Fe-rich micrometeorites and cosmic spherules nearly always contain high abundances of nickel, with a range of 5–25 wt percent, averaging 10 wt percent (Wittke et al. 2013). In contrast, YDB spherules are depleted in nickel, having an average concentration of .1 wt, with a range of 0–2 wt percent. For Si-rich cosmic microspherules and micrometeorites, more than 98 percent are enriched in MgO at >10 wt percent, averaging 29 percent, with a range of 1–55 percent, whereas ≈98.8 percent of YDB spherules contain < 10 percent MgO (Wittke et al. 2013). These results indicate that very few YDB spherules are cosmic in origin, and instead, their composition matches that of melted terrestrial material. In addition, the high concentrations of YDB spherules in sediments are consistent with that of the Cretaceous–Paleogene (K-Pg) impact but are far higher than found in polar ice (Wittke et al. 2013 and references therein). One study of cosmic influx in Antarctic ice found an average of only one spherule in each 67 kg of ice (or .014 spherules/kg), whereas the average number of spherules in YDB sediment is 955 avg. spherules/kg (Wittke et al. 2013). (2) Anthropogenic origin: fly ash spherules, a common anthropogenic contaminant, have been deposited only since the beginning of the Industrial Revolution, and hence, their distribution is typically restricted to sediment depths of less than ≈20 cm from the ground surface. They form at temperatures of <1,400 °C, well below 1,800 °C, the melting point of many common minerals found in YDB spherules. Unlike fly ash, YDB spherules are typically buried deeper than anthropogenic spherules, at an average depth of 2.5 m (max: 15 m. (3) Authigenic origin: this process can be rejected because YDB spherules possess surface morphology,

visible only under SEM examination, that indicates incomplete crystal formation. Such features are evidence that they were melted and then rapidly quenched, unlike authigenic spherules, which are unmelted and crystallize slowly over a long period. (4) Volcanism: compared to volcanic spherules, YDB spherules average 8× higher in Cr, 11× higher in K, 3× lower in Mg, and 2× lower in Na, showing that they are geochemically dissimilar (Wittke et al 2013). In addition, volcanic spherules are invariably Si-rich, without high concentrations of Fe, as is found in many YDB spherules. (5) Lightning: measurements of remanent magnetism indicate that YDB spherules cooled rapidly in Earth's ambient magnetic field (Wittke et al. 2013). This eliminates the possibility that YDB spherules formed by lightning, which generates a strong magnetic field that can be easily detected in lightning-melted materials (Nabelek et al. 2013).

Impact-Related Origin

The shapes, composition, and surface textures of most YDB spherules are similar to those formed in the Tunguska airburst in 1908, the Australasian Tektite Field at ≈680 kya, Meteor Crater at ≈50 kya, the Chesapeake Bay impact at ≈35 Ma, and the K-Pg impact ≈65 Ma (Wittke et al. 2013). After eliminating all other known possibilities, a cosmic impact is the only remaining plausible explanation for high-temperature–quenched YDB spherules.

Formation Mechanism

Based on all available evidence, YDB spherules formed when high-temperature, hypervelocity jets descended to the ground from atmospheric explosions and melted terrestrial sediment, whether located on land, in glacial ice as detritus, or as oceanic sediments. Following formation, the rising impact plume(s) dispersed the spherules into the atmosphere and distributed them widely across multiple continents.

High-Temperature, Melted Silica-Rich Glass

Characteristics

Found at six sites in North and South America and Asia, YDB meltglass, also called scoria-like glass, exhibits a wide range of colors: black, brown, red, blue, green, gray, tan, and/or white, ranging in clarity from opaque to transparent (Bunch et al. 2012). Meltglass shapes range from small, angular, glassy, shardlike particles to large masses of highly vesiculated glass. Sizes range in diameter from ≈300 μm to 11.75 mm, averaging 2.6 mm (Figure 8.1C). Although meltglass is generally enriched in silica, it exhibits a wide range in composition: FeO ranges from 0 to 82 wt percent, averaging 12 wt percent; SiO_2 from 1 to 100 wt percent, averaging 55 wt percent; and Al_2O_3 from 0 to 65 wt percent, averaging 13 wt percents. Some small glass inclusions had high percentages of other important minerals: up to 37 wt percent of P_2O_5; 38 wt percent of NiO; 41 wt percent of MgO; 49 wt percent of SO_3; and 60 percent of Cr_2O_3. YDB meltglass also contains some of the same high-temperature, melted minerals found in the spherules. For example, titanomagnetite melts at ≈1,400 °C, schreibersite at ≈1,400 °C, wollastonite at ≈1,500 °C, magnetite at ≈1,550 °C, hercynite at ≈1,700 °C, corundum at ≈1,800 °C, mullite at ≈1,800 °C, sillimanite at ≈1,800 °C, rutile at ≈1,840 °C, lechatelierite at ≈2,200 °C, and suessite at ≈2,300 °C (Bunch et al. 2012; Wu et al. 2013).

Distribution

Silica-rich YDB meltglass has been found in the United States (Arizona, Pennsylvania, New Jersey, New York, and South Carolina), as well as in Venezuela and northern Syria, an area spanning ≈50 million square kilometers (Bunch et al. 2012; Fayek et al. 2012; Firestone et al. 2007; Kinzie et al. 2014; Mahaney et al. 2010; Wittke et al. 2013). It has been found in high abundances only in the YDB layer and closely adjacent strata. In some sections investigated, small amounts of meltglass have been reworked upward and downward from the YDB layer by natural sedimentary and biogenic processes (Bunch et al. 2012).

Inconsistent Origins

Bunch et al. (2012) compared and contrasted potential origins of YDB meltglass and eliminated the following possibilities: (1) Cosmic origin: results indicate >90 percent of YDB high-temperature meltglass and spherules are geochemically dissimilar to cosmic-derived materials. (2) Anthropogenic origin: more than 75 percent of YDB objects have compositions different from anthropogenic objects, rejecting anthropogenesis as a potential origin. (3) Authigenic origin: this can be rejected because meltglass was once molten, by definition, unlike unmelted authigenic material. (4) Volcanic origin: approximately 85 percent of YDB objects are compositionally distinct from volcanic material, and furthermore, the YDB layer at all sites contains no volcanic ash and tephra, thus refuting this origin. (5) Origin by lightning: studies of remanent magnetism indicate that YDB meltglass could not have formed by lightning (Nabelek et al. 2013).

Impact-Related Origin

The shapes, composition, and surface textures of YDB meltglass are similar or identical to meltglass formed in the Tunguska airburst, the Australasian Tektite Field, Meteor Crater, and other existing impact craters (Bunch et al 2012).

Formation Mechanism

YDB meltglass composition is terrestrial (Bunch et al. 2012), consistent with having formed as ejecta that contained little or no impactor material. During the impact, molten glass would have been ejected into the atmosphere when the high-temperature, hypervelocity airburst jet and/or the impactor reached the ground, forming a shallow crater. Because 95 percent of ejecta travels less than 5 crater radii, most ejected glass would have fallen out rapidly near the area of impact (Bunch et al. 2012 and references therein). However, some meltglass may have been distributed over greater distances, as occurred with the Australasian tektite field that covers ≈10 percent of the planet, and for which no crater has been found (Bunch et al. 2012 and references therein). Remanent magnetic measurements and high formation temperatures (≈1,500 to 2,200 °C) *rule out formation mechanisms other than cosmic impact.*

Nanodiamonds

Characteristics

Twenty-one YDB sites on three continents contain multiple polytypes of nanodiamonds, including cubic diamonds, lonsdaleite-like crystals, and diamond-like carbon nanoparticles called n-diamond and i-carbon (Kinzie et al. 2014). Typical shapes are spherical to ovoid, with sizes ranging from 2 to 10 nm, although a few YDB nanodiamonds are up to 2.9 μm in diameter (Figure 8.2A). YDB nanodiamond concentrations in bulk sediment ranged from ≈60 to 500 ppb (avg: 200 ppb), and in fire-related YDB carbon spherules (discussed below), they ranged from ≈10 to 3900 ppb (avg: ≈750 ppb) (Kinzie et al. 2014). After extraction, the identification and characterization

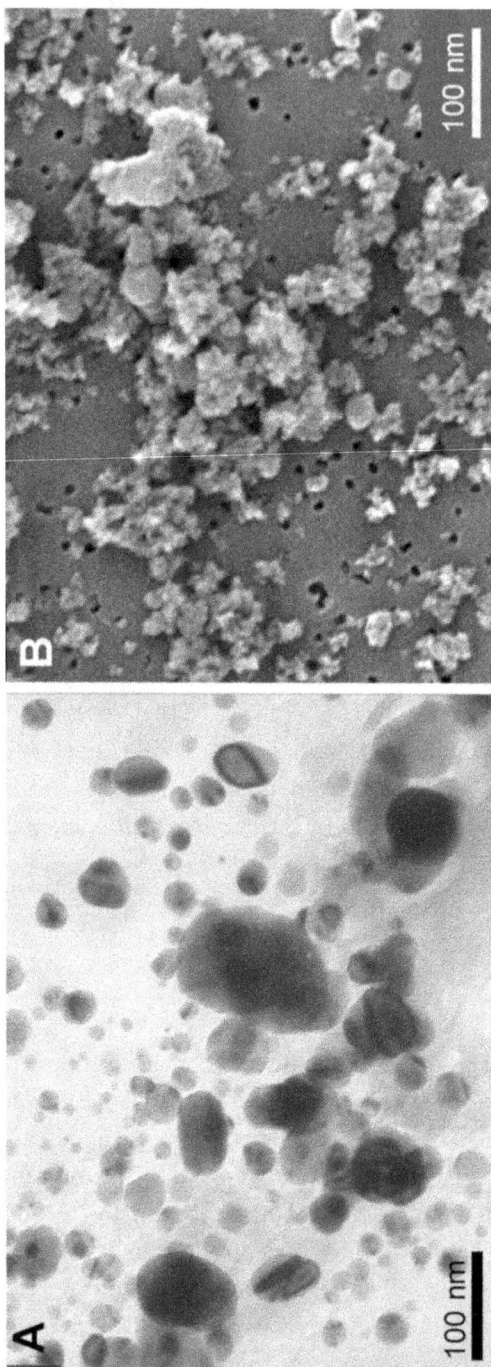

Figure 8.2. (A) TEM image of YDB nanodiamonds extracted from bulk sediments from Murray Springs, Arizona. (B) SEM image of aciniform carbon also from YDB bulk sediment at Murray Springs.

of YDB nanodiamonds requires high-resolution transmission electron microscopy (TEM), which is difficult and labor intensive.

Distribution

YDB abundance peaks in nanodiamonds have been reported for 24 dated stratigraphic sections in 10 countries across three continents, the same area as for YDB impact-related spherules (Kinzie et al. 2014). Peak abundances in nanodiamonds were exhibited at every YDB site tested.

Inconsistent Origins

(1) Cosmic origin: nanodiamonds are present in some cosmic dust particles and meteorites (Kinzie et al. 2014). However, based on carbon and nitrogen isotopic ratios ($\delta13C$ and $\delta15N$), YDB nanodiamonds are not of cosmic origin (Israde et al. 2012; Kinzie et al. 2014; Tian et al. 2011), meaning that they did not arrive in micrometeorites or cosmic dust and were not derived from the impactor itself. (2) Anthropogenic origin: outside of the laboratory, modern high-energy explosives are the only known, widespread anthropogenic process capable of producing large numbers of nanodiamonds. However, that process can be rejected, because YDB nanodiamonds are widely distributed on three continents and deeply buried up to 4 m, ruling out formation in modern times. (3) Authigenic origin: no known or plausible mechanisms form nanodiamonds authigenically. (4) Volcanic origin: cubic diamonds do occur rarely in terrestrial deposits, such as mantle-derived kimberlite pipes. However, such diamonds are not found in any known, non-impact-related geological column that is associated with coeval peaks in impact-related proxies. Furthermore, such diamonds are always associated with geochemically distinctive mantle-derived rocks, which are absent at all YDB sites. (5) Origin by wildfires: based on more than a century of laboratory experiments, there is no evidence that nanodiamonds can be produced in wildfires, or by any other natural, terrestrial conditions on Earth's surface. If nanodiamonds could be produced in natural fires, they should be common and ubiquitous in sediments of all ages, but instead, they range from nonexistent to extraordinarily rare, being found in high abundances only in known or proposed impact-related sedimentary layers (Bement et al. 2014; Kinzie et al. 2014; Tian et al. 2011). (6) Origin by lightning: there are no confirmed mechanisms for nanodiamond production through lightning.

Impact-Related Origin

Nanodiamonds are commonly associated with known impact events, including the K-Pg impact at 65 Ma and with the Tunguska airburst over Siberia in 1908, to which they are morphologically and compositionally similar. The $\delta13C$ and $\delta15N$ ratios indicate YDB nanodiamonds were produced from terrestrial carbon, as is the case for all known impact-related nanodiamonds.

Formation Mechanism

It was proposed that K-Pg nanodiamonds formed by carbon vapor deposition (CVD) when the impactor collided with carbon-rich limestone strata (Kinzie et al. 2014 and references therein). Kinzie et al. (2014) discussed several lines of evidence suggesting that YDB nanodiamonds may have formed within the impact cloud by CVD. This mechanism requires elemental carbon vapor and low-oxygen atmospheric conditions, both of which would be present in an impact fireball (Wen et al. 2007) but do not occur naturally on Earth. In support of CVD, Kinzie et al. (2014) reported experiments demonstrating that nanodiamond formation requires anoxia combined with elevated temperatures of 1,000 to 1,200 °C. These conditions mirror those associated with cosmic impact but do not result from any other natural mechanism.

Geochemical Enrichments

Characteristics

Anomalous geochemical concentrations have been found in the YDB layer at 27 YDB sites, using electron diffraction spectroscopy (EDS), X-ray fluorescence spectroscopy (XRF), and instrumental neutron activation analysis (INAA) (Firestone et al. 2007). Anomalous concentrations in YDB sediments and a Younger Dryas–age Greenland ice core were observed for nickel, cobalt, chromium, rare earth elements (e.g., lanthanum and cerium), and/or platinum group elements (e.g., iridium, platinum, and osmium) (Andronikov et al. 2015; Bunch et al. 2012; Firestone et al. 2007; LeCompte et al. 2012; Petaev et al. 2013; Wittke et al. 2013; Wu et al. 2013). At 23 YDB sites on four continents, these anomalous concentrations peak only in the YDB layer and are at normal crustal abundances in sediments above and below the YDB layer.

Distribution

One or more geochemical anomalies are present in the YDB layer dating to 12,800 ± 150 cal B.P. at ≈27 sites examined across four continents, spanning ≈50 million km².

Impact-Related Origin

The above anomalous elements in the YDB layer are known to be highly enriched in asteroids and are proposed to be enriched in comets (Firestone et al. 2007). The fact that their concentrations are anomalously high in the YDB layer at so many widely distributed sites supports a cosmic impact origin, rather than from unknown local elemental sources. The elemental enrichments could have resulted from two impact-related processes. First, these high concentrations could represent remnants of the vaporized impactor itself. Second, they could result from enriched target rocks ejected by impact(s) and widely distributed through the atmosphere.

Secondary Impact-Related Proxies

Fire-related: four kinds of material that result from high-temperature biomass burning have been found in peak abundances in the YDB layer across four continents. These are aciniform carbon, carbon spherules (with and without nanodiamonds), glass-like carbon (with and without nanodiamonds), and charcoal. A comparison of their relative abundances in the YDB layer compared with background concentrations provides evidence for an increase in biomass burning associated with the cosmic impact at the onset of Younger Dryas cooling (Firestone et al. 2007).

Aciniform Carbon

Description

"Soot" or "black carbon" refers primarily to elemental carbon components remaining after incomplete combustion. Soot includes all particulates collected above a flame in a fire, whereas aciniform carbon is a subcategory of soot. For YDB studies, the two terms are used interchangeably. Abundance peaks in aciniform carbon have previously been interpreted as definitive evidence for impact-related fires at the K-Pg impact boundary (Wolbach et al. 1985) and also serve as evidence for increased biomass burning at the time of the YDB impact event (Firestone et al. 2007).

Characteristics

The distinctive morphology of aciniform carbon enables quantification using scanning electron microscopy (SEM). Aciniform carbon consists of chainlike aggregates of 10–30 spherical units, each with diameters of 10–50 nm, arranged in necklace-like chains or "grape-like" aciniform clusters (Figure 8.2B) (Calcote 1981; Harris and Weiner 1985). In the YDB layer, typical sizes of aciniform carbon clusters are < 1 μm, ranging in abundance from ≈100 to 6,100 ppm and averaging ≈1,480 ppm (Firestone et al. 2007).

Preservation

Following deposition, aciniform carbon and soot are subject to relatively rapid oxidation, and consequently they are generally found only in sediments deposited under oxygen-deficient, reducing conditions. Soot is rarely found in sedimentary profiles, because its high surface-to-volume ratio results in rapid loss through oxidation over time. Soot was preserved globally at the K-Pg boundary, most likely because of rapid burial associated with the impact event, protecting it from oxidation. A similar, less intense burial process may have preserved aciniform carbon in the YDB layer at some sites.

Distribution

Aciniform carbon production is influenced by many variables, including fuel source, moisture levels, humidity, temperature, O_2 availability, and CO_2 concentrations above the fire. After formation, soot can be carried significant distances from the fire; hence, it is not necessarily an indicator of local fires. Aciniform carbon was found in the YDB layer at 7 of 15 sites tested across two continents (Firestone et al. 2007; Kennett et al. 2015).

Inconsistent Origins

(1) Cosmic origin: there is no reported evidence that aciniform carbon is delivered to Earth from space. (2) Anthropogenic origin: coal-fired power plants produce soot, but it is found in surface layers, whereas the YDB layer at most sites is buried and sealed >2 m below the surface, precluding migration of aciniform carbon downward. (3) Authigenic origin: aciniform carbon cannot be authigenically produced. (4) Volcanic origin: if trees are burned by an eruption, soot can be produced, but North American YDB layers contain no tephra, ash, or geochemical anomalies related to

volcanism. (5) Origin by lightning: this process is precluded, because aciniform carbon and soot are nonmagnetic.

Impact-Related Origin

YDB aciniform carbon is found with other proxies known to be associated with impact events, and this association has never been found in sedimentary contexts that can be attributed to any other source besides an impact event. Based on SEM observations by one of us (Wolbach), soot from both the YDB and K-Pg layers exhibits similar morphology and particle size distribution (Wolbach et al. 1985). K-Pg soot was found globally at more than 12 widely dispersed sites (Wolbach et al. 1990; Wolbach et al. 2003), and similarly, YDB soot has been found at seven North American sites, consistent with production during a major cosmic impact event.

Formation

YDB aciniform carbon likely formed through extensive biomass burning at temperatures higher than those of typical wildfires. Initially, it may have resulted directly from the YDB airburst/impacts and then subsequently from burning of biomass that was decimated by rapid climate change. An impact into or over the ice sheet would have produced little aciniform carbon from biomass burning, but some may have formed from vaporization of carbon-rich target rocks (e.g., limestone) or hydrocarbons trapped in target rocks, as is proposed for the K-Pg event. (Kinzie et al. 2014 and references therein).

Carbon Spherules Containing Nanodiamonds

These small, distinctive, black carbonaceous spheres form from boiling tree sap and by condensation of high-temperature, carbon-rich vapor. They commonly range in size from .15 to 2.5 mm and have an average YDB abundance of ≈250/kg (Figure 8.3A) (Firestone et al. 2007; Israde et al. 2012; Kinzie et al. 2014). At 20 sites on four continents, YDB carbon spherules exhibit peak abundances in response to widespread biomass burning (Kennett et al. 2015). They are easily separated from sediment using sieves or flotation and are readily identified, given their relatively large size, often shiny, smooth surfaces, and distinctive honeycomb interior ultrastructure and outer crust (Firestone et al. 2007). This structure is readily observed using a regular stereoscopic light microscope, but especially by using SEM. Because carbon spherules peak in abundance in the YDB layer at many

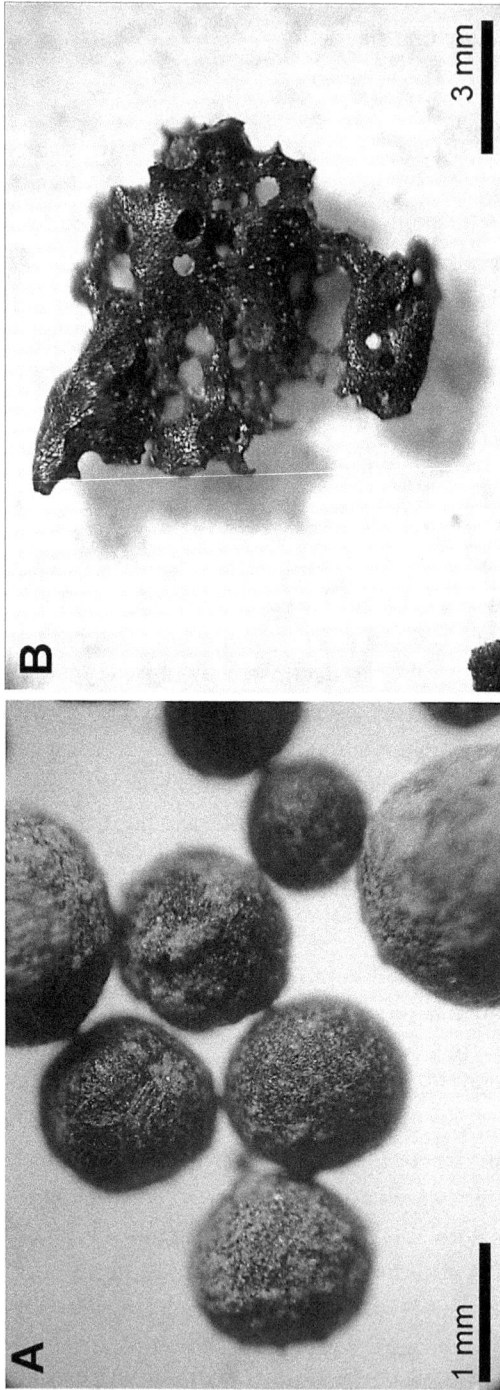

Figure 8.3. Photomicrographs of (A) carbon spherules from Gainey, Michigan, and (B) glass-like carbon from Santa Maira, Spain. Both of these materials from the YDB layer were found to contain nanodiamonds observed using high-resolution transmission electron microscopy.

sites, they are useful as a preliminary indicator of the location of the YDB layer prior to additional, more-detailed analyses for other proxies.

Carbon spherules are typically found in natural, high-temperature wildfires, so they are not uniquely diagnostic of an impact event. What makes YDB carbon spherules unusual is that they often contain nanodiamonds with the same characteristics as those found in sediments (see nanodiamond section above). Laboratory experiments indicate that these nanodiamond-rich carbon spherules require hypoxic atmospheres at 1,000 to 1,200 °C, conditions that do not exist in normal wildfires but occur during an impact event. Hence, those containing nanodiamonds most likely formed under high-temperature, hypoxic conditions at the time of the YDB impact.

Glass-Like Carbon Containing Nanodiamonds

These materials have the same composition as carbon spherules but lack the spherulitic shape and the honeycomb interior. Instead, these objects are composed of black, highly angular, smooth-textured carbon glass that can also exhibit conchoidal fracturing. They typically range in size from a few microns to several cm and average ≈1.0 g/kg (Figure 8.3B) (Firestone et al. 2007). As with carbon spherules, glass-like carbon forms from burning tree sap and can be common in all natural, high-temperature wildfires. What can be unique about this material when found in the YDB layer is that it can contain nanodiamonds, otherwise not found outside the layer at high concentrations.

Charcoal

Charcoal is a well-known product of natural wildfires and thus is not uniquely diagnostic of an impact event. However, the YDB layer at 20 synchronous sites on four continents contains a distinct abundance peak in charcoal (Kennett et al. 2015), indicating that fires were widespread and common at the time of the impact event, although some may represent human campfires. This pattern is also consistent with evidence from the K-Pg impact event (Firestone et al. 2007 and references therein). Charcoal in the YDB layer ranges in size from a few microns to several centimeters and exhibits average concentration values of 1.4 g/kg (Firestone et al. 2007).

Biomass Burning Processes at YDB

To produce the fire-related proxies observed to peak in the YDB layer in many locations, distal ejecta and secondary impacts would have ignited scattered fires on land. Such fires would have been widespread, but there is no evidence, or necessity, that they were ubiquitous (Marlon et al. 2009). Wildfires induced directly by an impact's thermal pulse would instantly ignite beneath the fireball, but because of the curvature of the Earth, these would be limited by distance from the fireball. For example, an airburst ≈5 km above Earth's surface would be directly visible only ≈250 km away, and thus incapable of starting fires farther away. The intensity of thermal radiation declines exponentially with distance, and so, even at distances of < 250 km, thermally induced fires would have occurred only near the fireball. In addition, high-temperature ejecta would have been capable of igniting wildfires at greater distances.

If multiple YDB airbursts occurred, impact-related fires would have been intense and numerous, but widely separated. As recorded in the Greenland Ice Sheet, there is strong independent evidence of a major peak in biomass burning at the onset of the Younger Dryas. The concentrations of wildfire-related aerosols (NH4, NOx) represent the largest such episode in the previous 386,000 years, the temporal limit of the record (Kurbatov et al. 2011 and references therein). This represents unequivocal evidence for major biomass burning apparently coeval with a Younger Dryas impact event.

The estimate of the annual area burned by wildfires across one hemisphere is ≈2,000,000 km², representing ≈2.7 percent of the land surface (Yang et al. 2014). Napier et al. (2013) speculated that the YDB impact event may have included ≈5,000 airbursts equal to or larger than the Tunguska airburst, which burned 500 km² of forest. Although there are many variables, if that estimated number is correct, then up to 2,500,000 km² could have burned in a single day, totaling ≈3 percent of Earth's surface. Thus, in just one day, such fires would have burned more area than all the current annual wildfires across one hemisphere, accounting for >300 times more biomass burning proxies at the Younger Dryas onset. It is also possible that the increase in biomass burning at the YDB resulted from an abundance of dead, dry biomass fuel. Major and abrupt environmental degradation resulting from the impact, in addition to abrupt cooling at the onset of the Younger Dryas, almost certainly would have been a major contributor to increased abundances of highly combustible fuel. Both these effects, high-temperature airbursts and combustible fuel, are proposed to have occurred over broad areas of Earth and could explain the wide distribution of evidence for biomass burning at the YDB.

Characteristics of the Younger Dryas Impact(s)

At present, there is insufficient evidence to determine the characteristics of the YDB impactor(s), but there are a number of clues. Here, we provide a brief overview of several possibilities that have previously been proposed.

What was it? Firestone et al. (2007) speculated that because YDB proxies are carbon-enriched and nickel-depleted, the impactor most likely was a comet, either fragmented or whole. Alternately, Petaev et al. (2013) discovered YDB platinum enrichment in an ice core recovered by the Greenland Ice Core Project (GISP2), leading them to suggest that the YDB impactor was an iron-rich, iridium-depleted iron meteorite. Offering a comet-related explanation, Napier et al. (2013) proposed that the Younger Dryas impact resulted from a comet swarm of sufficient size and magnitude to deposit widespread proxies, ignite wildfires, and cause megafaunal extinctions (Napier 2010). They noted that giant comets, called centaurs, enter Earth-crossing orbits approximately every 175,000 years, with each episode lasting a few thousand years (Napier et al. 2013). One of the largest centaurs, Chiron, is more than 200 km in diameter and currently orbits beyond Saturn. Such objects are known to undergo hierarchic disintegrations, during which multiple collisions with Earth are possible (Napier et al. 2015).

What size was it? For impacts in general, Toon et al. (1997), as cited in Firestone et al. (2007), concluded that an impact capable of continent-wide damage requires an impact by a comet that is >4 km wide. Previously, Chapman and Morrison (1994) loosely estimated an even lower threshold by predicting widespread catastrophes for impactors ranging from 500 m to 5 km. Pierazzo and Artemieva (2012) calculated that a 1-km to 10-km impactor would cause a global catastrophe, injecting enough dust into the stratosphere to alter climate, cause mass starvation, and trigger widespread epidemics. Pierazzo et al. (2010) reported model results indicating that an oceanic impact by a 1-km asteroid or comet could inject enough water vapor and aerosols to diminish ozone production for a period of years. More intense impacts produce greater vapor plume heights, corresponding to proportionally greater ozone destruction. This depletion would allow harmful levels of UVB radiation to reach Earth's surface, with potentially catastrophic consequences for terrestrial and marine ecosystems, possibly contributing to extinctions. A similarly sized object impacting a large continental ice sheet should have similar consequences.

For the Younger Dryas impact event, Firestone et al. (2007) suggested that the impactor originally had a diameter larger than 4 km. They proposed that before impacting Earth, the comet broke up in space (not Earth's atmosphere) to produce a comet swarm of unknown mass, but with some fragments as large as ≈2 km in diameter. In addition, multiple smaller fragments would have exploded as atmospheric airbursts, as occurred at Tunguska, Siberia, in 1908. Israde et al. (2012) suggested that the impactor was a fragmented object that originally was larger than several hundred meters in diameter.

As proposed by Napier et al. (2013), if the YDB cometary fragments equaled one-thousandth the mass of 200-km-wide centaur Chiron (that is, a fragment equivalent to a 20-km-wide object), those fragments could have produced ≈5,000 catastrophic, Tunguska-sized airburst/impacts over one hemisphere of the Earth within just a few hours.

Where did the impact occur? Based on the geographic distribution and concentration of proxies, along with the current lack of obvious YDB craters, Firestone et al. (2007) concluded that the largest of the comet fragments struck glaciated portions of eastern Canada. Those authors cited NASA experiments showing that multiple 2-km cometary fragments could have impacted the Laurentide Ice Sheet (up to ≈3 km thick), leaving shallow or no craters. In support of that, the Tunguska event and the Dakhleh event show that devastating airbursts can occur without leaving a visible crater (Firestone et al. 2007; Napier et al. 2013). The calculations of Napier et al. (2013) suggest that a highly devastating comet swarm could have occurred over one hemisphere of the planet without producing craters.

Conclusions

Of all the possible mechanisms that could account for the diverse assemblage of YDB proxies found variably at 32 sites on four continents, only a cosmic impact event could have produced all of them together. The ages of 22 YDB sites on four continents are statistically isochronous, within the limits of dating methodologies, indicating that a temporally singular impact event occurred, affecting at least one hemisphere. The evidence suggests that the impact event was environmentally catastrophic, abruptly changing ocean circulation, triggering severe Younger Dryas climate change, contributing to megafaunal extinctions, and causing human cultural shifts and population declines in people and animals, as discussed in a companion chapter in this volume.

9

POTENTIAL CONSEQUENCES OF
THE YDB COSMIC IMPACT AT 12.8 KYA

CLIMATE, HUMANS, AND MEGAFAUNA

JAMES P. KENNETT, DOUGLAS J. KENNETT,
MALCOLM A. LECOMPTE, AND ALLEN WEST

The Younger Dryas (YD) cooling episode (12.8 to 11.5 kya) anomalously punctuated the last deglacial episode, otherwise a time of increasing global warmth and the melting of vast Northern Hemisphere ice sheets. The YD episode marks an abrupt return to near-glacial conditions that caused broad environmental changes over the Northern Hemisphere and tropics. Conditions suddenly became colder (Alley 2004) and drier, with resulting major environmental changes that caused shifts in plant and animal biogeography (Peros et al. 2008), increased the atmospheric dust load (Taylor et al. 1993), contributed to megafaunal extinctions, and led to human cultural and population reorganizations (Haynes 1984, 2007). This extreme climatic episode has long been considered anomalous, and even a freak event (Broecker 2006), largely because of its timing during deglaciation and its magnitude and abruptness. Thus, the YD has remained enigmatic (e.g., Fiedel 2011), fueling much debate amongst earth scientists and archaeologists about its origin, consequences, and implications. Understanding what triggered the YD cold episode is crucial, because this event is often taken as a key example of strong nonlinearity in the climate system, leading to abrupt, millennial-scale climate change. In addition, such understanding appears to be crucial in helping solve the cause of extinction of most late Pleistocene megafauna, long debated but inadequately resolved.

Firestone et al. (2007) presented the hypothesis that the abrupt and enigmatic cooling marking the onset of the YD was triggered by the YD impact event at 12.8 kya. This event is posited to have triggered the YD episode of abrupt climate change, contributed to the end-Pleistocene megafaunal extinctions, and initiated human population reorganization/decline across the Northern Hemisphere. According to the Younger Dryas impact hypothesis, a major cosmic episode of multiple airbursts/impacts occurred at 12,800 ± 300 calendar years ago (95 percent probability), or 12,950 to 12,650 cal B.P. at 68 percent probability (Kennett et al. 2015). This event formed the widely distributed Younger Dryas Boundary layer (YDB) identified so far in nearly 40 stratigraphic sections on four continents, containing peak abundances in multiple, high-temperature, impact-related proxies. These include variable abundances of high-temperature, quenched spherules, high-temperature minerals and melt-glass, nanodiamonds, aciniform carbon, charcoal, carbon spherules, glass-like carbon, and anomalous concentrations of particular elements, including platinum, osmium, and nickel. An overview summary of the various proxies used to identify the YDB layer and their wide distribution, along with supporting source literature, is presented in chapter 8.

Bayesian statistical analyses of many dates from 23 sedimentary sequences over four continents established a modeled YDB age range of 12,835 to 12,735 cal B.P. (Kennett et al. 2015). This investigation also indicates synchroneity of the YDB layer at high probability (95 percent). This range overlaps that of a platinum peak recorded in the Greenland Ice Sheet and of the onset of the Younger Dryas climate episode in six key records, suggesting a causal connection between the impact event and the Younger Dryas. Due to its rarity and distinct characteristics, the YDB layer has been proposed to serve as a widespread correlation datum (Kennett et al. 2015).

The main purpose of this chapter is to provide a brief overview focusing on three of the potential major consequences of the YDB cosmic impact at 12.8 kya. These are YD climate and ocean change, human cultural shift and population decline, and the North American megafaunal extinction. There are many other environmental and biotic consequences not presented here, including evidence for widespread, major biomass burning at the onset of the YD over North America, as discussed in chapter 8, and as recently dramatically demonstrated in biomass burning proxies preserved in Greenland ice cores (Fischer et al. 2015).

Triggering of Younger Dryas Cooling

The abrupt onset of YD cooling over Greenland (Dansgaard et al. 1993; Grootes et al. 1993) is marked by a temperature decrease of about 10 °C ±

4 °C (Alley et al. 2003; Grachev and Severinghaus 2005) and represents the coldest interval of the YD. Remarkably, the onset of the YD climate episode occurred within a single year or less, corresponding to a major shift in atmospheric circulation and initial cooling (Steffensen et al. 2008). The cooling continued for another 180 years, likely due to climatic feedbacks (e.g., sea-ice expansion) triggered by the immediate atmospheric shift. Mid-latitude surface ocean temperatures also cooled by at least 4 °C (Kennett and Ingram 1995; Hendy et al. 2002). Continental climate changes appear to have been equally abrupt and broad, as recorded in varved sedimentary records in Germany (Brauer et al. 2008; Neugebauer et al. 2012) and as shown by dramatic vegetation shifts of >300 km in less than 100 years due to cooling and changes in moisture balance (Peros et al. 2008; Shuman et al. 2002). The onset in deposition of a widely distributed black mat over western North America with basal age of 12.8 kya (YD onset in Haynes 2007, 2008; and the YDB in Firestone et al. 2007) occurred in response to climate-driven, abrupt environmental change and impact-related biodegradation.

The conventional hypothesis, widely accepted to account for triggering abrupt YD cooling (12.8 kya), involves abrupt, massive diversion of overflow water of the enormous proglacial Lake Agassiz (~.05 to .30 sverdrups, defined as the measure of water volume above baseline flow). This flow was diverted from the Mississippi Basin (Kennett and Shackleton 1975; Teller et al. 2002; Flower et al. 2004) to the St. Lawrence Basin through newly opened eastern outlets (Lake Superior/St. Lawrence Seaway) and/or northwestern outlets into the Arctic Ocean through the Mackenzie River (Murton et al. 2010; Teller 2013). This plumbing shift is often considered to have resulted from critical retreat of the Laurentide Ice Sheet edge at the beginning of the YD (Kennett and Shackleton 1975; Broecker et al. 1989; Broecker 2006), forming conduits for outflow waters to the ocean (Figure 9.1). Although sources and paths of these waters are debated, evidence is increasing for widespread instability of the Laurentide Ice Sheet and its proglacial lakes (Teller et al. 2005), and even the Greenland ice sheet margins (Jennings et al. 2006) at the YD onset. This instability and outflow is indicated by changes in a wide range of environmental proxies (oxygen isotopes and other geochemistry; sediment parameters; biotic and others) from dated records in the Arctic Ocean and its margin (e.g., Maccalli et al. 2013; Murton et al. 2010; Not and Hillaire-Marcel 2012; Spielhagen et al. 2004) and near the ice sheets of North America and the north Atlantic (Figure 9.1). These regions include Lake Agassiz (Teller 2013), St. Lawrence

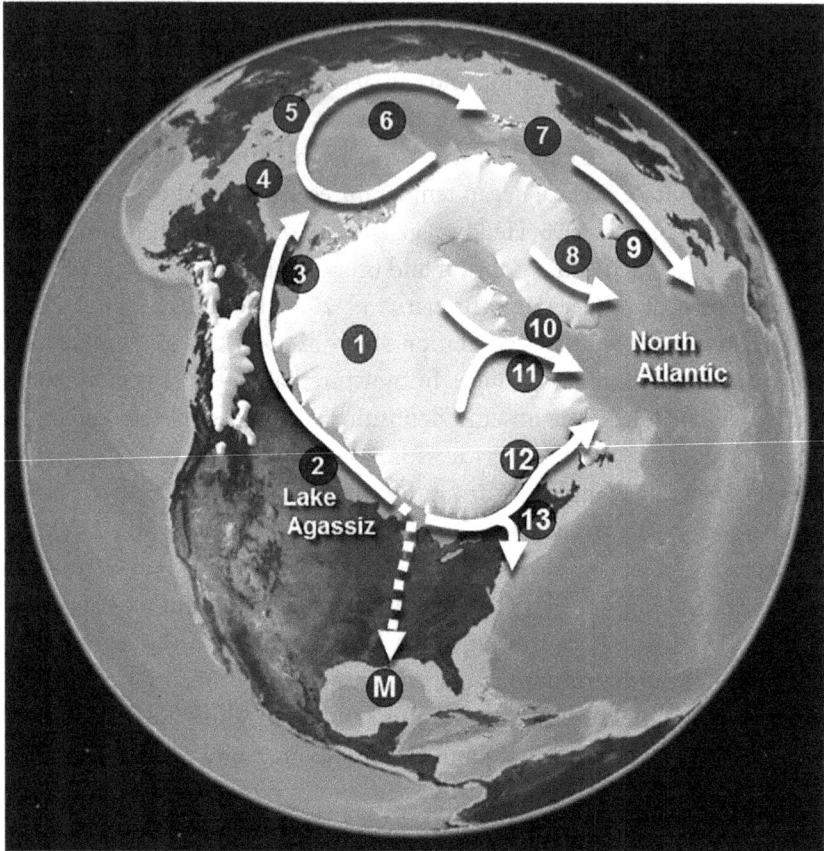

Figure 9.1. Evidence for YD outflow flooding, iceberg discharge, and their ocean effects around Laurentide and Greenland Ice Sheets. (*M*) denotes major drainage prior to 12.8 kya through the Mississippi River system into the Gulf of Mexico. After 12.8 kya, ice sheet drainage shifted to the Arctic and North Atlantic, throttling meridional overturning (oceanic conveyor) in the North Atlantic circulation and causing strong cooling at the YD episode. (*1*) Major collapse of the Keewatin Dome (Tarasov and Peltier 2005); (*2*) Lake Agassiz major drainage (Teller 2013); (*3*) Mackenzie Delta (Murton et al. 2010); (*4*) Alaska (Hill and Driscoll 2010); (*5*) Laptev Sea (Spielhagen et al. 2005); (*6*) Arctic Ocean (Poore at al. 1999; Polyak at al. 2004; Not and Hillaire-Marcel 2012); (*7*) Fram Strait (Maccali et al. 2013); (*8*) South Iceland (Thornalley et al. 2010); (*9*) Labrador Sea (Knutz et al. 2011); (*10*) Greenland (Jennings et al. 2006); (*11*) Hudson Strait (Miller and Kaufman 1990; Andrews et al. 1992, 1995; Rashid et al. 2011); (*12*) St. Lawrence Seaway (Carlson et al. 2007; Levac et al. 2015); (*13*) Lake Vermont and Champlain Sea (Cronin et al. 2008, 2012). Figure partially based on Tarasov and Peltier 2005, Figure 1.

Seaway and Lake Champlain (Carlson et al. 2007; Cronin et al. 2008; Cronin et al. 2012; see also Levac et al. 2015 for summary), Labrador Sea (Knutz et al. 2011); Hudson Strait (e.g., Rashid et al. 2011), Iceland (Thornalley et al. 2010), and Greenland (Jennings et al. 2006). In addition, modeling experiments by Tarasov and Peltier (2005) predicted major collapse of the Keewatin Ice Dome of the Laurentide Ice Sheet as the underlying cause of freshwater forcing of the YD cooling.

This diversion of continental interior drainage and its intensification in the early YD was of sufficient magnitude to freshen surface waters of the Arctic Ocean and, possibly, the northernmost Atlantic. The resulting cap of low-salinity surface waters strongly reduced thermohaline circulation (THC), leading to climatic feedbacks that led to abrupt YD cooling (Broecker et al. 1989; Clark et al. 2001; Teller et al. 2002). Reorganization of ocean circulation due to YD weakening of THC at the YD onset (Keigwin 2004; McManus et al. 2004) appears strongly connected with variations in strength of Atlantic meridional overturning circulation (MOC). This is indicated by a major change in a number of ocean-circulation proxies recorded in marine sediments (e.g., Robinson et al. 2005; Thornalley et al. 2010). In addition, an inferred maximum in atmospheric $\delta^{13}C$ recorded in *Cariaco* Basin sediments at 12.8 kya (Hughen et al. 1998) is generally interpreted to have resulted from a slowdown in MOC and a related decrease in ocean ventilation (Keigwin 2004).

The YDB impact hypothesis posits that the cosmic impact into the Laurentide Ice Sheet and the world's oceans triggered the abrupt onset of YD cooling through both short- and longer-term climate change mechanisms that returned broad areas of the earth to near-glacial conditions. The impact event thus represents both the triggering mechanism and the energy source necessary to shift the climate system into a major cooling mode with significant inertia to remain in that state. Initial cooling was caused by abrupt and major shifts in the atmosphere and cryosphere, including a reduction in solar radiation through a major dust-load increase (impact winter) and increased destabilization of the ice sheet margin. The cooling caused major changes in the oceans at high northern latitudes and changed global ocean circulation. Climatic feedbacks related to the ocean reorganization maintained cool climates for the duration of the YD, long after the cosmic impact. Available data suggests that YD cooling was not triggered solely by salinity-driven ocean circulation changes. Instead, the abrupt change in atmospheric circulation caused by the impact triggered initial cooling that was later reinforced in response to the ocean circulation changes. Thus, this hypothesis posits that the YD climate episode would not have taken place without the YD cosmic impact event.

Why did YD cooling that was triggered by the cosmic impact last for so long (>1,000 years) rather than only a few decades? Climatic responses and feedbacks normally resulting from a cosmic impact are expected to be relatively short-lived (Pierazzo and Artemieva 2012), whereas climatic response to the YDB impact appears anomalously long. This was because of the geological timing of the impact. Critically, this took place during the presence on North America of a major ice sheet and of sufficient volumes of outburst waters to rapidly reduce surface salinity in the high-latitude oceans and abruptly throttle MOC. This fundamental switch in ocean circulation (the oceanic conveyor) produced the necessary climatic feedbacks and global inertia for long-term maintenance of the cold climate of the YD. The inertia of the new climate system may have been supported by continued relatively low salinity of Arctic surface waters through continued ice sheet melting and the newly established outflow of Lake Agassiz waters to the Arctic.

The impact hypothesis as a trigger for the YD climate episode appears consistent with a wide range of observations and can explain a number of unresolved problems related to the enigmatic YD climate episode. These include the following:

- Anomalous in its timing, magnitude, and duration, because the YD cooling is not predicted by orbital forcing theory. Instead, it occurred near the maximum of Northern Hemisphere solar insolation that should have induced warming rather than cooling at the time of the YD episode (Lisiecki and Raymo 2005).
- Anomalous major cooling reversal during the transition from the last glacial to the present interglacial episode. In a long series of deglacial episodes through the late Quaternary, none shows evidence of an event that is identical to the YD. In addition, ice cores from Greenland and Antarctica exhibit a conspicuous decrease in atmospheric CH_4 during the YD with no similar episodes apparent in previous glacial terminations (Petit et al. 1999; Broecker 2006; and converse to conclusions of Cheng et al. 2009).
- Anomalous cooling marks the YD compared with other late Quaternary millennial-scale climate episodes because the strongest cooling occurred near the YD onset (Grootes et al. 1993) rather than near the end.

- Remarkable abruptness (one year or less) and magnitude of the on-set of YD climate change. Although other late Quaternary climatic changes were also abrupt (Steffensen et al. 2008), the YD onset was unusually rapid, representing an extreme event.
- Abruptness of the switch at 12.8 kya of Lake Agassiz outflow south-ward from the Mississippi Basin outlet to the newly opened outlets to the east and/or north (Broecker et al. 1989; Flower et al. 2004, 2011; Kennett and Shackleton 1975; Teller 2013).
- Coincidence of this sudden diversion from Lake Agassiz with an apparent lake failure marked by a major drop in its level by ~100 m with corresponding water loss of 9,500 km^3 (Leverington et al. 2000; Meissner and Clark 2006; Teller 2013; Teller et al. 2005).
- Vast extent of evidence for major destabilization and outflow along the ice sheet margins into the surrounding oceans at the onset of the YD. Increasing evidence supports broadly distributed major continental outflow from the ice sheet periphery, rather than via a single conduit from Lake Agassiz (Levac et al. 2015). This is consis-tent with the occurrence of an unusual trigger, capable of affecting more than just a restricted portion of the ice sheet. It is proposed that the impact shock into and/or over the ice sheet further desta-bilized the ice sheet's margins and breached the ice dams on Lake Agassiz and other proglacial lakes.
- Major collapse of the Keewatin Dome of the Laurentide Ice Sheet inferred at the onset of the YD (Tarasov and Peltier 2005).

Human Cultural Shift and Population Decline at the YDB

Firestone et al. (2007) proposed that the YDB impact at 12.8 kya caused the abrupt disappearance of the Paleoindian Clovis culture over North Amer-ica. Although it is now well established that human occupation of North America preceded Clovis people for at least 1,000 years (the pre-Clovis in-terval; e.g., Waters et al. 2011), the Clovis cultural complex represents the first well-established, widely distributed population in North America to leave a firm archaeological footprint (Haynes 2005). Abundant emblem-atic artifacts, representing a specific toolkit produced by these people, are widely scattered across the continent and represent widely shared cultural traditions of a highly successful hunting-and-gathering adaptation compa-rable to Upper Paleolithic traditions in Europe (Gamble 1999; Gamble et al. 2005). Available data indicate that the tenure of Clovis in North America was remarkably brief, within an interval of only ~200 years, ranging between ~13 and 12.8 kya, based on overlap of the most credible radiocarbon dates in 11 stratified archeological sites (Waters and Stafford 2007a, 2007b). Additional modern radiocarbon dating at new sites may require older extension of this range, but the termination of Clovis is well indicated at ~12.8 kya, coinciding with the onset of the YD climate episode and the YDB in numerous sites (Firestone et al. 2007).

Clovis-age radiocarbon chronology is well supported by clearly defined stratigraphic evidence at numerous sites, including Murray Springs and Lehner in Arizona (Haynes 2007), and Blackwater Draw in New Mexico (Haynes 1995). At these sites, and across much of western North America, Clovis artifacts occur up to, but not above, a datum of 12.8 kya (Haynes 2007), coinciding with the YDB impact layer and usually representing the base of a distinctive black layer that marks the onset of the YD climate episode. A similar stratigraphic succession occurs in eastern North America, as reflected at the Topper Paleoindian chert quarry in South Carolina, where the YDB layer dates to ≈12.84 kya (10,958 ±65 ^{14}C years, AA-100294; Goodyear and Steffy 2003; Anderson et al. 2016), but is not associated with a black layer.

The remarkable abruptness of loss of such a well-established, successful culture simultaneously over vast parts of North America is consistent with major environmental and ecological change caused by the YDB cosmic impact. This hypothesis is further supported by widespread evidence for an associated and near-synchronous major population decrease at the YD onset. Of 11 credibly well-dated Clovis sites containing artifacts (Waters and Stafford 2007a, 2007b), none contain post-Clovis artifacts immediately above the YDB layer, suggesting a disruption in activity and population decline. Anderson et al. (2011) presented multiple lines of evidence consistent with major decline in human populations at the onset of the YD. In southeastern and central North America, total numbers of known Paleoindian projectile points declined by half immediately after ~12.8 kya, a trend reflected across broad parts of North America (Figure 9.2) (Anderson et al. 2011; Faught et al. 1994). This is consistent with the Californian record, marked by a hiatus in human activity, with none known for the early and middle YD episode (Jones and Kennett 2012).

At the same time in the southeastern U.S., more than a dozen chert quarries, a vital Paleoindian resource, were suddenly abandoned, or nearly so (Anderson et al. 2011; LeCompte et al. 2012; Fig. 9.2). For example, a close

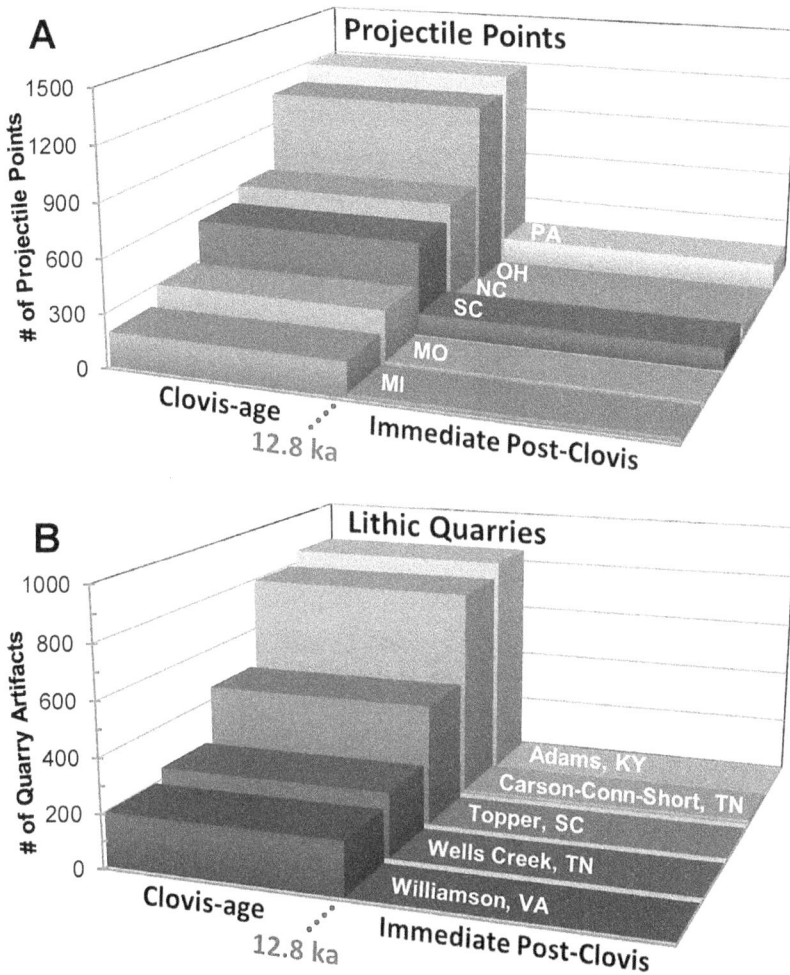

Figure 9.2. Changes in artifact numbers over the YD onset (12.8 kya). (*A*) Numbers of projectile points in different regions of eastern North America showing major decrease after 12.8 kya. (*B*) Numbers of artifacts in 5 Clovis-age quarries in the SE United States (projectile points, preforms, cores, and blades) attributed to Clovis and to immediate post-Clovis cultural traditions. Major declines in quarry usage occurred at end of Clovis cultural tradition. The immediate post-Clovis interval is considered equivalent to the early YD. Data are from North American Paleoindian Projectile Point Database, including the assigned archeological groups (see Faught et al. 1994 and Anderson et al. 2011 for details). Figure partially based on Anderson et al. 2011, Figure 7.

linkage between population decline and the YDB impact was found in South Carolina at the Topper Paleoindian chert quarry, which was abandoned by humans at the onset of the YD climate episode. There, LeCompte et al. (2012) found that YDB impact spherules were directly in contact with the upper surfaces of excavated Clovis artifacts, but no spherules were detected below the artifacts. This finding provides evidence that the impact event coincided with the start of a 500-year-long abandonment of the Topper quarry, a highly valued Paleoindian source of chert.

Later in the YD, beginning after ~12.6 kya, there was an apparent resurgence in population and/or settlements in many areas, as indicated by increases in projectile points, quarry usage, and human-related radiocarbon ages. Similarly, archaeological records suggest significant population declines at the onset of the YD in northern Europe (Gamble 1999; Gamble et al. 2005) and the Near East (Moore and Hillman 1992), with subsequent population rebound many centuries later (Anderson et al. 2011).

North American Megafaunal Extinction

Near the end of the Pleistocene, at least 35 mammal and 19 bird genera became extinct in North America. Almost all were large animals representing a wide diversity of herbivores and carnivores, and many would almost certainly have been widely distributed in vast numbers over the continent. This late Pleistocene megafaunal extinction included all the horses (Equids), camels (Camelids), mammoths (*Mammuthus*), mastodons (*Mammut*), giant ground sloths, saber-toothed cats, the short-faced bear, and the dire wolf, to name a few (Grayson and Meltzer 2003). For large animals then inhabiting North America south of Beringia, extinction was almost complete, with only a few taxa surviving. This major event caused irreversible changes in the terrestrial biota and related profound changes in the landscape of North America. Of the remaining large animals, some experienced population bottlenecks, including bison (McDonald 1981), as well as humans (e.g., Malhi et al. 2007; Schroeder et al. 2009). The extinction also led to opportunities in vacant habitats that resulted in migrations of certain taxa previously absent in North America or with limited biogeographic range, including moose, elk, and brown bear, now part of the modern iconic assemblage. This represents a major extinction not only because so many large and well-known animals were lost, but also because many of the extinct taxa had resided for millions of years in North America (MacFadden 2005). Horse evolution had continued without break in North America since the Eocene (~55 Ma), with the only known absence beginning at ~12.8 kya until their return from Europe ~500 years ago with Spanish explorers. Clearly, such extinctions are highly anomalous.

Currently there is no scientific consensus about the cause of the Late Pleistocene North American megafaunal extinctions, but there are four main hypotheses: a) Paleoindian overhunting, b) epidemic diseases, c) climate change, and d) the YDB cosmic impact event (Firestone et al. 2007; Kennett et al. 2008). The cause of the extinction has been long de-bated, since the Argentinean excavations of extinct megafauna conducted by Charles Darwin in 1832 during the voyage of the *Beagle*. Remarkably, more than 150 years ago, Darwin was the first to posit three of the current hypotheses as potential causes for extinction of South and North Ameri-can megafauna: climate, human hunting, or some unknown catastrophe (Darwin 1845:178–181). The potential roles of climate change and/or human overkill have long been debated, with limited success and with much con-troversy. Alley et al. (2003) identified the close coincidence of the megafau-nal extinctions with YD cooling onset but considered that climate change was unlikely the sole trigger, because the fauna had previously survived many similar shifts. Instead, those workers considered the cause as some combination of climate change with overhunting. However, the abruptness of this major extinction appears inconsistent with the hypotheses of only human overkill and climatic change. Instead, all four processes could have contributed to the extinction episode, but the YDB impact hypothesis is posited as the primary mechanism that caused the extinctions, principally by abruptly triggering impact winter, accompanied by extensive biomass burning. In addition, impacts into the Laurentide Ice Sheet and the world's oceans are proposed to have injected sufficient water into the stratosphere to cause severe damage to the Earth's ozone layer, resulting in the wide-spread collapse of terrestrial ecosystems (Pierazzo et al. 2010).

Human predation obviously can contribute to reduction in animal population numbers, but as previously mentioned, the Clovis culture dis-appeared and human populations declined abruptly, not gradually, at the onset of the Younger Dryas (Anderson et al. 2011). Yet this human decline appears to have coincided with the equally abrupt extinction of many of the abundant and widespread taxa making up the North American megafauna (Firestone et al. 2007; Kennett et al. 2008). Hence, it is difficult to argue that the Clovis peoples caused the extinction by overhunting when the people themselves also abruptly declined simultaneously with the other animal taxa.

The YDB impact hypothesis has been added as the potential extinction trigger, and so, the debate continues, especially because the climate and human overkill hypotheses remain inconsistent with many observations about the timing, magnitude, distribution, and environmental context of the animal extinctions. Furthermore, related inconsistencies have increased along with modern advances in accuracy and precision in dating the extinctions and through improvements in stratigraphic resolution and global correlation. In addition, there have been major improvements in determining relationships between the extinctions and paleoenvironmental changes through an expansion in proxies for those changes (e.g., Jones and Kennett 2012).

A substantial body of evidence now exists in support of the YDB cosmic impact at ~12.8 kya. This was a major event and of sufficient extent and magnitude to be well recorded in the YDB layer that is widely distributed over at least four continents (Kennett et al. 2015). Nevertheless, questions arise as to whether the environmental changes resulting from the impact were sufficiently large to cause the megafaunal extinctions over at least North America. The onset of the YD is clearly associated with abrupt and broad changes in vegetation (e.g., Peros et al. 2008; Shuman et al. 2002), sedimentation, widespread biomass burning, and abrupt cooling on the continent (see chapter 8 for a brief overview). Sufficient geologic and chronologic data now exist to support the hypothesis that megafaunal extinctions were caused by continental-scale ecosystem disruption, resulting from the cosmic impact at the onset of the YD. Firestone et al. (2007) and many later contributions recently summarized by Kennett et al. (2015) have consistently argued that the megafaunal extinction would not have occurred at or close to the YD onset without the YDB cosmic impact at ~12.8 kya. Instead, many of the now-extinct animals would have survived much longer, even to modern times.

The record of North American megafaunal extinction should exhibit several key characteristics (predictions) for consistency with the YDB impact hypothesis:

1) The megafaunal extinctions should be abrupt and synchronous with the YDB impact event, forming a primary extinction datum. The youngest, well-dated credible occurrence of numerous megafaunal taxa in stratigraphic sections, in particular the most abundant forms, coincides with the YDB layer (~12.8 kya), and in situ remains are not found in younger sediments, except in rare cases.

In comparison, the youngest known ages for less common taxa sometimes are older than 12.8 kya. These last occurrences likely do not reflect full ranges and have remained older than the YDB because of limitations in the fossil record, as recognized by Signor and Lipps (1982). The so-called Signor-Lipps effect recognizes that fossil ranges can terminate toward boundaries because of a variety of factors, producing an apparently gradual extinction, even if the event was abrupt and geologically instantaneous.

A prediction of megafaunal synchroneity does not require the age of every individual extinct animal to be equal to or older than 12.8 kya. The survival of a few extinct animals beyond the extinction boundary is to be expected, because isolated groups can temporarily survive in refugia. For example, reliable dating shows that dwarf mammoths survived into the Holocene in refugia on isolated Pribilof Islands off Alaska (Guthrie 2004), on Wrangel Island off Siberia (Vartanyan et al. 1995), and near the Great Lakes (Woodman and Athfield 2009). The impact hypothesis predicts that with future work the youngest age limit known for extinct megafaunal taxa will move closer to the YD onset (YDB), but not be younger, except in rare cases.

2) The primary extinction horizon, as defined, should exhibit broad distribution over North America, forming a biostratigraphic datum recognizable when the resolution of the fossil record is sufficiently high.

3) The primary extinction horizon should be synchronous, as determined using highly accurate, precise, and well-calibrated radiocarbon dating at high statistical probability.

4) The megafaunal extinction datum can be expected to continue exhibiting coincidence with evidence for continental-scale ecosystem disruption.

The testing of these criteria remains a challenge, mainly because of the observed and predicted abruptness of the events at or near the YD onset. Increasingly high stratigraphic resolution is required to help resolve age relations between the abrupt events, a difficulty exacerbated by the fact that many sites exhibit low rates of sedimentation combined with significant bioturbation.

The extinction and biogeographic chronologies for many extinct species remain poorly known, and well-dated faunal assemblages of YDB (12.8

kya) age are uncommon in North America. A plateau in the radiocarbon calibration curve over the onset of the YD episode increases difficulty in obtaining accurate ages. In addition, the majority of radiocarbon dates produced during the last 50 years to establish Late Pleistocene extinction chronology are not suitable, because of outdated preparation techniques and large error margins. Nevertheless, chronology building to test the age of the megafaunal extinction is well under way using modern radiocarbon techniques and approaches, such as for sequences of latest Pleistocene megafauna in the Willamette Valley, Oregon (Gilmour et al. 2015). This includes direct dating of biological materials (bone, dung) using appropriate chemical purification techniques. Results from modern improvements in accuracy of dating and critical examination of radiocarbon ages continue to support age of the abrupt megafaunal extinction near 12.8 kya (Waters and Stafford 2007; Kennett and Kennett 2008), including for the most common animals: horses, camels, mammoths, and mastodons (Grayson 2007:200). Bayesian statistical models as applied to this problem are also expected to assist with building a more robust extinction chronology of the North American extinct megafauna (Culleton and Kennett 2008).

In spite of age limitations, a solid body of biostratigraphic evidence already exists in strong support of the abrupt disappearance of many megafaunal taxa at the onset of the YD and the YDB impact layer. This coincidence is most clearly shown by the ranges of taxa in well-preserved sections broadly distributed over North America, including *Equus* (horse), *Camelops* (camel), and *Mammuthus* (mammoth) (Haynes 2008). The base of the black layer in fluvial sequences that began to be deposited at the time of the YDB impact event coincides with the extinction of many megafaunal taxa. Haynes (1998) reported that these occur directly below but never above this readily discernible layer at sites investigated. At Murray Springs, Arizona, Clovis-age artifacts and the remains of the extinct megafauna occur limited to a distinct 0.5-m-thick layer, well dated to between 13.0 and 12.8 kya. The remains of at least 10 extinct megafauna—mammoth, horse, camel, mastodon, Shasta ground sloth, short-faced bear, dire wolf, American lion, great bison, and tapir—range in depth up to the base of the black layer (Figure 9.3), and the youngest were in direct contact with the black mat shrouding their remains (Haynes 1984). Haynes (1998:6) stated that "the sudden extinction of the Pleistocene megafauna would be dramatically revealed by explaining that all were gone an instant before the black mat was deposited." This level was shown later to coincide exactly with the YDB cosmic impact layer at 12.8 kya (Firestone et al. 2007).

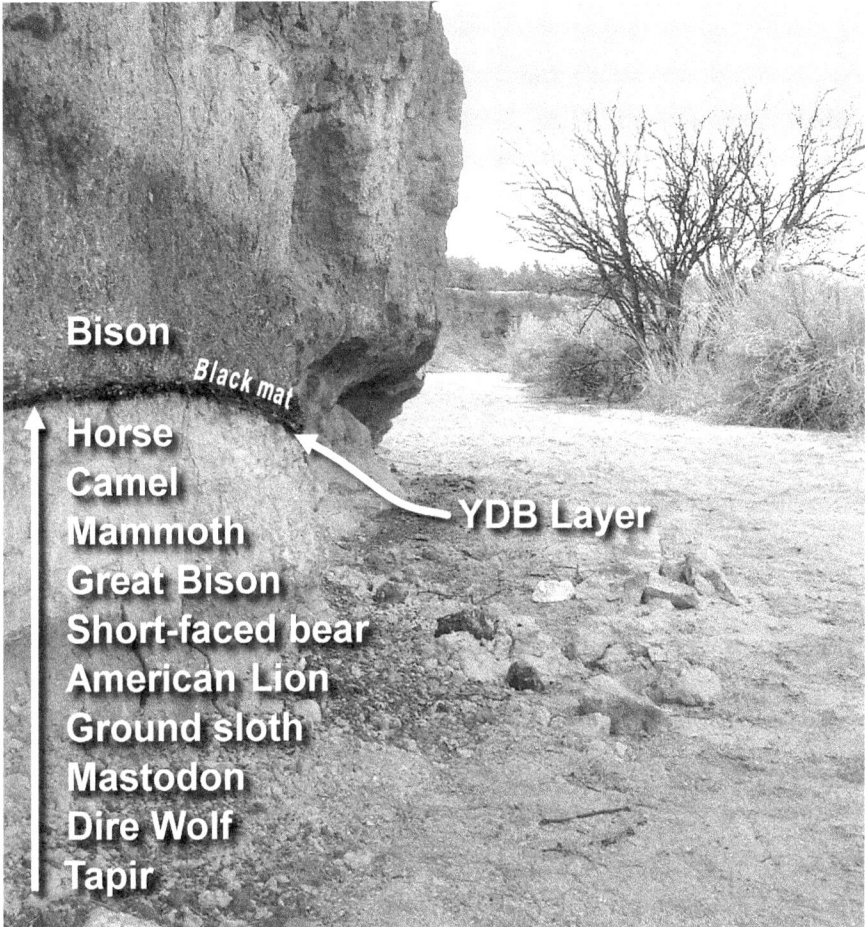

Figure 9.3. Megafaunal extinctions; biostratigraphic evidence at Murray Springs, Arizona. Bones of extinct megafauna extend up to the base of the black mat, which coincides with the YDB impact layer (Firestone et al. 2007). At this and nearby sites, the last appearances of these animals occurred precisely at the base of the black mat (Haynes 2007) and the YDB layer (Firestone et al. 2007); only a smaller species of bison survived following deposition of the YDB layer. Haynes (1998) wrote: "The sudden extinction of the Pleistocene megafauna would be dramatically revealed by explaining that all were gone in an instant before the black mat was deposited."

Conclusions

This chapter summarizes remarkable, widespread geological and archaeological consequences of a major cosmic collision (airbursts/impacts) with Earth 12,800 years ago (± 300 yrs; 95 percent probability) at the onset of the Younger Dryas cool episode. Massive energy release from this impact appears to have caused widespread biomass burning and other severe biotic and environmental changes, including widespread disruption of continental vegetation. A wide range of evidence is consistent with an impact of a comet cloud with Earth resulting in multiple widely distributed atmospheric aerial bursts. This was a cataclysmic event causing deposition of a thin Younger Dryas Boundary layer marked by peak abundances (anomalies) in a diverse assemblage of cosmic-impact-related materials found at nearly 40 sites over four continents (summarized in chapter 8). These impact proxies include high-temperature, quenched spherules, melt-glass, nanodiamonds, carbon spherules, and anomalously high concentrations of platinum, iridium, osmium, and nickel. The discovery of this layer led to the formulation by Firestone and colleagues of the YDB cosmic impact hypothesis. Bayesian statistical analysis of a large body of radiocarbon and other chronological data indicates that the YDB impact occurred between 12,835 and 12,735 cal B.P. This is synchronous within dating uncertainties across four continents, consistent with a single major cosmic event. We expect the YDB layer will serve as a widely distributed time marker horizon (datum) for identification and correlation of the onset of the YD climatic episode at 12,800 cal B.P. Furthermore, this datum will likely prove valuable in dating and correlating archeological, paleontological, and paleoenvironmental data between sequences, especially those with limited age control, including southeastern North America.

The cosmic impact event was closely associated with widespread biomass burning, continental hydrographic reorganization (plumbing change), outburst floods into the oceans surrounding the Laurentide Ice Sheet, major partial drainage of Lake Agassiz, and a resulting shift in ocean circulation and abrupt YD cooling. The YDB impact event also closely coincided with major extinction of the North American megafauna (including mammoths, ground sloths, saber-toothed cats, horses, and camels). Human populations also changed, as reflected by the abrupt loss of the widespread Stone Age Clovis culture and by a population decline over the continent that persisted for several hundred years during the early Younger Dryas climate episode.

The enigmatic Younger Dryas cooling episode (12.9–11.5 kya) is unique to late Quaternary deglacials; its timing is unexplainable by orbital forcing, because Northern Hemisphere insolation was increasing at that time. The abrupt onset of YD cooling coincided with, and was likely partially in consequence of, reduction in North Atlantic thermohaline circulation (THC). Triggering of YD cooling has often been primarily attributed to major diversion of freshwater outflow from the continental interior via newly opened outlets resulting from ice sheet melt-back. It seems, however, that an alternative primary trigger for YD cooling is necessary to account for problems related to the timing of outlet openings and the inferred magnitude of freshwater input into the surrounding oceans. The primary trigger for YD cooling may have instead been the YDB cosmic impact at 12.8 kya. YD cooling likely resulted from both short-term atmospheric processes due to the impact itself that reduced solar radiation and major longer-term reorganization of ocean and atmospheric circulation. The hypothesis posits that the impact caused partial destabilization of northern ice sheets and the opening of freshwater conduits; freshening of Arctic and northern Atlantic surface waters, and resulting strong reduction in North Atlantic THC. The impact hypothesis for YD triggering explains the timing enigma of the YD episode and is consistent with much existing data: 1) abrupt and dramatic switch in Lake Agassiz outflow at 12.8 kya away from the Mississippi River's southern outlet to newly opened outlets to the east and/or north; 2) a major and abrupt drop in ice-margin lake levels at precisely the time of the impact, and 3) evidence at the onset of YD cooling for partial destabilization and melting of the ice sheet margins. It is proposed that the YDB cooling episode would not have occurred in the absence of the YDB cosmic impact event. Thus, the YDB impact event supports the concept that cosmic impacts, even of limited geographic extent, can significantly and abruptly affect global climate change.

Near the end of the Pleistocene, at least 35 mammal and 19 bird genera became extinct over North America. Modern improvements in dating suggest that this extinction occurred abruptly at ~12.8 kya (11 radiocarbon kyrs). This hypothesis was tested by critically examining radiocarbon ages and extinction stratigraphy of these taxa. From a large data pool, radiocarbon dates were accepted only if they had low error margins, were preferably from directly dated biological materials (bone, dung), and were produced using modern chemical purification techniques. These data show that 16 animal genera and several other species became extinct close to 12.8 kya, including the most common animals: horses, camels, mammoths, and mastodons. Furthermore, the remains of extinct taxa are reportedly found up to, but not above, the YDB layer. The abruptness of this major extinction is inconsistent with the hypotheses of human overkill and climatic change. Extinction ages older than 12.8 kya for many less common species likely reflect limitations of the paleontological record as exemplified by the Signor-Lipps effect.

The broad environmental and ecological changes that mark the YDB also coincide with a remarkably abrupt loss of the well-established, successful Clovis culture over North America. Widespread evidence also exists of significant population declines and/or reorganizations at 12.8 kya, suggested by: (1) declines in Paleoindian projectile points; (2) near-to-total abandonment of 11 Paleoindian quarries; and (3) a sharp drop in cultural radiocarbon dates, most effectively shown using Bayesian analysis. These changes suggest deleterious effects of the YDB event on humans over broad areas of North America, including the southeastern United States.

10

REGIONAL MANIFESTATIONS OF LATE QUATERNARY CLIMATE CHANGE AND ARCHAEOLOGICAL SITE BURIAL ALONG THE SOUTH ATLANTIC COASTAL PLAIN

CHRISTOPHER R. MOORE, MARK J. BROOKS, I. RANDOLPH DANIEL JR., ANDREW H. IVESTER, JAMES K. FEATHERS, AND TERRY E. BARBOUR

Geoarchaeological evidence has continued to mount in support of regional-scale burial processes in the South Atlantic Coastal Plain (SACP). This includes a limited but pervasive signature of landform aggradation over the Holocene in a variety of depositional environments and geomorphic settings. These include linear sand ridges of mixed aeolian and fluvial origin, aeolian sand-sheets and dunes, levee and alluvial terrace deposits, and lacustrine Carolina bay sand rims. Burial processes include aeolian sedimentation, point bar or fluvial traction sediments deposited during large floods on elevated riverine terraces and levees, slopewash sedimentation on sloped surfaces, and combinations of all three. The recognition of regional-scale burial processes is important because of, and significant to, the commonality among archaeological sites, that is, shallow, sandy Coastal Plain sites with no discernible stratigraphy, due to little textural variation in sediments dominated by medium quartz sand.

The refinement and use of optically stimulated luminescence (OSL) data, particularly single-grain OSL, for archaeologically stratified sandy sites has led to greater understanding of site burial processes and evaluation of taphonomic, pedological, and anthropogenic processes that affect buried sites (Bateman et al. 2003, 2007; Boulter et al. 2006; Feathers, Holliday et al. 2006; Feathers, Rhodes, et al. 2006; Moore and Daniel 2011; Rink, Dunbar,

Doran et al. 2012; Rink et al. 2013). The results of these studies strongly indicate that vertically separated archaeological sequences can no longer all be explained as biomantles as described by Johnson (1990). Stratified archaeological sites do exist in the Coastal Plain with clear evidence for periods of Holocene sedimentation. For example, luminescence and radiocarbon (^{14}C) dates from archaeologically stratified sand ridges along the Tar River (Moore and Daniel 2011) correspond closely to Bond events 4–8, as well as the Younger Dryas chronozone, and are consistent with periods of active site burial in response to rapid climate change events as documented by high-resolution global and regional proxy records (Bond et al. 1997; Bond et al. 1999; Cronin et al. 2005; Mayewski et al. 2004; O'Brien et al. 2003; Overpeck and Webb 2000; Springer et al. 2008; Steig 1999; Viau et al. 2002; Viau et al. 2006; Willard et al. 2005). These burial events are discernible with close-interval analysis of archaeostratigraphy, sediment textural data, and OSL/^{14}C dating. Other researchers in the Southeast have also found evidence for coupling of the late Quaternary sedimentological record with abrupt climate and vegetation changes (e.g., Waters et al. 2009). These data suggest that rapid and short-lived climate change events in the SACP are dynamically linked to both human behavior/adaptation and geologic processes that led to burial and preservation of the archaeological correlates of those behaviors/adaptations (Moore 2009b).

Archaeologically stratified sand ridges have been identified within Coastal Plain riverine environments throughout the SACP (e.g., Curry 1992; Daniel 2002a, 2002b; Daniel and Moore 2011; Daniel et al. 2013; Daniels et al. 1969; Goodyear 1999; Gunn and Foss 1992; Moore and Daniel 2011; Moore 2009a, 2009b; Seramur 2004; Seramur and Cowan 2002, 2003; Seramur et al. 2003; Wagner and McAvoy 2004; Ward and Bachman 1987). Many of these landforms have been identified along the east and northeast side of Coastal Plain rivers (Daniels et al. 1969; Mallinson et al. 2008; Markewich and Markewich 1994; Markewich et al. 2015; Ivester and Leigh 2003; Ivester et al. 2001; Otvos and Price 2001; Soller 1988; Zayac et al. 2001) and have been interpreted elsewhere as coalescing parabolic and transverse dunes (Ivester et al. 2001; Ivester and Leigh 2003; Markewich and Markewich 1994; Moore and Brooks 2011; Moore and Daniel 2011).

Other common depositional environments in the SACP conducive to archaeological site burial are Carolina bay sand rims, floodplain environments such as fluvial terraces, and sloped landforms that are susceptible to slopewash. Recent investigations have documented the presence of buried archaeological deposits spanning the Late Pleistocene and Holocene within each of these depositional environments. For example, relict aeolian dunes have been identified in the Coastal Plain portion of southeastern Virginia with clear indications of intact archaeostratigraphy (Johnson 2013; McAvoy and McAvoy 1997). On the Tar River in North Carolina, combined aeolian and fluvial traction or point bar deposits have been investigated with numerous stratified sandy sites identified (e.g., Choate 2011; Daniel 2002a; Daniel et al. 2008, 2013; Daniel and Moore 2011; Moore 2009a, 2009b; Mc-Fadden 2009; Moore and Daniel 2011). In South Carolina, fluvial point bar deposits in the Lower Coastal Plain portion of the Pee Dee River (Steen 2000) and elsewhere (Brooks 1990), dune and slopewash deposits in the Upper Coastal Plain Sandhills region (Ivester et al. 2011), fluvial point bar deposits within the Upper Coastal Plain portion of the Savannah River Valley (Brooks and Sassaman 1990), and numerous lacustrine deposits in the form of Carolina bay sand rims scattered throughout the Coastal Plain (Brooks et al. 1996; Brooks et al. 2001; Brooks et al. 2010; Grant et al. 1998) are revealing evidence for a regional signature of landform aggradation and archaeological site burial.

Here, we evaluate the geologic context of multiple sandy sites along the SACP through the use of sedimentology, OSL, archaeostratigraphy, and ^{14}C dating in order to interpret depositional environment, determine the timing of depositional events, and relate these events to regional and global paleoclimate records. This is of critical importance in: 1) the evaluation of archaeological site formation processes at shallow, sandy Coastal Plain sites lacking visually observable, depositional, or archaeological stratigraphy; 2) linking site burial episodes to particular cultural or climate events; and 3) geomorphic reconstruction and dating of landforms.

The sites under consideration range from Virginia to South Carolina and are characterized by shallow, sandy deposits dominated by medium quartz sand (Figure 10.1). Many of these sites have very little textural variability and, as a result, lack visible depositional stratigraphy and exhibit only weak pedogenic overprinting. Sites that are discussed below include Cactus Hill (44SX202) in Virginia and Squires Ridge (31ED365) and Barber Creek (31PT259) along the Tar River in North Carolina. In South Carolina we evaluate evidence from the Johannes Kolb Site (38DA75) on the Pee Dee River; 38RD842 (a site located on Fort Jackson) in the Upper Coastal Plain, Carolina Bays, including Flamingo Bay (38AK469), Frierson Bay (38BR1319 and 38BR1320), and Johns Bay (38AL246) in the Central Savannah River

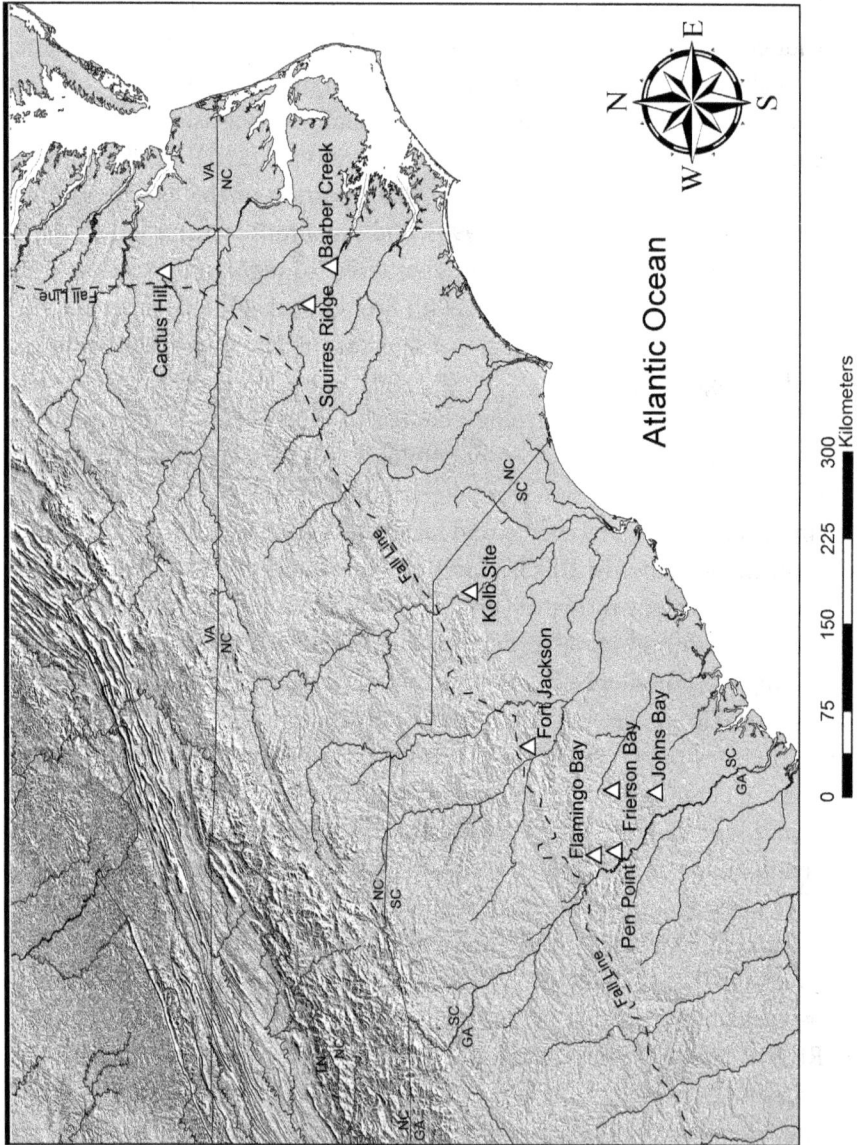

Figure 10.1. Map showing the location of study sites discussed in the text.

Atlantic Ocean

Fall Line

Cactus Hill

Squires Ridge

Barber Creek

VA
NC

VA
NC

Fall Line

Kolb Site

NC
SC

Fort Jackson

Flamingo Bay

Frierson Bay

Johns Bay

NC
SC

Pen Point

Fall Line

SC
GA

SC
GA

NC
GA

NC
GA

N
E
S
W

0   75   150   225   300

Kilometers

Area (CSRA); and Pen Point (38BR383), a lower terrace site on the Upper Coastal Plain portion of the Savannah River.

The Evidence

Cactus Hill

The Cactus Hill site (44SX202) is an archaeologically stratified sand body in the westernmost portion of the Coastal Plain in southeastern Virginia (Figure 10.1). The landform is about 25 km east of the Fall Line and occupies the first terrace on the east side of the Nottoway River in Sussex County, Virginia. Intensive archaeological investigations of the site (McAvoy and McAvoy 1997) have revealed a generally intact and stratified prehistoric sequence from Early Paleoindian through Woodland, with clear indications of buried surfaces or occupation floors covered in lithic debris and hearths preserved in layer-cake fashion over large portions of the site (Wagner and McAvoy 2004) (Figure 10.2). Numerous studies (Jones and Johnson 1997; MacPhail and McAvoy 2008; Wagner and McAvoy 2004) have shown that the main portion of the site is composed principally of aeolian sand derived from a backwater eddy of the Nottoway River floodplain with evidence of incremental sedimentation of dune sand since the Last Glacial Maximum. As is typical of all sandy sites discussed here, leached medium to fine sands dominate, with no visual evidence of depositional stratigraphy; however, micromorphology of the sediments has revealed ephemeral evidence of paleosols, limited periods of deflation followed by site burial events, and evidence for "small-scale bioturbation and overprinting of clay lamellae, suggesting site stratigraphy has been stable for a long time (Macphail and McAvoy 2008:675)." At Cactus Hill, as with other stratified sand ridges in the SACP, bioturbation is more accurately conceived as an overprint of relatively intact archaeostratigraphy evident from the excavations—severe in places, but not a primary mechanism of archaeological site burial.

A more significant vector for post-depositional disturbance processes relates to clear indications of anthropogenic disturbance in the form of pit digging for subsurface food storage and cooking by later prehistoric occupants of the site. Nevertheless, large portions of the site at Cactus Hill reveal distinct and unequivocal evidence of former occupation surfaces separated by thin lenses of sterile or nearly sterile sands and with temporally diagnostic hafted bifaces and luminescence age estimates generally

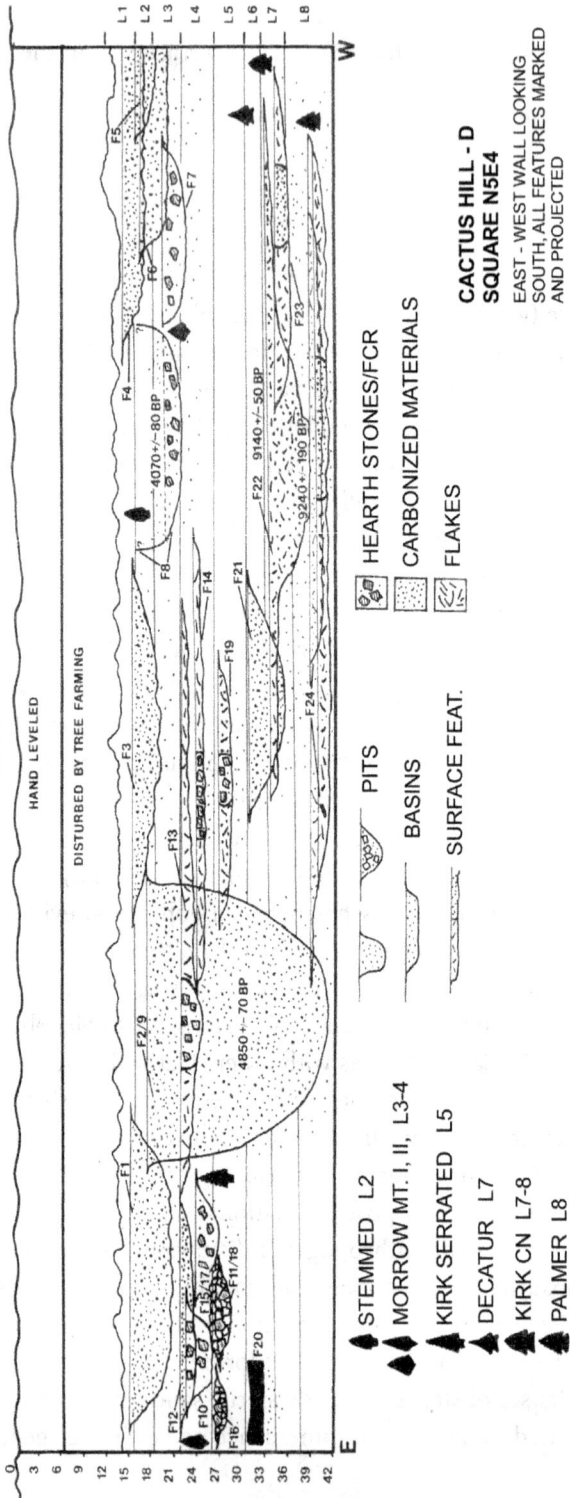

Figure 10.2. Backplot for Cactus Hill (44SX202) showing Features 1–24 in excavation unit N5E4 from Area D, radiocarbon dates, and associated temporally diagnostic hafted bifaces. View is facing south. Figure reprinted from McAvoy and McAvoy (1997) with permission of Joe McAvoy and the Virginia Department of Historic Resources.

found in correct chronostratigraphic order (Feathers, Rhodes, et al. 2006; McAvoy and McAvoy 1997; Wagner and McAvoy 2004). Luminescence age-estimates are also in broad agreement with radiocarbon ages (Tables 10.1 and 10.2) obtained from cultural features (Feathers, Rhodes, et al. 2006; McAvoy et al. 2000).

Tar River

Moving south, geoarchaeological investigations of sand ridges along the Tar River (Choate 2011; Daniel 2002a, 2002b; Daniel et al. 2008; Daniel et al. 2008 2013; McFadden 2009; Moore 2009a, 2009b; Moore and Daniel 2011; Seramur 2004; Seramur and Cowan 2002; Seramur et al. 2003) have provided additional evidence for incremental site burial through a combination of source-bordering aeolian and fluvial processes. Geoarchaeological work along the lower paleo-braidplain terrace of the Tar River has identified numerous sites with clear indications of buried surfaces and archaeological cultures spanning the Early Archaic through the Woodland period. Work at the Barber Creek Site (31PT259) and Squires Ridge (31ED365) have provided evidence consistent with episodic site burial very similar to that reported for Cactus Hill (Figure 10.3). At these sites, detailed analysis of piece-plotted artifacts, luminescence and radiocarbon dating, close-interval sedimentology, and refitting analysis all provide evidence consistent with incremental artifact burial. In particular, refitting analysis has identified multimodal and discontinuous distributions of larger plotted artifacts within relatively distinct soil stratigraphic zones defined by sedimentology and chronometric dating (Barbour 2015; Choate 2011; Daniel et al. 2008; Daniel et al. 2008, 2013; McFadden 2009; Moore 2009a; Moore and Daniel 2011). At Barber Creek, Choate (2011) identified three former occupation floors dating to the Early Archaic, Middle/Late Archaic, and Early/Middle Woodland periods. These are relatively discrete surfaces identified by the presence of larger artifacts and temporally diagnostic tools. Of particular note, each occupation floor is separated by a 4–10-cm absence of large artifacts, indicating a period of sedimentation.

Most recently, a detailed refitting study was undertaken (Barbour 2015) for piece-plotted artifacts from the Squires Ridge site (31ED365) and revealed evidence for at least two dense and stratigraphically distinct occupation zones with intervening stratigraphic zones containing fewer artifacts (Figure 10.4). Analysis of piece-plotted artifact distributions and refitting analysis suggest there are occupation surfaces or zones present at Squires Ridge dating to the Early/Middle Archaic, the Middle Archaic, the Middle/

Table 10.1. Dosimetry Data and Basis for Age for OSL Dates Discussed in the Text

Sample	Site	Method[e]	Depth (m)	^{238}U (ppm)	^{233}Th (ppm)	K (%)
UW435[a]	Cactus Hill	s-g	*1.25	1.19±.11	4.22±.80	2.03±.02
UW436[a]	Cactus Hill	s-g	*1.25	1.41±.11	2.93±.66	1.86±.06
UW697[a]	Cactus Hill	s-g	*.85	1.06±.12	7.28±1.07	1.99±.13
UW698[a]	Cactus Hill	s-g	*.7	.49±.10	6.02±.77	1.97±.02
UW617[a]	Cactus Hill	s-g	*.8	1.12±.10	3.46±.72	2.02±.06
UW699[a]	Cactus Hill	s-g	*.8	1.59±.13	5.10±.90	2.34±.08
UW700[a]	Cactus Hill	s-g	*.8	.66±.09	4.82±.85	1.95±.03
UW701[a]	Cactus Hill	s-g	*.8	.74±.10	5.19±.89	2.01±.01
UW618[a]	Cactus Hill	s-g	*1.2	1.09±.11	3.93±.78	2.08±.01
UW696[a]	Cactus Hill	s-g	*1.5	.80±.10	4.77±.85	2.08±.01
UW1907[a]	Barber Creek	s-g	.8	1.64±.13	5.22±.91	1.39±.03
UW1908[a]	Barber Creek	s-g	1	1.53±.12	3.74±.76	1.28±.04
UW1909[a]	Barber Creek	s-g	1.4	.31±.07	3.73±.74	1.36±.03
FS #2511[b]	Barber Creek	s-a	3.15	1.37 ±.04	7.3 ± 1.66	2.3 ±.49
FS #171[c]	Squires Ridge	s-a	.5	1.31 ±.10	4.52 ±.17	1.34 ±.07
FS #172[c]	Squires Ridge	s-a	.7	1.31 ±.10	4.52 ±.17	1.34 ±.07
FS #166[c]	Squires Ridge	s-a	.95	1.31 ±.10	4.52 ±.17	1.34 ±.07
UW2708[a]	Kolb	s-g	112	.64±.07	2.63±.62	.88±.03
UW2709[a]	Kolb	s-g	92.5	.73±.06	1.59±.44	.82±.03
UW2710[a]	Kolb	s-g	55	1.04±.08	1.47±.43	.76±.02
UW2711[a]	Kolb	s-g	81	1.17±.10	2.80±.65	.86±.04
UW2725[a]	Kolb	s-g	30	.77±.07	1.56±48	.89±.01
UW2726[a]	Kolb	s-g	40	.62±.07	2.46±.54	.96±.04
UW2727[a]	Kolb	s-g	50	.60±.06	1.28±.39	.72±.04
UW2728[a]	Kolb	s-g	80	.41±.07	3.00±.66	.77±.03
UW2729[a]	Kolb	s-g	100	.39±.06	1.96±.52	.81±.03
USU-934[d]	Fort Jackson	s-g	.3	4.5±.3	24.9±2.2	.09±.01
USU-935[d]	Fort Jackson	s-g	.4	3.8±.3	22.8±2.1	.09±.01
USU-936[d]	Fort Jackson	s-g	.5	4.6±.3	24.5±2.2	.09±.01
USU-937[d]	Fort Jackson	s-g	.6	5.7±.4	32.1±2.9	.11±.01

Total dose rate (Gy/ka)	Central age D_e (Gy)	σ_b (%)	Minimum age D_e (Gy)	FMM–most common component (Gy)	Age (ka)	% error	Basis for age[f]
2.63±.08	31.7±1.0	35±2	21.1±1.4	-	8.0±.6	7.5	MAM
2.43±.09	31.5±.8	28±2	24.9±1.1	-	10.3±.6	5.8	MAM
2.75±.14	47.1±1.3	34±2	32.4±1.3	-	11.8±.8	6.8	MAM
2.52±.08	41.1±1.0	30±2	31.4±1.2	-	12.5±.6	4.8	MAM
2.51±.09	48.4±2.0	40±3	42.8±3.1	-	19.3±1.0	5.2	CAM
2.74±.19	59. ±1.8	24±3	47.3±3.0	-	17.3±1.6	9.2	MAM
2.42±.08	56.0±2.4	25±4	48.1±9.1	-	19.8±3.8	19.2	MAM
2.52±.08	57.9±2.1	25±3	46.1±3.2	-	18.3±1.4	7.7	MAM
2.58±.08	53.2±1.8	25±3	41.1±6.8	-	20.6±.9	4.4	CAM
2.60±.08	70.3±1.6	28±2	31.4±2.8	-	27.0±1.1	4.1	CAM
2.01±.08	18.5±.9	44 ± 4	-	16.7±1.2	9.2 ±.7	7.1	CAM
1.91±.08	23.1±.8	30 ± 3	-	21.1±2.0	12.1 ±.7	6.2	CAM
1.72±.07	24.8±1.3	29 ± 4	-	31.4±2.2	14.5 ± 1.0	7.1	CAM
2.28 ±.2	38.9 ± 2.66	-	-	-	16.8 ± 1.9	11.3	CAM
1.88 ±.05	10.2 ±.09	19 ±.9	7.84 ±.42	8.65 ±.71	5.40 ±.16	3	MAM
1.93 ±.05	16.4 ±.13	17 ±.85	14.2 ±.83	16.6 ± 1.25	8.52 ±.25	3.1	MAM
1.97 ±.05	24.0 ±.60	9.8 ± .5	20.9 ± 1.00	24.4 ±.86	10.6 ±.57	5.4	CAM
1.28±.06	17.4±1.6	64±7	-	22.0±1.1	17.2±1.3	7.4	LC
1.37±.11	18.1±1.5	7	-	21.8±1.3	15.9±1.6	1.3	LC
1.22±.06	8.1±.8	61±8	-	7.9±.5	6.5±.5	8.3	LC
1.41±.07	11.1±.8	40±6	-	13.5±1.2	9.6±1.0	1.7	LC
1.31±.06	4.2±.5	76±10	-	3.0±.2	2.3±.2	8.4	LC
1.38±.07	4.5±.7	93±12	-	3.3±.3	2.4±.2	10.3	LC
1.08±.06	7.1±.6	65±7	-	3.9±.4	3.7±.4	11.9	LC
1.17±.06	11.0±1.0	68±7	-	12.4±1.2	10.6±1.2	11.1	LC
1.13±.06	14.7±1.2	56±7	-	13.8±1.5	12.3±1.5	12.5	LC
2.94 ±.19	10.17 ±.75	60.3 ± 6.1	5.56 ±.49	nc	3.45 ±.38	11.0	CAM
2.64 ±.17	14.71 ±.64	42.9 ± 3.4	7.69 ±.53	nc	5.57 ±.52	9.3	CAM
2.96 ±.19	20.08 ±.85	27.2 ± 3.9	nc	nc	6.78 ±.63	9.3	CAM
3.75 ±.24	26.24 ±.96	21.0 ± 3.5	nc	nc	6.99 ±.64	9.2	CAM

(continued)

Table 10.1—*Continued*

Sample	Site	Method[e]	Depth	^{238}U	$^{233'}Th$	K
USU-938[d]	Fort Jackson	s-g	.7	5.2±.4	28.5±2.6	.10±.01
UW2076[a]	Flamingo Bay	s-g	.35	1.44±.12	6.28±.78	.08±.01
UW2077[a]	Flamingo Bay	s-g	.5	1.41±.11	3.79±.69	.11±.03
UW2078[a]	Flamingo Bay	s-g	.65	1.43±.11	3.99±.71	.10±.01
UW2079[a]	Flamingo Bay	s-g	.8	1.58±.13	6.36±.93	.09±.01
UW2080[a]	Flamingo Bay	s-g	1	1.52±.13	5.71±.95	.16±.01
UW2731[a]	Flamingo Bay	s-g	1.58–1.95	1.45±.11	3.34±.72	.02±.02
UW2139[a]	Frierson Bay	s-g	.5	.91±.07	2.10±.50	.03±.02
UW2140[a]	Frierson Bay	s-g	.66	.95±.09	4.42±.74	.03±.01
UW2141[a]	Frierson Bay	s-g	.8	.98±.10	4.57±.83	.04±.01
UW2730[a]	Frierson Bay	s-g	2.45–2.75	3.45±.36	29.15±2.35	.02±.02
UW2142[a]	Johns Bay	s-g	60	.97±.08	2.52±.55	.04±0.02
UW2143[a]	Johns Bay	s-g	80	.78±.07	2.65±.57	.06±.01
UW2144[a]	Johns Bay	s-g	100	.60±.08	3.96±.69	.04±.01
UW2145[a]	Johns Bay	s-g	165–195	1.10±.11	5.46±.85	.03±.01
UW2146[a]	Johns Bay	s-g	255–285	2.00±.14	3.83±.71	.02±.01

Notes: *Cactus Hill depths are rather meaningless, due to the contour of the site. UW435 and UW436 are from Archaic layers, UW697 and UW698 are from the upper part of the pre-Clovis blade level; UW617, UW699, UW700, and UW701 are from the lower part of the pre-Clovis blade level; UW618 is below the pre-Clovis layer; and UW696 is from a buried A-horizon farther below the pre-Clovis layer.

[a]UW, University of Washington; James Feathers

[b]UGA, University of Georgia (Athens); George Brook

[c]USGS, Denver Colorado; Shannon Mahan

[d]USU, Utah State University; Tammy Rittenour

[e]s-g = single-grain; s-a = single-aliquot

[f]CAM = Central Age Model, MAM = Minimum Age Model, LC = Largest Component.

For UW, moisture content was taken as 6 ± 3%, typical for sandy sediments in temperate climates (Brady 1974). U, Th, and K values determined by UW by alpha counting, beta counting, and flame photometry. At USGS, UGA, USU, U, Th, and K values are determined by gamma spectrometry or ICP-MS. For the UGA sample, moisture content used for calculation was 10% ± 5%. For USGS samples, moisture value used in calculation was 55% of total saturation. For USU samples, moisture values were determined in situ as 4.3 ± 3.0% for USU-934, 4.5 ± 3.0% for USU-935, 4.0±3.0% for USU936, 3.1±3.0% for USU-937, and 3.4±3.0% for USU-938.

Total dose rate	Central age D_e (Gy)	σ_b (%)	Minimum age D_e (Gy)	FMM–most common component (Gy)	Age (ka)	% error	Basis for age[f]
3.37 ±.22	30.04 ±.95	16.2 ± 3.2	nc	nc	8.90 ±.79	8.9	CAM
.97±.07	10.5±.4	58±3	4.9±.3	10.6±.6	5.0±.5	9.9	MAM
.87±.06	14.1±.7	44±4	8.0±.6	13.2±.7	9.2±1.0	11.2	MAM
.88±.06	18.5±1.0	47±4	10.1±.9	18.5±1.3	11.5±1.3	11.7	MAM
.96±.07	21.4±.9	34±4	14.9±1.3	26.2±1.2	15.5±1.8	11.8	MAM
.96±.07	21.8±1.3	42±5	12.6±1.4	18.2±1.1	13.1±1.7	13.2	MAM
.71±.05	45.6±4.5	71±8	-	45.6±2.7	87.4±15.9	18.2	LC, FR>5
.58±.05	4.4±.2	54±4	2.3±.1	3.9±.2	4.0±.4	10.7	MAM
.73±.06	7.9±.6	41±7	4.7±.7	10.6±1.0	6.4±1.1	17.3	MAM
.75±.06	20.7±5.5	85±19	5.2±1.8	35.5±3.2	7.0±2.5	35.6	MAM
2.79±.15	59.9±4.9	56±7	-	89.8±5.3	35.3±2.9	8.1	LC, FR>5
.62±.06	9.0±.6	58±6	4.4±.5	9.8±.6	7.0±1.1	15.5	MAM
.60±.05	11.6±.6	51±4	5.6±.5	16.3±.6	9.3±1.2	12.5	MAM
.61±.05	15.6±.6	36±4	10.2±.8	19.9±1.2	16.7±2.0	12.1	MAM
.72±.06	24.2±.9	24±3	19.8±1.8	-	33.6±3.2	9.4	CAM
.87±.06	34.6±1.1	36±3	23.4±1.2	42.4±2.8	39.7 ± 3.0	7.7	CAM

Table 10.2. Radiocarbon and Calibrated Dates Discussed in the Text

Site Name	Site #	Method	Radiocarbon Age	Cal B.P.[a]	Beta Number
Cactus Hill	44SX202	Standard	4070 ± 80	4830–4410	Beta-80144
Cactus Hill	44SX202	Standard	4850 ± 70	5720–5465; 5345–5335	Beta-80184
Cactus Hill	44SX202	AMS	9140 ± 50	10,415–10,225	Beta-83012
Cactus Hill	44SX202	Standard	9240 ± 90	10,660–10,230	Beta-80182
Squires Ridge	31ED365	AMS	3990 ± 30	4525–4415	Beta-414621
Squires Ridge	31ED365	AMS	4690 ± 30	5575–5540; 5475–5435; 5425–5420	Beta-414622
Squires Ridge	31ED365	AMS	9010 ± 50	10,240–10,150; 9980–9970	Beta-283749
Squires Ridge	31ED365	AMS	9120 ± 30	10,280–10,230	Beta-399437
Flamingo Bay	38AK469	AMS	6140 ± 40	7160–6920	Beta-288775
Flamingo Bay	38AK469	AMS	6600 ± 40	7570–7430	Beta-283753
Flamingo Bay	38AK469	AMS	8170 ± 40	9260–9010	Beta-288776
Flamingo Bay	38AK469	AMS	9380 ± 50	10,720–10,500	Beta-288777

[a]INTCAL04 (2 sigma) calibration.

Late Archaic, and the Early Woodland (Barbour 2015). Refitting analysis (based on nearly 300 artifacts with at least one refit) indicates a high degree of archaeostratigraphic integrity for parts of the site with refit artifacts averaging only 3.5 cm in vertical displacement and with several clusters of lithic artifacts that appear to represent a buried surface or activity area.

Analysis and interpretation of multiple data sets, including ground-penetrating radar (GPR), OSL, and sedimentology have revealed sand ridges along the lower paleo-braidplain of the Tar River to consist of mixed fluvial/aeolian sediments in the upper sand unit (~1 m) (Moore 2009a). These sands overlie fluvial levee and relict braid-bar deposits. Sand ridges along the lower paleo-braidplain appear to have formed initially by braided or large-scale meandering (Leigh 2006, 2008; Leigh et al. 2004) of the Tar River (Moore and Daniel 2011). Archaeological evidence from cultures spanning the Holocene indicates sequentially buried deposits in this upper sand unit at Barber Creek and Squires Ridge through a combination of aeolian and fluvial overbank processes after the Tar River transitioned

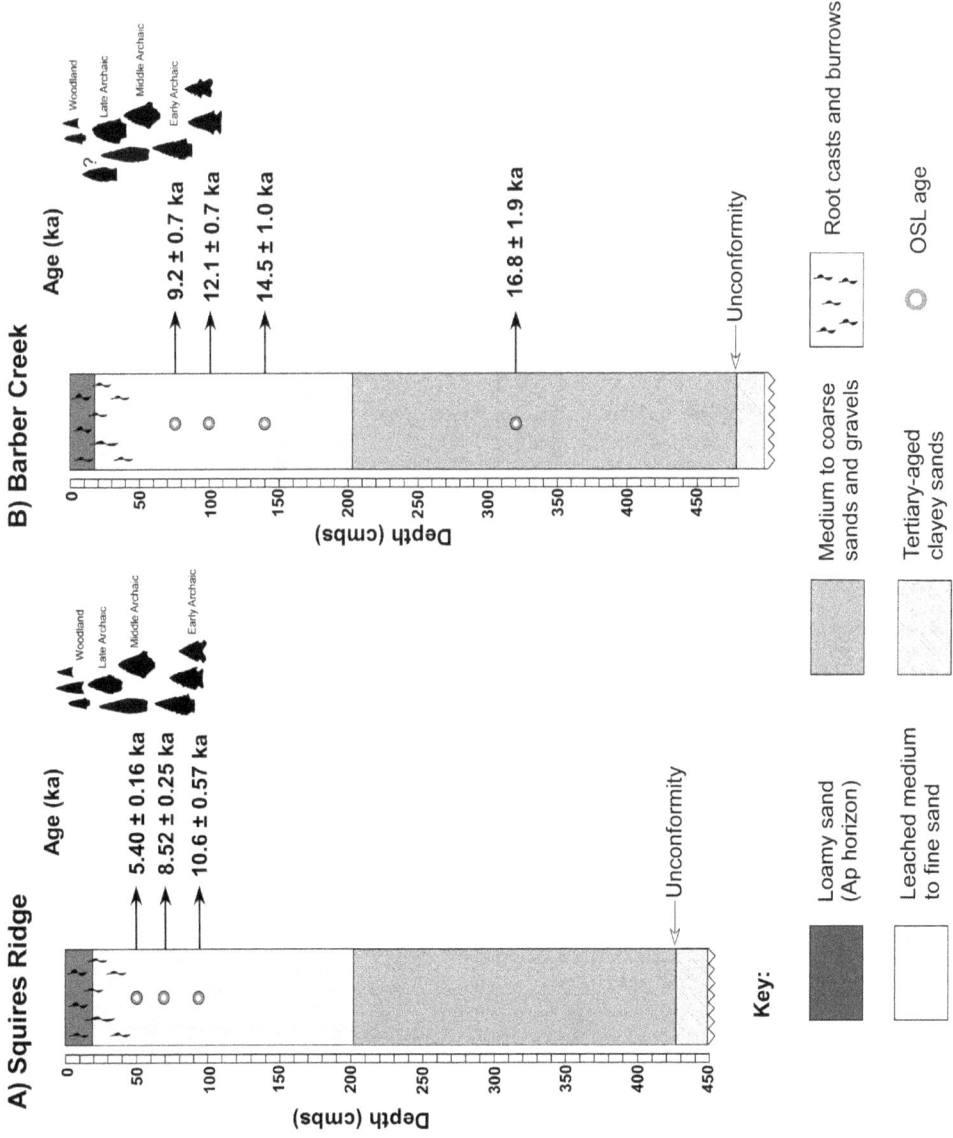

Figure 10.3. Lithostratigraphy, OSL geochronology, and generalized archaeostratigraphy for Squires Ridge (31ED365) and Barber Creek (31PT259) on the Tar River in North Carolina. OSL age-estimates for 31ED365 are single-aliquot and single-grain for 31PT259 (Moore and Daniel 2011).

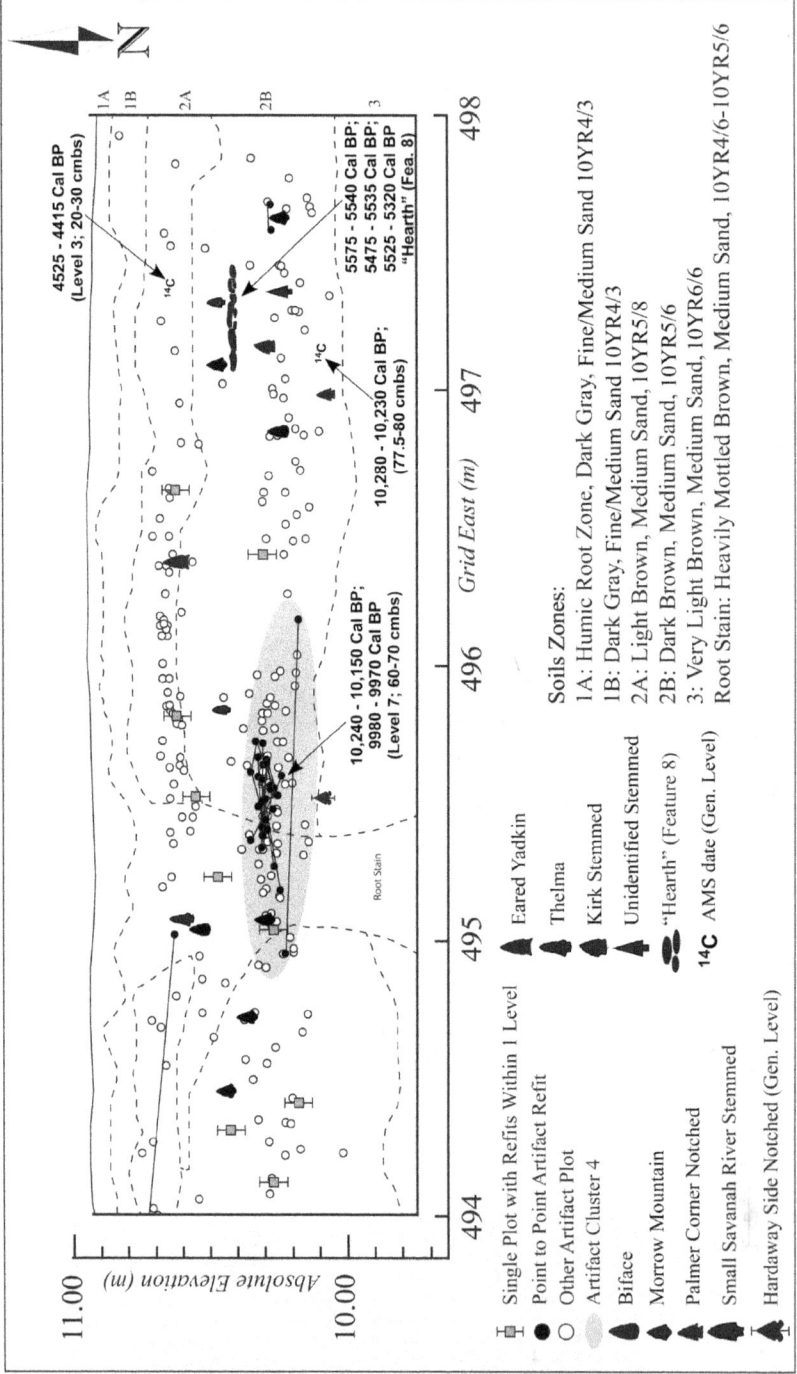

Figure 10.4. Backplot for Squires Ridge (31ED365) showing piece-plotted artifacts, temporally diagnostic hafted bifaces, artifact refits, and recent AMS dates from both feature- and general-level context.

Skewness (phi)

0.15

0.13

0.11

0.09

0.07

0.05

0.03

0.01

0.90   0.95   1.00   1.05   1.10   1.15   1.20   1.25   1.30

Standard Deviation (phi)

21.25

4525 - 4415 Cal BP

Eared-Yadkin

16.25

11.25

? 28.75

23.75

Late Archaic and Early Woodland

38.75

Middle Archaic and Late Archaic ?

Thelma 26.25

Guilford

Morrow Mt. 46.25

33.75

Savannah River

*5575 - 5540 Cal BP;
*5475 - 5535 Cal BP;
*5525 - 5320 Cal BP

Woodland

78.75

41.25 43.75
66.25 36.25 31.25
81.25
76.25   58.75 48.75 51.25

3.75

18.75

8.75

68.75 96.25
101.25
91.25 93.75 86.25
66.25

6.25

13.75

Kirk Stemmed

88.75

Early and Middle Archaic

Woodland Triangular

Ap horizon

71.25 98.75
83.75
103.75
53.75 63.75

1.25

Kirk/Palmer
Corner-Notched

73.75

10,280 - 10,230 Cal BP;
*10,240 - 10,150 Cal BP;
*9980 - 9970 Cal BP

Hardaway Side-Notched

108.75

106.25

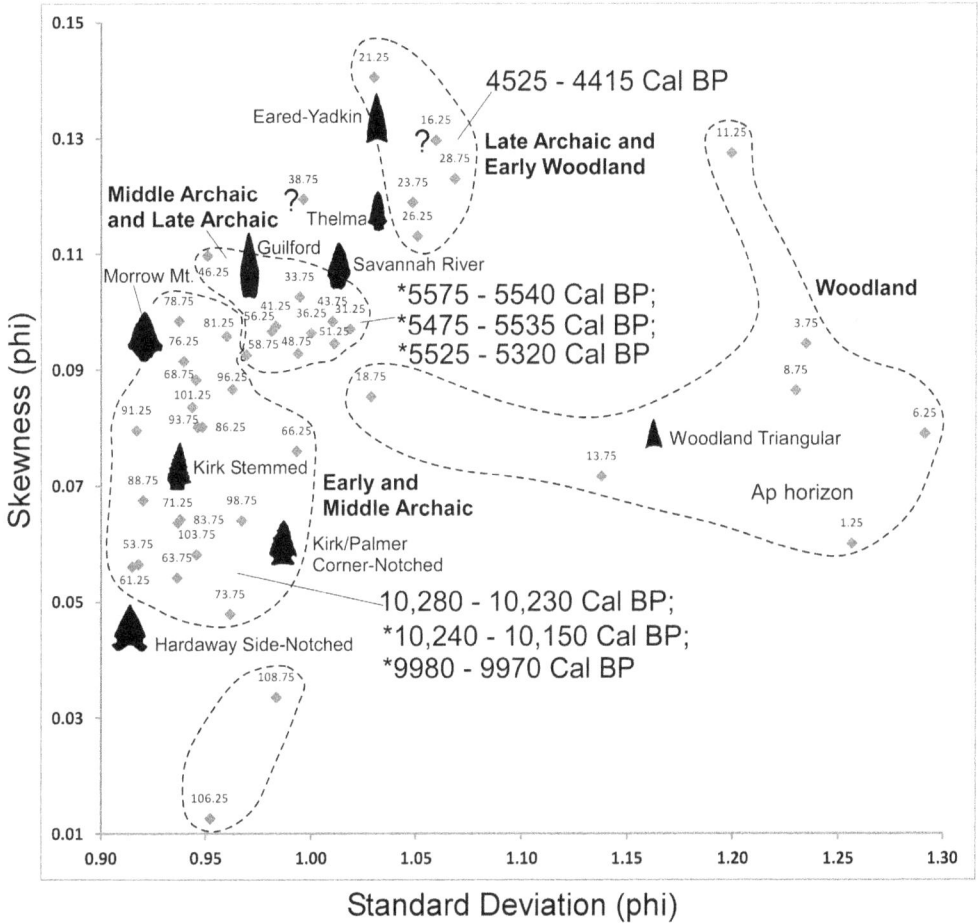

Figure 10.5. Bivariate plot of sorting and skewness (1/2 phi intervals) for sediments from Squires Ridge (31ED365; N546 E498) showing sedimentological stratigraphy, generalized archaeostratigraphy of temporally diagnostic hafted bifaces, and AMS dates.

to the modern incised and weakly meandering fluvial system. Single-grain OSL and radiocarbon age estimates for deposits at Barber Creek indicate aeolian sand-sheet deposition beginning during the Younger Dryas stadial event (ca. 12,900–11,700 cal. B.P.) and continuing episodically throughout much of the Holocene (Moore and Daniel 2011). Bivariate plots of close-interval grain-size data reveal distinct populations of samples by depth that represent periods of more-active sedimentation followed by stability, human occupation, and weak pedogenic development (Figure 10.5).

OSL age estimates and ^{14}C dates from Squires Ridge and Barber Creek in the upper 1 m of sand are consistent with ages determined through examination of temporally diagnostic artifacts, ^{14}C dating, and the overall archaeostratigraphy from each study site (Daniel and Moore 2011; Daniel et al. 2008; Daniel et al. 2013; Moore and Daniel 2011) (Figures 10.3–10.5; Tables 10.1 and 10.2). Cumulatively, these data show that lower paleo-braidplain aeolian/fluvial deposits along the Tar River (although shallow) likely contain the most complete paleoenvironmental record of climate change (for landforms along the Tar River) during the Late Pleistocene and Holocene.

Kolb (38DA75)

The Kolb site is located in the Great Pee Dee Heritage Preserve in South Carolina and lies within the Middle Coastal Plain portion of the Pee Dee River Valley. The landform sits on the first alluvial terrace overlooking the river. Geomorphically, the Kolb site is an overbank deposit (2–3 m thick) laid down immediately adjacent to the primary channel since the Late Pleistocene (Leigh 2001a). Since 1997, intensive archaeological fieldwork has been conducted at Kolb by the South Carolina Department of Natural Resources and the South Carolina Heritage Trust Program. Excavations have revealed evidence of intensive occupation, with stratified sequences including historic through Paleoindian and at depths of up to 1.2 m. Recent geoarchaeological investigations at the Kolb site by the authors have included close-interval sedimentology, analysis of archaeostratigraphy, and single-grain OSL dating (Figures 10.6–10.8). These data provide clear evidence of landform accretion and subsequent burial of occupation surfaces. Intact occupation floors are often found along with polymodal artifact density by level, changes in raw material use through time, and buried cultural features (Figure 10.9). Large Woodland pit features represent the largest and most obvious disturbance vector at Kolb, with other natural post-depositional processes playing a secondary but limited role. Single-grain luminescence age estimates obtained from two separate profiles provide ages in correct chronostratigraphic order and are broadly consistent with the observed archaeostratigraphy and stratigraphic breaks indicated by sedimentology (Figures 10.6 and 10.8; Table 10.1). Changes in sand fraction statistical parameters with depth are also consistent with periodic accretionary episodes, likely in the form of large flood events followed by periods of stability, weak pedogenic development, and anthropogenic occupation/disturbance (Figure 10.7).

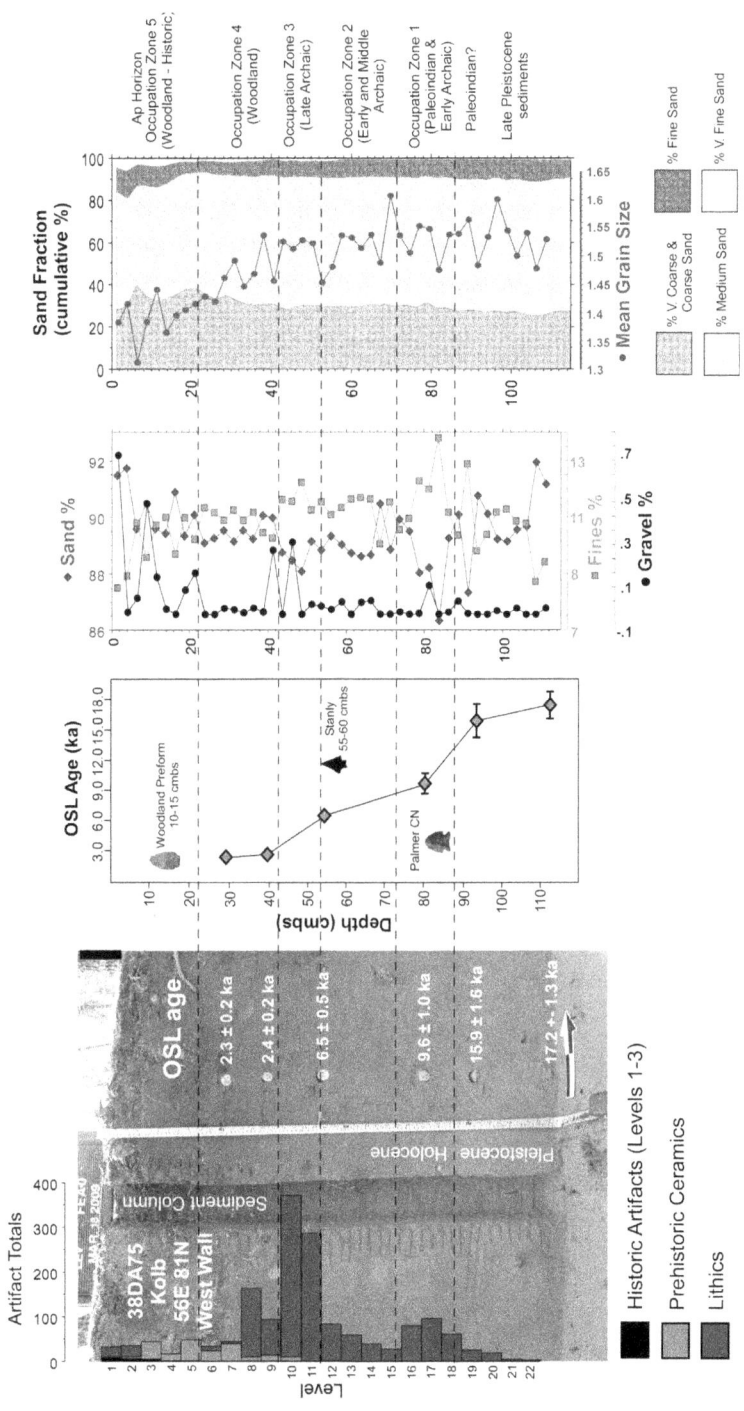

Figure 10.6. Archaeostratigraphy, sedimentological data, and single-grain OSL age-estimates for the Kolb Site (38DA75; 56E 81N) on the Pee Dee River in the Lower Coastal Plain of South Carolina.

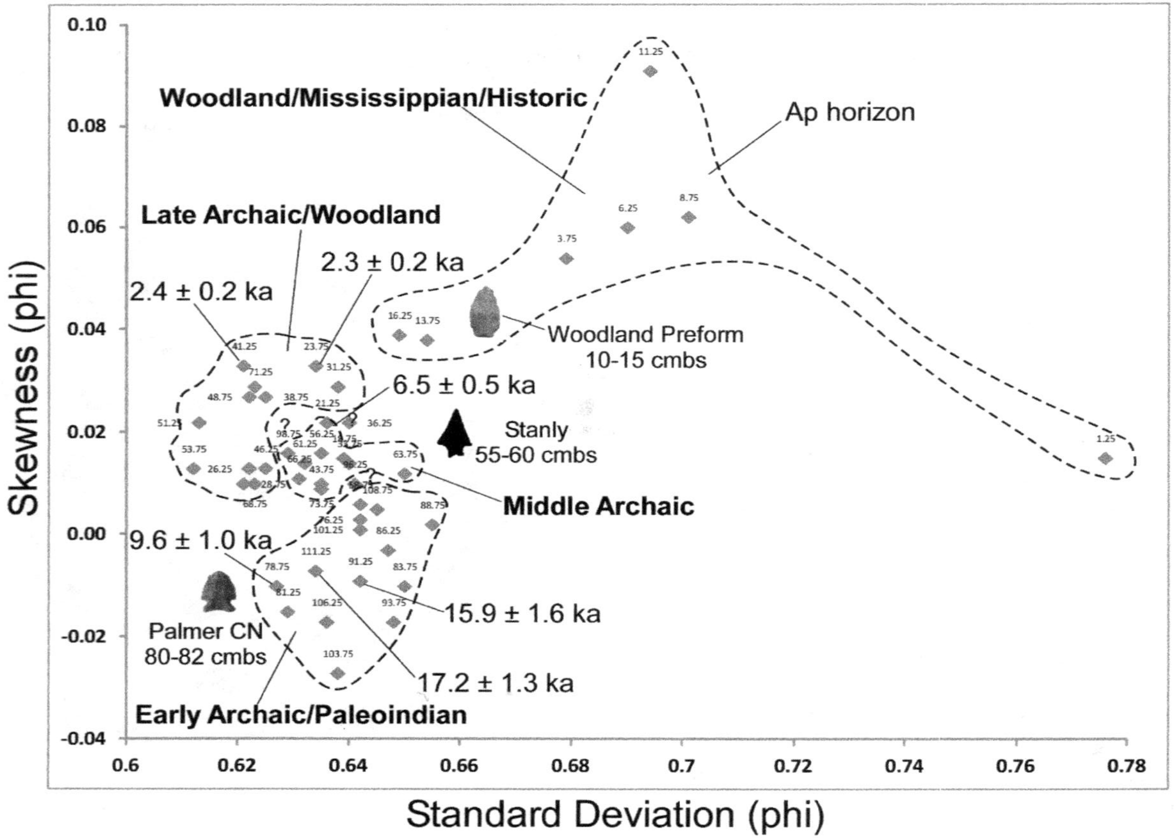

Figure 10.7. Bivariate plot of sorting and skewness (1/2 phi intervals) for sediments from Kolb (38DA75) showing sedimentological stratigraphy, generalized archaeo-stratigraphy of temporally diagnostic hafted bifaces, and singe-grain OSL age-estimates.

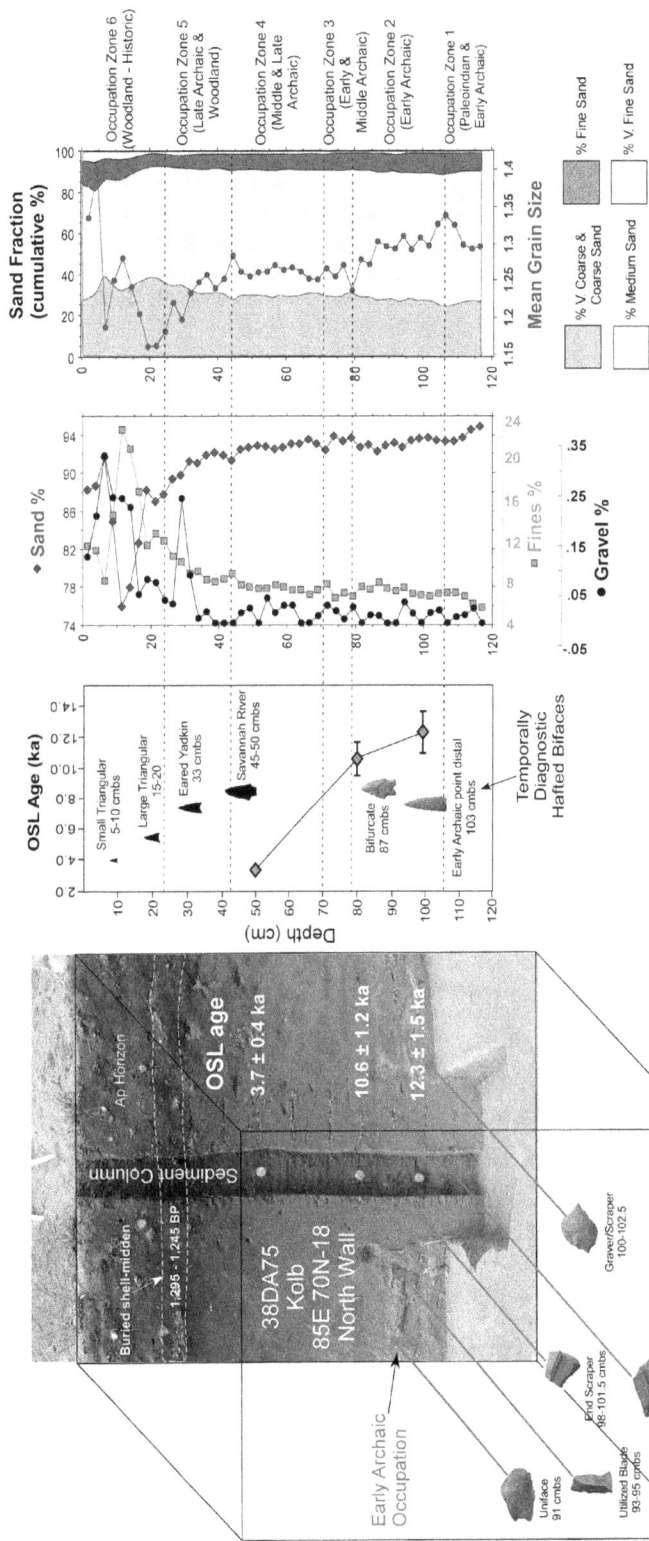

Figure 10.8. Archaeostratigraphy, sedimentological data, and single-grain OSL age estimates for the Kolb Site (38DA75; 85E 70N-18) on the Pee Dee River in the Lower Coastal Plain of South Carolina.

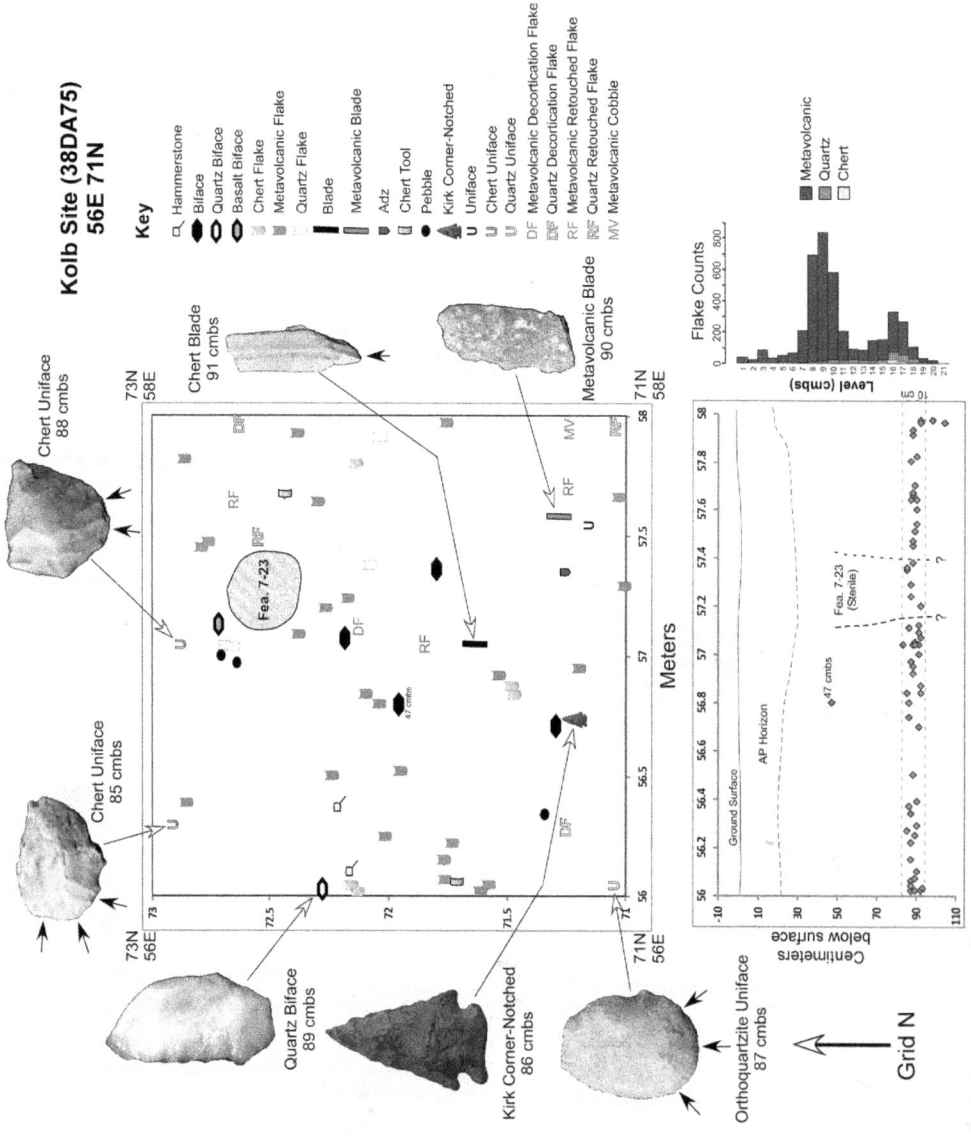

Figure 10.9. Artifact plan view and backplot for Kolb (38DA75; 56E 71N) showing piece-plotted artifacts with evidence of a buried Early Archaic occupation surface and multiple artifact density modes by level.

Fort Jackson (38RD852)

Geoarchaeological investigations at Fort Jackson have revealed evidence for periodic Holocene aeolian and colluvial deposition and archaeological site burial within an upland setting of the South Carolina Sandhills. Site 38RD842 is located on a broad upland with a gentle slope. Sandy loam underlies cover sands below 180 cm, with micaceous sand between 100 and 180 cm depth. Although other stratigraphic breaks are evident from an examination of grain-size data, multiple lines of evidence point toward stratigraphic breaks at ~70–72.5 cm and 37.5 cm below surface (Figure 10.10). The zone below 70 cm has more clay, the presence of clay lamellae, and a higher chroma than the overlying zone. Although these are primarily pedogenically produced differentiators, they might also mirror and accentuate primary lithologic differences. A low artifact count below ~70 cm suggests that the first site occupants in the early Holocene (based on an Early Archaic diagnostic point at 60–65 cm) occupied a surface at about 70 cm depth. The higher values of phosphorous and titanium and a peak in organic carbon at 67.5–70 cm (Ivester et al. 2011) indicate remnants of a stable early Holocene soil surface at about 70 cm depth. Based on a close examination of grain-size data, other potential surfaces exist at around 90 cm and 50 cm, with Late Woodland and historic occupation occurring within the recent Ap horizon in the upper 20 cm (Figure 10.11).

During the early to mid-Holocene, episodic to continuous accretion, perhaps in the form of minor localized aeolian redeposition supplemented with minor slopewash, raised the surface to about 37.5 cm, where a lithologic break occurs. This break, not obvious in the field, is manifest in several laboratory data sets: the overlying sediment (from 0 to 37.5 cm) is higher in coarse silt and has a more variable 90–63 μm fraction (Ivester et al. 2011). Sand is better sorted, more variably sorted, and more finely skewed above 37.5 cm. These indicators suggest that the top 37.5 cm of the soil profile are reworked aeolian materials. The indicators are similar to those seen in Holocene reactivated slipfaces overlying Ab horizons in riverine dunes (Ivester and Leigh 2003). It is possible that some of the reworking is due to slopewash, but the increase in coarse silt and small-scale vertical fluctuations in the coarse silt and very fine sand fractions suggest episodic deflation and aeolian transport of surrounding soil A horizons. It is more likely that the upper 37.5 cm at 38RD842 was reworked by aeolian deposition, given the landscape position—fairly level upland on a crest with

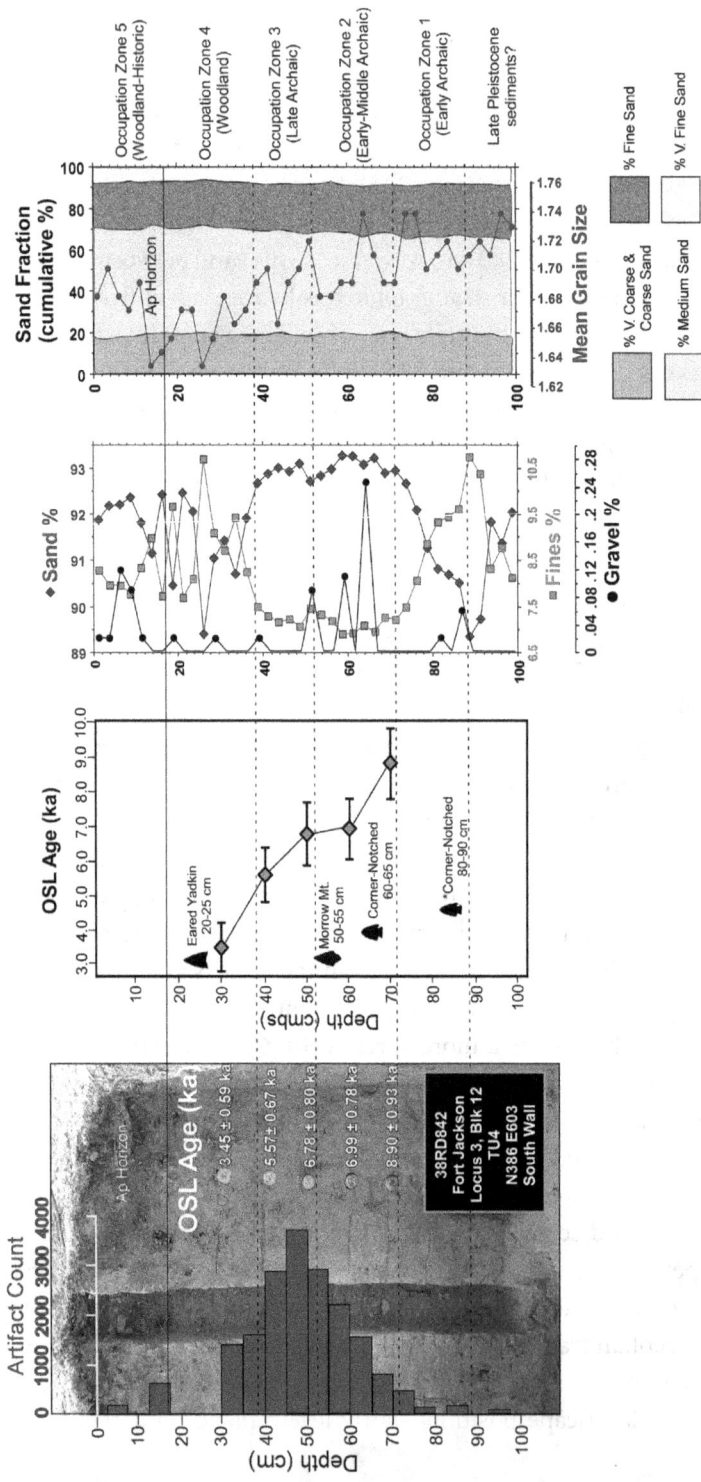

Figure 10.10. Archaeostratigraphy, sedimentological data, and OSL age estimates for site 38RD842 at Fort Jackson (Upper Coastal Plain portion of South Carolina).

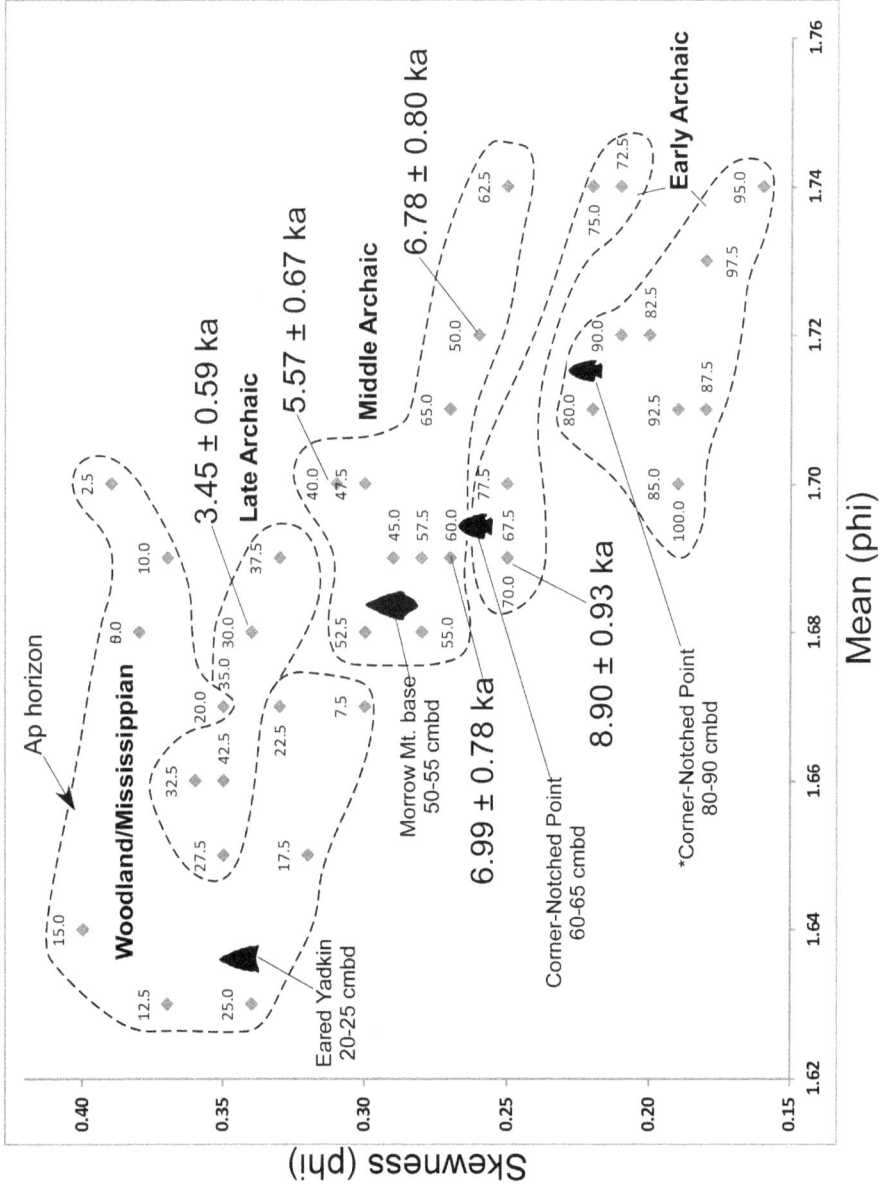

Figure 10.11. Bivariate plot of sorting and mean grain-size (1/2 phi intervals) for sediments from site 38RD842 at Fort Jackson showing sedimentological stratigraphy, generalized archaeostratigraphy of temporally diagnostic hafted bifaces, and singe-grain OSL age-estimates. OSL age-estimates provided courtesy of Audrey Dawson (project director).

little gradient for slopewash or runoff. In any case, the reworking could have been small scale and would not require widespread denudation of the landscape.

Single-grain luminescence dates (Figure 10.10) acquired for the site provide age estimates in proper chronostratigraphic order, ages consistent with temporally diagnostic artifacts, and evidence for a period of more rapid sedimentation during the most intensive occupation of the site during the Middle Archaic. The obvious question is whether or not this enhanced sedimentation is due to anthropogenic disturbance (e.g., trampling and removal of vegetation), changes in climate (e.g., drought), periods of enhanced fire, or some combination of all three. Although sedimentation processes are interpreted as primarily aeolian, a colluvial contribution may be evident from several very slight increases in very fine gravel in Zone 2 during the Early to Middle Archaic.

Carolina Bays

Carolina bays are shallow, oriented (NW–SE in the Carolinas), elliptically shaped lakes occurring in large numbers throughout the SACP (Johnson 1942; Kaczorowski 1977; Prouty 1952; Raisz 1934; Thom 1970). Carolina bays often have elevated sand rims composed of fine sand to gravel-sized sediments. Geological evidence of Carolina bays in the Central Savannah River Area (CSRA) indicate that these sediments were deposited by high-energy, lacustrine (lake) processes involving shoreface (water-laid) and aeolian (wind-blown) sedimentation (Brooks et al. 1996; Grant et al. 1998; Kaczorowski 1977). Geoarchaeological investigations at 38AK469 (Flamingo Bay), 38BR1319/1320 (Frierson Bay), and 38AL246 (Johns Bay) have provided evidence for site burial and archaeostratigraphic integrity with temporally diagnostic artifacts in proper chronostratigraphic order, buried cultural features, and single-grain OSL dates consistent with episodic burial (Moore et al. 2012) (Figure 10.12).

Site 38AK469 is located on the eastern sand rim of Flamingo Bay, a Carolina bay on the U.S. Department of Energy's (DOE) Savannah River Site (SRS) in the Upper Coastal Plain of South Carolina. Analysis of archaeostratigraphic data from Flamingo Bay indicates a shallow stratigraphic sequence with Mississippian and Woodland occupations within the historic plow zone (a plow zone significantly deflated by as much as 30 cm through historic land use practices), Late Archaic (Savannah River) occupations at the base or just below the plow zone, followed by Middle Archaic (Guilford and Morrow Mountain), Early Archaic (Kirk Corner-Notched), and

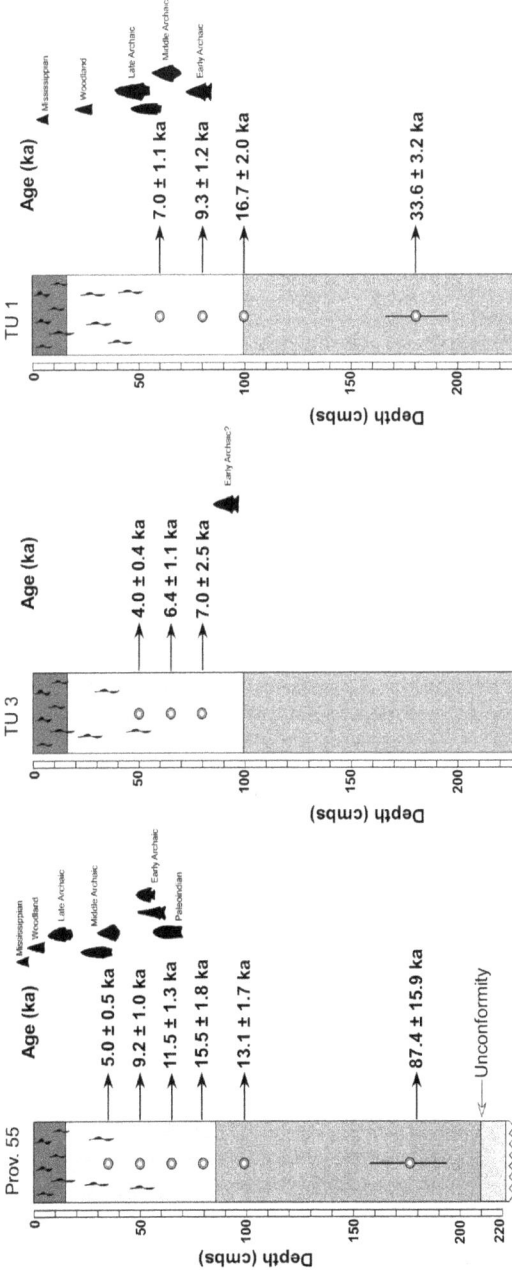
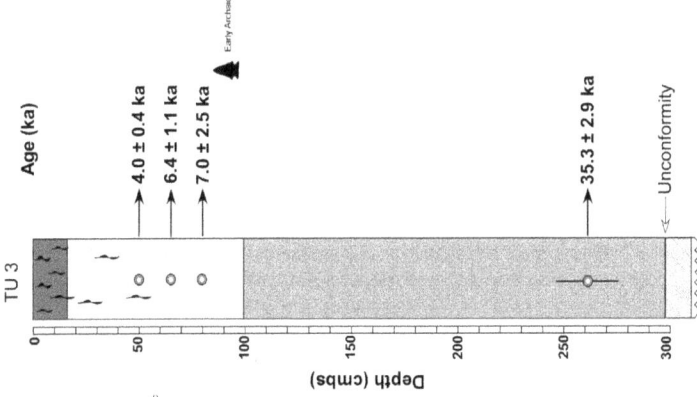
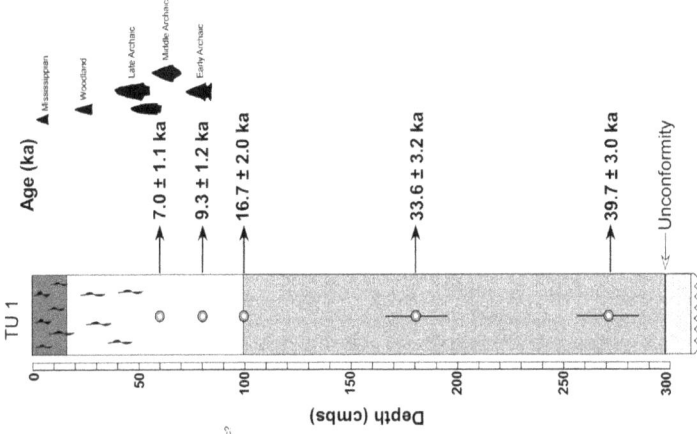

Figure 10.12. Lithostratigraphy, OSL geochronology, and generalized archaeostratigraphy for Flamingo Bay (38AK469), Frierson Bay (38BR1319 and 38BR1320), and Johns Bay (38AL246) in the Central Savannah River Area (CSRA) of South Carolina.

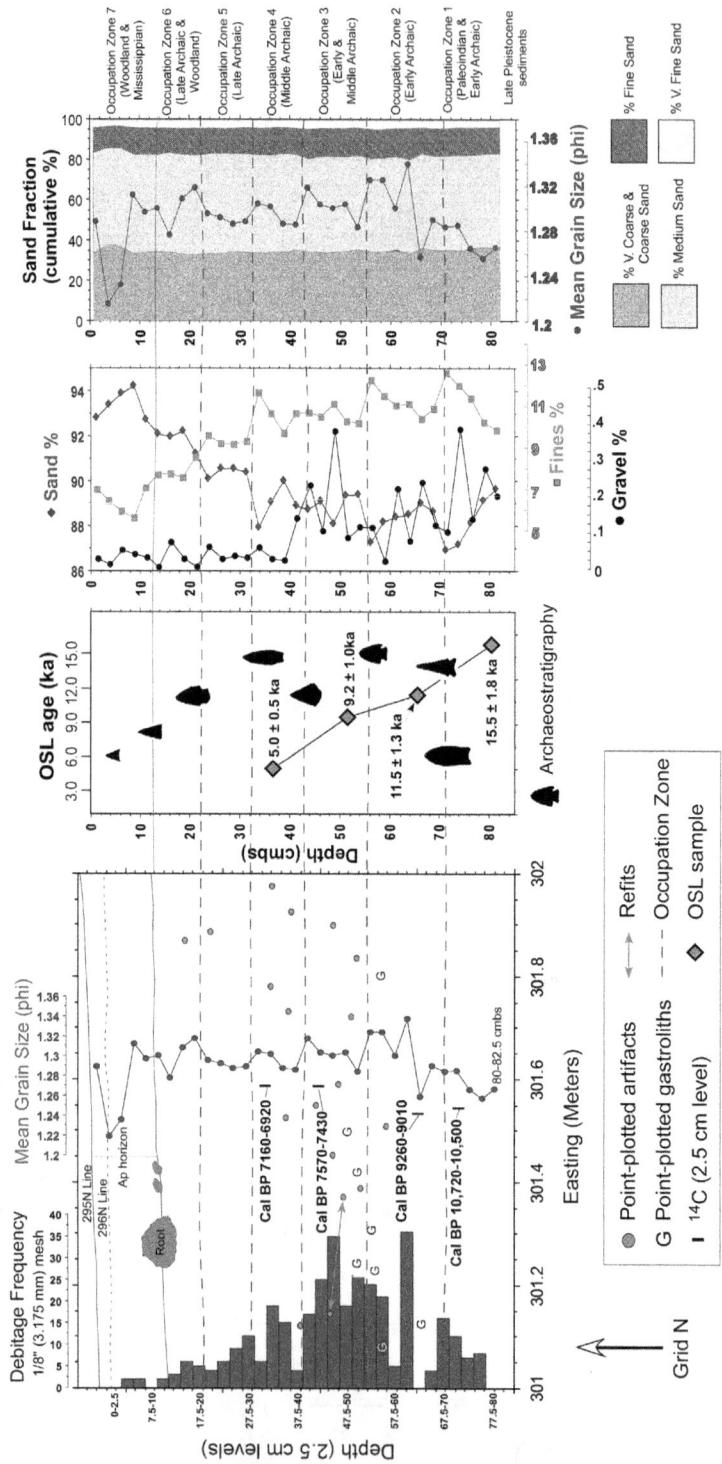

Figure 10.13. Backplot for Flamingo Bay (38AK469, PROV. 62) showing piece-plotted artifacts, temporally diagnostic hafted bifaces, artifact refits, 2.5 cm excavation artifact frequency data, general level AMS dates, and single-grain OSL age-estimates.

Paleoindian (Clovis) occupations (Moore and Brooks 2012) typically between 50 and 70 cm below surface (Figure 10.13).

An artifact refitting analysis was conducted for Flamingo Bay (38AK469), due to the extensive recovery and piece-plotting of broken cobbles, hammer stones, fire-cracked rock, numerous broken flakes, cores, and biface fragments. Out of a total of 267 piece-plotted artifacts, 13 refit groups were found. Average vertical displacement for these refits is only 5 cm, even though two refit pairs were vertically displaced 8 and 19 cm respectively. These displaced samples appear to be associated with a Middle Archaic pit feature and are vertically displaced by the activities of mid-Holocene hunter-gatherers at the site, rather than by post-depositional bioturbation or biomantle processes. Minimal vertical displacement of artifacts is consistent with an interpretation of archaeological site burial through periodic aeolian and colluvial or slopewash processes (Brooks et al. 1996, 2010).

In addition to the analysis of refit data, an analysis of 2.5-cm excavation data (collected with 3.2-mm mesh) has revealed archaeostratigraphic data that are both multimodal and discontinuous in vertical distribution. Data on lithic debitage frequency at 2.5-cm levels reveal five peak density modes with levels between devoid or nearly devoid of debitage (Figure 10.13). These data reveal microstratigraphic units masked by traditional arbitrary 10 cm excavation levels and suggest that archaeological integrity is relatively intact. Analysis of close-interval sand fraction data indicate *multisequal* soil stratigraphic zones that correlate well with artifact modes (Figure 10.13). Bivariate analysis of grain-size data also reveals distinct sedimentological units by depth that reflect cumulative periods of aeolian and colluvial sedimentation (Figure 10.14).

Luminescence dating is perhaps the most critical for establishing a landform geochronology. With respect to Flamingo Bay (38AK469), single-grain OSL dates ($n = 5$) provide minimum age model estimates (Galbraith and Roberts 2012) consistent with the observed archaeostratigraphy at the site. General-level AMS dates on carbonized nutshell also provide ages in broad agreement with the archaeology and with OSL ages (Table 10.2).

Pen Point (38BR383)

Pen Point is a stratified overbank alluvial site located on the U.S. Department of Energy's Savannah River Site in Barnwell County, South Carolina. The site sits on the edge of the first terrace of the Savannah River at its confluence with Pen Branch, a tributary of the Savannah River. Excavations by the Savannah River Archaeological Research Program (SRARP) in the

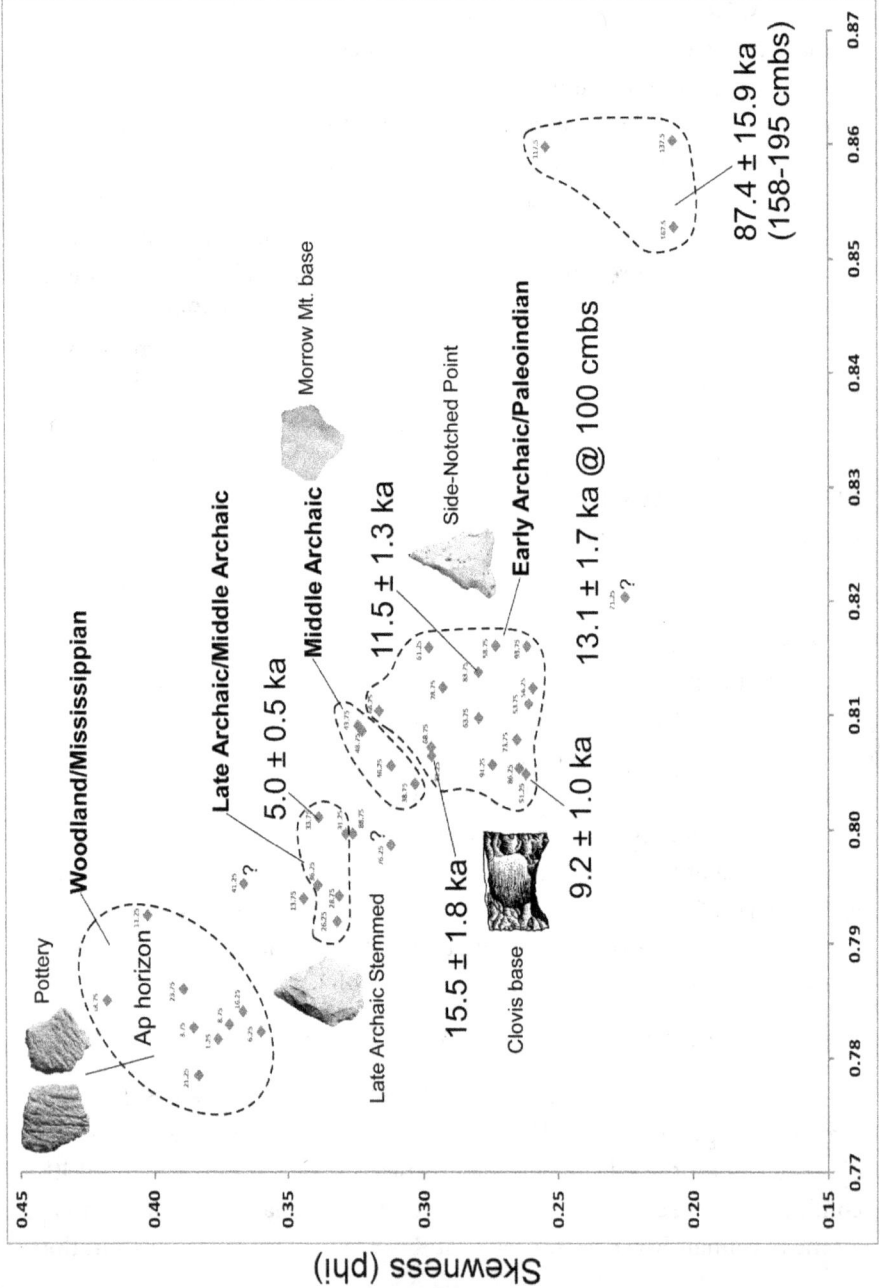

Figure 10.14. Bivariate plot of sorting and skewness (1/2 phi intervals) for sediments from Flamingo Bay (38AK469; PROV. 55) showing sedimentological stratigraphy, generalized archaeostratigraphy of temporally diagnostic hafted bifaces, and single-grain OSL age-estimates.

early to mid-1980s recovered over 90,000 artifacts, with clear evidence of archaeological stratigraphy from Woodland through Early Archaic contained within more than 1 m of alluvial sand (Brooks and Sassaman 1990) (Figure 10.15). "Pen Point contains two discrete early to mid-Holocene density modes within a distribution of low-density remains above, below, and between the observed modes" (Brooks and Sassaman 1990). Although excavated before the widespread use of luminescence dating, Pen Point revealed a wide range of Woodland and Archaic diagnostic points in correct chronostratigraphic order. In addition, a thick lens of lithic debris (Feature 14) was recovered that consisted of an intensive and laterally extensive lithic reduction event associated with numerous early Late Archaic Allendale hafted bifaces (Sassaman et al. 1990). Refitting analysis revealed numerous horizontal refits, with clear evidence of a rapidly buried occupation surface. This inference was supported by examination of close-interval sedimentology data revealing the presence of four discrete packages of fining-upward sediments indicating site burial by multiple large flood events (Brooks and Colquhoun 1991; Brooks and Sassaman 1990) (Figure 10.15). Artifacts were found to cluster in and around the tops of each of these fining-upward sequences. Estimates for periods of accretion and stability were calculated based on the position of numerous temporally diagnostic hafted bifaces and generally show increasingly longer periods of surface exposure and stability (from a few centuries to several millennia) before subsequent burial during periods of more active flooding (Brooks and Sassaman 1990).

Discussion

Sediment transport, and hence surface burial, is dependent upon an available sediment supply and a source of energy, usually variations of wind and water, depending on depositional environment. Away from the coast and tidal influence, deposition via water may be broadly divided into fluvial, lacustrine, and slopewash depositional environments, whereas deposition via wind (aeolian) may result in dunal, sand-sheet, or often hummocky source-bordering aeolian deposits. The morphology of aeolian deposits is conditioned by wind strength and direction(s), and the nature and structure of the vegetation cover (Markewich and Markewich 1994).

Sediment availability is usually dependent on vegetation cover, or relative lack thereof. During climatic intervals involving cooler, drier conditions, vegetation groundcover is typically sparse, and hence the sediments more available. Sands are more erodible than the cohesive silts and clays,

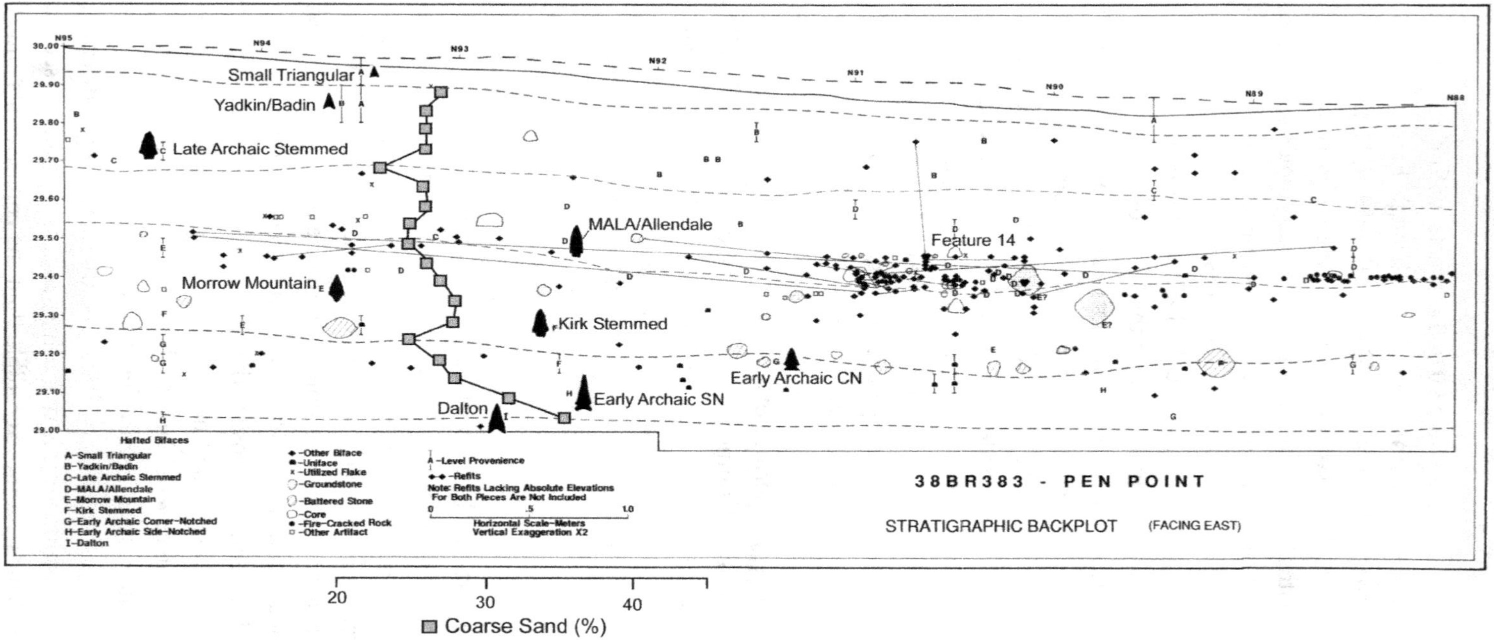

Figure 10.15. Backplot for Pen Point (38BR383) on the Savannah River in South Carolina showing piece-plotted artifacts, temporally diagnostic hafted bifaces, artifact refits, grain-size data, and interpreted fining-upward sequences representing the tops of major occupation surfaces.

making them generally more transportable as well. During more stable, warm, moist intervals, sediments tend to be vegetation-bound and less susceptible to erosion, and hence transport and deposition; however, extreme events can provide catastrophic exceptions.

Luminescence dating of shallow Quaternary-age sediments is becoming commonplace and is beginning to provide evidence needed for understanding the timing and nature of landform aggradation processes in the SACP (e.g., Feathers, Rhodes, et al. 2006; Waters et al. 2009). Below, we discuss the application of OSL dating in shallow sandy sites and evaluate the evidence presented thus far for regional-scale site formation processes likely operating on millennial time-scales and in response to regional if not global perturbations to the climate system.

OSL Dating of Sandy Sites

Given the increasing use and importance of OSL dating for estimating burial age of sediments within sandy archaeological sites, we would be remiss to not briefly discuss the method along with potential issues with interpreting OSL data. Generally speaking, OSL provides a measure of the amount of time sediments have been buried or the time since they were last exposed to sunlight (Huntley et al. 1985; Wintle 2008). During depositional events, exposure to light releases any acquired luminescence signal. After burial, sand grains begin to accumulate energy from natural background ionizing radiation (i.e., paleodose) within electron traps or defects in the crystalline structure of the sand grain. Paleodose is measured in the lab by artificially stimulating the acquired luminescence signal and calibrating it against laboratory irradiation. This produces an estimate of the paleodose, called the equivalent dose (De), which is then divided by the dose rate to determine time of burial (Feathers 2003). The goal of luminescence geochronology is to establish the timing of burial events (Aitken 1998).

OSL dating utilizes various mathematical age models to estimate burial age (Galbraith and Roberts 2012). Studies have shown that OSL ages in sandy sites may be significantly affected by post-depositional processes that create a mismatch between OSL age-estimates and those indicated by temporally diagnostic artifacts (Bateman et al. 2003; Bateman et al. 2007; Boulter et al. 2006; Feathers, Holliday, et al. 2006; Feathers, Rhodes, et al. 2006; Frederick et al. 2002). We note that in many cases, use of the minimum age model (MAM) has provided geochronologies consistent with those interpreted from the archaeological record (e.g., Feathers, Rhodes, et al. 2006; Moore and Daniel 2011; Moore et al. 2012; Rink, Dunbar, Doran et al. 2012; Rink et al. 2013). The consistency with which the use of MAM provides ages in agreement with the archaeostratigraphy in sandy sites may be related to the likely preferential movement of individual sand grains by ants and other burrowing animals. Recent experimental work by Rink et al. (2013) has shown that ants preferentially move older grains upward at a higher rate than they move younger grains downward through the solum. These older grains may produce age overestimates, particularly for single-aliquot OSL age estimates based on a weighted mean or central age model estimate (e.g., Wilder et al. 2007), or even when using MAM (Feathers and Tunnicliff 2011).

Evaluation of appropriate age models for archaeologically stratified sandy sites should take advantage of the temporal markers provided by particular artifacts (i.e., hafted bifaces and pottery), as well as where you have evidence of occupation floors, radiocarbon dates, and refit data indicating minimal vertical movement of larger artifacts. Single-grain (rather than single-aliquot) OSL dating should also be utilized if possible to provide age estimates of shallow and stratigraphically complex sandy sites (e.g., Feathers, Rhodes, et al. 2006). Single-grain OSL is preferable because it collects De data on many individual grains rather than averaging De values for clusters of grains, as is done with single-aliquot dating. Analysis of single-grain OSL data allows a more refined assessment of post-depositional processes, including distinguishing various populations of grains that represent upward or downward displacement, exhumation and reburial of zeroed grains, and/or the presence of partially bleached grains (Rink et al. 2013). This allows for the evaluation of post-depositional processes and the potential to mitigate the effects of limited bioturbation for determination of true burial age of the sediments and the artifacts contained within (Bateman et al. 2003; Bateman et al. 2007; Boulter et al. 2006; Rink et al. 2013).

Analysis of single-grain OSL data for sites in Florida has shown that the use of OSL age estimates (without consideration of the youngest grain population) consistently overestimates the age of buried Paleoindian and Archaic-bearing sediments, while evaluation of the youngest grains produced ages in good agreement with the expected age (Rink, Dunbar, Doran et al. 2012). This finding is consistent with MAM estimates for Cactus Hill (Feathers, Holliday, et al. 2006), sandy sites on the Tar River (Daniel et al. 2013; Moore 2009b; Moore and Daniel 2011), Flamingo Bay (Moore et al. 2012), and elsewhere (e.g., Feathers, Rhodes et al. 2006; Rink, Dunbar,

Doran et al. 2012, 2013) with the preferential upward movement of sand grains but not artifacts.

Linkages with the Regional and Global Climate Records

As a result of the analysis of several high-resolution regional sedimento-logical (e.g., Willard et al. 2005) and stalagmite (e.g., Springer et al. 2008) records, we now know that our "stable" Holocene climate has been punctuated with periods of rapid and synchronous change, including rapid changes in temperature, available moisture, and vegetation (e.g., Alley et al. 1997; Bard 2002; Bond et al. 1997; Bond et al. 1999; Bond et al. 2001; Cronin et al. 2005; Kidder 2006; Mayewski et al. 2004; O'Brien et al. 2003; Overpeck and Webb 2000; Springer et al. 2008; Steig 1999; Viau et al. 2002; Viau et al. 2006; Willard et al. 2005). Recent studies suggest periods of abrupt climate change during the Holocene, including departures in temperature and precipitation with millennial-scale cyclicity that operates independent of glacial/interglacial climate (Bond et al. 1997).

For example, extremely high-resolution isotopic and pollen data from Chesapeake Bay (Cronin et al. 2005; Willard et al. 2005), stalagmite records from West Virginia (Springer et al. 2008), and analysis of multiple global climate proxies (Bond et al. 1997; Bond et al. 1999; Bond et al. 2001; Mayewski et al. 2004) indicate that at least nine significant millennial-scale rapid climate change (RCC) events have occurred since the start of the Holocene (ca. 11,700 calendar years B.P.) (Figure 10.16). Specifically, these RCC events appear to be represented by the onset of colder and dryer conditions (i.e., Bond events) and are similar to, but less severe than, Dansgaard-Oeschger and Heinrich events recorded for the glacial period (Bond et al. 1997). These abrupt shifts in climate during the Holocene correspond to ice-rafting events recorded in North Atlantic marine sediments (Bond et al. 1997). Marine sediments preserve a record of ice-rafted debris in the form of lithic grains, including volcanic glass and hematite-stained grains (Bond et al. 2001). Timing of RCC events has been well established by analysis of multiple global proxy records of climate at approximately 2,800–2000- and 1,500-year intervals (Mayewski et al. 2004).

Based on an analysis of more than 3,000 ^{14}C dates from 700 different pollen diagrams for North America, Viau et al. (2002) argue that millennial-scale climate oscillations caused rapid and synchronous changes to vegetation composition across North America and that these changes are synchronous with changes in marine and ice-core records. Causes for

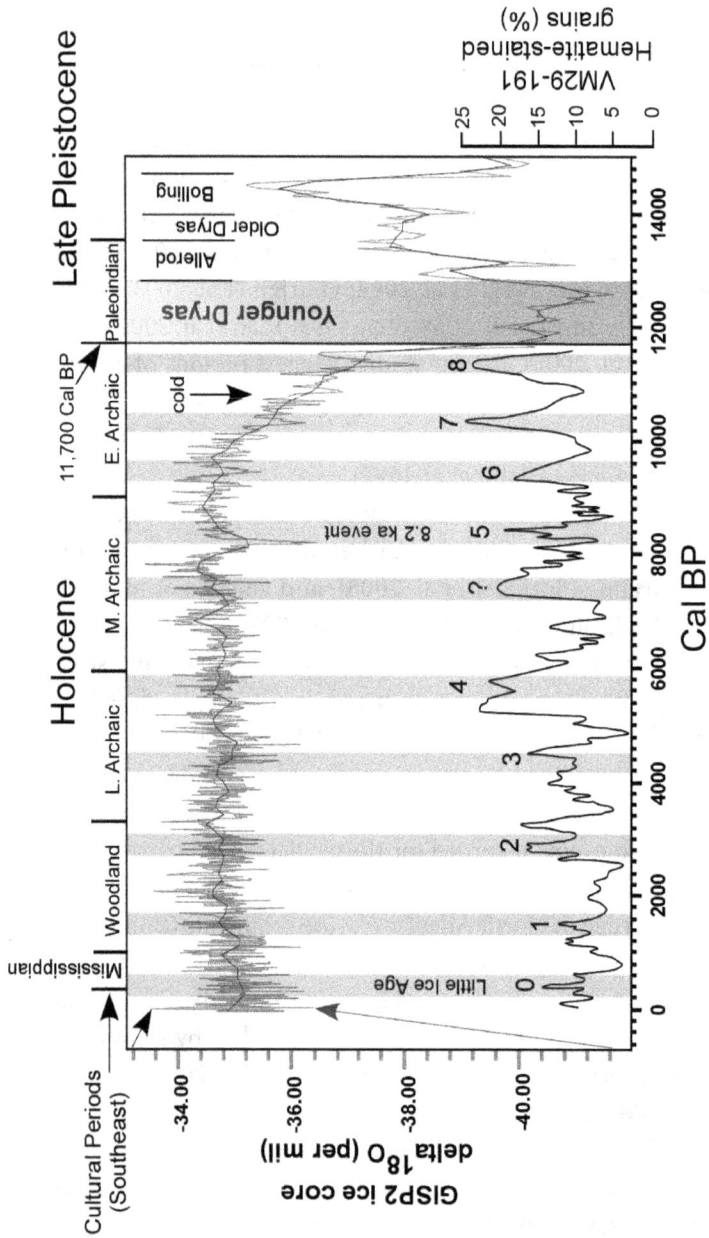

Figure 10.16. Periods of rapid climate change or Bond Events (light-colored bars) recorded for the Holocene as indicated by the abundance of hematite-stained lithic grains in marine cores from the North Atlantic (Bond et al. 1997, 1999, 2001). Also, shown is the GISP2 Oxygen Isotope curve for the last 15 kya and calibrated calendar-year intervals for cultural periods in the Southeast during the Holocene. GISP2 delta ^{18}O ice core data was provided by the National Snow and Ice Data Center, University of Colorado, Boulder and the WDC-A for Paleoclimatology, National Geophysical Data Center, Boulder, Colorado (Grootes et al. 1993).

these millennial-scale RCC events have been attributed to variability in solar irradiance and resulting atmospheric and ocean current reorganization during solar minima (Bond et al. 2001; Perry and Hsu 2000; Springer et al. 2008). North American droughts may have been brought about by weakened north/south pressure gradients and subsequent changes to the jet stream (Springer et al. 2008). This reorganization of pressure gradients over North America is attributed to cooling in both the Pacific and the Atlantic oceans during periods of reduced solar output (Springer et al. 2008; Viau et al. 2002).

Interestingly, reduced solar output (e.g., solar minima) is associated with every major drift-ice event (i.e., Bond event) recorded in North Atlantic marine sediments (Bond et al. 1997). Starting with the Little Ice Age (LIA), nine Bond events are indicated for the Holocene: 0) ~500, 1) ~1400, 2) 2800, 3) 4300, 4) 5900, 5) 8200, 6) 9500, 7) 10,300, and 8) 11,100 cal B.P. (Bond et al. 1997; Bond et al. 2001) (Figure 10.16). Another likely Bond event occurred at ca. 7500, based on analyses of marine core data, but was not reported by Bond et al. (1997, 2001). Episodes of reduced rainfall (i.e., megadroughts) are also indicated by high-resolution Sr/Ca and $\delta^{13}C$ analysis of stalagmites from West Virginia (Springer et al. 2008). These data indicate multiple time-scales and periodicities but with a dominant, 1,200-year periodicity, very similar to 1,500-year Bond events. The last ice-rafting event occurred during the LIA from 650–150 calendar years B.P. and is coincident with the Maunder solar minimum (Bond et al. 2001). Other researchers have found that solar forcing of 1,000- and 2,500-year oscillations is but one component of the 1,500-year ocean-forcing cycle (Debret et al. 2007). In this scenario, marine sediments, ice core studies, pollen analysis, and isotopic studies of sediments and stalagmites are reflecting the combined forcing from variation in solar output and oceanic circulation.

Several questions seem pertinent to this discussion regarding climate proxies, regional geomorphology, and archaeological site burial in the SACP: 1) are sedimentological, archaeostratigraphic, and chronometric signatures of climate instability preserved within relict sand bodies?; 2) are periods of landform aggradation linked with rapid climate change events?; 3) can we correlate depositional events and periods of rapid climate change given post-depositional disturbances common to shallow sandy sites?; and 4) what role does anthropogenic disturbance play in the site formation histories of these sites?

The linkages between periods of climate stress, sediment mobility, and site formation are complex. For example, periods of drought and increased fire may be followed by large floods where sediment (freed from vegetation) may more easily be transported by water to elevated terrace locations. It follows that vegetation removal through periods of drought and fire also increases the likelihood of significant slopewash events. The episodic nature of archaeological site burial in the SACP suggests a possible link between depositional events and rapid climate change events recorded in global and regional-scale climate proxy records. Combined OSL and radiocarbon dates from multiple sites along the SACP correspond closely to periods of climatic instability and suggest a possible link to pervasive and episodic climate change over the last 13,000 years. Along the Tar River in North Carolina, OSL dating has provided ages consistent with periods of rapid climate change corresponding to Bond events 4 through 8 and the Younger Dryas (Daniel et al. 2013; Moore 2009b; Moore and Daniel 2010; Moore and Daniel 2011).

Depositional processes for the sites discussed here are likely driven in part by *penecontemporaneous* hydrological and vegetation changes in response to periods of rapid climate change and ecosystem stress, and may be related to millennial-scale climatic cyclicity (e.g., RCC events), including periods of enhanced fire recorded in regional and global climate proxy records (Marlon et al. 2009; Viau et al. 2002). For example, at Barber Creek and Squires Ridge, grain-size analysis indicates five or six major depositional events since the Late Pleistocene (Moore 2009b; Moore and Daniel 2011) (Figure 10.5). Evidence from the Kolb Site and Flamingo Bay shows similar multisequal patterns (Figures 10.7, 10.11, and 10.14). Perhaps not coincidentally, this number of depositional events corresponds favorably with the number of RCC events indicated by global and regional climate records for the Holocene (e.g., Mayewski et al. 2004; Willard et al. 2005).

Significant and synchronous vegetation changes associated with Bond events (Viau et al. 2002) would have been conducive for sediment mobility through a variety of mechanisms. Aeolian sedimentation and deposition of flood deposits along river terraces, high-energy lacustrine processes at Carolina Bay sand rims, and periods of active slopewash and aeolian sedimentation in upland settings would likely have been facilitated by the onset of cooler and dryer or warmer and wetter climate events. In this scenario, depositional processes occur episodically, with pulses of sedimentation occurring primarily during these rapid and very short (i.e., three-to-five-century) periods of climatic disequilibrium. In many cases, maximum temperature and moisture deviations lasted less than a century (Alley et al.

1997). Grain-size data suggest that Late Pleistocene (i.e., Younger Dryas) and early Holocene events (e.g., 8.2 kya event) were higher amplitude. On the other hand, the lack of thick, archaeologically sterile levels indicates that individual depositional episodes, particularly during the mid-to-late Holocene, were centimeter-scale events. Minor displacement of artifacts, both above and below buried surfaces, during periods of landform stability also accounts for the lack of sterile deposits between shallowly stratified occupation surfaces. As demonstrated by 2.5-cm-level data from Flamingo Bay, arbitrary excavation levels typically used by archaeologists (usually 10 cm) likely miss these very thin sterile or nearly sterile layers representing more active periods of sedimentation (Figure 10.13).

Although the most significant periods of deposition appear to coincide with the Late Pleistocene and early Holocene, it is interesting to note that as much as 50 cm or more of deposition has occurred since the mid-Holocene at many of the sites discussed in this chapter. For example, well-stratified Middle Archaic through Woodland archaeological sequences and grain-size data at both Squires Ridge and Barber Creek on the Tar River, Fort Jackson, Kolb, and Pen Point indicate multiple periods of accretion over the last ~8,000 years. Deviations in grain size and trends (i.e., coarsening or fining upward) indicate only slightly smaller depositional packages for the mid-to-late Holocene compared to the early Holocene.

Coupled with the likely regional influence of climate events on archaeological site burial are the significant and spatially variable anthropogenic effects on landforms that include everything from intentional (or accidental) burning, trampling and resultant reduction of vegetation, and pit digging and subsurface storage or cooking. Increased use of fire by hunter-gatherers (e.g., Abrams and Nowacki 2008; Davis and Stevenson 2007; Patterson and Sassaman 1988; Taylor et al. 2011) during the mid-Holocene for driving game animals or clearing forests may also have been a factor in removing vegetation and freeing up sediments. These anthropogenic activities may make it difficult in some cases to infer sedimentological, archaeostratigraphic, and chronometric signatures of climate instability preserved within relict sand bodies.

While post-depositional processes such as bioturbation do not appear to be the primary burial mechanism, particularly for riverine sites, minor artifact displacement due to bioturbation is common (Figure 10.17). In some areas, bioturbation is extensive, with indication of significant ground disturbance and/or long-term processes that rejuvenate sediments (Thulman

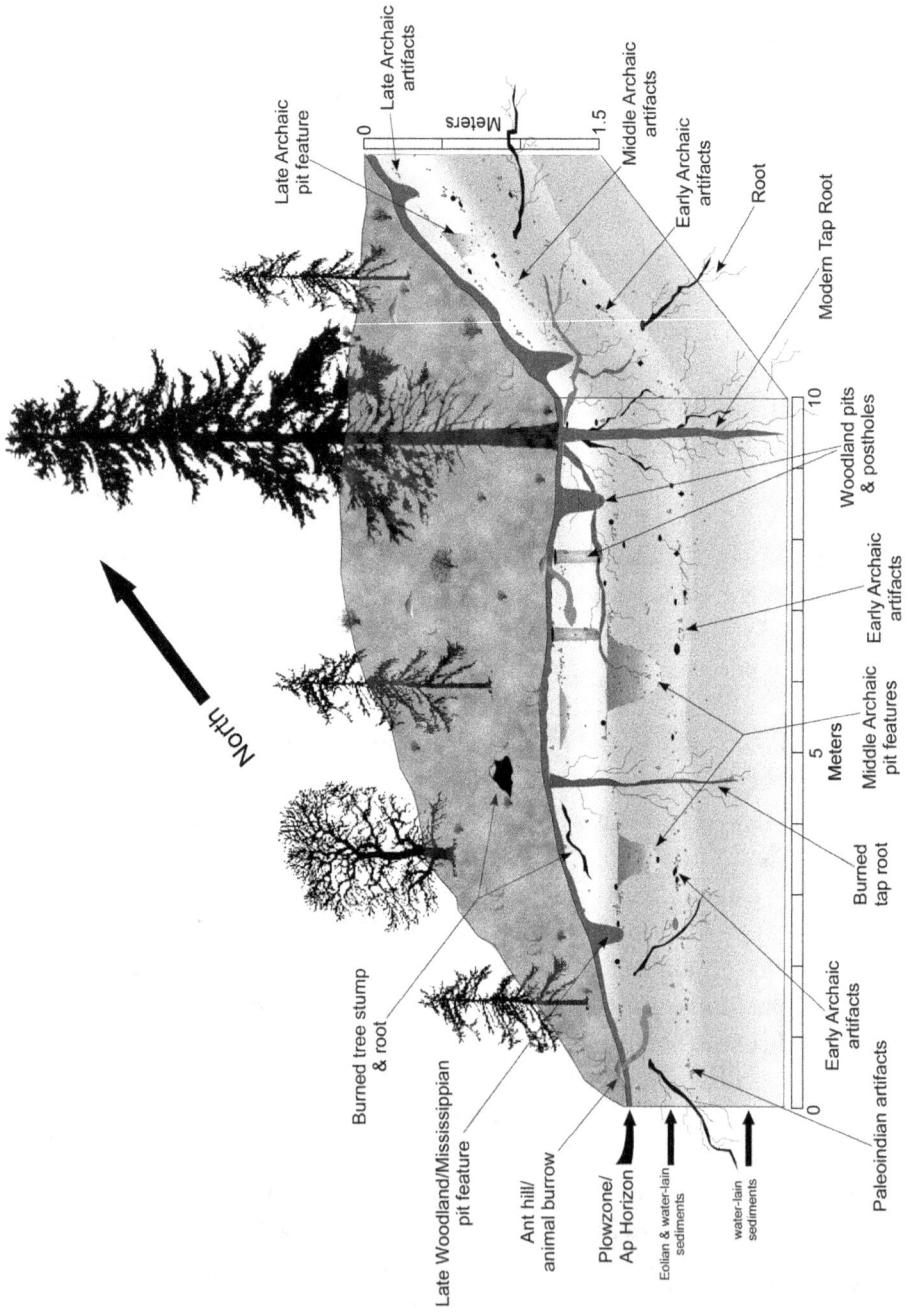

Figure 10.17. Generalized model showing likely soil, site formation, and taphonomic processes active within shallowly stratified sandy sites common in the South Atlantic Coastal Plain.

2012a). That said, sedimentological, archaeological, and chronometric age dating suggest that many SACP sites have particularly good archaeological stratigraphy, with relatively shallow but intact archaeological sequences in correct chronostratigraphic order. Polymodal artifact distributions, cobble clusters, pottery and lithic distributions, the vertical position of temporally diagnostic projectile points, close-interval grain-size data, and chronometric (OSL and ^{14}C) dating all suggest direct burial of occupation surfaces over the course of the Holocene. Biomantling processes are undoubtedly at work but in many cases appear to reflect translocation of sediments, not necessarily artifacts themselves (Rink et al. 2013; cf. Thulman 2012a). Occasional inversions of either temporally diagnostic artifacts or dates are to be expected but do not negate the broader pattern.

From our experience, the most pervasive post-depositional and post-occupational disturbances are anthropogenic in nature. These disturbances are from: 1) site inhabitants themselves; 2) historic/modern activities (i.e., land clearing and plowing); and 3) archaeological excavations in gross, arbitrary levels due to no observable depositional stratigraphy. The latter results in cross-cutting multiple surfaces due to small-scale (vertical and lateral) burial events. Thus, cm-scale excavation levels and/or piece-plotting are essential. This is shown most clearly by the experimental 2.5-cm-excavation-level data from Flamingo Bay where generally unimodal distributions of artifacts (from arbitrary 10-cm-level data) reveal themselves as multimodal and discontinuous when excavated in much thinner excavation levels. Another feature common to many of the sites discussed here is the presence of two or three stratigraphic zones or surfaces with multiple occupations/components, often with dense artifact concentrations (e.g., Squires Ridge, Kolb, Pen Point) (Figures 10.4, 10.6, 10.9, 10.13, and 10.15). These zones likely represent periods of long-term stable surfaces followed by more frequent sedimentation events.

Extensive excavations at Cactus Hill (McAvoy and McAvoy 1997), the Barber Creek and Squires Ridge sites on the Tar River (Daniel 2002a, 2002b; Daniel et al. 2008; Daniel et al. 2013; Moore 2009a, 2009b; Moore and Daniel 2011), and recent geoarchaeological investigations by the authors of this chapter at Kolb (38DA75), Fort Jackson (38RD842), Carolina bays in the CSRA, and earlier work at Pen Point (38BR383) by Brooks and Sassaman (1990), suggest that stratified sandy sites are common in the SACP and are formed through a mosaic of processes. These processes include aeolian, fluvial, and slopewash accretion, periods of deflation, long-term stable surfaces, and post-depositional processes such as bioturbation (e.g., Feathers, Holliday et al. 2006; Feathers, Rhodes, et al. 2006; MacPhail and McAvoy 2008; Wagner and McAvoy 2004) and anthroturbation. In particular geomorphic settings, site burial by up to 1 m of sand is typical of sites within the SACP with compressed but generally stratified cultural deposits spanning the Late Pleistocene and Holocene. OSL ages consistent with observed archaeostratigraphy confirm this general pattern.

Conclusions

The data presented here demonstrate that periods of sedimentation and archaeological site burial are pervasive features within particular geomorphic settings of the SACP. These data include evidence of intact archaeological occupation surfaces or zones, single-grain OSL and radiocarbon chronologies consistent with each other and with temporally diagnostic artifacts, artifact refit data showing minimal vertical displacement, and close-interval sedimentology indicating multisequal sedimentological facies. In fact, multiple data sets are consistent with a regional signature of landform aggradation with emplacement of approximately 1 m of sediments burying sites along stream terraces, slopewash environments, within Carolina bay sand rims, and source-bordering dunes. We recognize the role of bioturbation (particularly anthroturbation) as an overprint of these processes that may blur or distort our ability to interpret the archaeological record or link periods of sedimentation to high-resolution geologic proxies for climate change. Nevertheless, years of careful archaeological and geoarchaeological research have made several observations worth summarizing again here.

Archaeostratigraphic, sedimentological, and chronometric data suggest archaeological sites are buried/stratified within relict sand bodies with similar depths of burial for temporally diagnostic artifacts region-wide.

- Sedimentation processes have occurred episodically during the Holocene with subsequent burial and preservation of archaeologically stratified zones. These zones have archaeostratigraphic integrity and preserve a matrix of sediments, artifacts, botanicals, calcined bone, and carbon (i.e., wood charcoal and charred nutshell) that are recognizable and represent various and often distinct cultural, biological, and sedimentological inputs through time.
- Conflation of various archaeological components is common due to periods of long-term stable surfaces that were available

for occupation over multiple centuries to millennia. For example, many sandy sites in the SACP contain Paleoindian and Early Archaic components within the same stratigraphic zone or with very little separation (e.g., Cactus Hill, Kolb, and Flamingo Bay).

- Bioturbation is recognized as ubiquitous but highly variable in severity and as a secondary, post-depositional, process affecting sandy archaeological sites—not the primary mechanism for artifact burial within the sites investigated here. The varied influence of post-depositional disturbance requires careful interpretations of archaeostratigraphy and evaluations of both OSL age-models and radiocarbon chronologies.

- Based on analysis of archaeostratigraphy, sedimentology, and chronometric dating, periods of landform aggradation are plausibly linked to Holocene millennial-scale climatic cyclicity (e.g., Bond et al. 1997) and its related effects on the regional environment—providing a source of sediments for aeolian transport onto adjacent alluvial terraces, destabilization of slopes leading to increased slopewash, and increases in sediment availability for transport via large flood events as fluvial point bar deposits.

While the general climatic trend over the course of the Holocene on the SACP was apparently toward warmer, moister conditions with accompanying vegetation-bound sediments, the archaeological sites discussed in this synthesis clearly demonstrate that landforms throughout the region in diverse depositional environments were aggrading and burying occupation surfaces in the process. The regional extent of the pattern implicates climate, rather than local perturbations. Given the overall trend toward vegetation-bound sediments, the freeing up of those sediments for transport and subsequent landform aggradation was almost certainly episodic during intervals of vegetation destabilization. To our thinking, RCC events are implicated, but not conclusively demonstrated. In many cases, the chronologies for the landforms/sites in question are not yet sufficiently refined for direct correlation with RCC events (i.e., large sigmas associated with OSL dates).

Similarly, from the standpoint of possible behavioral responses to RCC events, one might expect lateral and vertical shifts in plant and animal communities, along with shifts in human settlement. Again, because very few archaeological sites are precisely dated, it is usually impossible to distinguish between diachronic and synchronic settlement variability within our broadly dated cultural periods. Until such time that we construct high-resolution climate/environment and cultural chronologies, correlating these records with any confidence will be impossible, and deriving causal relationships will continue to be a matter of "informed" speculation.

Directions for future research include the need for more geoarchaeological studies of stratified sandy sites, particular in Georgia, where data on such sites are lacking. These studies should include additional and close-interval single-grain OSL dating with appropriate evaluation of OSL data, age models, and archaeostratigraphy. Other lines of research include geochemistry, isotope analysis, palynology, and phytolith analysis (i.e., biogenic silica) of bulk sediments. Although extremely time-consuming, artifact refitting studies are perhaps the best method for evaluating site integrity.

The findings of this research have broad relevance to understanding landscape-scale geomorphology and archaeological site formation processes at other similar, typically shallow, sandy, and stratigraphically undifferentiated Coastal Plain archaeological sites. Many such sites are often considered by archaeologists as lacking integrity or by geologists as undifferentiated Quaternary alluvium. The underlying assumption is that shallow, late Quaternary Coastal Plain deposits lack interpretable archaeological and paleoenvironmental data due to extensive post-depositional disturbance and/or pedoturbation (e.g., Leigh 1998a, 1998b, 2001b, 2004; Michie 1990; Thulman 2012a). While these sites may be complex and difficult to interpret, this research demonstrates that shallowly buried sandy sites have the potential to provide valuable archaeological and paleoenvironmental data, particularly when appropriate methodological and analytical scales are applied. Accomplishing this requires the appropriate geosciences training of the archaeologist, or an archaeological background for geoscientist consultants. In either case, archaeologists should evaluate their own data on a case-by-case basis and not simply listen to the pronouncements of geomorphologists lacking a complete understanding of archaeological problems and realities.

Acknowledgments

We thank Carl Steen (Diachronic Research Foundation), Chris Judge (USC Lancaster), Sean Taylor (SC DNR), Ken Sassaman (UF), Joe McAvoy (Nottoway River Survey), Audrey Dawson (University of South Carolina), Allen West (GeoScience Consulting), Shannon Mahan (USGS Luminescence

Dating Laboratory), Tammy Rittenour (Department of Geology, Utah State University), George Brook (UGA Luminescence Dating Laboratory), Mike Johnson (Research Associate, Virginia Museum of Natural History), and the Virginia Department of Historic Resources for allowing us access to archaeological sites and data used in this chapter. Tammy Heron (SRARP) provided a technical edit of the manuscript.

11

MULTIPLE SCALES OF INTERACTION IN THE EARLY SIDE-NOTCHED HORIZON

KARA BRIDGMAN SWEENEY

Recent regional analyses of Early Archaic artifacts from throughout the Coastal Plain provide evidence for social boundaries and intergroup interactions within the Early Side-Notched horizon (11,200–10,500 cal. B.P.) (Bridgman Sweeney 2013; Faught and Waggoner 2012:154; Sherwood et al. 2004:546). Much of this discussion was anticipated by concepts first explored for a long-term research project to explore the complex and multiscalar relationship between artifact variation and cultural affiliation among Early Holocene populations (Bridgman Sweeney 2013). Here, I remodel those data, applying social network analysis (SNA) to a large database of side-notched artifacts already indicative of multiple and overlapping scales of social interaction.

Paleoindian Antecedents

Elsewhere (Bridgman Sweeney 2013), I have argued that large-scale sharing networks, facilitated by regular cross-drainage mobility, are reflected in the patterned variation of high frequencies of Early Archaic side-notched hafted tools (both bifaces and unifaces) made of Coastal Plain chert. These findings provide additional support for certain models of initial colonization, regionalization, and settlement for the Southeast (Anderson and Sassaman 2012; Smallwood 2012; Thulman 2006). It may be possible to trace the origins of subregional cultural traditions in the Early Side-Notched horizon to similar Paleoindian traditions, and to view the persistence of these subregional traditions as linked to settlement patterns well anticipated by the staging-area model (Anderson 1990, 1996; Anderson and Gillam 2001) for initial widespread colonization and settlement.

The staging-area hypothesis suggests that Clovis settlement was gradual, and that groups slowed their initial migration to establish territorial ranges based along resource-rich river drainages. According to this model, Clovis populations were "place-oriented," rather than "technology-oriented," and these staging areas were areas of habitual use that formed the foundations for early regionalization in the Southeast (Anderson 1990, 1996; Anderson and Sassaman 2012:50). As outlined in the staging-area hypothesis, interaction networks enabled Paleoindian groups to colonize North America despite low population density, while maintaining reproductive viability. These social networks may have been maintained by way of "loosely scheduled meetings" (Anderson and Gillam 2001:530) or occasional instances of social aggregation (Miller 2016). Such networks arguably also allowed for the development of subregional traditions (Anderson 1995; Anderson and Gillam 2001), such as those evidenced for the subsequent Early Side-Notched horizon.

Patterns of regionalization predicted by the staging-area hypothesis have been supported by recent studies of (post-Clovis) fluted points from throughout the Southeast (Smallwood 2012; Thulman 2006). One study of bifacial forms from sites in Tennessee, South Carolina, and Virginia lends support to the specific aspects of timing and directionality predicted by the staging-area model (Smallwood 2012). Another study considered Paleoindian bifaces from numerous Florida river drainages. Based on the degree of similarity between these regions, a "distance-decay" relationship was considered, such that the collective styles of closely related groups would be expected to be subtle and to vary in few aspects. This study identified the earliest evidence for regionalization in Florida points at the end of the Early Paleoindian period. This regional variation appears to have increased over time, as Florida Paleoindians apparently intensified their use of specific river drainage locations (Thulman 2006).

Recent research has demonstrated that possible Paleoindian aggregation locations tend to be located at the intersections of major rivers, at raw material sources, and at other physiographic boundaries (Miller 2016). Such place-based traditions were not only wholly unlike Paleoindian cultural expressions in the American West (Smallwood 2011); they laid the foundations for early regionalization in the Southeast. This GIS-based research also appears to support the staging-area hypothesis (Anderson and Sassaman 2012:50–51).

The Early Side-Notched Horizon

Early Archaic inhabitants of the Coastal Plain arguably were descendants of Paleoindian groups who were in place throughout the Southeast by ca. 13,000 cal B.P. (Waters and Stafford 2007:1122). Immediately prior to the Early Archaic period, the landscape of the lower Southeast was home to groups who had established areas of habitual use as well as variations on a shared technology by late Paleoindian times, during the Terminal Pleistocene.

Artifact type names (including Taylor, Bolen, and Big Sandy) have been proposed (Bullen 1958, 1975; Kneberg 1956; Michie 1966) to distinguish subregional variations in bifacial tool forms within the Early Side-Notched horizon. These typologies implicitly assume differences in cultural identity. As previously defined, these artifact types would seem to reflect distinct social groups who occupied South Carolina (Taylor Zone), Florida (Bolen Zone), and Alabama (Big Sandy Zone). This does not help to explain the origin of these tool forms, or their persistence over some seven centuries. Recently, a detailed analysis (Bridgman Sweeney 2013) of variation within each of these formal artifact types was conducted, with the goal of understanding the genesis and transformation of social boundaries for the earliest Archaic groups.

Subregional Trends in the Early Side-Notched Horizon

As part of a long-term research project (Bridgman Sweeney 2013), I developed a database of side-notched hafted bifaces with the goal of examining the variation within and between Early Archaic artifact types. A literature review would suggest that Taylor, Bolen, and Big Sandy side-notched forms all have relatively well-mapped and well-understood geographical zones (cf. Bissett 2003; Bullen 1975; Cambron and Hulse 1983; Michie 1996; Milanich 1994). However, the patterned variation of this artifact class had not been previously investigated at a broad regional scale. Therefore, detailed metric and nonmetric analyses conducted on bifaces recovered from these previously understood geographic zones were incorporated into the Early Side-Notched database to examine any recognizable patterned variation across these zones (Bridgman Sweeney 2013).

Both multiscalar and macroregional perspectives are essential to studies of Early Archaic groups. Therefore, the artifacts analyzed and incorporated into the Early Side-Notched database can consist of varying contexts of recovery. The database consists of assemblages from various archaeological sites and broader collection areas throughout the Coastal Plain, including portions of South Carolina, Georgia, Florida, and Alabama.

Analyses conducted for this database are currently restricted to tools made of chert (commonly known as Coastal Plain chert within the study area). While detailed petrologic surveys and analyses have been conducted in South Carolina and Florida, formal chert sourcing studies have not been completed for all portions of the Coastal Plain. It is still possible to provide a coarse-grained depiction of the locations of high-quality cherts in the region. Figure 11.1 presents the distribution of high-quality chert throughout the Coastal Plain. This map portrays information assembled from a variety of sources designed to provide state-level coverage of geological as well as archaeological information for Coastal Plain chert distribution (Goad 1979; Goodyear et al. 1985; University of South Alabama 2004; Upchurch et al. 1982a).

The density of Paleoindian and Early Archaic hafted bifaces in the Coastal Plain long has been linked to the availability of high-quality cherts (Austin and Mitchell 1999, 2010; Goad 1979; Goodyear et al. 1983; Goodyear et al. 1985; Upchurch et al. 1982a). High-quality Coastal Plain cherts are found south of the Fall Line in South Carolina, west into east-central and southwestern Georgia as well as southeastern Alabama, and south into the Tampa Bay region (after Goodyear et al. 1985). This is the approximate extent of my area of interest.

In South Carolina these cherts primarily are located in Allendale County, in the southwestern portion of the state (Daniel 1998; Goodyear 2010; Goodyear et al. 1985), where chert nodules up to 500 mm in diameter have been described (Smallwood 2010, 2012:693). In southwestern Georgia, between Albany and Bainbridge, cherts occur in large boulders, along the Flint River. Various Coastal Plain chert quarry clusters have been defined by researchers in Florida (Austin and Mitchell 1999, 2010; Austin et al. 2014; Goodyear et al. 1983; Upchurch et al. 1982a). A recent pilot study of quarry cluster sourcing of Florida bifaces (Bridgman Sweeney 2013; Robert Austin, personal communication 2005) identified very few examples of the use of nonlocal raw materials in side-notched tool manufacture throughout Florida's Coastal Plain. However, those few instances were possible indicators of cross-drainage mobility within the peninsula, specifically between the Aucilla and Hillsborough rivers.

A majority of the Early Side-Notched database consists of artifacts from numerous private collections, many of which currently are housed at the

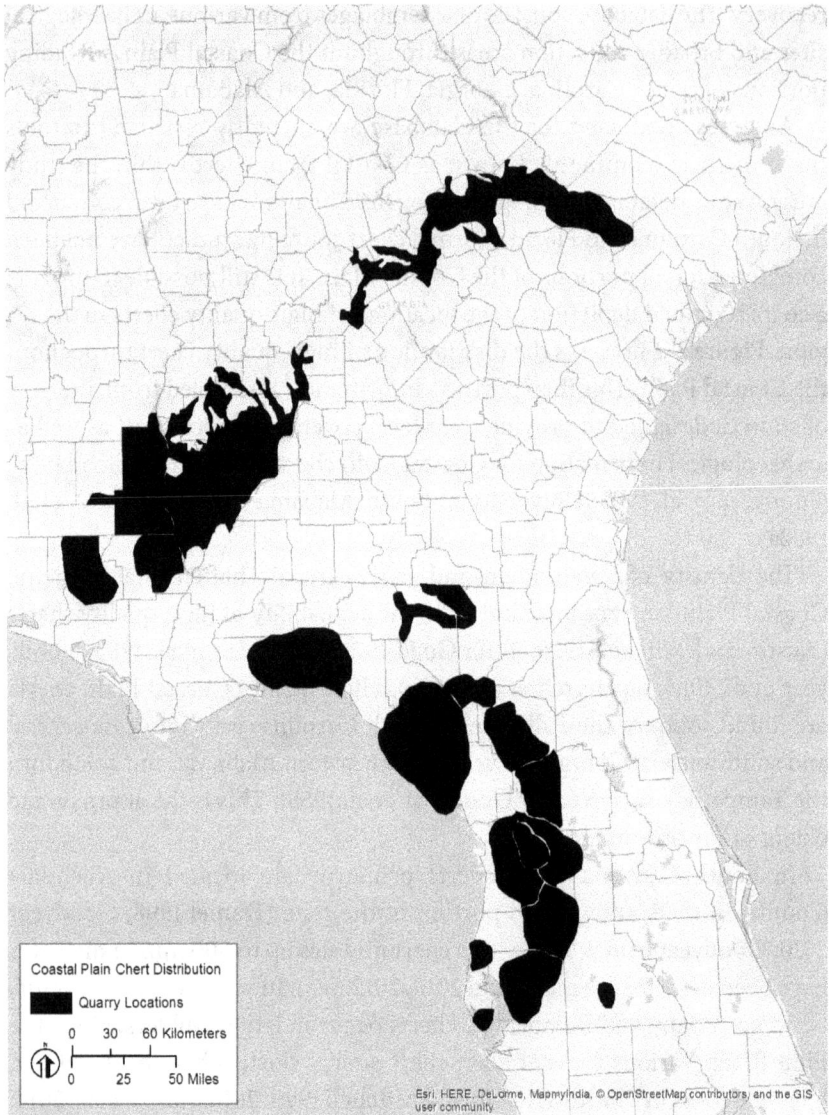

Figure 11.1. The distribution of high-quality Coastal Plain chert throughout the research area.

homes of individual artifact collectors, or in banks or local museums. Artifacts from excavated collections housed in curation facilities and at universities are also incorporated into the database. Suitable provenance information was available for all artifacts incorporated into the database to conduct a macroregional level of analysis regardless of their context of recovery from both private collections and formally excavated archaeological sites (Bridgman Sweeney 2013).

Both nominal and ratio-scale attributes were recorded for all analyzed artifacts. Nominal attributes of analyzed artifacts included: notch type, basal configuration, manufacturing condition, fracture type, basal grinding, cross section type, lateral condition, and beveling. Ratio-scale attributes of analyzed artifacts included: blade length, shoulder width, between-notch width, maximum thickness, basal concavity width, base width, base depth, auricle height, notch height, notch width, and shoulder length. Based on the detailed comparison of certain recorded attributes in the database, we are able to recognize patterning that can be geographically expressed (Bridgman Sweeney 2013).

The database consists of side-notched artifacts recovered from seven river drainage systems, including a total of 1,765 bifaces. These drainage systems include: the Santee-Cooper, Savannah-Ogeechee, Ocmulgee, Flint, Chattahoochee, Aucilla-Suwannee, and Tampa Bay. Each of the circled areas shown in Figure 11.2 is an analytical unit, as discussed below. While this area is not the full extent of the Early Side-Notched Horizon as a cultural expression, it does broadly correspond to the availability of Coastal Plain chert (see Figure 11.1).

Prior to the SNA data remodeling that is the focus of this research, numerous analytical and statistical techniques (both descriptive and inferential) were applied in the documentation of the Early Side-Notched database (Bridgman Sweeney 2013). Lithic analysis was conducted at the gross level of the individual hafted bifaces, and at the finer level of individual artifact attributes. These units were plotted through space, as well as in association to one another. County and site-level data (microscale) were aggregated to the level of individual river drainage systems (mesoscale), as well as to the level of the Coastal Plain watershed (macroscale) (following Knappett 2011). Descriptive and inferential statistical techniques were applied to all Early Side-Notched data sets, and percentile plots were designed to illustrate metric variation.

Specific geographic zones of apparent regionalization were identified within the Coastal Plain. These zones correspond to specific portions of the South Atlantic Slope and eastern Gulf Coast. Broadly speaking, areas of regional differentiation were identified, demarcated by a centrally located boundary zone along the Ocmulgee River, at the interface of the Atlantic and Gulf watersheds. Additionally, a high degree of variation for artifacts

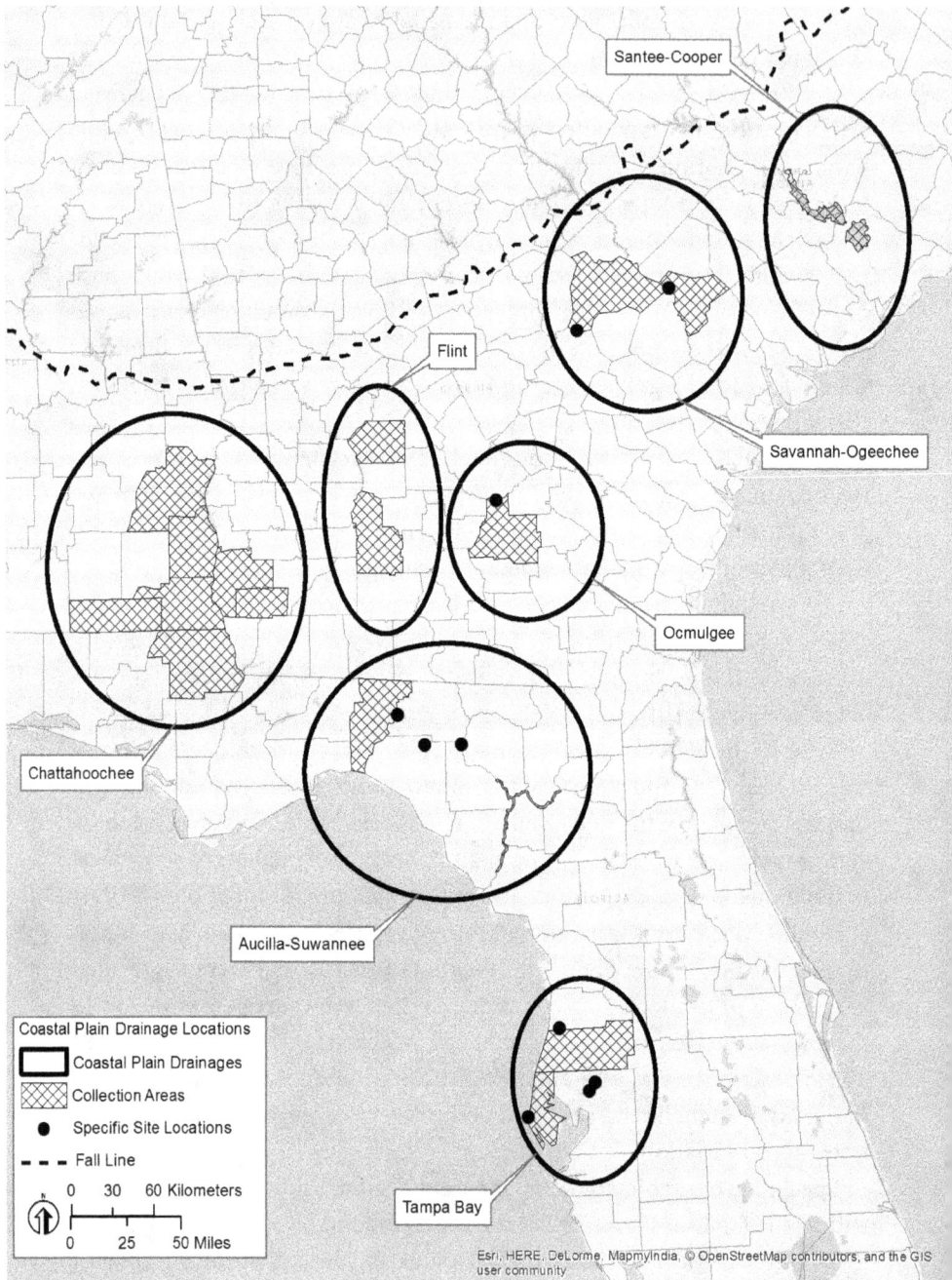

Figure 11.2. Research area in the Coastal Plain Southeast.

from the boundary zone was delineated, contrasting with the centers of zones where hafted biface types were defined.

The three classes of basal configuration observed in the Early Side-Notched database are incurvate, straight, and excurvate. These classes correspond to Ripley Bullen's (1975) use of the categories of concave, straight, and convex. Chi-square analyses demonstrated that side-notched tool base shape is directly correlated to geographic region (chi-square = 348.5599, with 12 degrees of freedom, and a probability of < .0001) (Bridgman Sweeney 2013:156–157). Basal configuration is presumed to remain relatively unchanged during the use-life of a tool, as basal configuration is typically not affected by resharpening. I argue that incurvate, straight, and excurvate base shape variations were coeval. At one Early Archaic site (the Jeanie's Better Back site, 8LF54), archaeologists (Austin and Mitchell 2010) recorded no distinctions in vertical distribution for variations in basal configuration, suggesting that these variations were contemporary.

The high degree of correlation between basal configuration of side-notched artifacts and geographic region provides support for the existence of distinct subregional traditions within the Early Side-Notched horizon. Basal configuration may therefore be seen as a reflection of social group affiliation. Side-notched tools may have implicitly communicated information about social boundaries, their variation in form referencing other people-groups and places (after Hendon 2000; Hodder 2012; Potter 2004; Tilley 1994; Wiessner 1982; Williams 1982). A high relative degree of variation in basal configuration in samples from the Ocmulgee River drainage was interpreted as an amalgam of multiple base-shape traditions from throughout the region.

Further investigations of these data continued with the presumption of a Taylor Zone (after Michie 1966), a Bolen Zone (after Bullen 1958, 1975), and a Big Sandy Zone (after Kneberg 1956). In order to test the hypothesis that these zones are geographically distinguishable (relative to measurable shifts in the patterned variation of associated side-notched tool forms), approximate central points (*sensu* core areas) were designated within zones, and boundary areas were defined at zonal intersections. Patterning in the centers of zones where side-notched hafted biface types (including Taylor, Bolen, and Big Sandy) were defined was compared to patterning in the boundary area where these zones intersect.

The approximate center of the Taylor Zone is Allendale County; the Strong Collection (n = 411 hafted bifaces) assemblage is from the core of the Taylor Zone. The approximate center of the Bolen Zone is the

Aucilla-Suwannee River drainage; the Hendrix Collection (n = 268 hafted bifaces) assemblage is from the core of the Bolen Zone. Large frequencies of hafted bifaces were not available for study from the center of the Big Sandy Zone. The Feronia Site Complex (in Coffee County, Georgia) in the Ocmulgee River drainage is situated at the intersection of the Taylor, Bolen, and Big Sandy zones (see Figure 11.2, in which the Feronia Site Complex is the only site location designated within the Ocmulgee River drainage). Therefore, those assemblages from Feronia (n = 37 hafted bifaces) and Coffee County (n = 37) were assigned special status due to their provenance at a boundary area.

Percentile plots of all ratio-scale data from the centers of the Taylor and Bolen zones were created to allow comparison with data from the Ocmulgee boundary area on the same graphs. In general, biface data from the centers of the Taylor and Bolen zones were seen to display low variance (Figure 11.3).This patterning is to be expected if these localities in fact represent the centers of respective social group ranges. More variation would then be expected for inferred boundary areas. In order to test this hypothesis, variation from the three sample subsets was compared, and the most evidence for variation was found for a number of ratio-scale attributes in samples from the Ocmulgee boundary area. Specific tests of the hypothesis included tests for normality and Levene's test of equality of variance (Gastwirth et al. 2009; Levene 1960) to compare multiple sample variances (cf. Kvamme at al. 1996:124).

That the Ocmulgee boundary area produced the most variation in basal configuration relative to the Taylor and Bolen zones is suggestive of a coalescence of various cultural and technological traditions in this zone. Variation in basal configuration in the Ocmulgee boundary samples may be interpreted in light of the probable permeability of social boundaries (after Kelly 1995; Woodburn 1968). Perhaps this patterning also lends support to the notion that groups throughout the region aggregated along the Ocmulgee River.

The Feronia Site Complex is located far from any known source of lithic raw material; this is atypical of Early Archaic site placement (cf. Daniel 2001). Specifically, while roughly 99 percent of the lithic artifacts recovered at the Feronia sites are manufactured from Coastal Plain chert, the closest source of that material is located approximately 83 km to the northwest (Blanton and Snow 1986, 1989; Goad 1979:6, 9). The position of the Ocmulgee River at the interstream divide of the Atlantic and Gulf watersheds would have made it an ideal point of aggregation. Periodic aggregation

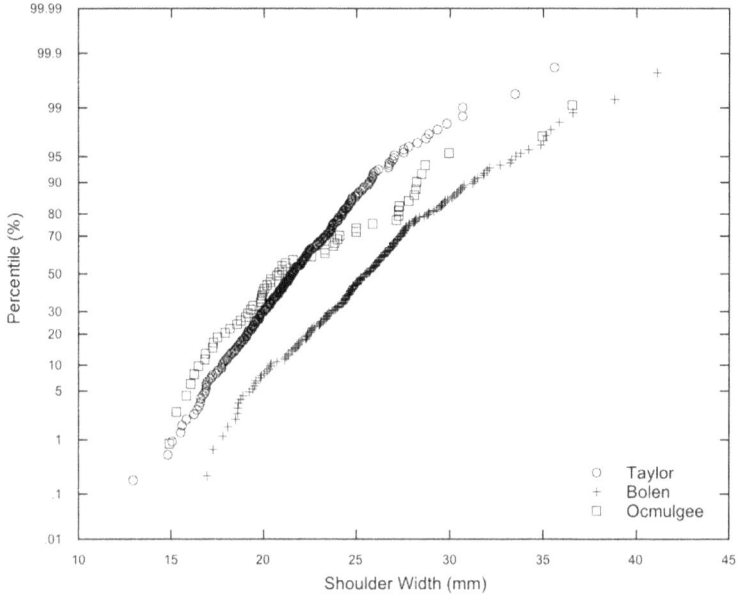

Figure 11.3a. Normal distribution percentile plot for hafted biface shoulder width.

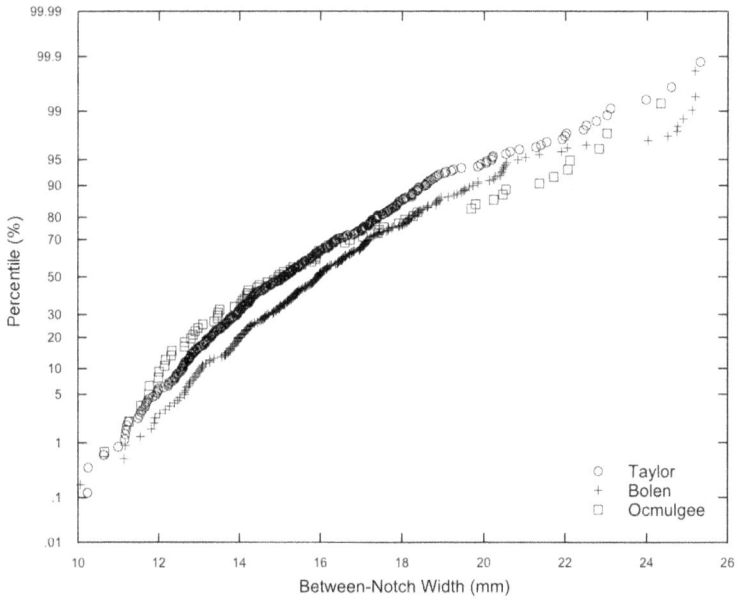

Figure 11.3b. Normal distribution percentile plot for hafted biface between-notch width.

would have helped to maintain the larger collective, and frequent social networking among neighboring macrobands is advantageous in times of resource stress, as well as a form of social storage in anticipation of such times (cf. Kelly 1995; Whallon 2006).

A Network Analysis of the Early Side-Notched Horizon

Social network analysis is arguably in its exploratory stage of application in archaeology, with increasing contributions over the past decade (Brughmans 2013; Collar et al. 2015; Gjesfjeld 2015; Knappett 2011, 2013; Mills et al. 2015; Pearce 2014). Network perspectives allow archaeologists to "translate" archaeological data into network data, and to represent dynamic social processes, including the relationships that are key components of networks (Collar et al. 2015:4). This is an important shift in perspective from spatial relations, which emphasize geographic space, to social relations and a focus on intergroup influences and interactions (Mills et al. 2015).

As a methodological toolkit, SNA is especially well suited to the study of large databases, including lithic assemblages. Material culture is produced by people in relational contexts (Mills et al. 2015). Since tools and other objects are made in communities of practice, and their technological reproduction is related to learning (Knappett 2011), the flow of goods and/ or ideas may be archaeologically visible in the form of specific artifact attributes. SNA methods can enhance regional analysis, as they can emphasize relational connections among social entities, depending on the resolution of the archaeological data (cf. Mills et al. 2015). The capability of network approaches to visually represent multiscalar relationships in these data is advantageous for analysis and communication (Collar et al. 2015).

Using patterning in basal configuration as a proxy for social group affiliation, I sought to gauge the level of cross-drainage transhumance. During the course of this remodeling effort, I retained the spatial component of the social networks throughout the Coastal Plain, explicitly prioritizing the spatial along with the relational network patterning (following Knappett 2011:11).

Typically in a social network analysis, nodes are people or key actors, and ties are the relationships or interactions among those groups, such that a network can be said to have two components: a list of actors and a list of interactions between actors. Theoretically, a proper social network analysis for the Coastal Plain at the Pleistocene–Holocene transition could be designed to reflect time-transgressive trends in colonization and regionalization. Ideally, it would be possible to model the various relational contexts that can be obscured by coarse-grained regional analysis of limited classes of material culture. Admittedly, there are certain clear challenges in the direct application of SNA to material culture, but attention to the interactions among social groups at varying scales can only enhance regional analyses (cf. Mills et al. 2015).

The value of SNA (or network reconstruction or synthesis, following Knappett 2013) is that social relations can be well mapped using edges and vertices. This is because people live in social fields that rarely have boundaries that can be well understood by drawing circles on maps (Mills et al. 2015; Terrell 2013), such as those depicted in Figure 11.4. On the basis of numerous ethnographic studies (cf. Kelly 1995; Yellen and Harpending 1972), there is every reason to presume that the earliest Archaic group membership patterns were relatively fluid, with flexible social group structure and relatively permeable social boundaries.

It is important to explicitly define this network. Perhaps at most we can define it as: a set of drainage locations within the Coastal Plain, where side-notched artifacts made of Coastal Plain chert have been found. Nodes (or "players") in the social network in consideration here include the seven (previously) mapped drainages, from Santee-Cooper south to Tampa Bay, and west to the Chattahoochee along the Alabama/Georgia border. Ocmulgee is arguably the "key" player (or central node) in this network.

Table 11.1 shows raw data for percentages of biface base shape per Coastal Plain drainage. I modified these tabular data, and here we see there are 21 possible connections out of seven drainages for base shape similarity; this includes direct cases of drainage-to-drainage interaction (where no sense of directionality is being implied). For example, between the Santee-Cooper and the Savannah-Ogeechee River drainages, there is an overall difference of 14.08, which is a sum of the difference for each of three base shapes.

The bold-faced cells shown here are marking those samples with the lowest degrees of difference. This is essentially a measurement of the relative centrality of each interdrainage tie. This test is a more robust way to demonstrate the regional connections between drainages with respect to basal configuration. Additionally, this technique allows for the production of new forms of output that can be used to explore regional patterns in materiality.

Figure 11.5 depicts relative tie strength for similarity of base shape (and I am using basal configuration as a proxy for social group affiliation, as

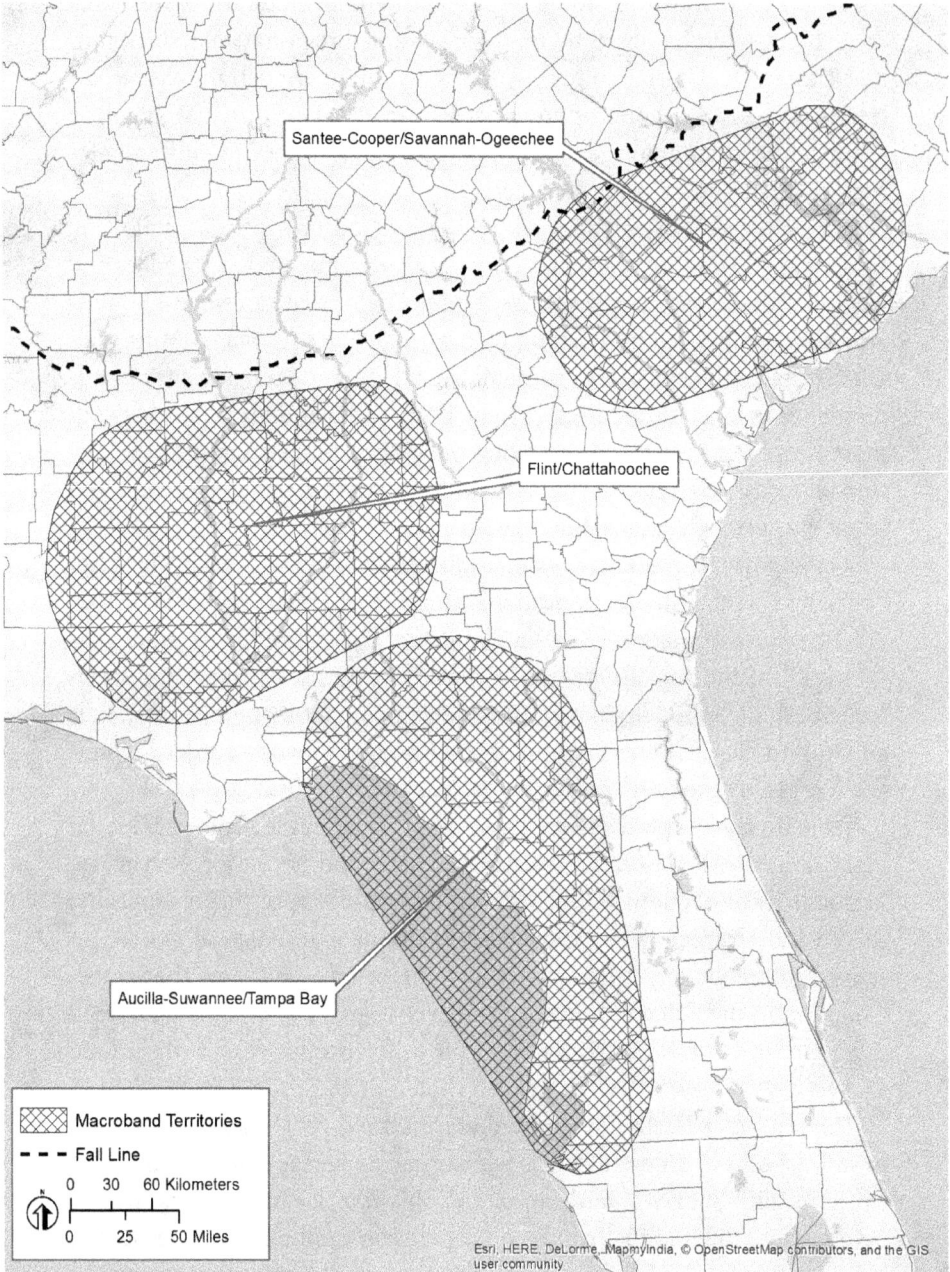

Figure 11.4. Proposed Coastal Plain macroband territories (Bridgman Sweeney 2013:313).

Table 11.1. A Quantification of Coastal Plain Inter-drainage Interactions

Drainage	Percent		
	Incurvate	Straight	Excurvate
Santee-Cooper [SC]	71.88	26.56	1.56
Savannah-Ogeechee [SO]	66.27	25.13	8.6
Ocmulgee [O]	43.94	46.97	9.09
Flint [F]	32.98	64.89	2.13
Chattahoochee [C]	41.33	54.93	3.73
Aucilla-Suwannee [AS]	18.28	47.8	33.92
Tampa Bay [TB]	18.18	46.75	35.06
DRAINAGE–DRAINAGE INTERACTION	Difference		Sum of Difference
SC—SO	**5.61**	**1.43**	**7.04**	**14.08**
SC—O	27.94	20.41	7.53	55.88
SC—F	38.90	38.33	0.57	77.80
SC—C	30.55	28.37	2.17	61.09
SC—AS	53.60	21.24	32.36	107.20
SC—TB	53.70	20.19	33.50	107.39
SO—O	22.33	21.84	0.49	44.66
SO—F	33.29	39.76	6.47	79.52
SO—C	24.94	29.80	4.87	59.61
SO—AS	47.99	22.67	25.32	95.98
SO—TB	48.09	21.62	26.46	96.17
O—F	10.96	17.92	6.96	35.84
O—C	**2.61**	**7.96**	**5.36**	**15.93**
O—AS	25.66	0.83	24.83	51.32
O—TB	25.76	0.22	25.97	51.95
F—C	**8.35**	**9.96**	**1.60**	**19.91**
F—AS	14.70	17.09	31.79	63.58
F—TB	14.80	18.14	32.93	65.87
C—AS	23.05	7.13	30.19	60.37
C—TB	23.15	8.18	31.33	62.66
AS—TB	**0.10**	**1.05**	**1.14**	**2.29**

Note: Entries in bold mark those samples with the lowest degrees of difference.

previously noted). Data from Table 11.1 were mapped on a graduated symbol scale, such that the greatest differences (or least similarities) are displayed as thinner, more dotted lines, and the least differences (or greatest similarities) are displayed as thicker, solid lines, using Jenks Natural Breaks Classification Method. A total of five classifications was produced; the very weakest link was removed for production of this graphic.

Some patterning is intuitive based solely on geography. For example, I see the least difference (or highest tie strength) between Aucilla-Suwannee and Tampa Bay. In the tabular data I recorded the most relative difference between the regions of Santee-Cooper and Tampa Bay. These are the most geographically disparate regions of the analysis, and they have such a weak tie strength that there is no line to represent their relationship on Figure 11.5.

The "circles on maps" technique, as previously shown, can seem to suggest bounded entities, and I would like to explicitly avoid such a classification of these social groups (after Parkinson 2006). Instead, I designated center points (or centroids, *sensu* core areas) within each river drainage, drawing the lines of relationships between and among the river drainages. This is a significant shift away from "zonal" understandings of social network structures (Rivers et al. 2013).

Using this technique, I found that the same level of tie strength connects Ocmulgee to each of the following: Savannah-Ogeechee, Flint, Aucilla-Suwannee, and Tampa Bay. Weaker network ties are indicated between the Ocmulgee and the Santee-Cooper. This may suggest that groups along the Santee-Cooper had more social networking connections with the Piedmont region than with the drainages of the Coastal Plain, and for the purposes of aggregation, Santee-Cooper groups may have done so along the Fall Line (as others have postulated) (Anderson 1996; Anderson and Hanson 1988; Anderson et al. 2009; Daniel 1998). It is also possible that Coastal Plain chert tools found in Santee-Cooper reflect movement by groups more typically connected to the Savannah-Ogeechee River drainage.

As Figure 11.5 presents numerous instances of weak (and less strong) ties throughout the drainages of the Coastal Plain, it is worth noting that the strength of weak ties (as first discussed by Granovetter 1973) is that you can focus more attention on the relationships between groups, instead of within the primary groups in consideration. This approach can allow for a more relational (and less "zonal") understanding of the social collectivities that most regularly interacted.

It is important to note that while material culture may not be a particular

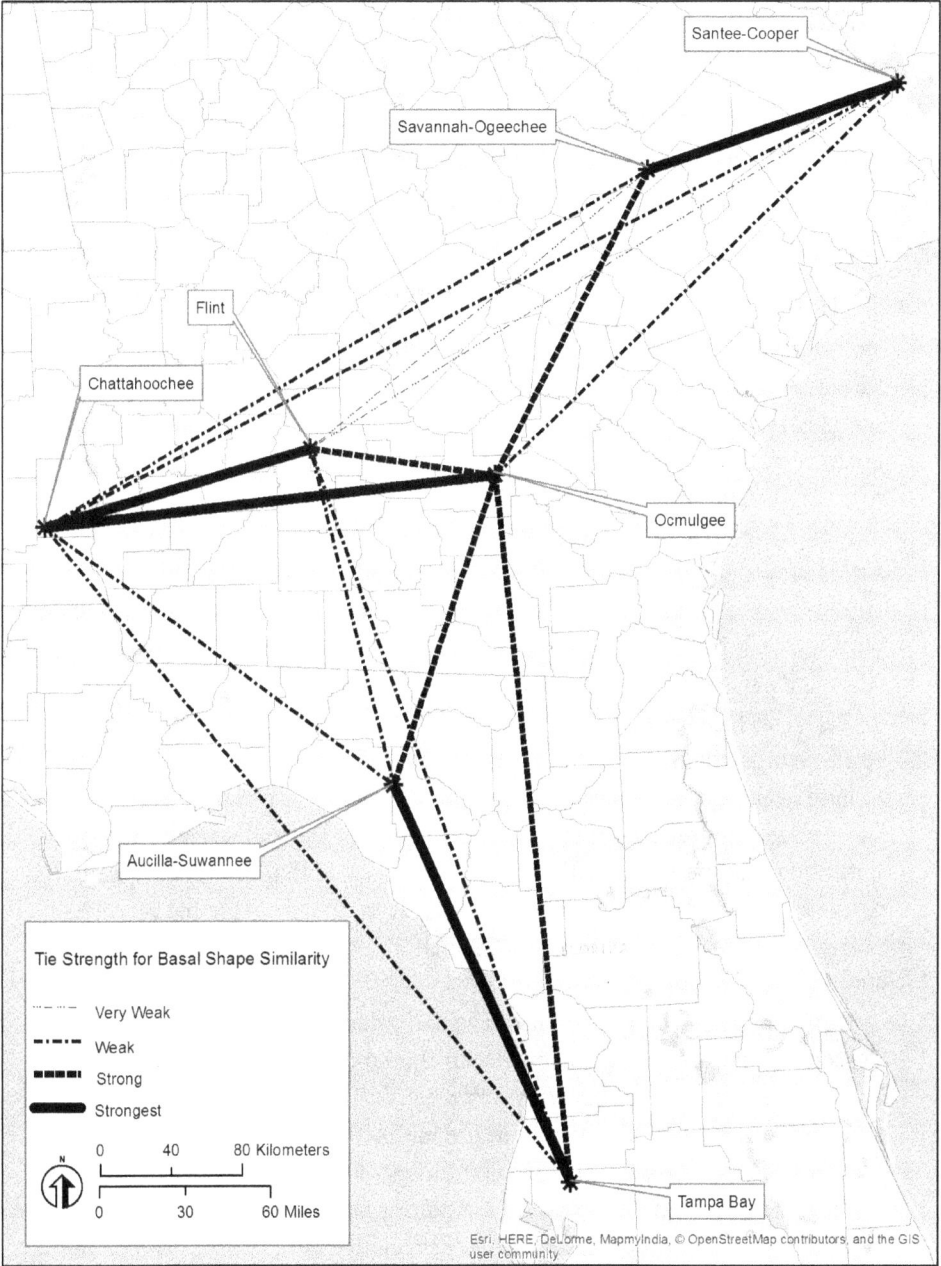

Figure 11.5. Relative tie strength for the Early Side-Notched database, based on percentage of basal configuration.

strength of social network analysis, it is worth evaluating whether links are stronger in one direction than another (Knappett 2013; Rivers et al. 2013). The view of the Coastal Plain in Figure 11.6 is of a reduced network, limited to connections with the Ocmulgee River drainage. The weakest tie strength is to the northeast of the Ocmulgee River drainage; the highest tie strength is actually to the west, with the Chattahoochee River drainage. The Ocmulgee River drainage should be viewed as a persistent node of intercultural contact (after Wallis and Randall 2014:13), beginning at the onset of the Archaic period if not before.

While there have been some recent attempts to model antecedent Paleoindian regionalization and social organization (Anderson 1990, 1996; Miller 2011; Smallwood 2012; Thulman 2006), the social boundaries potentially reflected by subregional traditions within the Early Side-Notched horizon have been underexplored. Some models for Early Archaic settlement have been presented that take social networks into account, but it is vital to remember that social networks serve more than mating purposes. Interaction networks serve both biological and social reproduction (after Anderson and Gillam 2001), and the benefits of a large regional social network go well beyond demographic concerns and the search for suitable marriage partners.

Early Archaic groups may have created kinscapes, or "maps" of social relationships, through which they negotiated their ties to one another and to land over great distances (after Bender 1999:36). For instance, ethnographies of certain hunter-gatherer societies point to the humanization of the natural landscape through the use of place names that reference specific associations with current use, historic use, or mythical or totemic activities and events (after Basso 1983; Gould 1969, 1971, 1978; Tilley 1994; Woodburn 1968).

Early Archaic groups also may have had totemic ties to land, reckoning descent to specific points of interest in the landscape, such as individual river drainages or chert quarries (after Gould 1978). They also likely had kin-based relationships to places in the landscape such as burial grounds, former home sites, and locations where rites of initiation were performed (after Hitchcock and Bartram 1998). Additionally, ritual acts such as long-distance gifting and the manufacture of specially crafted bifaces can be interpreted as biographical processes. These can be read as historical productions, since they were connected to people whose own biographies could be traced to different times and places (after Pauketat 2013; Sassaman 2011). In this way, places throughout the landscape of the Coastal Plain may well

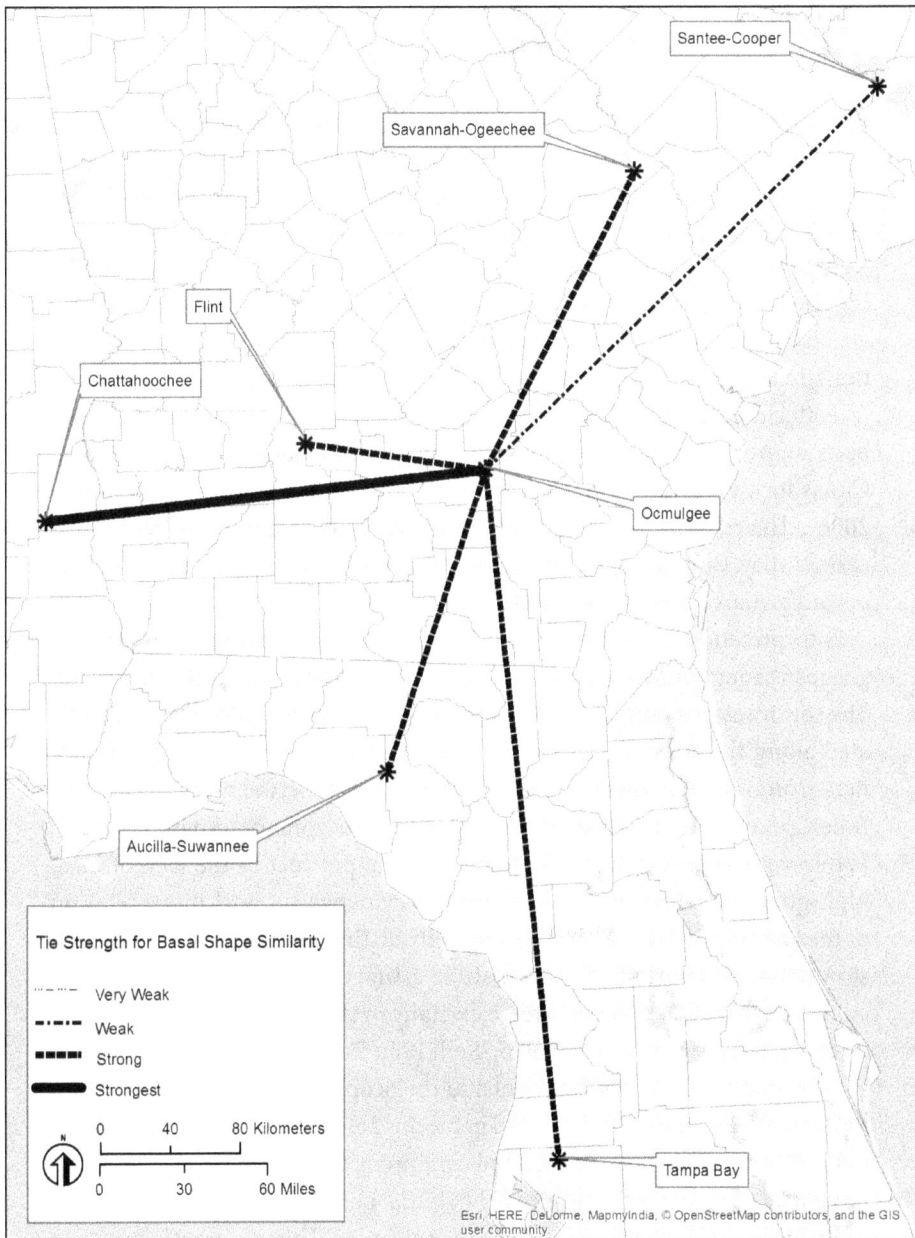

Figure 11.6. Relative tie strength with Ocmulgee River connections, based on percentage of basal configuration.

have been integral parts of social and historical memories, expressing multiple scales of social identities and relationships, and relating at once to social group organization, practice, and process (after Hendon 2000; Morphy 1995).

No adequate term exists to denote the great regional scale of social interaction presented here for the Early Archaic Southeast. Perhaps, in the spirit of the related concept of landscape as kinscape, we can imagine the broader landscape of the Coastal Plain Southeast as a *bandscape,* a collectivity composed of multiple macrobands that were engaged in broadly similar cultural traditions. Certainly, patterned variation in side-notched artifacts lends itself to an appreciation of macroregional social reproduction greater than that typically described by anthropologists.

Patterns of regionalization predicted by the staging-area hypothesis have been supported by recent studies of fluted points (that apparently postdate Clovis forms) from throughout the Southeast (Smallwood 2012; Thulman 2006). The reuse of places inhabited by Paleoindian and more recent ancestors may well have provoked historical memory among Early Archaic period groups (after Bender 2002).

Interpretation of the Ocmulgee River drainage as a boundary area for groups throughout the region may be justified (Blanton and Snow 1989). The southwestern portion of the proposed Ocmulgee boundary area is situated along the Atlantic–Gulf drainage divide (Figure 11.7). Hafted-biface data from the Ocmulgee boundary area, situated between the Taylor and Bolen zones, produced the most variance in the zone-boundary test case. While a great deal of this variation may be a product of the lack of local high-quality raw material, other lines of evidence support interpretation of the Ocmulgee River as archaeologically distinct. For instance, pitted egg stones found as part of Ocmulgee River artifact suites are similar to forms commonly found at Florida sites, especially in the Aucilla-Suwannee River drainage (Blanton and Snow 1986; Neill 1971; Purdy 1981:23, 30).

Information exchange well outside the scope of the co-resident group may have been embedded in social gatherings along the Ocmulgee River, as part of feasts, trade fairs, or planned ceremonies (after Fitzhugh et al. 2011). Its central position between areas of habitual use made the Ocmulgee River drainage an ideal location for social aggregation. This apparently was true despite the local absence of high-quality lithic raw materials. The location of the Feronia Site Complex suggests that aggregation may have occurred at any zonal interface, whether at the Piedmont/Coastal Plain (Fall Line), or at the interface of the Atlantic and Gulf watersheds (Blanton and Snow 1989),

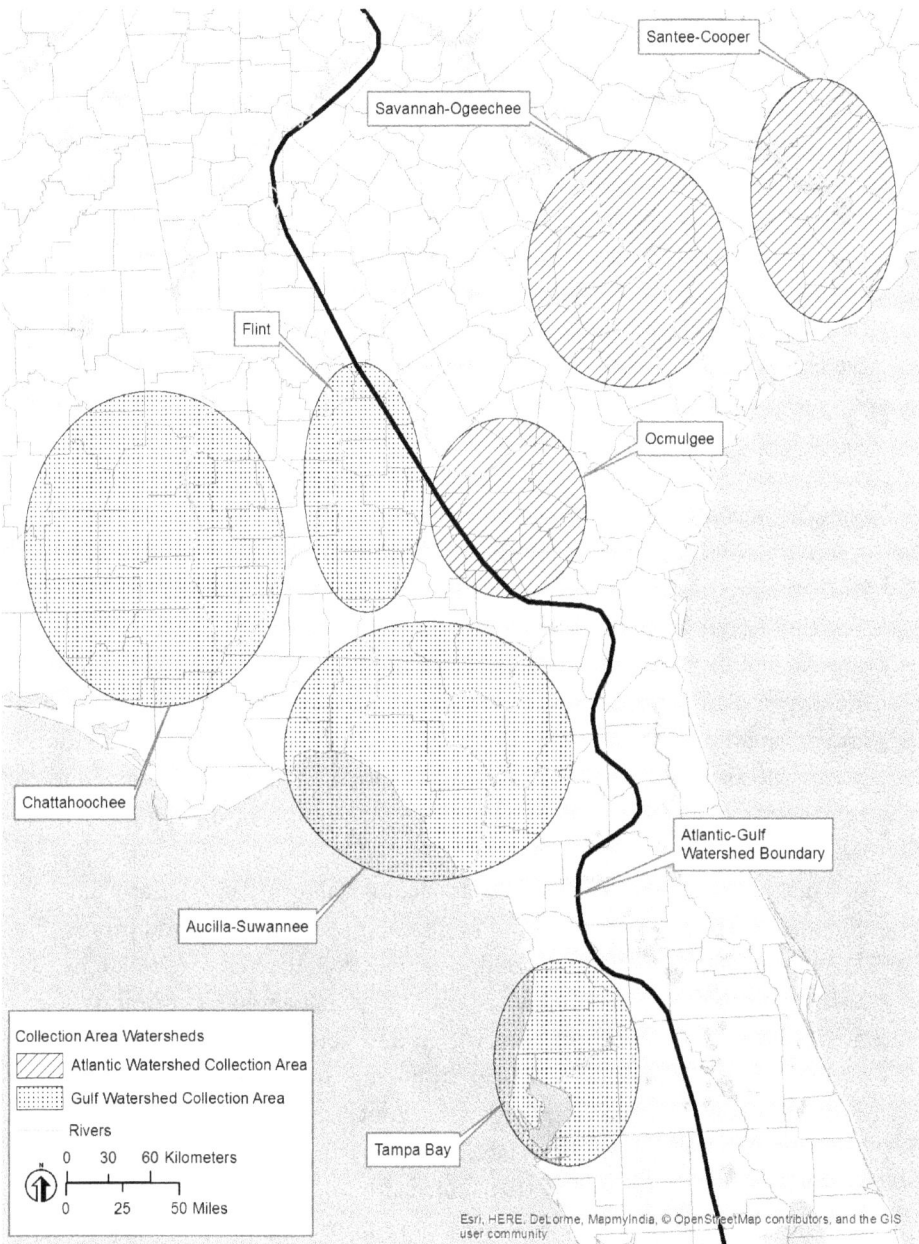

Figure 11.7. The Atlantic/Gulf watershed boundary in the context of Coastal Plain drainages.

and that the key was aggregation in places that would have been easy to find, describe, and re-locate (after Miller 2016:711). That social aggregation is highly indicated for Ocmulgee in spite of the absence of locally available cherts underscores the primary importance of social group interactions during the Early Archaic (after Sassaman 2011).

Ethnographically, aggregations are most commonly seen to occur in the course of other activities where mobility patterns intersect, or where concentrations of specific resources draw groups together (Fitzhugh et al. 2011). Perhaps Early Archaic groups from throughout the Coastal Plain viewed the Ocmulgee River drainage as a key destination, as what is sometimes ethnographically described as a kind of "super waterhole" (after Hiatt 1968:100).

Conclusions

Network techniques can provide a level of validation and visualization to results obtained by other means. Here, I have attempted not so much a network analysis as a network reconstruction or synthesis for the Early Side-Notched horizon (following Knappett 2013). In applying a macroregional approach to the linkages of patterned variation in material culture, to social identity and affiliation, I am documenting place-based traditions in local and more extensive regional landscapes. This analysis suggests that specific places within the Coastal Plain served as focal points for settlement and aggregation beginning with Paleoindian colonization of the region (Anderson 1990; Miller 2011, 2016).

I suggest that what we see in the archaeological record of the Early Side-Notched horizon is a reflection of multiscalar social and cultural process. The subregional technological traditions evident in the Early Side-Notched horizon arguably trace ancestry to post-Clovis Paleoindian cultural traditions, and reflect movement both within and between habitual use areas. Several lines of ancillary evidence, supported by this remodeling of the Early Side-Notched database, suggest that zonal interfaces such as the physiographic "hinge" area of the Atlantic–Gulf drainage divide were points of social aggregation for widely distributed groups. This analysis reveals at once the complexity of social processes responsible for archaeologically recognized boundaries, and the apparent permeability of such boundaries at the Pleistocene–Holocene transition.

12

DISCERNING EARLY ARCHAIC BOLEN
TERRITORIES USING GEOMETRIC
MORPHOMETRICS

DAVID K. THULMAN

Diagnostic artifacts are constantly used by archaeologists to identify the age of a site, establish cultural connections, and recreate prehistoric social organization. Given their ubiquitous use, it is problematic that many artifact types are ambiguously defined and open to dispute (Buchanan and Collard 2010; Lenardi and Merwin 2010; Thulman 2012b). This is in part because artifact types were traditionally established by the subjective assessment of experts in the 1950s and 1960s (e.g., Bullen 1975; Cambron and Hulse 1983; Ritchie 1971). Artifact types, especially projectile points, are identified almost exclusively by shape, and most typologies rely mainly on impressionistic inferences. The typologies based on shape are rarely subjected to rigorous testing because it is difficult, if not impossible, to evaluate the efficacy of subjective categories (Thulman 2012b).

In this chapter I analyze the shape and examine the distribution of the Bolen point, an Early Archaic diagnostic artifact (Figure 12.1), which I define as a side- or corner-notched point with a ground base. The goals are to establish a more rigorous typology and investigate the artifact's spatial and temporal distribution in north central Florida (the study area; Figure 12.2) for the purpose of reconstructing prehistoric social organization in the area. This analysis is part of a larger effort to understand the transition in point shapes from lanceolate-shaped points used in eastern North America in the Late Paleoindian period (ca. 10,500–10,000 B.P.; 12,450–11,500 cal B.P.) to notched points in the Early Archaic period (ca. 10,000–9000 B.P.; 11,500–10,100 cal B.P.)(Anderson et al. 1996). Such an effort requires a

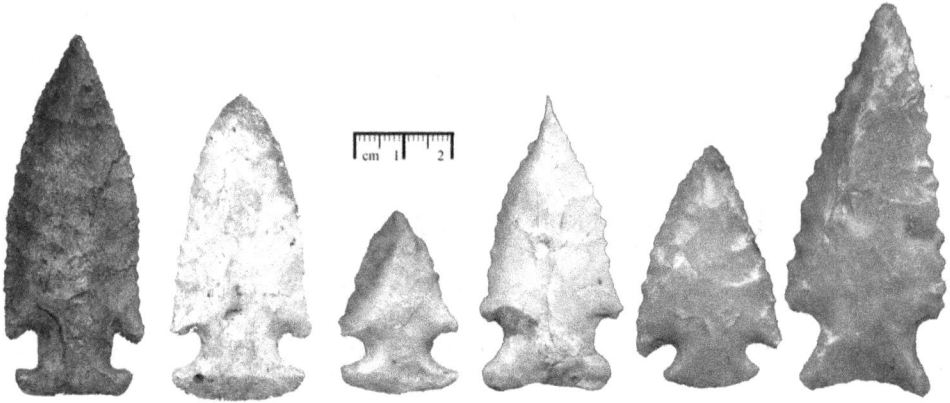

Figure 12.1. Five Bolen points showing the basal variation.

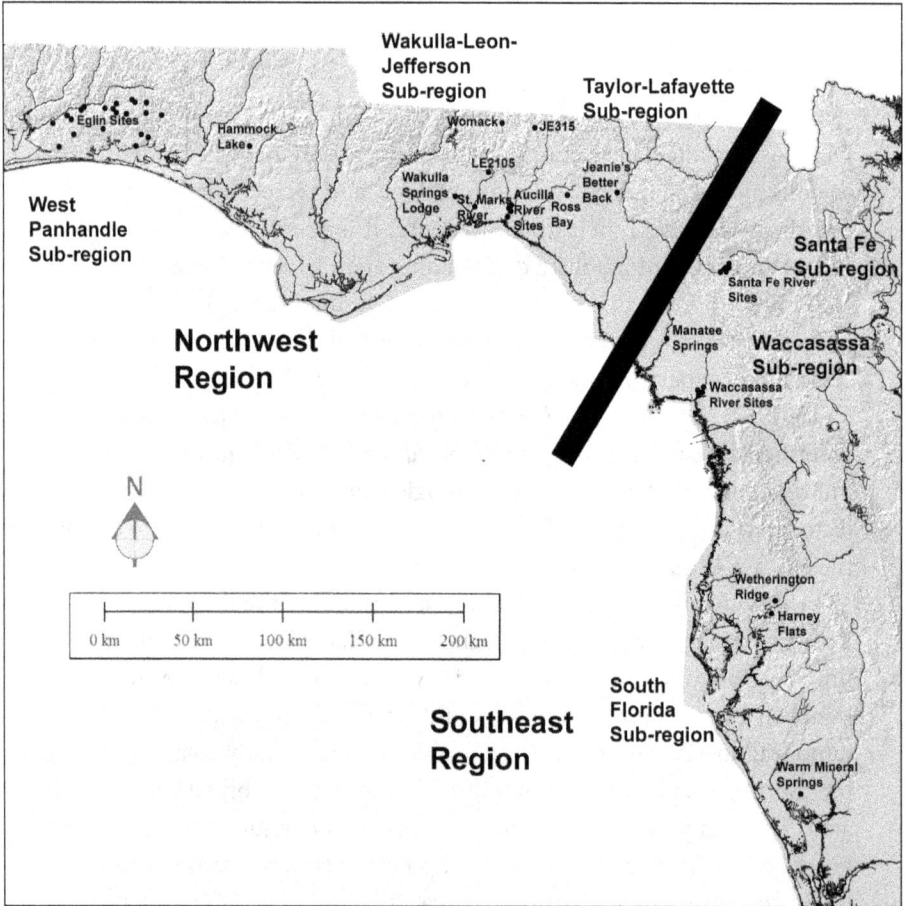

Figure 12.2. Locations of all the sites, localities, regions, and sub-regions in the study area used in this analysis.

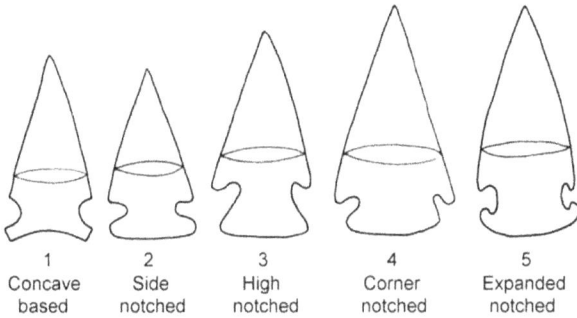

Figure 12.3. Bullen's five Bolen basal subtypes. Modified from Bullen (1975:51–52).

better understanding of the temporal and spatial distribution of these early notched forms.

The Bolen point was named for the Bolen Bluff site on Paynes Prairie, south of Gainesville, in Alachua County, Florida (Bullen 1958). Later, in his classic book on Florida point typology—*A Guide to the Identification of Florida Projectile Points*—Bullen (1975:51–52) expanded the definition and identified two types of Bolens based on whether the blade was beveled or plain (i.e., unbeveled; Lipo et al. 2012). Each Bolen type was divided into the same five subtypes that described the basal shape: concave, side-notched, high-notched, corner-notched, and expanded notched (Figure 12.3).

Two previous efforts have analyzed the shape and size of Bolen points in Florida. Bissett (2003) analyzed the attributes in a sample of 200 corner- and side-notched Bolen points from a single collection, 145 of which had location information. Sweeney's (2013) large-scale analysis of 2,020 Early Archaic side-notched points used attributes similar to Bissett's. Both studies found regional variation in one or two attributes within the physiographic province of the Coastal Plain of the Southeast, including parts of north and peninsular Florida covered in the present study. However, neither study presented a coherent description of the shape variation—not because it was not present, but because their methods do not facilitate comprehensive analysis of shape.

The present study examined 329 notched points with ground bases, which are hallmarks of Early Archaic Bolen points (Purdy 1981:24). The study focuses on the shape of the base of the Bolen point but takes a different analytical approach by employing landmark-based geometric morphometrics (LGM) to analyze the two-dimensional shapes. LGM is contrasted with traditional morphometric analyses usually used in archaeology, which focus on combinations of linear and angular measurements, ratios, and categorical data (Shott and Trail 2010; Thulman 2012). LGM allows the analyst to consider the entire shape, independent of size, as a single unit without having to break it down into a set of linear and angular measurements or categorical designations (Slice 2007; Zelditch et al. 2012).

The results of the LGM analysis identified four varieties of Early Archaic notched points that are statistically significantly different: two side-notched and two corner-notched varieties, which do not correspond well with Bullen's five subtypes. Side-notched and corner-notched varieties of points were used concurrently in the earliest dated Bolen sites in Florida, ca. 10,000 [14]C B.P. (11,500 cal B.P.; Faught et al. 2003). Further, the distributions of the early side- and corner-notched types show a definite spatial pattern, with significantly higher percentages of corner-notched points to the west and side-notched points to the south and east of the Suwannee River. These patterns cannot be easily attributed to different adaptive strategies and likely represent established traditions of artifact manufacture.

Most qualitative typologies of artifacts, and Bullen's typology of Florida points in particular, were developed by looking at an assemblage of points and identifying examples that appear to be exemplars of different types (Milanich 2004). These exemplars are usually distinctive in shape, but their usefulness for categorizing points that fall between the exemplars can be problematic (Buchanan and Collard 2010; Lenardi and Merwin 2010; Thulman 2012b). The strength of our inferences in this regard should consider the entire assemblage of points, not just the exemplars; and characterizing the entire assemblage requires that we *focus* on the variation in the assemblage. In short, where do all the in-betweeners fit in the typology?

The typology developed here is used to infer the basal shape the makers intended to produce when they made Bolen points. Our understanding of how people learn to make things (e.g., Bril and Roux 2005; Lave and Wenger 1991) and how ideas are transmitted and manifested in material culture (e.g., Thulman 2014) has advanced greatly in the last few decades by anthropologists (e.g., Boyd and Richerson 1985; Henrich and Boyd 1998; Henrich 2001) and archaeologists (e.g., O'Brien et al. 2014; Eerkens et al. 2006) investigating the spatial and temporal transmission of ideas manifested in material culture. The notion of ideational models is commonly employed as units of analysis (Lyman and O'Brien 2010; Mesoudi and

O'Brien 2008) and is used here to model the differences in point types and their distributions.

Learning is fundamentally a social process, and deciding what to copy, whom to copy, when to imitate, and when to experiment all involve individual assessments of appropriate behavior (Henrich 2010). To illustrate the learning process, imagine a group of people of all ability levels making a particular kind of artifact, which I will refer to as a social learning group (SLG). An SLG can vary from a small, tightly constrained membership to a loose confederation of members who share information directly or indirectly, many of whom may never meet. The key is that each member is trying to make the same type of artifact. It is important to emphasize that an SLG has no necessary corollary in traditional notions of prehistoric hunter-gatherer organization, such as band, macroband, or clan. An SLG is inferred from the distribution of similar shapes (and their discrimination from other shapes) and models of how those shapes are learned and created. Projecting an SLG onto another organization is fraught with peril and supposition.

In prehistoric societies, each member of the SLG likely had an idiosyncratic notion, or ideational model (*sensu* Deetz 1977), of how to make the artifact; there was no single common ideational model. A new member of a Bolen point social learning group unsure of how to proceed would probably follow one of two learning strategies: copy what the most successful hunter was making, thinking that would increase his own chances of success, or would make the version that most of his SLG members were making, thinking it unlikely the majority would make the wrong choice (Henrich 2010; Henrich and Boyd 1998). Either decision strategy usually leads to a single version for a group (Boyd and Richerson 1985). Generally, once a choice is made, it should be maintained through time and space as ideas and information are transmitted through generations within the SLG and lead to what we interpret as archaeological cultures or traditions (Henrich 2010). This process of learning could also lead to the development of regional variations as each SLG makes different choices in which design to adopt and transmit. Whereas two SLGs may start with the same design, over time they can embark on different trajectories that lead to distinctly different designs. Once established, the variation can be maintained in the SLG even in areas where groups with different ideas mix (McElreath 2004; McElreath et al. 2003); interaction among social learning groups making different artifact designs in similar environmental conditions does not necessarily result in a blended design (Henrich and Boyd 1998; McElreath 2004).

These variations in artifact shape can be a useful proxy for identifying SLGs (Thulman 2006). The goal in this analysis is discerning the SLG's ideational model, which here is the consensus of what shape the Bolen point makers thought a Bolen point should have, as well as how it should have been made and used. As discussed above, the ideational models were personal; each maker had his own idea of what to make. However, our available analytical tools cannot reconstruct these idiosyncratic models; we can only estimate the consensus model. This consensus model is a convenient proxy for analyzing the variation, but I do not assert that it is a reconstruction of the original idea any particular maker held. Nevertheless, it does represent an approximation of what SLG members were thinking. Figure 12.4 illustrates a model of how that consensus can inferred from the variation in a group of Bolen point makers in two social groups. The light gray shapes represent the ideational models of Bolen point makers in each group, and the black shapes represent the variation of the actual points produced by those makers. The dark gray shapes labeled 1 and 2 are the mean or consensus ideational shapes, and they are inferred from the average shape of all the points produced by a group of point makers. The key to figuring out the makers' original intent when they were making Bolen points is to work with the part of the point that best preserves the ideational model at manufacture. I believe the base of the Bolen point best preserves the model, because once completed it was less likely to have been intentionally modified, unlike the blade, which was often resharpened or broken through use (O'Brien et al. 2014; Thulman 2006, 2012b).

Several assumptions that relate to inferring social groups from artifact variation are warranted about the manufacture of Bolen points. First, the maker's intent was initially to produce a bilaterally symmetrical tool, although through resharpening and damage during use the tool may have ended up asymmetric. We do not know, but it is likely, that Bolen points were initially used both as knives and projectile points, although some blades on the points were modified for use as drills or borers (Goodwin et al. 2013:118–128). I discern no clear indication of intention to make asymmetrical blades or bases in Bolen points other than those created during manufacture due to raw material heterogeneities or the imperfect translation of idea to finished product, and there is some evidence that symmetry is important for predictable projectile trajectories (Lipo et al. 2012). Second, the ideational form must be inferred from the average of all shapes in each

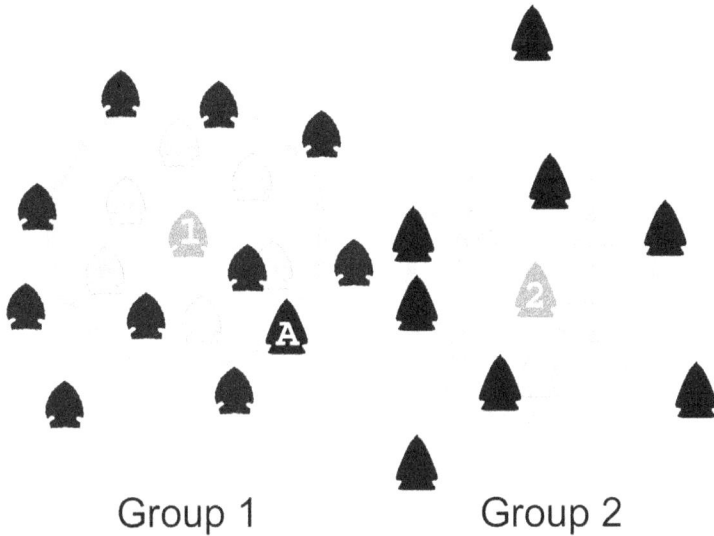

Figure 12.4. Illustration of the range of variation of ideational models and artifacts of two social learning groups making points. The light gray shapes represent the ideational models and the black shapes represent the makers' attempts to makes their ideational models, i.e., the actual artifacts. The dark gray shapes, labeled *1* and *2*, are the mean or consensus ideational model for each group, which are estimated by the average shape of all the actual artifacts. The artifact labeled *A* represents an attempt to make a Group 2 point that is actually closer in shape to a Group 1 point.

unit of the analysis, because no single artifact is a perfect manifestation of the ideational form. Third, variation in the shape of notching on the base of a Bolen point has no obvious functional advantage. Fourth, the variation in Bolen points was not caused by different raw materials. Fifth, the base of a point was made to fit existing hafts, so the size of the bases varied, but the intended shape of the haft was invariant.

A morphometric analysis simply means an analysis of shape, as opposed to size, manufacturing technique, or raw material choice. In this case the analysis is focused on shape differences and similarities. Shape is defined as an invariant geometric configuration of points or locations on an artifact that is unchanged in regard to translation, rotation, and size (Bookstein 1991; Zelditch et al. 2012). The mathematical basis for LGM has been well explored in the last 25 years and was developed to understand biological processes related to shape, like speciation (Adams et al. 2013), although it is becoming more common in archaeological analysis (e.g., Azevedo et al. 2014; Buchanan et al. 2014; Charlin et al. 2014).

Given the assumption that the ideational form was bilaterally symmetric, using one half of the base is required for an appropriate statistical analysis (Bookstein 1996; Klingenberg et al. 2002). One half of the base can be created by averaging both sides of the base or using only one side, which is what was done here. My intent was to use the side that best preserved the maker's intent, meaning they had the (1) best-preserved notch and base, (2) most uniform notch and base, and (3) the longer basal end or smaller notch (a longer basal end or smaller notch is a better indication of the maker's intent, because the longer ends could always be shortened and smaller notches could be enlarged). Images of 329 Bolen points were collected from 50 sites and localities. The sites were grouped from west to east by general subregions (Figure 12.2).

The best landmark (LM) configurations and number of LMs for discriminating shapes were determined through exploratory data analysis (Whallon 1982). All but five of the points from the sites and localities were scanned on a flatbed scanner at 600 dpi. Four LMs were initially placed on the image: the most distal point of the notch (LM 1), the point representing the left end of the minimum basal width (LM 2), the leftmost point on the basal end (LM 3), and the midpoint of the base (LM 4), which was determined as the intersection of a line drawn perpendicular from the midpoint of the minimum basal width. Two curves were then drawn using the curve tool in *tpsDig2* (Rohlf 2013). Five equally spaced points were interpolated for each curve (Figure 12.5). The top curve was drawn from LM 2 to LM 3 (LMs 5–9), and the bottom curve was drawn from LM 3 to LM 4 (LMs 10–14).

Differentiating groups in the population of 329 Bolen points was an iterative process of testing different combinations of LMs with statistical tests to evaluate the coherence of the groupings. I initially sorted the points based on a cursory inspection, then examined the entire group in a principal components analysis (PCA; Zelditch et al. 2012) to look for concentrations of individual artifacts. Individual artifacts were examined based on the PCA and reallocated to a different group as appropriate. Group allocations were tested with a discriminant function analysis (DFA; Klecka 1980; Kovarovic et al. 2011; McGarigal et al. 2000). All the analyses were run in *MorphoJ* v.1.05d, a freeware program that is specifically designed to analyze shape data (Klingenberg 2011).

The DFA is the workhorse of the analysis, but it must be used cautiously to avoid misleading results. DFA maximizes the variation among groups and minimizes variation within groups, but a statistically significant DFA

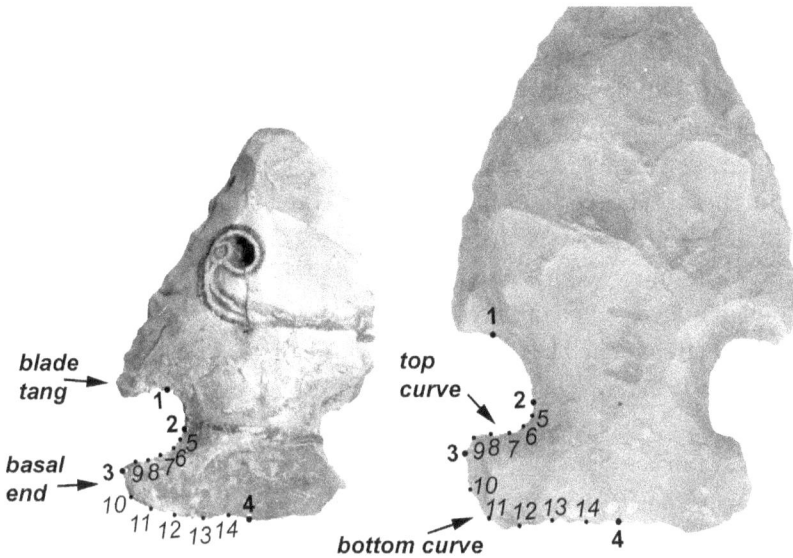

Figure 12.5. Representative Bolen points showing assigned landmarks (LM1–4) and the top (LMs 5–9) and bottom (LMs 10–14) curves.

result alone does not mean the difference between groups is salient (Kovarovic et al. 2011). Statistical significance in this context depends on the absolute and relative sample sizes of each group, multivariate normality of the data, and equality of the covariance matrices for each group (Klecka 1980; McGarigal et al. 2000; Mitteroecker and Bookstein 2011). Relative sample sizes of 4:1 dramatically affect the calculation of the correct classification rate (White and Ruttenberg 2007). Thus, if possible, group sizes should be close in size (no more than 2:1), and each group should be at least three times the number of variables. These requirements were met here.

Although mean shapes may be significantly different, the groups may not be good at discriminating the individual specimens. The efficacy of the DFA must be tested, which is best done by cross-validation through a jackknifing technique that produces a classification table (Kovarovic et al. 2011). The correct classification rate must be corrected to account for the number of correct classifications expected simply by chance. For example, for two groups of 50 artifacts (100 total), at least 50 of the artifacts would be properly classified simply through random assignment. The kappa statistic (McGarigal et al. 2000; Titus et al. 1984) calculates the percentage of correct classifications above chance by comparing the percentage of expected correct classifications due to chance with the actual classifications. Kappa ranges between 1 (perfect association) and 0 (no association). Landis and Koch (1977:165) designate a kappa statistic of .61–.8 as a general, albeit arbitrary, range for a "substantial" strength of association. A high chance-corrected percentage rate near the uncorrected percentage is another indication the classification was successful (Titus et al. 1984).

In a biological analysis of species, the gold standard is 100 percent correct classifications to justify separate species (Hammer and Harper 2005), although a lower rate is typically accepted. No specific level of adequate discrimination for archaeological data to justify concluding artifact shapes are distinctly different has been established, especially when the shapes are similar, but I used a 70 percent chance-corrected kappa statistic in this analysis as an acceptable minimum standard for proper allocation; if kappa was lower than 70 percent, then the typology was suspect.

Analysis and Results

The initial division produced two groups that generally coincided with accepted notions in the Southeast of Early Archaic side-notched (SN) and corner-notched (CN) categories. The same iterative process was used to determine whether these categories could be further divided. In the end, four groups were distinguished and unimaginatively labeled Side Notch A and B (SN A and SN B) and Corner Notch A and B (CN A and CN B)(Table 12.1). The use of the catchall terms SN and CN is simply meant to keep this proposed typology in the traditional overall cultural historical nomenclature used in the Southeast. It is not my intent, nor is it likely possible, to change the SN and CN designations. The consensus shapes of these varieties are illustrated in Figure 12.6 and should be compared to Bullen's five varieties in Figure 12.3. The consensus shapes were created in the *tpsSuper* v. 1.14 program (Rohlf 2003) by aligning the images of the points in a group by stretching and squeezing them to fit the consensus shape of the LMs. Because only the left side of the base was used to define the types, only the LMs on that side were used to align the specimens. The spread of variation for the CN A and SN A varieties is illustrated in Figures 12.7 and 12.8.

All the groups reported here were statistically significantly different in the DFA at $\alpha = .05$ ($p < .0001$, whether measured by the Mahalanobis distance or the Procrustes distance). The CN and SN groups were best differentiated using LMs 2, 3, 4, and the top and bottom curves–LMs 5–14: 13 LMs in total). The data were permuted 10,000 times, and the jackknife

Table 12.1. The Classification Tables for the Discriminant Analyses for the Corner- and Side-Notched Categories and the Two Subtypes in the Side- and Corner-Notched Categories

CLASSIFICATION OF CORNER AND SIDE NOTCHED BOLENS

Group	Corner-Notched	Side-Notched	Total	Percent	Kappa
Corner-Notched	154	20	174	89%	71%
Side-Notched	27	128	155	83%	

CLASSIFICATION OF SIDE-NOTCHED A AND SIDE-NOTCHED B BOLENS

	Side-Notched A	Side-Notched B	Total	Percent	Kappa
Side-Notched A	74	9	83	89%	78%
Side-Notched B	11	61	72	85%	

CLASSIFICATION OF CORNER-NOTCHED A AND CORNER=NOTCHED B BOLENS

	Corner-Notched A	Corner-Notched B	Total	Percent	Kappa
Corner-Notched A	101	10	111	91%	75%
Corner-Notched B	10	53	63	84%	

Note: The rows in each section of the table show how many of the specimens of each type were properly and improperly allocated. For example, in the top section, 108 of the total number of Corner-Notched points were properly allocated to the Corner-Notched category, and 11 of the 119 were misallocated to the Side-Notched category, which is a 91% correct allocation rate.

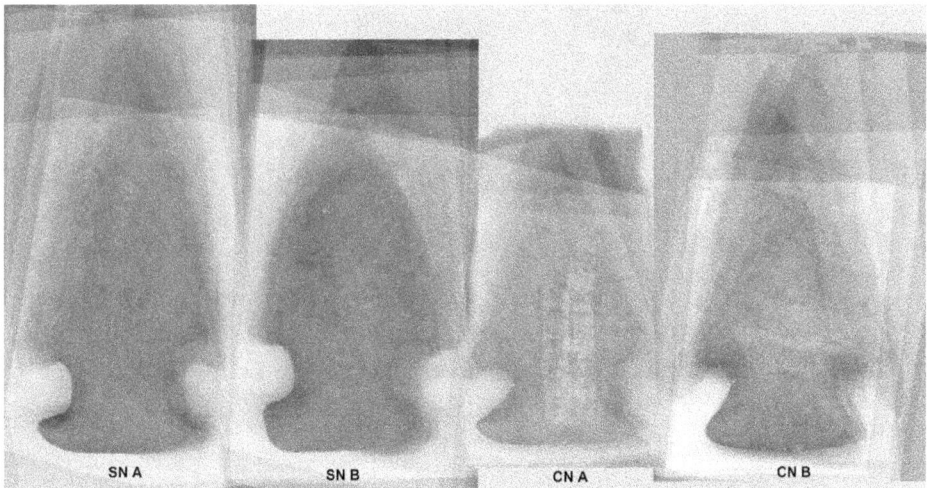

Figure 12.6. Consensus shapes of SN A, SN B CN A, and CN B.

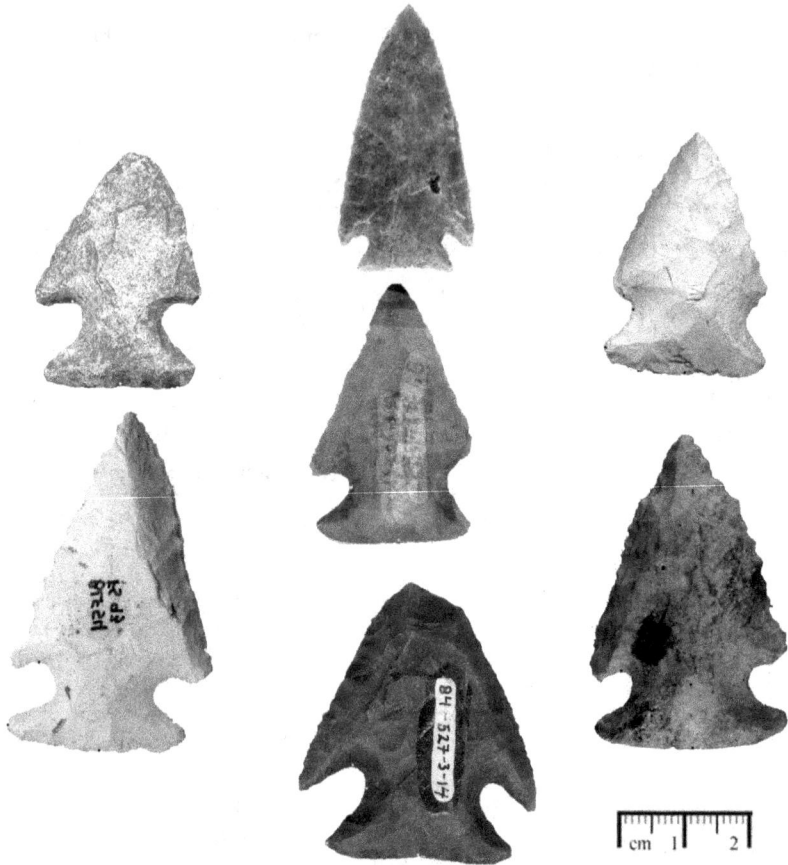

Figure 12.7. Range of variation for CN A. The center image is the consensus shape. The points are arranged per their approximate locations in a between-groups principal components analysis.

cross-validation tests showed that 20 CN points were misallocated to the SN category (89 percent success rate), and 27 SN were misallocated (81 percent success rate). The kappa statistic indicates these rates are 71 percent above chance and close enough to the uncorrected rate to indicate the association is sound.

The SN group was further divided into SN A and SN B types, which were differentiated based on the morphology of the base (LMs 2, 3, 4 and the bottom curve: eight LMs in total). Seventy-four of a total of 83 (89 percent) of SN A points were appropriately allocated, whereas 61 of 72 (85 percent) of SN B points were appropriately allocated. The CN group was

Figure 12.8. Range of variation for SN A. The center image is the consensus shape. The points are arranged per their approximate locations in a between-groups principal components analysis.

divided using the morphology of the top curve (LMs 2, 3, 4 and the top curve: eight LMs in total). Ninety-one percent (101 of 111) of CN A points were appropriately allocated, and 84 percent (53 of 63) of CN B were appropriately allocated. Kappa for the SN and CN groups was 78 and 75 percent, respectively, so the allocations were appropriate.

Temporal and Spatial Variation

Only the SN A and CN A varieties have been dated in Florida. A Bayesian analysis of the eight ^{14}C dates in OxCal (Ramsey 2009) indicates the early phase of Bolen was between about 11,600 and 10,900 cal B.P., although there is great uncertainty in the estimate. Two of the eleven dated Bolens are SN A from Page-Ladson Unit C (Carter and Dunbar 2006); the rest are CN A. Finding both CN and SN points together in the earliest Early Archaic period makes Florida unique in the Southeast (Faught et al. 2003), where sites from the same time period have produced only SN points (Sherwood et al. 2004; Stafford and Cantin 2009).

The spatial variation of the SN and CN categories shows a regional distribution with the Suwannee River as the approximate dividing boundary (Figure 12.2). The gross CN and SN categories are divided between a region to the west of the river and a region to the east and south in the study area (Table 12.2): 64 percent of the points found in the east and south region are SN points (88 of 141 total), whereas only 36 percent of the points found in the west region are SN (67 of 188). This trend holds in the subregions, with the percentages of SN points in the three subregions in the east and south region ranging from 58 to 71 percent, and 31 to 40 percent in the west region. The same spatial variation holds for the SN A and CN A varieties (Table 12.2). These distributions are significant using the chi-square test (SN—CN: $\chi^2 = 16.8413$, $df = 1$, $p < .0001$; SNA—CNA: $\chi^2 = 14.8818$, $df = 1$, $p < .001$).

Discussion

This analysis should be viewed as heuristic, and at least the details may change with more or different data. Nonetheless, because these types were based on a model of social learning and group differentiation, the value of the typology developed here can be assessed by whether it makes sense in inferring social groups. The Early Archaic people in north-central Florida can be conceptualized as occupying both spatial and temporal distributions,

Table 12.2. The Percentage of All Side-Notched, Side-Notched A (Early Period), and Side-Notched B (Late Period) by Region and Subregion

Region	Subregion	SN	CN	Percentage SN	SN A	CN A	Percentage SN A
Southeast	Santa Fe R.	41	28	59%	17	7	71%
	Waccasassa R.	32	23	58%	18	14	56%
	Tampa Area	5	2	71%	4	2	67%
	TOTAL	78	53	60%	39	23	63%
Northeast	Western Panhandle	8	18	31%	0	11	0%
	Wakulla-Leon-Jefferson	31	61	34%	21	45	32%
	Lafayette-Taylor	28	42	40%	21	32	40%
	Total	67	121	36%	42	88	35%

and their larger social organization, which would have affected the development of types of Bolen points, could have taken several forms.

The Environmental and Chronological Setting of the Bolen Period

The early Holocene environment in this area of Florida is only broadly understood, but it was likely initially drier than present conditions, with lower water tables and fewer potable water supplies (Dunbar 2002; Russell et al. 2009; Thulman 2009). The Bolen surface in unit C at the Page-Ladson site (Figure 12.2), which during occupation was on the water's edge of a sinkhole, is about 5 m below present river water levels (Carter and Dunbar 2006). The Gulf of Mexico was more than 130 km from the modern coast, which means the area covered by this study was far inland. Today, the study area, which is in the coastal plain physiographic region of Florida (Schmidt 1997), has low relief (sea level to about 35 m) dominated by sandy soils thinly overlying karst bedrock. The area has small rivers incised in the bedrock, numerous sinkholes, and some springs that provide conduits to the aquifer. Today, some coastal springs discharge large amounts of water (>2.3 $m^{3\text{-s}}$), but in Bolen times they likely did not flow (Faure et al. 2002; Thulman 2009). The coastal plain is dominated by pine flatwoods, with swamps in the few floodplains, around some sinkholes, and areas of perched water tables (Brown et al. 1990; Thulman 2009). Swamps and wetlands, which dominate much of Florida today, did not begin to develop until about 8500 B.P. (ca. 9500 cal B.P.; Watts and Hansen 1988). Stone tool resources consisting mainly of Coastal Plain cherts are common, but scattered, throughout the area (Thomas et al. 2013). The only exception was in the western pan-handle, where Tallahatta quartzite was the most common tool stone; cherts are present, but rare, in that region (Thomas et al. 2013). In sum, during the Bolen period in the study area, people were likely focused around scattered reliable water sources far from the coast but could access locally available lithic and food sources (Thulman 2009). The Bolen-era environment was likely undifferentiated throughout the area, making extensive travel for rare resources unnecessary.

Inferring Social Phenomena from the Typology

The two types of coincident Bolen hafts could be explained from several phenomena. First, the variation could be illusory, and with a large enough sample, we would no longer be able to discriminate distinctive groups. As discussed below, this seems unlikely, but it is a possibility. In such a case "Bolen" would have been a unitary phenomenon, unchanging through time and space, but with lots of variation in the shape of the base. That could happen under the learning model described above if the intergenerational transmission of knowledge was rigid, meaning little change was tolerated as grandfather taught father taught son. It is also possible that the Bolen people throughout the regions were in regular contact and adopted designs from one another. In such circumstances, a single broadly variable Bolen-type would have developed throughout the area, or at least in the areas of regular contact, and been maintained through time. Second, the variation could be due to functional differences; that is, the differences in the hafts were a result of the need to attach each point to a haft differently. Third, the variation could be temporal. For example, Florida could follow the gener-ally accepted side-notch-to-corner-notch temporal change posited for the rest of the Southeast. In all three of these scenarios, we would expect to find a relatively equal percentage of CN A and SN A points throughout the study area. However, if the variance is due to different ideational models used by different SLGs that were spatially constrained in the study area, then we would expect to find regional variation in the percentages.

We can infer from these regional distributions that the basal configu-rations did not reflect functional differences, because, given that the re-gions were likely essentially homogeneous in environment and resource availability, the point types were not evenly distributed in the regions. This inference does not necessarily conflict with the seasonal rounds inferred for Early Archaic groups by Anderson and Hanson (1988) along rivers in parts of Georgia, and North and South Carolina, or the patterns of raw material use found by Daniel (2001) in generally the same region. They used different data (site and raw material distributions) in a significantly different physiographic region. I think the most parsimonious explanation for the Florida data is that the variation is social, rather than reflecting an adaptation to different environmental conditions, meaning the forms were made by distinct social learning groups carrying on distinct point-making traditions.

Conclusions

Several interesting questions are raised by this work. How would the regions change with more sites, including sites outside of Florida, or a larger sample? It is possible that the patterns reported here result from a small sample size, although that seems unlikely because the regional patterns are reflected in all of the subregions? Could these regional territories be discerned back into the Paleoindian period or forward in time? Both avenues of research suffer from a lack of dated sites and an incomplete understanding of the predicate and subsequent forms of the points that were used during those times. What kind of communication did Bolen people have with others in the Southeast? I am presently exploring that issue by analyzing contemporaneous sites further to the north.

In the study reported here I have tried to demonstrate the utility of accurate, quantitative point typologies based on a large data set and grounded in a theory of learning that accounts for temporal and spatial variation in shape. This kind of work would not be easy, and perhaps would be impossible, without being able to parse subtle but statistically significant differences in shape using LGM that we might expect to be present among distinct but closely interacting social groups. It is unclear whether these distinctions would be found using traditional morphometric analysis. Large data sets allow us to evaluate all of the variation illustrated in Figures 12.7–12.8, and testing the efficacy of typologies against the underlying hypotheses for the variation (i.e., how would we expect variation to arise through these models of cultural transmission, and what does it tell us about human behavior?) is the best way to determine a typology's value.

13

FROM THE SAVANNAH TO THE SANTEE RIVER

EARLY ARCHAIC MOBILITY AND RAW MATERIAL UTILIZATION IN THE COASTAL PLAIN OF SOUTH CAROLINA

JOSEPH E. WILKINSON

The field of prehistoric archaeology has a very short history when compared to the expanse of time that it studies. The cultural history of North America extends back at least 13,000 years, and many would argue much farther, while prehistoric archaeology, with few exceptions, has only been around roughly a century. To complicate the already overwhelming task of studying prehistory, biological and geological processes at work over long expanses of time ensure that much of the cultural remains of prehistoric peoples vanish from the record. Among the remains that survive the test of time are stone tools, which can have a great deal to tell us about the people who created and used them. One of the stories that stone tools can tell us, relates to the tracing of people as they moved across the landscape. This can be studied particularly if the geologic locations of the raw materials from which these tools are made are known.

The present study is based on the analysis of stone tools from private artifact collections forming a transect across the Coastal Plain of South Carolina stretching from the Savannah River to the Santee River drainage (Figure 13.1). Because the lithic raw materials used for tools are well known, it is possible to gain some sense of the distances prehistoric peoples moved. This study seeks to gain additional insight into the settlement organization of Early Archaic cultures and their subsistence strategies by examining stone-tool-using behavior across and within this zone.

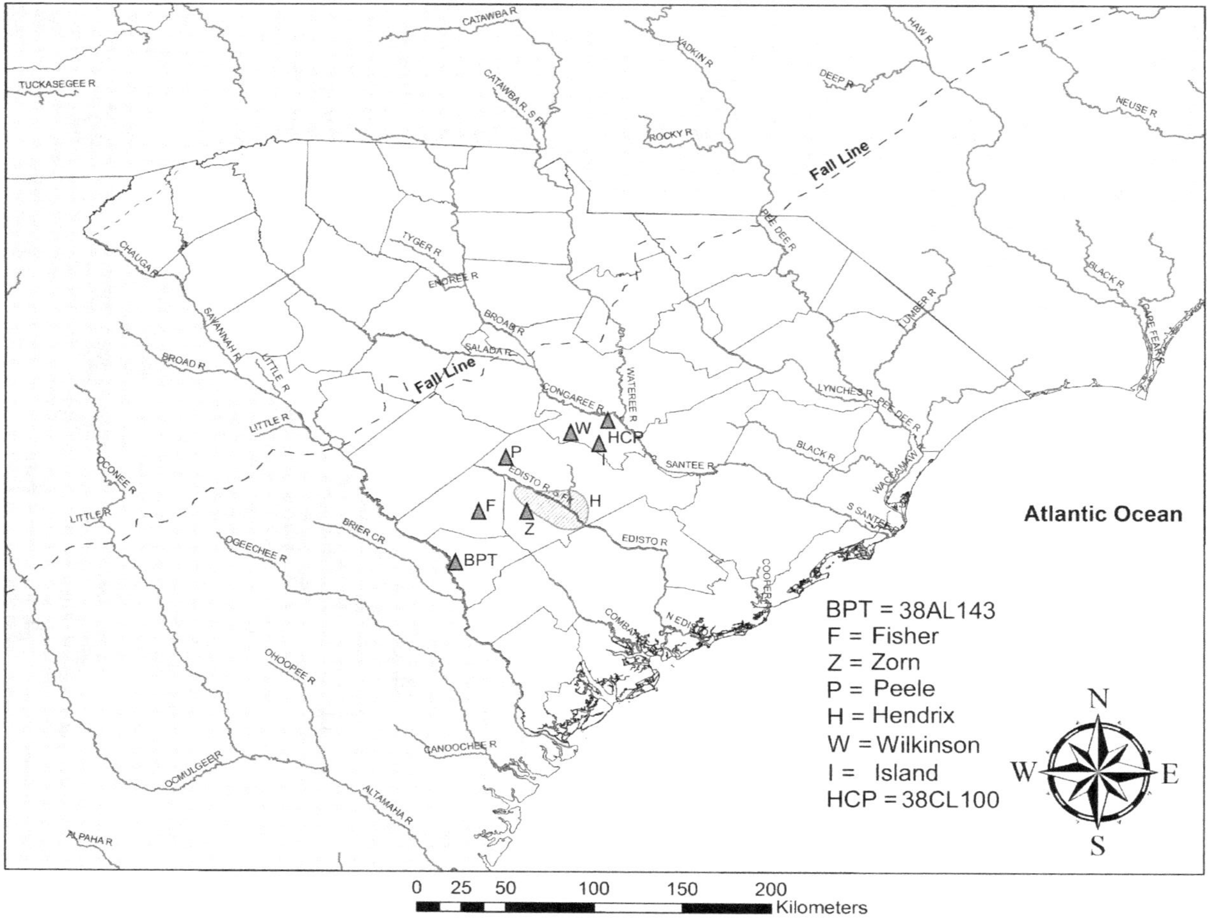

Figure 13.1. Transect of private collections studied by Goodyear and Wilkinson 2014b (page 15:Figure 2).

The Early Archaic

The Early Archaic is an archaeological period following the fluted-point Paleoindian cultures coinciding with the beginning of the Holocene, or the modern-day environment. Radiocarbon and stratigraphic evidence indicates it lasted roughly 2,500–3,000 years, with distinct subphases based on projectile point changes (Anderson and Hanson 1988; Anderson and Sassaman 1996, 2012:5; Bense 1994; Broyles 1971; Coe 1964; Daniel 1998, 2001; Dejarnette et al. 1962; Goodyear 1999, 2014; Goodyear et al. 1990; Goodyear et al. 1993; Sassaman 1996; Tuck 1974). Although it had some continuity with Paleoindian stone tool technology, it also brought with it a more diverse lithic toolkit, which included notched projectile points suitably adapted for hunting the new dominant species of fauna, such as white-tailed deer, as well as an expansion in unifacial tool forms, and the addition of the adze (Figure 13.2) (Anderson and Sassaman 1996; Coe 1964; Daniel 1998; Goodyear 1974; Morse and Goodyear 1973; Sassaman et al. 2002; Sassaman et al. 2005). The Early Archaic is of interest to archaeologists because it occurred during the Pleistocene–Holocene transition, which has long been the subject of a great deal of investigation worldwide (Ellis et al. 1998; Goodyear 1999; Meeks and Anderson 2012; Morse et al. 1996; Watts 1980). The Early Archaic begins just after the end of the Younger Dryas, about 11,600 calendar years ago, with the onset of more modern climatic conditions. Based on the greatly increased numbers of archaeological sites and artifacts from previous Paleoindian cultures, it appears to represent something of an extensive population expansion all over the Southeast (Anderson and Sassaman 1996, 2012; Morse et al. 1996:328). For the purposes of this study, I have defined the temporal boundaries of the Early Archaic to include everything post-Dalton, to prior to Morrow Mountain. This was done to encompass the entirety of what could be considered to be Early Archaic hafted-biface technology up to the onset of Morrow Mountain points, with its adoption of unambiguous socketed stemmed points (Sassaman 2010).

Previous Models

In the South Atlantic area of the Southeast, some attempts have been made by archaeologists to model Early Archaic settlement systems. These have tended to focus on large sites located on the major rivers. The inter-riverine zones, or the landscape between the major rivers, have tended to be

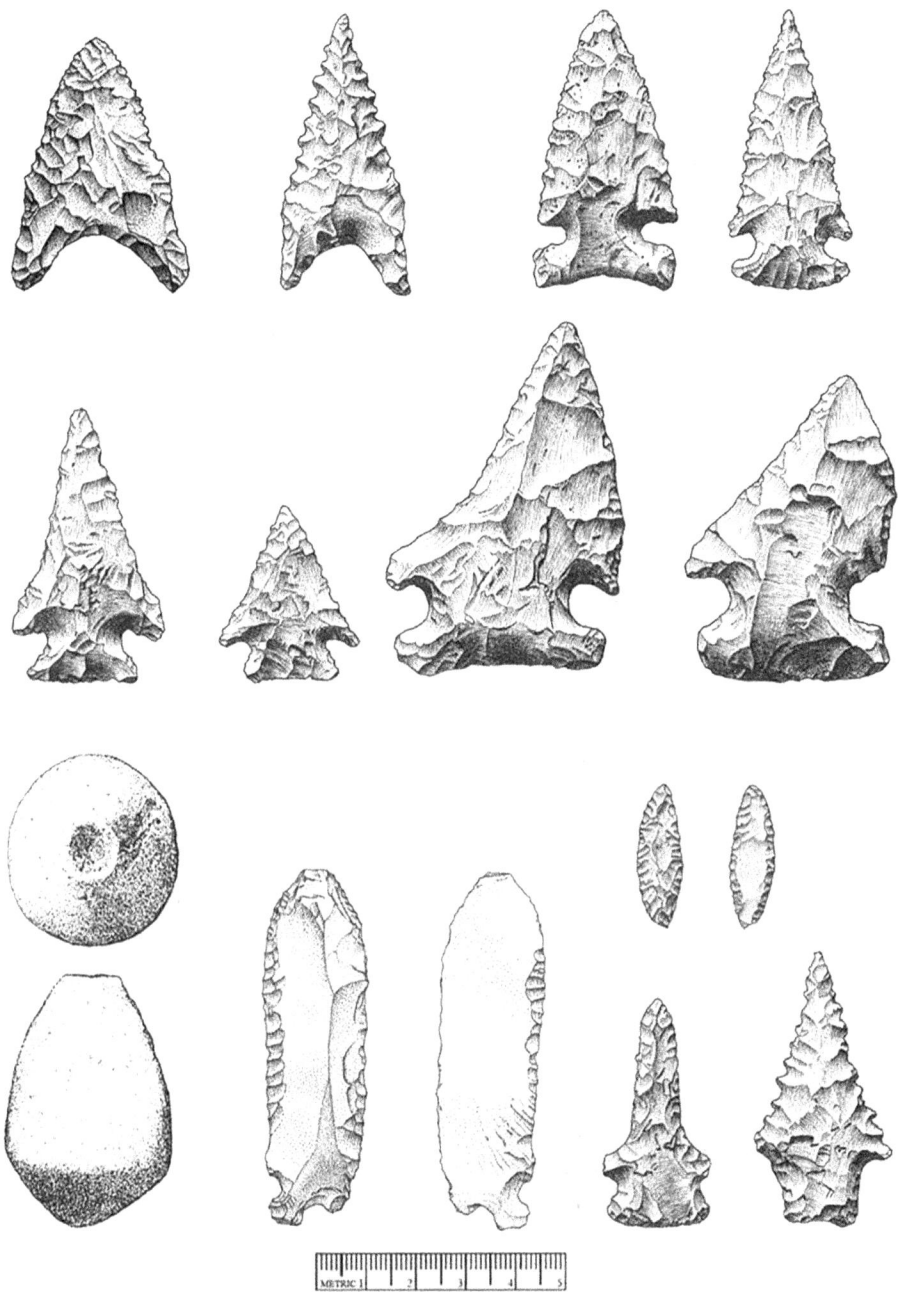

Figure 13.2. Early Archaic stone tool diversity (courtesy of Dr. Al Goodyear and the Southeastern Paleoamerican Survey).

understudied (Anderson and Hanson 1988; Anderson and Schuldenrein 1983; Daniel 1998, 2001; Sassaman et al. 1988; Sassaman 1996). In contrast, Daniel (2001) examined Kirk and Palmer corner-notched points in private and state-owned collections along the Yadkin–Pee Dee drainage in both North and South Carolina and compared the riverine transect to a transect across drainages in North Carolina. Until recently, no one has extensively studied the Upper and Middle Coastal Plain of South Carolina between the major rivers, the Savannah, and the Congaree/Santee. This inter-riverine zone is not well surveyed and, with few exceptions, lacks significant site excavations (Anderson et al. 1979; Goodyear and Wilkinson 2014a, 2014b; cf. Sassaman et al. 2005). Another significant factor in this zone is the absence of naturally available toolstone. While large-scale systematic surveys are lacking, a number of private artifact collections have been made, which have great potential for examining diagnostic artifacts and their raw materials. A good illustration of this kind of analysis can be seen in the study by Sassaman et al. (2005) of the Zorn collection located in Bamberg County, midway between the major rivers.

Anderson and Schuldenrein (1983) analyzed the excavated Early Archaic assemblages at the Rucker's Bottom site and compared it to nine other excavated assemblages and 88 surface-collected sites. Their analysis indicated that Early Archaic hunter-gatherers became more residential and focused their subsistence strategies around the major river drainages, and it was so argued based on the diversity of stone tools present on extralocal raw materials such as Allendale chert. Their study focused its attention on unambiguously typed Palmer and Kirk points and determined that more rapid movement of extralocal raw materials was present within the riverine zone, while the absence of extralocal raw materials in the inter-riverine Piedmont suggested slower movement or infrequent use. As a result of this determination, they concluded that Early Archaic movement was concentrated along the riverine zone. Much has been learned about Early Archaic typology since this publication, but the focus on the Savannah River Valley has created a biased effect on the interpretations of Early Archaic subsistence and settlement strategies on the South Carolina Coastal Plain.

Anderson and Hanson (1988) proposed that Early Archaic hunter-gatherers centered their settlement around major river drainages with their abundant resources. They argued that movement up and down the drainage from the Coastal Plain to the Piedmont occurred for the seasonal exploitation of plants and animals where a spectrum of foraging behaviors would be present (Binford 1980). During the spring and summer seasons, resource availability would be more abundant and widespread, and thus a more dispersed pattern of foraging is expected. The winter season would have fewer plant resources available. In the fall higher deer concentrations might be expected in upland mast-producing forests, likely resulting in fall and winter hunting camps. The Coastal Plain, with its abundance of surface water and larger riverine zones, would support more biodiversity and would also have a longer growing season for plant resources, due to its warmer average temperatures for longer periods of time compared to the Piedmont. Their model proposed a system of bands and macrobands within which people would organize themselves during seasonal exploitations of different plant and animal resources. Large aggregations of people occurred primarily for the purposes of exchanging mates and information, likely along the Fall Line in winter base camps. Their analysis focused on social-structure factors and the effects each had on the organization of mobility and subsistence.

This model has been tested and supported by the work of Sassaman (1996), which utilized the statewide collector database, a product primarily of the work of Tommy Charles at the South Carolina Institute of Archaeology and Anthropology (SCIAA) (Charles 1981, 1983, 1986). Sassaman utilized the database to examine several transects both along major river drainages and across them in the different geographic regions of the state. While Sassaman (1996) used the database to map the extent of different hafted-biface types, in what could perhaps be called cultural ranges (1996:Fig. 4.1), the transects studied only Kirk and Palmer corner-notched points (1996:Figs. 4.3–4.6). His analysis of corner-notched hafted bifaces seems to support the arguments proposed by Anderson and Hanson (1988). He does, however, note that although the Anderson and Hanson model seemed to be the most accurate explanation of Early Archaic mobility, it did not explain the cross-drainage movement of Allendale chert artifacts specifically on the Coastal Plain. Sassaman's analysis focused on hafted bifaces only and did not include an analysis of all types of Early Archaic hafted bifaces or other Early Archaic tool forms present.

Daniel's (2001) examination of the Early Archaic period offers a different interpretation of Early Archaic settlement and subsistence behavior. Daniel studied Kirk and Palmer corner-notched bifaces in a transect along the Yadkin–Pee Dee River drainage in North Carolina and South Carolina and compared them to a cross-drainage transect in North Carolina. Daniel's analysis indicated a pattern of raw material dependence on high-quality North Carolina Uwharrie Mountain rhyolites. His interpretation indicates a lithic-raw-material-centered settlement system, which implies that hunter-gatherers during the Early Archaic focused their geographic movement around the raw materials they utilized for the manufacture of their stone tools. In that sense, their settlement system was "lithic centered." Daniel's analysis was also limited to corner-notched hafted bifaces without considering other tool types.

Raw Materials

One aspect of this study that has allowed for reliable interpretations regarding mobility is the restricted geographic range of the geologic occurrences of various toolstones. The geographical position of the present transect is situated in such a way that both ends of the transect are located in the geographic vicinity of very different lithic raw material sources, with a barren zone in between. The zone between the major rivers is lacking in lithic raw material, with the exception of quartz, which can be found as small cobbles in small isolated occurrences among the smaller river systems present on the Coastal Plain.

The raw materials present on the southwesternmost end of the transect occur along the Savannah River in Allendale County. These materials include the famous Allendale chert quarries, quartz from river gravels, and a variety of orthoquartzite for which no evidence of quarrying has been found (Goodyear and Charles 1984). Extensive quarries of the Allendale chert have been identified and explored archaeologically (Goodyear 2012, 2017; Goodyear and Charles 1984; Novick 1978; Upchurch 1984b).

On the northeasternmost end of the transect, a variety of different raw materials are present. Some Coastal Plain cherts are present that have a varying range of quality and availability. Black Mingo chert is available along the Congaree, Wateree, and Santee rivers. One quarry of this material has been identified and reported archaeologically along the Congaree River (Goodyear and Wilkinson 2014a). Wyboo chert is available along the Santee River, and at least one known quarry has been investigated and reported (Costello and Goodyear 2014; Costello and Steffy 2013). Another raw material source available in a range of places along the Santee River drainage is orthoquartzite. This raw material is a sandstone cemented together with silica, which allows for the manufacture of stone tools. The western most known occurrence occurs in Calhoun County (Goodyear and Wilkinson 2015). Unlike the orthoquartzite found in Allendale County, these sources were extensively utilized throughout prehistory, as it is often present in private collections in this locale (Goodyear 2014; Goodyear and Wilkinson 2014a, 2014b, 2015). Also present in this geographic region is quartz, which has been transported fluvially from the Piedmont.

Other raw materials present in the study are various metavolcanics from the Uwharrie Mountain vicinity (Daniel 1998, 2001; Daniel and Butler 1996; Moore and Irwin 2006; Novick 1978; Steponaitis et al. 2006). These materials were heavily transported fluvially down the Pee Dee River in the northeastern portion of South Carolina's Coastal Plain (Young 2010). Also sometimes present among artifact assemblages are varieties of Ridge and Valley cherts from northern Georgia and Tennessee (Goodyear et al. 1990; Novick 1978; Upchurch 1984b). No known geologic sources of this material have yet been identified within modern South Carolina state lines.

The Present Study

In recent years several large private collections have been identified in Allendale, Barnwell, Bamberg, Orangeburg, and Calhoun counties, forming a transect from the Savannah River to the Congaree River (Figure 13.1) (Goodyear and Wilkinson 2014b:Fig. 2). Given the lack of knowledge for the inter-riverine zone, these collections were analyzed with a view toward documenting the Early Archaic hafted bifaces by type and raw material. Large, well-provenienced private collections were utilized, which, according to Sassaman et al. (2005:35) are useful for "comparative analyses at the scales of locality, river drainage, or subregion." Not only were Early Archaic hafted bifaces studied, but all time-sensitive stone tools were also inventoried (Goodyear and Wilkinson 2014b). These collections yielded a total of 5,010 typed hafted bifaces ranging from the Paleoindian through the Mississippian period. Throughout the analysis of Early Archaic tools, both metric and nonmetric attributes of hafted bifaces and unifaces were recorded, and documented with drawings and photographs. This study included 744 Early Archaic typed hafted bifaces, and 482 unifaces (Wilkinson 2014). Table 13.1 documents the largest collections studied across this transect.

Hafted Biface Results

Traditional cultural historical types were used for the analysis of hafted bifaces, such as: Hardaway and Taylor side-notched, Kirk and Palmer corner-notched, Kirk Stemmed, bifurcates, and Stanly (Figure 13.3) (Anderson

Table 13.1. Large Private Collections Studied in This Transect and the
Frequencies of Early Archaic Hafted Bifaces

Zone	Sites/Collections	Hafted Biface Sample N	No. of Early Archaic Hafted Bifaces	EA % of Collection
I	38AL135 Charles Site	700+	18	
	38AL143 Big Pine Tree		105	
II	Hendrix Barnwell	40	12	30.77
	Lorene Fisher	400	13	3.25
	Harrold Keel	196	19	9.69
	Jenkins	88	22	25
	Porter	79	4	5.06
	Tommy Sanders	166	14	8.43
III	Hendrix Bamberg	769	120	15.6
	Zorn	1329	82	6.17
IV	Peele	367	30	8.17
	Hendrix Orangeburg	34	5	14.71
V	Island	725	96	13.24
	Wilkinson	65	11	16.92
	G. Lee Thomas	64	11	17.19
VI	38CL100 High Creek	428	140	32.71
	John Hydrick	87	3	3.45
	Ruffin	73	9	12.33
	G. Lee Thomas	72	7	9.72
	38CL17 Buycke's Bluff	28	13	46.43

1991; Broyles 1971; Cable 1996; Coe 1964; Daniel 1998; Dejarnette et al. 1962; Goodyear et al. 1993; Michie 1966, 1996; Sassaman et al. 2002; Tuck 1974). Also recorded were projectile point fragments, and well-made weathered preforms. Various types of flake tools and unifaces were recorded, such as: hafted end scrapers, end scrapers, side scrapers, side-end scrapers, Edgefield scrapers, gravers, drills, Waller knives, etc. (Coe 1964; Daniel 1998; Michie 1968, 1973; Sassaman et al. 2002). Other tools recorded in this transect were adzes and bolas.

In order to understand the distribution of these artifacts across the inter-riverine zone, this transect was divided into 20-km-wide zones beginning

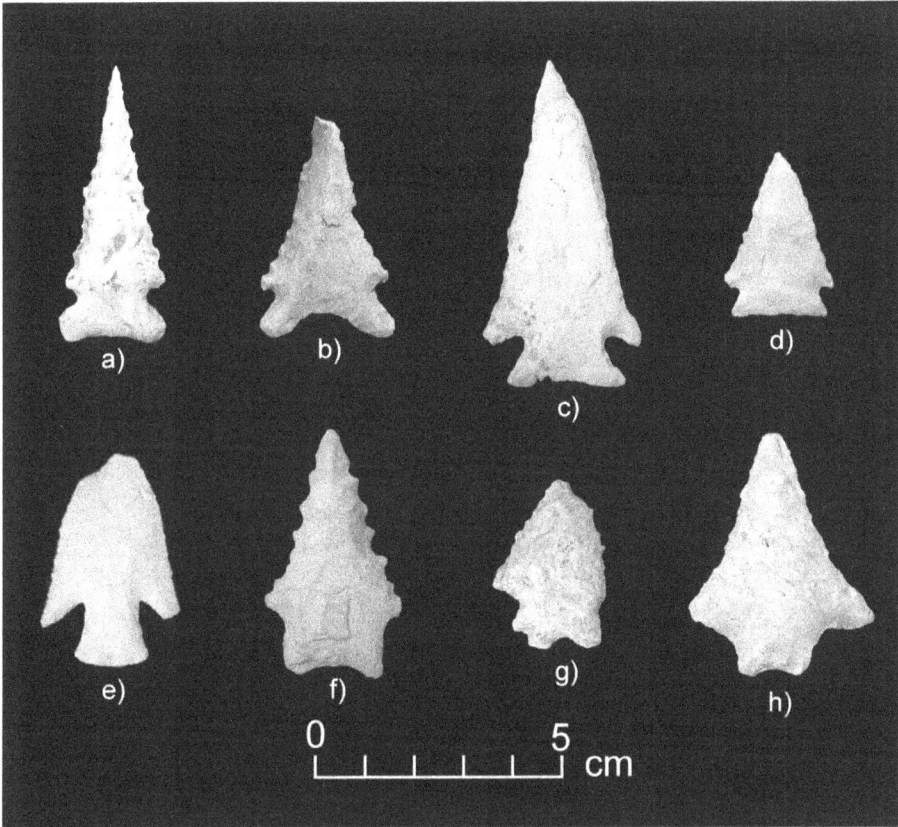

Figure 13.3. Examples of commonly accepted point types from the private collections studied: (*a*) Taylor side notched from the Big Pine Tree site (38AL143). (*b*) Van Lott side notched from the Harrold Keel Collection. (*c*) Kirk corner notched from the Dennis Hendrix collection. (*d*) Palmer corner notched from the Jerry Morris collection. (*e*) Hardin stemmed from the Dennis Hendrix collection. (*f*) Kirk Stemmed from the Buycke's Bluff site (38CL17). (*g*) Bifurcate from the Kat Salley collection (38CL100). (*h*) Stanly from the Dennis Hendrix collection.

at the Savannah River, extending northeast to the Congaree/Santee River (Figure 13.4). Others such as Binford (2001) and Surovell (2009:130) have estimated that the maximum distance a hunter-gatherer could walk in a day would be 20 km (Gingerich 2012; Goodyear 2014:5). With this idea in mind, the transect was divided into six 20-km zones, river to river, in order to measure time and distance to raw-material sources. The incidence of raw material use per 20-km zone was then examined by the different commonly accepted notch type horizons: side, corner, and post-Kirk hafted bifaces.

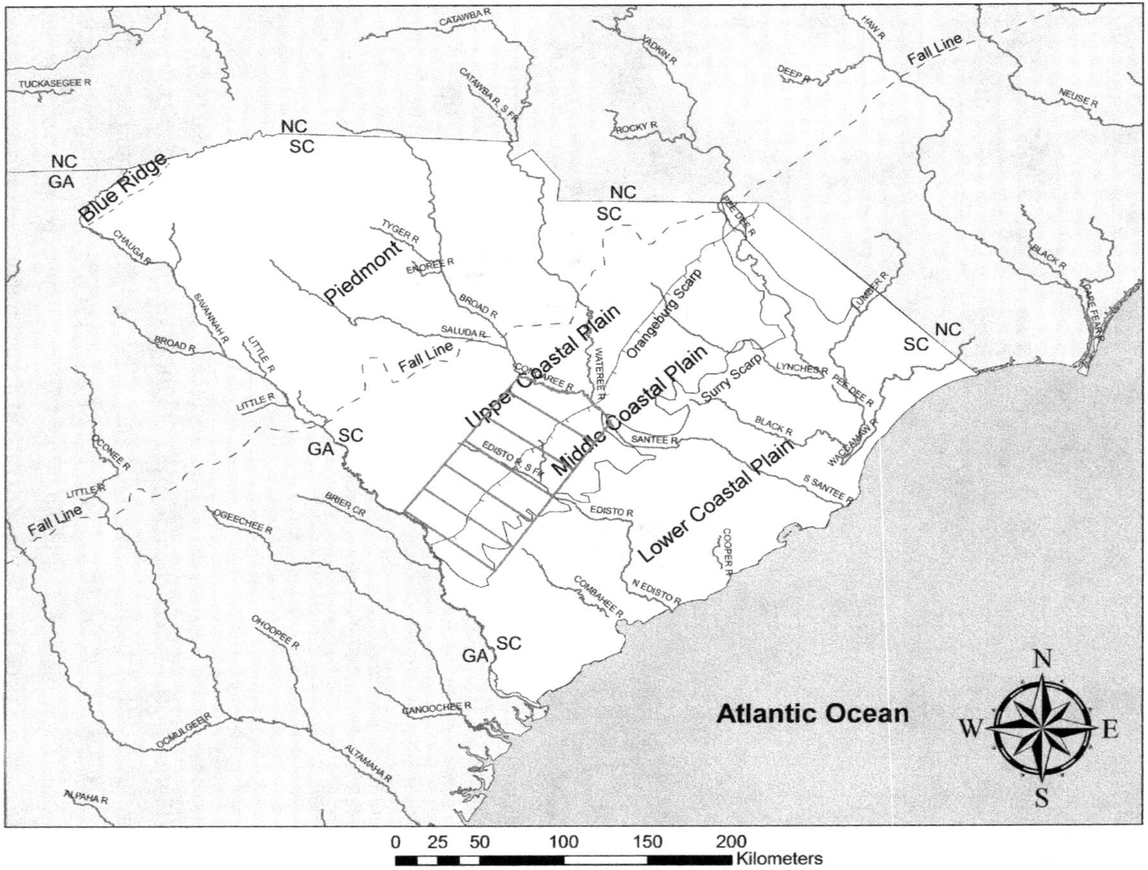

Figure 13.4. Map of the twenty kilometer zones that divided the private collections for this study between the Savannah river and the Congaree/Santee river.

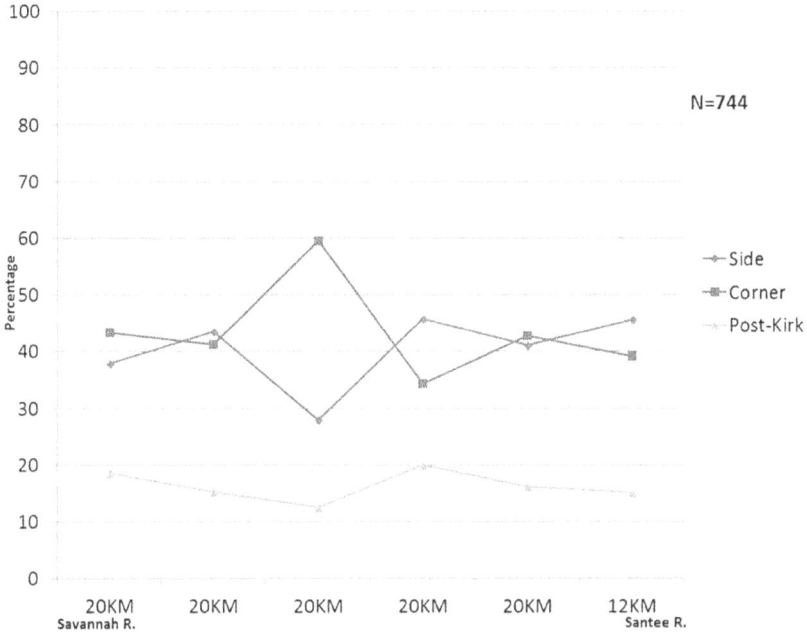

Figure 13.5. Hafted biface type frequency by zone.

Post-Kirk here is meant to include stemmed points such as Kirk Stemmed and Stanly, as well as basally notched bifurcate types.

Of the 744 typed Early Archaic hafted bifaces, corner-notched bifaces were the most abundant, at 45.97 percent. Side-notched bifaces were present at 38.58 percent, and post-Kirk hafted bifaces summed to 15.46 percent of the study. This decline in post-Kirk hafted bifaces has previously been observed by other archaeologists, such as Anderson (1991) and Sassaman (1996). The results of this study show the same pattern. Plotting the frequencies of each notch type per zone across the Coastal Plain illustrates this, with the exception of the last zone, where side-notched points are seen to be more abundant than corner (Figure 13.5). The fourth zone has a very small sample of typed Early Archaic hafted bifaces, which causes the percentages for that zone to be less reliable, a problem to be remedied in the near future.

Next to be examined were the raw materials used for all of the Early Archaic types, moving from raw material quarry sources across the inter-riverine zone, which has been described as a raw material "desert." Thus, every stone artifact in the inter-riverine zone had to have been brought in;

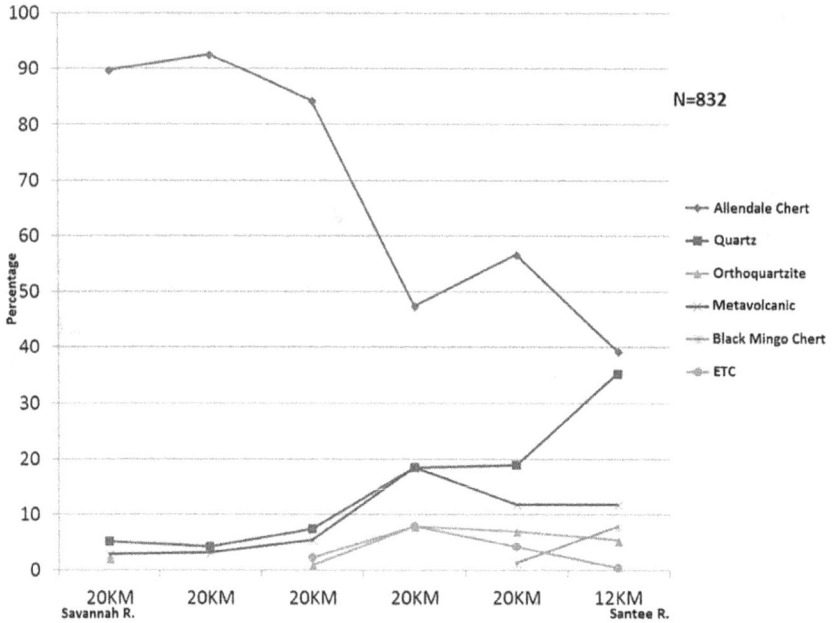

Figure 13.6. Overall raw material use across the Coastal Plain throughout all of the Early Archaic.

for example, Allendale chert is predominantly used over other materials across the transect (Figure 13.6).

When looking at raw material use per notch point cluster, across the transect from the Savannah River to the Congaree/Santee rivers, another pattern emerges. While Allendale chert is still heavily utilized for side-notched bifaces, quartz and other materials local to the Congaree/Santee River Valley see an increase in utilization. This is especially apparent by the heavier utilization of quartz (Figure 13.7). Corner-notched bifaces show a different pattern. Allendale chert is the dominant material, while other exotics and metavolcanics show an increase in utilization over more readily available local raw materials (Figure 13.8). Post-Kirk hafted bifaces show a similar pattern to corner-notched points, in that exotics are present more frequently than are locally available materials (Figure 13.9).

In order to examine local versus exotic material use, the transect was divided into two larger zones. The first zone consisted of the first three 20-km zones from the Savannah River out onto the Coastal Plain, while the second consisted of the last three zones stretching from the middle of the transect to the Congaree/Santee rivers. This division represents the shift in

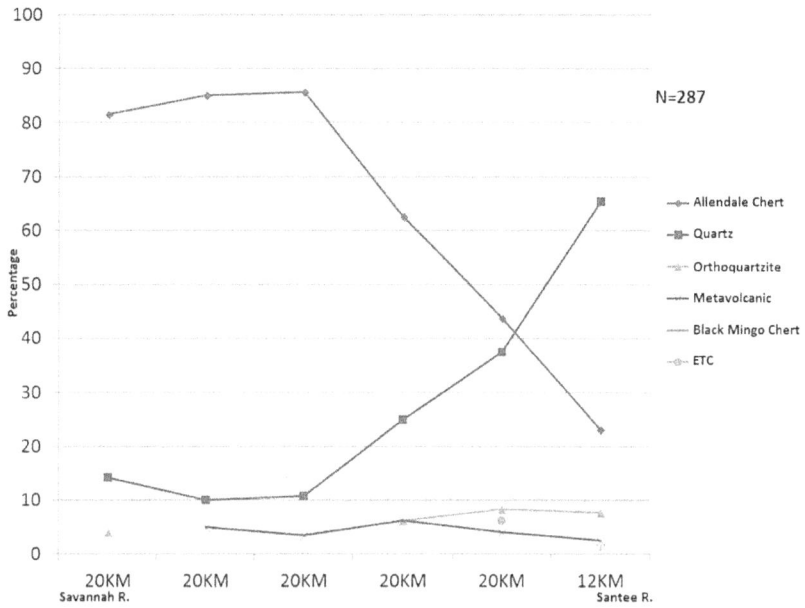

Figure 13.7. Side-notched raw material use by zone.

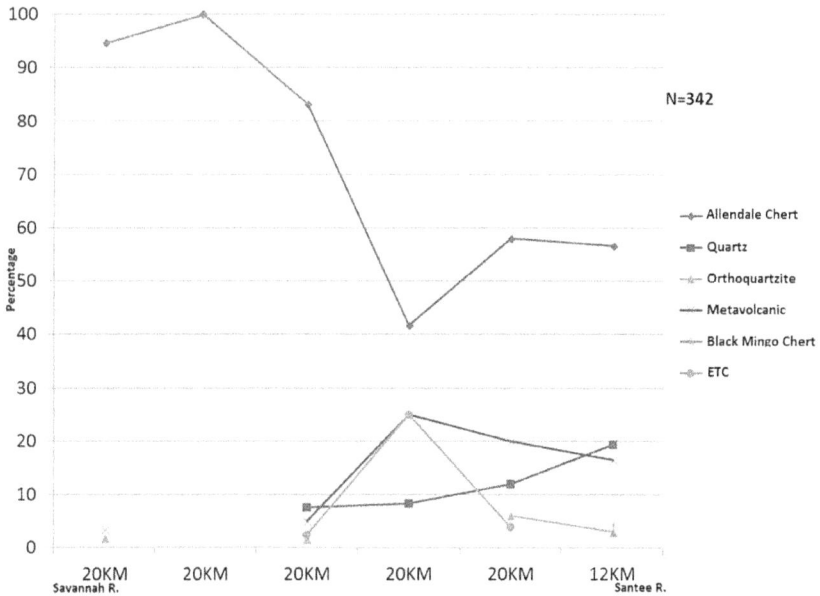

Figure 13.8. Corner-notched raw material use by zone.

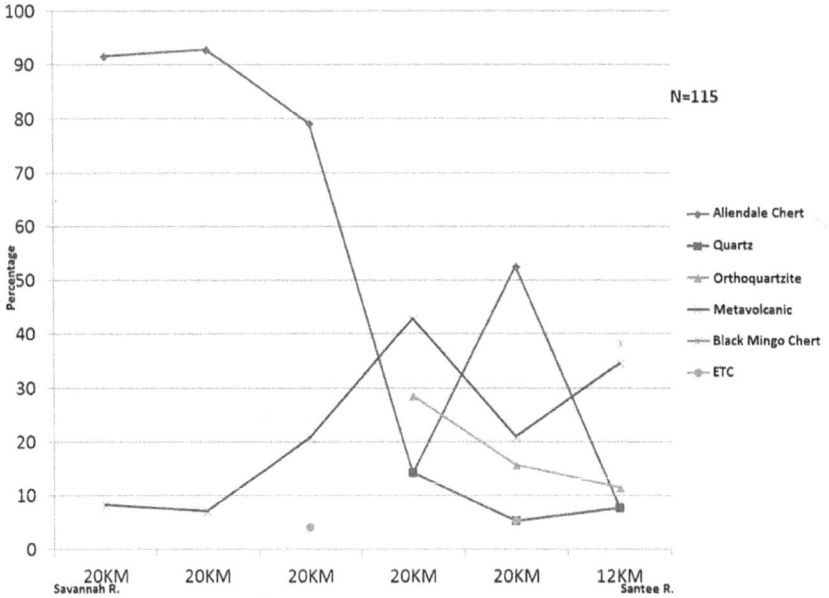

Figure 13.9. Post-Kirk raw material use by zone.

time and energy needed to acquire new lithic raw materials while foraging in the inter-riverine zone. In the first half of the transect, or the first 60 km, the use of local Allendale chert predominates. Of the Early Archaic hafted bifaces, 84.14 percent were made on Allendale chert, and 11.72 percent made on quartz, both of which are locally available in the Savannah River drainage. Only 4.14 percent of hafted bifaces are made of exotic materials imported to this zone (Table 13.2). From side-notched bifaces, through corner-notched bifaces, to post-Kirk bifaces, there is a steady increase in the number of exotics imported into this zone, as expressed in Table 13.2.

For the second half of the transect, there is a significant shift in raw-material utilization. Upon reaching a relatively close proximity of the Congaree/Santee River drainage, and its associated raw-material sources, local raw-material utilization drops to only 42.41 percent for all Early Archaic hafted bifaces. People who produced side-notched bifaces are the dominant users of local materials, with 61.27 percent local use, while those producing corner-notched bifaces maintained an exotic dependence, with only 21.71 percent of local materials used. Post-Kirk biface manufacture falls between those patterns, with 42.31 percent local use. Table 13.2 also expresses these changes. The percentages observed here resemble percentages previously

Table 13.2. Local versus Exotic Raw Material Use by Hafted Biface Type in Two Large 60-Km Zones, Evenly Dividing the Transect across the Coastal Plain

	Side		Corner		Post-Kirk		Typed		Overall	
	N	%	N	%	N	%	N	%	N	%
FIRST 60KM										
Local	141	97.24	202	94.84	54	87.1	397	94.3	423	94.63
Exotic	4	2.76	11	5.17	9	14.52	24	5.7	24	5.37
SECOND 52KM										
Local	87	61.27	28	21.71	22	42.31	137	42.41	150	38.96
Exotic	55	38.73	101	78.29	30	57.69	186	57.59	235	61.04

observed by Goodyear (2014:Tables7–9) in his study of the Congaree, Wateree, and Santee (COWASEE) river basin. The materials local to the Congaree/Santee River basin—quartz, orthoquartzite, Black Mingo, and Wyboo cherts—were infrequently utilized as compared to exotic materials for Early Archaic hafted bifaces in this zone. This infrequent use is likely the result of these materials being of a lesser quality for knapping as compared to Allendale chert or Uhwarrie rhyolites, and therefore less desirable. Quartz cobbles present locally in river gravels tend to be small, and orthoquartzite is known to be more brittle, like Black Mingo and Wyboo cherts, which are extremely fossiliferous and difficult to work.

Uniface Results

Throughout the analysis of Early Archaic artifacts from these private collections, the presence of unifacial tools was abundant. The comprehensive and systematic analysis of unifacial tools has not yet been attempted for the Early Archaic across the state of South Carolina, with the exception of the collector database compiled by Tommy Charles of SCIAA (1981, 1983, 1986). The present study included at a minimum the type and raw material of each uniface, and in the case of formalized types have been analyzed in detail. Unifacial tools are present in varying frequencies throughout the inter-riverine zone and occur with the hafted bifaces. Because most formalized and expedient unifaces are found in both Paleoindian and Early Archaic assemblages, specific temporal placement of these artifacts was not possible, due to the surface nature of the collections. The formalized and expedient unifaces analyzed in this study are believed to be at least Early Archaic in age, due to evidence from excavations that these tool types do

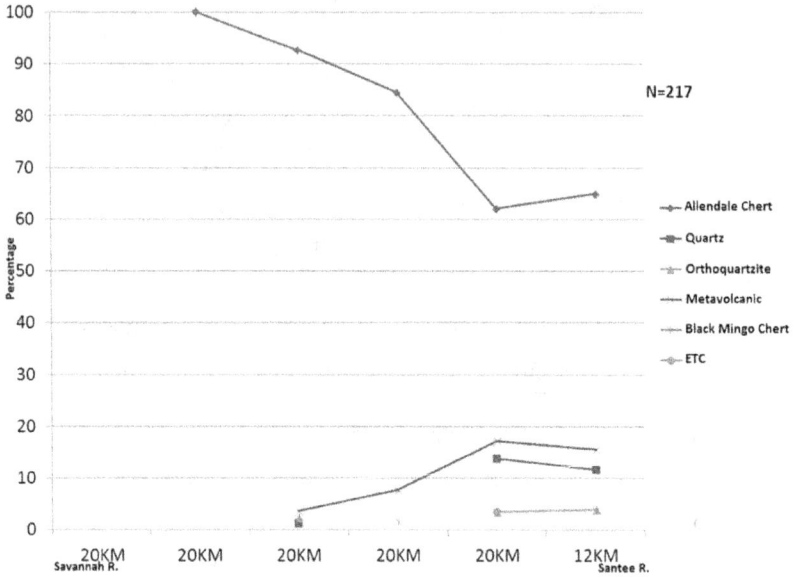

Figure 13.10. Hafted endscraper raw material use by zone.

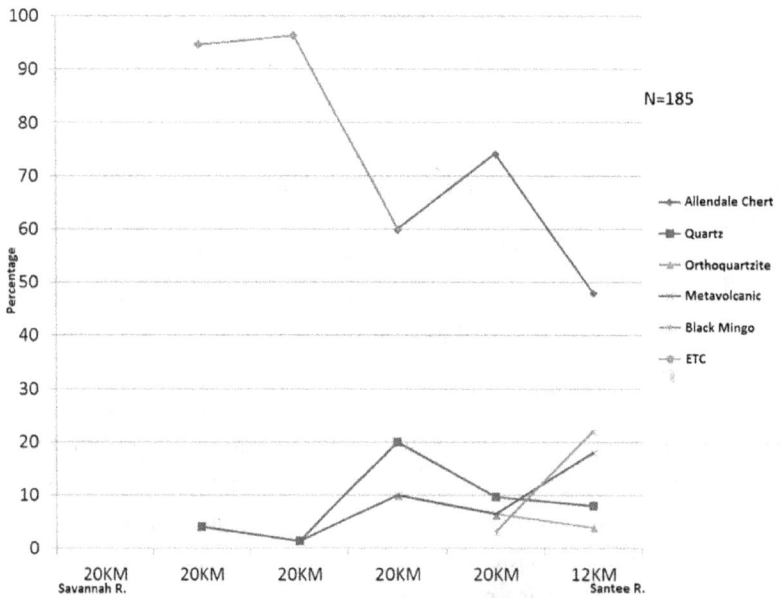

Figure 13.11. Sidescraper raw material use by zone.

Table 13.3. Uniface Types by Zone

Uniface Type	Zone 1	Zone 2	Zone 3	Zone 4	Zone 5	Zone 6	Totals
Hafted endscraper	Present	15	83	13	29	77	217
Sidescraper		24	70	10	31	50	185
Endscraper		1	3	3	2	16	25
Side-endscraper		2	13		5	1	21
Bilateral Sidescraper		4				2	6
Spokeshave		2	1				3
Limace			2				2
Graver		1	6	1	3	6	17
3-Sided uniface				2			2
Turtleback/circular/ thumbnail Scraper				2	2		4
Totals		49	178	31	72	152	482

not extend later in time into the Middle Archaic (Coe 1964; Daniel 1998; Sassaman et al. 2002; Sassaman et al. 2005). Given the much lower frequencies of Paleoindian hafted bifaces, compared to the relatively high frequencies of Early Archaic hafted bifaces and diagnostic tools, it is assumed for the sake of this study that the majority of the unifacial tools studied fall within the Early Archaic time period (Daniel and Goodyear 2015, 2017; Goodyear, personal communication 2015; Sassaman et al. 2005).

It should be noted that the first 20-km zone along the Savannah River contained an abundance of unifaces, such as those from the Big Pine Tree Site (38AL143) that were not included in this study. The only collections examined were quarry sites on the Savannah River in Allendale County, where an overwhelming number of expedient unifaces and quarry discards were found. The results of the analyses of unifaces and other tools were geographically located from the second 20-km zone through all the zones stretching to the northeast toward the Congaree and Santee rivers.

The most frequent unifacial tool type present was the hafted endscraper, easily recognized by its steep unifacial flaking on the end of an often teardrop-shaped flake (Coe 1964; Daniel 1998; Sassaman et al. 2005). Hafted endscrapers were present with 217 examples, which is nearly half (45.02 percent) of the total of 482 unifaces present. The second-most abundant unifacial tool type was the sidescraper, with 185 (38.38 percent) examples present. The distribution of these two tool types by raw material across the coastal plain is expressed in Figures 13.10 and 13.11. These figures illustrate the dominance of Allendale chert, which mirrors the raw material utilization for hafted bifaces throughout the Early Archaic. These unifacial tools are quantified with the remaining unifacial tool types in Table 13.3.

Other Tools

Other tool types were present that are known to occur throughout the Early Archaic. These include Edgefield scrapers, adzes, bolas (commonly called egg stones), drills, and Waller knives (Table 13.4). The Edgefield scraper has a unifacially flaked bit with a side-notched hafting element that is created with either bifacial or unifacial flaking (Bridgman Sweeney et al. 2008; Michie 1968, 1973; Sassaman et al. 2002). Well-made flaked adzes, which often exhibit grinding on the lateral edges and bit, have been excavated in South Carolina in Early Archaic assemblages (Sassaman et al. 2002). Similar adzes have been excavated outside of this state farther west in Dalton assemblages (Goodyear 1974; Morse and Goodyear 1973). Temporal placement of these Dalton assemblages as compared to the side-notched hafted bifaces here in South Carolina suggests contemporaneity (Goodyear, personal communication 2015). Bolas are ground stone objects that often resemble the shape of an egg, often having a flat or slightly concave ground feature on the smaller end. (Figure 13.2) Bolas have also been excavated in Early Archaic contexts at the Topper site (38AL23) in Allendale County and have been suspected to be associated with Taylor side-notched hafted bifaces (Goodyear, personal communication 2015). Drills are commonly associated with Early Archaic assemblages (Figure 13.2) and, due to their weathered appearance and their skillful manufacture, were included in this study (Daniel 1998:Figs. 4.3 and 4.44). Care was taken not to mistake an Early Archaic drill for a drill from the Late Archaic, which are known to occur in Savannah River hafted-biface assemblages (Sassaman et al. 2005:Fig. 9 a–d). Waller knives are expediently notched flakes (Figure 13.2) and are believed to belong to the Early Archaic based on the notched hafting elements and the weathering especially evident on Allendale chert (Goodyear et al. 1993). The presence of these tools is quantified in Table 13.4.

Discussion

Altogether, these data would indicate that more than just hunting was taking place in the inter-riverine zone, as indicated by the number of hafted bifaces. These points are characteristically resharpened, indicating use as knives, and were strategies to extend tool life. The unifacial tools would suggest that craft activities beyond just hide processing were also taking place. The presence of hafted adzes, some of which are fragmentary, would indicate that Early Archaic peoples were bringing heavy-duty woodworking

Table 13.4. Other Tool Types by Zone

Other Tools	Zone 1	Zone 2	Zone 3	Zone 4	Zone 5	Zone 6	Totals
Edgefield scraper	7	8	22		5	3	45
Adze	7	2	5	1	1	6	22
Bola	4	1			1	4	10
Kirk drill					3	1	4
Waller		3	5		1		9
Totals	18	14	32	1	11	14	

tools into the inter-riverine zone and using them there. Considering the totality of all of the collections examined and their proveniences, with the exception of the Island Site (38CL102), there were no large Early Archaic sites present. "Large" should be understood to mean sites with high densities of hafted bifaces and unifacial tools. This is in contrast with dense riverine sites like Big Pine Tree (38AL143) on the Savannah, and High Creek Plantation (38CL100) on the Congaree/Santee.

The contrast between local and exotic raw materials use patterns that are apparent between the side-notched and corner-notched hafted bifaces seems significant. In the case of side-notched hafted bifaces near the Congaree/Santee, while Allendale chert hafted bifaces are still present, they are eclipsed by hafted bifaces made of local materials such as quartz, orthoquartzite, and the local Black Mingo and Wyboo cherts. This is parallel to what Goodyear (2014:Table 8) found in the Congaree, Wateree, and Santee river drainage study. However, the high percentage of Allendale chert and high-quality rhyolites among the corner-notched hafted bifaces in the Congaree/Santee basin seems to suggest that by corner-notch times neighboring bands in South Carolina and North Carolina may have been using this riverine zone as a locality for aggregation. This also parallels what Goodyear (2014) found for corner-notched hafted bifaces and is consistent with Daniel's model of the Uwharrie and Allendale bands (Daniel 1998, 2001).

In Goodyear's (2014) extensive study down the Congaree, Wateree, and Santee river drainage, he found that the corner-notched hafted bifaces were almost identical to the pattern of exotic-raw-material utilization of Clovis. In this study he used the local-versus-exotic index as an indication of residence time in the COWASEE river drainage. The assumption is that higher percentages of locally utilized materials indicate that people were spending more time in the COWASEE river drainage. More time means more broken bifaces and discarded tools, and a need to replace them with local materials. While several collections analyzed here were also included in his study, our percentages both include collections independent from each study. Our percentages of local versus exotic materials for the Early Archaic hafted bifaces in this zone are almost exactly identical to each other, indicating that this pattern has some validity.

The model proposed by Daniel is very similar to a recognized pattern witnessed in Clovis. Daniel and Goodyear (2015, 2018) have argued that Clovis hunter-gatherers in the Carolinas organized themselves into macrobands that centered themselves on the major silicate resources in the Uwharrie vicinity as well as the Allendale and Brier Creek cherts of the Savannah River locale (Daniel and Goodyear 2015, 2017; Goodyear 2018). Goodyear has argued that Clovis technological organization depended on high-quality toolstone, which would allow flexibility in meeting the diverse needs of regionally mobile Paleoindian hunter-gatherers (Goodyear 1979). This required flexibility arose from the nature of high regional mobility among Paleoindians, who might travel great distances away from desired raw-material sources.

The Early Archaic is known to have some continuity with Paleoindian lithic technology, both of which were focused on highly curated strategies (Binford 1979). High regional mobility was also present among Early Archaic hunter-gatherers, as evidenced by the high percentages of exotic materials present in the Congaree/Santee river drainages throughout the Early Archaic. The raw-material utilizations of Clovis and corner-notched bifaces are identical in this region, both a result of the use of exotic materials from the Uwharrie and Allendale clusters (Goodyear 2014). Given the high regional mobility of Early Archaic hunter-gatherers, and the similarities in exotic raw-material utilization with Clovis, a dependence on a flexible toolkit seems apparent. In other words, Early Archaic hunter-gatherers relied on high-quality lithic raw materials for maintainable and dependable toolkits (Bleed 1986), similar to their Paleoindian predecessors.

A closer examination of the raw materials utilized during the Early Archaic is necessary. When examining Figure 13.6, the dominance of Allendale chert across the inter-riverine is obvious. As the transect approaches the vicinity of the Congaree/Santee rivers, the local materials from that locale appear on the graph. If the materials local to the Congaree/Santee such as Black Mingo and Wyboo cherts, quartz, and orthoquartzite are equal in quality to Allendale chert, why are those materials not traveling as far across the inter-riverine toward the Savannah River? In order for the argument to stand that Allendale chert and Uwharrie rhyolites are of a higher quality than the raw materials present in the Congaree/Santee locale, the

Table 13.5. Hafted Biface Types by Raw Material from the Andy Shull Collection

	Metavolcanic	Allendale Chert	Quartz	Orthoquartzite	Black Mingo Chert	Other Local	Other Exotic	Totals
Side	24	10	42	4	1		2	83
Corner	58	19	19	3	1	4	5	109
Post-Kirk	30	2	3	3	1	2		41
Totals	112	31	64	10	3	6	7	233

Table 13.6. Local versus Exotic Raw Material Use in the Andy Shull Collection

	Local Percentage		Exotic Percentage		Metavolcanic Percentage		Allendale Percentage	
	Total N	%	Total N	%	Total N	%	Total N	%
Side	49	59.04	34	40.96	24	28.92	10	12.05
Corner	27	24.77	82	75.23	58	53.21	19	17.43
Post-Kirk	9	21.95	32	78.05	30	73.17	2	4.88

pattern of Uwharrie rhyolites should mirror the dominance of Allendale chert beyond the Congaree/Santee.

Others have noted the shift of raw material utilization during the Early Archaic from Allendale chert to metavolcanics, and vice versa, when crossing the Congaree/Santee river drainage divide (Daniel 2001; Sassaman 1996). For the present study an additional collection was examined from the Black River drainage approximately 40 km east/northeast of the Congaree/Santee River drainage. The Black River drainage is lacking in raw-material sources just like the inter-riverine between the Savannah and the Congaree/Santee rivers. This collection came from a multitude of sites along this drainage and contained a total of 233 typed hafted bifaces from the Early Archaic. The totals of these hafted bifaces are presented in Table 13.5 according to the side, corner, and post-Kirk designations. Table 13.6 expresses the differences in local versus exotic material utilization between the notch horizons and shows the higher frequencies of metavolcanics throughout those horizons when compared to Allendale chert. Exotic raw materials such as Allendale chert and the various metavolcanics from the Uwharries are still dominant in the Black River drainage. Perhaps the most significant change in the pattern of local versus exotic raw-material use is the higher dependence on exotics seen in the post-Kirk horizon. In agreement with data presented by Sassaman (1996:Figs. 4.5 and 4.6), this collection is evidence of the shift from Allendale chert to Uwharrie metavolcanics as the dominant exotic raw material.

Broader Implications

Given this pattern of raw material distribution, care must be taken not to assume that these distributions are the necessary result of cultural territories. Raw-material quality, when analyzed with regard to a specific tool type and its use-life, should become apparent by its geographic distribution. This is to say that hafted bifaces, for example, made on different raw materials, will be transported only as far as the raw material's quality and the tool's use-life can maintain utility. Raw-material quality will determine the extent to which a tool can travel, assuming of course that all tools of a specific type (such as hafted bifaces) are made and used at a steady rate with similar use-lives. Considering this assumption, Daniel's model (2001), as he cautions us (1998:194–195), does not exclusively reflect territorial boundaries, but foraging ranges of probable macrobands made possible by the extent that high-quality raw materials such as Allendale chert and Uwharrie rhyolites maintain utility. Lesser-quality raw materials should have reduced utility, which is reflected in the reduced geographic dispersion of artifacts made from raw materials local to the Congaree/Santee river drainage as expressed in Figure 13.6. If Early Archaic foraging strategies were centered on high-quality raw-material sources such as Allendale chert, why would lesser-quality local materials be utilized? The fact that tools of the materials local to the Congaree/Santee river drainage do not tend to be found far from the locality in which they occur geologically, seems to suggest that they are in fact more expediently used.

A lithic-centered mobility strategy, however, also does not seem likely, and the Anderson and Hanson (1988) model of major river drainage dependence does not seem entirely adequate either, given the cross-drainage distribution of Allendale chert and Uhwarrie rhyolite artifacts. A geographically extensive analysis of raw-material distribution ranges needs to be taken into account, and hafted biface types need to be examined for their geographic ranges as well. Only when these comprehensive distributions are established will we be able to see a clearer picture of Early Archaic settlement strategies.

Conclusions

Much is left to be learned about the Early Archaic, and early prehistory in general. A comprehensive analysis of Early Archaic artifacts across the Coastal Plain perhaps creates more questions than it answers. Comprehensive studies such as this are useful in generating a more regionally complete sample of settlement behavior, which in turn allows for a more accurate interpretation of past cultural organizations and strategies. Finally, it seems clear from the results of analyzing these large, well-provenienced private collections that there is a significant story that can be told using such data. In the near-absence of intensive site surveys in the zone between the major rivers, as well as the lack of excavations, private collections can provide the information needed to flesh out the variation in past behavior as prehistoric peoples went into and across the major interfluves.

Acknowledgments

This case study has been influenced by a number of people over a several-year period. First and foremost, my parents, Robert and Belinda Wilkinson, have sacrificed and supported me throughout my life in countless ways, making my education possible. To them both I owe a great deal of love and thanks for all they have done and continue to do to support me. A great deal of thanks is owed to Albert Goodyear, whose encouragement and mentorship have made the beginning of my archaeological career and this chapter possible. Numerous individuals at the South Carolina Institute of Archaeology and Anthropology have encouraged and supported me; and to them, much thanks is owed. These include Karen Smith, Keith Stephenson, Christopher Moore, Keith Derting, Nena Rice, Steve Smith, and Susan Davis, as well as others who have contributed in some way to my development. Numerous individuals within the collecting and avocational communities have graciously granted access to their collections for study. The Salley family, notably Ms. Kat Salley and Ms. Jane Salley, have been very generous in allowing me to study their collections. Dennis Hendrix is thanked for allowing me to spend a considerable amount of time with his collection. Steve Williams has been a wonderful friend, has graciously allowed me to borrow his collections, and has provided insights from his flintknapping experience. Ms. Lorene Fisher has provided both access to her collection and a meal or two on my trips to her property. Another great friend, Andy Shull, has been both generous and patient in allowing me access to his collection on numerous occasions. Numerous other collectors who have granted me access to their collections and to whom I am also thankful include John Hydrick, the Jenkins collection at the Barnwell Museum, Harrold Keel, Jerry Morris, Adam and Susan Ruffin, Tommy Sanders, G. Lee Thomas, Gene Porter, and my father, Robert Wilkinson. It is with great thanks that I acknowledge these individuals, and my great appreciation for their help.

14

Late Pleistocene/Early Holocene Archaeology of the Southeastern Atlantic Slope

DAVID G. ANDERSON

Thirty years ago papers addressing early human occupation in the lower Southeast appeared only rarely, primarily because few professional archaeologists were concentrating on the subject. When the first peoples arrived and what they did once they got here have always been considered legitimate subjects for archaeological research. Most fieldwork and analysis, however, was directed to the major mound- or shell-midden-building cultures of the later Archaic, Woodland, Mississippian, and Historic periods, sites easily detected and yielding dramatic information and artifact return for comparatively little effort, at least when compared to the time it took to locate and excavate well-preserved earlier occupations. The chapters in this volume demonstrate that the situation has changed dramatically. A vibrant multidisciplinary community of scholars is now in place, routinely collecting and integrating archaeological and paleoenvironmental information on the earliest Americans. The fact that many of the contributors to this volume are in early stages of what promise to be long and distinguished careers means the future looks bright.

Some questions remain unchanged, such as when people first got here or how early occupations are identified. New research themes are emerging, however, and some old ones are receiving far greater attention. Relationships between climate change and human settlement, always a major consideration in hunter-gatherer research, has increased markedly as global warming has come to be accepted as a major challenge facing modern civilization. Studies examining sea level fluctuations and human occupation on the now-submerged continental shelf have proceeded to the point where analyses are targeting underwater locations where early settlements might be located (Anderson and Bissett 2015; Faught 2004a, 2004b, 2014; Harris, this volume; Harris et al. 2013; Sain 2016). Archaeologists are increasingly exploring how change in the global climate system affected human occupations throughout prehistory in the region, acquiring lessons useful for dealing with sea level rise happening now (e.g., Anderson et al. 2013, 2017; Sanger 2010; Sassaman 2016; Sassaman et al. 2014, 2016; Thompson and Worth 2011). The shoreline movement early populations experienced impacted all aspects of culture, including settlement, perceptions of landscape stability, burial practices, and cosmology, and we can expect no less to occur in the years to come in our own societies (Anderson and Bissett 2015; Sassaman 2012, 2013, 2016; Sassaman et al. 2014, 2016; Smallwood et al., this volume; Smallwood et al. 2015).

Early Paleoindian Pre-Clovis Occupations in the Southeast

When people first arrived in the Southeast remains an enduring subject of research and debate, and several of the chapters herein (e.g., Ensor, Goodyear and Sain, and Hemmings et al.) present evidence for a great antiquity to human settlement in the region, well before 13,000 cal yr B.P., when Clovis points occur widely. Such claims, flying in the face of most accepted archaeological and genetic evidence about the nature and timing of New World colonization, which places it no more than a few thousand years before Clovis (e.g., Goebel 2015; Goebel et al. 2008; Haynes 2015; Meltzer 2009; Raghavan et al. 2015; Waters and Stafford 2013), need to be carefully considered. It is a truism in science that extraordinary claims require extraordinary evidence, and that is certainly the case in archaeology, a field that has grappled with fantastic claims throughout its history (Feder 2011; Williams 1991). That does not mean early occupations do not exist, just that they require careful documentation. For the past 15 years, in fact, I have argued that our regional cultural sequence needs to reflect their existence, with Early Paleoindian assemblages corresponding to materials >13,250 cal yr B.P., Middle Paleoindian from 13,250 to 12,850 cal yr B.P., and Late Paleoindian from 12,850 to 11,700 cal yr BP, the latter corresponding to the Younger Dryas (Anderson 2001:152–156; Anderson and Sassaman 2012:5; Anderson et al. 2015:8–9; see also Waters and Stafford 2013, who argue that the pre-Clovis era should be known as the "Exploration" period). At present, however, given the existence of only three extensively excavated, dated, and reported *pre*-Clovis sites in the region—Cactus Hill (McAvoy and McAvoy 1997, 2015), Page-Ladson (Halligan et al. 2016; Webb 2006), and Topper (King 2012, 2016; Sain 2015)—with Vero a fourth now undergoing a comparable level of examination (Hemmings et al., this volume), about all that can be said with certainty is that human settlement in the Southeast had happened by ca. 14,000 to 15,000 years ago, but was minimal or at least archaeologically all but invisible or unrecognized until Clovis times, around 13,000 years ago, when hundreds of sites are identified by the presence of diagnostic projectile points (Anderson 2005; Anderson et al. 2015; Goodyear 2005a).

To determine when people first arrived in the Southeast, assemblages predating Clovis must be sought—and excavated, analyzed, and reported in such a way that they can be thoroughly evaluated, something that requires the publication of comprehensive site reports and, wherever possible, articles in major peer-reviewed journals. Site reports linked to well-curated assemblages, including both field and analysis records, represent the primary intellectual product of our profession. In-depth reporting is critical to evaluate what was done and found at a site and provides an essential guide to the analysis of associated assemblages for generations of subsequent scholars. Journal articles, furthermore, provide useful and informative synopses of major research projects and findings and are often far more carefully peer reviewed than site reports. By the very nature of their brevity, however, journal articles should be considered a complement to, and never a substitute for, site reports. Both journal articles and site reports thus need to be produced whenever possible for sites used to support extraordinary claims, such as when people first arrived in the Southeast, and what they were doing here. While these guidelines for reporting are directed to pre-Clovis assemblages, the same philosophy should guide archaeological research on sites of every period.

Few Paleoindian sites in the Southeast meet these admittedly steep reporting and associated curatorial requirements, although their numbers are growing, particularly for Early Paleoindian assemblages. The best-documented of these are Page-Ladson in Florida (Halligan et al. 2016; Webb 2006), Cactus Hill in Virginia (McAvoy and McAvoy 1997, 2015), Topper in South Carolina (Goodyear 2005a; King 2012, 2016; Sain 2015), and Big Eddy in Missouri (Lopinot et al. 1998, 2000), although arguably much more research and reporting needs to occur at all of them. The Debra L. Friedkin site in Texas (Waters et al. 2011), like Page-Ladson, sets the standard for the kind of rigorous peer-reviewed journal publication that needs to occur before claims can be considered likely substantiated—articles about both sites have appeared in the journal *Science* with extensive supplementary materials—and even then not all scholars are convinced these are pre-Clovis in age (e.g., Morrow et al. 2012). The chapters in this volume describing possible pre-Clovis industries are thus a necessary step, but not the final word, in the process of documenting such assemblages in the Southeast. Much remains to be done before Early Paleoindian assemblages will be accepted as uncritically as Middle and Late Paleoindian and Early Archaic sites are at present. Only when we have multiple, well-dated assemblages in secure stratigraphic context, and ideally artifacts unequivocally accepted as diagnostic temporal markers permitting the recognition of early assemblages in surface context, will our understanding of Early Paleoindian occupations in the region grow as rapidly as it has for Middle and Late Paleoindian assemblages in recent decades.

We need to keep an open mind, however, and not be dogmatic about what assemblages and dates are possible. When unusual industries are reported, what we need are thorough studies directed to evaluating whether the purported artifacts are humanly produced or not, and how they got into the deposits where they have been found (matters that Ensor and Goodyear and Sain, this volume, all consider). Detailed studies have been conducted with Pre-Clovis materials from Topper (King 2012, 2016; Goodyear and Sain this volume; Sain 2015), and while humanly created artifacts are present below Clovis, how they arrived in the ancient deposits remains to be fully determined and, as a result, the assemblage remains controversial (cf. Fiedel 2013, 2016; Goodyear 2005a; Waters et al. 2009; Wheat 2012). Goodyear and I have argued for years about the pre-Clovis materials at Topper, and we respect each other's efforts to understand the nature of the assemblage. He has been open and collegial in this regard, to the point of allowing my graduate students to work at the site and with the materials. First, Megan Hoak King (2012, 2016) conducted master's research, and subsequently Doug Sain (2015, 2016) undertook his doctoral research on the pre-Clovis deposits. King's (2012, 2016) thesis demonstrated unequivocally that there are humanly created chert flakes in the pre-Clovis deposits, but neither her work nor Sain's, which yielded similar results with a far larger sample, has answered the question as to how they got there. Both studies, importantly, have shown how ambiguous specimens can be differentiated from humanly created artifacts, although this same work has also shown that for many items no unequivocal determination can be made.

There is a lesson to be learned from this . . . we can disagree with our colleagues while maintaining positive working relationships and a common desire to find the truth. My own approach when it comes to dealing with ambiguous artifacts is that until they have been evaluated through thorough analysis, to adopt a modification of Yoffee's rule (1993:69) regarding early state-level societies . . . if you can argue about whether something is a state or not (or in this case an artifact or not), it is better to be conservative and assume the negative, that it isn't. Human agency is even more unlikely if the geological content is ambiguous or of great antiquity, or if large quantities of heavily weathered chert or other potential tool stone are present, increasing the likelihood that some or all of the "artifacts" are actually chance creations or geofacts. In this regard, local-, subregional-, and regional-scale geomorphological and geological research is critical if we are to efficiently find early sites and understand whether and how possible artifacts occur within them (Waters 2004; Waters et al. 2009; Moore et al., this volume). Working with geoarchaeologists is essential to effective site interpretation, a lesson I learned early in my career from Joe Schuldenrein when examining assemblages at Rucker's Bottom in the Richard B. Russell Reservoir on the upper Savannah River (Anderson and Schuldenrein 1983, 1985; Schuldenrein, this volume). Many of the sites and assemblages proposed as pre-Clovis in age in the Southeast, in my opinion, need to be more thoroughly excavated, evaluated, and reported.

One way to advance our understanding is to revisit sites excavated long ago and reexamine them using modern procedures. Hemmings, Adovasio, and colleagues' work at Vero is an exemplary multidisciplinary investigation of this kind, documenting what was done in the early twentieth century and what remains from this locality, which was the center of a firestorm of debate over its antiquity in the early twentieth century by some of the top scientific minds of the day, most of whom dismissed the possibility that Pleistocene-age deposits were present (Meltzer 2015:253–292). That decision, the recent work has shown, was woefully in error and highlights the need to leave portions of deposits behind where possible, so they can be reexamined by subsequent generations with different procedures and perspectives. Prior to the Folsom discovery, archaeological sites of inferred Pleistocene age were not readily accepted in the Americas, and even after Pleistocene occupations were recognized, knowledge of Paleoindian lifeways only slowly advanced. It has been only 20 years since the Monte Verde discovery affirmed the existence of pre-Clovis populations (Dillehay 1996;

Meltzer et al. 1997), and, barring fortuitous discoveries, it likely will take several more generations of research before we begin to understand when and where Early Paleoindian peoples were present and what they were doing in the region.

Morphological and Distributional Analyses

Another major theme explored in recent years in the Southeast is the analysis of temporally diagnostic artifacts, typically hafted bifaces, showing how such data can be used to delimit group ranges and interaction patterns over space and time (chapters by Bridgman Sweeney, Smallwood et al., Thulman, and Wilkinson, this volume). For every major excavation conducted and reported in the region, there are hundreds of locations where points have been found, allowing for the assemblages to be placed in a far broader context. As the authors of these chapters have done, making the data collected during such analyses available for inspection and use is, fortunately, well-established professional practice in the region, employing outlets like DINAA (the Digital Index of North American Archaeology) and PIDBA (the Paleoindian Database of the Americas), or in online supplementary materials, or in hard copies in curation repositories (e.g., Anderson 2018; Anderson et al. 2010, 2017; Wells et al. 2014; White 2014).

Artifact morphology is being used to delimit subregional cultural traditions, with clusters of similar points on the landscape and variability between clusters likely reflecting band ranges and multiband interaction patterns within Early Archaic side- and corner-notched forms on the South Atlantic Slope (chapters by Sweeney, Thulman, Wilkinson, this volume), much as Thulman (2006) did for Middle and Late Paleoindian fluted and lanceolate assemblages in Florida. Network analysis and cultural transmission theory are used to delimit areas of greater or lesser similarity of forms and, hence presumably, interaction. The variability in morphology delimited in the studies herein is likely paralleled over the entire region, meaning we are rapidly moving toward being able to see subregional cultural interaction at multiple scales, what Sweeney calls bandscapes, with a high degree of precision and replicability (see also White 2012, 2014). We have, in fact, come a long way from the rather static macroband boundaries and group territories intuitively drawn on maps a few decades ago (Anderson 1990, 1995; Anderson and Hanson 1988; Daniel 1998, 2001). For the first time we are becoming aware that mobility patterns, including fluidity of movement between groups, changed over time, even during the periods specific point forms were in use. These analyses are showing us which measurements to collect to untangle behaviorally meaningful variability in notched point morphology. The incidence and occurrence of these point forms over time on the landscape are also being used to document how populations responded to changes in climate and sea level, leading to new settlement models like the Dalton Piedmont Transhumance Model, reflecting Late Paleoindian period population movements away from unstable coastal areas into the interior (Smallwood et al. 2015, this volume). Most importantly, these analyses highlight what can be done with private collections and how much valuable information resides within them and remains to be documented, demonstrating that even areas where archaeologists haven't done much work have still seen a lot of coverage by avocationals. Documenting such collections is an ongoing responsibility that both groups can share, to the benefit of our understanding of the past (e.g., Anderson and Miller 2017; Thulman 2012b, this volume; White 2014).

Specialized/Paleoenvironmental Analyses

Several chapters highlight the superb geoarchaeological and paleoenvironmental research that is routinely being undertaken on many early southeastern sites, with a landscape perspective increasingly used to place occupations at specific sites into a larger regional framework. As Moore et al. herein demonstrate, the sediment matrix or geological context is just as important as the more traditional artifacts categories found within it, and multiple lines of evidence, when collected and integrated, can provide highly credible descriptions of site deposits. Harris and colleagues' work on the paleolandscapes of the southeastern continental shelf, tied with sea level reconstructions, is telling us exactly where we need to look offshore to find early sites. I have no doubt unequivocal evidence for human occupations of Middle and perhaps even Early Paleoindian age will be found in the near future on the continental shelf; the depth of the water will provide minimum ages for these sites, that is, when they would have been submerged. Likewise Austin et al.'s chapter on the quarry cluster approach provides a good overview of the history and importance of sourcing analyses in Florida, with lessons to be considered throughout the region, not the least of which is that continual refinement of the variability that occurs within sources is necessary, as well as the documentation of new sources, to provide data useful to questions about group lithic raw material procurement and mobility strategies.

The chapters on the Younger Dryas Cosmic Impact hypothesis (LeCompte et al., Kennett et al.) provide an excellent overview of possible causes of the Younger Dryas onset and its effects on plant and animal, including human, populations in the Southeast and beyond. Whatever the cause, there is no doubt that the Younger Dryas was a significant climatic excursion that began and also apparently ended rapidly, with well-dated beginning and ending points, which is why we use them to anchor our archaeological chronologies, specifically to bound the Late Paleoindian period. The argument about whether an impact occurred is highly contentious at present, but the scientific method will yield viable answers given a few more years or decades of research. The onset of the Younger Dryas is associated with major changes in Paleoindian lifeways in the Southeast, roughly coeval with the ending of Clovis, the final extinction of megafauna, and changes in group range and subsistence (e.g., Anderson 2001; Anderson et al. 2010, 2011; Meeks and Anderson 2012; Smallwood et al. 2015, this volume). Whether an extraterrestrial object impact occurred at the onset of the Younger Dryas or not, they certainly occurred at other points in time in Earth's history (Anderson 2000). Wherever possible, archaeologists should facilitate sampling at possible boundary zones by specialists and assure that proper quality control occurs. Environmental change during the Younger Dryas appears to have profoundly shaped settlement in both the Georgia and South Carolina areas, something likely due in part to rapidly changing sea levels (Smallwood et al., this volume; Smallwood et al. 2015; see also Anderson and Bissett 2015). What happened elsewhere in the Southeast during this interval will need to be addressed with additional localized studies.

Conclusions

The chapters in this volume make clear that our understanding of terminal Pleistocene/early Holocene lifeways has markedly improved in recent decades. The evaluation, refinement, and replacement of settlement models is ongoing. The likelihood that individual band ranges occupied entire river valleys or even larger areas during the Early Archaic (e.g., (Anderson and Hanson 1988; Daniel 1998, 2001), for example, is probably unrealistic, given that people would have been in the region for at least 3,000 years by this point. Much larger populations were likely present, something indicated by dramatic increases in the numbers of sites and artifacts over the course of the Late Paleoindian and Early Archaic periods (Anderson 1990:198–201, 1996:160–163). Increased use of local materials is also evident, suggesting movement was becoming progressively restricted as populations grew and group ranges contracted. Fluid movement between individual bands may have still occurred, but the area each band or group occupied was likely growing smaller, something we can evaluate using collections data.

Questioning our fundamental assumptions about early settlement also remains important (Speth et al. 2013). Early occupations in the Southeast are widely assumed to have been tethered to major drainages, interior water sources like sinks and Carolina bays, or specific raw material sources. But was this really the case? We also need to think diachronically, examining change within as well as between periods. During Middle Paleoindian Clovis times, for example, was there an initial settlement into and then movement out of posited staging areas associated with the filling of the regional landscape, coupled with changes in toolkits over time (e.g., Anderson 1990; Smallwood 2010, 2011, 2012)? For the early Younger Dryas, is evidence for population decline or reorganization occurring uniformly across the region, or, as some have argued (Miller and Gingerich 2013a, 2013b; Smallwood et al. 2015, this volume; Tune 2016), is settlement change more pronounced in coastal than in interior areas? We need to be thinking about various ways of measuring the numbers and locations of people on the landscape, even if only in relative terms. Numbers of sites, diagnostic artifacts, or radiocarbon dates have been suggested as possible population proxies, and other measures, such as changes in the degree of similarity of point forms evident from morphological analyses, are being used to document population location and change over time (Thulman 2006). It may ultimately be possible to recognize individual knappers or kin groups, given that we are now beginning to resolve knapping communities and group ranges using these approaches.

To conclude, this volume represents one more testament to Albert C. Goodyear's long and productive career, which, given his infectious enthusiasm for Pleistocene archaeology, will undoubtedly continue for many years to come. The Topper site, perhaps his greatest archaeological discovery, contains one of the most remarkable Clovis assemblages found in North America, and a wealth of earlier and later materials as well. Work has been under way there for over three decades, highlighting the importance of

long-term research programs and careers to the understanding of early occupations in the Southeast. Al has helped mentor several generations of Paleoindian researchers—including me, 40 years ago when I was his research
assistant—and his work will inspire more generations to come.

Acknowledgments

Al Goodyear, Chris Moore, Joe Schuldenrein, Andrew White, Joe Wilkinson, and Judith Knight offered advice and suggestions that aided in the
preparation of this chapter, and they have my thanks.

15

MIGRATIONS AND THE EARLY HUMAN ECOLOGY
OF THE SOUTHEASTERN ATLANTIC SLOPE

A Long View

JOSEPH SCHULDENREIN

The late Karl Butzer's seminal volume *Archaeology as Human Ecology* (1982) fortified the centrality of the "human ecosystem" for understanding the dynamic symbiosis between human behavior and environmental change. Those relationships have, arguably, finite beginnings in space and time with archaeology and landscape histories as joint, reinforcing signatures. The timelines and trajectories of those beginnings remain fluid, reflecting the growing databases that push back human chronologies and refine the environmental circumstances accounting for human mobility, settlement, and adaptation. The question of the initial peopling of the Southeastern Atlantic Slope and its environmental correlates serves as the anchor for the present volume. Butzer visualized the study of human ecology as key to modeling linked human mobility and landscape selection and utilization. His book served as "an introduction to the methodology and theoretical framework for such a study" (Butzer 1982:xi). Some 35 years later, the present volume demonstrates unequivocally that, for the Southeast at least, we are no longer in the introductory stages of such research. Moreover, these advances not only are methodological but beg to be framed in a theoretical context that was presciently visualized at that time. I make specific reference to the pointed application of scientific method, which, when accompanied by monumental technological advances, has produced uniquely archaeological frameworks. The latter have structured the collection of massive data sets, thereby opening up new avenues for more reliable archaeological inference, hypothesis testing, and increasingly secure interpretation.

The sophistication that the present contributions bring to bear on trends in early southeastern prehistory did not emerge in a vacuum. As an Old World geoarchaeologist trained in the arenas of the European and Near Eastern Paleolithic, my introduction to Southeastern prehistory was born of collaborative associations with David G. Anderson, the late Victor Carbone, and others in the 1980s. Their perspicacious recognition of the intimate connections between archaeology and environment, and the need to incorporate the hard sciences into dynamic models of settlement geography and changing landscapes, was visionary for that time. Those perspectives coincided with the groundswell of Cultural Resource Management (CRM) projects, the attendant exponential enrichment of the archaeological database, and the need to make sense of it all. The latter objective underscored the imperative not only for structuring complex human/landscape relationships but also for more concrete objectives: recognizing site settlement patterning and developing empirical tools for deciphering the systematics of site preservation for land-use management and planning purposes. Applications of geomorphology, paleo-ethnobotany, faunal analyses, human osteology, and trace element analysis (among other subspecialties) crystallized an "inter-disciplinary imperative" in archaeology. Applications of these methods not only restructured our understanding of the systematics of human adaptation; they also streamlined survey, testing, and large-scale excavation strategies more efficiently as the reach of the National Historic Preservation Act (1966) expanded across the United States.

Those of us who came of professional age in those last two decades of the twentieth century were the beneficiaries of a revolution in archaeological thinking, one in which the traditional pedagogy was questioned. The work of Lewis Binford (1968) and his students called attention to the need to redirect archaeological thinking from issues of chronology building and monumental site excavation to anthropological frameworks that stressed behavioral correlates of the material culture record, a shift to analysis of the archaeological remains of non-elite populations, and an appreciation of the role of environment in fashioning adaptive strategies across time and space. Interdisciplinary scientific research became de rigueur. Similar thematic changes had been introduced in geography departments some 30 years earlier, and budding geoarchaeologists profited from an increased emphasis on scientific method in cultural and physical geography largely through the efforts of Carl Sauer. A review of these early theoretical frameworks in anthropological archaeology and scientific method is germane to any understanding of the synthetic thread joining scientific method, technology, and the systematics of early human migrations.

Scientific Method and Archaeological Inference: Advances and Limitations

At its core, scientific method utilizes observation and techniques for investigating natural phenomena and integrating such observations with previous, and similarly acquired, bodies of knowledge (Kuhn 1961). Combining scientific method with archaeological data collection and interpretation was elegantly laid out by Watson (1976:379), who posited that archaeological inference is grounded on "principles of cultural behavior, the accumulation and alteration of material, and archaeologists' methods." In this exposé Watson argues that archaeology is best classed a science by its logical connections to other hard sciences and the potential to structure new laws of human and cultural change. Empirically and functionally, the past half-century has demonstrated that the convergence of scientific method and archaeological inference is expanding the limits of interpretation because of the versatility of technologies that maximize knowledge yield from spheres as diverse as paleo-genetics to site discovery.

The present set of essays underscores both the levels and applications of technological sophistication that emerged from initial interdisciplinary efforts. Geographic information systems (GIS), digital elevation modeling (DEM), digital and spectral imagery (e.g., LIDAR), remote sensing technology, and numerous other survey and testing tools, as well as integrative database software, have accelerated data processing and interpretive domains in ways unimagined in the earlier years when interdisciplinary studies were visualized only as potentially helpful in modelng human ecological constructs. Progressive technological advances practiced by an expanding array of archaeological scientists and concomitant growth of the database have revolutionized our understanding of the Early Amerindian timelines. This volume centers on the pivotal issues for today's research on human arrivals to the Southeast and the adaptive strategies signaled by the visible archaeological record from earliest arrivals (Late Pleistocene/pre-Clovis) and well into postglacial times (early Holocene/Early Archaic). Our constructs of Late Pleistocene site geography have progressed from dots on a map to regional clusters mapped onto discrete ancient biomes and landscapes. This trend extends from terrestrial to submarine landscapes with site concentrations abounding as new terrain models expand.

The contributions in this volume converge around several themes that highlight the latest trends in Southeastern archaeology. Each integrates the material culture record with scientific method. Thus, we have an emphasis on the Younger Dryas event and its impacts on population movement (Kennett and LeCompte; LeCompte, Hemmings, et al.); earliest arrivals and pre-Clovis contexts from a chrono-stratigraphic perspective (Hemmings et al; Ensor; Goodyear and Sain); demographics, climate and sea level rise (Harris; Smallwood et al.); and demography, lithics, and quarry signatures (Wilkinson; Bridgman; Ensor; Austin et al.; Thulman). A most compelling integrative piece underscores the unifying applications of scientific technologies (^{14}C/OSL, climate, geomorphology, sedimentology) to explain preservation settings as they link archaeological configurations to their presence on the ground (Moore et al.). The subtext of that piece is that site formation process must gird any interpretation of the archaeological record. Implicit in all of these pieces is a collective claim that failures to reach interpretive consensus should at the very least direct researchers to frame testable hypotheses that will take us to tenable interpretations. The message, as Dave Anderson points out, is not only the facility and familiarity that southeastern archaeologists have with sophisticated scientific methodologies, but that these investigative approaches enhance their understanding of the interpretive possibilities afforded by technology and interdisciplinary co-operation. The application of methods to evolving interpretive and epistemological issues reflects the strong academic training and applied uses that the present generation of researchers brings to the table.

Progressive applications of the latest archaeological science technologies are almost naturally paired with investigations of early human dispersals. Such pairings converge around an epistemological issue that needs to be viewed on multiple scales and from the perspectives of inductivist vs. deductivist thinking. In the 1970s anthropological archaeologists argued for a deductivist approach to data collection in advance of interpretive modeling. The argument was that "abstraction" was a dangerous potential outcome of data collection methods and strategies that were simply not sufficiently sophisticated or systematized to furnish explanatory models (i.e., Fritz and Plog, 1970). Data collection at the time was recognized to be little more than happenstance, with poor survey and sampling strategies that, at best, hinted at simple archaeological patterning without recognition of sources of variability. Thus, expanding questionable collection methods to generate regional models of, for example, population expansion, is an inherently dangerous exercise. How, for example, could we advance theories of Late Pleistocene population movements across the Southeast when relevant data were sparse, collection strategies were still in their infancy, applications of high-tech approaches were still experimental, and the human ecological approach was still in an embryonic stage and not universally accepted by old-school archaeologists? That situation has changed monumentally in the past half century. This set of papers shows us how approaches to data collection and multiple reinforcing data sets can converge around verification of certain explanatory postulates (if not truths). Examples put forth in this volume (and related works recently published) include the critical role of the Younger Dryas in tempering our ideas of the trajectories and timing of human expansions across the landscapes; site-landform correlations and chrono-stratigraphic relations that are repetitive across the broader physiographic zones of the Southeast (i.e., inner and outer Coastal Plains); and underwater explorations off the Atlantic and Gulf Coasts that facilitate submerged landscape reconstructions with such precision that modeling continental shelf settlement patterning is no longer just a theoretical possibility but a testable empirical project (see Harris, this volume). Legitimate transgressive-regressive sea level/landscape constructs are a realistic objective, with timelines indexed by a broad array of dating methods. By extension, submerged preservation settings can be identified by projecting mapped terrestrial landform configurations with the use of submarine vehicles and underwater dive teams. Such exercises may, in conjunction with terrestrial stratigraphic records, lay to rest the pre-Clovis argument, the cause-and-effect relationships of the Younger Dryas on the human ecology of the earliest human groups, and, just as significantly, map out the migratory pathways followed by succeeding Clovis (post-Clovis/transitional??) and Early Archaic populations.

My sole cautionary note in this regard concerns an over-reliance on regional biases in data collection and interpretation. It is my experience both in the Southeast and elsewhere in North America and the Old World that regionally accepted investigative and interpretive techniques and perspectives severely limit the creative range of methodological exploration and synthetic data assembly. That is a discussion for another place and time, but my own approaches as a "non-regional" practitioner will filter through elsewhere in this presentation. The balance of this discussion examines some of the more salient aspects of early southeastern human ecology and archaeology that I have gleaned from this volume, related synthetic works over the past decades, and my own experiences working in this most fascinating corner of the archaeological universe.

The Southeastern Atlantic Slope: An Ideal Geoarchaeological Laboratory?

Geoarchaeological research across North America is arguably at a stage where pivotal issues address preservation contexts more than baseline archaeological discovery. This is not to say that it is beyond the pale that, for example, pre-Clovis assemblages may extend up to the Late Glacial Maximum (LGM) (Anderson 2005; Anderson and Sassaman 2012), but simply that discoveries significantly antecedent to that time frame are not very likely. As the present volume illustrates, dominant foci consider mobility patterns, landscape utilization, landform configurations, resource exploitation (for raw material procurement and subsistence), climate change, and submerged (continental shelf) geography as the key elements for charting patterns of human distributions. Just as significant is the reconstruction of geomorphic processes that account for the differential maintenance of the archaeological record.

   In this connection, I would advance the notion that the physiography of the Southeast is probably the most hospitable region of the Eastern Woodlands for mapping out surviving person–landscape records in prehistory. If we consider the eastern seaboard generally, we note that there is a widening curvilinear expanse spanning continuous physiographic zones from New England to Georgia and Florida. In general, landform, topographic, and hydrographic zonations are continuous along the Atlantic Slope; they extend from mountainous and rugged terrain to graded hilly landforms that flatten out to more extended coastal plains. While baseline structures for these configurations are orogenic, they are modified extensively by glacial process that has dramatically fashioned landform configurations everywhere north of New York State. Postglacial meltwater and drainage overhauls have modified topographic gradients and hydrography in the mid-Atlantic, and these down-latitude gradational geomorphic processes culminate in lower surface attrition rates for the Southeast. For the latter zone, graded surfaces are accompanied by wider stream channels and more laterally extensive and geomorphically complex alluvial basin configurations. Such settings are ideal for teasing out settlement patterns in response to changing terminal Pleistocene/early Holocene geomorphic processes and preservation signatures, because of the lower-energy, down-latitude postglacial modifications. The Southeast features substantially reduced erosional-depositional balances and more stabilized channels with attendant sub-basins; the latter are prone to more optimal registration of landform-sediment signatures and archaeological site maintenance.

Next, this same down-latitude progression can be invoked to explain the diminution of an urbanized geography. Not only does the latter place constraints on the application of earth science techniques to archaeology because of the extensive overprint of made lands, but hand in hand with that condition, limitations are imposed on the fragmentary distributions of archaeological sites. Major drainage lines in the Northeast (Delaware, Hudson, and Connecticut rivers) are not only shorter, but the effects of nineteenth- and twentieth-century industrialization has left a geoarchaeological record that is incomparably more discontinuous, and harder to piece together than that of the Southeast, where the systematics of fluvial geomorphology play out against a backdrop of relatively pristine natural landscapes. As a rule, the hydrodynamics of upstream erosion, midstream sediment mobilization, and downstream discharge are readily tied to geographically dictated trends of prehistoric alluvial stratification and site sealing. Accordingly, the relatively pristine and graded southeastern terrain invites synthetic modeling of the linked systematics of fluvial sedimentation from the Ridge-Valley through Piedmont and then Coastal Plain reaches of the trunk streams (Schuldenrein 1996). The lessons I learned from the Southeast allowed me to transplant the integrated geoarchaeological spatial dynamics of an intact landscape to one that was compromised by the urban overprint in the Northeast (Schuldenrein 1994).

It follows that the southeastern model exemplifies an almost textbook case in which Late Quaternary floodplain/terrace complexes help structure predictive modeling for archaeological site distributions and expectations. The paradigm exemplifies the traditional, three-zone construct of drainage basin hydrography articulated by Schumm (1977). The basin charts the systematics of stream behavior by subdividing the drainage into discrete hydrographic zones based on stream dynamics and the mechanics of sediment transfer. Zones are tracked from the head of the stream downstream to its mouth. Functionally, the upstream zone (Zone 1) is characterized by erosion as the river strips the slopes and mobilizes sediment to a second segment (transfer zone 2) where a knick point serves to bridge erosional process into a sediment "transfer zone," effectively the central portion of the drainage; here sediment accretion and landform construction are dominant processes (i.e., creation of Pleistocene/Holocene terraces). Zone 3 marks the settling out of the sediment load "deposition zone," as the stream gradient diminishes and thence debouches onto the Coastal Plain. In Zone 3, the channel anastomoses and splays out, discharging large volumes of sediment and creating landscapes that combine both terrestrial, estuarine, and marine elements. At this point the fluvial system is most visibly affected by changing base levels. This simple model of stream dynamics may be readily applied to site-landform geography and the time-space systematics of archaeological preservation (see discussion in Schuldenrein 1994, 2004). Archaeologically, at the upstream zone, small, residual prehistoric sites were exposed at bluff tops, where minimal soil cover was stripped by incipient streams (Zone 1), stratified multicomponent sites were preserved in terrace floodplain complexes (Zone 2), and more complex multisubsistence zone sites were found in the deposition segment (Zone 3). The latter served as the most diverse but richest archaeological preservation contexts insofar as streams abutted marine landscapes, and, not surprisingly, eco-tonal subsistence environments were preserved. In the Southeast these Coastal Plain sites feature intricate landscape and stratigraphic signatures (Brooks and Sassaman 1990; Schuldenrein and Blanton 1995). Coastal Plain geoarchaeological models have been further refined by subsequent geoarchaeological studies in which climate projections and systems geomorphology were overlain and conjoined into increasingly more sophisticated exemplars.

On an extraregional level this type of geoarchaeological model building is also applicable to the considerably more intricate site-landform settings of the U.S. Midwest where the Mississippi Basin's fluvial landscapes are geomorphically leaps and bounds more disjointed and uneven than those of the Southeast and, for that matter, the Northeast. The extent of the primary midcontinental drainage basin, its high rates of deposition, stream channel anastomosing, and irregular lateral array of basin landform segments render archaeological preservation signatures eminently richer but significantly more unpredictable. Those complexities hold true for all three zones in the Schumm model because zonation the length of the trunk is variably disrupted by localized (rather than purely regional) hydrographic controls. The interdigitations of alluvial sediments and later prehistoric occupation horizons are infinitely more difficult to disentangle, although considerable progress has been made here in recent years (see Knox 2006 and references).

Viewed in terms of a feedback loop, the holistic perspective I gleaned from the Southeast paradigm was an ability to restructure the more complex dynamics linking fluvial systematics and archaeological preservation trends elsewhere in the Eastern Woodlands. This was achieved by factoring in how trunk streams trenching through and carrying more complex bedload and sediment loads from glacial materials produced a considerably more "loaded" geoarchaeological signature for both Holocene alluvial landscape construction and archaeological site architecture. Those variables, in my estimation, play out in the most complex geoarchaeological contexts in the central and lower Mississippi valleys. It is not coincidental that, arguably, the broadest range of preservation settings is present in this reach of the midcontinent.

Geoarchaeological Challenges: Non-Stratigraphy, Anomalous Landforms, Sea Level Rise

Another example of this type of inductivist transposition can be invoked from the Old World to explain site formation process in sandy locations at both Coastal Plain and Piedmont locations in the Southeast (for relevant examples, see Moore, this volume). Paradoxically, that analogy cross-cuts both environmental zonation and depositional landscapes; it is keyed directly to the dynamics of sediment mobility, aeolian activity, and surface transformation. For purposes of stark contrasts, I would draw attention to desertic Upper Pleistocene Paleolithic open-air sites wherein subtle lithostratigraphy is the product of ancient land surface attrition. Reference is made to desert pediment plains, essentially long-term surfaces undergoing net sediment removal over tens of thousands of years. In a recent project in Iraq, I noted no primary stratigraphic relationships separating Acheulean and Upper Paleolithic artifact components. Mixed assemblages were the product of ongoing, downward collapse (Schuldenrein 2015). Site formation process mimics a model put forth by Moore and Leigh for the Southeast, with elegant step-wise removal of non-weathered alluvial and aeolian sediment bodies subject to "net zero" accretion (and no recognizable stratigraphic discontinuities). Here is a case where dissimilar landscapes have undergone analogous site formation transformations to provide palimpsests of non-primary assemblages in a way that had puzzled New and Old World archaeologists alike for years.

Across the Middle Atlantic and Southeastern Coastal areas, there remains the question of the origins and antiquity of the ellipsoid Carolina Bays. Provisional assessments of antiquity place their evolution on the order of 100–70 kya, or perhaps earlier (between MIS 5e and 5a; Lisieki and Raymo 2005). Cyclical processes are attributable to terrestrial origins and subsequent effects of combined lacustrine, aeolian, and colluviation process (Brooks et al. 2010; Leigh 2008; Markewich et al. 2015). Linkages to later terrestrial events have also been proposed, including a tie to the extraterrestrial Younger Dryas comet event (12,900 B.P.), but the latter hypothesis has come under increased criticism. It is significant that arrays of deep depressions, principally along Coastal Plain margins on the Atlantic Slope, find correlates in the emergence of the extensive lake basins in the desert regions the Near East. Prominent examples are taken from the Jordan rift valley, where nearly a century's worth of baseline geoarchaeological research has culminated in fixing the aging of Upper Pleistocene Lake Lisan, now estimated at 80,000 B.P. (see Picard 1943; Stein et al. 1997). Over the past three decades, deep and broad basins have been identified east of the rift in the Hasa basin in Jordan (Schuldenrein 1998; Schuldenrein and Clark 2003). Most recently, the complex of semicontinuous lake basins in the Arabian desert (Petraglia et al. 2012; Schuldenrein 2015) have also been explored. Across the greater Near East and well into the Arabian Peninsula and possibly into South Asia, these basin complexes are linked to prehistoric occupations around their peak high stands (ca. 40,000 B.P.), with secondary high stands around the LGM (ending 20,000–18,000 B.P.) where recessional phases are tied to classic tufa (spring) deposits dated to regional Epipaleolithic cultures. The tool kits of the latter may represent the waning moist phases of MIS 2, or a renewed moist phase wherein springs represented refugia to which populations gravitated at the onset of a prominent (regional) desiccation phase. Are the springs a moist or drying signal? Do they herald drastic climatic transformations wherein the springs represent migrations to surviving oases, where the Paleolithic hunter-gatherers gave way to pre-agricultural societies of the Natufian phase (ca. 10,000 B.P.)? Is there a global-scale connection between the terminal Pleistocene disappearance of the lakes, the turn to pre-agricultural societies in the heartland of ancient Near Eastern civilizations, and the pairing of Coastal Bay transformation to the initial peopling of the New World per the pre-Clovis populations? There are plausible arguments to be made that this time frame was a global phenomenon marking the rapid rise in sea level during the transition from MIS 1 to MIS 2.

Back to the New World, we are now in a position to reconstruct sea level curves in the Northeast; a recent (provisional) mid-Atlantic model was linked to archaeological manifestations off the coast of New York City

(Schuldenrein et al. 2013, revised from Neuman et al. 1969). It should be possible to merge the higher-latitude sea level plots with the Southeast and Middle Atlantic and New England data sets. Obviously, these models are tempered by glacio-eustatic and isostatic considerations, but these have been accommodated in earlier Late Quaternary sea level constructs. Regionally based sequences are beginning to incorporate archaeologically dated sediments to account for climatic or structural rebound, with attendant implications for the changing maps of early human settlements along the Atlantic Coast. Taken together, a comprehensive and well-dated western Atlantic coast master sequence is within reach. A corollary to this is the generation of working hypotheses on the expansion of early peopling of eastern North America, recognition of mobility patterns between regions, identifications of subsistence networks and strategies, and, ironically, the development of baselines for predicting the deleterious effects of potential sea level rise in this age of accelerated climate change. Indeed, the human ecology of the past can be considered as useful a barometer as any for predicting the nature of catastrophic damage. It can also help to guide scheduling plans for escapes to the interior in advance of calamity.

The Younger Dryas Question

The Younger Dryas was a global phenomenon. Its geoarchaeological manifestations are also apparent in the Near East, and its effects have promoted widespread controversy surrounding the Natufian dilemma (Bar-Yosef et al. 2002; Byrd 2005;). In the Levant earlier archaeological observations of a steep drop in settlement density suggested that a "dry" phase accounted for a reconfiguration of settlement during the Early Natufian. The archaeological record denotes a displacement of sites to areas of relatively steady water availability (i.e., oases). Within several hundred years the Late Natufian witnessed a redistribution of settlements to former patterns. Reference is made to demographic patterns reminiscent of those prevailing during the moister phases of the earlier (pre-Natufian) Epipaleolithic. These cyclical trends have been attributed to recurrent phases of climatic amelioration wherein moister landscapes emerged outside of former refugia as more hydrographic settings began to extend into the desert margins. Years of research and an increase in the number of radiocarbon dates and geological investigations showed that for the Late Natufian, at least, ostensibly moister climatic pulses represented an environmental response to the Younger Dryas dry pulse. The recognition of that event, coupled with the

refinements in landscape and settlement reconstructions, facilitated explanations for the cause-and-effect dynamics of the Younger Dryas on a questionable scale. Of considerable interest in this regard, of course, is the fact
that the Younger Dryas is coincident with the later Paleoindian period, and
it should be possible to identify the effects of this singular event, and controls on cyclic climate patterns, on a global scale. How reliably can we (inductively) extend the range of regional and extraregional climatic change,
and can we extend such hypotheses to refine ideas and the geography of
population migrations and human ecology?

New Frontiers in Human Migration Modeling

The past 20 years of bioanthropological and paleoanthropological research
have resulted in a complete transformation of ancient templates of human
origins and the subsequent trajectories of cultural expansion (Anton and
Swisher 2004; Carotenuto et al. 2008; Shea 2011). Previously, the prevailing
wisdom was confined to looking at narrow, genus-based diffusion paradigms, largely centered on East African and South African successions.
Now we are finding that the chronology of human origins extends across
the African continent, with DNA studies used to fingerprint migratory patterns (Disotell 2013).

Migration studies are of increasing relevance to the more regional models developed in the present volume, as they implicate coupling between
lithic technologies and parallel trends in stone tool manufacturing in locations as far afield as Africa, India, and China for the Acheulean (Petraglia
et al. 2012). Most recently there are more than coincident replications of
assemblages bridging these areas using the corridor of the Arabian Peninsula (Petraglia et al. 2012). Many of these newly recognized diffusion trends
may simply be a function of differential areal investigations, in many cases
dictated by political concerns. And the tethering of these developments
to more-detailed environmental reconstructions is increasingly corrobo-
rated by refinements in the Marine Isotope Stage (MIS) chronologies and
advances in stable isotope analyses. Taken together, these trends point to
transitions in vegetation communities independent of purely climatic constructs, thus providing closer linkages to the connections between ecological zonation and climate change on a variety of scales.

Such advances bring about some provocative new theories on migration for later time frames, those equivalent to, or even antecedent to pre-
Clovis. Did Upper Paleolithic populations "cruise" (analogy intentional)

into eastern North America with a ready-made and sophisticated chipped tool tradition (Solutrean)? Was a variant of that tradition refined in the Eastern Shore of the Delmarva peninsula, or were these simply independent developments attributable to local or regional artisans developing new manufacturing technologies on locally available cherts (Bradley and Stanford 2004)? While these are the most recent examples, analogous questions have actually been pondered for over a century, going back to the age of the antiquarians at the turn of the twentieth century in North America. In the Middle Atlantic region, national luminaries such as C. C. Abbott, W. H. Holmes, and Henry Mercer considered the morphological similarities between artifacts known as "turtlebacks" and Late Acheulean handaxes (Meltzer 1991). The artifact type was found, in large numbers, at a Late Archaic village in eastern Pennsylvania, as well as in other locales nearby. In nearly all cases this and similar hypotheses were debunked through closer analyses of supplementary lithic assemblages, and, in the case of Mercer, "hypotheses" were dismissed because of the unique weathering of the local source material (rhyolite) (Schuldenrein et al. 1991). In the present volume, arguments have been advanced for the presence of Middle to Upper Paleolithic traditions (or variants thereof) at Capps (Ensor). Old World archaeologists have argued that in order to promote such far-reaching hypotheses, the researcher must investigate substantially larger assemblages with Levallois toolkits and hallmarks of the reduction technique to promote a compelling case on techno-typological grounds (Dibble et al. 2016). I don't see the evidence for this at either Vero or Capps-Shelley, but the questions are most certainly legitimate.

Conclusions

I have been privileged to "cut my geoarchaeological teeth" in the southeastern United States. Over the years I have been invited back on a number of projects across the region that have afforded me the opportunity to examine more complex and increasingly older prehistoric sites. The methodological advances in this part of the world are astounding, and the level of professionalism undertaken by the new generation of practitioners is even more so. As the contributions in this volume attest, there are no questions too complex to be addressed. The Southeast remains cutting-edge for archaeological science, both nationally and on a global scale. My only cautionary note is that researchers continue to promote advancement by looking at investigative strategies in other parts of the world in order to stay afloat with contemporary trends in archaeological technology. They have lots to learn, but, I dare say, they have at least as much to teach. I suspect that in several years many of these human ecological issues surrounding the early peopling of the Southeast will be promoted to the hypothesis-testing stage, and possibly even answered. If the past is any indicator of the future, the state of archaeological research in this unique corner of the world will continue to be in the forefront of global archaeological practice. And that speaks volumes about the state of affairs.

Acknowledgments

I extend my appreciation to Al Goodyear and Chris Moore for inviting me to contribute this chapter, and to the SEAC 2014 conference from which it emerged. The chapter benefited extensively from conversations with Dave Anderson over the course of its preparation.

REFERENCES CITED

Abbott, Charles C.
1872   *The Stone Age in New Jersey*. Salem Press, Salem.

Abrams, Marc D., and Gregory J. Nowacki
2008   Native Americans as Active and Passive Promoters of Mast and Fruit Trees in the Eastern USA. *Holocene* 18:1123–1137.

Adams, Dean, F. James Rohlf, and Dennis Slice
2013   A Field Comes of Age: Geometric Morphometrics in the 21st Century. *Hystrix, the Italian Journal of Mammalogy* 24(1):7–4.

Adovasio, James M., C. Andrew Hemmings, and Anne Marjenin
2014   The Old Vero Man Site (8RI009): Current Investigations Suggest Pleistocene Human Occupation. Paper presented at the 71st Annual Meeting of the Southeastern Archaeological Society, Greenville, South Carolina.

Adovasio, James M., David R. Pedler, Jesse Donahue, and Robert Stuckenrath
1999   No Vestige of a Beginning nor Prospect for an End: Two Decades of Debate on Meadowcroft. In *Ice Age Peoples of North America: Environments, Origins, and Adaptations of the First Americans*, edited by Robson Bonnichsen and Karen L. Turnmire, pp. 416–431. Oregon State University Press, Corvallis.

Agenbroad, Larry D.
2005   North American Proboscideans: Mammoths: The State of Knowledge, 2003. *Quaternary International* 126–128:73–92.

Aitken, Martin J.
1998   *An Introduction to Optical Dating: The Dating of Quaternary Sediments by the Use of Photon-Stimulated Luminescence*. Oxford University Press, New York.

Alley, Richard B.
2000   Ice-Core Evidence of Abrupt Climate Changes. *Proceedings of the National Academy of Sciences* 97:1331–1334.
2004   Abrupt Climate Changes: Oceans, Ice, and Us. *Oceanography* 17:1 Abrupt Climate Changes: Oceans, Ice, and Us. *Oceanography* 94–206.

Alley, Richard B., Jochem Marotzke, William D. Nordhaus, Jonathan T. Overpeck, Dorothy M. Peteet, Roger A. Pielke Jr., Raymond T. Pierrehumbert, Peter B. Rhines, Thomas F. Stocker, Lynne D. Talley, and John M. Wallace
2003   Abrupt Climate Change. *Science* 299:2005–2010.

Alley, Richard B., Paul A. Mayewski, Todd Sowers, Minze Stuiver, Kendrick C. Taylor, and
Peter U. Clark
1997   Holocene Climatic Instability: A Prominent, Widespread Event 8200 yr Ago.
            Geology 25:483–486.
Anderson, David G.
1990   The Paleoindian Colonization of Eastern North America: A View from the
            Southeastern United States. In *Early Paleoindian Economies of Eastern North
            America*, edited by Kenneth B. Tankersley and Barry L. Isaac, pp. 163–216.
            Research in Economic Anthropology Supplement 5. JAI Press, Greenwich.
1991   The Bifurcate Tradition in the South Atlantic Region. *Journal of Middle At-
            lantic Archaeology* 7:91–106.
1995   Paleoindian Interaction Networks in the Eastern Woodlands. In *Native
            American Interaction: Multiscalar Analyses and Interpretations in the Eastern
            Woodlands*, edited by Michael S. Nassaney and Kenneth E. Sassaman, pp.
            1–26. University of Tennessee Press, Knoxville.
1996a   Modeling Regional Settlement in the Archaic Period Southeast. In *Archae-
            ology of the Mid-Holocene Southeast*, edited by Kenneth E. Sassaman and
            David G. Anderson, pp. 157–176. University Press of Florida, Gainesville.
1996b   Models of Paleoindian and Early Archaic Settlement in the Lower South-
            east. In *The Paleoindian and Early Archaic Southeast*, edited by David G.
            Anderson and Kenneth Sassaman, pp. 29–57. University of Alabama Press,
            Tuscaloosa.
2000   Epilogue. In *The Years without Summer, Tracing A.D. 536 and Its Aftermath*,
            edited by Joel Gunn, pp. 169–170. BAR International Series 872. Archaeo-
            press, Oxford.
2001   Climate and Culture Change in Prehistoric and Early Historic Eastern North
            America. *Archaeology of Eastern North America* 29:143–186.
2005   Pleistocene Human Occupation of the Southeastern United States: Research
            Directions for the Early 21st Century. In *Paleoamerican Origins: Beyond Clo-
            vis*, edited by Robson Bonnichsen, Bradley T. Lepper, Dennis Stanford, and
            Michael R. Waters, pp. 29–43. Texas A&M University Press, College Station.
2018   Using CRM Data for "Big Picture" Research. In *New Perspectives in Cultural
            Resource Management*, edited by Francis P. McManamon, pp. 197–212. Rout-
            ledge Press, New York.
Anderson, David G. and Thaddeus G. Bissett
2015   The Initial Colonization of North America: Sea Level Change, Shoreline
            Movement, and Great Migrations. In *Mobility and Ancient Society in Asia
            and the Americas: Proceedings of the Second International Conference on
            "Great Migrations,"* edited by Michael Frachetti and Robert Spengler, pp.
            59–88. Springer, New York.
Anderson, David G., Thaddeus G. Bissett, and Stephen J. Yerka
2013   The Late Pleistocene Human Settlement of Interior North America: The Role
            of Physiography and Sea-Level Change. In *Paleoamerican Odyssey*, edited
            by Kelly E. Graf, Caroline V. Ketron, and Michael R. Waters, pp. 183–203.

Center for the Study of the First Americans, Texas A&M University, College Station.

Anderson, David G., Thaddeus G. Bissett, Stephen J. Yerka, Joshua J. Wells, Eric C. Kansa, Sarah W. Kansa, Kelsey Noack Myers, R. Carl DeMuth, and Devin A. White

2017   Sea-level Rise and Archaeological Site Destruction: An Example from the Southeastern United States Using DINAA (Digital Index of North American Archaeology). *PLOS ONE* 12 (11): e0188142. https://doi.org/10.1371/journal. pone.0188142.

Anderson, David G., and J. Christopher Gillam

2001   Paleoindian Interaction and Mating Networks: Reply to Moore and Moseley. *American Antiquity* 66(3):530–535.

Anderson, David G., Albert C. Goodyear, James P. Kennett, and Allen West

2011   Multiple Lines of Evidence for Possible Human Population Decline/Settlement Reorganization during the Early Younger Dryas. *Quaternary International* 242:570–583.

Anderson, David G., and Glen T. Hanson

1988   Early Archaic Occupations in the Southeastern United States: A Case Study from the Savannah River Basin. *American Antiquity* 53:262–286.

Anderson, David A., Jerald Ledbetter, Lisa O'Steen, Daniel T. Elliott, Dennis Blanton, Glen T. Hanson, and Frankie Snow

2009   Paleoindian and Early Archaic in the Lower Southeast: A View from Georgia. In *Ocmulgee Archaeology, 1936–1986*, edited by David J. Hally. University of Georgia Press, Athens.

Anderson, David G., Sammy T. Lee, and A. Robert Parler Jr.

1979   *Cal Smoak, Archeological Investigations along the Edisto River in the Coastal Plain of South Carolina*. Occasional Papers No. 1, Archeological Society of South Carolina, Inc. Columbia.

Anderson, David G., and D. Shane Miller

2017   PIDBA (Paleoindian Database of the Americas): Call for Data. *PaleoAmerica* 4(1):3–7.

Anderson, David G., D. Shane Miller, Stephen J. Yerka, J. Christopher Gillam, Erik N. Johanson, David T. Anderson, Albert C. Goodyear, and Ashley M. Smallwood

2010   PIDBA (Paleoindian Database of the Americas) 2010: Current Status and Findings. *Archaeology of Eastern North America* 38:63–90.

Anderson, David G., Lisa D. O'Steen, and Kenneth E. Sassaman

1996   Environmental and Chronological Considerations. In *The Paleoindian and Early Archaic Southeast*, pp. 3–15. University of Alabama Press, Tuscaloosa.

Anderson, David G., and Kenneth E. Sassaman

2012   *Recent Developments in Southeastern Archaeology: From Colonization to Complexity*. Society of American Archaeology Press, Washington, D.C.

Anderson, David G., and Kenneth E. Sassaman (editors)

1996   *The Paleoindian and Early Archaic Southeast*. University of Alabama Press, Tuscaloosa.

Anderson, David G., and Joseph Schuldenrein
1983   Early Archaic Settlement on the Southeastern Atlantic Slope: A View from the Rucker's Bottom Site, Elbert County, Georgia. *North American Archaeologist* 4(3):177–210.
Anderson, David G., and Joseph Schuldenrein (editors)
1985   *Prehistoric Human Ecology along the Upper Savannah River: Excavations at the Rucker's Bottom, Abbeville and Bullard Site Groups.* Interagency Archaeological Services–Atlanta. Atlanta, Georgia: National Park Service, Russell Papers.
Anderson, David G., Ashley M. Smallwood, and D. Shane Miller
2015   Pleistocene Human Settlement in the Southeastern United States : Current Evidence and Future Directions. *PaleoAmerica* 1 7–51. doi:http://dx.doi.org/10.1179/2055556314Z.00000000012.
Anderson, Derek
2011   The 2010 4 × 4 Meter Unit at Topper: Preliminary Lithic and Spatial Analyses. *Legacy* 15(1):16–19.
2018   A Mass Analysis of Paleoindian and Early Archaic Debitage from the Hillside Deposits at the Topper Site, South Carolina. In *In the Eastern Fluted Point Tradition*, Vol. 2, edited by Joseph A. M. Gingerich, in press. University of Utah Press.
Anderson, Derek T., Ashley M. Smallwood, Albert C. Goodyear, and Sarah E. Walters
2016   The Paleoindian and Early Archaic Hilltop Occupations at the Topper Site. *Tennessee Archaeology* 8(1–2):102–113.
Andrefsky, William Jr.
1987   Diffusion and Innovation from the Perspective of Wedge-Shaped Cores in Alaska and Japan. In *The Organization of Core Technology*, edited by Jay K. Johnson and Carol A. Morrow, pp. 13–44. Westview Press, Boulder.
Andrews, John T., Anne E. Jennings, Michael Kerwin, Matthew Kirby, William Manley, Gifford H. Miller, Gerard Bond, and Brian McLean
1995   A Heinrich-Like Event, H-0 (DC-0): Source(s) for Detrital Carbonate in the North Atlantic during the Younger Dryas Chronozone. *Paleoceanography* 10(5):943–952.
Andrews, John T., and Katherine Tedesco
1992   Detrital Carbonate-Rich Sediments, Northwestern Labrador Sea: Implications for Ice-Sheet Dynamics and Iceberg Rafting (Heinrich) Events in the North Atlantic. *Geology* 20:1087–1090.
Andronikov, Alexandre, Dante S. Lauretta, Irina E. Andronikva, and R. J. Maxwell
2011   On the Possibility of a Late Pleistocene, Extraterrestrial Impact: LA-ICP-MS analysis of the Black Mat and Usselo Horizon Samples. Abstract for a poster presented at the 74th Meteoritical Society Meeting, London.
Andronikov, Alexandre, Eugenija Rudnickaite, Dante S. Lauretta, Irinia E. Andronikova, Donatas Kaminskas, Petras Šinkūnas, and Monika Melešytė
2015   Geochemical Evidence of the Presence of Volcanic and Meteoritic Materials in Late Pleistocene Lake Sediments of Lithuania. *Quaternary International* 386(2):18–29. DOI: 10.1016/j.quaint.2014.10.005.

Antón, Susan C., and Carl C. Swisher III

2004   Early Dispersals of Homo from Africa. *Annual Review of Anthropology* 33:271296.

Aplin, Graeme

2007   World Heritage Cultural Landscapes. *International Journal of Heritage Studies* 13:427–446. doi:10.1080/13527250701570515.

Austin, Robert J.

1995   Stone Tool Technology and Use. In *Yat Kitischee: A Prehistoric Coastal Hamlet, 100 B.C.–A.D. 1200*, edited and compiled by Robert J. Austin, pp. 176–218. Report prepared for the Board of County Commissioners of Pinellas County, Florida by Janus Research. On file, Florida Division of Historical Resources, Tallahassee.

1996   Lithic Procurement and Mobility Strategies on the Lake Wales Ridge. *Florida Anthropologist* 49:211–223.

1997   *The Economics of Lithic-Resource Use in South-Central Florida*. Ph.D. dissertation, Department of Anthropology, University of Florida. University Microfilms, Ann Arbor.

1998   A Technological and Functional Analysis of Lithic Artifacts from the Narvaez/Anderson Site, 8PI54, with Comments on Time Allocation and Craft Specialization. In *The Narvaez/Anderson Site (8PI54), a Safety Harbor Culture Shell Mound and Midden, A.D. 1000–1600*, edited by Terrance L. Simpson, pp. 87–200. Central Gulf Coast Archaeological Society, Tampa.

2004   Chipped Stone Artifacts from the Miami Circle Excavations at Brickell Point. *Florida Anthropologist* 57:85–132.

2006   *Knife and Hammer: An Exercise in Positive Deconstruction: The I-75 Project and Lithic Scatter Research in Florida*. Special Publication No. 16. Florida Anthropological Society, Tallahassee.

2008   *Lithic Artifacts from the Cutler Site, 8DA2001*. Report on file, Archaeological and Historical Conservancy, Davie, Florida.

2013   Lithic Acquisition and Use at Pineland. In *The Archaeology of Pineland: A Coastal Southwest Florida Village Complex, A.D. 50–1710*, edited by William H. Marquardt and Karen J. Walker, pp. 657–717. Institute of Archaeology and Paleoenvironmental Studies, Monograph No. 4. University of Florida, Gainesville.

2015   The Ritual Uses of Lithic Raw Materials during the Woodland Period, Fort Center, Southern Florida. *Journal of Field Archaeology* 40:413–427.

Austin, Robert J., and Jon C. Endonino

2004   Lithic Artifacts: Spatial and Temporal Variability. In *Multidisciplinary Investigations at West Williams, 8HI509: An Archaic Period Site Located within Florida Gas Transmission Company's Bayside Lateral Pipeline Corridor, Hillsborough County, Florida*, compiled by Robert J. Austin, pp. 287–292. Prepared for Florida Gas Transmission Company by Southeastern Archaeological Research, Inc. On file, Florida Division of Historical Resources, Tallahassee.

2011   *Archaeological Data Recovery at Montverde, 8LA243: A Terminal Archaic through St. Johns II Site on Lake Apopka, Lake County, Florida.* Prepared for Roper Real Estate by Southeastern Archaeological Research, Inc. On file, Florida Division of Historical Resources, Tallahassee.

Austin, Robert J. and Richard W. Estabrook

2000   Chert Distribution and Exploitation in Peninsular Florida. *Florida Anthropologist* 53:116–130.

Austin, Robert J., Greg S. Hendryx, Jon Simon Suarez, Geoff DuChemin, and Debra Wells

2015   *NRHP Evaluation of 12 Archaeological Sites at the Rodman Bombing Range, Putnam County, Florida, under the Jurisdiction of NAS Jacksonville.* Report prepared by Southeastern Archaeological Research, Inc. for Naval Facilities Engineering Command Southeast and Ecology and Environment, Inc. On file, Florida Division of Historical Resources, Tallahassee.

Austin, Robert J., Nicholas Linville, and Matthew Betz

2012   *Phase II Test Excavation at 8HR880 and Historical Background Research at 8HR883, Mosaic Fertilizer's Ona Mine, Hardee County, Florida.* Report prepared for Mosaic Fertilizer LLC by Southeastern Archaeological Research, Inc. On file, Florida Division of Historical Resources, Tallahassee.

Austin, Robert J. and Scott E. Mitchell

1999   *Archaeological Investigations at Jeanie's Better Back (8LF54), an Early Archaic Site in Lafayette County, Florida.* Prepared by Southeastern Archaeological Research, Inc., for Florida Department of Transportation, District Two, Lake City, Florida.

2010   Reconstructing the Life Histories of Bolen Hafted Bifaces from a North Florida Archaeological Site. *Early Georgia* 38(1):3–27.

Austin, Robert J., Sam B. Upchurch, James S. Dunbar, Richard W. Estabrook, Jon C. Endonino, and Adam Burke

2014   The Quarry Cluster Approach to Chert Provenance Studies, with Examples from Florida. Paper presented at the 71st Annual Southeastern Archaeological Conference, Greenville, South Carolina.

Azevedo, Soledad de, Judith Charlin, and Rolando González-José

2014   Identifying Design and Reduction Effects on Lithic Projectile Point Shapes. *Journal of Archaeological Science* 41:297–307.

Baker, D. W., P. J. Miranda, and K. E. Gibbs

2008   Montana Evidence for Extra-terrestrial Impact Event That Caused Ice-Age Mammal Die-Off. American Geophysical Union, Spring Meeting 2008, abstract #P41A-05.

Baldwin, Wayne E., Robert A. Morton, Thomas R. Putney, Michael P. Katuna, M. Scott Harris, Paul T. Gayes, Neal W. Driscoll, Jane F. and William C. Schwab

2006   Migration of the Pee Dee River System Inferred from Ancestral Paleochannels Underlying the South Carolina Grand Strand and Long Bay Inner Shelf. *Bulletin of the Geological Society of America* 118:533–549. doi:10.1130/B25856.1.

Balsillie, James H., and Joseph F. Donoghue,

2004   *High Resolution Sea-Level History for the Gulf of Mexico since the Last Glacial*

Maximum. Report of Investigations No. 103. Florida Geological Survey, Tallahassee.

Barbour, Terry E.

2015   Reconstructing the Culture History of the Multicomponent Site Squires Ridge (31ED365) within the Northern Coastal Plain of North Carolina. Unpublished Master's thesis, Department of Anthropology, East Carolina University.

Bard, Edouard

2002   Abrupt Climate Changes over Millennial Time Scales: Climate Shock. *Physics Today* 55:32–38.

Bard, Edouard, Bruno Hamelin, and Doriane Delanghe-Sabatier

2010   Deglacial Meltwater Pulse 1B and Younger Dryas Sea Levels Revisited with Boreholes at Tahiti. *Science* 327:1235–1237. doi:10.1126/science.1180557.

Bar-Yosef, Ofer, and Anna Belfer-Cohen

2002   Facing Environmental Crisis: Societal and Cultural Changes at the Transition from the Younger Dryas to the Holocene in the Levant. In *The Dawn of Farming in the Near East*, edited by René T. J. Cappers and Sytze Bottema, pp. 55–66. ex oriente, Berlin.

Basso, Keith H.

1983   "Stalking with Stories": Names, Places, and Moral Narratives among the Western Apache. In *Text, Play, and Story: The Construction and Reconstruction of Self and Society*, edited by Edward M. Bruner, pp. 19–55. American Ethnological Society, Washington, D.C.

Bateman, Mark D., Claire H. Boulter, Andrew S. Carr, Charles D. Frederick, Duane Peter, and Michael Wilder

2007   Detecting Post-depositional Sediment Disturbance in Sandy Deposits Using Optical Luminescence. *Quaternary Geochronology* 2:57–64.

Bateman, Mark D., Charles D. Frederick, Manoj K. Jaiswal, Ashok K. Singhvi

2003   Investigations into the Potential Effects of Pedoturbation on Luminescence Dating. *Quaternary Research Reviews* 22:1169–1176.

Beets, C. J., Mukul Sharma, Cornelius Kasse, and Sjoerd Bohncke

2008   Search for Extraterrestrial Osmium at the Allerod–Younger Dryas Boundary. Abstract #V53A-2150, American Geophysical Union, Fall Meeting, San Francisco.

Belknap, Daniel F., and John C. Kraft

1977   Holocene Relative Sea-Level Changes and Coastal Stratigraphic Units on the Northwest Flank of the Baltimore Canyon Trough Geosyncline. *Journal of Sedimentary Research* 47:610–629. doi:10.1306/212F71F8–2B24–11D7–8648000102C1865D.

1981   Preservation Potential of Transgressive Coastal Lithosomes on the U.S. Atlantic Shelf. *Marine Geology* 42:429–442. doi:http://dx.doi.org/10.1016/0025–3227(81)90173–0.

Bement, Leland C., Andrew S. Madden, Brian J. Carter, Alexander R. Simms, Andrew L. Swindle, Hanna M. Alexander, Scott Fine, and Mourad Benamara

2014   Quantifying the Distribution of Nanodiamonds in Pre- Younger Dryas to

Recent Age Deposits along Bull Creek, Oklahoma Panhandle, USA. *Proceedings* of the *National Academy of Sciences USA* 111(5):1726–1731.

Bender, Barbara

1999   Subverting the Western Gaze: Mapping Alternative Worlds. In *The Archaeology and Anthropology of Landscape: Shaping Your Landscape,* edited by Peter J. Ucko and Robert Layton, pp. 31–45. Routledge, London.

2002   Time and Landscape. *Current Anthropology* 43 suppl.:S103–S112.

Bense, Judith A.

1994   *Archaeology of the Southeastern United States: Paleoindian to World War I.* Academic Press, San Diego.

Bense, Judith A. (editor)

1987   *Final Report: The Midden Mound Project.* Report of Investigations 6. Office of Cultural and Archaeological Research, University of West Florida, Pensacola.

Benson, Robert

2007   *Cultural Resources Survey of the Turkey/Byrd Watershed, Approximately 4,500 Acres in the Long Cane Ranger District, Sumter National Forest, Edgefield and McCormick Counties, South Carolina.* Francis Marion and Sumter National Forests Cultural Resources Management Report 07–09. Southeastern Archaeological Services. Athens, Georgia.

Binford, Lewis R.

1968   *New Perspectives in Archeology.* Aldine, Chicago.

1979   Organization and Formation Processes: Looking at Curated Technologies. *Journal of Anthropological Research* 35(3):255–273.

1980   Willow Smoke and Dogs' Tails: Hunter-Gatherer Settlement Systems and Archaeological Site Formation. *American Antiquity* 45(1):4–20.

2001   *Constructing Frames of Reference: An Analytical Method for Archaeological Theory Building Using Ethnographic Data Sets.* University of California Press, Berkeley and Los Angeles.

Bissett, Thaddeus G.

2003   Morphological Variation of Bolen Haftable Bifaces: Function and Style among Chipped-Stone Artifacts from the Early Holocene Southeast. Master's thesis, Department of Anthropology, Florida State University, Tallahassee.

Blackwelder, Blake W., Orrin H. Pilkey, and James D. Howard

1979   Late Wisconsinan Sea Levels on the Southeast U.S. Atlantic Shelf Based on In-Place Shoreline Indicators. *Science* 204:618–620. doi:10.1126/science.204.4393.618.

Blanton, Dennis B., and Frankie Snow

1986   Paleo-Indian and Early Archaic Lithic Assemblage Composition in South Georgia: Evidence from the Feronia Locality. Paper presented at the annual Southeastern Archaeological Conference, Nashville, Tennessee.

1989   Paleo-Indian and Early Archaic Occupations at the Feronia Locality in South-Central Georgia. Paper presented at the 54th Annual Meeting of the Society for American Archaeology, Atlanta, Georgia.

Bleed, Peter
1986   The Optimal Design of Hunting Weapons: Maintainability or Reliability. *American Antiquity* 51(4):737–747.
Boëda, Eric, Antoine Lourdeau, Christelle Lahaye, Gisele Daltrini Felice, Sibeli Viana, Ignacio Clemente-Conte, Mario Pino, Michel Fontugne, Sirlei Hoeltz, Niède Guidon, Anne-Marie Pessis, Amélie Da Costa, and Marina Pagli
2013   Late-Pleistocene Industries of Piaui, Brazil: New Data. In *Paleoamerican Odyssey*, edited by Kelly E. Graf, Caroline Ketron, and Michael R. Waters, pp. 445–465. Center for the Study of the First Americans, Department of Anthropology, Texas A&M University, College Station.
Bond, Gerald, Bernd Kromer, Juerg Beer, Raimund Muscheler, Michael N. Evans, William Showers, Sharon Hoffman, Rusty Lotti-Bond, Irka Hajdas, and Georges Bonani
2001   Persistent Solar Influence on North Atlantic Climate during the Holocene. *Science* 294:2130–2136.
Bond, Gerald, William M. Showers, Maziet Cheseby, Rusty Lotti, Peter Almasi, Peter de-Menocal, Paul Priore, Heidi Cullen, Irka Hajdas, and Georges Bonani
1997   A Pervasive Millennial-Scale Cycle in North Atlantic Holocene and Glacial Climates. *Science* 278:1257–1266.
Bond, Gerald, William Showers, Mary Elliot, Michael Evans, Rusty Lotti, Irka Hajdas, Georges Bonani, and Sigfus Johnson
1999   The North Atlantic's 1–2 kya Climate Rhythm: Relation to Heinrich Events, Dansgaard/Oeschger Cycle and the Little Ice Age. In *Mechanisms of Global Climate Change at Millennial Time Scales*, edited by Peter Clark, Richard Webb, and Lloyd Keigwin, pp. 35–58. Geophysical Monograph Series Vol. 112. American Geophysical Union, Washington, D.C.
Bookstein, Fred L.
1991   *Morphometric Tools for Landmark Data: Geometry and Biology.* Cambridge University Press, Cambridge.
1996   Combining the Tools of Geometric Morphometrics. In *Advances in Morphometrics*, edited by Leslie F. Marcus, Marco Corti, Anna Loy, Gavin J. P. Naylor, and Dennis E. Slice, pp. 131–151. Plenum Press, New York.
Bordes, François
1961   *Typologie du Paléolithique ancien et moyen.* 2 vols. Mémoires de l'Institut de Préhistoire de l'Université de Bordeaux 1. Delmas, Bordeaux.
Boulter, Claire H., Mark D. Bateman, Andrew S. Carr, and Charles D. Frederick
2006   Assessment of Archaeological Site Integrity of Sandy Substrates Using Luminescence Dating. *Society of Archaeological Sciences Bulletin* 29:8–12.
Boyd, Robert, and Peter J. Richerson
1985   *Culture and the Evolutionary Process.* University of Chicago Press, Chicago.
Bradley, Bruce A.
1997   Sloan Site Biface and Projectile Point Technology. In *Sloan: A Paleoindian Dalton Cemetery in Arkansas*, edited by Dan F. Morse, pp. 53–57. Smithsonian Institution Press, Washington, D.C.

Bradley, Bruce A., Michael B. Collins, and Andrew Hemmings
2010   *Clovis Technology.* Archaeological Series 17. International Monographs in Prehistory, Ann Arbor.

Bradley, Bruce A., and Dennis J. Stanford
2004   The North Atlantic Ice-Edge Corridor: A Possible Palaeolithic Route to the New World. *World Archaeology* 36(4): 459–478.

Brady, Nyle C.
1974   *The Nature and Properties of Soils.* Macmillan, New York.

Brauer, Achim, Gerald H. Haug, Peter Dulski, Daniel M. Sigman, and Jörg F. W. Negendank
2008   An Abrupt Wind Shift in Western Europe at the Onset of the Younger Dryas Cold Period. *Nature Geoscience* 1:520–523.

Bridgman Sweeney, Kara
2013   A Complex Web of History and Artifact Types in the Early Archaic Southeast. Ph.D. dissertation, Department of Anthropology, University of Florida, Gainesville.

Bridgman Sweeney, Kara, and Albert C. Goodyear III, Tommy Charles, and Erika Shofner
2008   Achieved and Received Wisdom in the Archaeology of Edgefield Scrapers. Paper presented at the 65th Meeting of the Southeastern Archaeological Conference, Charlotte.

Bril, Blandine, and Valentine Roux (editors)
2005   *Stone Knapping: The Necessary Conditions for a Uniquely Hominin Behaviour.* McDonald Institute for Archaeological Research, Cambridge.

Broecker, Wallace S.
2006   Was the Younger Dryas Triggered by a Flood? *Science* 312:1146–1148.

Broecker, Wallace S., Michael Andree, Willy Wolfli, H. Oeschger, Georges Bonani, James Kennett, and Dorothy Peteet
1988   The Chronology of the Last Deglaciation: Implications to the Cause of the Younger Dryas Event. *Paleoceanography* 3:1–19.

Broecker, Wallace, and George Denton
2012   The Role of Ocean-Atmosphere System Reorganizations in Glacial Cycles. *Quaternary Science Reviews* 9:305–341.

Broecker, Wallace S., James P. Kennett, Benjamin P. Flower, James T. Teller, Sue Trumbore, Georges Bonani, and Willy Wolfi
1989   Routing of Meltwater from the Laurentide Ice Sheet during the Younger Dryas. *Nature* 341:318–321.

Brown, Randall, Early L. Stone, and Victor W. Carlisle
1990   Soils. In *Ecosystems of Florida*, edited by Ronald L. Myers and John J. Ewel, pp. 35–69. University of Central Florida Press, Orlando.

Bronk Ramsey, C.
2009   Bayesian Analysis of Radiocarbon Dates. *Radiocarbon* 51(1):337–360.

Brooks, Mark J.
1990   A Point-Bar Site on the South Edisto River in the Upper Coastal Plain of South Carolina: Depositional History and Environmental Implications. *South Carolina Antiquities* 22(1&2):17–25.

Brooks, Mark J., and Donald J. Colquhoun
1991   Late Pleistocene–Holocene Depositional Change in the Coastal Plain of the Savannah River Valley: A Geoarchaeological Perspective. *Early Georgia* 19(2):1–20.
Brooks, Mark J., and Kenneth E. Sassaman
1990   Point Bar Geoarchaeology in the Upper Coastal Plain of the Savannah River Valley, South Carolina: A Case Study. In *Archaeological Geology of North America*, Centennial Special Volume 4, edited by Norman P. Lasca and Jack E. Donahue, pp. 183–197. Geological Society of America, Boulder.
Brooks, Mark J., Barbara E. Taylor, and John A. Grant
1996   Carolina Bay Geoarchaeology and Holocene Landscape Evolution on the Upper Coastal Plain of South Carolina. *Geoarchaeology* 11:481–504.
Brooks, Mark J., Barbara E. Taylor, and Andrew H. Ivester
2010   Carolina Bays: Time Capsules of Culture and Climate Change. *Southeastern Archaeology* 29(1):146–163.
Brooks, Mark J., Barbara E. Taylor, Peter A. Stone, and L. R. Gardner
2001   Pleistocene Encroachment of the Wateree River Sand Sheet into Big Bay on the Middle Coastal Plain of South Carolina. *Southeastern Geology* 40:241–257.
Broyles, Bettye J.
1971   *Second Preliminary Report: The St. Albans Site, Kanawha County, West Virginia*. Report of Archeological Investigations No. 3. West Virginia Geological and Economic Survey, Morgantown.
Brughmans, Tom
2013   Thinking through Networks: A Review of Formal Network Methods in Archaeology. *Journal of Archaeological Method and Theory* 20:623–662.
Bryan, Kirk
1950   *Flint Quarries—The Sources of Tools and, at the Same Time, the Factories of the American Indian*. Papers of the Peabody Museum of American Archaeology and Ethnology Vol. 17, No. 3. Harvard University, Cambridge.
Buchanan, Briggs, and Mark Collard
2010   A Geometric Morphometrics-Based Assessment of Blade Shape Differences among Paleoindian Projectile Point Types from Western North America. *Journal of Archaeological Science* 37(2):350–359.
Buchanan, Briggs, Michael J. O'Brien, and Mark Collard
2014   Continent-Wide or Region-Specific? A Geometric Morphometrics-Based Assessment of Variation in Clovis Point Shape. *Archaeological and Anthropological Sciences* 6(2):145–162.
Bullen, Ripley P.
1958   *The Bolen Bluff Site on Paynes Prairie, Florida*. Contributions of the Florida State Museum, Social Sciences No. 4. University of Florida, Gainesville.
1975   *A Guide to the Identification of Florida Projectile Points*. Rev. ed. Kendall Books, Gainesville.

Bunch, Ted E., Robert E. Hermes, Andrew M. T. Moore, Douglas J. Kennett, James C. Weaver, James H. Wittke, Paul S. DeCarli, James L. Bischoff, Gordon C. Hillman, George A. Howard, David R. Kimbel, Gunther Kletetschka, Carl P. Lipo, Sachiko Sakai, Zsolt Revay, Allen West, Richard B. Firestone, and James P. Kennett

2012   Very High-Temperature Impact Melt Products as Evidence for Cosmic Airbursts and Impacts 12,900 Years Ago. *Proceedings of the National Academy of Sciences USA* 109(28):11066–11067.

Burke, Adam M.

2014   The Wayne's Sink Site (8JE1508/8TA280): A PXRF Analysis of Lithic Materials from a Submerged Quarry in the Aucilla River, Florida. Master's thesis, Anthropology Department, Indiana University of Pennsylvania, Indiana, Pennsylvania.

Butzer, Karl W.

1982   *Archaeology as Human Ecology: Method and Theory for a Contextual Approach.* University of Chicago, Chicago.

Byrd, Brian F.

2005   Reassessing the Emergence of Village Life in the Near East. *Journal of Archaeological Research* 13(3): 231–290.

Cable, John S.

1996   Haw River Revisited: Implications for Modeling Late Glacial and Early Holocene Hunter-Gatherer Settlement Systems in the Southeast. In *The Paleoindian and Early Archaic Southeast*, edited by David G. Anderson and Kenneth E. Sassaman, pp. 107–148. University of Alabama Press, Tuscaloosa.

Cable, John S., and Charles E. Cantley (assemblers)

1979   *An Intensive Archeological Survey of the South Carolina 151 Highway Widening Project.* Research Manuscript series. University of South Carolina, Institute of Archeology and Anthropology, Columbia.

Calcote, Haetwell F.

1981   Mechanisms of Soot Nucleation in Flames—a Critical Review. *Combustion and Flame* 42:215–242.

Callahan, Errett

1979   *The Basics of Biface Knapping in the Eastern Fluted Point Tradition: A Manual for Flintknappers and Lithic Analysts.* Archaeology of Eastern North America Vol. 7, No. 1. Eastern States Archaeological Federation, Washington, Connecticut.

Cambron, James W., and David C. Hulse

1983   *Handbook of Alabama Archaeology, Part I: Point Types*, edited by David L. DeJarnette. Archaeological Research Association of Alabama, Tuscaloosa.

Canouts, Veletta

1981   *Woodland Occupation in the Upper Coastal Plain of South Carolina: An Archeological Reconnaissance of the Carolina Power and Light Company's Lake Robinson to Sumter 230-kV Transmission Line Corridor.* University of South Carolina Scholar Commons, Research Manuscript Series, South Carolina Institute of Archaeology and Anthropology, Columbia.

Carlson, Anders E., Peter U. Clark, Brian A. Haley, Gary P. Klinkhammer, Kathleen Simmons, Edward J. Brook, and Katrin J. Meissner

2007   Geochemical Proxies of North American Freshwater Routing during the Younger Dryas Cold Event. *Proceedings of the National Academy of Sciences USA* 104:6493–6494.

Carotenuto, Francesco, Nikoloz Tsikaridze, Lorenzo Rook, David Lordkipanidze, Laura Longo, Silvana Condemi, and Pasquale Raia

2008   Venturing out Safely: The Biogeography of Homo Erectus Dispersal out of Africa. *Journal of Human Evolution* 95:1–12.

Carter, Brinnen C., and James S. Dunbar

2006   Early Archaic Archaeology. In *First Floridians and Last Mastodons: The Page-Ladson Site in the Aucilla River*, edited by S. David Webb, pp. 493–515. Springer, Dordrecht.

Carter, George F.

1957   *Pleistocene Man at San Diego*. Johns Hopkins Press, Baltimore.

Chamberlin, Rollin T.

1917   Interpretation of the Formations Containing Human Bones at Vero, Florida. *Journal of Geology* 25(1):25–39.

Chapman, Clark R., and David Morrison

1994   Impact on the Earth by Asteroids and Comets: Assessing the Hazard. *Nature* 367:33–40.

Charles, Tommy

1981   *Dwindling Resources: An Overture to the Future of South Carolina's Archaeological Resources*. Notebook 13. South Carolina Institute of Archaeology and Anthropology, University of South Carolina, Columbia.

1983   *Thoughts and Records from the Survey of Private Collections of Prehistoric Artifacts throughout South Carolina: A Second Report*. Notebook 15. South Carolina Institute of Archaeology and Anthropology, University of South Carolina, Columbia.

1986   *Fifth Phase of the Collectors Survey*. Notebook 18. South Carolina Institute of Archaeology and Anthropology, University of South Carolina, Columbia.

Charles, Tommy, and James L. Michie

1992   South Carolina Paleo Point Database. In *Paleoindian and Early Archaic Research in the Lower Southeast: A South Carolina Perspective*, edited by David G. Anderson, Christopher Judge, and Kenneth E. Sassaman, pp. 381–389. Council of South Carolina Professional Archaeologists, Columbia.

Charlin, Judith, Marcelo Cardillo, and Karen Borrazzo

2014   Spatial Patterns in Late Holocene Lithic Projectile Point Technology of Tierra del Fuego (Southern South America): Assessing Size and Shape Changes. *World Archaeology* 46(1): 78–100.

Cheng, Hai, R. Lawrence Edwards, Wallace S. Broecker, George H. Denton, Xinggong Kong, Yongjin Wang, Rong Zhang, and Xienfeng Wang

2009   Ice Age Terminations. *Science* 326:248–252.

Choate, Brian C.

2011   Stratigraphic Investigations at Barber Creek (31PT259): Reconstructing the

Culture-History of a Multicomponent Site in the North Carolina Coastal Plain. Unpublished aster's thesis, Department of Anthropology, East Carolina University.

Clark, Graham
1969   *World Prehistory: A New Synthesis*. Cambridge University Press, Cambridge.

Clark, Peter U., Shawn J. Marshall, Garry K. C. Clarke, Steven W. Hostetler, Joseph M. Licciardi, and James T. Teller
2001   Freshwater Forcing of Abrupt Climate Change during the Last Glaciation. *Science* 293:283–287.

Coe, Joffrey Lanning
1964   *The Formative Cultures of the Carolina Piedmont*. Transactions of the American Philosophical Society Vol. 54, Part 5. American Philosophical Society, Philadelphia.

Cole, John R., Laurie R Godfrey, Robert E. Funk, James T. Kirkland, and William A. Starna
1977   On "Some Paleolithic Tools from Northeast North America." *Current Anthropology* 3:541–546.

Coleman, Dennis D.
1972   Illinois State Geological Survey Radiocarbon Dates III. *Radiocarbon* 14:149–154.

Collar, Anna, Fiona Coward, Tom Brughmans, and Barbara J. Mills
2015   Networks in Archaeology: Phenomena, Abstraction, Representation. *Journal of Archaeological Method and Theory* 22:1–32.

Collins, Michael B.
1999   *Clovis Blade Technology*. University of Texas Press, Austin.

Collins, Michael B., Dennis J. Stanford, Darrin L. Lowery, and Bruce A. Bradley
2013   North America before Clovis: Variance in Temporal/Spatial Cultural Patterns, 27,000–13,000 cal yr BP. In *Paleoamerican Odyssey*, edited by Kelly E. Graf, Caroline V. Ketron, and Michael R. Waters, pp. 521–539. Center for the Study of the First Americans, Texas A&M University, College Station.

Colquhoun, Donald J.
1974   Cyclic Surficial Stratigraphic Units of the Middle and Lower Coastal Plains, Central South Carolina. In *Post-Miocene Stratigraphy, Central and Southern Atlantic Coastal Plain*, edited by Robert Q. Oaks and Jules R. DuBar, pp. 179–190. Utah State University Press, Logan.
1995   A Review of Cenozoic Evolution of the Southeastern United States Atlantic Coast North of the Georgia Trough. *Quaternary International* 26:35–41.

Colquhoun, Donald J., Gerald H. Johnson, Pamela C. Peebles, Paul F. Huddlestun, and Thomas Scott
1991   Quaternary Geology of the Atlantic Coastal Plain. In *Quaternary Nonglacial Geology: Conterminous US*, edited by Robert B. Morrison, pp. 629–650. Geological Society of America, Boulder.

Conley, Mary C., Mark G. Anderson, Laura Geselbracht, Robert Newton, Katherine Weaver, Analie Barnett, and John Prince

2015   South Atlantic Bight Marine Assessment: Species, Habitats and Ecosystems, Nature Conservancy Eastern U.S. Division Boston. Electronic Document, http://nature.ly/marineSAtlanticBightERA, Accessed July 1, 2015.

Cooke, Charles Wythe
1936   *Geology of the Coastal Plain of South Carolina*. Bulletin 867. U.S. Department of the Interior, Washington, D.C.

Copeland, Charles W.
1968   *Geology of the Alabama Coastal Plain: A Guidebook*. Issue 47. Geological Survey of Alabama, University of Alabama, Tuscaloosa.

Costello, Robert C., and Albert C. Goodyear
2014   Revisiting the 38CR33 Lithic Assemblage: Evidence of a Wyboo Chert Processing Site in Clarendon County, South Carolina. *South Carolina Antiquities* 46:45–47.

Costello, Robert C., and Kenneth E. Steffy
2013   Wyboo Chert and Its Prehistoric Utilization. *South Carolina Antiquities* 45:84–87.

Cotterell, Brian, and Johan Kamminga
1987   The Formation of Flakes. *American Antiquity* 52:678–708.

Crabtree, Don E.
1972   *An Introduction to Flintworking*. Occasional Papers of the Museum No. 28. Idaho State University, Pocatello.

Crane, Horace R., and James B. Griffin
1972   University of Michigan Radiocarbon Dates XIV. *Radiocarbon* 14:155–194.

Cronin, Thomas M., Patricia Manley, Stefanie Brachfield, Tom Manley, Debra A. Willard, Jean-Pierre Guilbault, John A. Rayburn, Robert Thunell, and Melissa Berke
2008   Impacts of Post-Glacial Lake Drainage Events and Revised Chronology of the Champlain Sea Episode 13–9 ka. *Palaeoceanography, Palaeoclimatology, Palaeoecology* 262:46–60.

Cronin, Thomas M., John A. Rayburn, Jean-Pierre Guilbault, Robert Thunell, and David A. Franzi
2012   Stable Isotope Evidence for Glacial Lake Drainage through the St. Lawrence Estuary, Eastern Canada, ~13.1–12.9 ka. *Quaternary International* 260:55–65.

Cronin, Thomas M., Barney J. Szabo, Thomas A. Ager, Joseph E. Hazel, and James P. Owens
1981   Quaternary Climates and Sea Levels of the U.S. Atlantic Coastal Plain. *Science* 211:233–40. doi:10.1126/science.211.4479.233.

Cronin, Thomas M., Robert Thunell, Gary S. Dwyer, Casey Saenger, Michael E. Mann, Cheryl D. Vann, and Robert R. Seal II
2005   Multiproxy Evidence of Holocene Climate Variability from Estuarine Sediments, Eastern North America. *Paleoceanography* 20:1–21.

Culleton, Brendan J., and Douglas J. Kennett
2008   Evaluating the Paleoindian Radiocarbon Record at the Onset of the Younger Dryas: Sensitivity Analyses and Bayesian Chronology-Building. American Geophysical Union, Fall Meeting 2008, San Francisco, abstract #PP23D-03.

Curry, Dennis C.

1992   Burial of Late Archaic Coastal Plain Sites as a Result of Eolian Deposition. *Maryland Archaeology* 28:17–26.

Daniel, I. Randolph

1998   *Hardaway Revisited: Early Archaic Settlement in the Southeast.* University of Alabama Press, Tuscaloosa.

2001   Stone Raw Material Availability and Early Archaic Settlement in the Southeastern United States. *American Antiquity* 66(2):237–266.

2002a   Stratified Early-Middle Holocene Remains in the North Carolina Coastal Plain. *Southeastern Archaeological Conference Special Publication* 7:6–11.

2002b   *Geoarchaeological Investigations at Barber Creek (31PT259), Greenville, North Carolina.* Report prepared under a Historic Preservation Fund Grant from the United States Department of Interior and administered by the North Carolina Division of Archives and History.

Daniel, I. Randolph, and J. Robert Butler

1996   An Archaeological Survey and Petrographic Description of Rhyolite Sources in the Uwharrie Mountains, North Carolina. *Southern Indian Studies* 45:1–37.

Daniel, I. Randolph, and Albert C. Goodyear III

2006   An Update on the North Carolina Fluted-Point Survey. *Current Research in the Pleistocene* 23:88–90.

2015   North Carolina Clovis. In *Clovis: On the Edge of a New Understanding*, edited by Ashley M. Smallwood and Thomas A. Jennings, pp. 319–331. Texas A&M University Press, College Station.

2018   Clovis Macrobands in the Carolinas. In *In the Eastern Fluted Point Tradition, Volume 2*, edited by Joseph A. M. Gingerich. University of Utah Press, Salt Lake City.

Daniel, I. Randolph Jr. and Christopher R. Moore

2011   Current Research into the Paleoindian and Archaic Periods in the North Carolina Coastal Plain. *North Carolina Archaeological Council Publication* 30:95–119.

Daniel, I. Randolph Jr., Christopher R. Moore, and E. Christopher Canyor

2013   Sifting the Sands of Time: Geoarchaeology, Culture Chronology, and Climate Change at Squires Ridge, Northeastern North Carolina. *Southeastern Archaeology* 32:253–270.

Daniel, I. Randolph Jr., Keith C. Seramur, Tara L. Potts, and Mathew W. Jorgenson

2008   Searching a Sand Dune: Shovel Testing the Barber Creek Site. *North Carolina Archaeology* 57:50–77.

Daniel, I. Randolph Jr., and Michael Wisenbaker

1987   *Harney Flats: A Florida Paleo-Indian Site.* Baywood, Farmingdale, New York.

Daniels, Raymond B., Erling E. Gamble, and Stanley W. Boul

1969   Eolian Sands Associated with Coastal Plain River Valleys—Some Problems in Their Age and Source. *Southeastern Geology* 11:97–110.

Dansgaard, Willi, Sigfús J. Johnsen, Henrik B. Clausen, Dorothe Dahl-Jensen, Niels S. Gundestrup, Claus Uffe Hammer, Christine S. Hvidberg, Jørgen P. Steffensen, Árny E. Sveinbjörnsdottir, Jean Jouzel, and Gerard Bond
1993   Evidence for General Instability of Past Climate from a 250-kyr Ice-Core Record. *Nature* 364:218–220.
Darwin, Charles
1969[1845]   *The Voyage of the Beagle.* Harvard Classics. Collier and Son, New York.
Daulton, Tyrone, Nicholas Pinter, and Andrew Scott
2010   No Evidence of Nanodiamonds in Younger-Dryas Sediments to Support an Impact Event. *Proceedings of the National Academy of Sciences USA* 107(37):16043–16047.
Davis, Basil A. S., and Anthony C. Stevenson
2007   The 8.2 ka Event and Early–Mid Holocene Forests, Fires and Flooding in the Central Ebro Desert, NE Spain. *Quaternary Science Reviews* 26:1695–1712.
Debénath, André, and Harold L. Dibble
1994   *Handbook of Paleolithic Typology: 1. Lower and Middle Paleolithic of Europe.* Museum of Archaeology and Anthropology, University of Pennsylvania, Philadelphia.
Debret, Maxime, Viviane Bout-Roumazeilles, Francis Grousset, Marc Desmet, Jerry F. McManus, Nicolas Massei, David Sebag, Jean R. Petit, Yoann Copard, and Alain Trentesaux
2007   The Origin of the 1500-Year Climate Cycles in Holocene North-Atlantic Records. *Climate of the Past Discussions* 3:569–575.
Deetz, James
1977   *In Small Things Forgotten: The Archaeology of Early American Life.* Anchor Press/Doubleday, Garden City.
DeJarnette, David L.
1975   *Archaeological Salvage in the Walter F. George Basin of the Chattahoochee River in Alabama.* University of Alabama Press, Tuscaloosa.
DeJarnette, David L., Edward B. Kurjack, and James Cambron
1962   Excavations at the Stanfield-Worley Bluff Shelter. *Journal of Alabama Archaeology* 8(1–2):1–124.
Delcourt, Hazel R., and Paul A. Delcourt
1985   Quaternary Palynology and Vegetational History of the Southeastern United States. In *Pollen Records of Late-Quaternary North American Sediments,* edited by Vaughn M. Bryant and Richard G. Holloway, pp. 1–37. American Association of Stratigraphic Palynologists Foundation, Dallas.
Derev'anko, Anatoliy P. (editor and compiler)
1998   *The Paleolithic of Siberia: New Discoveries and Interpretations.* University of Illinois Press, Urbana.
Devoe, Rick
2015   *South Carolina Cooperative Agreement: Atlantic Offshore Wind Energy Development: Geophysical Mapping and Identification of Paleolandscapes and Historic Shipwrecks Offshore South Carolina.* Bureau of Energy Management, Washington, D.C.

Dibble, Harold L.
1995   Biache Saint-Vaast, Level IIA: A Comparison of Analytical Approaches. In *The Definition and Interpretation of Levallois Technology*, edited by Harold Dibble and Ofer Bar-Yosef, pp. 93–116. Monographs in World Archaeology 23. Prehistory Press, Madison.

Dibble, Harold L., Simon J. Holdaway, Sam C. Lin, David R. Braun, Matthew J. Douglass, Radu Iovita, Shannon P. McPherron, Deborah I. Olszewski, and Dennis Sandgathe
2016   Major Fallacies Surrounding Stone Artifacts and Assemblages. *Journal of Archaeological Method and Theory* 23(2): 1–39.

Dillehay, Thomas D.
1996   *Monte Verde: A Late Pleistocene Settlement in Chile: 2. The Archaeological Context and Interpretation.* Smithsonian Institution Press, Washington, D.C.
2000   *The Settlement of the Americas: A New Prehistory.* Basic Books, New York.
2009   Probing Deeper into First American Studies. *Proceedings of the National Academy of Sciences* 106(4): 971–978.

Disotell, Todd R.
2013   Phylogenetic Relationships (Biomolecules). In *Handbook of Paleoanthropology, Volume 3*, pp. 1807–1824. Springer, New York.

Dixon, Raoul M.
1983   The First Big Game Hunters: A Preliminary Report. *Nevada Archaeologist* 4(1):26–33.

Donahue, Brian T., Paul T. Gayes, David B. Scott, and Francine M. G. McCarthy
1995   The Late Pleistocene–Early Holocene Marine Transition in South Carolina: An Exposed Forest Floor on the SC Mid-Shelf. *Geological Society of America Abstracts with Programs* 27:202.

Dragoo, Don W.
1973   Wells Creek—An Early Man Site in Stewart County, Tennessee. *Archaeology of Eastern North America* 1(1):1–56.

Drennan, Robert D.
2009   *Statistics for Archaeologists.* 2nd ed. Springer, New York.

Dromgoole, Sarah
2010   Revisiting the Relationship between Marine Scientific Research and the Underwater Cultural Heritage. *International Journal of Marine and Coastal Law* 25:33–61. doi:10.1163/157180809 × 12583617932149.

DuBar, Jules R., Susan S. DuBar, Lauck W. Ward, Blake W. Blackwelder, William H. Abbot, and Paul F. Huddlestun
1980   Cenozoic Biostratigraphy of the Carolina Outer Coastal Plain. In *Excursions in Southeastern Geology: Geological Society of America 1980 Annual Meeting Field Trip Guidebook,* edited by Robert W. Frey, pp. 179–233. Geological Society of America, Atlanta.

Dunbar, James S.
1988   Cutler Site Lithic Artifact Analysis. Unpublished notes and date sheets on file at the Aucilla Research Institute, Jefferson County, Florida.

2002   Chronostratigraphy and Paleoclimate of Late Pleistocene Florida and the
            Implications of Changing Paleoindian Land Use. Unpublished master's the-
            sis, Department of Anthropology, Florida State University, Tallahassee.
2006   Paleoindian Archaeology. In *First Floridians and Last Mastodons: The Page-
            Ladson Site in the Aucilla River*, edited by S. David Webb, pp. 403–438.
            Springer, Dordrecht.
2012   *Artifact and Specimen Documentation for Case FWSW100FF6661-JF.* Report
            prepared for the Florida Fish and Wildlife Conservation Commission, Tal-
            lahassee.
2016   *Paleoindian Societies of the Coastal Southeast.* University Press of Florida,
            Gainesville.

Dunbar, James S., Glen H. Doran, and Jack Rink
2010   Paleoindian Sites Revisited: Known Sites and New Perspectives. Report on
            file, Florida Division of Historical Resources, Tallahassee.

Dunbar, James S., and C. Andrew Hemmings
2004   Florida Paleoindian Points and Knives. In *New Perspectives on the First
            Americans*, edited by Bradley T. Lepper and Robson Bonnichsen, pp. 65–72.
            Center for the Study of the First Americans, Texas A&M University Press,
            College Station.

Dunbar, James S., and Christine L. Newman
2003   *Assessment and Documentation of Cultural Resources in Goethe State Forest,
            Levy County, Florida I, II, and III.* CARL Archaeological Program, Florida
            Bureau of Archaeological Research, Tallahassee.

Dunbar, James S., and Pamela K. Vojnovski
2007   Early Floridians and Late Mega-mammals: Some Technological and Dietary
            Evidence from Four North Florida Paleoindian Sites. In *Foragers of the Ter-
            minal Pleistocene in North America*, edited by Renee B. Walker and Boyce N.
            Driskell, pp. 167–202. University of Nebraska Press, Lincoln.

Dunbar, James S., and Ben I. Waller
1983   A Distribution Analysis of the Clovis/Suwannee Paleo-Indian Sites of Flori-
            da—A Geographic Approach. *Florida Anthropologist* 36:18–30.

Dunbar, James S., S. David Webb, and Michael K. Faught
1991   Inundated Prehistoric Sites in Apalachicola Bay, Florida and the Search for
            the Clovis Shoreline. In *Paleoshorelines and Prehistory: An Investigation of
            Method*, edited by Lucille Lewis Johnson and Melanie Stright, pp. 117–146.
            CRC Press, Boca Raton, Florida.

Eerkens, Jelmer W., Robert L. Bettinger, and Richard McElreath
2006   Cultural Transmission, Phylogenetics, and the Archaeological Record. In
            *Mapping Our Ancestors: Phylogenetic Approaches in Anthropology and Pre-
            history*, edited by Carl P. Lipo, Michael J. O'Brien, Mark Collard, and Stephen
            J. Shennan, pp. 169–208. Transaction, Piscataway.

Ellis, Christopher, Albert C. Goodyear, Dan F. Morse, and Kenneth B. Tankersley
1998   Archaeology of the Pleistocene–Holocene Transition in Eastern North
            America. *Quaternary International* 49/50:151–166.

Emanuel, William H.
1968   The American "Hand-Axe." *Tennessee Archaeologist* 24(1):8–28.

Emery, Kenneth O.
1972   Eastern Atlantic Continental Margin: Some Results of the 1972 Cruise of the
            R. V. Atlantis II. *Science* 178:298–301. doi:10.1126/science.178.4058.298.

Endonino, Jon C.
2007   A Reevaluation of the Gainesville, Ocala, and Lake Panasoffkee Quarry
            Clusters. *Florida Anthropologist* 60:77–96.

Engelhart, Simon E., William R. Peltier, and Benjamin P. Horton
2011   Holocene Relative Sea-Level Changes and Glacial Isostatic Adjustment of
            the U.S. Atlantic Coast. *Geology* 39:751–754. doi:10.1130/G31857.1.

Ensor, H. Blaine
1981   *Gainesville Lake Area Lithics: Chronology, Technology, and Use.* Archaeologi-
            cal Investigations in the Gainesville Lake Area of the Tennessee-Tombigbee
            Waterway Vol. 3. Report of Investigations No. 13. Office of Archaeological
            Research, University of Alabama.
2008   Capps: A Levallois-Like Prepared Core Technology in the Southeastern
            United States. Paper presented at the 65th Annual Meeting of the Southeast-
            ern Archaeological Conference, Charlotte, North Carolina.
2013   Capps: A Levallois-Like Technology in North America. Paper presented at
            the Paleoamerican Odyssey Conference, October 17–19, Santa Fe.
2014   Development of a New Paradigm for Early Settlement of the Americas: Data
            from the Gulf Coastal Plain and Beyond. Paper presented at the 71st Annual
            Meeting of the Southeastern Archaeological Conference. Greenville, South
            Carolina.

Ensor, H. Blaine, and Floyd B. Largent
1997   Recent Survey and Archaeological Research in the Vicinity of Fort Rucker,
            Southeastern Alabama. *Journal of Alabama Archaeology* 43(1):48–83.

Erlandson, Jon M.
2001   The Archaeology of Aquatic Adaptations: Paradigms for a New Millennium.
            Journal of Archaeological Research 9:287–350.

Estabrook, Richard W.
2011   *Social Landscapes of Transegalitarian Societies: An Analysis of the Chipped
            Stone Artifact Assemblage from the Crystal River Site (8CI1), Citrus County,
            Florida.* Ph.D. dissertation, Department of Anthropology, University of
            South Florida, Tampa. ProQuest.

Estabrook, Richard W., and J. Raymond Williams
1992   Analysis of Lithic Materials from the Rattlesnake Midden Site (8HI981),
            Tampa Bay, Florida. *Florida Anthropologist* 45:39–51.

Evans, Amanda M., Joe Flatman, and Nicholas Flemming (editors)
2014   *Prehistoric Archaeology on the Continental Shelf: A Global Review.* Springer,
            New York.

Fairbanks, Richard G.
1989   A 17,000-Year Glacio-Eustatic Sea Level Record: Influence of Glacial Melt-

ing Rates on the Younger Dryas Event and Deep-Ocean Circulation. *Nature* 342:637–642.

Faith, J. Tyler

2011   Late Pleistocene Climate Change, Nutrient Cycling, and the Megafaunal Extinctions in North America. *Quaternary Science Reviews* 30:1675–1680.

Faith, J. Tyler, and Todd A. Surovell

2009   Synchronous Extinction of North America's Pleistocene Mammals. *Proceedings of the National Academy of Sciences* 106 (49):20641–20645.

Faught, Michael K.

2004a   The Underwater Archaeology of Paleolandscapes, Apalachee Bay, Florida. *American Antiquity* 69:275–289. doi:10.2307/4128420.

2004b   Submerged Paleoindian and Archaic Sites of the Big Bend, Florida. *Journal of Field Archaeology* 29:273–290. doi:10.2307/3250893.

2014   Remote Sensing, Target Identification and Testing for Submerged Prehistoric Sites in Florida: Process and Protocol in Underwater CRM Projects. In *Prehistoric Archaeology on the Continental Shelf: A Global Review*, edited by Amanda Evans, Joe Flatman, and Nicolas Flemming, pp. 37–52. Springer, New York. doi:10.1007/978-1-4614-9635-9.

Faught, Michael K., David G. Anderson, and Anne Gisiger

1994   North American Paleoindian Database—an Update. *Current Research in the Pleistocene* 11:32–35.

Faught, Michael K. and Joseph F. Donoghue

1997   Marine Inundated Archaeological Sites and Paleofluvial Systems: Examples from a Karst-Controlled Continental Shelf Setting in Apalachee Bay, Northeastern Gulf of Mexico. *Geoarchaeology* 12:417–458. doi:10.1002/(SICI)1520-6548(199708)12:5<417:AID-GEA1>3.0.CO;2-2.

Faught, Michael K., and Amy E. Gusick

2011   Submerged Prehistory in the Americas. In *Submerged Prehistory*, edited by Jonathan Benjamin, Clive Bonsall, Catriona Pickard, and Anders Fischer, pp. 145–157. Oxbow Books, Oxford.

Faught, Michael K., Michael Hornum, Brinnen Carter, R. Christopher Goodwin, and S. David Webb

2003   Earliest Holocene Tool Assemblages from Northern Florida with Stratigraphically Controlled Radiocarbon Estimates (Sites 8LE2105 and 8JE591). *Current Research in the Pleistocene* 20:16–18.

Faught, Michael K., and James C. Waggoner Jr.

2012   The Early Archaic to Middle Archaic Transition: An Argument for Discontinuity. *Florida Anthropologist* 65(3):153–175.

Faure, Hugues, Robert C. Walter, and Douglas R. Grant

2002   The Coastal Oasis: Ice Age Springs on Emerged Continental Shelves. *Global and Planetary Change* 33(1–2):47–56.

Fayek, Mostafa, Lawrence M. Anovitz, Lawrence F. Allard, and Sharon Hull

2012   Framboidal Iron Oxide: Chondrite-Like Material from the Black Mat, Murray Springs, Arizona. *Earth and Planetary Science Letters* 319:251–258.

Feathers, James K.
2003   Use of Luminescence Dating in Archaeology. *Measurement and Science Technology* 14:1493–1509.

Feathers, James K., Vance T. Holliday, and David J. Meltzer
2006   Optically Stimulated Luminescence Dating of Southern High Plains Archaeological Sites. *Journal of Archaeological Science* 33:1661–1665.

Feathers, James K., Edward J. Rhodes, Sebastien Huot, and Joseph M. McAvoy
2006   Luminescence Dating of Sand Deposits Related to Late Pleistocene Human Occupation at the Cactus Hill Site, Virginia, USA. *Quaternary Geochronology* 1:167–187.

Feathers, James K., and Jon Tunnicliff
2011   Effect of Single-Grain versus Multi-Grain Aliquots in Determining Age for K-feldspars from Southwestern British Columbia. *Ancient TL* 29:53–58

Feder, Kenneth L.
2011   *Frauds, Myths, and Mysteries: Science and Pseudoscience in Archaeology*. McGraw Hill, New York.

Fenneman, Nevin M.
1916   Physiographic Divisions of the United States. *Annals of the Association of American Geographers* 6:19–98.

Ferring, C. Reid
2001   *The Archaeology and Paleoecology of the Aubrey Clovis Site (41DN479) Denton County, Texas.* Report prepared for the U.S. Army Corps of Engineers Fort Worth District. Center for Environmental Archaeology, Department of Geography, University of North Texas, Denton.

Fiedel, Stuart J.
2009   Sudden Deaths: The Chronology of Terminal Pleistocene Megafaunal Extinction. In *American Megafaunal Extinctions at the End of the Pleistocene*, edited by Gary Haynes, pp. 21–37. Springer, New York.

2011   The Mysterious Onset of the Younger Dryas. *Quaternary International* 2:262–266.

2013   Is That All There Is? The Weak Case for Pre-Clovis Occupation of Eastern North America. In *In the Eastern Fluted Point Tradition*, edited by Joseph A. M. Gingerich, pp. 333–354. University of Utah Press, Salt Lake City.

2016   Foreword. In *The Distribution of Paleoindian Debitage from the Pleistocene Terrace at the Topper Site: An Evaluation of a Possible Pre-Clovis Occupation (38Al23)*, by Megan H. King, pp. i–ii. Occasional Papers 3. Southeastern Paleoamerican Survey, South Carolina Institute of Archaeology and Anthropology, University of South Carolina, Columbia.

Fiedel, Stuart J., and Gary Haynes
2004   A Premature Burial: Comments on Grayson and Meltzer's "Requiem for Overkill." *Journal of Archaeological Science* 31:121–131.

Finkl, Charles W., Jacob E. Becerra, Victoria Achatz, and Jeffrey L. Andrews
2008   Geomorphological Mapping along the Upper Southeast Florida Atlantic Continental Platform: I: Mapping Units, Symbolization and Geographic In-

formation System Presentation of Interpreted Seafloor Topography. *Journal of Coastal Re*search 24:1388–1417. doi:10.2112/08a-0007.1.

Firestone, Richard B., Allen West, James P. Kennett, Luann Becker, Ted E. Bunch, Zsolt S. Revay, Peter H. Schultz, Tamas Belgya, Douglas J. Kennett, Jon M. Erlandson, O. J. Dickenson, Albert C. Goodyear, R. Scott Harris, George A. Howard, Johan B. Kloosterman, Paul Lechler, Paul A. Mayewski, Jenna Montgomery, Robert Poreda, Thomas Darrah, Shane S. Que Hee, A. R. Smith, Adrienne Stich, William Topping, James H. Wittke, and Wendy S. Wolbach
2007 Evidence for an Extraterrestrial Impact 12,900 Years Ago That Contributed to the Megafaunal Extinctions and the Younger Dryas Cooling. *Proceedings of the National Academy of Sciences USA* 104(41):16016–16021.

Fischer, Hubertus, Simon Schüpbach, Gideon Gfeller, Matthias Bigler, Regine Röthlisberger, Tobias Erhardt, Thomas F. Stocker, Robert Mulvaney, and Eric W. Wolff
2015 Millennial Changes in North American Wildfire and Soil Activity over the Last Glacial Cycle. *Nature Geoscience* 8:723–727.

Fisher, N. I.
1993 *Statistical Analysis of Circular Data*. Cambridge University Press, New York.

Fitzhugh, Ben, S. Colby Phillips, and Erik Gjesfjeld
2011 Modeling Variability in Hunter-Gatherer Information Networks: An Archaeological Case Study from the Kuril Islands. In *Information and Its Role in Hunter-Gatherer Bands*, edited by Robert W. Whallon, William A. Lovis, and Robert K. Hitchcock, pp. 85–115. UCLA Cotsen Institute of Archaeology, Los Angeles.

Fladmark, Knut R.
1979 Routes: Alternate Migration Corridors for Early Man in North America. *American Antiquity* 44:55–69.

Flower, Benjamin P., Carlie Williams, Heather W. Hill, and David W. Hastings
2011 Laurentide Ice Sheet Meltwater and the Atlantic Meridional Overturning Circulation during the Last Glacial Cycle: A View From the Gulf of Mexico. *American Geophysical Union,* doi: 10.1029/2010GM001016.

Flower, Benjamin P., David W. Hastings, Heather W. Hill, and Terrence M. Quinn
2004 Phasing of Deglacial Warming and Laurentide Ice Sheet Meltwater in the Gulf of Mexico. *Geology* 32(7):597–600.

Ford, James A., Philip Phillips, and William G. Haag
1955 *The Jaketown Site in West-Central Mississippi*. Anthropological Papers Vol. 45, Pt. 1. American Museum of Natural History, New York.

Fort Pierce [Florida] *News*
1915 State Geologist Studies Fossils Found Here. 19 February 1915.
1916 State Geologist Finds First Fossilized Human Bone at Vero. 18 February 1916.

Fraser, Sarah B., and George R. Sedberry
2008 Reef Morphology and Invertebrate Distribution at Continental Shelf Edge Reefs in the South Atlantic Bight. *Southeastern Naturalist* 7:191–206. doi:10.1656/1528 7092(2008)7[191:RMAIDA]2.0.CO;2

Frederick, Charles D., Mark D. Bateman, and Robert Rogers
2002 Evidence for Eolian Deposition in the Sandy Uplands of East Texas and the

Implications for Archaeological Site Integrity. *Geoarchaeology: An International Journal* 17:191–217.

Frederick, Charles D., Michael D. Glasscock, Hector Neff, and Christopher M. Stevenson
1994   *Evaluation of Chert Patination as a Dating Technique: A Case Study from Fort Hood, Texas.* United States Army Fort Hood, Archeological Resource Management Series, Research Report 32. Mariah and Associates, Inc. Austin, Texas.

Fritz, John M., and Fred T. Plog
1970   The Nature of Archaeological Explanation. *American Antiquity* 35(4):405–412.

Galbraith, Rex F., and Richard G. Roberts
2012   Statistical Aspects of Equivalent Dose and Error Calculation and Display in OLS Dating: An Overview and Some Recommendations. *Quaternary Geochronology* 11:1–27.

Galparsoro, Ibon, Pedro Liria, Irati Legorburu, Juan Bald, Guillem Chust, Pablo Ruiz-Minguela, Germán Peréz, Javier Marqués, Yago Torre-Enciso, Manuel González, and Angel Borja
2012   A Marine Spatial Planning Approach to Select Suitable Areas for Installing Wave Energy Converters (WECs), on the Basque Continental Shelf (Bay of Biscay). *Coastal Management* 40(1):1–19. doi:10.1080/08920753.2011.637483.

Gamble, Clive
1999   *The Paleolithic Societies of Europe.* Cambridge University Press, Cambridge.

Gamble, Clive, William Davies, Paul Pettitt, Lee Hazelwood, and Martin Richards
2005   The Archaeological and Genetic Foundations of the European Population during the Late Glacial: Implications for "Agricultural Thinking." *Cambridge Archaeological Journal* 15:193–223.

Garrison, Ervan G., Wendy Weaver, Sherri L. Littman, Jessica C. Hale, and Pradeep Srivastava
2012   Late Quaternary Paleoecology and Heinrich Events at Gray's Reef National Marine Sanctuary, South Atlantic Bight, Georgia. *Southeastern Geology* 48(4):165–184.

Gastwirth, Joseph L., Yulia R. Gel, and Weiwen Miao
2009   The Impact of Levene's Test of Equality of Variances on Statistical Theory and Practice. *Statistical Science* 24(3):343–360.

Gehrels, W. Roland, and Ian Shennan
2015   Sea Level in Time and Space: Revolutions and Inconvenient Truths. *Journal of Quaternary Science* 30:131–143. doi:10.1002/jqs.2771.

Gilbert, M. Thomas P., Dennis L. Jenkins, Anders Gotherstrom, Nuria Nauveran, Juan J. Sanchez, Michael Hofreiter, Philip F. Thomsen, Jonas Binladen, Thomas F. G. Higham, Robert M. Yohe II, Robert Parr, Linda S. Cummings, and Eske Willerslev
2008   DNA from Pre-Clovis Human Coprolites in Oregon, North America. *Science* 320:786–789.

Gilmour, Daniel M., Virginia L. Butler, Jim E. O'Connor, Edward B. Davis, Brendan J. Culleton, Douglas J. Kennett, and Gregory Hodgins

2015   Chronology and Ecology of Late Pleistocene Megafauna in the Northern Willamette Valley, Oregon. *Quaternary Research* 83:127–136.

Gingerich, Joseph A. M.

2012   Late Pleistocene Human Adaptations in Eastern North America: Evidence of Universal Adaptations. Unpublished Ph.D. dissertation, Department of Anthropology, University of Wyoming, Laramie.

Gjesfjeld, Erik

2015   Network Analysis of Archaeological Data from Hunter-Gatherers: Methodological Problems and Potential Solutions. *Journal of Archaeological Method and Theory* 22(1):182–205.

Goad, Sharon I.

1979   *Chert Resources in Georgia: Archaeological and Geological Perspectives.* Wallace Reservoir Project Contribution 3. University of Georgia Laboratory of Archaeology Series Report No. 21, Athens.

Goebel, Ted

2015   Clovis Culture Update. In *Clovis: On the Edge of a New Understanding*, edited by Ashley M. Smallwood and Thomas A. Jennings, pp. 335–352. Texas A&M University Press, College Station.

Goebel, Ted, Michael R. Waters, and Dennis H. O'Rourke

2008   The Late Pleistocene Dispersal of Modern Humans in the Americas. *Science* 319:1497–1502.

Goman, Michelle, and David S. Leigh

2004   Wet Early to Middle Holocene Conditions on the Upper Coastal Plain of North Carolina, USA. *Quaternary Research* 61:256–264. doi:10.1016/j.yqres.2004.02.007.

Goodwin, R. Christopher, William P. Barse, and Charlotte Pevny

2013   *Adapting to Climate Change at the Pleistocene–Holocene Transition: Data Recovery of Five Late Paleoindian to Early Archaic Sites along Florida's Cody Scarp (8LE2105, 8LE2102, 8JE880/8LE2909, 8JE872, and 8JE878).* FMSF Survey #20082R. R. Christopher Goodwin and Associates, Inc., New Orleans.

Goodyear, Albert C. III

1974   *The Brand Site: A Techno-Functional Study of a Dalton Site in Northeast Arkansas.* Research Series No. 1. Arkansas Archaeological Survey, Fayetteville.

1979   *A Hypothesis for the Use of Cryptocrystalline Raw Materials among Paleoindian Groups of North America.* Research Manuscript Series 156. South Carolina Institute of Archaeology and Anthropology, University of South Carolina, Columbia.

1982   The Chronological Position of the Dalton Horizon in the Southeastern United States. *American Antiquity* 47:382–395.

1983   A Hypothesis for the Use of Cryptocrystalline Raw Materials among Paleoindian Groups of North America. In *Eastern Paleoindian Lithic Resource Use*, edited by Christopher J. Ellis and Jonathan C. Lothrop, pp. 1–9. Westview Press, Boulder.

1999   The Early Holocene Occupation of the Southeastern United States: A Geo-archaeological Summary. In *Ice Age People of North America: Environments, Origins, and Adaptations*, edited by Robson Bonnichsen and Karen L. Turnmire, pp. 432–481. Oregon State University Press, Corvallis.

2000   The Topper Site 2000: Results of the 2000 Allendale Paleoindian Expedition. *Legacy* 5(2):18–25.

2005a   Evidence of Pre-Clovis Sites in the Eastern United States. In *Paleoamerican Origins: Beyond Clovis*, edited by Robson Bonnichsen, Bradley T. Lepper, Dennis Stanford, and Michael R. Waters, pp. 103–112. Center for the Study of the First Americans, Department of Anthropology, Texas A&M University, College Station.

2005b   Summary of the Allendale Paleoindian Expedition—2003 and 2004 Field Seasons. *Legacy* 9 (1/2):4–11.

2006   Recognizing the Redstone Fluted Point in the South Carolina Paleoindian Point Database. *Current Research in the Pleistocene* 23:100–103.

2010a   Lithic Raw Material Studies in South Carolina and Their Implications for Paleoindian Mobility. *South Carolina Antiquities* 42:40–41.

2010b   Instrument-Assisted Fluting as a Technochronological Marker among North American Paleoindian Points. *Current Research in the Pleistocene* 27:86–88.

2012   2011 Activities of the Southeastern Paleoamerican Survey. *Legacy* 16(1):6–10.

2013   Update on the 2012–2013 Activities of the Southeastern Paleoamerican Survey. *Legacy* 17(1):10–12.

2014   Paleoindian in COWASEE: Time, Typology, and Raw Material Selection. *South Carolina Antiquities* 46:3–20.

2016   The Search for the Earliest Humans in the Land Recently Called South Carolina. In *Archaeology in South Carolina*, edited by Adam King, pp. 1–13. University of South Carolina Press, Columbia.

2018   The Allendale-Brier Creek Clovis Complex of the Central Savannah River Valley. In *In the Eastern Fluted Point Tradition*, Vol. 2, edited by Joseph A. M. Gingerich, in press. University of Utah Press, Salt Lake City.

Goodyear, Albert C. III, and Tommy Charles
1984   *An Archaeological Survey of Chert Quarries in Western Allendale County, South Carolina*. Research Manuscript Series 195. South Carolina Institute of Archaeology and Anthropology, University of South Carolina, Columbia.

Goodyear, Albert C. III, Tommy Charles, and James L. Michie
1993   Early Prehistoric Peoples of South Carolina. *South Carolina Antiquities* 25:23–29.

Goodyear, Albert C. III, James L. Michie, and Tommy Charles
1989   The Earliest South Carolinians. In *Studies in South Carolina Archaeology: Essays in Honor of Robert L. Stephenson*, edited by Albert C. Goodyear III and Glen T. Hanson, pp. 19–52. Anthropological Studies 9. South Carolina Institute of Archaeology and Anthropology, University of South Carolina, Columbia.

1990   *The Earliest South Carolinians: The Paleoindian Occupation of South Caro-*

lina. Occasional Papers No. 2. Archaeological Society of South Carolina, Columbia.

Goodyear, Albert C. III, D. Shane Miller, and Ashley M. Smallwood
2007   Introducing Clovis at the Topper Site, 38AL23, Allendale County, South Carolina. Paper presented at the 72nd Annual Meeting of the Society for American Archaeology, Austin.

Goodyear, Albert C., Douglas A. Sain, Megan Hoak King, Derek T. Anderson, Elizabeth Bell, and M. Scott Harris
2013   Topper, an Early Paleoamerican Site in South Carolina. Paper presented at the Paleoamerican Odyssey Conference, Santa Fe.

Goodyear, Albert C. III, and Kenneth E. Steffy
2003   Evidence of a Clovis Occupation at the Topper Site, 38AL23, Allendale County, South Carolina. *Current Research in the Pleistocene* 20:23–25.

Goodyear, Albert C., Sam B. Upchurch, and Mark J. Brooks
1980   Turtlecrawl Point: An Inundated Early Holocene Archeological Site on the West Coast of Florida. In *Holocene Geology and Man in Pinellas and Hillsborough Counties, Florida*, compiled by Sam B. Upchurch, pp. 24–33. Guidebook No. 22. Southeastern Geological Society, Tallahassee.
1993   Turtlecrawl Point: Lessons from an Inundated Prehistoric Site on Boca Ciega Bay, Florida. Paper presented at the 45th Annual Meeting of the Florida Anthropological Society, Clearwater, Florida.

Goodyear, Albert C. III, Sam B. Upchurch, Mark J. Brooks, and Nancy N. Goodyear
1983   Paleo-indian Manifestations in the Tampa Bay Region, Florida. *Florida Anthropologist* 36(1&2):40–66.

Goodyear, Albert C. III, Sam B. Upchurch, Tommy Charles, and Alan B. Albright
1985   Chert Sources and Paleoindian Lithic Processing in Allendale County, South Carolina. *Current Research in the Pleistocene* 2:47–49.

Goodyear, Albert C. III, and Joseph E. Wilkinson
2014a   Prehistory at High Creek Plantation: A Black Mingo Chert Source and Quarry in Calhoun County, South Carolina. *South Carolina Antiquity* 46:35–43.
2014b   Across the Coastal Plain: Examining the Prehistoric Archaeology of the Inter-Riverine Zone through Private Collections. *Legacy* 18(2):15–17.
2015   Documenting Orthoquartzite Tool Stone in the Beaver Creek Locality in Calhoun County, S.C. Paper presented at the 41st Meeting of the Archaeological Society of South Carolina, Columbia.

Gould, Richard A.
1969   *Yiwara: Foragers of the Australian Desert*. Collins, London.
1971   The Archaeologist as Ethnographer: A Case from the Western Desert of Australia. *World Archaeology* 3(2):143–177.
1978   The Anthropology of Human Residues. *American Anthropologist* 80(4):815–835.

Grachev, Alexei M., and Jeffrey P. Severinghaus
2005   A Revised +10 ± 4 °C Magnitude of the Abrupt Change in Greenland Temperature at the Younger-Dryas Termination Using Published GISP2 Gas Iso-

tope Data and Air Thermal Diffusion Constants. *Quaternary Science Reviews* 24:513–519.

Granovetter, Mark S.
1973   The Strength of Weak Ties. *American Journal of Sociology* 78(6):1360–1380.

Grant, John A., Mark J. Brooks, and Barbara E. Taylor
1998   New Constraints on the Evolution of Carolina Bays from Ground-Penetrating Radar. *Geomorphology* 22:325–345.

Grayson, Donald K.
1987   An Analysis of the Chronology of Late Pleistocene Mammalian Extinctions in North America. *Quaternary Research* 28:281–289.
2006   Late Pleistocene Faunal Extinctions. In *Handbook of North American Indians, Volume 3, Environment, Origins, and Population*, edited by Douglas H. Ubelaker, pp. 208–218. Smithsonian Institution, Washington, D.C.
2007   Deciphering North American Pleistocene Extinctions. *Journal of Anthropological Research* 63:185–213.

Grayson, Donald K., and David J. Meltzer
2002   Clovis Hunting and Large Mammal Extinction: A Critical Review of the Evidence. *Journal of World Prehistory* 16:313–359.
2003   A Requiem for North American Overkill. *Journal of Archaeological Science* 30:585–593.

Green, Andrew N., J. Andrew G. Cooper, and Leslee Salzmann
2014   Geomorphic and Stratigraphic Signals of Postglacial Meltwater Pulses on Continental Shelves. *Geology* 42:151–154. doi:doi:10.1130/G35052.1.

Grootes, Pieter M., Minze Stuiver, James W. White, Sigfus Johnsen, and Jean Jouzel
1993   Comparison of Oxygen Isotope Records from the GISP2 and GRIP Greenland Ice Cores. *Nature* 366:552–554.

Guidon, Niéde, and Geogette Delibrias
1986   Carbon-14 Dates Point to Man in the Americas 32,000 Years Ago. *Nature* 321:769–771.

Gunn, Joel D., and John E. Foss
1992   Copperhead Hollow (38CT58): Middle Holocene Upland Conditions on the Piedmont-Coastal Plain Margin. *South Carolina Antiquities* 24:1–17.

Guthrie, R. Dale
2003   Rapid Body Size Decline in Alaskan Pleistocene Horses before Extinction. *Nature* 426:169–171.
2004   Radiocarbon Evidence of Mid-Holocene Mammoths Stranded on an Alaskan Bering Sea Island. *Nature* 429:746–749.

Halligan, Jessi J., Michael R. Waters, Angelina Perotti, Ivy J. Owens, Joshua M. Feinberg, Mark D. Bourne, Brendan Fenerty, Barbara Winsborough, David Carlson, Daniel C. Fisher, Thomas W. Stafford Jr., and James S. Dunbar
2016   Pre-Clovis Occupation 14,550 Years Ago at the Page-Ladson Site, Florida and the Peopling of the Americas. *Science Advances* 2(5):e1600375. Doi.org/10.1126/sciadv1600375.

Hammer, Øyvind, and David A. T. Harper
2005   *Paleontological Data Analysis*. Wiley-Blackwell, Malden.
Harris, M. Scott, Paul T. Gayes, Jack L. Kindinger, James G. Flocks, David E. Krantz, and
        Patricia Donovan
2005   Quaternary Geomorphology and Modern Coastal Development in Re-
        sponse to an Inherent Geologic Framework: An Example from Charleston,
        South Carolina. *Journal of Coastal Research* 211:49–64. doi:10.2112/00–015.1.
Harris, M. Scott, Katherine E. Luciano, Kacey L. Johnson, Sharon Kate McMullen, Brian
        Kennedy, Leslie Sautter, Norman S. Levine, Anjana Shah, George R. Sed-
        berry, and Ashley Deming
2011   Geologic Mapping of Surficial Sediments and Near-Surface Stratigraphy
        with Multiple Remote-Sensing Techniques; Describing and Monitoring
        Tidal Regions in Central South Carolina. Abstracts with Programs—Geo-
        logical Society of America 43:66.
Harris, M. Scott, Leslie Sautter, George R. Sedberry, Katherine E. Luciano, Eric E. Wright,
        Kacey L. Johnson, and Amy N. S. Siuda
2014   Regional Quaternary Landscape Evolution of the Southeastern U.S. Conti-
        nental Shelf and Adjacent Coastal Plain. Abstracts with Programs—Geologi-
        cal Society of America 46:33.
Harris, M. Scott, Leslie R. Sautter, Kacey L. Johnson, Katherine E. Luciano, George R.
        Sedberry, Eric E. Wright, and Amy N. S. Siuda
2013   Continental Shelf Landscapes of the Southeastern United States since the Last
        Interglacial. *Geomorphology* 203:6–24. doi:10.1016/j.geomorph.2013.02.014.
Harris, M. Scott, Kristina Poston, and Katherine Luciano
2010   High Resolution Sediment Profiles of the Topper Archaeological Site
        (38AL23) in Allendale County, South Carolina. Poster program, South Caro-
        lina Academy of Sciences 2010 Annual Meeting, Paper 50-NSCB.
Harris, Stephen J., and Anita M. Weiner
1985   Chemical Kinetics of Soot Particle Growth. *Annual Review of Physical Chem-
        istry* 36:31–52.
Hayes, Miles O.
1994   The Georgia Bight Barrier System. In *Geology of Holocene Barrier Island Sys-
        tems,* edited by Richard A. Davis Jr., pp. 233–304. Springer, Berlin.
Haynes, C. Vance
1973   The Calico Site: Artifacts or Geofacts? *Science* 181:305–310.
1984   Stratigraphy and Late Pleistocene Extinction in the United States. In *Qua-
        ternary Extinctions: A Prehistoric Revolution*, edited by Paul S. Martin and
        Richard G. Klein, pp. 345–353. University of Arizona Press, Tucson.
1995   Geochronology of Paleoenvironmental Change, Clovis Type Site, Blackwater
        Draw, New Mexico. *Geoarchaeology* 10(5):317–388.
1998   Arizona's Famous Clovis Sites Could Be Displayed or Public. *Mammoth
        Trumpet* 13(2):3–6.
2005   Clovis, Pre-Clovis, Climate Change, and Extinction. In *Paleoamerican Ori-
        gins: Beyond Clovis*, edited by Robson Bonnichsen, Bradley T. Lepper, Den-

nis Stanford, and Michael R. Waters, pp. 113–132. Texas A & M, College Station.

2007   Quaternary Geology of the Murray Springs Clovis Site. In *Murray Springs: A Clovis Site with Multiple Activity Areas in the San Pedro Valley, Arizona*, edited by C. Vance Haynes and Bruce B. Huckell, pp. 16–56. University of Arizona Press, Tucson.

2008   Younger Dryas "Black Mats" and the Rancholabrean Termination in North America. *Proceedings of the National Academy of Sciences USA* 105(18):6520–6525.

Haynes, C. Vance Jr., Jennifer Boerner, Kenneth Domanik, Dante Lauretta, Jesse Ballenger, and Julia Goreva

2010   The Murray Springs Clovis Site, Pleistocene Extinction, and the Question of Extraterrestrial Impact. *Proceedings of the National Academy of Sciences USA* 107(9):4010–4015.

Haynes, Gary

2002   The Catastrophic Extinction of North American Mammoths and Mastodons. *World Archaeology* 33:391–416.

2009   Introduction to the Volume. In *American Megafaunal Extinctions at the End of the Pleistocene*, edited by Gary Haynes, pp. 1–20. Springer, New York.

2015   The Millennium before Clovis. *PaleoAmerica* 1(2):134–162.

Hendon, Julia A.

2000   Having and Holding: Storage, Memory, Knowledge, and Social Relations. *American Anthropologist* 102(1):42–53.

Hendy, Ingrid L., James P. Kennett, E. Brendan Roark, and B. Lynn Ingram

2002   Apparent Synchroneity of Submillenial Scale Climate Events between Greenland and Santa Barbara Basin, California from 30–10 ka. *Quaternary Science Reviews* 2:1167–1184.

Henrich, Joseph

2001   Cultural Transmission and the Diffusion of Innovations: Adoption Dynamics Indicate That Biased Cultural Transmission Is the Predominate Force in Behavioral Change. *American Anthropologist* 103(4):992–1013.

2010   The Evolution of Innovation-Enhancing Institutions. In *Innovation in Cultural Systems: Contributions from Evolutionary Anthropology*, edited by Michael J. O'Brien and Stephen J. Shennan, pp. 99–120. MIT Press, Cambridge.

Henrich, Joseph, and Robert Boyd

1998   The Evolution of Conformist Transmission and the Emergence of Between-Group Differences. *Evolution and Human Behavior* 19(4):215–241.

Hiatt, Lester R.

1968   Ownership and Use of Land among the Australian Aborigines. In *Man the Hunter*, edited by Richard B. Lee and Irven DeVore, pp. 99–110. Aldine, Chicago.

Hibben, Frank C.

1941   *Evidence of Early Occupation at Sandia Cave*. Miscellaneous Collections Vol. 99, No. 23. Smithsonian Institution, Washington, D.C.

Hill, David F., Stephen D. Griffiths, William R. Peltier, Benjamin P. Horton, and Torbjö
E. Törnqvist
2011   High-Resolution Numerical Modeling of Tides in the Western Atlantic, Gulf
of Mexico, and Caribbean Sea during the Holocene. *Journal of Geophysical
Research* 116:C10014. doi:10.1029/2010JC006896.

Hill, Jenna C., and Alan Condron
2014   Subtropical Iceberg Scours and Meltwater Routing in the Deglacial Western
North Atlantic. *National Geosci*ence 7:806–810. doi:10.1038/ngeo2267.

Hill, Jenna C., and Neal W. Driscoll
2010   Iceberg Discharge to the Chukchi Shelf during the Younger Dryas. *Quaternary Research* 74:57–62.

Hitchcock, Robert K., and Laurence E. Bartram
1998   Social Boundaries, Technical Systems, and the Use of Space and Technology
in the Kalahari. In *The Archaeology of Social Boundaries*, edited by Miriam
T. Stark, pp. 12–49. Smithsonian Institution Press, Washington, D.C.

Hodder, Ian
2012   *Entangled: An Archaeology of the Relationships between Humans and Things.*
Wiley-Blackwell, West Sussex.

Holen, Steven R., Thomas A. Deméré, Daniel C. Fisher, Richard Fullagar, James B. Paces,
George T. Jefferson, Jared M. Beeton, Richard A. Cerutti, Adam N. Rountrey,
Lawrence Vescera, and Kathleen A. Holen
2017   A 130,000-Year-Old Archaeological Site in Southern California, USA. *Nature*
544:479–486.

Holliday, Vance T., and D. Shane Miller
2013   The Clovis Landscape. In *Paleoamerican Odyssey*, edited by Kelly E. Graf,
Caroline V. Ketron, and Michael R. Waters, pp. 221–245. Texas A&M Press,
College Station.

Holmes, William H.
1919   *Handbook of Aboriginal Antiquities: Pt. I: The Lithic Industries.* Bureau of
American Ethnology Bulletin 60. Smithsonian Institution, Washington, D.C.

Horton, Benjamin P.
2007   Late Quaternary Relative Sea-Level Changes in Mid-Latitudes. In *Encyclo-
pedia of Quaternary Science,* edited by Scott Elias, pp. 3064–3072. Elsevier
Science, Amsterdam.

Hovers, Erella
2009   *The Lithic Assemblages of Qafzeh Cave.* Oxford University Press, Oxford.

Hrdlička, Ales
1917   Preliminary Report on Finds of Supposedly Ancient Human Remains at
Vero, Florida. *Journal of Geology* 25(1):43–51.

Hughen, Konrad A., Jonathan T. Overpeck, Scott J. Lehman, Michaele Kashgarian, John
Southon, Larry C. Peterson, Richard B. Alley, and Daniel M. Sigman
1998   Deglacial Changes in Ocean Circulation from an Extended Radiocarbon
Calibration. *Nature* 391:65–68.

Huntley, David J., Dorothy I. Godfrey-Smith, and Michael L. W. Thewalt
1985   Optical Dating of Sediments. *Nature* 313:105–107.

Hurst, Vernon J., and Arthur R. Kelly
1961   Patination of Cultural Flints. *Science* 134(3474):251–256.
Hussey, Tristram C.
1993   A 20,000-Year History of Vegetation and Climate at Clear Pond Northeastern South Carolina. Master's thesis, University of Maine, Orono.
Imbrie, John, and Katherine P. Imbrie
1979   *Ice Ages: Solving the Mystery*. Harvard University Press, Cambridge.
Indian River Farmer
1914   What They Are Doing at Vero. 5 November.
Israde-Alcántara, Isabel, James L. Bischoff, Gabriela Domínguez-Vázquez, Hong-Chun Li, Paul S. DeCarli, Ted E. Bunch, James H. Wittke, James C. Weaver, Richard B. Firestone, Allen West, James P. Kennett, Chris Mercer, Sujing Xie, Eric K. Richman, Charles R. Kinzie, and Wendy S. Wolbach
2012   Evidence from Central Mexico Supporting the Younger Dryas Extraterrestrial Impact Hypothesis. *Proceedings of the National Academy of Sciences* 109(13):E738–E747.

Ives, David J.
1975   *The Crescent Hills Prehistoric Quarrying Area*. Museum Brief No. 22. Museum of Anthropology, University of Missouri, Columbia.
Ivester, Andrew H., Mark J. Brooks, and Christopher R. Moore
2011   Geomorphological Investigations: Archaeological Sites 38RD841/842/844, Fort Jackson, South Carolina. Unpublished manuscript on file at University of West Georgia, Carrollton.
Ivester, Andrew H., and David S. Leigh
2003   Riverine Dunes on the Coastal Plain of Georgia, USA. *Geomorphology* 51:289–311. doi:10.1016/S0169-555X(02)00240-4.
Ivester, Andrew H., David S. Leigh, and Dorothy I. Godfrey-Smith
2001   Chronology of Inland Eolian Dunes on the Coastal Plain of Georgia, USA. *Quaternary Research* 55:293–302.
Jennings, Anne E., Morten Hald, Laryn M. Smith, and John T. Andrews
2006   Freshwater Forcing from the Greenland Ice Sheet during the Younger Dryas: Evidence from Southeastern Greenland Shelf Cores. *Quaternary Science Reviews* 25:282–298.
Jennings, Thomas A.
2008   San Patrice: An Example of Late Paleoindian Adaptive Versatility in South-Central North America. *American Antiquity* 73:539–559.
2010   Exploring the San Patrice Lanceolate to Notched Hafting Transition. In *Exploring Variability in Early Holocene Hunter-Gatherer Lifeways*, edited by Stance Hurst and Jack L. Hofman, pp. 153–166. University of Kansas Publications in Anthropology 25. University of Kansas, Lawrence.
Johnson, Donald L.
1990   Biomantle Evolution and the Redistribution of Earth Materials and Artifacts. *Soil Science* 149:84–102.
Johnson, Douglas W.
1942   *The Origin of the Carolina Bays*. Columbia University Press, New York.

Johnson, Gerald H., Todd Beach, M. Scott Harris, and Julie Herman
1993   Late Cenozoic Environments along the James River, Southeastern Virginia. Paper presented at the 24th Annual Virginia Geological Field Conference, Williamsburg.

Johnson, Jay K.(editor)
1981   *Lithic Procurement and Utilization Trajectories: Analysis, Yellow Creek Nuclear Power Plant Site, Tishomingo County, Mississippi, Vol. II.* Archeological Papers of the Center for Archaeological Research No. 1. University of Mississippi, Oxford.

Johnson, Michael F.
2013   Cactus Hill, Rubis-Pearsall, and Blueberry Hill: One Is an Accident, Two Is a Coincidence, Three Is a Pattern—Predicting "Old Dirt" in the Nottoway River Valley of Southeastern Virginia, U.S.A. Unpublished Ph.D. dissertation, Department of Archaeology, University of Exeter.

Jones, Kevin B., and Gerald H. Johnson
1997   Geology of the Cactus Hill Archaeological Site (44SX202), Sussex County, Virginia. In *Archaeological Investigations of Site 44SX202, Cactus Hill, Sussex County, Virginia*, Appendix C, edited by Joseph M. McAvoy and Lynn D. McAvoy. Virginia Department of Historic Resources, Richmond.

Jones, Scott
2002   Smashing Success: Pleistocene Lithic Replication in South Carolina. *Bulletin of Primitive Technology* (Spring) 2002: 44–51.

Jones, Terry L., and Douglas J. Kennett
2012   A Land Impacted? The Younger Dryas Boundary Event in California. In *Contemporary Issues in California Archaeology,* edited by Terry L. Jones and Jennifer E. Perry, pp. 37–48. Routledge, New York.

Josselyn, Daniel W.
1965   The Lively Complex: Announcing a Pebble Tool Industry in Alabama. *Journal of Alabama Archaeology* 11(2):103–122.

Journal of Geology
1917   Symposium on the Age and Relations of the Fossil Human Remains Found at Vero, Florida. 25(1):1–3.

Kaczorowski, Ray T.
1977   The Carolina Bays: A Comparison with Modern Oriented Lakes. Technical Report No. 13-CRD, Coastal Research Division, Department of Geology, University of South Carolina, Columbia.

Karabanov, Eugene, Brandy Glett, Angie McManus, Albert Goodyear, Paul Gayes, Douglas Williams, and Allendale Coring Group
2002   Sedimentary Framework for the Allendale-Topper Site. Poster program for the North-Central Section (36th) and Southeastern Section (51st), Geological Society of America Joint Annual Meeting, 3–5 April, Lexington, Kentucky.

Keigwin, Lloyd D.
2004   Radiocarbon and Stable Isotope Constraints on Last Glacial and Younger
           Dryas Ventilation in the Western North Atlantic. *Paleoceanography* 19(4):PA
           4012. doi.org/10.1029/2004PA001029.
Kelly, Robert L.
1995   *The Foraging Spectrum: Diversity in Hunter-Gatherer Lifeways.* Smithsonian
           Institution Press, Washington, D.C.
Kemp, Andrew C., Christopher E. Bernhardt, Benjamin P. Horton, Robert E. Kopp, Chris-
           topher H. Vane, W. Richard Peltier, Andrea D. Hawkes, Jeffrey P. Donnelly,
           Andrew C. Parnell, and Niamh Cahill
2014   Late Holocene Sea- and Land-Level Change on the U.S. Southeastern Atlan-
           tic Coast. *Marine Geology* 357:90–100. doi:10.1016/j.margeo.2014.07.010
Kennett, Douglas J., James P. Kennett, G. James West, Jon M. Erlandson, John R. John-
           son, Ingrid L. Hendy, Allen West, Brendan J. Culleton, Terry L. Jones, and
           Thomas W. Stafford Jr.
2008   Wildfire and Abrupt Ecosystem Disruption on California's Northern Chan-
           nel Islands at the Ållerød–Younger Dryas Boundary (13.0–12.9 ka). *Quater-
           nary Science Reviews* 27(27–28):2530–2545.
Kennett, Douglas J., James P. Kennett, Allen West, Chris Mercer, Shane S. Que Hee, and
           Leland Bement
2009   Nanodiamonds in the Younger Dryas Boundary Sediment Layer. *Science*
           323(5910):94.
Kennett, Douglas J., James P. Kennett, Allen West, G. James West, Ted E. Bunch, Brendan J.
           Culleton, Jon M. Erlandson, Shane S. Que Hee, John R. Johnson, Chris Mer-
           cer, Feng Shen, Marilee Sellers, Thomas W. Stafford, Adrienne Stich, James
           C. Weaver, James H. Wittke, and Wendy S. Wolbach
2009   Shock-Synthesized Hexagonal Diamonds in Younger Dryas Boundary Sedi-
           ments. *Proceedings of the National Academy of Sciences USA* 106(31):12623–
           12628.
Kennett, James P., and B. Lynn Ingram
1995   A 20,000-Year Record of Ocean Circulation and Climate Change from the
           Santa Barbara Basin. *Nature* 377:510–514.
Kennett, James P. and Douglas J. Kennett
2008   Late Pleistocene Megafaunal Extinction Consistent with YDB Impact Hy-
           pothesis at Younger Dryas Onset. American Geophysical Union, Fall Meet-
           ing 2008, San Francisco. Abstract #PP23D-02.
Kennett, James P., Douglas J. Kennett, Brendan J. Culleton, J. Emili Aura Tortosa, James
           L. Bischoff, Ted E. Bunch, I. Randolph Daniel Jr., Jon M. Erlandson, David
           Ferraro, Richard B. Firestone, Albert C. Goodyear III, Isabel Israde-Alcan-
           tara, John R. Johnson, Jésus F. Jordá Pardo, David R. Kimbel, Malcolm A.
           Lecompte, Neal H. Lopinot, William C. Mahaney, Andrew M. T. Moore,
           Christopher R. Moore, Jack H. Ray, Thomas W. Stafford Jr., Kenneth B. Tank-
           ersley, James H. Wittke, Wendy S. Wolbach, and Allen West
2015   Bayesian Chronological Analysis Consistent with Synchronous Age of

12,835–12,735 cal BP for Younger Dryas Boundary on Four Continents. *Proceedings of the National Academy of Sciences USA* 112(32):E4344–E4353.

Kennett, James P., and Nicholas J. Shackleton

1975   Laurentide Ice Sheet Meltwater Recorded in Gulf of Mexico Deep-Sea Cores. *Science* 188:147–150.

Kidder, Tristram R.

2006   Climate Change and the Archaic to Woodland Transition (3000–2500 ca. B.P.) in the Mississippi River Basin. *American Antiquity* 71(2):195–231.

Kimball, Larry R.

1996   Early Archaic Settlement and Technology: Lessons from Tellico. In *The Paleo-Indian and Early Archaic Southeast*, edited by David G. Anderson and Kenneth E. Sassaman, pp. 149–186. University of Alabama Press, Tuscaloosa.

King, Megan Hoak

2012   The Distribution of Paleoindian Debitage from the Pleistocene Terrace at the Topper Site: An Evaluation of a Possible Pre-Clovis Occupation (38AL23). Unpublished master's thesis, Department of Anthropology, University of Tennessee, Knoxville.

2016   *The Distribution of Paleoindian Debitage from the Pleistocene Terrace at the Topper Site: An Evaluation of a Possible Pre-Clovis Occupation (38Al23).* Occasional Papers 3. Southeastern Paleoamerican Survey, South Carolina Institute of Archaeology and Anthropology, University of South Carolina, Columbia.

Kinzie, Charles R., Shane S. Que Hee, Adrienne Stich, Kevin A. Tague, Chris Mercer, Joshua J. Razink, Douglas J. Kennett, Paul S. DeCarli, Ted E. Bunch, James H. Wittke, Isabel Israde-Alcántara, James L. Bischoff, Albert C. Goodyear, Kenneth B. Tankersley, David R. Kimbel, Brendan J. Culleton, Jon M. Erlandson, Thomas W. Stafford, Johan B. Kloosterman, Andrew M. T. Moore, Richard B. Firestone, J. Emili Aura Tortosa, Jesus F. Jordá Pardo, Allen West, James P. Kennett, and Wendy S. Wolbach

2014   Nanodiamond-Rich Layer across Three Continents Consistent with Major Cosmic Impact at 12,800 cal BP. *Journal of Geology* 122(5):475–506.

Klecka, William R.

1980   *Discriminant Analysis.* Sage, Beverly Hills.

Klingenberg, Christian Peter

2011   MorphoJ: An Integrated Software Package for Geometric Morphometrics. *Molecular Ecology Resources* 11(2):353–357.

Klingenberg, Christian Peter, Marta Barluenga, and Axel Meyer

2002   Shape Analysis of Symmetric Structures: Quantifying Variation among Individuals and Asymmetry. *Evolution* 56(10):1909–1920.

Knappett, Carl

2011   *An Archaeology of Interaction: Network Perspectives on Material Culture and Society.* Oxford University Press, Oxford.

Knappett, Carl (editor)

2013   *Network Analysis in Archaeology: New Approaches to Regional Interaction.* Oxford University Press, Oxford.

Kneberg, Madeline
1956   Some Important Projectile Types Found in the Tennessee Area. *Tennessee Archaeologist* 13(1):55–56.

Knox, James C.
2006   Floodplain Sedimentation in the Upper Mississippi Valley: Natural versus Human Accelerated. In *The Human Role in Changing Fluvial Systems: Proceedings of the 37th Binghamton Symposium in Geomorphology*, Columbia, edited by L. Allan James and W. Andrew Marcus. *Geomorphology* Special Issue 79(3):286–310. Elsevier, Amsterdam.

Knutz, Paul C., Marie-Alexandrine Sicre, Hanne Ebbesen, Sarah Christiansen, and Antoon Kuijpers
2011   Multiple-Stage Deglacial Retreat of the Southern Greenland Ice Sheet Linked with Irminger Current Warm Water Transport. *Paleoceanography* 26:1–18.

Koldehoff, Brad
1987   The Cahokia Flake Tool Industry. In *The Organization of Core Technology*, edited by Jay K. Johnson and Carol A. Morrow, pp. 151–186. Westview Press, Boulder.

Koldehoff, Brad, and John A. Walthall
2004   Settling In: Hunter-Gatherer Mobility during the Pleistocene-Holocene Transition in the Central Mississippi Valley. In *Aboriginal Ritual and Economy in the Eastern Woodlands: Essays in Honor of Howard Dalton Winters*, edited by Anne-Marie Cantwell, Lawrence A. Conrad, and Jonathan E. Reyman, pp. 49–72. Scientific Papers 30. Illinois State Museum, Springfield.

2009   Dalton and the Early Holocene Midcontinent: Setting the Stage. In *Archaic Societies of the Midcontinent*, edited by Thomas E. Emerson, Dale L. McElrath, and Andrew C. Fortier, pp. 317–375. State University of New York, Albany.

Kovach, Warren L.
2011   *Oriana–Circular Statistics for Windows, Version 4*. Kovach Computing Services, Pentraeth, Wales.

Kovarovic, Kris, Leslie C. Aiello, Andrea Cardini, and Charles A. Lockwood
2011   Discriminant Function Analyses in Archaeology: Are Classification Rates Too Good to Be True? *Journal of Archaeological Science* 38(11):3006–3018.

Kraft, John C., Stanley E. Aschenbrenner, and George Rapp
1977   Paleogeographic Reconstructions of Coastal Aegean Archaeological Sites. *Science* 195:941–947.

Krieger, Alex
1964   Early Man in the New World. In *Prehistoric Man in the New World*, edited by Jesse D. Jennings and Edward Norbeck, pp. 23–84. University of Chicago Press, Chicago.

Krupa, Amanda J., and Victor T. Mullen Jr.
2005   *Literature Review and Assessment of Geological Logs to Determine the Extent of a Dense Limestone Layer in the Upper Portion of the Biscayne Aquifer in the Pennsuco Wetlands, Miami-Dade County, Florida*. Technical Publication HESM-1. South Florida Water Management District, West Palm Beach.

Kuhn, Thomas S.
1961 The Function of Measurement in Modern Physical Science. *Isis* 52(2):161–193.
Kurbatov, Andrei V., Paul A. Mayewski, Jorgen P. Steffensen, Allen West, Douglas J. Kennett, James P. Kennett, Ted E. Bunch, Mike Handley, Douglas S. Introne, Shane S. Que Hee, Chris Mercer, Merilee Sellers, Feng Shen, Sharon B. Sneed, James C. Weaver, James H. Wittke, Thomas W. Stafford Jr., John J. Donovan, Sujing Xie, Joshua J. Razink, Adrienne Stich, Charles R. Kinzie, and Wendy S. Wolbach
2011 Discovery of a Nanodiamond-Rich Layer in the Greenland Ice Sheet. *Journal of Glaciology* 56:749–759.
Kvamme, Kenneth L., Miriam T. Stark, and William A. Longacre
1996 Alternative Procedures for Assessing Standardization in Ceramic Assemblages. *American Antiquity* 61(1):116–126.
Landis, J. Richard, and Gary G. Koch
1977 The Measurement of Observer Agreement for Categorical Data. *Biometrics* 33(1): 159–174.
Lave, Jean, and Etienne Wenger
1991 *Situated Learning: Legitimate Peripheral Participation.* Cambridge University Press, Cambridge.
Leakey, Louis S. B.
1935 *The Stone Age Races of Kenya.* Oxford University Press, Oxford.
1979 Calico and Early Man. In *Pleistocene Man at Calico*, edited by Walter C. Schuiling, pp. 91–96. San Bernardino County Museum Association. Redlands, California.
LeCompte, Malcolm A., Albert C. Goodyear, Mark N. Demitroff, David Batchelor, Edward K. Vogel, Charles Mooney, Barrett N. Rock, and Alfred W. Seidel
2012 Independent Evaluation of Conflicting Microspherule Results from Different Investigations of the Younger Dryas Impact Hypothesis. *Proceedings of the National Academy of Sciences USA* 109(44):E2960–E2969.
Lee, Thomas E.
1957 The Antiquity of the Sheguiandah Site. *Canadian Field-Naturalist* 71(3):117–148.
Leigh, David S.
1998a Evaluating Artifact Burial by Eolian versus Bioturbation Processes, South Carolina Sandhills, USA. *Geoarchaeology* 13:309–330.
1998b *Geomorphic Reconnaissance of the Overhills Tract at Fort Bragg with Special Emphasis on Bioturbation and Burial of Artifacts in Upland Sands.* Report submitted to Southeastern Archaeological Services, Athens, Georgia.
2001a *Geomorphology of the Kolb Site.* Report prepared for Diachronic Research Foundation, Columbia, South Carolina.
2001b Buried Artifacts in Sandy Soils: Techniques for Evaluating Pedoturbation versus Sedimentation. In *Earth Sciences and Archaeology*, edited by Paul Goldberg, Vance T. Holliday, and C. Reid Ferring, pp. 269–295. Kluwer Academic/Plenum, New York.

2004   *Geomorphic Processes Influencing Archaeological Site Burial at Fort Bragg.* Final report submitted to the Fort Bragg Cultural Resources Office, Fort Bragg, North Carolina.

2006   Terminal Pleistocene Braided to Meandering Transition in Rivers of the Southeastern USA. *Catena* 66:155–160. doi:10.1016/j.catena.2005.11.008.

2008   Late Quaternary Climates and River Channels of the Atlantic Coastal Plain, Southeastern USA. *Geomorphology* 101:90–108. doi:10.1016/j.geomorph.2008.05.024.

Leigh, David S., Pradeep Srivastava, and George A. Brook

2004   Late Pleistocene Braided Rivers of the Coastal Plain, USA. *Quaternary Science Reviews* 23:65–84.

Lenardi, Michael, and Daria Merwin

2010   Towards Automating Artifact Analysis: A Study Showing Potential Applications of Computer Vision and Morphometrics to Artifact Typology. In *Morphometrics for Nonmorphometricians*, edited by Ashraf M. T. Elewa, pp. 289–306. Springer-Verlag, Heidelberg.

Levac, Elisabeth, Michael Lewis, Vanessa Stretch, Kate Duchesne, and Thomas Neulieb

2015   Evidence for Meltwater Drainage via the St. Lawrence River Valley in Marine Cores from the Laurentian Channel at the Time of the Younger Dryas. *Global and Planetary Change* 130:47–65.

Levene, Howard

1960   Robust Tests for Equality of Variances. In *Contributions to Probability and Statistics: Essays in Honor of Harold Hotelling*, edited by Ingram Olkin, Sudhish G. Ghurye, Wassily Hoeffding, William G. Madow, and Henry B. Mann, pp. 278–292. Stanford University Press, California.

Leverington, David W., Jason D. Mann, and James T. Teller

2000   Changes in the Bathymetry and Volume of Glacial Lake Agassiz. *Quaternary Research* 54:174–181.

Lipo, Carl P., Robert C. Dunnell, Michael J. O'Brien, Veronica Harper, and John Dudgeon

2012   Beveled Projectile Points and Ballistics Technology. *American Antiquity* 77(4):774–788.

Lisiecki, Lorraine E., and Maureen E. Raymo

2005   A Pliocene–Pleistocene Stack of 57 Globally Distributed Benthic $\delta^{18}O$ Records. *Paleoceanography* 20(1):PA1003. Doi.org/10.1029/2004PA001071.

Lopinot, Neal H., Jack H. Ray, and Michael D. Conner

1998   *The 1997 Excavations at the Big Eddy Site (23CE426) in Southwest Missouri.* Special Publication No. 2. Southwest Center for Archaeological Research, Missouri State University, Springfield.

2000   *The 1999 Excavations at the Big Eddy Site (23CE426).* Special Publication No. 3. Center for Archaeological Research, Southwest Missouri State University, Springfield.

Lowery, Darrin L.

1989   The Paw Paw Cove Paleoindian site complex, Talbot County, Maryland. *Archaeology of Eastern North America* 17:143–163.

2002   *A Time of Dust: Archaeological and Geomorphological Investigations at the*

Paw Paw Cove Paleo-Indian Site Complex in Talbot County, Maryland. Maryland Historical Trust, Crownsville, Maryland.

2005   Archaeological Survey of the Fishing Bay and the Fairmount Wildlife Management Areas within Dorchester and Somerset County, Maryland. Monograph on file at the Maryland Historical Trust, Crownsville, Maryland.

2007   *Phase I Archaeological Survey of Miles Point in Talbot County, Maryland*. Maryland Historical Trust, Crownsville, Maryland.

2009   Geoarchaeological Investigations at Selected Coastal Archaeological Sites along the Delmarva Peninsula. Unpublished Ph.D. dissertation, Department of Geology, University of Delaware, Newark.

Lowery, Darrin, Margaret Jodry, and Dennis Stanford

2012   Clovis Coastal Zone Width Variation: A Possible Solution for Early Paleoindian Population Disparity along the Mid-Atlantic Coast, USA. *Journal of Island and Coastal Archaeology* 7(1):53–63. doi:10.1080/15564894.2011.611853.

Lowery, Darrin L., Michael A. O'Neal, John S. Wah, Daniel P. Wagner, and Dennis J. Stanford

2010   Late Pleistocene Upland Stratigraphy of the Western Delmarva Peninsula, USA. *Quaternary Science Reviews* 29:1472–1480.

Lowery, Darrin L., John Wah, and Rick Torben

2011   Post–Last Glacial Maximum Dune Sequence for the "Parsonburg" Formation at Elliott's Island, Maryland. *Current Research in the Pleistocene* 28:103–104.

Lundelius, L. Ernest Jr., Russell W. Graham, Elaine Anderson, John Guilday, J. Alan Holman, David W. Steadman, and S. David Webb

1983   Terrestrial Vertebrate Faunas. In *Late-Quaternary Environments of the United States: 1. The Late Pleistocene*, edited by Herbert Edgar Wright and Stephen C. Porter, pp. 311–353. University of Minnesota Press, Minneapolis.

Lyman, R. Lee, and Michael O'Brien

2010   Cultural Traits as Units of Analysis. *Philosophical Transactions of the Royal Society B: Biological Sciences* 365(1559):3797–3806.

Maccalli, Jenny, Claude Hillaire-Marcel, Jean Carignan, and Laurie C. Reisberg

2013   Geochemical Signatures of Sediments Documenting Arctic Sea-Ice and Water Mass Export through Fram Strait since the Last Glacial Maximum. *Quaternary Science Reviews* 64:136–151.

MacFadden, Bruce J.

2005   Fossil Horses—Evidence for Evolution. *Science* 307(5716):1728–1730.

Macphail, Richard I. and Joseph M. McAvoy

2008   A Micromorphological Analysis of Stratigraphic Integrity and Site Formation at Cactus Hill, an Early Paleoindian and Hypothesized Pre-Clovis Occupation in South-Central Virginia, USA. *Geoarchaeology* 23:675–694.

Mahan, E. C.

1964   Redstone. In *Handbook of Alabama Archaeology, Point Types Part I*, edited by James W. Cambron and David C. Hulse, p. A75. Archaeological Research Association of Alabama, Tuscaloosa.

Mahaney, William C., Volli Kalm, David H. Krinsley, Pierre Tricart, Stéphanie Schwartz, James Dohm, Kyeong J. Kim, Barbara Kapran, Michael W. Milner, Roelf Beukens, Sal Boccia, Ronald G. V. Hancock, Kris M. Hart, and Brian Kelleher
2010   Evidence from the Northwestern Venezuelan Andes for Extraterrestrial Impact: The Black Mat Enigma. *Geomorphology* 116(1–2):48–57.

Malhi, Ripan S., Brian M. Kemp, Jason A. Eshleman, Jerome Cybulski, David Glenn Smith, Scott Cousins, and Harold Harry
2007   Mitochondrial Haplogroup M Discovered in Prehistoric North Americans. *Journal of Archaeological Science* 34:642–648.

Mallinson, David J., Stephen J. Culver, Stanley R. Riggs, E. Robert Thieler, David Foster, John Wehmiller, Kathleen M. Ferrill, and Jessica Pierson
2010   Regional Seismic Stratigraphy and Controls on the Quaternary Evolution of the Cape Hatteras Region of the Atlantic Passive Margin, USA. *Marine Geology* 268:16–33. doi:10.1016/j.margeo.2009.10.007.

Mallinson, David J., Shannon A. Mahan, and Christopher R. Moore
2008   High-Resolution Shallow Geologic Characterization of a Late Pleistocene Eolian Environment Using Ground Penetrating Radar and Optically Stimulated Luminescence Techniques: North Carolina, USA. *Southeastern Geology* 45:161–171.

Mallinson, David J., Stanley Riggs, Kathleen Farrell, David S. Foster, D. Reide Corbett, Benjamin Horton, and John F. Wehmiller
2005   Late Neogene and Quaternary Evolution of the Northern Albemarle Embayment (Mid-Atlantic Continental Margin, USA). *Marine Geology* 217:97–117. doi:10.1016/j.margeo.2005.02.030.

Mardia, Kanti V., and Peter E. Jupp
2000   *Directional Statistics.* 2nd ed. Wiley, Chichester.

Markewich, Helaine W., Ronald J. Litwin, Douglas A. Wysocki, and Milan J. Pavich
2015   Synthesis on Quaternary Aeolian Research in the Unglaciated Eastern United States. *Aeolian Research* 17:139–191. doi:10.1016/j.aeolia.2015.01.011.

Markewich, Helaine W., and William Markewich
1994   *Overview of Pleistocene and Holocene Inland Dunes in Georgia and the Carolinas—Morphology, Distribution, Age, and Paleoclimate.* Bulletin 2069. United States Geological Survey, Washington, D.C.

Marlon, Jennifer R., Patrick J. Bartlein, Megan K. Walsh, Sandy P. Harrison, Kendrick J. Brown, Mary E. Edwards, Philip E. Higuera, Mitchell J. Power, R. Scott Anderson, Christy Briles, Andrea Brunelle, Christopher Carcaillet, Mark Daniels, Feng S. Hu, Martin Lavoie, Colin Long, Thomas Minckley, Pierre J. H. Richard, Andrew C. Scott, David S. Shafer, Willy Tinner, Charles E. Umbanhowar Jr., and Cathy Whitlock
2009   Wildfire Response to Abrupt Climate Change in North America. *Proceedings of the National Academy of Sciences USA* 106:2519–2524.

Martin, Paul S.
1973   The Discovery of America. *Science* 179:969–974.
2006   *Twilight of the Mammoths: Ice Age Extinctions and the Rewilding of America.* University of California Press, Berkeley.

Mayewski, Paul A., Eelco E. Rohling, J. Curt Stager, Wibjörn Karlén, Kirk A. Maasch, L. David Meeker, Eric A. Meyerson, Francoise Gasse, Shirley van Kreveld, Karin Holmgren, Julia Lee-Thorp, Gunhild Rosqvist, Frank Rack, Michael Staubwasser, Ralph R. Schneider, and Eric J. Steig

2004 Holocene Climate Variability. *Quaternary Research* 62:243–255.

McAvoy, Joseph M., James C. Baker, James K. Feathers, Richard L. Hodges, Lucinda Mc-Weeney, and Thomas R. Whyte

2000 *Summary of Research at the Cactus Hill Archaeological Site, 44SX202, Sussex County, Virginia.* National Geographic Society, Washington, D.C. (grant report #6345–98).

McAvoy, Joseph M., and Lynn D. McAvoy

1997 *Archaeological Investigations of Site 44SX202, Cactus Hill, Sussex County, Virginia.* Research Report Series No. 8. Virginia Department of Historic Resources, Richmond.

2003 *The Williamson Clovis Site, 44DW1, Dinwiddie County, Virginia: An Analysis of Research Potential in Threatened Areas.* Research Report Series No. 13. Virginia Department of Historic Resources, Richmond.

2015 *Nottoway River Survey, Part-II, Cactus Hill and Other Excavated Sites.* Nottoway River Publications, Sandston, Virginia.

McBride, Randolph A., John B. Anderson, Ilya V. Buynevich, William Cleary, Michael S. Fenster, Duncan Fitzgerald, M. Scott Harris, Christopher Hein, Antonio H. F, Klein, Baozhu Liu, Jao T. de Menezes, Morten Pejrup, Stanley R. Riggs, Andrew Short, Gregory W. Stone, Davin J. Wallace, and Ping Wang

2013 Morphodynamics of Barrier Systems: A Synthesis. In *Treatise on Geomorphology*, edited by John F. Shroder and Douglas J. Sherman, pp. 166–244. Academic Press, San Diego.

McDonald, Jerry N.

1981 *North American Bison: Their Classification and Evolution.* University of California Press, Berkeley.

2000 *An Outline of the Pre-Clovis Archaeology of SV-2, Saltville, Virginia, with Special Attention to a Bone Tool Dated 14,510 yr B.P.* Jeffersonia Contributions from the Virginia Museum of Natural History 9, Martinsville.

McElreath, Richard

2004 Social Learning and the Maintenance of Cultural Variation: An Evolutionary Model and Data from East Africa. *American Anthropologist* 106(2):308–321.

McElreath, Richard, Robert Boyd, and Peter Richerson

2003 Shared Norms and the Evolution of Ethnic Markers. *Current Anthropology* 44(1):122–129.

McFadden, Bruce J., Barbara A. Purdy, Krista Church, and Thomas W. Stafford Jr.

2012 Humans Were Contemporaneous with Late Pleistocene Mammals in Florida: Evidence from Rare Earth Elemental Analyses. *Journal of Vertebrate Paleontology* 32(3):708–716.

McFadden, Maureen

1982 Petrology of Porcellanites in the Hawthorn Formation, Hamilton County,

Florida. Master's thesis, Department of Geology, University of South Florida, Tampa.

McFadden, Paulette S.

2009   Geoarchaeological Investigations of Dune Formation and Artifact Deposition at Barber Creek (31PT259). Unpublished master's thesis, Department of Anthropology, East Carolina University.

McGarigal, Kevin, Sam Cushman, and Susan Stafford

2000   *Multivariate Statistics for Wildlife and Ecology Research*. Springer, New York.

McManus, Jerry F., Roger Francois, Jeanne M. Gherardi, Lloyd D. Keigwin, and Susan Brown-Leger

2004   Collapse and Rapid Resumption of Atlantic Meridional Circulation Linked to Deglacial Climate Changes. *Nature* 428(6985):834–837.

Mead, Jim I., and David J. Meltzer

1984   North American Late Quaternary Extinctions and the Radiocarbon Record. In *Quaternary Extinctions: A Prehistoric Revolution*, edited by Paul S. Martin and Richard G. Klein, pp. 440–450. University of Arizona Press, Tucson.

Meeks, Scott C., and David G. Anderson

2012   Evaluating the Effect of the Younger Dryas on Human Population Histories in the Southeastern United States. In *Hunter-Gatherer Behavior: Human Response during the Younger Dryas*, edited by Metin I. Eren, pp. 111–138. Left Coast Press, Walnut Creek, California.

Meissner, Katrin J., and Peter U. Clark

2006   Impact of Floods Versus Routing Events on the Thermohaline Circulation. *Geophysical Research Letters* 33: L15704. Doi.org/10.1029/2006GL026705.

Meltzer, David J.

1991   On "Paradigms" and "Paradigm Bias" in Controversies over Human Antiquity in America. In *The First Americans: Search and Research*, edited by Tom Dillehay and David Meltzer, pp. 13–49. CRC Press, Boca Raton, Florida.

2009   *First Peoples in a New World: Colonizing Ice Age America*. University of California Press, Berkeley.

2015   *The Great Paleolithic War: How Science Forged an Understanding of America's Ice Age Past*. University of Chicago Press, Chicago.

Meltzer, David J., and Robert C. Dunnell (editors)

1992   *The Archaeology of William Henry Holmes*. Smithsonian Institution Press, Washington, D.C.

Meltzer, David J., Donald K. Grayson, Gerardo Ardila, Alex W. Barker, Dena F. Dincauze, C. Vance Haynes, Francisco Mena, Lautaro Nunez, and Dennis J. Stanford

1997   On the Pleistocene Antiquity of Monte Verde, Southern Chile. *American Antiquity* 62(4):659–663.

Meltzer, David J., and Jim I. Mead

1983   The Timing of Late Pleistocene Mammalian Extinctions in North America. *Quaternary Research* 19:130–135.

Mesoudi, Alex, and Michael O'Brien

2008   The Cultural Transmission of Great Basin Projectile-Point Technology I: An Experimental Simulation. *American Antiquity* 73(1):3–28.

Michie, James L.
1966   The Taylor Point. *Chesopiean* 4(5–6):123–124.
1968   The Edgefield Scraper. *Chesopiean* 6(2):30–31.
1973   The Edgefield Scraper: Its Inferred Antiquity and Use. *Chesopiean* 11(1):2–10.
1977   Early Man in South Carolina. Senior honors thesis, Department of Anthropology, University of South Carolina, Columbia.
1980   *An Archeological Survey of Congaree Swamp: Cultural Resources Inventory and Assessment of a Bottomland Environment in Central South Carolina.* Research Manuscript Series 163. South Carolina Institute of Archeology and Anthropology, University of South Carolina, Columbia.
1990   Bioturbation and Gravity as a Potential Site Formation Process: The Open Air Site 38GE261, Georgetown County, South Carolina. *South Carolina Antiquities* 22:27–46.
1996   The Taylor Site: An Early Occupation in Central South Carolina. In *The Paleoindian and Early Archaic Southeast*, edited by David G. Anderson and Kenneth E. Sassaman, pp. 238–269. University of Alabama Press, Tuscaloosa.

Milanich, Jerald T.
1994   *Archaeology of Precolumbian Florida.* University of Florida Press, Gainesville.
2004   History of the Ripley Bullen Projectile Point Typology. Electronic Document. http://www.flmnh.ufl.edu/flarch/bullen/Original_Milanich_Bullen_PP_Forward_2004.pdf. Accessed January 1, 2015.

Miller, D. Shane
2010   *Clovis Excavations at Topper 2005–2007: Examining Site Formation Processes at an Upland Paleoindian Site along the Middle Savannah River.* Southeastern Paleoamerican Survey, Occasional Paper No. 1. South Carolina Institute of Archaeology and Anthropology, University of South Carolina, Columbia.
2011   Rivers, Rocks and Eco-Tones: Modeling Clovis Landscape-Use in the Southeastern United States. Paper presented at the 76th Annual Meeting of the Society for American Archaeology, Sacramento.
2016   Modeling Clovis Landscape Use and Recovery Bias in the Southeastern United States Using the Paleoindian Database of the Americas (PIDBA). *American Antiquity* 81(4):697–716.

Miller, D. Shane, and Joseph A. M. Gingerich
2013a   Paleoindian Chronology and the Eastern Fluted Point Tradition. In *In the Eastern Fluted Point Tradition, Volume 1,* edited by Joseph A. M. Gingerich, pp. 9–37. University of Utah Press, Salt Lake.
2013b   Regional Variation in the Terminal Pleistocene and Early Holocene Radiocarbon Record of Eastern North America. *Quaternary Research* 79:175–188.

Miller, Gifford H., and Darrell S. Kaufman
1990   Rapid Fluctuations of the Laurentide Ice Sheet at the Mouth of Hudson Strait: New Evidence for Ocean/Ice-Sheet Interactions as Control on the Younger Dryas. *Paleoceanography* 5:907–919.

Miller, Stephen J. Yerka, J. Christopher Gillam, Eric N. Johanson, Derek T. Anderson, Albert C. Goodyear, and Ashley M. Smallwood
2010   PIDBA (Paleoindian Database of the Americas) Current Status and Findings. *Archaeology of Eastern North America* 38:63–90.

Mills, Barbara J., Matthew A. Peeples, W. Randall Haas Jr., Lewis Borck, Jeffery J. Clark, and John M. Roberts Jr.
2015   Multiscalar Perspectives on Social Networks in the Late Prehispanic Southwest. *American Antiquity* 80(1):3–24.

Minshall, Herbert L.
1976   *The Broken Stones.* Copley Books, San Diego.

Mitchell, Neil C., and John M. Huthnance
2008   Oceanographic Currents and the Convexity of the Uppermost Continental Slope. *Journal of Sedimentary Research* 78:29–44. doi:10.2110/jsr.2008.006.

Mitteroecker, Phillip, and Fred Bookstein
2011   Linear Discrimination, Ordination, and the Visualization of Selection Gradients in Modern Morphometrics. *Evolutionary Biology* 38:100–114.

Mittwede, Steven K.
1988   Spherulites in the Spring Branch Rhyolite, Western Saluda County, South Carolina. *South Carolina Geology* 32(1 & 2):21–25.

Mixon, Robert B.
1985   Stratigraphic and Geomorphic Framework of Uppermost Cenozoic Deposits in the Southern Delmarva Peninsula, Virginia and Maryland. US Geological Survey Professional Paper 1067G.

Montet-White, Anta
1968   *The Lithic Industries of the Illinois Valley in the Early and Middle Woodland Period.* Anthropological Papers Vol. 35. University of Michigan, Ann Arbor.

Moon, Steven Elliott
1999   Patterns of Paleoindian Land Use on the Eastern Gulf Coastal Plain of Southeastern Alabama: New Evidence from the Artifact Collector Community. Unpublished master's thesis, Iowa State University, Ames.

Moore, Andrew M. T., and Gordon C. Hillman
1992   The Pleistocene to Holocene Transition and Human Economy in Southwest Asia: The Impact of the Younger Dryas. *American Antiquity* 57:482–494.

Moore, Christopher R.
2009a   Geoarchaeology and Geochronology at the Owens Ridge Site (31ED369). *North Carolina Archaeological Society Newsletter* 18(4):1–5.

2009b   Late Quaternary Geoarchaeology and Geochronology of Stratified Eolian Deposits, Tar River, North Carolina. Unpublished Ph.D. dissertation, Coastal Resources Management, East Carolina University, Greenville, North Carolina.

Moore, Christopher R., and Mark J. Brooks
2011   Evidence for Widespread Eolian Activity in the Coastal Plain Uplands of North and South Carolina Revealed by High-Resolution LiDAR Data. Poster presented at the 60th Annual Meeting of the Southeastern Section, Geological Society of America, Wilmington, North Carolina. Available online at

https://www.academia.edu/8156689/Evidence_for_Widespread_Eolian_Activity_in_the_Coastal_Plain_Uplands_of_North_and_South_Carolina_Revealed_by_High-Resolution_LiDAR_Data

2012a   An in situ Clovis Assemblage from a Carolina Bay Sand Rim, Aiken County, South Carolina. *South Carolina Antiquities* 44:110–112.

2012b   Geoarchaeological and Paleoenviromental Research. In *Annual Review of Cultural Resource Investigations by the Savannah River Archaeological Research Program: Fiscal Year 2012*, pp. 72–83. Savannah River Archaeological Research Program, South Carolina Institute of Archaeology and Anthropology, University of South Carolina, Columbia.

Moore, Christopher R., Mark J. Brooks, Andrew H. Ivester, Terry Ferguson, and James K. Feathers

2012   Radiocarbon and Luminescence Dating at Flamingo Bay (38AK469): Implications for Site Formation Processes and Artifact Burial at a Carolina Bay. *Legacy* 16 (1):16-21.

Moore, Christopher R., Mark J. Brooks, Larry R. Kimball, Margaret E. Newman, and Brian P. Kooyman

2016   Early Hunter-Gatherer Tool Use and Animal Exploitation in the Southeast: Protein and Microwear Evidence from the Central Savannah River Valley. *American Antiquity* 81(1):132–147.

Moore, Christopher R., and I. Randolph Daniel Jr.

2010   Site Formation Processes and Climatic Disequilibrium: Geoarchaeological Evidence for Rapid and Episodic Climate Change Events in the North Carolina Coastal Plain. Poster presented at the 66th Annual Meeting of the Southeastern Archaeological Conference, Mobile, Alabama.

2011   Geoarchaeological Investigations of Stratified Sand Ridges along the Tar River, North Carolina. In *The Archaeology of North Carolina: Three Archaeological Symposia*, edited by Charles R. Ewen, Thomas R. Whyte, and R. P. Stephen Davis Jr., pp. 1–42. Publication 30. North Carolina Archaeological Council, Raleigh.

Moore, Christopher R., and Jeffrey D. Irwin

2006   Quarries and Artifacts. In *Stone Quarries and Sourcing in the Carolina Slate Belt*, Research Report No. 25, edited by Vincas P. Steponaitis, Theresa E. McReynolds, Jeffrey D. Irwin, and Christopher R. Moore, pp. 16–41. Research Laboratories of Archaeology, University of North Carolina, Chapel Hill.

Moore, Christopher R., Allen West, Malcolm A. LeCompte, Mark J. Brooks, I. Randolph Daniel Jr., Albert C. Goodyear, Terry A. Ferguson, Andrew H. Ivester, James K. Feathers, James P. Kennett, Kenneth B. Tankersley, Victor A. Adedeji, and Ted E. Bunch

2017   Widespread Platinum Anomaly Documented at the Younger Dryas Onset in North American Sedimentary Sequences. *Nature Scientific Reports* 7:44031. Doi.org/10.1038/srep44031(2017).

Morphy, Howard

1995   Landscape and the Reproduction of the Ancestral Past. In *The Anthropol-*

ogy of Landscape: Perspectives on Place and Space, edited by Eric Hirsch and Michael O'Hanlon, pp. 184–209. Clarendon Press, Oxford.

Morrow, Juliet E., Stuart J. Fiedel, Donald L. Johnson, Marcel Kornfeld, Moye Rutledge, and W. Raymond Wood

2015   Pre-Clovis in Texas? A Critical Assessment of the Buttermilk Creek Complex. *Journal of Archaeological Science* 39(12):3677–3682.

Morse, Dan F.

1997   *Sloan: A Paleoindian Dalton Cemetery in Arkansas*. Smithsonian Institution, Washington, D.C.

Morse, Dan F., David G. Anderson, and Albert C. Goodyear III

1996   The Pleistocene–Holocene Transition in the Eastern United States. In *Humans at the End of the Ice Age: The Archaeology of the Pleistocene–Holocene Transition*, edited by Lawrence G. Straus, Berit Valentin Eriksen, Jon M. Erlandson, and David R. Yesner. Plenum Press, New York.

Morse, Dan F., and Albert C. Goodyear III

1973   The Significance of the Dalton Adze in Northeast Arkansas. *Plains Anthropologist* 18: 315–322.

Murton, Julian B., Mark D. Bateman, Scott R. Dallimore, James T. Teller, and Zhirong Yang

2010   Identification of Younger Dryas Outburst Flood Path from Lake Agassiz to the Arctic Ocean. *Nature* 464:740–743.

Muto, Guy

1976   *The Cascade Technique: An Examination of a Levallois-Like Reduction System in Early Snake River Prehistory*. Ph.D. dissertation, Washington State University, Pullman.

Nabelek, Ladislav, Gunther Kletetschka, Jaroslav Kadlec, Allen West, Ted E. Bunch, Helena Svitavska-Svobodova, and James Wittke

2013   Magnetism of Microspheres from the Proposed Younger Dryas Impact Event 12,900 Years Ago. Poster presented at 44th Lunar and Planetary Science Conference, The Woodlands, Texas. LPI Contribution No. 1719, p.1707.

Napier, William M.

2010   Palaeolithic Extinctions and the Taurid Complex. *Monthly Notices of the Royal Astronomical Society* 405:1901–1906.

2015   Giant Comets and Mass Extinctions of Life. *Monthly Notices of the Royal Astronomical Society* 448:27–36.

Napier, William M., David Asher, Mark Bailey, and Duncan Steel

2015   Centaurs as a Hazard to Civilization. *Astronomy and Geophysics* 56:6–30.

Napier, William M., Ted E. Bunch, James P. Kennett, James H. Wittke, Kenneth B. Tankersley, Gunther Kleteschka, George A. Howard, and Allen West

2013   Reply to Boslough et al.: They Ignore Decades of Comet Research. *Proceedings of the National Academy of Sciences USA* 110(45):E4171. Doi.org/10.1073/pnas.1315467110.

Neill, Wilfred T.

1971   A Florida Paleoindian Implement of Ground Stone. *Florida Anthropologist* 24:61–70.

Nelson, Nels C.
1918   Chronology in Florida. *Anthropological Papers of the American Museum of Natural History* 22(2):75–103.

Neugebauer, Ina, Achim Brauer, Nadine Dräger, Peter Dulski, Sabine Wulf, Birgit Plessen, Jens Mingram, Ulrike Herzschuh, and Arthur Brande
2012   A Younger Dryas Varve Chronology from the Rehwiese Palaeolake Record in NE-Germany. *Quaternary Science Reviews* 36:91–102.

Neuman, W. S., D. H. Thurber, H. S. Zeiss, A. Rokach, and L. Musich
1969   Late Quaternary Geology of the Hudson River Estuary: A Preliminary Report. *Transactions of the New York Academy of Sciences* 31: 548–570.

Nichols, Maynard M., Gerald H. Johnson, and Pamela C. Peebles
1991   Modern Sediments and Facies Model for a Microtidal Coastal Plain Estuary, the James Estuary, Virginia. *Journal of Sedimentary Research* 61:883–899. doi:10.1306/D42677F8-2B26-11D7-8648000102C1865D.

Nikitina, Daria L., James E. Pizzuto, Reed A. Schwimmer, and Kelvin W. Ramsey
2000   An Updated Holocene Sea-Level Curve for the Delaware Coast. *Marine Geology* 171:7–20. doi:10.1016/S0025-3227(00)00104-3.

Not, Christelle, and Claude Hillaire-Marcel
2012   Enhanced Sea-Ice Export from the Arctic during the Younger Dryas. *Nature Communications* 3:647.

Novick, A. Lee
1978   Prehistoric Lithic Material Sources and Types in South Carolina: A Preliminary Statement. *South Carolina Antiquities* 10(1):422–437.

Nunn, Cece.
2010   Discoveries Might Reveal Origins of Southeastern N.C.'s First Inhabitants. *Star News Online.* Available online at http://www.starnewsonline.com/news/20100509/discoveries-might-reveal-origins-of-southeastern-ncs-first-inhabitants.

O'Brien, Michael J., Matthew T. Boulanger, Briggs Buchanan, Mark Collard, R. Lee Lyman, and John Darwent
2014   Innovation and Cultural Transmission in the American Paleolithic: Phylogenetic Analysis of Eastern Paleoindian Projectile-Point Classes. *Journal of Anthropological Archaeology* 34:100–119.

O'Brien, Suzanne R., Paul A. Mayewski, L. David Meeker, Debra A. Meese, Mark S. Twickler, and Sallie I. Whitlow
2003   Complexity of Holocene Climate as Reconstructed from a Greenland Ice Core. *Science* 5244:1962–1964.

Odell, George H.
1996   Economizing Behavior and the Concept of "Curation." In *Stone Tools: Theoretical Insights into Human Prehistory*, edited by George H. Odell, pp. 51–80. Plenum Press, New York.

Ojeda, German, Paul T. Gayes, Robert F. Van Dolah, and William C. Schwab
2004   Spatially Quantitative Seafloor Habitat Mapping: Example from the Northern South Carolina Inner Continental Shelf. *Estuary and Coastal Shelf Science* 59:399–416. doi:10.1016/j.ecss.2003.09.012.

O'Steen, Lisa D.
1996   Paleoindian and Early Archaic Settlement along the Oconee Drainage. In *The Paleoindian and Early Archaic Southeast*, edited by David G. Anderson and Kenneth E. Sassaman, pp. 92–106. University of Alabama Press, Tuscaloosa.

Otvos, Ervin G.
2014   The Last Interglacial Stage: Definitions and Marine Highstand, North America and Eurasia. *Quaternary International* 383:158–173. doi:10.1016/j.quaint.2014.05.010.

Otvos, Ervin G., and David M. Price
2001   Late Quaternary Inland Dunes of Southern Louisiana and Arid Climate Phases in the Gulf Coast Region. *Quaternary Research* 55:150–158.

Overpeck, Jonathan, and Robert Webb
2000   Nonglacial Rapid Climate Change Events: Past and Future. *Proceedings of the National Academy of Sciences USA* 97:1335–1338.

Paquay, François S., Steven Goderis, Greg Ravizza, Frank Vanhaeck, Matthew Boyd, Todd A. Surovell, Vance T. Holliday, C. Vance Haynes Jr., and Philippe Claeys
2009   Absence of Geochemical Evidence for an Impact Event at the Bølling-Allerød/Younger Dryas Transition. *Proceedings of the National Academy of Sciences USA* 106(51):21505–21510.

Parish, Ryan M.
2011   The Application of Visible/Near-Infrared Reflectance (VNIR) Spectroscopy to Chert: A Case Study from the Dover Quarry Sites, Tennessee. *Geoarchaeology* 26:420–439.

Parish, Ryan, and Ellis Durham
2015   The Problems with Visual Identification of Dover and Fort Payne Chert. *Southeastern Archaeology* 34:71–83.

Parish, Ryan Michael, George Hammond Swihart, and Ying Sing Li
2012   Evaluating Fourier Transform Infrared Spectroscopy as a Non-Destructive Chert Sourcing Technique. *Geoarchaeology* 28:289–307.

Parish, Ryan, and Michael Jeu
2016   A Chert Type Database for the Southeast. Paper presented at the 73rd Annual Meeting of the Southeastern Archaeological Conference, Athens.

Parkinson, William A.
2006   Tribal Boundaries, Stylistic Variability, and Social Boundary Maintenance during the Transition to the Copper Age on the Great Hungarian Plain. *Journal of Anthropological Archaeology* 25:33<n<58.

Parry, William J., and Robert L. Kelly
1987   Expedient Core Technology and Sedentism. In *The Organization of Core Technology*, edited by Jay K. Johnson and Carol A. Morrow, pp. 285–304. Westview Press, Boulder.

Parsons, Brian, Donald J. P. Swift, and Kenneth Williams
2003   Quaternary Facies Assemblages and Their Bounding Surfaces, Chesapeake Bay Mouth: An Approach to Mesoscale Stratigraphic Analysis. *Journal of Sedimentary Research* 73:672–690. doi:10.1306/012103730672.

Paskevich, Valerie F. and N. K. Soderberg
1997   Navigation and Geophysical Data Collected Onboard the R/V FAY from 1975–1976: U.S. Geological Survey Open-File Report 97–512, CD-ROM. U.S.G.S. Open File Rep. 97–512 CD-ROM.

Patterson, William A. III, and Kenneth E. Sassaman
1988   Indian Fires in the Prehistory of New England. In *Holocene Human Ecology of Northeastern North American.* Edited by George P. Nicholas, pp. 107–135. Plenum Press, New York.

Pauketat, Timothy R.
2013   Bundles of/in/as Time. In *Big Histories, Human Lives: Tackling Problems of Scale in Archaeology,* edited by John Robb and Timothy R. Pauketat, pp. 35–56. School for Advanced Research Press, Santa Fe.

Pearce, Eiluned
2014   Modelling Mechanisms of Social Network Maintenance in Hunter-Gatherers. *Journal of Archaeological Science* 50:403–413.

Pearson, Charles, Richard A. Weinstein, Sherwood M. Gagliano, and David B. Kelly
2014   Prehistoric Site Discovery on the Outer Continental Shelf, Gulf of Mexico, United States of America. In *Prehistoric Archaeology on the Continental Shelf: A Global Review,* edited by Amanda M. Evans, Joseph C. Flatman, and Nicholas C. Flemming, pp. 53–27. Springer, New York.

Peltier, William R.
2002   On Eustatic Sea Level History: Last Glacial Maximum to Holocene. *Quaternary Science Reviews* 21:377–396. doi:10.1016/S0277-3791(01)00084-1.
2004   Global Glacial Isostasy and the Surface of the Ice-Age Earth: The Ice-5g (Vm2) Model and Grace. *Annual Review of Earth and Planetary Sciences* 32:111–149. doi:10.1146/annurev.earth.32.082503.144359
2015   Home Page: William R. Peltier, Paleo-topography dataset for ICE-6G(VM5a) model, Electronic document, http://www.atmosp.physics.utoronto.ca/~peltier/data.php. Accessed 7.28.15.

Perino, Gregory H.
1960   The Micro-Drill Industry at Cahokia. *Central States Archaeological Journal* 7:117–120.

Peros, Matthew C., Konrad Gajewski, and André E. Viau
2008   Continental-Scale Tree Population Response to Rapid Climate Change, Competition, and Disturbance. *Global Ecology and Biogeography* 17:658–669.

Perry, Charles A. and Kenneth J. Hsu
2000   Geophysical, Archeological, and Historical Evidence Support a Solar-Output Model for Climate Change. *Proceedings of the National Academy of Sciences USA* 97(23):12433–12438.

Petaev, Michail I., Shichun Huang, Stein B. Jacobsen, and Alan Zindler
2013   Large Pt Anomaly in the GISP2 Ice Core Points to a Cataclysm at the Onset of Younger Dryas. *Proceedings of the National Academy of Sciences USA* 110(32):12917–12920.

Petit, Jean-Robert, Jean Jouzel, Dominique Raynaud, Nartiss I. Barkov, Jean-Marc Barnola, Isabel Basile, Michael Bender, Jerome Chappellaz, Mary Davis, Gilles Delaygue, Marc Delmotte, Vladimir M. Kotlyakov, Michel Legrand, Vladimir Y. Lipenkov, Claude Lorius, L. Pépin, Catherine Ritz, Eric Saltzman, and Michel Stievenard
1999   Climate and Atmospheric History of the Past 420,000 Years from the Vostok Ice Core, Antarctica. *Nature* 399:429–436.
Petraglia, Michael D., Abdullah Alsharekh, Paul Breeze, Chris Clarkson, Rémy Crassard, Nick A. Drake, Huw S. Groucutt, Richard Jennings, Adrian G. Parker, Ash Parton, Richard G. Roberts, Ceri Shipton, Carney Matheson, Abdulaziz al-Omari, and Margaret-Ashley Veall
2012   Hominin Dispersal into the Nefud Desert and Middle Palaeolithic Settlement along the Jubbah Palaeolake, Northern Arabia. *PLoS ONE* 7(11):e49840
Pettigrew, Devin B., John C. Whittaker, Justin Garnett, and Patrick Hashman
2015   How Atlatl Darts Behave: Beveled Points and the Relevance of Controlled Experiments. *American Antiquity* 80(3):590–601.
Picard, L.
1943   Structure and Evolution of Palestine. *Bulletin of the Geology Department of Hebrew University, Jerusalem*, No. 4 (204): 1–134.
Pierazzo, Elisabetta, and Natalia Artemieva
2012   Local and Global Environmental Effects of Impacts on Earth. *Elements* 8:55–60.
Pierazzo, Elisabetta, Rolando R. Garcia, Douglas E. Kinnison, Daniel R. Marsh, Julia Lee-Taylor, and Paul Jozef Crutzen
2010   Ozone Perturbation from Medium-Size Asteroid Impacts in the Ocean. *Earth and Planetary Science Letters* 299:263–272.
Pigati, Jeffrey S., Claudio Latorre, Jason A. Rech, Julio L. Betancourt, Katherine E. Martinez, and James R. Budahn
2012   Accumulation of Impact Markers in Desert Wetlands and Implications for the Younger Dryas Impact Hypothesis. *Proceedings of the National Academy of Sciences USA* 109(19):7208–7212.
Pinter, Nicholas, and Scott E. Ishman
2008   Impacts, Mega-Tsunami, and Other Extraordinary Claims. *GSA Today* 18(1):37–38.
Polyak, Leonid, William B. Curry, Dennis A. Darby, James Bischoff, and Thomas M. Cronin
2004   Contrasting Glacial/Interglacial Regimes in the Western Arctic Ocean as Exemplified by a Sedimentary Record form the Mendeleev Ridge. *Palaeogeography, Palaeoclimatology, Palaeoecology* 203:73–93.
Poore, Richard Z., Lisa Osterman, William B. Curry, and Rebecca L. Phillips
1999   Late Pleistocene and Holocene Meltwater Events in the Western Arctic Ocean. *Geology* 27(8):759–762.
Potter, Emma-Kate, and Kurt Lambeck
2004   Reconciliation of Sea-Level Observations in the Western North Atlantic dur-

ing the Last Glacial Cycle. *Earth* and *Planetary Science Letters* 217:171–181. doi:10.1016/S0012–821X(03)00587–9.

Potter, James M.

2004   The Creation of Person, the Creation of Place: Hunting Landscapes in the American Southwest. *American Antiquity* 69(2):322–338.

Prouty, William F.

1952   Carolina Bays and Their Origin. *Geological Society of America Bulletin* 63:167–224.

Purdy, Barbara A.

1981   *Florida's Prehistoric Stone Technology: A Study of the Flint-Working Techniques of Early Florida Stone Implement Makers.* University Press of Florida, Gainesville.

2013   The Container Corporation of America Site (8MR154), Marion County, Florida: A Narrative Account and Visual Evidence of Humans in America before Clovis. Paper presented at the Paleoamerican Odyssey Conference, Santa Fe.

Purdy, Barbara A. and David E. Clark

1987   Weathering of Inorganic Materials: Dating and Other Applications. *Advances in Archaeological Method and Theory* 11:211–253.

Putney, Thomas R., Michael P. Katuna, and M. Scott Harris

2004   Subsurface Stratigraphy and Geomorphology of the Grand Strand, Georgetown and Horry Counties, South Carolina. *Southeastern Geology* 42:217–236.

Raemsch, Bruce E.

1977a   Some Paleolithic Tools from Northeast North America. *Current Anthropology* 18:97–99.

1977b   Some Early Man Cultures of the Catskill Region. In *Archaeology and Geochronology of the Susquehanna and Schoharie Regions*, edited by John R. Cole and Laurie R. Godfrey, pp. 1–13. Proceedings of the Yager Conference at Hartwick College, Oneonta, New York.

Raghavan, M., Matthias Steinrücken, Kelley Harris, Stephan Schiffels, Simon Rasmussen, Michael DeGiorgio, Anders Albrechtsen, Cristina Valdiosera, María C. Ávila-Arcos, Anna-Sapfo Malaspinas, Anders Eriksson, Ida Moltke, Mait Metspalu, Julian R. Homburger, Jeff Wall, Omar E. Cornejo, J. Víctor Moreno-Mayar, Thorfinn S. Korneliussen, Tracey Pierre, Morten Rasmussen, Paula F. Campos, Peter de Barros Damgaard, Morten E. Allentoft, John Lindo, Ene Metspalu, Ricardo Rodríguez-Varela, Josefina Mansilla, Celeste Henrickson, Andaine Seguin-Orlando, Helena Malmström, Thomas Stafford Jr., Suyash S. Shringarpure, Andrés Moreno-Estrada, Monika Karmin, Kristiina Tambets, Anders Bergström, Yali Xue, Vera Warmuth, Andrew D. Friend, Joy Singarayer, Paul Valdes, Francois Balloux, Ilán Leboreiro, Jose Luis Vera, Hector Rangel-Villalobos, Davide Pettener, Donata Luiselli, Loren G. Davis, Evelyne Heyer, Christoph P. E. Zollikofer, Marcia S. Ponce de León, Colin I. Smith, Vaughan Grimes, Kelly-Anne Pike, Michael Deal, Benjamin T. Fuller, Bernardo Arriaza, Vivien Standen, Maria F. Luz, Francois Ricaut, Niede Guidon, Ludmila Osipova, Mikhail I. Voevoda, Olga L. Posukh, Oleg

Balanovsky, Maria Lavryashina, Yuri Bogunov, Elza Khusnutdinova, Marina Gubina, Elena Balanovska, Sardana Fedorova, Sergey Litvinov, Boris Malyarchuk, Miroslava Derenko, M. J. Mosher, David Archer, Jerome Cybulski, Barbara Petzelt, Joycelynn Mitchell, Rosita Worl, Paul J. Norman, Peter Parham, Brian M. Kemp, Toomas Kivisild, Chris Tyler-Smith, Manjinder S. Sandhu, Michael Crawford, Richard Villems, David Glenn Smith, Michael R. Waters, Ted Goebel, John R. Johnson, Ripan S. Malhi, Mattias Jakobsson, David J. Meltzer, Andrea Manica, Richard Durbin, Carlos D. Bustamante, Yun S. Song, Rasmus Nielsen, Eske Willerslev

2015   Genomic Evidence for the Pleistocene and Recent Population History of Native Americans. *Science* 349(6250):aab3884. DOI: 10.1126/science.aab3884.

Raines, Gary L., Graeme F. Bonham-Carter, and Laura Kemp

2000   Predictive Probabilistic Modeling Using ArcView GIS. *ArcUser* April–June:45–48.

Raisz, Erwin

1934   Rounded Lakes and Lagoons of the Coastal Plains of Massachusetts. *Journal of Geology* 2:839–848.

Ramsay, Peter, and J. Andrew G. Cooper

2002   Late Quaternary Sea-Level Change in South Africa. *Quaternary Research* 57:82–90. doi:10.1006/qres.2001.2290.

Rashid, Harunur, David J. W. Piper, and Benjamin P. Flower

2011   The Role of Hudson Strait Outlet in Younger Dryas Sedimentation in the Labrador Sea. *Geophysical Monograph Series* 193:93–110.

Ray, Jack H.

1998   Chert Resource Availability and Utilization. In *The 1997 Excavations at the Big Eddy Site (23CE426) in Southwest Missouri*, edited by Neal H. Lopinot, Jack H. Ray, and Michael D. Conner, pp. 221–265. Special Publication No. 2. Center for Archaeological Research, Southwest Missouri State University, Springfield.

Reimer, Paula J., Edouard Bard, Alex Bayliss, J. Warren Beck, Paul G. Blackwell, Christopher Bronk Ramsey, Caitlin E. Buck, Hai Cheng, R. Lawrence Edwards, Michael Friedrich, Pieter M. Grootes, Thomas P. Guilderson, Haflidi Haflidason, Irka Hajdas, Christine Hatté, Timothy J. Heaton, Dirk L. Hoffmann, Alan G. Hogg, Konrad A. Hughen, K. Felix Kaiser, Bernd Kromer, Sturt W. Manning, Mu Niu, Ron W. Reimer, David A. Richards, E. Marian Scott, John R. Southon, Richard A. Staff, Christian S. M. Turney, Johannes van der Plicht

2013   IntCal13 and Marine13 Radiocarbon Age Calibration Curves 0–50,000 Years Cal BP. *Radiocarbon* 55:1869–1887.

Renaud, Etienne B.

1936   When Did Early Man First Reach America's Shores? *Science News-Letter* 29:39–46

Riggs, Stanley R., William G. Ambrose, Jeffrey W. Cook, Scott W. Snyder, and Stephen W. Snyder

1998   Sediment Production on Sediment-Starved Continental Margins; The Interrelationship between Hardbottoms, Sedimentological and Benthic Community Processes, and Storm Dynamics. *Journal of Sedimentary Research* 68:155–168.

Riggs, Stanley R., Dorthea Ames, D. Randall Brant, and Eric D. Sager
2000   The Waccamaw Drainage System: Geology and Dynamics of a Coastal Wetland, Southeastern North Carolina. Division of Water Resources, North Carolina Department of Environment and Natural Resources, Raleigh.

Rink, W. Jack, James S. Dunbar, and Kevin E. Burdette
2012   The Wakulla Springs Lodge Site (8Wa329): 2008 Excavations and New OSL Dating Evidence. *Florida Anthropologist* 65:5–24.

Rink, W. Jack, James S. Dunbar, Glen H. Doran, Charles Frederick, and Brittney Gregory
2012   Geoarchaeological Investigations and OSL Dating Evidence in an Archaic and Paleoindian Context at the Helen Blazes Site (8Br27), Brevard County, Florida. *Florida Anthropologist* 65:87–109.

Rink, W. Jack, James S. Dunbar, Walter K. Tschinkel, Christina Kwapich, Andrea Repp, William Stanton, and David K. Thulman
2013   Subterranean Transport and Deposition of Quartz by Ants in Sandy Sites Relevant to Age Overestimation in Optical Luminescence Dating. *Journal of Archaeological Science* 40:2217–2226.

Ritchie, William A.
1971   *New York Projectile Points: A Typology and Nomenclature.* Rev. ed. University of the State of New York, Albany.
1977   Summary. In *Archaeology and Geochronology of the Susquehanna and Schoharie Regions*, edited by John R. Cole and Laurie R. Godfrey, pp. 115–119. Proceedings of the Yager Conference at Hartwick College, Oneonta, New York.

Rivers, Ray, Carl Knappett, and Tim Evans
2013   What Makes a Site Important? Centrality, Gateways, and Gravity. In *Network Analysis in Archaeology: New Approaches to Regional Interaction,* edited by Carl Knappett, pp. 125–150. Oxford University Press, Oxford.

Robinson, Guy S., Lida P. Burney, and David A. Burney
2005   Landscape Paleoecology and Megafaunal Extinction in Southeastern New York State. *Ecological Monographs* 75:295–315.

Rogers, Jeffrey C., and Robert V. Rohli
1991   Florida Citrus Freezes and Polar Anticyclones in the Great Plains. *Journal of Climate* 4:1103–1113.

Rohlf, F. James
2003   *tpsSuper, Superimposition and Image Averaging.* Department of Ecology and Evolution, State University of New York at Stony Brook.
2013   *tpsDig2, Digitize Landmarks and Outlines.* Department of Ecology and Evolution, State University of New York at Stony Brook.

Rohli, Robert V., and Jeffrey C. Rogers
1993   Atmospheric Teleconnections and Citrus Freezes in the Southern United States. *Physical Geography* 14(1):1–15.

Roll, Tom E., Michael P. Neeley, Robert J. Speakman, and Michael D. Glascock
2005   Characterization of Montana Cherts by LA-ICP-MS. In *Laser Ablation ICP-*

MS in Archaeological Research, edited by Robert J. Speakman and Hector Neff, pp. 59–74. University of New Mexico Press, Albuquerque.

Root, Matthew J., Jerry D. William, Marvin Kay, and Lisa K. Shifrin

1999   Folsom Ultrathin Biface and Radial Break Tools in the Knife River Flint Quarry Area. In *Folsom Lithic Technology, Explorations in Structure and Variation*, edited by Daniel S. Amick, pp. 144–168. Archaeological Series 12. International Monographs in Prehistory, Ann Arbor.

Roy, Kevin, and William R. Peltier

2015   Glacial Isostatic Adjustment, Relative Sea Level History and Mantle Viscosity: Reconciling Relative Sea Level Model Predictions for the U.S. East Coast with Geological Constraints. *Geophysical Journal International* 201(2):1156–1181. doi:10.1093/gji/ggv066.

Russell, Dale A., Fredrick J. Rich, Vincent Schneider, and Jean Lynch-Stieglitz

2009   A Warm Thermal Enclave in the Late Pleistocene of the South-Eastern United States. *Biological Reviews* 84:173–202.

Sain, Douglas A.

2011   *Clovis Blade Technology at the Topper Site (38AL23): Assessing Lithic Attribute Variation and Regional Patterns of Technological Organization.* Southeastern Paleoamerican Survey, Occasional Papers 2. South Carolina Institute of Archaeology and Anthropology, University of South Carolina, Columbia.

2015   *Pre Clovis at Topper (38AL23): Evaluating the Role of Human versus Natural Agency in the Formation of Lithic Deposits from a Pleistocene Terrace in the American Southeast.* Ph.D. dissertation, Department of Anthropology, University of Tennessee, Knoxville.

2016   A Model for Paleoamerican Coastal Zone Preference for the Atlantic Slope of Eastern North America since the Last Glacial Maximum. *Journal of Island and Coastal Archaeology* DOI: 10.1080/15564894.2016.1220436.

2018   *Pre-Clovis at Topper (38AL23): Evaluating the Role of Human versus Natural Agency in the Formation of Lithic Deposits from a Pleistocene Terrace in the American Southeast.* Southeastern Paleoamerican Survey, Occasional Papers 6. South Carolina Institute of Archaeology and Anthropology, University of South Carolina, Columbia, in press.

Sain, Douglas A., and Albert C. Goodyear III

2012   A Comparison of Clovis Blades at the Topper and Big Pine Tree Sites, Allendale County, South Carolina. In *Contemporary Lithic Analysis in the Southeast, Problems, Solutions, and Interpretations*, edited by Philip J. Carr, Andrew P. Bradbury, and Sarah E. Price, pp. 42–54. University of Alabama Press, Tuscaloosa.

Sandgathe, Dennis M.

2005   An Analysis of the Levallois Reduction Strategy Using a Design Theory Framework. Unpublished Ph.D. dissertation. Department of Archaeology, Simon Fraser University, Burnaby, British Columbia.

Sanger, Matthew C.

2010   Leaving the Rings: Shell Ring Abandonment and the End of the Late Archaic. In *Trend, Tradition, and Turmoil: What Happened to the Southeastern*

Archaic? edited by David Hurst Thomas and Matthew C. Sanger, pp. 201–215. Proceedings of the Third Caldwell Conference, St. Catherines Island, Georgia, May 9–11, 2008. Anthropological Papers of the American Museum of Natural History, New York.

Sassaman, Kenneth E.

1996   Early Archaic Settlement in the South Carolina Coastal Plain. In *The Paleoindian and Early Archaic Southeast*, edited by David G. Anderson and Kenneth E. Sassaman, pp. 58–83. University of Alabama Press, Tuscaloosa.

2010   *The Eastern Archaic Historicized*. AltaMira, Lanham.

2011   History and Alterity in the Eastern Archaic. In *Hunter-Gatherer Archaeology as Historical Process*, edited by Kenneth E. Sassaman and Donald H. Holly Jr., pp. 187–208. University of Arizona Press, Tucson.

2012   Futurologists Look Back. *Archaeologies* 8:250–268.

2013   Drowning Out the Past: How Humans Historicize Water as Water Historicizes Them. In *Big Histories, Human Lives Tackling Problems of Scale in Archaeology*, edited by John Robb and Timothy R. Pauketat, pp. 171–191. School for Advanced Research Press, Sante Fe.

2016   A Constellation of Practice in the Experience of Sea-Level Rise. In *Knowledge in Motion: Constellations of Learning across Time and Space*, edited by Andrew P. Roddick and Ann B. Stahl, pp. 271–298. University of Arizona Press, Tucson.

Sassaman, Kenneth E., Mark J. Brooks, Glen T. Hanson, and David G. Anderson

1990   *Native American Prehistory of the Middle Savannah River Valley: A Synthesis of Archaeological Investigations on the Savannah River Site, Aiken and Barnwell Counties, South Carolina*. Savannah River Archaeological Research Papers 1, South Carolina Institute of Archaeology and Anthropology, University of South Carolina, Columbia.

Sassaman, Kenneth E., I. Randolph Daniel Jr., and Christopher R. Moore

2002   *G. S. Lewis-East: Early and Late Archaic Occupations along the Savannah River, Aiken County, South Carolina*. Savannah River Archaeological Research Papers 12. Savannah River Archaeological Research Program, South Carolina Institute of Archaeology and Anthropology, University of South Carolina, Columbia.

Sassaman, Kenneth E., Glen T. Hanson, and Tommy Charles

1988   Raw Material Procurement and the Reduction of Hunter-Gatherer Range in the Savannah River Valley. *Southeastern Archaeology* 7:79–94.

Sassaman, Kenneth E., Paulette S. McFadden, Micah P. Monés, Andrea Palmiotto, and Asa R. Randall

2014   Northern Gulf Coastal Archaeology of the Here and Now. In *New Histories of Precolumbian Florida*, edited by Neill J. Wallis and Asa R. Randall, pp. 143–162. University Press of Florida, Gainesville.

Sassaman, Kenneth E., Paul G. Nystrom Jr., and Sonny Zorn

2005   Hills on the Plain: Archaeology and Geology of the Zorn Sites, Bamberg County, South Carolina. *South Carolina Antiquity* 31(1–2):1–42.

Sassaman, Kenneth E., Neill J. Wallis, Paulette S. McFadden, Ginessa J. Mahar, Jessica
A. Jenkins, Mark C. Donop, Micah P. Monés, Andrea Palmiotto, Anthony
Boucher, Joshua M. Goodwin, and Cristina I. Oliveira

2016   Keeping Pace with Rising Sea: The First 6 Years of the Lower Suwannee Archaeological Survey, Gulf Coastal Florida. *Journal of Island and Coastal Archaeology* 12(2):1730199. doi.org/10.1080/15564894.2016.11.63758.

Schmidt, Matthew W., and Jean Lynch-Stieglitz

2011   Florida Straits Deglacial Temperature and Salinity Change: Implications for
Tropical Hydrologic Cycle Variability during the Younger Dryas. *Paleoceanography* 26(4):PA4205. doi:10.1029/2011PA002157.

Schmidt, Walter

1997   Geomorphology and Physiography of Florida. In *The Geology of Florida*, edited by Anthony F. Randazzo and Douglas S. Jones, pp. 1–12. University Press
of Florida, Gainesville

Schmunk, Robert B.

2015   NASA GISS: Panoply 4 netCDF, HDF and GRIB Data Viewer Electronic
Document NASA GISS. URL http://www.giss.nasa.gov/tools/panoply/. Accessed July 1, 2015.

Science Applications, Inc.

1981   *A Cultural Resources Survey of the Continental Shelf from Cape Hatteras to
Key West. Volume 1: Introduction and Physical Environment.* Report sub-
mitted by Science Applications, Inc. to the Bureau of Land Management,
McLean

Schobernd, Christina M., and George R. Sedberry

2009   Shelf-Edge and Upper-Slope Reef Fish Assemblages in the South Atlantic
Bight: Habitat Characteristics, Spatial Variation, and Reproductive Behavior.
Bulletin of Marine Science 84:67–92.

Schroeder, Kari B., Mattias Jakobsson, Michael H. Crawford, Theodore G. Schurr, Simina
M. Boca, Donald F. Conrad, Raul Y. Tito, Ludmilla P. Osipova, Larissa A.
Tarskaia, Sergey I. Zhadanov, Jeffrey D. Wall, Jonathan K. Pritchard, Ripan
S. Malhi, David G. Smith, and Noah A. Rosenberg

2009   Haplotypic Background of a Private Allele at High Frequency in the Americas. *Molecular Biology and Evolution* 26:995–1016.

Schuldenrein, Joseph

1994   Alluvial Site Geoarcheology of the Middle Delaware Valley: A Fluvial Systems Paradigm. *Journal of Middle Atlantic Archaeology* 10:1–21.

1996   Geoarchaeology and the Mid-Holocene Landscape History of the Greater
Southeast. In *Archaeology of the Mid-Holocene Southeast*, edited by Kenneth
E. Sassaman and David G. Anderson, pp. 3–27. University Press of Florida,
Gainesville.

1998   Geomorphology and Stratigraphy of Prehistoric Sites along the Wadi al-Hasa. In *The Archaeology of the Wadi Al-Hasa, West-Central Jordan: 1: Surveys,
Settlement Patterns and Paleoenvironments*, edited by Nancy R. Coinman,
pp. 205–228. Arizona State University, Tempe.

2015   Refining Landscape Contexts for Open-Air, Lower and Middle Paleolithic

Sites: A Case Study from Muthanna Province, Southern Iraq. *Journal of Archaeological and Anthropological Sciences* 7(2):257–273.

Schuldenrein, Joseph, and Dennis B. Blanton

1997   Prehistory and Holocene Floodplain Evolution along the Inner Coastal Plain of Virginia: A Case Study from the Chickahominy Drainage. In *Proceedings of the Second International Conference on Pedoarchaeology*, edited by Albert C. Goodyear, John E. Foss, and Kenneth E. Sassaman, pp. 75–95. University of South Carolina Press, Columbia.

Schuldenrein, Joseph, and Geoffrey A. Clark

2003   Prehistoric Landscapes and Settlement Geography along the Wadi Hasa, West-Central Jordan. Part II: Towards a Model of Palaeoecological Settlement for the Wadi Hasa. *Environmental Archaeology* 8:1–16.

Schuldenrein, Joseph, Eva Hulse, and Rona Winter-Livneh

2013   Geoarchaeological Reconstruction of Old Place Neck, NJ–NY Expansion Project, Staten Island, Richmond County, New York. Report prepared for Extell Development Company.

Schuldenrein, Joseph, Robert G. Kingsley, James A. Robertson, Linda Scott-Cummings, and Daniel R. Hayes

1991   Archaeology of the Lower Black's Eddy Site, Buck County, Pennsylvania: A Preliminary Report. *Pennsylvania Archaeologist* 61(1):19–75.

Schumm, Stanley A.

1977   *The Fluvial System*. Blackburn Press, Caldwell, New Jersey.

Schuur, Catherine, John A. Goff, James A. Austin Jr., and Craig S. Fulthorpe

2000   Tracking the Last Sea-Level Cycle : Sea Floor Morphology and Shallow Stratigraphy of the Latest Quaternary New Jersey Middle Continental Shelf. *Marine Geology* 170:395–421.

Scott, Andrew C., Nicholas Pinter, Margaret E. Collinson, Mark Hardiman, R. Scott Anderson, Anthony P. R. Brain, Selena Y. Smith, Federica Marone, and Marco Stampanoni

2010   Fungus, Not Comet or Catastrophe, Accounts for Carbonaceous Spherules in the Younger Dryas "Impact Layer." *Geophysical Research Letters* 37(14):L14302. doi.org/10.1029/2010GL043345

Sedberry, George R., and Robert F. Van Dolah

1984   Demersal Fish Assemblages Associated with Hard Bottom Habitat in the South Atlantic Bight. *Environmental Biology of Fishes* 11:241–258.

Sellards, Elias H.

1915   The Pebble Phosphates of Florida. In *Seventh Annual Report*, pp. 25–116. Florida Geological Survey, Tallahassee.

1916a   On the Discovery of Fossil Human Remains in Florida in Association with Extinct Vertebrates. *American Journal of Science*, 4th ser. 42(247):1–18.

1916b   Human Remains and Associated Fossils from the Pleistocene of Florida. In *Eighth Annual Report,* pp. 121–160. Florida State Geological Survey, Tallahassee.

1917a   Further Notes on Human Remains from Vero, Florida. *American Anthropologist* 19(2):239–251.

1917b   Review of the Evidence on Which the Human Remains Found at Vero Are Referred to the Pleistocene. In *Ninth Annual Report,* pp. 69–84. Florida State Geological Survey, Tallahassee.

1919   Literature Relating to Human Remains and Artifacts at Vero, Florida. Florida State Geological Survey. In *Twelfth Annual Report*, pp. 1–4. Florida Geological Survey, Tallahassee.

1952   *Early Man in America.* University of Texas Press, Austin.

Seramur, Keith C.

2004   *Geoarchaeology of Site 31HT435 Harnett County, North Carolina.* Report submitted to New South Associates, Inc. in response to widening of NC87, Federal AID Project No. HBF-87 (4), State Project 8.T540302, TIP Project No. 2238.

Seramur, Keith C., and Ellen A. Cowan

2002   *Geoarchaeology of Site 31PT259 at the Confluence of Barber Creek and the Tar River Pitt County, Greenville, North Carolina.* Report prepared for I. Randolph Daniel Jr., Department of Anthropology, East Carolina University, Greenville, North Carolina.

2003   Site Formation Processes of Buried Cultural Horizons in the Sandhills of North Carolina: An Example from the Horses Grazing Site (31MR205). *North Carolina Archaeology* 52:101–118.

Seramur, Keith C., Ellen A. Cowan, D. J. Hettinger, and I. Randolph Daniel Jr.

2003   Interpreting Site Formation Processes at a Stratified Archaeology Site in a Sand Dune on the Atlantic Coastal Plain. Paper presented at the 33rd Annual Meeting of the Middle Atlantic Archaeological Conference, Virginia Beach, VA.

Shackleton, Nicholas J., and Neil D. Opdyke

1973   Oxygen Isotope and Palaeomagnetic Stratigraphy of Equatorial Pacific Core V28–238: Oxygen Isotope Temperatures and Ice Volumes on a 105 Year and 106 Year Scale. *Quaternary Research* 3(1):39–55. doi:10.1016/0033-5894 (73)90052-5.

Sharrock, Floyd W.

1966   *Prehistoric Occupation Patterns in Southwest Wyoming and Cultural Relationships with the Great Basin and Plains Culture Areas.* Anthropological Papers No. 77. Department of Anthropology, University of Utah, Salt Lake City.

Shea, John J.

2011   Stone Tool Analysis and Human Origins Research: Some Advice from Uncle Screwtape. *Evolutionary Anthropology* 20:48–53.

2013   Lithic Modes A–I: A New Framework for Describing Global-Scale Variation in Stone Tool Technology Illustrated with Evidence from the East Mediterranean Levant. *Journal of Archaeological Method and Theory* 20:151–186.

Sherwood, Sarah C., Boyce N. Driskell, Asa Randall, and Scott C. Meeks

2004   Chronology and Stratigraphy at Dust Cave, Alabama. *American Antiquity* 69(3):533–554.

Sherwood, Sarah C., and Paul Goldberg

2006   The Micromorphological Evaluation of Feature 91, Topper Site (38AL23),

Allendale County, South Carolina. Report on file at the South Carolina Institute of Archaeology and Anthropology, University of South Carolina, Columbia.

Shott, Michael, and Brian Trail
2010   Exploring New Approaches to Lithic Analysis : Laser Scanning and Geometric Morphometrics. *Lithic Technology* 35(2):195–220.

Shuman, Bryan, Thompson Webb III, Patrick Bartlein, and John W. Williams
2002   The Anatomy of a Climatic Oscillation: Vegetation Change in Eastern North America during the Younger Dryas Chronozone. *Quaternary Science Reviews* 21:1777–1791.

Signor, Philip W. III, and Jere H. Lipps
1982   Sampling Bias, Gradual Extinction Patterns and Catastrophes in the Fossil Record. *Geological Society of America* 190:291–296.

Simpson, Ruth D.
1989   *An Introduction to the Calico Early Man Site Lithic Assemblage.* Quarterly No. 36, No. 3, San Bernardino County Museum Association, Redlands, California.

Skoglund, Pontus, and David Reich
2016   A Genomic View of the Peopling of the Americas. *Current Opinion in Genetics and Development* 41:27–35. doi:10.1016/j.gde.2016.06.016.

Slice, Dennis E.
2007   Geometric Morphometrics. *Annual Review of Anthropology* 36(1):261–281.

Smallwood, Ashley M.
2010   Clovis Biface Technology at the Topper Site, South Carolina: Evidence for Variation and Technological Flexibility. *Journal of Archaeological Science* 37:2413–2425.
2011   *Clovis Technology and Settlement in the American Southeast.* Ph.D. dissertation, Department of Anthropology, Texas A&M University, College Station.
2012   Clovis Technology and Settlement in the American Southeast: Using Biface Analysis to Evaluate Dispersal Models. *American Antiquity* 77:689–713.
2015   Context and Spatial Organization of the Clovis Assemblage from the Topper Site, South Carolina. *Journal of Field Archaeology* 40(1):69–88.

Smallwood, Ashley M., Thomas A. Jennings, David G. Anderson, and R. Jerald Ledbetter
2015   Testing for Evidence of Paleoindian Responses to the Younger Dryas in Georgia, USA. *Southeastern Archaeology* 34:23–45.

Smallwood, Ashley M., D. Shane Miller, and Douglas Sain
2013   Topper Site, South Carolina: An Overview of the Clovis Lithic Assemblage from the Topper Hillside. In *In the Eastern Fluted Point Tradition*, Vol. 1, edited by Joseph A. M. Gingerich, pp. 280–298. University of Utah Press, Salt Lake City.

Smith, Bruce D.
1975   *Middle Mississippian Exploitation of Animal Populations.* Anthropological Papers 57. Museum of Anthropology, University of Michigan, Ann Arbor.

Smith, Heather, Ashley M. Smallwood, and Thomas DeWitt
2015   A Geometric Morphometric Exploration of Clovis Fluted Point Shape Vari-

ability. In *Clovis: On the Edge of a New Understanding*, edited by Ashley M. Smallwood and Thomas A. Jennings. Texas A&M University Press, College Station.

Soller, David R.

1988   Geology and Tectonic History of the Lower Cape Fear River Valley, Southeastern North Carolina. *U.S. Geological Survey Professional Paper 1466-A.*

Southerlin, Bobby

2012   A Brief Distributional Assessment of Metavolcanic Artifacts and Sources in the Long Cane District of the Sumter National Forest or Let There Be (Rhyo-) Light. Paper presented at the 38th Annual Conference on South Carolina Archaeology, Columbia.

Speer, Charles A.

2015   LA-ICP-MS Analysis of Clovis Period Projectile Points from the Gault Site. *Journal of Archaeological Science* 52:1–11.

Speth, John D., Khori Newlander, Andrew A. White, Ashley K. Lemke, and Lars E. Anderson

2013   Early Paleoindian Big-Game Hunting in North America: Provisioning or Politics? *Quaternary International* 285:111–139.

Spielhagaen, Robert F., Karl-Heinz Baumann, Helmut Erlenkeuser, Norbert R. Nowaczyk, Niels Nørgaard-Pedersen, Christoph Vogt, and Dominik Weiel

2004   Arctic Ocean Deep-Sea Record of Northern Eurasian Ice Sheet History. *Quaternary Science Reviews* 23:1455–1483.

Springer, Gregory S., Harold D. Rowe, Ben Hardt, R. Lawrence Edwards, and Hai Cheng

2008   Solar Forcing of Holocene Droughts in a Stalagmite Record from West Virginia in East-Central North America. *Geophysical Research Letters* 35:L17703

St. Lucie Tribune

1913   Fossil Remains in Florida. 21 February 1913.

Stafford, Russell C., and Mark Cantin

2009   Archaic Period Chronology in the Hill Country of Southern Indiana. In *Archaic Societies: Diversity and Complexity across the Midcontinent*, edited by Thomas E. Emerson, Dale L. McElrath, and Andrew C. Fortier, pp. 287–313. SUNY Press, Albany.

Stahlman, Patricia, and Frank J. Vento

2012   Early Prehistoric Site Potential on Atlantic Coast Barrier Islands: St. Catherines Island, Georgia: A Proxy Study. Poster presented at the 69th Annual Meeting of the Southeastern Archaeological Conference, Baton Rouge, Louisiana.

Stanford, Dennis, and Bruce Bradley

2000   The Solutrean Solution: Did Some Ancient Americans Come from Europe? *Scientific American Discovering Archaeology* 2:54–55.

Stanford, Dennis J.

1991   Clovis Origins and Adaptations: An Introductory Perspective. In *Clovis Origins and Adaptations*, edited by Robson Bonnichsen and Karene L. Turnmire, pp. 1–14. Center for the Study of the First Americans, Oregon State University, Corvallis.

Starna, William A.
1977   On Some Paleolithic Tools from Northeast North America. *Current Anthro-pology* 3:541–546.

Ste. Claire, Dana
1987   The Development of Thermal Alteration Technologies in Florida: Implications for the Study of Prehistoric Adaptation. *Florida Anthropologist* 40:203–208.

Steen, Carl
2000   *Archaeology and History at the Johannes Kolb Site–38DA75*. Report prepared for the South Carolina Department of Natural Resources Heritage Trust Program, Columbia.

Steffensen, Jørgen P., Katrine K. Andersen, Matthias Bigler, Henrik B. Clausen, Dorthe Dahl-Jensen, Hubertus Fischer, Kumiko Goto-Azuma, Margareta Hansson, Sigfus J. Johnsen, Jean Jouzel, Valérie Masson-Delmotte, Trevor Popp, Sune O. Rasmussen, Regine Röthlisberger, Urs Ruth, Bernhard Stauffer, Marie-Louise Siggaard-Andersen, Àrny E. Sveinbjornsdottir, Anders Svensson, and James W. C. White
2008   High-Resolution Greenland Ice Core Data Show Abrupt Climate Change Happens in Few Years. *Science* 321:650–651.

Steig, Eric J.
1999   Mid-Holocene Climate Change. *Science* 286:1485–1487.

Stein, Mordechai, Abraham Starinsky, Amitai Katz, Steven L. Goldstein, Malka Machlus, and Alexandra Schramm
1997   Strontium Isotopic, Chemical, and Sedimentological Evidence for the Evolution of Lake Lisan and the Dead Sea. *Geochimica et Cosmochimica Acta* 61(18):3975–3992.

Steponaitis, Vincas P., Jeffrey D. Irwin, Theresa E. McReynolds, and Christopher R. Moore (editors)
2006   *Stone Quarries and Sourcing in the Carolina Slate Belt*. Research Report No. 25. Research Laboratories of Archaeology, University of North Carolina, Chapel Hill.

Stewart, Thomas Dale
1946   A Re-examination of the Fossil Human Skeletal Remains from Melbourne, Florida with Further Data on the Vero Skull. *Smithsonian Miscellaneous Collections* 106 #10.

Strasser, Thomas F., Eleni Panagopoulou, Curtis N. Runnels, Priscilla Murray, Nicholas C. Thompson, Panagiotis Karkanas, Floyd W. McCoy, and Karl W. Wegmann
2010   Stone Age Seafaring in the Mediterranean: Evidence from the Plakias Region for Lower Palaeolithic and Mesolithic Habitation of Crete. *Hesperia* 79:145–190.

Surovell, Todd A.
2009   *Toward a Behavioral Ecology of Lithic Technology: Cases from Paleoindian Archaeology*. University of Arizona Press, Tucson.

Surovell, Todd, Vance T. Holliday, Joseph A. M. Gingerich, Caroline V. Ketron, C. Vance Haynes, Ilene Hilman, Daniel P. Wagner, Eileen Johnson, and Philippe Claeys

2009   An Independent Evaluation of the Younger Dryas Extraterrestrial Impact Hypothesis. *Proceedings of the National Academy of Sciences USA* 104:18155–18158.

Suther, Bradley E.

2013   *Stratigraphy, Paleohydrology, and Soil Variability in Late Quaternary River Valleys of the Southeastern Atlantic Coastal Plain, USA.* Ph.D. dissertation, Department of Geography, University of Georgia, Athens.

Suther, Bradley E., David S. Leigh, and George A. Brook

2011   Fluvial Terraces of the Little River Valley, Atlantic Coastal Plain, North Carolina. *Southeastern Geology* 73–93.

Swift, Donald J. P.

1970   Quaternary Shelves and the Return to Grade. *Marine Geology* 8:5–30.

Talwani, Pradeep

2003   Letter Report on Field Trip to Topper on May 31, 2002. On file at South Carolina Institute of Archaeology and Anthropology, Columbia.

Tankersley, Kenneth B.

2004   The Concept of Clovis and the Peopling of North America. In *The Settlement of the American Continent: A Multidisciplinary Approach to Human Biogeography*, edited by C. Michael Barton, Geoffrey A. Clark, David R. Yesner, and Georges A. Pearson, pp. 49–63. University of Arizona Press, Tucson.

Tarasov, Lev, and William R. Peltier

2005   Arctic Freshwater Forcing of the Younger Dryas Cold Reversal. *Nature* 435:662–665.

Taylor, Barbara E., Fred J. Rich, Mark J. Brooks, Andrew H. Ivester, and Christopher O. Clement

2011   Late Pleistocene and Holocene Vegetation Changes in the Sandhills, Ft. Jackson, South Carolina. *Southeastern Geology* 48:147–163.

Taylor, Kendrick C., Gregg W. Lamorey, Georgia A. Doyle, Richard B. Alley, Pieter M. Grootes, Paul A. Mayewski, James W. C. White, and Lisa K. Barlow

1993   The Flickering Switch of Late Wisconsin Climate Change. *Nature* 361:432–436.

Teller, James T.

2002   Reply to Comment by Paul F. Karrow. *Quaternary Science Reviews* 21:2119–2122.

2013   Lake Agassiz during the Younger Dryas. *Quaternary Research* 80:361–369.

Teller, James T., Matthew Boyd, Zhirong Yang, Phillip S. G. Kor, and Amir M. Fard

2005   Alternative Routing of Lake Agassiz Overflow during the Younger Dryas: New Dates, Paleotopography, and Re- evaluation. *Quaternary Science Reviews* 24:1890–1905.

Terrell, John Edward

2013   Social Network Analysis and the Practice of History. In *Network Analysis in*

Archaeology: New Approaches to Regional Interaction, edited by Carl Knappett, pp. 17–41. Oxford University Press, Oxford.

Thieler, E. Robert, David S. Foster, Emily A. Himmelstoss, and David J. Mallinson
2014   Geologic Framework of the Northern North Carolina, USA Inner Continental Shelf and Its Influence on Coastal Evolution. *Marine Geology* 348:113–130. doi:10.1016/j.margeo.2013.11.011.

Thom, Bruce G.
1970   Carolina Bays in Horry and Marion Counties, South Carolina. *Geological Society of America Bulletin* 81:783–814.

Thomas, Prentice, James Morehead, L. Janice Campbell, Philip Bourgeois, Lee Thomas, and Erica Meyer
2013   Data Recovery at 8WL68 within Test Area D-84, Cultural Resources Management Support, Eglin Air Force Base, Walton County, Florida. Report available from the Florida Bureau of Archaeological Research, Tallahassee.

Thompson, Victor D., and John E. Worth
2011   Dwellers by the Sea: Native American Adaptations along the Southern Coasts of Eastern North America. *Journal of Archaeological Research* 19:51–101.

Thornalley, David J. R., I. Nick McCave, and Harry Elderfield
2010   Freshwater Input and Abrupt Deglacial Climate Change in the North Atlantic. *Paleoceanography* 25(1):PA1201. doi: 10.1029/2009PA001772.

Thulman, David K.
2006   *A Reconstruction of Paleoindian Social Organization in North Central Florida.* Ph.D. dissertation, Department of Anthropology, Florida State University, Tallahassee.
2009   Freshwater Availability as the Constraining Factor in the Middle Paleoindian Occupation of North-Central Florida. *Geoarchaeology* 24(3):243–276.
2012a   Bioturbation and the Wakulla Springs Lodge Site Artifact Distributions. *Florida Anthropologist* 65:25–34.
2012b   Discriminating Paleoindian Point Types from Florida Using Landmark Geometric Morphometrics. *Journal of Archaeological Science* 39(5):1599–1607.
2014   The Role of Nondeclarative Memory Systems in the Inference of Long-Term Population Continuity. *Journal of Archaeological Method and Theory* 21(4):724–749.

Tian, He, Dominique Schryvers, and Philippe Claeys
2011   Nanodiamonds Do Not Provide Unique Evidence for a Younger Dryas Impact. *Proceedings of the National Academy of Sciences USA* 108(1):40–44.

Tilley, Christopher
1994   *A Phenomenology of Landscape: Places, Paths, and Monuments.* Berg, Oxford.

Titus, Kimberly, James A. Mosher, and Byron K. Williams
1984   Chance-Corrected Classification for Use in Discriminant Analysis: Ecological Applications. *American Midland Naturalist* 111(1):1–7.

Toon, Owen B., Kevin Zahnle, Richard P. Tukco, David Morrison, and Curt Covey
1997   Environmental Perturbations Caused by the Impacts of Asteroids and Comets. *Reviews of Geophysics* 35:41–78.

Tuck, James A.

1974   Early Archaic Horizons in Eastern North America. *Archaeology of Eastern North America* 2(1):72–80.

Tune, Jesse W.

2016   The Clovis–Cumberland–Dalton Succession: Settling into the Midsouth United States during the Pleistocene to Holocene Transition. *PaleoAmerica* 2:261–273.

University of South Alabama

2004   *Ocala Chert Distribution.* Electronic document, http://www.geoarchaeology. southalabama.edu/ocala_distribution.html, accessed October 10, 2012.

Upchurch, Sam B.

1984a   Geology and Lithic Materials at the Harney Flats Archaeological Site (8HI507), Hillsborough County, Florida. Report on file, Florida Division of Historical Resources, Bureau of Archaeological Research, Conservation and Collections Section, Tallahassee.

1984b   Petrology of Selected Lithic Materials from the South Carolina Coastal Plain. In *An Archeological Survey of Chert Quarries in Western Allendale County, South Carolina* by Albert C. Goodyear and Tommy Charles, pp. 125–140. South Carolina Institute of Archaeology and Anthropology, Research Manuscript Series 195. University of South Carolina, Columbia.

2015   Silicification and Epikarst Development of the Miocene Tampa Member, Arcadia Formation, in the Caladesi Quarry Cluster, Pasco and Hernando Counties, Florida. In *A Field Guide to Honeymoon Island Beach Nourishment,* compiled by Bryan Carrick, pp. 28–37. Guidebook No. 64. Southeastern Geological Society, Tallahasse.

Upchurch, Sam B., Richard N. Strohm, and Mark G. Nuckels

1982a   *Methods of Provenance Determination of Florida Cherts.* Report prepared for the Florida Division of Archives, History, and Records Management by the Department of Geology, University of South Florida, Tampa.

1982b   Silicification of Miocene Rocks from Central Florida. In *Miocene of the Southeastern United States,* edited by Thomas M. Scott and Sam B. Upchurch, pp. 251–284. Special Publication No. 25. Florida Bureau of Geology, Tallahassee.

Van De Plassche, Orson, Alex J. Wright, Benjamin P. Horton, Simon E. Engelhart, Andrew C. Kemp, David Mallinson, Robert E. Kopp

2014   Estimating Tectonic Uplift of the Cape Fear Arch (South-Eastern United States) Using Reconstructions of Holocene Relative Sea Level. *Journal of Quaternary Science* 29:749–759. doi:10.1002/jqs.2746.

van Hoesel, Annelies, Wim Z. Hoek, Freek Braadbaart, Johannes van der Plicht, Gillian M. Pennock, and Martyn R. Drury

2012   Nanodiamonds and Wildfire Evidence in the Usselo Horizon Postdate the Allerød-Younger Dryas Boundary. *Proceedings of the National Academy of Sciences USA* 109(2):7648–7653.

Van Peer, Philip
1992   *The Levallois Reduction Strategy*. Monographs in World Archaeology No. 13. Prehistory Press, Madison.

VanPool, Todd L., and Robert D. Leonard
2011   *Quantitative Analysis in Archaeology*. Wiley-Blackwell, Malden.

Van Riet-Lowe, Clarence
1945   The Evolution of the Levallois Technique in South Africa. *Man* 45:49–59.

Varmer, Ole
2014a   Closing the Gaps in the Law Protecting Underwater Cultural Heritage on the Outer Continental Shelf. *Stanford Environmental Law Journal* 33:251–286.
2014b   *Underwater Cultural Heritage Law Study*, OCS Study Bureau of Ocean Energy Management, Washington, D.C.

Varmer, Ole, Jefferson Gray, and David Alberg
2010   United States: Responses to the 2001 UNESCO Convention on the Protection of the Underwater Cultural Heritage. *Journal of Maritime Archaeology* 5129–141. doi:10.1007/s11457-010-9070–1.

Vartanyan, Sergey L., Khikmat A. Arslanov, T. V. Tertychnaya, and Sergey B. Chernov
1995   Radiocarbon Dating Evidence for Mammoths on Wrangel Island, Arctic Ocean, until 2000 BC. *Radiocarbon* 37(1):1–6.

Vega, Anthony J., and Mark S. Binkley
1994   Origins of Tropical Cyclones Striking the U.S. Mainland, 1960–1989. *National Weather Digest* 19(1):14–26.

Vento, Frank J., and Patty A. Stahlman
2011   Development of a Late Pleistocene–Holocene Genetic Stratigraphy Framework for St. Catherines Island: Archaeological Implications. In *Geoarchaeology of St. Catherines Island, Georgia*, edited by Gale A. Bishop, Harold B. Rollins, and David Hurst Thomas, pp. 99–112. Anthropological Papers No. 94. American Museum of Natural History, New York.

Viau, André E., Konrad Gajewski, Michael C. Sawada, and Philippe Fines
2006   Millennial-Scale Temperature Variations in North America during the Holocene. *Journal of Geophysical Research* 111, D09102. (Downloadable data grids at: http://www.ncdc.noaa.gov/paleo/pubs/viau2006/viau2006.html).

Viau, André E., Konrad Gajewski, Philippe Fines, David E. Atkinson, and Michael C. Sawada
2002   Widespread Evidence of 1500 Yr Climate Variability in North America during the Past 14000 Yr. *Geology* 30:455–458.

Voorhies, Michael R.
1974   Late Miocene Terrestrial Mammals, Echols County, Georgia. *Southeastern Geology* 15(4):223–235.

Waggoner, James C., and Scott Jones
2007   Validating "Daltonite" within the Greater Classification of Lithic Resources in the Interior Coastal Plain. *Early Georgia* 35(1):45–62.

Wagner, Daniel P., and Joseph M. McAvoy
2004   Pedoarchaeology of Cactus Hill, a Sandy Paleoindian Site in Southeastern Virginia, U.S.A. *Geoarchaeology* 19:297–322. doi:10.1002/gea.10120.

Wah, John S.

2003   The Origin and Pedogenic History of Quaternary Silts on the Delmarva Peninsula in Maryland. Unpublished Ph.D. dissertation, Department of Environmental Science and Technology, University of Maryland, College Park.

Wallis, Neill J., and Asa R. Randall (editors)

2014   New Approaches to Ancient Florida. In *New Histories of Pre-Columbian Florida*, pp. 1–17. University Press of Florida, Gainesville.

Walthall, John A.

1998   Rockshelters and Hunter-Gatherer Adaptation to the Pleistocene/Holocene Transition. *American Antiquity* 63(2):223–238.

Ward, Henry H., and David C. Bachman

1987   Eolian Burial of Woodland Sites on the Delaware Coastal Plain. *Journal of Middle Atlantic Archaeology* 3:103–110.

Waters, Michael R.

2004   The Role of Geoarchaeology in the Search for the First Americans. In *New Perspectives on the First Americans*, edited by Bradley T. Lepper and Robson Bonnichsen, pp. 187–192. Center for the Study of the First Americans, Texas A&M University Press, College Station.

Waters, Michael R., Steven L. Forman, Thomas A. Jennings, Lee C. Nordt, Steven G. Driese, Joshua Feinberg, Joshua L. Keene, Jessi Halligan, Anna Lindquist, James Pierson, Charles T. Hallmark, Michael B. Collins, and James Weiderhold

2011   The Buttermilk Creek Complex and the Origins of Clovis at the Debra L. Friedkin Site, Texas. *Science* 331:1599–1603.

Waters, Michael R., Steven L. Forman, Thomas W. Stafford Jr., and John Foss

2009   Geoarchaeological Investigations at the Topper and Big Pine Tree Sites, Allendale County, South Carolina. *Journal of Archaeological Science* 36(7):1300–1311.

Waters, Michael R., and Thomas W. Stafford Jr.

2007a   Redefining the Age of Clovis: Implications for the Peopling of the Americas. *Science* 315:1122–1126.

2007b   Response to Comment on "Redefining the Age of Clovis: Implications for the Peopling of the Americas." *Science* 317:320c.

2013   The First Americans: A Review of the Evidence for the Late-Pleistocene Peopling of the Americas. In *Paleoamerican Odyssey*, edited by Kelly E. Graf, Caroline V. Ketron, and Michael R. Waters, pp. 541–560. Center for the Study of the First Americans, Texas A&M University, College Station.

Waters, Michael R., Thomas W. Stafford, H. Gregory McDonald, Carl Gustafson, Morten Rasmussen, Enrico Cappellini, Jesper V. Olsen, Damian Szklarczyk, Lars J. Jensen, M. Thomas, P. Gilbert, and Eske Willerslev

2011   Pre-Clovis Mastodon Hunting 13,800 Years Ago at the Manis Site, Washington. *Science* 334:351–353. doi:10.1016/j.jas.2008.12.020.

Watson, Richard A.

1976   Inference in Archaeology. *American Antiquity* 41(1):58–66.

Watts, William A.
1980   Late-Quaternary Vegetation History at White Pond on the Inner Coastal
            Plain of South Carolina. *Quaternary Research* 13:187–199.
Watts, William A., and Barbara C. S. Hansen
1988   Environments of Florida in the Late Wisconsin and Holocene. In *Wet Sites
            Archaeology*, edited by Barbara A. Purdy, pp. 307–323. Telford Press, West
            Caldwell.
Webb, S. David
1981a   Late Pleistocene Vertebrates as Climatic Indicators. In *Cultural Resource Sur-
            vey of the Continental Shelf from Cape Hatteras to Key West: 1. Introduction
            and Physical Environment*, pp. 73–81. Report submitted by Science Applica-
            tions, Inc. to the Bureau of Land Management, McLean, Virginia.
19181b   *A Cultural Resources Survey of the Continental Shelf from Cape Hatteras to
            Key West: 1. Introduction and Physical Environment.* Report Submitted to the
            Bureau of Land Management, McLean, Virginia.
Webb, S. David (editor)
2006   *First Floridians and Last Mastodons: The Page-Ladson Site in the Aucilla
            River.* Springer, Dordrecht, The Netherlands.
Wehmiller, John F., Linda L. York, and Michelle L. Bart
1995   Amino Acid Racemization Geochronology of Reworked Quaternary Mol-
            lusks on U.S. Atlantic Coast Beaches: Implications for Chronostratigraphy,
            Taphonomy, and Coastal Sediment Transport. *Marine Geology* 124:303–337.
            doi:10.1016/0025–3227(95)00047–3.
Weigel, Robert D.
1962   *Fossil Vertebrates of Vero, Florida.* Special Publication No. 10. Florida Geo-
            logical Survey, Tallahassee.
Wells, Joshua J., Eric C. Kansa, Sarah Whitcher Kansa, Stephen J. Yerka, David G. Ander-
            son, Kelsey Noack Myers, R. Carl DeMuth, and Thaddeus G. Bissett
2014   Web-Based Discovery and Integration of Archaeological Historic Proper-
            ties Inventory Data: The Digital Index of North American Archaeology (DI-
            NAA). *Literary and Linguistic Computing* 29(3):349–360.
Wen, Bin, Jijun J. Zhao, and Tingju Li
2007   Synthesis and Crystal Structure of N-Diamond. *International Materials Re-
            view* 52(3):131–151.
West, Larry T.
2004   Profile Description of Topper Site Backhoe Trench 17, July 1, 2004. On file at
            South Carolina Institute of Archaeology and Anthropology, Columbia.
Wettstein, Carol A., Chris V. Noble, and James D. Slabaugh
1986   *Soil Survey of Indian River County, Florida. Soil Conservation Service, Flor-
            ida. Dept. of Agriculture and Consumer Services, University of Florida.* Ag-
            ricultural Experiment Station, University of Florida. Institute of Food and
            Agricultural Sciences, University of Florida.
Whallon, Robert
1982   Variables and Dimensions: The Critical Step in Quantitative Typology. In
            Essays on Archaeological Typology, edited by Robert Whallon and James A.

Brown, pp. 127–161. Center for American Archaeology Press, Evanston, Illinois.

2006   Social Networks and Information: Non-"utilitarian" Mobility among Hunter-Gatherers. *Journal of Anthropological Archaeology* 25(2):259–270.

Wheat, Amber

2012   Survey of Professional Opinions regarding the Peopling of the Americas. *SAA Archaeological Record* 12(2):10–14.

White, Andrew

2012   *The Social Networks of Early Hunter-Gatherers in Midcontinental North America*. Ph.D. dissertation, Department of Anthropology, University of Michigan, Ann Arbor.

2014   Changing Scales of Lithic Raw Material Transport among Early Hunter-Gatherers in Midcontinental North America. *Archaeology of Eastern North America* 42:51–75.

White, J. Wilson, and Benjamin I. Ruttenberg

2007   Discriminant Function Analysis in Marine Ecology: Some Oversights and Their Solutions. *Marine Ecology Progress Series* 329:301–305.

Wierhold, James E., and Charlotte D. Pevny

2014   Fundamentals in Practice: A Holistic Approach to Microwear Analysis at the Debra L. Friedkin Site, Texas. *Journal of Archaeological Science* 48:104–119.

Wiessner, Polly

1982   Risk, Reciprocity, and Social Influences on !Kung San Economics. In *Politics and History in Band Societies*, edited by Eleanor Leacock and Richard B. Lee, pp. 61–84. Cambridge University Press, Cambridge.

Wilder, Michael, Charles D. Frederick, Mark D. Bateman, and Duane E. Peter

2007   Geoarchaeological Investigations in the Flats of the Osceola Plain, Highlands and Polk Counties, Florida. *Florida Anthropologist* 60:97–116.

Wilkinson, Joseph E.

2014   Across the Coastal Plain: Looking at Early Archaic Hafted Bifaces by Raw Material and Geography. Paper presented at the Southeastern Archaeological Society Conference, presented in the symposium Early Human Life on the Southeastern Coastal Plain. Greenville, South Carolina.

2017   Modeling Early Archaic Mobility and Subsistence: Evaluating Resource Risk across the South Carolina Landscape. Master's thesis, Department of Anthropology, University of South Carolina, Columbia.

Willard, Debra A., Christopher E. Bernhardt, David A. Korejwo, and Stephen R. Myers

2005   Impact of Millennial-Scale Holocene Climate Variability on Eastern North America Terrestrial Ecosystems: Pollen-Based Climate Reconstruction. *Global and Planetary Change* 47:17–35.

Willey, Gordon R.

1966   *Introduction to North American Archaeology: 1: North and Middle America*. Prentice-Hall, Englewood Cliffs.

Williams, Nancy

1982   A Boundary Is to Cross: Observations on Yolngu Boundaries and Permission. In *Resource Managers: North American and Australian Hunter-Gather-*

ers, edited by Nancy Williams and Eugene S. Hunn, pp. 131–153. Westview Press, Boulder.

Williams, Stephen
1991   *Fantastic Archaeology: The Wild Side of North American Prehistory*. University of Pennsylvania Press, Philadelphia.

Willig, Judith A.
1991   Clovis Technology and Adaptation in Far Western North America: Regional Pattern and Environmental Context. In *Clovis Origins and Adaptations*, edited by Robson Bonnichsen and Karen L. Turnmire, pp. 91–119. Center for the Study of the First Americans, Oregon State University, Corvallis.

Wintle, Ann G.
2008   Fifty Years of Luminescence Dating. *Archaeometry* 50:276–312.

Witthoft, John
1967   The Art of Flint Chipping. *Archaeological Society of Maryland Journal* 3(1):123–144.

Wittke, James H., James C. Weaver, Ted E. Bunch, James P. Kennett, Douglas J. Kennett, Andrew M. T. Moore, Gordon C. Hillman, Kenneth B. Tankersley, Albert C. Goodyear, Christopher R. Moore, I. Randolph Daniel Jr., Jack H. Ray, Neal H. Lopinot, D. Ferraro, Isabel Israde-Alcántara, James L. Bischoff, Paul S. DeCarli, Robert E. Hermes, Johan B. Kloosterman, Zsolt Revay, George A. Howard, David R. Kimbel, Gunther Kletetschka, Ladislav Nabelek, Carl P. Lipo, Sachiko Sakai, Allen West, and Richard B. Firestone
2013   Evidence for Deposition of 10 Million Tonnes of Cosmic Impact Spherules across Four Continents 12,800 Years Ago. *Proceedings of the National Academy of Sciences USA* 110(23):E2088–E2097.

Wolbach, Wendy S., Iain Gilmour, and Edward Anders
1990   Major Wildfires at the Cretaceous–Tertiary Boundary. In *Global Catastrophes in Earth History*, edited by Virgil L. Sharpton and Peter Ward. Geological Society of America Special Paper 247: 391–400.

Wolbach, Wendy S., Roy S. Lewis, and Edward Anders
1985   Cretaceous Extinctions: Evidence for Wildfires and Search for Meteoritic Material. *Science* 230:167–170.

Wolbach, Wendy S., Susanna Widicus, and Frank T. Kyte
2003   A Search for Soot from Global Wildfires in Central Pacific Cretaceous–Tertiary Boundary and Other Extinction and Impact Horizon Sediments. *Astrobiology* 3:91–97.

Woodburn, James
1968   Stability and Flexibility in Hadza Residential Groupings. In *Man the Hunter*, edited by Richard B. Lee and Irven L. DeVore, pp. 49–55. Aldine, Chicago.

Woodman, Neal, and Nancy Beavan Athfield
2009   Post-Clovis Survival of American Mastodon in the Southern Great Lakes Region of North America. *Quaternary Research* 72(3):359–363.

Wormington, H. Marie
1957   *Ancient Man in North America*. Denver Museum of Natural History, Popular Series 4. Peerless, Denver.

Wu, Yingzhe, Mukul Sharma, Malcolm A. LeCompte, Mark Demitroff, and Joshua D. Landis

2013 Origin and Provenance of Spherules and Magnetic Grains at the Younger Dryas Boundary. *Proceedings of the National Academy of Sciences USA* 110(38):E3557–E3566.

Wyckoff, Don G., James L. Theler, and Brian J. Carter

2003 *The Burnham Site in Northwestern Oklahoma: Glimpses beyond Clovis?* Oklahoma Anthropological Society Memoir 9. Sam Noble Oklahoma Museum of Natural History, Norman.

Yang, Jia, Hanqin Tian, Bo Tao, Wei Ren, John Kush, Yongqiang Liu, and Yuhang Wang

2014 Spatial and Temporal Patterns of Global Burned Area in Response to Anthropogenic and Environmental Factors: Reconstructing Global Fire History for the 20th and Early 21st Centuries. *Journal of Geophysical Research: Biogeosciences,* 119:1–15.

Yellen, John, and Henry Harpending

1972 Hunter-Gatherer Populations and Archaeological Inference. *World Archaeology* 4:244–253.

Yoffee, Norman

1993 Too Many Chiefs? (Or, Safe Texts for the '90s). In *Archaeological Theory: Who Sets the Agenda?* edited by Norman Yoffee and Andrew Sherratt, pp. 60–78. Cambridge University Press, Cambridge.

Young, Christopher K.

2010 A Study of the Availability and Selection of Stone Tool Raw Materials in Relation to the Johannes Kolb Archaeological Site (38DA75). *South Carolina Antiquities* 42:27–34.

2012 Lithic Sourcing in the Great Pee Dee River Region. Paper presented at the 77th Annual Meeting of the Society for American Archaeology, Memphis.

2013 Lithic Raw Material Procurement in Relation to the Johannes Kolb Site (38DA75). *South Carolina Antiquities* 45:82–84.

Zayac, Tracy, Fredrick J. Rich, and Lee Newson

2001 Paleoecology and Depositional Environments of the McClelland Sandpit Site, Douglas, Georgia. *Southeastern Geology* 40:259–272.

Zelditch, Miriam Leah, Donald L. Swiderski, and H. David Sheets (editors)

2012 *Geometric Morphometrics for Biologists, Second Edition: A Primer.* Academic Press, Amsterdam.

Contributors

A. Victor Adedeji received his PhD in physics from Auburn University. He has been teaching physics at the college level for more than 20 years inside and outside the United States. His research interests are in the deposition and characterization of low-D composite electronic materials for harsh environment applications and chromogenic materials for energy conservation applications. He studies the electrical and optical characteristics and the materials' dynamic surface morphology with SEM and EDS.

James M. Adovasio, PhD, DSc, received his undergraduate degree in anthropology from the University of Arizona and doctorate in anthropology from the University of Utah. He is currently director of archaeology at Harbor Branch Oceanographic Institute, Florida Atlantic University, and is the principal investigator of the re-excavation at the Old Vero Man Site in Florida. He achieved world acclaim as an archaeologist in the 1970s with his excavation of Pennsylvania's Meadowcroft Rockshelter. During his career, he has specialized in the analysis of perishable materials (basketry, textiles, cordage, etc.) and the application of high-tech methods in archaeological research.

David G. Anderson is professor in the Department of Anthropology at the University of Tennessee, Knoxville. He has written over 50 books and monographs and over 150 papers encompassing Paleoindian through recent historic tenant farmstead assemblages, including work at the Mattassee Lake, Rucker's Bottom, and Topper sites.

Robert J. Austin received his PhD in anthropology from the University of Florida in 1997 and has been a practicing archaeologist for nearly 40 years. He has conducted fieldwork throughout Florida, the eastern and western United States, the Caribbean, and Africa. He is currently an independent cultural resource consultant.

Terry E. Barbour is a PhD student in anthropology at the University of Florida. He is a member of the Laboratory of Southeastern Archaeology team and is currently part of its Lower Suwannee Archaeology Survey in the Big Bend region of Florida, where his dissertation research is focused.

Kara Bridgman Sweeney, PhD, (instructor of anthropology, Georgia Southern University) is an anthropological archaeologist. Her research is based on modeling the cultural traditions of the Pleistocene–Holocene transition, with particular emphasis on the Early Side-Notched Horizon in the Southeastern Coastal Plain.

Mark J. Brooks, PhD, conducts geoarchaeological research in the southeastern U.S. Coastal Plain, focusing on integrated studies of archaeological site formation, climate and landscape change, and early hunter-gatherer adaptations. He retired from the University of South Carolina in 2014 but continues to pursue his research interests.

Ted E. Bunch received his PhD from the University of Pittsburgh. He retired from NASA after 35 years of research primarily in space and planetary science, hypervelocity impact, and meteorites. He is adjunct professor at Northern Arizona University, continues research in the effects of comet impact with the Earth, and is CEO of Space Science Consulting Services LLC.

Adam M. Burke earned his MA in applied archaeology from Indiana University of Pennsylvania in 2014 and is a current doctoral student in the Department of Anthropology at Texas A&M University. His research interests include using geochemical methods to source toolstone, lithic technological organization, and Paleoindian mobility and settlement patterns in the southeastern United States.

I. Randolph Daniel Jr. received his PhD in 1994 from the University of North Carolina at Chapel Hill. He is professor in the Department of Anthropology at East Carolina University where he has worked since 1996. His research interests include the archaeology of prehistoric hunter-gatherers in the southeastern United States, particularly hunter-gatherer adaptations at the end of the last Ice Age.

James S. Dunbar was awarded a BA at the University of Florida and an MA and PhD at Florida State University and was employed by the Bureau of Archaeological Research before retiring after 35.5 years of service. He is now the principal investigator of ongoing research of archaeology projects taking place in Wakulla Springs State Park.

Jon C. Endonino is assistant professor of anthropology at Eastern Kentucky University. Dr. Endonino's research interests include lithic technology and sourcing, interaction and exchange, and the origins of mortuary mounds during the Late Archaic in Florida.

H. Blaine Ensor is currently principal archaeologist at Historic Properties Consultants, a small private cultural resources management firm in Murphysboro, Illinois. Over the past 40 years he has worked in cultural resource management specializing in prehistoric lithic analysis and serving as principal investigator, project manager, and research archaeologist at various universities and private companies. Most recently he has focused on Clovis and potential pre-Clovis sites in the southeastern United States.

Richard W. Estabrook holds a BA from Stony Brook University in New York and earned his MA and PhD from the University of South Florida, Tampa. He has worked as a cultural resources consultant for the past 30 years in the U.S. and Canada, but with a strong focus on the southeastern U.S. His research interests include sourcing toolstones, use-wear analysis, and stone tool replication and use.

James K. Feathers received his PhD in anthropology from the University of Washington in 1990. After postdoctoral work at the Smithsonian Institution and the University of Maryland, he became director of the Luminescence Dating Laboratory at the University of Washington in 1993, a position he still holds. Under his direction the laboratory has dated more than 3000 sediment and ceramic samples from all seven continents.

Albert C. Goodyear is research affiliate with the South Carolina Institute of Archaeology and Anthropology and director of the Southeastern Paleoamerican Survey. He has been pursuing prehistoric research on the Southeastern Coastal Plain for over 40 years, including chert types and sources, Paleoindian from Clovis through Dalton, Pre-Clovis, and the proposed Younger Dryas Boundary Impact hypothesis.

M. Scott Harris received his PhD in geology from the University of Delaware and has been working on Coastal Plain and Continental Shelf geology and geoarchaeology for 30 years. He has conducted field work in the eastern and western United States, Greece, and Ethiopia. Dr. Harris currently serves as associate professor of geology and within the archaeology program at the College of Charleston.

C. Andrew Hemmings received his bachelor's degree at the University of Arizona and both graduate degrees from the University of Florida. After a postdoctoral research position at the University of Texas he has been active in terrestrial and underwater Paleoindian research across the Americas for the last 10 years.

Andrew H. Ivester, PhD, is a physical geographer with interests in geomorphology, soil science, and environmental change. He has worked on geoarchaeological projects throughout the eastern U.S. and in southern Africa. He is currently adjunct faculty in the Department of Geosciences at the University of West Georgia where he teaches courses in geography, geology, and environmental science.

Thomas A. Jennings is director of the Antonio J. Waring, Jr. Archaeological Laboratory at the University of West Georgia. His research interests include Paleoindian and Archaic technologies and geoarchaeology of the Plains and Southeast.

Douglas J. Kennett (BA, 1990; MA, 1994; PhD, 1998, University of California, Santa Barbara) is professor of environmental archaeology in the Department of Anthropology at Penn State University. He has held faculty positions at California State University Long Beach (1998–2001) and the University of Oregon (2001–2011). His current interests include the study of human sociopolitical dynamics under changing environmental conditions, human impacts on ancient environments, and behavioral response to abrupt climate change in the past.

James P. Kennett is a marine geologist who has worked on a broad range of marine and terrestrial geological subjects for over 50 years. These include Cenozoic climatic history and, more recently, the climate role in archaeology. He is emeritus professor in earth and marine sciences at the University of California, Santa Barbara.

Malcolm A. LeCompte received a PhD in atmospheric, planetary, and astrophysical sciences in 1984 from the University of Colorado, Boulder. After a postdoctoral appointment to the Harvard College Observatory, he pursued a 23-year career in terrestrial planet remote sensing. In 2009, he retired from Elizabeth City State University (ECSU), having been director of research at its Center of Excellence in Remote Sensing Education and Research. Since his retirement, his research has been focused on the investigation of quaternary earth impacts.

Christopher R. Moore, PhD, is a geoarchaeologist at the Savannah River Archaeological Research Program. His research interests include site formation processes and geochronology of stratified sites in the Southeastern Coastal Plain, paleoenvironmental reconstruction, early hunter-gatherer adaptations, lithic technology, and immunological blood residue analysis.

Douglas A. Sain is an archaeologist at Terracon Consultants. He specializes in lithic technology and Paleoindian archaeology. He has been involved in archaeological projects throughout the southeast, south central, and western United States. His research explores human origins in North America, the organization of lithic technology, and the dynamics of prehistoric settlement subsistence systems.

Joseph Schuldenrein is president and principal of Geoarcheology Research Associates (GRA). He has been involved in geoarchaeological research and heritage projects throughout the world at locations as diverse as South Asia, the Mediterranean Basin, and the urban landscapes of the United States. He has worked extensively in the U.S. Southeast and is proud to have collaborated with some of that region's foremost researchers.

Ashley M. Smallwood is associate professor of anthropology at the University of West Georgia. She studies Clovis technology in the American Southeast, with a focus on the adaptive context of stone tool production. Her current research focuses on identifying the signatures of southeastern Paleoindian technology and the organization of the lithic industry in order to culturally define Paleoindian lifeways.

David K. Thulman received his PhD in anthropology from Florida State University and JD from George Washington University. He is assistant professorial lecturer at George Washington University, specializing in ethical issues and reconstructions of prehistoric social organization in eastern North America.

Sam B. Upchurch received his education at Vanderbilt University and Northwestern University where he specialized in geochemistry, sedimentary petrology, and sedimentology. He served as professor and chairman of the Geology Department at the University of South Florida. He has recently retired from SDII Global Corporation where he served as vice president and senior principal geologist. He specializes in karst hydrogeology and the origin and provenance of chert.

Anthony J. Vega is professor in the Biology and Geoscience Department at Clarion University. His background includes a BA in physical geography from the University of New Orleans, an MS in geoscience (meteorology) from Mississippi State University, and a PhD in synoptic climatology from Louisiana State University. Dr. Vega has authored numerous books and textbooks on climatology and has extensive peer-reviewed publications. His research centers on atmospheric teleconnections, tropical cyclone climatology, paleoclimatolgoy, and mid-tropospheric flow variations and resulting surface climate variations.

Frank J. Vento has conducted geoarchaeological investigations in the U.S. and abroad for more than 35 years. He is a licensed professional geologist. Dr. Vento received his PhD in geology and MA in anthropology from the University of Pittsburgh. Dr. Vento is professor emeritus of Clarion University of Pennsylvania and currently serves as president of Quaternary Geological and Environmental Consultants, LLC. Dr. Vento has completed more than 12 million in grants and contracts. His research is primarily centered on fluvial, karst and coastal geomorphology, and reconstructing paleoenvironments.

Allen West, PhD, is a retired geophysicist, author, and former owner of a consulting company to resource exploration companies in the Middle East, North America, and South America. He is cofounder of the Comet Research Group and has coauthored more than 50 peer-reviewed scientific papers and conference presentations.

Joseph E. Wilkinson is a graduate student in anthropology at the University of South Carolina. His research interests include the study of Paleoindian and Early Archaic cultures and their lithic technologies within South Carolina and across the broader Southeast, landscape archaeology, and hunter-gatherer subsistence modeling.

Wendy S. Wolbach received her PhD in chemistry from The University of Chicago in 1990. She is currently professor of chemistry at DePaul University in Chicago, where she teaches and conducts research on the geochemistry of sedimentary rocks associated with large impacts and mass extinctions.

INDEX

Ripley P. Bullen Series
Florida Museum of Natural History

Tacachale: Essays on the Indians of Florida and Southeastern Georgia during the Historic Period, edited by Jerald T. Milanich and Samuel Proctor (1978)

Aboriginal Subsistence Technology on the Southeastern Coastal Plain during the Late Prehistoric Period, by Lewis H. Larson (1980)

Cemochechobee: Archaeology of a Mississippian Ceremonial Center on the Chattahoochee River, by Frank T. Schnell, Vernon J. Knight Jr., and Gail S. Schnell (1981)

Fort Center: An Archaeological Site in the Lake Okeechobee Basin, by William H. Sears, with contributions by Elsie O'R. Sears and Karl T. Steinen (1982)

Perspectives on Gulf Coast Prehistory, edited by Dave D. Davis (1984)

Archaeology of Aboriginal Culture Change in the Interior Southeast: Depopulation during the Early Historic Period, by Marvin T. Smith (1987)

Apalachee: The Land between the Rivers, by John H. Hann (1988)

Key Marco's Buried Treasure: Archaeology and Adventure in the Nineteenth Century, by Marion Spjut Gilliland (1989)

First Encounters: Spanish Explorations in the Caribbean and the United States, 1492–1570, edited by Jerald T. Milanich and Susan Milbrath (1989)

Missions to the Calusa, edited and translated by John H. Hann, with an introduction by William H. Marquardt (1991)

Excavations on the Franciscan Frontier: Archaeology at the Fig Springs Mission, by Brent Richards Weisman (1992)

The People Who Discovered Columbus: The Prehistory of the Bahamas, by William F. Keegan (1992)

Hernando de Soto and the Indians of Florida, by Jerald T. Milanich and Charles Hudson (1992)

Foraging and Farming in the Eastern Woodlands, edited by C. Margaret Scarry (1993)

Puerto Real: The Archaeology of a Sixteenth-Century Spanish Town in Hispaniola, edited by Kathleen Deagan (1995)

Political Structure and Change in the Prehistoric Southeastern United States, edited by John F. Scarry (1996)

Bioarchaeology of Native American Adaptation in the Spanish Borderlands, edited by Brenda J. Baker and Lisa Kealhofer (1996)

A History of the Timucua Indians and Missions, by John H. Hann (1996)

Archaeology of the Mid-Holocene Southeast, edited by Kenneth E. Sassaman and David G. Anderson (1996)

The Indigenous People of the Caribbean, edited by Samuel M. Wilson (1997; first paperback edition, 1999)

Hernando de Soto among the Apalachee: The Archaeology of the First Winter Encampment, by Charles R. Ewen and John H. Hann (1998)

The Timucuan Chiefdoms of Spanish Florida, by John E. Worth: vol. 1, *Assimilation*; vol. 2, *Resistance and Destruction* (1998; first paperback edition, 2020)

Ancient Earthen Enclosures of the Eastern Woodlands, edited by Robert C. Mainfort Jr. and Lynne P. Sullivan (1998)

An Environmental History of Northeast Florida, by James J. Miller (1998)

Precolumbian Architecture in Eastern North America, by William N. Morgan (1999)

Archaeology of Colonial Pensacola, edited by Judith A. Bense (1999)

Grit-Tempered: Early Women Archaeologists in the Southeastern United States, edited by Nancy Marie White, Lynne P. Sullivan, and Rochelle A. Marrinan (1999; first paperback edition, 2001)

Coosa: The Rise and Fall of a Southeastern Mississippian Chiefdom, by Marvin T. Smith (2000)

Religion, Power, and Politics in Colonial St. Augustine, by Robert L. Kapitzke (2001)

Bioarchaeology of Spanish Florida: The Impact of Colonialism, edited by Clark Spencer Larsen (2001)

Archaeological Studies of Gender in the Southeastern United States, edited by Jane M. Eastman and Christopher B. Rodning (2001)

The Archaeology of Traditions: Agency and History Before and After Columbus, edited by Timothy R. Pauketat (2001)

Foraging, Farming, and Coastal Biocultural Adaptation in Late Prehistoric North Carolina, by Dale L. Hutchinson (2002)

Windover: Multidisciplinary Investigations of an Early Archaic Florida Cemetery, edited by Glen H. Doran (2002)

Archaeology of the Everglades, by John W. Griffin (2002; first paperback edition, 2017)

Pioneer in Space and Time: John Mann Goggin and the Development of Florida Archaeology, by Brent Richards Weisman (2002)

Indians of Central and South Florida, 1513–1763, by John H. Hann (2003)

Presidio Santa María de Galve: A Struggle for Survival in Colonial Spanish Pensacola, edited by Judith A. Bense (2003)

Bioarchaeology of the Florida Gulf Coast: Adaptation, Conflict, and Change, by Dale L. Hutchinson (2004; first paperback edition, 2020)

The Myth of Syphilis: The Natural History of Treponematosis in North America, edited by Mary Lucas Powell and Della Collins Cook (2005)

The Florida Journals of Frank Hamilton Cushing, edited by Phyllis E. Kolianos and Brent R. Weisman (2005)

The Lost Florida Manuscript of Frank Hamilton Cushing, edited by Phyllis E. Kolianos and Brent R. Weisman (2005)

The Native American World Beyond Apalachee: West Florida and the Chattahoochee Valley, by John H. Hann (2006)

Tatham Mound and the Bioarchaeology of European Contact: Disease and Depopulation in Central Gulf Coast Florida, by Dale L. Hutchinson (2007)

Taíno Indian Myth and Practice: The Arrival of the Stranger King, by William F. Keegan (2007)

An Archaeology of Black Markets: Local Ceramics and Economies in Eighteenth-Century Jamaica, by Mark W. Hauser (2008; first paperback edition, 2013)

Mississippian Mortuary Practices: Beyond Hierarchy and the Representationist Perspective, edited by Lynne P. Sullivan and Robert C. Mainfort Jr. (2010; first paperback edition, 2012)

Bioarchaeology of Ethnogenesis in the Colonial Southeast, by Christopher M. Stojanowski (2010; first paperback edition, 2013)

French Colonial Archaeology in the Southeast and Caribbean, edited by Kenneth G. Kelly and Meredith D. Hardy (2011; first paperback edition, 2015)

Late Prehistoric Florida: Archaeology at the Edge of the Mississippian World, edited by Keith Ashley and Nancy Marie White (2012; first paperback edition, 2015)

Early and Middle Woodland Landscapes of the Southeast, edited by Alice P. Wright and Edward R. Henry (2013; first paperback edition, 2019)

Trends and Traditions in Southeastern Zooarchaeology, edited by Tanya M. Peres (2014)

New Histories of Pre-Columbian Florida, edited by Neill J. Wallis and Asa R. Randall (2014; first paperback edition, 2016)

Discovering Florida: First-Contact Narratives from Spanish Expeditions along the Lower Gulf Coast, edited and translated by John E. Worth (2014; first paperback edition, 2016)

Constructing Histories: Archaic Freshwater Shell Mounds and Social Landscapes of the St. Johns River, Florida, by Asa R. Randall (2015)

www.ingramcontent.com/pod-product-compliance
Lightning Source LLC
Chambersburg PA
CBHW050623280326
41932CB00015B/2499